An Integrated Approach
to Communication Theory and Research

LEA'S COMMUNICATION SERIES
Jennings Bryant/Dolf Zillmann, General Editors

For a complete list of other titles in LEA's Communication Series, please contact Lawrence Erlbaum Associates, Publishers.

An Integrated Approach to Communication Theory and Research

Edited by

Michael B. Salwen
Don W. Stacks
University of Miami

LEA

LAWRENCE ERLBAUM ASSOCIATES, PUBLISHERS
1996   Mahwah, New Jersey

Lawrence Erlbaum Associates, Inc., Publishers
10 Industrial Avenue
Mahwah, NJ 07430

Portions of chapter 11 are reprinted from *Public Opinion, the Press, and Public Policy* (pp. 146–152), by J.
D. Kennamer (Ed.), 1992, Westport, CT: Greenwood
Publishers. Copyright 1992 by Greenwood Publishers,
an imprint of Greenwood Publishing Group, Inc., Westport, CT.

Cover design by Gail Silverman

Library of Congress Cataloging-in-Publication Data

An Integrated approach to communication theory and research / Michael B. Salwen and Don W. Stacks, ed.
        p.   cm.
    Includes bibliographical references and index.
    ISBN 0-8058-1630-5 (alk. paper). — ISBN 0-8058-
1631-3 (pbk. : alk. paper)
    1. Communications—Methodology. 2. Mass me-
dia—Methodology. I. Salwen, Michael Brian. II.
Stacks, Don W.
    P91.1558   1996
    302.2'01—dc20
                                                96-2786
                                                  CIP

Contents

Preface

THE INTEGRATIVE PROCESS

This volume focuses on *integrating* theory and research in communication study. The terms "theory" and "research" are often linked together, like bread and butter, bagel and cream cheese, or speech communication and mass communication. It is stating the obvious to say that theory and research should be similarly linked together. Despite the obviousness of this statement, it comments on our field that a volume such as this that links communication theory and research in the same chapters is needed.

Our purpose in editing this volume is to provide both seasoned scholars and beginning students unfamiliar with the state of theory and research in various areas of communication study to provide with a taste, a sampler if you will, of current theory *and* research in communication. To explicate the integration process, the chapter contributors, experts in their respective areas, offer sample studies in the form of hypothetical studies, published studies, or unpublished research, showing how theory and research are integrated in their particular areas.

The idea for this book grew out of a series of informal discussions between the coeditors by the water cooler, in the photocopy room, in the hallway, by the coffee machine, and outside faculty mailboxes. In these discussions, we complained about the difficulty of teaching communication students communication theory *and* research. As with many programs, theory and research are taught in the University of Miami's School of Communication as separate courses. This clean curricular separation, however, bears no resemblance to how the courses are actually taught. Faculty who teach communication theory often digress into a discussion on research methods to make sense of exemplar studies. This is no small matter; sometimes an entire theory class is devoted to discussions of research methods. Likewise, faculty who teach research methods have—out of necessity—had to bring discussion of theory into their courses. It was clear that the teachers were not to blame for this situation; the curriculum was at fault. In attempting to alleviate the problem of linking theory and research in communication study, we were astounded to find that no single volume attacked the problem of linking theory and research in communication study; some volumes examine the human and speech communication areas, whereas others focus on the mass communication areas—but none could be found that combine both areas under the rubric *communication*.

We do not claim that this book will resolve the difficulties regarding the distinction between theory and research in general, and communication theory and research in particular. We are not arguing for a wholesale revamping in communication curriculum to integrate theory and research, for we realize how easy it is to advocate curricular change but how difficult it is to exercise change in practice. The purpose is simply to explicitly recognize that theory and research are related and must be addressed together even in courses that involve largely theory or largely research.

While the book was in progress, we extended the integration process to address issues regarding the integration of mass and speech communication, what we call human communication. To do otherwise would have defied our purpose of leaving the reader with an appreciation of current theory and research in the various areas of communication study. It is important that all communication scholars, no matter what their areas, have some familiarity with the broader field. The state of communication study is such that most researchers are trained in either mass or human communication and, as a result, have a certain way of approaching communication or are more familiar with one area than the other.

In editing the book we wrestled with the best way of organizing the various theoretical approaches to communication. We originally opted for the traditional bifurcation of *communication* into mass communication and human communication, and, to some extent, we have followed this course. Part I examines general questions related to theory and research methodology. Part II examines important theoretical approaches to mass communication. Part III does the same with human communication approaches.

As we quickly learned, this bifurcation does not lend itself well to communication study. As we enter the 21st century, with new media technologies that do not fit neatly into either mass communication or human categories, the bifurcation promises to raise more problems. Therefore, while we were editing the book, we invited Kathleen Reardon and Emmeline G. de Pillis to write a lead chapter for an additional section, Part IV, to cover chapters that we were having particular difficulty classifying into sections, those that crossed the traditional divide between mass and human communication.

Even in the sections in which we classified chapters as mass or human communication, we recognize that others might have classified them differently. Our decisions were admittedly subjective, but not arbitrary. The decisions were based partly on how the contributors approached their chapters. In this regard, we might have placed the chapters in different sections had they been written in different ways. For example, it might seem traditional to place advertising and public relations back to back (the two are often grouped together, like theory and research); but we decided that the advertising chapter took a more traditional mass communication approach, while the public relations chapter addressed issues involving organizational communication, and therefore we placed it in Part IV, *Integrated Approaches*. Likewise, persuasive communication is an area of interest in both mass and human communication, but the chapter contributors took more of what we regarded as a human communication approach. Similarly, as the contributors of the chapter on the spiral of silence themselves noted, the model involves the interaction of both human communication as well as mass communication. But because of the chapter's emphasis on mass communication, it was placed in the mass communication section. The political communication chapter also took a largely mass communication approach.

Our point here—by noting our difficulties in classifying the chapters—is to emphasize the *artificiality* of the bifurcation. As editors, we treated the bifurcation as a convenient means of organizing a book, for a book must have organization. And practically speaking, despite the noted occasional problems, most chapters fit the bifurcation fairly well. Further, the bifurcation reflects a reality of communication study today which we would have been foolish to ignore. Still, our decision to bifurcate mass and human communication should not blind us to the similarities shared by all the areas of communication study.

In keeping with the difficulty in distinguishing mass and human communication, we invited Tony Atwater and Gustav W. Friedrich, former heads of leading mass (Association for Education in Journalism and Mass Communication) and human (Speech Communication Association) communication associations, respectively, to offer their thoughts in the final section, Part V, on where communication theory and research is going.

We are not so naive as to believe that this book will lead to a unified field of *communication* study, or even the utopian goal of a discipline of communication, and perhaps these goals are not even desirable. If the book succeeds in furthering understanding among scholars and students regarding the mass–human communication divide and different approaches to integrating theory and research in different areas of communication, that will be a small triumph. We also realize, after working and arguing this project between ourselves, that to become a discipline we need more cross-communication, more dialogue with our brothers and sisters who examine different areas of a larger area. To this end, we hope that some of the material presented piques scholarly interest, challenges theorists and researchers to look at the broader scope of communication study (which, based on many of the chapters, has taken the first steps toward integrating the many areas of communication presented), and begin to work together in formulating a truly grounded *communication* approach to *communication* theory and research.

—*Michael B. Salwen*
—*Don W. Stacks*

I

Studying "Theory"—Doing "Research"

1

Integrating Theory and Research: Starting With Questions

Don W. Stacks
Michael B. Salwen
University of Miami

Toward the end of their academic careers, most graduate students are required to demonstrate their ability to integrate theory and research methodology in their field of study by completing a project, thesis, or dissertation. Students of communication, particularly those concentrating on mass communication, have been so inculcated with the practice and application of their field that they often find this task daunting—and sometimes irrelevant.

This is a perhaps understandable reaction to theory (the rationale we extend to understand the world around us) and research (ways to test or make sense of that rationale from either quantitative or qualitative approaches) from those whose lifetimes involved a certain respect for "common sense." But as Albert Einstein (1960) warned against a blind reliance on common sense:

> Conclusions obtained by purely rational processes are, so far as reality is concerned, entirely empty. It is because he recognized this, and especially because he impressed it upon the scientific world, that Galileo became the father of modern physics and in fact of the whole modern natural science. (p. 81)

The thesis or dissertation process might seem intimidating, especially as critics harp on such seemingly trivial matters as measuring tools, study designs, statistical or interpretative procedures, tests for reliability and validity, units of analysis, metaphor, meaning, and historical significance. But theory and research, despite the fact that their qualities seem mysitcal to the initiate, are by no means extraneous to understanding the communication process—whether it be an understanding of the theoretical or applied aspects of communication. The purpose of the thesis or dissertation exercise is to master a skill that has its own common sense standards that differ from traditional standards.

The purpose of the thesis or dissertation is more than simply to master the content. It involves learning via a mode of conceiving and conceptualizing in which hypotheses or research questions are derived from theory. The hypotheses or research questions are then tested in a manner adhering to agreed-upon standards for gathering evidence, be they quantitative or qualitative in nature.

Mastering narrow and perhaps esoteric bodies of research and conducting research based on the literature has, admittedly, little value for students unless they plan to continue in that area. But mastering theoretically based research skills are immensely valuable to the student, scholar, or practitioner who plans to generate or consume primary or secondary research in the future.

WHERE NO ONE HAS GONE BEFORE

Theory organizes and refines our ideas, like a map for exploring unexplored territories. Imagine exploring new lands without at least examining the maps and writings of past explorers to see what rivers and lands they traversed. Although we do not put complete faith in old adventurers' maps and writings, we would be foolish to ignore what others have done.

The novice researcher or the seasoned scholar, excited by a new idea while in the bath, almost always emerges from the bathroom proclaiming that "no one has ever thought of this before." That researcher is like the explorer who believes no one has ever gone, or tried to go, where he or she plans to go. Even cursory investigation, however, usually reveals that others have gone—or tried to go—where the novice researcher plans to go. Theoretically driven research involves building and testing on the knowledge of previous explorers.

In this opening chapter, we examine the link between theory and research methodology, and integrate these two primal aspects of academic study in communication. Our approach is simple: The *research process* itself is integrated. One cannot conduct good research without theory and good theory development requires good verification.

THE COMMUNICATION PROCESS

The research process in communication begins with a good question, perhaps later developed into a hypothesis, tested in the most rigorous and appropriate way. Research, then, advances the theory behind the question/hypothesis, leading to refinements in the research, and so forth.

Few explorers discovered new lands or routes without some knowledge of those who went before them. Each explorer makes new headway for the next. But metaphors are never perfect, and the communication process studied by communication researchers is not exactly like finding a new land: As far as the communication process is concerned, there is no final "place" to be discovered, where a theoretical "flag" can be planted. Yet there is something to be gained by acquiring knowledge about a process that may never be completely understood.

The integration of theory and research methodology and the communication process are similar processes. Each begins with information gleaned from some source, and integrates that information into a message of some form (e.g., verbal or nonverbal) or some medium (e.g., interpersonal or mass mediated) that conveys meaning. Information takes on different forms at different times in both processes; sometimes it merely exists, much like background noise or something noted in the environment; sometimes it consists of symbols and signs, such as the words on this page, only written in a language you may not understand (French, Greek, Latin). Either way, there is no intent, it is just there. To some, to be considered communication, the information must be intentionally sent *and* intentionally received (Burgoon & Ruffner, 1978). Dittman (1972) pointed out that a message may be subliminal—not consciously received—and yet still impact our thoughts, attitudes, and behaviors. Burgoon and Ruffner (1978) argued that communication has not occurred unless both source and receiver perceive a message to be intentional. Others (Malandro, Barker, & Barker, 1989; Hickson & Stacks, 1993) considered communication to occur if either sender or receiver perceive intent. Either way, information often leads to communication, depending on how the researcher has defined *communication*.[1]

Perhaps the phrase *human communication* is all too often used to describe all communication. This is not feasable when it is necessary to distintinguish mass mediated communication from nonmediated communication. The research process begins when the researcher reviews the literature relevant to the question or hypothesis of interest, yielding the *literature review*. Previous theory and research form the basis for a new approach, model, or theory that interprets communication differently. Thus, information is basic to both the communication and the theory–research process; it begins the process by pointing to something new, either in the environment (such as Newton's apple leading us to gravity) or in a specific literature (such as theories of how the brain operates coming from neurophysiological studies).

We all are familiar with the cliche that "knowledge is power." But what does this really mean? Knowedge about the communication processes has very practical applications for a variety of purposes—persuading other people to do what you want, for good or evil purposes; teaching elementary students; launching an information campaign to reduce AIDS risk behaviors; selling soap; educating the public about some important issue; brainwashing the people, aggrandizing all power and becoming an absolulte dictator; and so forth.

---

[1]The distinction between human communication and mass communication is somewhat arbitrary yet historical. Throughout this book we will use human communication when focusing on those approaches and theories that have emerged from the speech communication and interpersonal communication approaches. *Mass communication* is used to describe approaches and theories that focus on mediated messages and channels of communication (e.g., newspaper, radio, television). Obviously, the two areas overlap in a variety of areas as seen in Part IV, which examines areas that have extended beyond this traditional dichotomy.

Thanks to our explorer-researchers, we have refined many of our ideas about human and mass communication processes. With some historical perspectives, we see that the communication process was once guided by naive theories, some as simple as those used to understand language acquisition. Language was once conceived as arising from physical exertion (*yo-he-ho*), from imitation of nature sounds (onomatopoeic, e.g., *bow-wow*), or when the mouth and vocal organs tried to pantomime body gestures (Gray & Wise, 1959). The mass communication process was once guided by a simplistic notion of a direct and universal "hypodermic-needle" effects model on a malleable and passive audience (Severin & Tankard, 1992, pp. 90–108). This model, too, is now in disrepute.

Today we can look back on the earlier generation of communication researchers who gave us various language acquisition and hypodermic-needle models of communication and wonder how they could have ever been so naive. Perhaps future generations will see us in much the same way.

THE RESEARCH PROCESS

We begin our journey by fleshing out the relationship between theory and research. In exploring this relationship we focus on the asking of "good" research questions that lead to important hypotheses. We then examine how the question dictates the methodology used to test the theoretical relationships. Finally, we examine the research process as a whole, coming full circle to understanding and predicting communication.

The research process begins by asking research questions. Research questions are drawn from the systematic study of an area of communication interest. Whereas a systematic study of the literature is necessary, "good" questions are also derived from old-fashioned common sense.

Questions can be derived either deductively or inductively. The scientific method gives more credence to the inductive process, or hypothetico-deductive logic, in which questions are induced from general principles. That is, they take a law-like approach, much like that found in Berger and Calebrese's (1975) interpersonal communication model of uncertainty reduction. Deduction, on the other hand, arives at truth and questions from rationale observation (Westley, 1958). Deduction can be as simple and elegant as the syllogism, "All humans are mortal; Judy is a human; therefore, Judy is mortal" or as complex as the rule-based, practical syllogism, "Jim wants good grades; to get good grades he must study; therefore Jim must study to get good grades." The two examples differ in their range of generality (cf., Stacks, Hickson, & Hill, 1991). The former has low generalizability, it is simple logic in a lawlike manner; the latter is midrange and more practical, and it requires a mediating factor.

Deduction is the way of everyday common sense and rationalism. But induction has its own logic. The logic of induction serves to restrain the dangers of total reliance on common sense that Albert Einstein warned against.

At one time, it seemed eminently sensible to thinkers that the earth was the center of the universe. After all, common wisdom told us that God placed humankind above all others, and by simply looking up at the skies it appeared that the heavens surrounded the Earth. From this observation, we deduced that humans must be in the center.

Induction forces us to challenge our notions of common sense. Long ago we learned that the Earth is not the center of our universe and that the Earth is round. The danger with a total reliance on induction is that it assumes that the theory and research methodology and not the researcher—who after all is a rational human being—can apply his or her reason to understanding the communication process (cf., Stacks & Hocking, 1992). This sometimes leads to a belief that the observations (data) are real—a philosophical stance sometimes called *logical positivism*, which some critics brand as *blind empiricism*.

In reality, most researchers maintain a dialectic between induction and deduction, drawing on each as needed. The researcher is a human being, not a machine, involved in the theory development process and does not shy away from making cautious "creative leaps" (Tichenor & McLeod, 1989, p. 16). Diehard logical positivists fear that without total reliance on hypothetico-deductive logic, researchers will draw back to a simple rationalism of their forebearers, who believed that the earth was the center of the universe. On the other hand, we do not want to bend over backwards too far in the other direction and abandon blind empiricism for blind humanism.

While contemporary social science has been influenced by logical positivism, few social scientists today adhere to the strict logical positivism espoused by Wittgenstein and the Vienna Circle of Scientists of the 1920s (Bergman, 1967). They posited a rigid and uncompromising form of empiricism that only recognized truths validated through specified procedures of observation. Questions that cannot meet these rigid standards are rejected as inappropriate for scientific study. Whereas critics often attack logical poisitivism as if they were attacking modern social science, their criticisms are aimed at a largely "dead horse" philosophy that few contemporary social science researchers adhere to (Hanfling, 1981, p. 171).[2]

ASKING QUESTIONS

The question-asking process in theory and research is more complex than simply generating the research question or questions guiding a particular study. Communication researchers ask questions in each step of the theory and research process.

An early stage in the theory–research process is concerned with defining the variables being studied. This stage is concerned with asking questions of definition that establish the phenomenon under study. This involves questions of fact. For example, what is *mass communication*? How does it differ from *human (speech) communication*? Are there differences in persuasibility in mass and speech communication? Are there similarities?

After researchers establish what is being studied, questions then focus on the relationships that communication variables have with the phenomenon under study.

---

[2]Social science today reflects an epistemological view that can be more properly described as logical empiricism than logical postivism (Carnap, 1953). Logical positivism has its intellectual roots in the physical sciences, where universal laws underlie theory; social science involves recurring regularities that are more rule-based (Stacks et al., 1991). Rather than being grounded in universal laws, logical empiricism puts forth lawlike statements that do not have to be universally true (Miller & Berger, 1978). The arguments of the 1970s regarding which philosophical approach is best have been supplanted by a growing movement toward triangulation, or theory and research that employs a combination of approaches.

These are *questions of variable relations*; in answering them we seek to establish if two or more variables are related to each other in observable ways; and, if so, how.

Some questions are not factually oriented; instead they relate to considerations that focus more on the goodness or value of the variables being studied and the study as a whole. These are *questions of value* that examine the aesthetic or normative features of communication. These questions examine how appropriate or inappropriate communication is, its value, or its beauty. Questions of value are related to the next category of question—*questions of policy*.

Questions of policy focus on how the communication phenomena under study affect how communication should be practiced (Stacks & Hocking, 1992). Questions of policy are especially important to media practitioners. They wrestle with ethical concerns that, in their quest for profits, they are doing the right thing. In this regard, applied communication researchers should heed the warnings of "critical scholars" who fear that communication research is often used merely to sell communication goods like commodities without regard for the social good (Bottomore, 1984).

We turn now to a more in-depth examination of each of these types of questions asked by researchers in the theory and research process.

Questions of Fact

All research, once the basic theoretical framework is established, begins with some form of definition, of elaborating the primitive terms in theory. Theory attempts to define the phenomena under study using terms and phrases, often loosely, to communicate meaning. At a gut level, most communicators believe they know what they mean by the symbols (words) they use; most message receivers also believe they know what was meant in the communicator's selection of symbols. But once we finish describing our theoretical frameworks, and roll up our sleeves for the nitty-gritty research work, we often find arguments between communicators and message receivers over what our seemingly obvious terms meant.

Of importance to theory and research is the ability to take an abstract concept and define it in such a way as to be testable. Until a concept has been defined in a certain agreed-on manner that meet criteria of reliability (it is consistent) and validity (it measures what we think it measures), the concept is nothing more than a primitive term (it is so basic that it could take on multiple meanings, such as *love, aggressiveness*, or *power*) with imprecise meaning. We now have to define our concepts in terms that are precise, measurable, reproducible, and demonstrate that our measures of the variables really represent what we tried to theoretically explain.

Some questions of definition in the physical sciences, such as of the quark (the smallest unit in the physical universe), were once only potentially definable. Until recently there was no method with which to test for their existence. Quarks were always theoretically defined in such a way as to be *potentially* observable (definable). Quarks were finally observed, but not until the equipment necessary to measure their existence was finally invented. The same is true in communication. Concepts such as attitudes, beliefs, and values are all abstractions requiring theoretical definitions that allow for *potential* observation and measurement.

Questions of definition also stipulate how a phenomenon is to be measured. This is called an *operational definition*. Operational definitions bridge the gap between theory and method by constructing a *variable* (something that can be observed, measured) from a theoretical abstraction. Suppose we have a theory that predicts that media violence is related to aggression. *Media violence* could take on many forms: channels, such as MTV, news coverage, or prime time shows, on the one hand or messages, such as depictions of physical abuse or harsh language on the other. The operational definition defines the concept in such a way that the researcher can test for the presence or absence (dichotomous measure) or degree (continuous measure) of media violence. Likewise, our theory must operationally define aggression.

The question of definition is found in all research, qualitative or quantitative. Some definitions obtained from previous research are called *reportative*; they have a conventional meaning, one well understood by others researching in the area. Other definitions are *stipulative*; they are unique to the particular theoretical approach being tested. Whenever we use stipulative definitions, we must be sure that they are clearly and usefully defined in ways that make them operable (cf., Stacks & Hocking, 1992, pp. 8–9). Much like with the observation of the quark, recent physics theory has been advanced by the observation of the black hole, long ago hypothesized to exist but only with the advent of the Hubble Telescope were astronomers able to actually see it.

Questions of Variable Relations

Questions of variable relations stem from questions of definition. Once the theoretical phenomenon has been demonstrated to be potentially observable (i.e., operationally defined), we now move to examine the relations between and among variables. Questions of variable relations assume that for every action there is a potential reaction. That is, based upon theory, changes in one variable have some hypothesized change with other variable(s).

Questions of variable relations might ask how a change—whether manipulated or natural in one variable—might have some predictable change in another variable; or what happens when one variable is combined with another; or how an array of variables change when one or many other variables change. How can we even speculate on variable relations? Speculations do not come out of thin air. Researchers examine a good deal of research by others and come to believe—based on theory development—that such variable relations exist.

Questions of variable relations are the building blocks of research that help us discover objective ways of understanding the world. In communication research predicting relationships often takes methodological form in experiments (which provide the only way to establish causal relationships between variables), survey research, and manifest content analysis (the actual content being analyzed). Experiments are most amenable to quantitative analysis, which usually examines how a number of people are affected by the concepts under study. Some questions are tested by qualitative methods, such as latent content analysis (ideas or themes related to or underlying the content being analyzed) or in-depth interview methodology.

Questions of variable relations serve an important role in communication research. They establish whether theoretical concepts can be verified across a diverse population.

They also provide researchers a way of objectively measuring whether predicted differences or relationships occur. Does watching violent television produce violence in viewers? Is there a difference between the way countries use satellite technology? Do superiors communicate differently with subordinates? Do quality circles yield increased worker morale and productivity? Each of these questions has terms or concepts that have been defined. Each concept is potentially testable and can be verified or refuted according to some criteria.

As will be discussed in later chapters, an empirical observation of variable relations does not necessarily mean that one variable causes the other. For example, during the 19th century an Italian prison physician, Ceasare Lombroso, claimed that he had discovered a biological cause for crime. He even produced empirical evidence for his theory. Through correlational research, Lombroso found that Italian criminals tended to have dark skins, sloping foreheads, jutting chins, and long arms. This was a potentially remarkable discovery. On closer inspection, however, it was found that the physical traits of criminals described by Lombroso were actually descriptions of those of people from the poor, southern region of Italy, especially Sicily. Sociologists took Lombroso's same data and applied a more plausible theoretical interpretation—that poverty and the ills associated with poverty, not physical traits, is associated with crime (Pick, 1986).

Questions of Value

Questions of value ask about subjective evaluations on such matters as goodness, beauty, rightfulness, or appropriateness. Although questions of value could be operationally defined to be empirically tested, for the most part their answers lie *within* the individual and generally accepted ethical norms.

Much research in rhetorical criticism, media content, interpersonal relations, international mass communications, journalism ethics, and feminist theory address questions of value. Although all theoretically driven research involves questions of value to varying degrees, some communication researchers working in areas such as feminism, cultural studies, critical theory, and so forth, are often explicit about the values underlying their research.

Questions of value lead the researcher to re-examine the original questions of fact or conceive and devise important steps in theory construction and validation. Even Paul F. Lazarsfeld, whom some critics wrongly describe and deride as a diehard logical positivist, was concerned about values (Pasanella, 1994). His landmark mass communication studies focused on ways to study voting and increase voter turnout—an important issue of value in a democratic society. Similarly, the landmark experimental research on attitude change by Carl Hovland and his colleagues at Yale University were motivated by a desire to counter Nazi propaganda and motivate American soldiers to fight for their country during World War II (Hovland, Janis, & Kelly, 1953).

Much international and intercultural communication research has been guided by questions of value. Underlying the study of cross-national and cross-cultural communication is the belief that if we could only use communication effectively to break down the cultural and national barriers that separate people we could achieve peace and understanding. This optimistic, and perhaps naive, view reached its pinnacle during the 1960s, when, according to some interpretations, Canadian scholar Marshall

McLuhan espoused the centrality of electronic media as a means to better the world. McLuhan predicted that the new electronic communication would turn the world into a "global village" breaking down all barriers of misunderstanding.[3]

The science fiction-humor writer Douglas Adams addressed the issue of a universe in which all races could communicate with each other in his *Hitchhiker's Guide to the Galaxy* (a four-part trilogy!). Unlike many science fiction writers, Adams addressed how alien races could communicate with each other. Thanks to a remarkable little fish called the babel fish, which you stick in your ear, you can understand all languages. The result of the babel fish was enhanced social communication throughout the Galaxy. The outcome, however, was far from the peace-through-communcation model that some communication researchers might expect:

> The practical upshot of all this is that if you stick a babel fish in your ear you can instantly understand anything said to you in any form of language. The speech patterns you actually hear decode the brain wave matrix which has been fed into your mind by your babel fish.
> . . . [T]he poor babel fish, by effectively removing all barriers to communication between different races and cultures, has caused more and bloodier wars than anything else in the history of creation. (Adams, 1979, pp. 59–61)

Questions of Policy

Policy questions ask whether some action or policy should be implemented. Most researchers do not have the political power to implement policy, so questions of policy often concern researchers as advocates for or against certain causes. For example, based upon research and common sense judgments of right or wrong, researchers might advocate that the U.S. government continue or refrain from broadcasting propaganda messages to Cuba through Radio Martí.

When researchers pose questions of policy, they typically have answered—or at least addressed—questions of definition, fact, and value—all of which impact on the final policy decision. But they also bring to the policy debate appeals to reason based on right and wrong. For example, in addition to empirical research findings, advocates for the continuation of Radio Martí will point to political oppression in Cuba and argue that messages over Radio Martí will provide what they believe is truthful information to Cubans. They might also use empirical data to support their views, such as the results of surveys of recent Cuban emigres. On the other hand, critics of Radio Martí will point to data that show that Radio Martí is ineffective—either because it is not being heard or is not believed—and appeal to the moral incorrectness of intrusion in other cultures as well as ascribing questionable or bad motives to the U.S. government.

Mass communication researchers have especially been interested in policy concerning such matters as media violence, journalism ethics, and so forth. According to the tenets of traditional democratic theory, the *raison d'étre* of mass communication is to create an informed public for a functioning democracy (Berelson, 1952; Sabine, 1952). The economic goals of mass media in most capitalist systems, however, means that mass media industries are usually motivated by profit. This profit motive was not

---

[3]For critical analyses of the myth of globalization, see Ferguson (1992) and Curtin (1993).

unforeseen or regarded as uniformly bad, according to some liberal thinkers, so long as there are sufficient checks to ensure that mass media provide some acceptable level of information for an enlightened public while the media industries also earn reasonable profits. The only problem is that often the profit goal supersedes the enlightenment goal, resulting in a dearth of useful information. As the social critic and rock star Bruce Springsteen (1992) observed in his song "57 Channels (and Nothin' On)" about the information revolution in cable television:

> *Man came by to hook up my cable TV*
> *We settled in for the night my baby and me*
> *We switch 'round and 'round 'til half-past dawn*
> *There was fifty-seven channels and nothin' on.*

Human communication researchers are generally less concerned with policy questions; they tend to focus more on questions of variable relations and value (especially when in rhetorical research which focuses on the value of a speech or rhetorical campaign). However, research in freedom of speech tends to look at policy and the law that inhibits or enhances our expressions.

Questions of policy do not fall into "basic" theory or research. Rather, they are asked when we feel we have tested the theories sufficiently to recommend a course of action to lawmakers and other policy-making institutions. Most communication policy questions have dealt with the media, although more are coming to be asked in organizational communication research.

"Good Questions"

Defining what research questions are is quite simple. In so doing we have relied on the reportative definition of questions used by Stacks and Hocking (1992), who in turn relied on Miller and Nicholson's (1976) approach to communication theory and research methodology. To varying degrees, each of the questions posed can be verified in the literature, assessed for its value, and even establish a research policy. Determining when a "good" question has been asked is not as simple. Just because a question is of interest to the researcher does not mean that it is good. It could be trivial (it affects no one). It could be useless (others have already asked similar questions and found no clear response). It could be irrelevant (it doesn't deal with communication). It could be impossible to test. Or, it could be significant and extend our knowledge of how and why we communicate. A good research question stems from a well-conceived theoretical approach to how humans communicate. Further, a good research question almost always dictates the method most appropriate to answer that question.

As with good theory, a good research question will lead to other significant questions. The relationship between theory and research methodology is more than a two-sided sword where one side proposes a view of the world and the other tests that view. Theory and research work hand-in-hand. Sometimes it is the research methodology that alters the way the question is posed and tested which, in turn, produces new theory. In this regard specific research methods are as heuristic as theory. Theory and research methodology involve a single integral process by which we attempt to better understand how and why people communicate or fail to communicate.

THE REST OF THE BOOK

In the rest of the book, the reader should keep in mind the questions each approach asks. Look closely at how they are answered, how they are tested. What stage of theoretical development do they reflect? How significant are the questions asked? What methods are required to answer them? How sophisticated are they? These questions may not yield answers until later. However, we believe that a basic understanding of the major questions being asked by communication researchers should provide the impetus to better understand where the communication discipline is and where it may be going. It should also provide the information necessary to formulate and state good research questions based on an understanding of communication research.

REFERENCES

Adams, D. (1979). *The hitchhiker's guide to the galaxy.* New York: Pocket Books.

Berelson, B. (1952). Democratic theory and public opinion. *Public Opinion Quarterly, 16,* 313–330.

Berger, C. R., & Calabrese, R. J. (1975). Some explanations in initial interaction and beyond: Toward a developmental theory of interpersonal communication. *Human Communication Research, 1,* 99–112.

Bergman, G. (1967). *The metaphysics of logical positivism.* Madison: University of Wisconsin Press.

Bottomore, T. (1982). *The Frankfurt school.* Chichester, Sussex: E. Harwood.

Burgoon, M., & Ruffner, M. (1978). *Human Communication.* New York: Holt, Rinehart & Winston.

Carnap, R. (1953). Testability and meaning. In H. Feigl & M. Brodbeck (Eds.), *Readings in the philosophy of science* (pp. 47–52). New York: Appleton-Century-Crofts.

Curtin, M. (1993). Beyond the vast wasteland: The policy discourse of global television and the politics of American empire. *Journal of Broadcasting & Electronic Media, 37,* 127–145.

Dittman, A. T. (1972). *Interpersonal messages of emotion.* New York: Springer.

Einstein, A. (1960). The method of science. In E.H. Madden (Ed.), *The structure of scientific thought* (pp. 80–93). Boston: Houghton-Mifflin. (Original work published 1933)

Ferguson, M. (1992). The mythology about globalization. *Journal of Communication, 7,* 69–93.

Gray, G. W., & Wise, J. M. (1959). *The bases of speech.* New York: Harper & Row.

Hanfling, O. (1981). *Logical positivism.* New York: Columbia University Press.

Hickson, M. L., & Stacks, D. W. (1993). *NVC: Nonverbal communication studies and applications* (3rd ed.). Dubuque, IA: William Brown.

Hovland, C. I., Janis, I. L., & Kelley, H. H. (1953). *Communication and persuasion.* New Haven, CT: Yale University Press.

Malandro, L., Barker, L. L., & Barker, D. (1989). *Nonverbal communication* (2nd ed.). Reading, MA: Addison-Wesley.

Miller, G. R., & Berger, C. R. (1978). On keeping the faith in matters scientific. *Western Journal of Speech Communication, 42,* 44–57.

Miller, G. R., & Nicholson, H. (1976). *Communication inquiry: A perspective on a process.* Reading, MA: Addison-Wesley.

Pasanella, A. K. (1994). *The mind traveller: A guide to Paul F. Lazerfeld's research papers.* New York: Freedom Forum Media Studies Center.

Pick, D. (1986). The faces of anarchy: Lombroso and the politics of criminal science in post-unification Italy. *History Workshop, 21,* 60–86.

Sabine, G. (1952). The two democratic traditions. *Philsophical Review, 61,* 451–474.

Severin, W. J., & Tankard, J. W., Jr. (1992). *Communication theories: Origins, methods, and uses in the mass media* (2nd ed.). New York: Longman.

Stacks, D. W., Hickson, M. L., & Hill, S. R. (1991). *An introduction to communication theory*. Dallas, TX: Holt, Rinehart & Winston.

Stacks, D. W., & Hocking, J. E. (1992). *Essentials of communication research*. New York: HarperCollins.

Springsteen, B. (1992). 57 channels (and nothin' on). *On human touch* [compact disk]. New York: Columbia.

Tichenor, P. J., & McLeod, D. M. (1989). The logic of social and behavioral science. In G. H. Stempel, III, & B. H. Westley (Eds.), *Research methods in mass communication* (pp. 19–29). New York: Prentice-Hall.

Westley, B. H. (1958). Journalism research and scientific method: II. *Journalism Quarterly, 35*, 307–316.

2

Thinking About Theory

Steven H. Chaffee[1]
Stanford University

Theorizing about human communication is a very common human activity. We could not live effective lives if we did not formulate, and act upon, general suppositions about why people say what they say, for example, or how what we say affects other people. Indeed, understanding communication has such obvious survival value that one might imagine theorizing to be a genetically inherited propensity throughout our species.

Research on human communication, on the other hand, is a rare activity, one that requires a number of intellectual skills that are developed only through academic discipline. Basic to almost all of these skills is the decidedly uncommon activity of *theorizing for research*. That is the subject of this chapter; to a great extent it is the purpose of this entire book.

Most readers will be familiar with two meanings of *theory*: theory as abstract ideas and theory as predictable findings. Neither of these quite describes the underlying process of theorizing as it will be described here. This chapter will emphasize a third meaning, one built around concept explication—a kind of thinking that connects the

[1]The author is indebted to Richard F. Carter, Jack M. McLeod, and Byron Reeves for many of the ideas underlying this chapter. Among those who commented helpfully on an earlier draft are Ben Detenber, Glenn Leshner, Dennis Kinsey, Jim Coyl, Bob Meeds, Andrew Mendelsohn, Ekaterina Ognianova, Jane B. Singer, and Charlie Wood.

other two notions of theory to one another. These three interconnected ideas are diagrammed in Fig. 2.1. The terms in boxes represent the elements of one's theory, and the terms outside the boxes (in italics) represent one's theorizing.

THEORY AS ABSTRACT IDEAS

The most popular meaning of "theory" in this field is an abstract scheme of thought about communication. The ancient tradition of rhetorical theory provides many examples. Media criticism, based on abstract suppositions about how communication ought to serve society, provides more. Professional "rules of thumb" about how best to design a newspaper, to concoct a TV commercial, or to tell a joke, are also theories in this sense. In each of these examples, theorizing involves imagined events; observing these events is not as a rule deemed necessary. Observation is, though, the main business of empirical research, and it takes us to the second meaning of "theory."

THEORY AS PREDICTABLE FINDINGS.

In the academic field of communication research, the term "theory" is sometimes applied to a consistent research result. This is a positivist view of knowledge, favored by cataloguers of findings such as Berelson and Steiner (1964). For example, studies indicate reliably different patterns of communication behavior in relation to knowledge among people located in different socioeconomic strata. Individuals who do not know much about an issue are unlikely to seek information about it, for instance, but when an argument reaches them they may be more readily persuaded than are those with a stronger backlog of knowledge. Researchers use replicated findings like these to predict what to expect in a new study, and professional communicators use them in planning how to communicate with different publics.

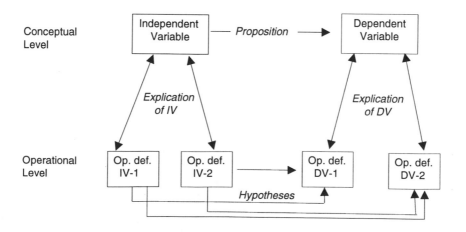

FIG. 2.1.   A schematic view of theorizing.

Concept explication comes into play at this point, where predictable findings from past studies are compared with the abstract terms of a general theory. Are the two related? This kind of question requires us to theorize. The answers determine where our research will lead in the long run.

To connect predictable results to abstract notions requires some assumptions, the most basic of which is that both kinds of theory should relate to the same phenomena. We assume not only that generalizable principles about communication exist, but that they can be studied directly and expressed in a common language if we work hard enough to achieve it.[2] The ongoing linkage between the intellectual world of abstract theory and the observable world of replicable findings is called *empirical theory*.

Within the framework of empirical theory, there are both horizontal and vertical connections (represented by arrows in Fig. 2.1). Each of these entails a different kind of thinking. The horizontal connection—the *proposition*—refers to thinking at the *conceptual level*. It involves both abstract concepts and a relationship between them. For example, John Milton and Thomas Jefferson, in arguing for freedom of expression, asserted in somewhat different terms that "truth will [win] out" (Milton, 1949) if opposing beliefs are allowed to contest freely in "the marketplace of ideas." Translating this into the language of research, a policy of constraint versus freedom to express contrasting viewpoints is an independent variable (it is manipulated as either constraint or freedom), and the emergence of truth is a dependent variable (it is observed or measured for the effect of that policy on it). The mental arrow connecting the two is a causal (albeit rather hazy) one. The argument, though, is almost purely rhetorical, not intended to be tested in a scientific sense.[3]

At the bottom of Fig. 2.1 is a second set of horizontal lines representing the parallel proposition but at the *operational level*. Here, replicable findings enter the picture; a theory should presumably produce a reliable result in the real world, or we should not have much use for it. In mainstream communication research, however, mere findings are not considered theories in themselves. Rather they are physical operations (either observations or manipulations), designed to indicate variation in the more abstract ideas postulated at the conceptual level. That is, the observable phenomena at the operational level are only part of one's theorizing and then only to the extent that they are connected to abstract concepts. Predicted relationships between operational definitions are called *hypotheses*. When a hypothesis has been deduced from a larger proposition, research to test the hypothesis can be interpreted as a test of the larger proposition as well. A major purpose of theorizing, then, is to foster hypothesis-testing research; communication scientists try to design studies that bear upon questions that go beyond the literal limits of their evidence.

---

[2]This is not always so. For some aspects of communication, there may be no general principles to discover, or they may be so abstract as to elude observation or verbal expression. An assumption is not a fact, just an untested premise that we accept for the time being; it enables us to proceed in a line of inquiry. If research based on one assumption produces no consistent results, and hence no generalization, it is sensible to discard it and start anew. Kuhn (1970) notes that anomalous results in a program of research lead to a shift from one scientific paradigm to an alternative set of assumptions.

[3]President Thomas Jefferson, who considered himself a scientific thinker, claimed to have empirical evidence that supported the theory. In his Second Inaugural address (1984) he praised the American people for "the discernment they have manifested between truth and falsehood." The public, he asserted, "may safely be trusted to hear everything true and false, and to form a correct judgment between them."

These assumptions about concepts, their operational definitions, and the parallel propositions and hypotheses in a complex theoretical scheme, are generally accepted among empirical scientists who study communication processes.[4] The outlines of Fig. 2.1 should be discernible to the reader throughout this book, although the terms and empirical content of concepts and hypotheses will vary from chapter to chapter.

Fig. 2.1 also calls attention to the vertical arrows, which represent *explication* of the concepts and their operational definitions. The diagram is drawn in causal form, with arrows indicating which idea leads to which. Horizontally, theory-building and theory-testing both lead logically from the independent (causal) variable on the left, to the dependent (criterion) variable on the right. Vertically, the arrows lead in both directions because—over time—that is how explication works for the researcher. While later chapters are concerned mainly with causal propositions and hypotheses, this chapter concentrates more on the ongoing dialectic between a communication variable's conceptual and operational manifestations.

When an empirical scholar theorizes about communication, thinking can run upward *or* downward. Often one begins by reading about and discussing an idea and then thinks downward toward operational definitions. After some research on these measures, the scholar may rethink the conceptual meaning in light of new findings. In writing these ideas into a research report, it is common to reinterpret the research literature, seeing matters with sharpened eyes. Research, then, is not so much the production of a single study as it is an engagement of the researcher in a long-term commitment to imagine, and then try to find out, what is going on when humans communicate with one another. The reciprocating arrows running up and down in Fig. 2.1 represent this continuing activity.

AN EXAMPLE: VIDEO GAMES AND VIOLENCE

To make things more concrete, let's use Fig. 2.1 as an outline to theorize and study a communication process. Consider the possible effects of violence in video games, a topic of current public concern. Most people come to this topic by observing disturbing amounts of violence—in both video games and daily life. The idea of doing research, and thereby doing some good as well, has occurred to quite a few communication researchers. How to proceed?

Organized thinking usually begins at the conceptual level. A first step (as indicated by the first downward arrow) might be to analyze what is meant by "violence" and "video games," and then to look for operational definitions. The beginning of a definition might, for example, emerge from an inventory of current video games on the market, grouping games into different types and noting the extent to which each involves violence. Surveys of manufacturers, of game stores or arcades, or of young people who play a lot of video games, could provide a starting point. This early empirical work should, in turn, lead back up to a clarified conceptual definition of the independent variable. Now that we have examined a fair amount of the violence in video games, just what does it mean?

---

[4]These assumptions are not shared throughout the entire academic field of communication. Some empiricists stay very close to their data, and trust only replicable findings, not more general theories. More commonly, many theorists do not intend their writings to be subjected to empirical testing. Indeed, many scholars do not accept the premise that communication phenomena follow lawful patterns at all. Because they make radically different starting assumptions, they conduct research that is markedly distinct in nature from what is described in this chapter.

We probably cannot observe the "content" of a video game without playing it—without experiencing the game directly. (Indeed, an attempt to classify video game content might lead to the conclusion that video games do not themselves "contain" violence, but they do bring violent experiences into their players' lives.) From our experience, and from discussing similar experiences with other players, an intuitive sense of some possible effects of violent video games might emerge. After playing such a game for a time, a person may feel different: perhaps a bit energized, perhaps tired, perhaps hostile, perhaps happy or relieved of cares, and so forth. Grounded in players' reports of these self-observations (at the operational level), as the investigators, we might begin to conceptualize one or more possible effects of interest, as represented by Fig. 2.1's right-side upward arrows.

Next comes some reading of a relevant literature, such as child psychology, on postulated effects. Prior studies have tested such theorized processes as arousal, social learning, catharsis, and disinhibition, in relation to television and film violence. What have they found? We might next design an experiment to test a proposition about the arousing, or modeling, or cathartic, or disinhibiting, effect of playing violent video games as compared with non-violent alternatives. Laboratory procedures contrived to observe these effects would represent added downward arrows on the right-hand side of Fig. 2.1 which by now can be regarded as outlining the dynamic general process of theorizing and not just the video game-aggressiveness cycle.

Research is of course much more complicated than this. Indeed, the example here, of effects of violent video games, has been successfully pursued by only a few investigators to date. This chapter aims to ease the process of research, by breaking down the steps represented by the vertical arrows in Fig. 2.1.

ANOTHER EXAMPLE: GENDER AND FAMILY INTERACTION

To explore how concept explication proceeds, let's consider a more universal example. Most of us as we grow up become conscious of interacting differently with our mothers and our fathers. As we reflect upon this difference, we begin to theorize, trying to generalize our family experience to the world beyond the home. We may decide that our interaction patterns are due to age differences, or role relationships, or gender. Each conception refers to a different interpretation outside one's own family—that is, it implies a different kind of theory.

As we begin the process of research, each theory points us in a distinct direction for study. We are no longer considering the totality of our own communication with our parents, but the specific concept of, say, gender effects on interaction *as it applies to everyone*. The researcher who selects gender interaction as a domain of inquiry will soon discover a large number of prior studies, a number of competing conceptualizations, and some conflicting or anomalous (i.e., nonreplicated) findings. (Once we focus on a limited domain, this wealth of viewpoints stimulates theorizing, although at first it may be disconcerting.) Another researcher, looking instead at age as the critical concept for theorizing about parent–child interaction patterns, would read a different set of results and theoretical explanations, and conduct a different kind of study. As we move beyond our own parents and personal experience, the naive theorist is succeeded by the disciplined investigator.

At home watching television, we may notice *varieties of interaction.* The television set in the living room displays more instances of communication between parents and children, which could also be ascribed to gender (or to age). The whole household may share in watching a popular situation comedy that features families and their problems, an experience that could provide inspiration for several different studies. We might examine sex-role differentiation in television, and compare it to real life. Does television portray family interaction patterns accurately? This question could lead to a separate survey of how people typically interact at home, for comparison. Or we might study whether homes where a particular situation comedy is often watched conform more closely to the television norm than do households where there is less exposure to this television model. Another research direction might be to interview people regarding the extent to which they see television families as the norm. Do they take television as reality, or as fiction? (A likely answer: "some of both.") Next, research could attempt to relate these perceptions to expectations within each family, regarding the behavior of different members.

What is going on in these sketchy (and sometimes fanciful) examples is an ongoing interplay between ideas and real-world studies. This entire process, including the seminal idea, the literature review, the research, and the hypotheses, constitutes theorizing. Let's look at this process more carefully, considering how a single concept evolves.

CONCEPT EXPLICATION

Most students new to research would like to work toward completing a project, such as a thesis or research report. In theorizing, though, one does not simply begin at a clearly marked starting point, proceed through a series of discrete steps, and eventually finish. Self-contained reports, such as theses and journal articles, flow from one's research; but in a rich program of study, the background work of theorizing is never finished, and each stage impinges on others. Nonetheless, it is possible to describe some definable phases in thinking through one's plan for a study, a process usually called *concept explication.*[5] The following sequence orients the beginner whose immediate goal is to get some results worth reporting.

Preliminary Identification. Before we can do much with an idea, it needs a name. Most often, of course, the chosen concept already has a name (or several) in the literature. Sometimes, though, current usage proves inadequate, and a new or modified name is needed. Results of communication research are presented mostly via words, and the ideas a word represents should remain consistent throughout a program of study.[6] Disciplined use of words encourages other scholars to employ the same terminology so that a growing body of research can be cumulative. Identification of a concept by giving it a preliminary name is a key starting point.

McCombs and Shaw (1972), for example, launched a major subfield of mass communication research when they coined the term "agenda setting." The same idea had been broached as "status conferral" by Lazarsfeld and Merton (1948), who lumped

---

[5]For a philosophical anlaysis of explication primarily in the physical sciences, consult Hempel (1952). Regarding its applicability to communication research, see Chaffee (1991).

[6]Research is often presented with numerical entries in tables, but a number is of little interest outside the confines of a specific study unless it is connected to a concept.

effects on the "status of an issue" with the more commonplace idea of the social "status of an individual." As a result the theory that media coverage can elevate the political importance of an *issue* escaped most students of media effects, until McCombs and Shaw revived it under a new name. It is important, when choosing the label for a new idea, to school yourself in the way people use the terms under consideration.

New ideas are often identified by novel usages of terms already in common use within the field. There is no rule of thumb, except to devise a working title that you can easily use to explain what you have in mind and how it differs from other, more familiar concepts. Sometimes this is best accomplished by resurrecting an obscure or archaic term, such as "heterophily" (Rogers, 1983). Sometimes acronyms, which use the first letter of each word in a technical phrase to create a memorable abbreviated "word,", can be devised—often with a touch of whimsy. An example is the method called signaled stopping technique (SST), introduced by researchers at the University of Washington (Carter, Ruggels, Jackson, & Heffner, 1973) about the time a Seattle aircraft plant lost a huge contract to build a supersonic transport (also SST).

An oxymoron (a combination of words that are mutually contradictory) can stimulate thought about relationships between its constituent terms. Examples include such phrases as "public opinion" and "mass communication," which juxtapose macroscopic and microscopic referents. Oxymorons do not lend themselves to clear explication, which would expose their inherent ambiguities. But an oxymoron can provide a distinctive rubric to describe a subfield of research. For example, "attitude change" mixes the idea of change with the term "attitude," normally defined as a stable motivational trait, to emphasize the difficulty of bringing about this kind of change. The analogous term "opinion change" does not evoke the same sense of persuasive power, because opinions are imagined as less deep-rooted, fixed, and emotional than attitudes (Hovland, Janis, & Kelley, 1953).

Another approach is to accept a popular term in the communication industry, but to explicate it from a new perspective. Steuer (1992), for example, showed that the oxymoron "virtual reality" can direct a coherent program of research if it is conceptualized as a perception of the person rather than a technological device.

Occasionally in science a concept comes to be known by the name of its discoverer or inventor. This eponymic honor is usually bestowed by usage among colleagues, not by oneself. Osgood (1952) may have missed his chance at immortality by giving his data collection tool the unique (and somehow euphonious) name, the "semantic differential." Likert (1932), less elegantly, entitled his rather similar procedure "summated ratings"—and it is known to practically everyone today as a "Likert scale."

The point is that a good deal of care should go into choosing of a name for one's concept, devising a label that is both distinctive and memorable. A considerable number of poor choices have been made over the years; the ideas involved have often been lost along with their names. The first task of concept naming, however, is not salesmanship but focusing attention on the essential features of the idea as you develop it into a tool for your own research. Tichenor, Olien, and Donohue's (1970) term "knowledge gap," which refers to effects of communication on variance (rather than central tendency) in a social system, is not just a felicitous catch-phrase. It pithily calls attention to a potential societal dysfunction, and has been used to organize dozens of innovative studies (Rogers, 1976).

Preliminary Definition.   Explication involves more than simply looking a term up in a dictionary, or tracing its etymology, although those are useful early steps.[7] For research, we need to study the ways other researchers have been using the concept—what they mean by it, and how it is represented in their studies. At this point we are leaving the world of common language, and joining a discipline of scholars who make distinctions that are not required in everyday usage.

Because a communication concept is likely to be rich in meanings, explication itself involves hypotheses. That is, an empirical definition is itself a kind of proposition, one that is tested at an early stage in a research program. The everyday phrase "attention to television," for example, is represented by very different operational definitions in experiments on psychophysiological responses (Reeves, Thorson, & Schleuder, 1986) and field surveys on cumulative learning (Chaffee & Schleuder, 1986). In a laboratory experiment, *a participant's attention elicited by a televised stimulus* is largely reflexive and automatic, dictated by the immediate situation. Survey researchers, on the other hand, ask how much *a respondent pays attention while watching television* habitually over time. Entirely   different research procedures are used when investigators are studying these different conceptions of attention in television viewing, and the theories in question are if anything even more different. The fact that "attention" or "watching television" might be indistinguishable verbally does not mean that they refer to the same kinds of human events in the two research traditions. Nonetheless, the survey questioning method is useful to validate the laboratory manipulation (Reeves et al, 1986).

Communication research makes special demands on our conceptual tools because much of what we mean by "communication" is not observed directly; it is imagined. In the last example, for instance, the difference between attention one voluntarily pays to television, and that which is elicited even from an unmotivated viewer, is not directly observable; it is inferred based upon distinct theories and supportive evidence.

Some components of the communication process can, however, be experienced directly. We can for example keep track of the words we say or read, and of the reactions we and others have to them. These real-life experiences are *percepts*, meaning that we perceive them in ourselves and others. They provide the raw data for our theorizing about communication in broader ways. If we had no concrete percepts, it would be hard to imagine doing communication research at all. Concepts connect percepts, which everyone has, to theories, which communication scientists build and test.

Observation.   Like everyone else, students of communication spend a great deal of time observing human activity. But we would never learn much new about communication by simply observing what goes on naturally around us. Communication scholars go to extraordinary efforts to gather evidence that would not otherwise enter their lives. I have at times noted my colleagues and students engaged in these kinds of activities; although they do not seem bizarre to me, they might to a visitor not used to communication research work:

---

[7]A dictionary tells what the term means in popular usage. An unabridged dictionary gives its specialized meanings in some esoteric contexts. An etymology indicates the purposes the word served when people invented it, and when others adapted it to new meanings.

- Reading through very old newspapers, keeping a careful record of statements of a certain kind.
- Hiding behind a one-way mirror, observing children watching television.
- Editing a video presentation that incorporates material from several different sources, to be shown to college students in an experimental laboratory.
- Calling randomly selected telephone numbers, and asking the adult who has had the most recent birthday what she thinks about a current news issue.
- Sitting in the corner of a meeting room, making tallies of who says what to whom, in a group brought together to work on a contrived problem.

The reader should by this point recognize these procedures as *operational definitions*, or, more exactly, as operations whose purpose is to satisfy requirements set forth in a definition. Each has been painstakingly arranged because the investigator thinks of it as representing some more general concept, not because the evidence being gathered would be terribly important in and of itself. Communication researchers spend much of their workdays defining their concepts operationally. Digging through archives, coding messages, running participants through an experiment, and interviewing respondents in a survey, are all time consuming. But a thousand hours spent categorizing utterances of husbands on TV, or measuring the pulse rates of sophomores who are being shown an erotic film, or asking people how they decided which way to vote, may be pointless if the resultant data do not serve a conceptual purpose. Explication can save many wasted hours. Theorizing, although it may be challenging, is certainly more pleasant work than most data collection activities.

Primitive and Derived Terms.   Conceptualization is built of words, and we must find the best place to start building. At some point in the explication process, it is useful to consider which terms are *primitive*, words that we take as commonly understood, or as givens (Hempel, 1952). The existence and acceptability of these few concepts are assumed, which means they are not questioned within the program of research that is built upon them.[8]

Primitive terms differ at various levels of analysis. Commonly, one essential given is the individual. To get on with our work, we usually assume that we know what a person is when we see one.[9] Some branches of communication research also assume the existence of supra-individual entities, such as families or communities or organizations or societies. These terms are often *derived* from the primitive term "person." That is, some researchers define an organization, say, as a combination of persons with specific boundary conditions added.[10] Similarly, the term "word" is often treated as a primitive term, and concepts like "sentence" or "message" are then derived from it.

---

[8]In other words, the primitive terms of an established tradition may very well be challenged. Kuhn's (1970) concept of a paradigm shift to a new scientific tradition could be described as a rejection of one set of primitive terms, and their replacement with a new set.

[9]The conceptual and operational definition of "human being" can be quite controversial in some fields, such as zoology or medical ethics. Scientists attempting to define the beginning or end of life, or the distinctions among higher primates, use a different set of primitive terms from those employed in communication research.

Time, and space, are also common primitive terms. We conventionally define people in relation to one another in these terms, such as saying that *two people together* constitutes a "couple." The term "together" here refers to juxtaposition in time and space; two people must be together in one place for a reasonably long time before we consider them a couple. Time and space are conveniences, and we would be foolish to expend a lot of time and effort on their definition. They would then cease to be convenient.[11] Explication includes stating the assumptions made about primitive terms and the terms derived from them for our convenience.

Validity.   Validity is the most general criterion of communication research. When we operationalize a concept, we try to evaluate its validity in terms of our explication. That is, does the operational definition represent the concept as we have defined it? Are we measuring what we intend to measure?

The same question applies to theory testing. When we test a hypothesis (a particular statement relating two operational definitions) to what extent does it represent a valid test of the more general proposition relating the two concepts? Explication relating each concept to its operational definition is central to this evaluation of a theory via hypothesis testing.[12]

The distinction between internal and external validity (Campbell & Stanley, 1966) can be applied to both the measurement of a single concept and the testing of a theory involving two or more concepts. Internal validity refers to what is done, what is found, and what is inferred *within a single study.* Has each concept been operationalized in a way that is reliable and appropriate to its explication? Has the hypothesis been tested so that alternative explanations for the findings have been ruled out?

External validity refers to the *generalizability* of a particular study to other settings, times, or units of study (e.g., persons). Is each operationalization consistent with the larger universe of measures that might represent the concept in question? Are inferences from a study applicable to conditions other than those which obtain in it? In theorizing such questions are considered in connection with research evidence from each study.

Reliability.   Reliability is a statistical criterion for evaluating the usefulness of an operational procedure. It refers to the replicability of a result across a series of observations or studies. Whereas validity refers to the relationship between the conceptual definition and its operational definition, reliability has to do with operational definitions. In practice, research procedures to maximize reliability sometimes do so at some expense to validity; this is a matter of balance: Some degree of reliability is necessary to validity.

---

[10]In other studies, though, an organization may simply be treated as a primitive term without saying exactly who or what comprises it.

[11]In some sciences, including some areas of communication science, considerable effort is given over to explication of time or space (e.g., Kline, 1978).

[12]"Validity" does not mean "truth," and truth is not a criterion for communication research. We usually intend our propositions to be true, but only after surviving many tests might a scientific statement come to be accepted as lawful. Very few communication theories ever reach this status. Truth is not so hard to abandon in explication as it is in other aspects of theorizing, however. Most of us can accept the assumption that there is no *true* definition for a concept, no one operationalization that *truly* represents the abstract concept best.

For example, consider the problem of measuring people's use of radio news. One possible question wording is, "Did you listen to news on the radio yesterday?" This is likely to produce fairly reliable reports, because most people can remember yesterday clearly. But that reliable item might not be especially valid as an indicator of a given person's habits; yesterday might have been an unusual day, either for the person or in the news. On the other hand, many people listen to radio news only when commuting to work; if they happen to be interviewed on a Sunday about listening "yesterday" they will report not listening, even though they may do so five days a week. If radio-listening habits are the focus of one's research interest, a more valid question might be, "How many days a week do you typically listen to news on the radio?" The person may not have the long-term recall and mathematical skills to give a precisely correct (i.e., highly reliable) answer, yet the vaguer measure might be more useful for the researcher.

Validity is evaluated in terms of one's explication, whereas reliability can be estimated for any operational procedure whether it represents a larger concept or not. The explication of a concept, in turn, is located within the larger theoretical structure outlined in Fig. 2.1. What this means in the example of radio news listening is that the choice between a highly specific question ("yesterday") and a more general question ("typically") depends on how the measure is to be employed. If the study's purpose is a descriptive survey, the "yesterday" question is probably preferable, because across a large number of responses random effects such as days of the week and other specific circumstances tend to average out. That is, the aggregate data yield the best (most reliable) estimate of what typically occurs. If the purpose is to test hypotheses about other variables that might predict radio listening, or about possible effects of radio news on individuals, then the more general measure that estimates most validly the typical radio use of each individual may be preferable.

Unit of Analysis.   A basic question that can be surprisingly tricky is, "For what class of entities does this concept vary?" Is it an attribute of individual persons, of aggregates such as communities or nations, of messsages, of events, or of some other unit? Units of analysis should be the ones talked about in your theorizing and the ones that are observed and described in empirical work. Inconsistency in the unit of analysis is a common error in communication research. On the one hand, it is risky to draw psychological inferences about individuals from observing patterns in aggregates, a practice often called the "ecological fallacy." Conversely, there are pitfalls in treating aggregated individual observations as if they represent some higher-order entity, as is done in polling when a large number of personal interviews are combined to say something about "the public's" opinion.

Study of media audiences is plagued by shifting units of analysis. A newspaper is almost always read by one person at a time, but television sets tend to be viewed by several people at once; it is very difficult to calibrate the two activities on a common scale. Newspaper or magazine circulation is usually calculated by the number of copies that are sold; as a rule the number that are read is lower, and the total number of readers is higher. Television ratings are calculated by household, and include such attributes as "woman aged 18–49" without much evidence that the woman so described watches television, or the specific program in question. Advertising is planned at the level of the market, which may be a local newspaper's circulation zone, a radio station's signal range, or a television network's specific segment of the national market.

These shifts in units of analysis cause few problems for the media marketing industry, which is mainly interested in reliable descriptive data. So long as numbers are compiled in the same way from place to place and from month to month, they can be compared across space or time. One can determine, for example, if newspaper reading is declining, or if more people watch television on weeknights than on weekends. But shifting units of analysis create difficulties in theorizing, when a researcher tries to match audience figures to some motivation or media effect. A common unit for television viewing is time spent with the medium, for example, but if that metric were applied to the newspaper a slow reader might be ranked above someone who has actually processed more words but in a shorter time. Using words as the unit of analysis for television, on the other hand, misses much of what TV, a rich audio visual medium, provides. Comparing the relative impact of these different media is similarly difficult. For example, if we ask whether the newspaper or television has greater impact on voters, should this be tested using time spent, or words processed, or some other method of assessing the independent variable? When the unit of analysis changes from one concept to another in the same theoretical structure, theory testing becomes very slippery business.

Relationship to Time.   Another basic query in theorizing concerns time. If a concept is an attribute of individuals, does it vary across persons at a given point in time (cross-sectional variance), or across times for a given person (process variance)? "Attitude," for example, is a cross-sectional concept whereas "attitude change" is a process concept. Many social attitudes do not seem to change within the same individual, so they are of limited applicability for theorizing and research on communication processes. Fear of crime is cross-sectionally correlated with heavy television use, for instance, but that does not guarantee that depriving a person of television would allay his fear of being a crime victim. In theorizing, it is essential to keep the many cross-sectional findings separate from the rarer studies in which process variance (change) has actually been observed. Experimental tests are generally preferred for effects hypotheses because time is controlled by the experimenter, and differences can be unambiguously attributed to processes set in motion by the communication intervention.

Many concepts are attributes of a social aggregate, rather than individual units of analysis. Examples that are sometimes related to communication factors include presidential popularity, crime rates, and fashions. These may vary across time either because individual members of the aggregate are changing ("process variance"), or because they are being replaced by new members who are different ("invasion and succession") even though no individual has changed. In the latter situation, causal theorizing may not be applicable. Newspaper reading, for example, has gradually declined in the United States as new generations reared on television have entered adulthood; the change in the aggregate has not been much due to any tendency for individuals to abandon their newspaper habits, but rather to a disinclination among young people to start reading. Hence, attempts to explain "why people are dropping the newspaper" miss the mark; very few individuals are doing that, so there are no reasons why. It is also instructive that, while newspaper reading is positively correlated cross-sectionally with people's education levels, the historical decline in readership has occurred even while the median level of education among American adults has increased by nearly two years. To account for the decline, then, requires more than a set of individual-level predictor variables.

LITERATURE REVIEW

One of the most ominous terms one encounters upon entering a field of research is *review of the literature*. In the long run, literature search does involve a good deal of work—searching out relevant studies, reading them, and synthesizing them into a coherent whole. But it is better characterized as a number of episodes of literature-searching; not all of this is done at any one time, and certainly not all of it is completed before we begin theorizing in anticipation of our own study.[13] While many good research ideas occur when we are reading other people's research, theorizing usually begins before much effort is put into a broad-scale search for related studies. Explication can help to bound a search on a concept, by sorting out those few writings that deal with the idea being developed.

Once a concept is defined preliminarily, reading studies related to it becomes a surprisingly pleasant and rewarding phase of research. The trick is to skim quickly past articles that involve the term being used but not the same meaning, at the same time looking for research involving the concept even though the name is not the same. Occasionally a very rich review of a literature closely related to the concept of interest is found. The bibliography of a well-crafted research article or book chapter can provide an excellent start.

Failure to find prior syntheses of research literature may be either a good sign or a bad one. If the reason that no one has previously analyzed research on a concept is that it is a novel idea, that can be heartening. It suggests that you may be on to something new and different—a scholar's ideal. But the absence of prior research may instead mean that the concept has not been very fruitful for other investigators; if so, you could be heading into a blind alley. In any event, it is helpful in constructing an analysis of the literature to know what, if anything, has been done on the subject by others with an idea that is similar to your own.

Meaning Analysis.   It is not necessary—nor possible—to track down every existing study. But a literature review will be more productive if you find examples of the full *variety* of meanings of your concept that communication scholars use. A good exercise at this stage in theorizing is to sort out the various meanings and terms into groups. Some usages may be discarded early on, but sometimes the category system itself can be a theoretical analysis. Linz and Malamuth (1993), for example, were able to organize an immense variety of studies by keying on three terms that at first blush might seem to refer to the same kind of messages: *obscenity*, *pornography*, and *erotica*.

---

[13]Published research articles and unpublished dissertations are organized to be read in a logical sequence, and hence give the impression that the work they describe was performed in the same sequence. This is almost never the case. The origination point of most communication research, if it could be located in the final published report, would be typically found 30% to 40% of the way into the text.

They found that each of these terms tends to be favored within one of three distinct intellectual traditions, which they called conservative-moralist, feminist, and liberal, respectively. This meaning analysis enabled them to compare the three traditions and to identify more subtle distinctions in theorizing and research generated from each viewpoint. It also served to pinpoint the distinctly feminist context of their own experiments on effects of pornography.

Operational Contingencies.   A literature review can organize studies alongside one another and explore differences among them. This becomes more possible as the literature review proceeds and focuses on details of those findings most relevant to your theorizing. This is done through attention to operational contingencies.

Each study in the published literature has been conducted under specific conditions, such as its historical time, place, and research method. These are necessary contingencies for doing the study at all; they constrain the operational definition of a concept in each instance. Theorizing ordinarily extends well beyond a specific measure in a particular context. For example, an investigation of the capacity of television to inform people finds very different operational measures of information in studies of politics versus health practices, and different results with children versus adults. Sorting out the literature in terms of these operational contingencies helps you comprehend the potential range of measures, and to adjudicate conflicting findings. Television news exposure is, for example, consistently found to be a strong correlate of political knowledge in studies of children and adolescents (Atkin, 1981), but only rarely in surveys of adults (McLeod & McDonald, 1985). Information encountered in a political campaign is less likely to be accepted than is information from a public health campaign. These study differences can become an important part of theorizing about the more general phenomenon.

Operational contingencies vary between studies, but they are usually not variables within a given study. To take advantage of them, organize the literature review according to those operational features that seem to make a difference in results. This kind of literature review can produce hypotheses based on between-studies variables. For example, Martin, McNelly, and Izcaray (1976) examined more than a dozen surveys of mass media use in western hemisphere nations. They found some studies reporting high correlations between use of various mass media and the person's education and income. In a second group of studies, education and income were not correlated with film attendance, nor with radio nor TV use. When the literature was divided in this way the first set of studies turned out to be almost entirely rural surveys, and the second group all urban. This led to an empirical analysis comparing urban dwellers who had recently moved to the city versus those who had always lived there; the results for these two subsamples paralleled those in the two groups of prior studies, which in turn helped them to clarify the meaning of the entire literature on the subject of socioeconomic status (SES) and media use.

Identification of operational contingencies that affect relationships between concepts is a product of synthesis, not just of reading and abstracting each study. Simply to paraphrase an unorganized string of studies one at a time, or even to group research reports in terms of their general conclusions, will not help identify operational contingencies that divide a literature.

Synthesis.   A literature review often becomes a study in itself. Some of the most useful advances in communication research have been analytic literature reviews. Rogers's monumental volume *Diffusion of Innovations* (1964, 1983), for example, began as the literature review section of his doctoral dissertation. By organizing and synthesizing thousands of studies of diffusion around a set of conceptual distinctions and empirical generalizations, Rogers founded an entire subdiscipline within communication research. His literature analysis became the main product of his theorizing, enabling other scholars to locate their specific diffusion studies in a larger theoretical context.

Empirical Definition.   The continuing process of theorizing is a kind of working understanding with oneself that both guides the literature review and prevents it from going on indefinitely. In practice the scholar begins by reading a few studies, then moves to explication, refines the preliminary definition, and returns to the literature search with a sharper definition. To read in advance the entire body of work loosely connected to a topic is usually much too time consuming to be practical. Explication helps to restrict efforts to those studies relevant to the concept being formulated—and only those studies.

Empirical definition is accomplished by gradually developing *rules of inclusion and exclusion.* That is, abstract meanings become translated, through empirical research, into statements of the conditions required by the explicated concept. Festinger (1957), for example, experimented for a number of years on the concept of cognitive dissonance. He viewed dissonance as conceptually similar to the overlapping concept called cognitive conflict, but the two conditions led to different theoretical predictions for communication behavior. Eventually he concluded that the boundary between the two was the making of a decision; specifically, conflict became defined as pre-decisional and dissonance as post-decisional (Festinger, 1964). This helped him to adjudicate the literature and focus his students on either dissonance or conflict without confusing the two streams of research.

EMPIRICAL STUDY

There is no clear cut demarcation between literature analysis and empirical study. Conceptual ideas continue to change throughout a program of research; surprising results should generate a revised interpretation of the prior literature. New theorizing is as important to this process as are new findings.

Once a scholar has collected a set of data, there is a tendency to become exclusively operational in one's thinking. If you do so, bear in mind that the larger goal is to use your data to advance your theorizing. Given the centrality of concept explication to this process, it makes sense to begin by considering each variable in its own right.

Univariate Analysis.   Presuming one has in hand a synthesis of the research literature on one's concept, the first empirical step is univariate analysis. In content analysis and survey research, and no less for dependent variables in controlled experiments, descriptive statistics such as the mean, variance, skewness, and reliability of each measure deserve careful examination. Even here we are in a sense testing hypotheses by comparing what we find to what others have found with similar measures in prior studies. Are the estimates of communication activity higher, or lower, than expected? Is the distribution of values normal, so that you can safely use the variable in correlational analyses? Does the range seem more restricted than you expected based on prior studies? How does the measure vary across time, and how might this affect the kinds of theories you should relate it to?

These operational questions are more closely related to theorizing than they might appear. Communication process theories are often couched in extensive terms that assume that every variable covers a wide range of possible values across units of analysis, and for the same unit over time. For example, the hypothesis, "Increased exposure to television violence heightens tendencies toward aggressive behavior," assumes that a person's television violence exposure and her aggressiveness can both increase. The companion formulation, "Decreased exposure reduces aggressive tendencies" assumes that both can go down. But do they? Very few studies empirically examine individuals whose habitual exposure to televised violence changes significantly, up or down; television use is a habit that is constrained by lifestyle, by preferences of others watching television in the same household, and by what is available to watch. These constraints in turn limit theorizing, or at least force the theorist to be more specific as to precisely what proposition is at stake and how much to expect of evidence bearing on an ambitious hypothesis.

Bivariate Analysis.   The next step in data analysis, and hence in theorizing, is to look for variables that are associated empirically with each measure of interest. This should be arranged in parallel with a literature review section on the same correlates. Prior research can indicate two kinds of correlates: within each study and across studies. Correlations within studies are usually reported as such, whereas only the person reviewing the literature is in a position to note patterns across studies.

One common bivariate question is whether indicators of SES correlate in a consistent way with a particular form of communication. Many media use studies, for example, report correlations with education, income, or occupational status. New data can be evaluated in this context: Have you found roughly the same patterns of correlations as in prior studies? Most present U.S. surveys find SES negatively correlated with time spent watching television. But in some developing countries the reverse is true—the television set is a luxury only the well-to-do can afford; indeed, that was also the case in the United States in the early 1950s. Even though theorizing about television's effects may not involve consideration of the person's SES, it is important to know how the two measures correlate to compare the tests to others' findings. Thus, we should keep SES factors in mind when theorizing about the specific process of interest if testing hypotheses with contemporary U.S. data. Empirical measures are affected by the social structure in which the data are collected; such contextual factors may need to be controlled in statistical analysis.

The seemingly inconsistent pattern of SES–television correlations across the history of empirical studies can be described by considering bivariate and univariate relationships together. When television use is very low (i.e., few people in the society have access to television reception), the SES–television correlation should be positive. As the mean level rises (i.e., as television use diffuses throughout the society), the correlation gradually flattens and then reverses. When almost everyone can watch television, it tends to be used most heavily by those in the lower socioeconomic brackets. The same historical pattern would probably be found for almost any major technological innovation, from the sewing machine to the typewriter to the word processor. Initially these "new toys" are prized possessions of the elite few, in homes of the rich and offices of supervisors. Eventually, though, they become work stations, often symbolic of the low estate of women in the work force. Evidence on such a general proposition regarding the social meaning of technological innovations is very unlikely to be shown within any single study. It is offered here more as conjecture than as an established finding, to remind the reader that theorizing persists long after even a great deal of research has seemingly been completed.

Construct Validation.   Ultimately one asks not just that an operational definition work in a loose pragmatic sense, but that it work the way one's theorizing has predicted. This is a question that arises rather late in a program of research. Successful theory testing is, however, far from the end of one's efforts. If a suspect measure "works" for your purposes better than a measure you felt passed all interim tests (e.g., reliability) better, you still have empirical work to do. You need to figure out what the "successful" operationalization contains that is missing from the other measure, and begin to build upon that. The term *construct* is used to refer to a concept that has acquired both empirical and theoretical meaning through a coherent program of study. Construct validation refers to consistency throughout a theoretical structure, conceptual and operational, including the linking explications.[14] This pursuit may send you back to even the earliest stages in this outline.

CONCLUSION

This chapter outlines the steps that lie ahead for those undertaking a commitment to study some facet of human communication. The discussion has constantly shifted between theory and method, and between the conceptual and the operational levels of thinking, because that is how theorizing is done.[15] The agenda of activities may seem imposing, and certainly one implication here is that communication research is an extensive, long-run, and demanding activity.

Balanced against the sheer volume of work that one undertakes in entering this field is the framework for organizing one's research and thinking that has been outlined here. Reading prior literature, explicating central concepts, collecting and analyzing data, and writing research conclusions, are activities that occupy the scholar's time at different points in the research process. Theorizing provides a sense of the relationship of these parts to one another, and to the whole, that can make the work of communication research both intellectually productive and enjoyable.

---

[14]Cook and Campbell (1979) take the position that construct validity relates primarily to explication, but most methods texts emphasize instead that constructs are validated to the extent that they enter into relationships with other constructs as predicted by the overall theory.

[15]A succinct summary of this chapter might be: "Theorizing is never done."

REFERENCES

Atkin, C. K. (1981). Communication and political socialization. In D. D. Nimmo & K. R. Sanders (Eds.), *Handbook of political communication* (pp. 299–328). Beverly Hills: Sage.

Berelson, B., & Steiner, G. (1964). *Human behavior: An inventory of scientific findings.* New York: Harcourt, Brace and World.

Campbell, D. T., & Stanley, J. C. (1966). *Experimental and quasi-experimental designs for research on teaching.* Chicago: Rand McNally.

Carter, F., Ruggels, W. L., Jackson, K. M., & Heffner, M. B. (1973). Application of signaled stopping technique to communication research. In Peter Clarke (Ed.), *New models for mass communication research*(pp. 15–43). Beverly Hills: Sage.

Chaffee, S. H. (1991). *Communication concepts 1: Explication.* Newbury Park, CA: Sage.

Chaffee, S. H., & Schleuder, J. (1986). Measurement and effects of attention to media news. *Human Communication Research, 13*, 76–107.

Cook, T. D., & Campbell, D. T. (1979). *Quasi-experimentation: Design & analysis issues for field settings.* Chicago: Rand McNally.

Festinger, L. (1957). *A theory of cognitive dissonance.* Stanford, CA: Stanford University Press.

Festinger, L. (1964). *Conflict, decision and dissonance.* Stanford, CA: Stanford University Press.

Hempel, C. G. (1952). *Fundamentals of concept formation in empirical science.* Chicago: University of Chicago Press.

Hovland, C. I., Janis, I. L., & Kelley, H. H. (1953). *Communication and persuasion: Psychological studies of opinion change.* New Haven: Yale University Press.

Jefferson, T. (1984). Letter to Judge John Tyler. In M. D. Patterson (Ed.), *Thomas Jefferson: Writings.* New York: Library of America.

Kline, F. G. (1978). Time in communication research. In P. M. Hirsch, P. V. Miller, & F. G. Kline (Eds.), *Strategies for communication research* (pp. 187–204). Beverly Hills, CA: Sage.

Kuhn, T. S. (1970). *The structure of scientific revolutions* (2nd ed.). Chicago: University of Chicago Press.

Lazarsfeld, P. F., & Merton, R. K. (1948). Mass communication popular taste, and organized social action. In L. Bryson (Ed.), *The communication of ideas* (pp. 95–118). New York: Harper and Brothers.

Likert, R. (1932). A technique for the measurement of attitudes. *Archives of Psychology, 22,* 5–55.

Linz, D., & Malamuth, N. (1993). *Communication concepts 5: Pornography.* Newbury Park, CA: Sage.

Martin, R. R., McNelly, J. T., & Izcaray, F. (1976). Is media exposure unidimensional? A socioeconomic approach. *Journalism Quarterly, 53*, 619–625.

McCombs, M. E., & Shaw, D. E. (1972). The agenda setting function of mass media. *Public Opinion Quarterly, 36,* 176–187.

McLeod, J. M., & McDonald, D. (1985). Beyond simple exposure: Media orientations and their impact on political processes. *Communication Research, 10,* 155–174.

Milton, J. (1949). *Areopagitica.* (J. W. Hales, Ed.). London: Oxford University Press.

Osgood, C. E. (1952). The nature and measurement of meaning. *Psychological Bulletin, 49,* 197–237.

Reeves, B., Thorson, E., & Schleuder, J. (1986). Attention to television: Psychological theories and chronometric measures. In J. Bryant & D. Zillmann (Eds.), *Perspectives on media effects* (pp. 251–279). Hillsdale, NJ: Lawrence Erlbaum Associates.

Rogers, E. M. (1964). *Diffusion of innovations.* New York: Free Press.

Rogers, E. M. (1983). *Diffusion of innovations* (3rd ed.). New York: Free Press.

Rogers, E. M. (1976). Communication and development: The passing of the dominant paradigm. *Communication Research, 3,* 213–240.

Steuer, J. (1992). Defining virtual reality: Dimensions determining telepresence. *Journal of Communication, 42,* 73–93.

Tichenor, P. J., Donohue, G. A., & Olien, C. N. (1970). Mass media and differential growth in knowledge. *Public Opinion Quarterly, 34,* 158–170.

3

Thinking Quantitatively

Michael J. Beatty
Cleveland State University

What are the components of competent interpersonal communication? What factors contribute to perceptions of political candidates' credibility? What vocal characteristics are associated with confidence? Communication scholars seek to answer or uncover clues pertaining to these and a myriad of other questions about communication. Sometimes research is conducted for the purpose of testing existing theories, or to produce data to construct new ones. At other times, research is designed to answer immediate, practical questions or to provide information critical to problem solving.

Underlying any research project, regardless of its intended purpose, are assumptions about what constitutes knowledge. These assumptions, known as *epistemological assumptions*, are foundational in the development of criteria for assessing the value or worth of data generated by research. Over the past 40 years, many communication scholars have embraced epistemological assumptions consistent with a scientific approach to the study of communication. Adopting a scientific perspective inevitably leads to the subject matter of this chapter, thinking quantitatively.

This chapter explores how quantitatively oriented communication scholars think—and why they think as they do. Earlier chapters focused on establishing a theoretical base for communication study; this chapter and the next explore how scholars test their theories. Perhaps quantitative thinking within a scientific paradigm can best be appreciated against the backdrop of alternative ways of answering questions about communication. As a starting point, let us examine nonscientific alternatives along with the reasons why they are rejected by scholars working from a scientific perspective.

UNSCIENTIFIC SOURCES OF KNOWLEDGE
ABOUT COMMUNICATION

The alternatives to science knowledge acquisition are intuition, tradition, common sense, personal experience, authority, and rationalism (Kerlinger, 1986). Scientists do not assert that these widespread sources of opinion are without value. At times, each provides reasonably accurate and informative perspectives to questions. Knowledge sources must be evaluated more rigorously than by casually observing that they are sometimes accurate; a stopped watch displays time accurately twice in a 24 hour period—but it is nevertheless stopped. Scientists consider the *potential* for being misled when assessing the merits of any method for gaining knowledge, looking for logical weaknesses, as well as dependence on subjective human judgments. Mindful of these criteria for evaluating knowledge sources, we will examine each unscientific approach.

Intuition

Intuition commonly functions as a source of unscientific information about communication. By *intuition*, we mean vague feelings, sometimes referred to as *gut reactions*. When we distrust a person without reason, enter into a contract because we "have a good feeling about it," or feel that the media are too liberal, we are using intuition.

One problem with intuition as a knowledge source is that our intuitions are often wrong. To illustrate, when we ask college students what they would do if they learned that their spouse was having an affair, almost all report that they would terminate the marriage. However, research shows that in most instances the relationships do not end after infidelity is discovered, and in the cases that do, it the unfaithful spouse who usually initiates divorce proceedings. Complicating matters, our memories are often highly selective; we conveniently forget when we are wrong, thereby leading to a false confidence in intuition.

A second problem arises because intuitions are feeling-based. Mood—and a host of other psychological and physiological factors—influence intuition. For example, ample evidence shows that we tend to evaluate opposite sex strangers more positively when our first encounter takes place in an aesthetically pleasing, comfortable room than when initial meetings occur in an ugly, uncomfortable space (Maslow & Mintz, 1956). Research also shows that most people are unaware of contextual effects on intuition. Finally, ask five people to make predictions based on intuition and we are likely to receive five different answers. We simply cannot place enough confidence in intuition to accept it as a source of information about communication.

Tenacity

A second source of information, known as *tradition* or *tenacity*, includes unquestioned belief in superstitions, truisms, and myths. These forms of knowledge are often passed from generation to generation through cultural mechanisms such as family, media, and religious and educational institutions. As an information source, tenacity is pervasive. Like intuition, however, many tenaciously held beliefs are inaccurate. For instance, at one time everyone held tenaciously to the beliefs that the Earth was flat; that the sun revolved around the earth; that applying leeches to the ill was good medical practice; and that Salem, Massachusetts was plagued with witches. Scientific breakthroughs in medicine, physics, and genetics, to name a few disciplines, continually expose the erroneous nature of previously held beliefs. Moreover, across and within cultures there is considerable variance in perspectives: What seems obvious to one social group is often rejected as ludicrous by another. Tenacity, like intuition, is an unacceptable way to answer communication questions.

Common Sense

Common sense, a third unscientific way of knowing, consists of generating what appear to be obvious answers to communication questions. Appeals to this source of knowledge are accompanied by prefacing or supporting remarks such as "it's obvious that . . .," "everybody knows . . .," "any halfway intelligent person can see that . . .," or "it's just common sense." Common sense, however, is often wrong; people often disagree about what constitutes the common sense thing to do in a particular situation. Furthermore, communication problems abound for which common sense provides no insight. This is particularly true for complex problems. For example, although some children raised by verbally abusive parents become verbally abusive parents as adults, many do not. What factors inhibit or encourage intergenerational transfer of parenting behaviors? There exist no common sense answers to such questions.

Personal Experience

Personal experience is often used as a knowledge source. We posses a wealth of personal experiences and—while experience is an extremely valuable resource—there are three reasons to be cautious about deriving knowledge claims about communication based on experiences. First, personal experience is both subjective and uncontrolled, leaving us susceptible to misperception and misinterpretations of events. While we are limited in the amount of information we can process, the quantity of stimuli in any given situation is virtually unlimited. As noted earlier, we often attend to events and stimuli selectively: We simply do not—cannot—pay attention to every sound; we don't notice everything there is to see; some things go undetected. Rather, we attend to some stimuli and block out others, some of what we do hear, we hear incorrectly, yielding an experience that is necessarily incomplete and often inaccurate as well.

Second, we selectively remember characteristics of experience. Anyone who has ever studied for a college examination realizes that some of the subject matter, although we read it and perhaps even hear it in lecture, was somehow inaccessible on exam day.

Thus, our memories of events are incomplete and often inaccurate. Problematic also is that selectivity is often driven by strong preconceptions. That is, we often attend, perceive, accept, and recall data that confirm our beliefs and attitudes whereas we tend to ignore, distort, discount, and forget data which disconfirm our attitudes and beliefs.

Finally, even if we could hone our perceptual skills so that all stimuli could be processed accurately, and fully retrieved on demand, our conclusions would not necessarily be consistent with the experiences of others. Factors such as communication competence level, physical attractiveness, vocal characteristics, social status, media use, and so forth might lead to different outcomes, even if we said and did everything identically. Overall, personal experience falls short of the mark as a knowledge source.

Authority

A fifth unscientific source of knowledge, *authority*, consists of appealing to experts for answers to our questions. We are surrounded by experts and authorities: professors, physicians, attorneys, journalists, economic advisors, stockbrokers, marriage counselors, automobile mechanics, and news anchors, to name but a few. Although experts frequently provide valuable service, there is often disagreement among them, and, of course, they can be wrong. A more important issue for our discussion, however, concerns how the experts gained their knowledge in the first place. If their knowledge was acquired through intuition, tenacity, or experience, it is subject to many of the caveats already mentioned. Assuming that an expert's knowledge is the product of scientific inquiry, it is the scientific inquiry—not the expert—that is source of the knowledge. Well informed experts can disseminate knowledge but they are not acceptable as progenerators of it.

Rationalism

A final unscientific way of deriving answers is through *rationalism,* or logic, usually in the form of deduction. Accordingly, knowledge takes the form of conclusions, which are deduced from premises. For example, suppose that (a) supportive messages usually produce positive emotions in receivers and that (b) positive emotional experiences usually produce interpersonal attraction. Applying logic we would conclude, therefore, that supportive messages usually produce interpersonal attraction.

Two major problems are associated with rationalism as a source of knowledge. First, we must consider how the truth of the premises was determined. Logic cannot produce premises, and without valid premises, sound conclusions cannot be deduced. Second, if we apply logic in this form to syllogisms consisting of premises that are not absolutely true, erroneous conclusions can be deduced even when strictly adhering to the rules of deduction. Reconsider our example. For convenience suppose that by *usually*, we mean 70 percent of the time. Thus, the probability of supportive statements resulting in positive receiver affect is .70, and the probability of positive emotions leading to interpersonal attraction is also .70. What then is the probability that supportive messages lead receivers to be attracted to the source of those messages? The correct answer is calculated by multiplying the probabilities for the two separate premises (i.e., .70 × .70 = .49). To say that one of two events is more likely to occur than the other requires a probability greater than .50. In contrast to the logically drawn conclusion, our calculation indicates that if we had to predict whether supportive statements produce interpersonal attraction, the more accurate prediction would be that, more often than not, supportive messages do not produce interpersonal attraction.

Logicians have devised methods under the rubric of quantifiable logic for syllogisms in which premises vary in the degree to which they hold true. However, logic itself does not provide those crucial probability estimates; nor does it produce the premises. While logic is an essential tool used by scientists, it alone is insufficient as a knowledge source because its use requires existing knowledge in the form of premises.

THINKING QUANTITATIVELY IN A SCIENTIFIC PERSPECTIVE

As hinted throughout this brief review of the unscientific sources of knowledge, we need a more precise and objective approach to generating knowledge. This leads us to consideration of the scientific perspective to knowledge acquisition and the role of quantitative thinking within that perspective.

Regardless of field of study, the activities of scholars committed to a scientific approach to generating answers to questions, whether theoretical or practical in nature, can almost always be described in terms of a five-step process known as the *scientific method*. It is, therefore, instructive to briefly review the steps with special focus on how they differ from unscientific ways of gaining knowledge and how quantitative thinking is central to performing those steps. The scientific method consists of the following five steps: (a) observe a phenomenon that needs to be explained; (b) construct provisional explanations or pose hypotheses; (c) design an adequate test of the hypotheses; (d) execute the test; and (e) accept, reject, or modify our hypotheses based on the outcome of our test.

Curiosity

The first step describes a basic characteristic of scientific thinking, curiosity. We notice that some people enjoy public speaking whereas others experience considerable apprehension and dread at the mere prospect of it. We notice, for instance, that some people seem to imitate what they see in the media, while others do not. We notice that some achieve more popularity in social situations than do others. When we focus on such observations and feel compelled to explain them, we have engaged in the first step of the scientific method. As noted in chapter 2, at this point, scholars engage in an exhaustive survey of existing research seeking an existing explanation. If one cannot be found, they move to the next step.

Conceptualizing

It is at the second step, constructing provisional explanations, that we begin to differentiate scientific from unscientific thinking. Not having found an explanation for a phenomenon, scholars look for clues in existing research. Under a scientific framework, input from intuition, tradition, experience, common sense, experts, and logic might be incorporated during the construction of provisional explanations, but we do not, at this point, accept the validity of those explanations. Suppose that we felt compelled to explain why people differ regarding fear of public speaking. Assume that a review of the research literature provides no insight whatsoever. When we think about the times we made presentations to an audience, it seems that we were most nervous when we were unprepared. Our provisional explanations begins to take shape. We suspect that preparation underlies confidence. This explanation squares with conclusions drawn from other unscientific sources. Based on our personal experiences we propose a tentative hypothesis: Speakers who are prepared will experience less fear while delivering a speech than speakers who are unprepared.

Operationalizing

Upon constructing a hypothesis, the scientist moves to the third step, constructing an adequate test of it. This phase further differentiates scientific and unscientific thinking and, furthermore, the role of quantitative thinking becomes profoundly evident.

In the simplest sense, quantitative thinking means attaching numerical values to concepts. Actually, we think quantitatively every day. When we request an estimate for automobile repair, ask about salary on a job interview, or inquire about delivery time for a new purchase, we expect quantitative answers. Responses such as "the cost will be reasonable," "the salary is good," and "it won't take too long" are usually unsatisfactory; they are vague responses and do not facilitate our decision making. We want the answers regarding costs to be quantified in terms of dollars and those concerning time to be quantified in terms of days or hours. Clearly, such estimates will be somewhat inaccurate. We understand that quantified answers are only estimates and we expect them to be imperfect. Obviously, precise estimates are ideal. However, we know that reasonably accurate estimates are more useful in our decision making and planning than no estimate at all.

Returning to our speaking example, an adequate test of the hypothesis involves comparing the fear levels of prepared and unprepared speakers. However, several practical questions arise with respect to designing our test. Exactly how much preparation is required to achieve a "prepared" state? Do we mean an hour, a day, a week? Should we include groups of speakers engaged in various amounts of preparation? How many prepared and unprepared speakers should we sample to provide a fair test? How should we determine speakers' levels of nervousness? Do we think that people are either nervous or calm (a dichotomous meansure) or do we think there are degrees of nervousness (a continuous measure)? Should we ask people to report their degree of nervousness on a scale ranging from 1 to 10 (a self-report measure) or should we monitor some physiological response during speeches (a direct observation measure)? How long should the presentations be; how large the audience?

The preceding list of questions are but a few examples of the types of decisions requiring quantitative thinking. While methods for dealing with these types of design questions are the subject matter of entire series of books and sequences of courses, our focus is only on the significance of quantitative approaches to making these important choices.

Characteristic of scientific endeavor are detailed and specific definitions of crucial variables. These definitions are termed *operational definitions*. Carefully describing the type and duration of preparation and the other variables in our study provides a clear picture of our experiment for others. In this way, other researchers interested in the phenomenon we investigated can comprehend exactly what we meant by *preparation, audience*, and so forth. Furthermore, clear operational definitions permit others to replicate our study. That is, they can conduct it for themselves, checking our results or making small modifications in the design to fit their interpretations of our results.

In addition to being specific, scholars operating under a scientific perspective are obligated to provide evidence for the *validity* and *reliability* of operational definitions. Therefore, in our public speaking study, we would be obligated to show that the questionnaire we used to measure nervousness does in fact measure nervousness (is valid) and does so consistently time after time (is reliable). We would be obligated to show that the speakers in our study actually prepared for the duration we assert. Likewise, we would be obligated to show that the audience size and speaking task were representative of what we normally expect in public speaking situations. (Would we accept as a "typical public speaking situation" a person sitting at a desk, speaking for one minute about the weather to one other person?) There are bound to be numerous reasonable and, therefore, valid ways to operationalize variables. Clearly, no single study will include all possible ways to define variables. Key, however, to scientific inquiry is the researcher's acceptance of the responsibility for providing clear, valid, operational definitions. This is not to say that we must agree with researchers' decisions. We are free to define the same variables in other ways, provided that we can present valid evidence for our definitions. Of importance is the public nature of those definitions, the clarity of which are greatly enhanced when expressed in quantitative terms (e.g., "The audience consisted of 24 undergraduate college students, 12 males and 12 females.").

Designing and Executing the Test

Another feature of the scientific method are tests of hypotheses that take care to control the influences of other, extraneous variables. Within a scientific paradigm, the researcher accepts the responsibility to ensure that the observed effects are not due to some other variable. Suppose that in our public speaking study the unprepared speakers all happen to have clinical neuroses, whereas the prepared group was emotionally stable. In such a case we could never be completely sure whether preparation really was the cause of nervousness during public speaking. That is, neurotic individuals might always experience fear whether they prepared or not. Conversely, unprepared emotionally stable individuals might not experience nervousness during a speech although their performance might suffer. Therefore, scientists must rule out *all* competing explanations.

If we suspected that individuals' neurotises might *confound* our findings we could control for its effects through matching, covariance, randomization, or experimental control. For example, we could administer a "neuroses test" to all speakers and make sure that stable and people with neuroses were equally represented in both prepared and unprepared conditions.[1] If we were able to place speakers in the prepared and unprepared speech situations so that the set of neuroses scores in one speech situation was the same as that in the other, we would be using a *matched design* for the study.

A second way to control for neuroticism effects would be to employ a statistical technique called *covariance analysis*. A comprehensive explanation of this technique is beyond the scope of this chapter.[2] Briefly, however, it permits researchers to estimate the effects of one variable (such as preparedness) on another (such as nervousness during speaking) over and beyond any effect to a variable that needs to be controlled (such as existence of neuroses).

Although the preceding methods of controlling variables are widely used in the behavioral sciences, they are restricted in some significant ways. Specifically, researchers must suspect that a particular variable will contaminate the results (through a review of existing literature) and that a limited number of variables can be controlled through matching or covariance analysis. The most powerful form of controlling differences among people in a sample is *randomization*. If we select a sufficiently large sample (e.g., 200 speakers) and randomly assign them to either the prepared or unprepared condition, we will have distributed the extraneous variables so that they are equally represented in both speaking conditions. In other words, rather than actively controlling for extraneous variables, we randomly assign participants to the different conditions on the assumption that the effects of all extraneous variables (both known and unknown) are equally distributed among participants in different groups.

Another way to neutralize extraneous variables is through *experimental control,* holding certain factors constant. For instance, in our study, we might make sure that all speeches were delivered in the same room, under similar conditions (e.g., lectern versus no lectern, audience size and feedback, etc.). An appropriate test of the effects of any variable requires testing under comparable conditions. If the unprepared group, in fact, performs in a cold room, without a lectern, to an inattentive, unresponsive audience but the prepared group speaks from behind a lectern, in a comfortable room, to a receptive audience, the effects of preparation have not been fairly and adequately tested. Indeed, the different conditions, singularly or in combination, cannot be ruled out and therefore remain as competing explanations for the speakers' levels of nervousness.

Scientific scholars, thinking about tentative explanations quantitatively, provide clear definitions of variables, offer evidence for their validity, and exert control over as many extraneous factors as possible. They attempt to provide fair and adequate tests of their hypotheses. Once accomplished, they execute the study.

Analysis and Interpreting Data

The final stage of the scientific process calls for the rejection, acceptance, or modification of the explanation based on an analysis of the data. During this step the role of quantitative thinking is paramount because the analyses of the data are based on statistical procedures.

---

[1]There are a variety of tests available for measuring variables. See, for example Miller (1983) or Rubin, Palmgreen, & Sypher (1994).

[2]See, Kerlinger (1986), Stacks & Hocking (1992), and Wimmer & Dominic (1994) for more comprehensive treatments.

The Concept of Variance.   To understand why statistical analyses are essential to a scientific approach to communication research, consider the alternative to our nervousness public speaking study. We have strong validity evidence for our variables and we accomplished control through randomization in our study's design. Furthermore, the study was conducted without fault. Therefore, we examine the nervousness scores, which we will assume ranged from 0 to 100, for prepared and unprepared speakers, and we observe that, although the average score for the prepared group is lower than that of the unprepared group, there is considerable dispersion, termed *variance*, among nervousness scores within each group. That is, we note that some prepared speakers report nervousness scores as low as 0 but others report scores as high as 52. Similarly, the scores reported by unprepared speakers range from 50 to 100. Furthermore, as our inspection of the data shows, a few prepared speakers were *more* nervous than some of the unprepared speakers. What should we conclude about the test of our hypothesis that preparation determines speakers' nervousness?

Before a scientific interpretation of the data can be offered, we must be attentive to possible sources of the variance in scores within prepared and unprepared groups of speakers? The categories that follow apply to all sorts of studies. However, it would be instructive to relate each to our sample study. Part of the variance in scores is attributable to *sampling error.* Despite our efforts to assign speakers to prepared and unprepared groups on a random basis, some differences between comparison groups are bound to happen in any study due to chance. Part of the variance is attributable to *measurement error.* No matter how rigorously we measure variables, our estimates of them are inherently imperfect. Our questionnaires, for example, might include words or phrases that are interpreted by some respondents in a manner different than we intended. Part of the variance is attributable to *design error.* Although substantial effort is expended to collect data under conditions that approximate the contexts and situations of interest, data collection environments are always imperfect. Perhaps the speaking task was too short to stimulate fear in some of the participants. Finally, some of the variance could represent *real error.* If preparation is not a determinant or is only one of the determinants of nervousness, our hypothesis is at least partially in error.

Statistical Significance and Magnitude of Effects   In light of the aforementioned set of issues, how can the test of the hypothesis be interpreted in an objective and adequate manner? Statistical analyses provide systematic procedures for accounting for the sources of variance or error in data. The various statistical tests permit researchers to separate the effect of the explanatory variable or variables (preparedness in our example) from the effects of the error sources.

Through statistical analyses we are able to estimate the probability that our findings are due to chance, instead of the explanatory variable or variables. These probability estimates are known as *significance* levels—frequently reported in the form, $p < .05$, which means that the probability of the findings being due to chance is less than 5 in 100 (or 1 in 20). This particular level, referred to as the .05 level of statistical significance, has traditionally served as the standard for accepting data as evidence for the hypothesis in most social science disciplines. When scholars refer to their findings as statistically significant, they mean the probability that their observed pattern of results is due to chance is no more than 5 in 100.

There are two basic mistakes, however, that researchers can make when interpreting statistical tests. They can claim a hypothesized difference exists when it truly does not (called *Type I error*) or they can claim a hypothesized difference does not exist when it actually does (called *Type II error*). Researchers try to avoid each by first ensuring that they have enough observations (participants) to adequately have sampled the population they are observing and examining by statistical means the *power* of their tests (which indicates whether or not a nonsupported hypothesis failed to be supported because there were no actual differences or because there were insufficient participants to adequately test whatever relationship was hypothesized). In general, the larger the sample size, the more powerful the statistical tests.

Furthermore, we can estimate the portion of the effect that is specifically attributable to the explanatory variable(s). When scholars report "variance explained" (or "accounted for"), the square of correlation coefficients (r^2), eta (η) or omega square (ω^2), or the d statistic, they are informing us about the relative magnitude of the explanatory variable(s)' impact. That is, how much the variables explain—or do not explain (i.e., $1 - r^2$ = variance unexplained)—the changes in the variables of interest.

In sum, the linchpin of quantitative thinking is statistical analysis. Although the example used throughout this chapter depicts an admittedly simplistic conceptualization of a complex communication problem, it served only to illustrate a process. In reality, statistical analyses have been designed to handle multiple explanatory and outcome variables, as well as complex relationships between and among variables.[3]

Depending on the outcome of our statistical analysis, we are positioned to interpret the results of our test and evaluate our hypothesis. Perhaps we found that the difference in nervousness scores was statistically significant, and that virtually all of the difference between the average nervousness scores for the two groups was attributable to whether the speakers were prepared. In other words, strong support for the hypotheses, indicating evidence for our explanation. Perhaps the differences were statistically significant but the variance explained in nervousness scores due to preparation was small. Assuming we were attentive to sources of error discussed above, we might modify our hypothesis by suggesting that preparation affects nervousness but additional variables must be studied to better explain why some people are nervous and others are confident during public speaking. Perhaps we found that our results were not significant: The differences between prepared and unprepared speakers large enough to reject chance as a plausible explanation. Because there are numerous criteria regarding research design and statistical analysis that must be satisfied before it can be concluded that a variable or set of variables has no effect on another, scholars usually conclude that they failed to support the hypothesis in such cases. Thinking quantitatively about the analyses of hypotheses makes it possible to clearly articulate the bases for evaluations of hypotheses and the theoretical speculation from which they emerged.

CONCLUDING REMARKS

At the outset of this chapter, the point was made that the aim of research was to answer questions about communication. Research conducted from a scientific point of view is well-rooted in the field of communication and has been a rich source of information

---

[3]For an excellent overview, see Williams (1992).

about a broad range of subject matter. Although numerous processes contribute to the formation of ideas, questions, and hypotheses about communication, scientific endeavor is required to verify or validate those hypotheses. Regardless of how intriguing a particular notion about communication might be, untestable hypotheses are of little use to scholars building theories of communication from a scientific perspective.

Adopting a scientific perspective commits scholars to thinking quantitatively in several ways. It requires us to think quantitatively when defining and measuring concepts, describing relationships between variables in precise mathematical terms, and assessing the merit of hypotheses.

This chapter should not be construed as suggesting that a quantitative approach to communication inquiry is easily accomplished or is somehow objective, straightforward, and always accurate in its conclusions. Without question, the history of social science, communication included, is replete with findings that were later amended or substantially qualified in some way. On the contrary, quantifying communication concepts is a messy business often rewarded by criticism and controversy. However, scientific progress is inevitably incremental, requiring programs of research which refine and extend prior work. Rarely, if ever, are single studies sufficient as sources of scientifically derived knowledge. Instead, hypotheses are retested employing different samples, operational definitions, and research designs. As mentioned, many times findings do not hold up across studies.

Indeed, the vast majority of scholars who are committed to a scientific perspective are painfully aware that quantitative methods are often imperfect. However, we also recognize that quantitative analysis is an indispensable tool in the study of human communication and, as with any tool, its ultimate value depends on the motivations and competence of its user. From a scientific perspective, deeper and more comprehensive understanding of human communication will follow deeper and more comprehensive understanding and application of all aspects of scientific methodology.

REFERENCES

Kerlinger, F. N. (1986). *Foundations of behavioral research* (3rd ed.). New York: Holt, Rinehart & Winston.

Maslow, A. H., & Mintz, N. L. (1956). Effects of esthetic surroundings: I. Initial effects of three esthetic conditions upon perceiving "energy" and "well–being" in faces. *Journal of Psychology, 41*, 247–254.

Miller, D. C. (1983). *Handbook of research design and social measurement.* New York: Longman.

Rubin, R. B., Palmgrreen, P., & Sypher, H. E. (Eds.). (1994). *Communication research measures.* New York: Guilford.

Stacks, D. W., & Hocking, J. E. (1992). *Essentials of communication research.* New York: HarperCollins.

Williams, F. N. (1992). *Reasoning with statistics.* New York: Holt, Rinehart & Winston.

Wimmer, R. D., & Dominick, J. R. (1994). *Mass media research: An introduction* (4th ed.). Belmont, CA: Wadsworth.

4

Thinking Qualitatively:
Hermeneutics in Science

James A. Anderson
University of Utah

This chapter redraws the science of human inquiry in the image of an old but now re-emerging paradigm often called "qualitative research" but is, perhaps, better called "hermeneutic empiricism" or simply "hermeneutic science." This is the science of Charles Sanders Peirce, Max Weber, George Herbert Mead, John Dewey, and Talcott Parsons and the researchers in the Chicago School.[1]

Communication scholars employing a hermeneutic science approach seek to test their theories in light of daily events, in commonly-placed situations, framed by the interaction of their participants. This approach focuses on the "accounts of everyday life" (Stacks, Hickson, & Hill, 1991, p. 306). *Hermeneutics* is the method through which theorists seek to discover the "conscious experience of communication."

ASSUMPTIONS

To understand qualitative thinking we must first examine its general philosophical approach and the phenomenological assumptions undergirding hermeneutic research. Qualitative approaches to research progress from some combination of the following underlying assumptions:

Multiple Domains of Experience.   Human engagement of the phenomenal world occurs across multiple domains (Roth, 1987). We are first of all material entities in a physical world. We are also living organisms giving expression to the principles of animation. But, we inhabit yet another domain—the domain of the sign. It is within this semiotic domain that we make sense of ourselves, our world, and our manner of being in it (Peirce, 1931, 1932, 1958; Popper & Eccles, 1977).

A Grant of Understanding.   Hermeneutic theories generally hold that human behavior is organized in action signs which are understandable as indicative of what is being done. Human behavior is always a symbolic expression never simply an objective fact (Parsons, 1937; Schutz, 1965; Weber, 1974).

The Centrality of Communication.   The peculiar human character arises within the semiotic domain through the practices of communication. It is managed through the iconic, discursive and performative practices which are the resources for our communicative efforts. A study of human behavior, then, is a study of communication (Bakhtin, 1986; Bellah, Madsen, Sullivan, Swindler, & Tipton, 1985; Habermas, 1981/1984).

A Focus on Relationships Rather Than Separate Entities.   "Sum of the parts" arguments and methods in which individual characteristics are examined and then "added up" to make the whole are not appropriate. Human behavior is understood as dialogic emerging in the interaction between self and other (Miller, 1982; Goffman, 1959).

The Acceptance of Agency.   Hermeneutic theories, while emphasizing the collective and the relational, acknowledge the contribution of the particular individual as an active, performing initiator, albeit one who is also an agent of collective understanding. Evidence and claim must preserve the contribution the individual makes (Newell, 1986).

An Emphasis on Historic Performances.   Historic here does not mean "of the past;" it refers to the study of actual performances of identified, contributing actors. It is the researcher's job to detail the performance, the circumstances of its presentation, all that which constitutes the historical frame. The researcher, then, is often directed towards the participant–observation method of ethnography—(Anderson, 1991; Anderson & Goodall, 1994). There is no requirement, however, to employ those methods.

The Subjectivity of Analysis.   The scientific study of the human condition is itself an expression of that condition (Bohman, 1991). Hermeneutic science would hold that truth is a human accomplishment within the semiotic domain. This truth construction accommodates the characteristics of the phenomenal world but is not determined by them (Weber, 1974; Schutz, 1965). Hermeneutic theories then—as with all theories—must be empirically adequate. From the qualitative approach, we are true to ourselves in the human truths expressed in local performances by social agents—here nominated as scientists—making politically significant and ethically accountable choices (Anderson, 1992; Harding, 1985).

[1]An excellent introduction into the varieties of and issues in qualitative research is in Denzin and Lincoln's (1994) *Handbook of Qualitiative Research*; Anderson (1987) and Lindlof (1994) are two contemporary methods books which also provide useful guides to other literature.

A COMPARISON OF PRACTICAL CHARACTERISTICS

We can see the practical consequences of these seven assumptions by offering a quick comparison between the qualitative research of hermeneutic science and the quantitative research of more objectivist frames. Such a comparison can be conducted on any number of terms, the most relevant for our purposes are: the reality criterion, the unit of analysis, measurement, focus of analysis, logic, explanation, and knowledge.

Quantitative research is derived from the material criterion of the real (Anderson, in press) with its emphasis on the objective character of phenomena and the independence between the knowing subject and the object of knowledge. It is this independence that centers objective measurement as the method of choice. Qualitative research is derived from a semiotic or pragmatic criterion of the real with its emphasis on the meaningfulness of things and the interaction between knowing subject and known object. It is this interaction which centers participation as the research method of choice. Both, however, are equally empirical in privileging our experiencing of the phenomenal world over its formal analysis.

The unit of analysis in qualitative research is discourse, whether the captured discourse of conversations, the produced discourse of interviews or the constructed discourse of field notes. One's measurement of that discourse is interpretive, the textual warranting of claim. The logic that governs the interpretation is discursive, the logic of language in use. Qualitative research's focus is on critical instances (Anderson, 1987), the meaningful order of things (Goodall, 1989), and collective understandings (Wagner, 1981). Explanation is rhetorical in the sense that it moves the significance of claim within an audience (Conquergood, 1991). And finally, knowledge is actional in that it is recognized in its instrumentality.

In quantitative research the unit of analysis is a quantity whether that quantity is a unity, as in types and categories, or an amount, as in elements, attributes, conditions, or states. One's measurement involves the literal quantification of the object or state as a function of numbers. Once quantified, the focus is on the presence or absence of categories or objects or states, their ordered values, and their rates of occurrence. The logic, then, is the logic of mathematics. Explanation intends to be categorically and transcendentally true. It is, therefore, archival ("one for the books," as they say). Finally knowledge moves toward the propositional, enduring and ahistorical.

Table 4.1 provides a summary of these characteristics with the corresponding values for quantitative research. The text that follows extends our discussion of the qualitative side of these comparisons by offering a short investigation into the nature of the practice of qualitative research.

NATURE

Studies within the domain of qualitative research often begin with interests in how something is done, the social value of an activity or symbolic resource, the meaning of an action or text, or the requirements of some consequential accomplishment. It is assumed that these interests are best explored in the everyday contexts of the actions, texts, and accomplishments. There is a resistance to—if not an outright rejection of— formal, decontextualized, or recontextualized approaches. The place of analysis is the "lifeworld;"

TABLE 4.1

Characteristics of Qualitative and Quantitative Methodologies

Characteristic	Qualititative	Quantitative
Reality Criterion	Semiotic	Material
Unit of Analysis	Discourse	Quantity
Measurement	Interpretive	Literal
Focus	Social Action: Its Critical Instances and Meanings	Objects and States Categories, Orders, and Rates
Logic	Discursive	Mathematical
Explanation	Rhetorical	Archival
Knowledge	Actional	Propositional

and the first task is to enter the researcher into the meaning production sites, of interest. At this stage of the research we are concerned with the strategies and tactics of field methods (see, for example, Erlandson, Harris, Skipper, & Allen, 1993; Lofland, 1975;).

Chase, Anderson, and Larson (1990), for example, were interested in the meanings television news programs had for avid news watchers. Given their qualitative approach, they assumed that some of the crucial meanings were called into place in the practices of news watching. In this part of the study, they were concerned with the manner by which the text of the news was engaged at the point of reception. Fifty people who had identified themselves as avid news viewers were visited at their homes on 2 or 3 occasions (some of the separate visits were combined) to introduce the study, have an extended conversation about the news, and to view the news together while the informant talked about her or his viewing engagement practices. The method used to enter the field was that everyday context of engaging the news.

Reading and Writing

Once the scene has been entered, the researcher works back and forth between reading and writing the scene. Reading involves the processes of making the scene sensible as a more or less coherent unity of action. Let's examine the three (reading, constructing, and action) in reverse order.

Unity of Action. The assumption of a (more or less) coherent unity exemplifies qualitative research's top down character. This character sees human actions as more than opportunistic behaviorism or deterministic cognitivism; they are meaningful acts intentionally orientated in a larger action. For the participants of Chase, Anderson, and Larson's study, one action they were involved in was watching television news. They were not just "watching television;" nor did they just "have the television set on." Their understanding of the meaningfulness of what they were doing was governed by the notion of watching the news.

Constructing the Scene. Making the scene sensible involves the conjoint intentionalities of the agent(s) of the scene and the agent(s) of the research. When we read the sentences on this page we make sense of the textual resources provided in accordance with the local characteristics of personal identity, as well as the cultural characteristics of the subjectivity of engagement. In that intersection of resource and engagement, the text is made sensible. (We might say that it is activated toward some end.) In the same way, when the researcher reads the scene, her or his identity and subjectivity is present in the reading. She or he is the instrument of the work of interpretation.

Probably no other characteristic of qualitative research evokes so much controversy and confusion as the recognition that we are implicated in the explanations we provide. For the radical hermeneuticist (Caputo, 1987), this recognition is a four square stance against even the possibility of objectivity. For the much less reconstructed grounded theorist (Glaser & Strauss, 1967, the classic reference), this amounts to a recognition that, of course, someone has to do it.

Methods of Reading.   Finally—and first—there is some process, some method of reading which the researcher put in place. Qualitative research of the empirical sort[2]—a distinction which separates it from cultural analysis or critical studies (Blaikie, 1993; see also chapter 3, this volume)—organizes those processes hierarchically according to the directness of the researcher's experience in the action under analysis.

Remembering, then, that the experience of interest is in the meaning of things, participation is a method of reading, but participation as a member is the privileged form. Conversations about (often called long-form interviews) and walking one through (sometimes called protocol analysis) are types of interactive reading that occupy the middle rungs of the hierarchy. One-way observation or the analysis of tapes are lower yet. Collecting artifacts, member-made photographs, maps, and written materials are forms of noninteractive reading that are perhaps the furthest removed from direct participation.

Concurrent with, but also extending beyond reading, are the multiple processes of writing. These processes can be further divided as "writing down" and "writing up."[3] Taking photographs, making maps, recordings, transcriptions, site notes and field notes are forms of writing *down* the scene. This writing down archives the scene and creates the *specimens*—what Lanigan (1992) called the *capta*—for analysis.

These twin processes of reading and writing down produce the research text archived in experience, in collection, and in discursive products of various sorts. This text is read, in some method of intimacy in a process of meaning attribution and written *up* in the interpretations of representational description, referential analysis, and critique. We will spend a moment with each of those elements in the example that follows. The text that follows alternates between an exemplar product of qualitative research and a discussion of the methods which led to its production.

---

[2]Empiricism is the philosophical position that the phenomenal world is most validly contacted through experience (as opposed to, say, formal analysis). It has many forms. Naive empiricism holds that we have an unmediated contact with the phenomenal world. Direct experience, therefore, is wholly trustworthy. Constructive empiricism (van Fraassen, 1980) holds that experience is mediated by belief, language, and so on, but there is an underlying substrata which always remains trustworthy. Hermeneutic empiricism holds that the phenomenal world appears in collectively constructed frameworks of understanding.

[3]The difference between *writing down* and *writing up* is useful for understanding the different writing tasks. Writing down privileges experience, writing up, interpretation. My thanks to Tom Lindlof for pointing out these terms.

The Terminator

For several years my daughter has managed a riding stable which provides instruction in the equestrian arts for children and adults. Her work in teaching adults how to stay on a horse while it is leaping over jumps of various heights has centered her in a social group with little else in common but their love of horses. I am not a horseman, but being a man of the American West I do own a pick-up truck. That makes me more than occasionally useful for hauling feed, gear, and horse trailers up into the mountains for trail rides and summer encampments. It also gives me my ticket for belonging to the group.

The principal moves of hermeneutic science, I think, can be demonstrated in the story of a gathering of some members of the equestrian group in celebration of the 1993 Super Bowl. The Super Bowl, as all but the most media deprived know, is the championship game of U.S. professional football and its timing in late January, as much as anything, has positioned it as a social occasion. At most of these social gatherings, the television set is nearly always on, but the game is watched by only a minority of the guests and rarely by anyone to its conclusion. Those who truly wish to watch the game either don't go to such parties or they record it on their VCRs at home.

The Super Bowl party of the equestrian group was no different. It was a small group of three couples and two singles or eight adults, along with the two children of the host couple. The timing of the party in early evening, and the fact that they were also students of riding brought the children into the party as full members if clearly part of the serving class.

The home of our hosts, Karen and Brad, is a turn of the century, two-story victorian following the traditional layout of the private rooms upstairs, the public rooms up front on the first floor, and the kitchen way to the back. One can see the restoration vision of its owners in the work in progress, but its completion is a bit down the road given the limits of time and money.

In this house, as in many houses, a major resource of space—here, the whole front parlor—has been given over to what is no longer television but a video center. The video centerpiece in this house is a 54-inch Mitsubishi monitor. It is fed by a broadcast antenna and a cable drop and is connected to both video tape and laser disk machines. A sound system, modest by current standards—and I might add since upgraded—augments the one in the monitor.

Method of Intimacy

The primary claims advanced by qualitative methods have to do with the structures and boundaries of meaningfulness in semiotically organized systems of performance and discourse. That meaningfulness, while locally produced by historical agents, is neither private nor personal but under the governance of collective effort.

Let me parse those sentences for you. "Semiotically organized systems of perform-ance and discourse" refers to qualitative research's assumption that human action and discourse[4] are intentionally[5] rather than randomly produced. Watching television news, therefore, is a meaningful activity for those who produce it. It has an internal organization and boundaries of where it ends or intersects with something else.

The meaningful character of performance and discourse is the sign of what is being done; its semiotic disposition. As a sign (words, symbols, and icons are also signs) it can be used in conjunction with other signs. For example, when I write to reveal myself as the author as I do in footnote 4 in the preceding paragraph and here, I put one discursive sign in play with another.

For something that you do to be meaningful to me takes only my intention to accomplish its meaningfulness. For something that you do to stand on a common ground of meaning between us requires our joint discipline of sign usage—yours in its performance and mine in its interpretation.[6] We cannot accomplish this discipline without collective resources of significance, or the mechanisms by which we can coordinate our efforts.

What a researcher observes in any particular performance or discursive product is one, local, improvised expression within a system of performance or discourse. The researcher's explanatory responsibility is not only what was done in the particular, but also how it was a meaningful expression within a system of significant action.

The interpretive task, then, is to get to the expression, and, consequently, some part of the system of significance, through an intimate knowledge of the details of performance. Unfortunately, qualitative procedures produce prodigious amounts of textual materials. Ethnographic studies will produce site notes, field notes and episodes; a single 30-minute interview takes 10 to 12 pages to transcribe; the protocol analysis of a single informant will triple that amount. Add to this any collected items and the scope of the problem begins to emerge.

The methods of intimacy, despite their soft-sounding name, represent as much hard work as the field methods that precede them. They require close readings, extensive indexing, a critical illumination of the allusions and figures in discourse and performance, a sensitivity to similarities and differences as well as a deep cultural understanding to contextualize the materials.

A tour of the restoration work and a discussion of the many steps to come is the common starting place for all the guests. As game time approached, we—mostly the men—spent several minutes tweaking the set for the perfect picture.

Once the game started, the party clearly broke by gender with all but one of the men watching the game and drinking a rough and not quite ready Australian cabernet. The women were in the kitchen playing a board game called "True Colors" in which players nominate one another as the one most likely to do this or that slightly outrageous act. It is sort of a bourgeois "Truth or Dare" in which the action is all talk. They were drinking a fruity California white.

---

[4]Discourse is generally defined as any extended language use, so this writing is an example of academic discourse of the textbook genre and its production, as good or bad as it may be, intends that end. It is not the discourse I would use on the soccer field nor am I permitted to use it unmarked at home. But the discourse of home and soccer field is equally intentional and produced as discourse, domestic and sporting.

[5]The concept of intentionality here does not suggest a causal linkage between some prior mental state and behavior produced, although that link may be present. It refers to the way things are meaningful as intentional objects of consciousness. Although I am in grave danger of this note's escaping from me, this intentionality deals with the manner in which meaning is accomplished.

[6]It is this requirement for a joint discipline which privileges participant forms of observation. I can certainly watch a video tape of some action and create an analysis of it. I have no basis, however, for any claim as to the meaningfulness of the action for the performers other than an appeal to common usage.

The lone non-football-watching male was the sole escort male—the others being part-nered or married—and seemed to be confused about where he should be. As a result he scuttled back and forth between the kitchen where the women and children were playing and the front room where the other men were watching the game. He was tolerated but effectively disenfranchised by both groups. He, by the way, was drinking beer.

By the start of the second half, the dominance of one team over the other was clear and the outcome moved from doubt. Nearly everyone was in the kitchen putting together a potluck supper. We got into a discussion of recent films, particularly of the high tech/violence genre. (I don't know how we got to this discussion but Brad, our host, is a gun collector.) Terminator and Terminator II were proposed as two of the better exemplars having both story and superior special effects—Terminator was rated as having the better story and Terminator II the better effects of the set.

I remarked that I had seen neither of the films. (I am bored by such films; I prefer a different kind of trash.) "Well, you really ought to," Brad replied. "In fact, I have both of them here." After a surprisingly easy discussion, the group chose films over football and it was decided that "Jim really ought to see Terminator before Terminator II."

Sue and her escort, with better things to do than watch a film with more settled folk, took their leave with thanks and praise. The audience for this film, therefore, was to be two couples, one married and one partnered, two adults of opposite gender attending the party without their partners and two female children, Lisa and Sarah. Lisa was aged 12 and looking forward into young womanhood. Sarah was 11 and hanging on to her childhood despite the imminent treachery of her body.

Meaning Attribution

Qualitative researchers have generally rejected the doctrine of meaning realism (Quine, 1980, Roth, 1987). Applied here, this doctrine holds that content is a "meaning delivery system," which, if done competently, unproblematically produces a common meaning in all auditors of that content. Meaning realism would hold, for example, that you and I could watch a video tape of a family dinner scene (a) in which the actions of the family would naturally produce the intended and unintended (or unconscious) mean-ings of the family members and (b) from which the two of us would derive a meaning common to each other and true to the performances. In short, actions and words have literal meanings that can be engaged by any competent reader.

Meaning realism is a necessary part of any objectivist project and its rejection by many qualitative researchers is an affirmation of the subjective stance of qualitative research. The subjective stance is a matrix of collective accomplishments that establish warrants upon which particular truth claims can be rested. Individual claim makers speak from this foundation, but their work is collectively authenticated and is not idiosyncratic or solipsistic. *Subjectivity*, then, is not the same as the "effect of the subject." It is the process by which action or discourse—as the subject of interpreta-tion—-is brought into meaningfulness through a particular interpretive method, itself made sensible in the matrix of reality accomplishments which produce a recognizable research activity (the subjective stance of analysis). The valid interpretation is true to its method and matrix.

For instance, in the example, I have been working a particular description because I want to make a statement about the audiences of our mass media. The description is true to the facts of the case, but I am certainly assured that those facts do not have the same meaning for the other members of the party. My writing is the *method* by which that meaning for the party is constructed.

But "my writing" is not simply "my" writing. It is responsive to the demands of my participation as a good party-goer, sensitive to relational and political outcomes, and governed by the conventions of narrative construction as well as the theoretical frames by which we understand audiences. While I do the writing, I do it as an agent of our culture and the collective enterprise of research. My agency and agentry create the subjectivity of the analysis.

Could someone else read and write the party toward a different end? Absolutely. This is a necessary outcome of the rejection of meaning realism and the acceptance of meaning attribution. The relationship between facts and their interpretation is permissive not deterministic (Madison, 1990); no one explanation is determined but not every explanation is permitted. The argument from the facts must be compelling, It must resonate—ring true to the scene and the reader's experience as well.

This audience helped itself to seconds on food and arranged itself in a double semi-circle one behind the other. In a very natural but almost sacred way, Brad stepped to the apex of this configuration removed the laser disc with practiced care and inserted it in the machine. His technology was on display and it was to display the technological brilliance of the film. That sacred instant was just a flicker of a pose, a strobe of movement, a posture in which the sense of the moment is delivered and we are returned immediately to the ordinary. "I prefer the laser to tape," Brad was saying. "It gives a much better picture and the sound will blow you away."

Terminator opens with what reviewers are wont to call a "gritty scene of death and destruction." The time is the future. Robotic intelligence has taken control of the earth. The human dream is the hands of a pitiful group of rag-tag warriors whose only hope is the last remnant of the great man theory, a charismatic leader who has some key to resurrection. Robotic intelligence, being what it is, has determined to reach back into the past and execute this leader's mother, thereby vaporizing his future. The humans, operating on their own intelligence have sent an operative into the past to assassinate the executioner. He arrives naked in history, due to some quirk in the time machine—but not without significance, and steals the trousers of a transient.

In the audience, I am struck by what has *not* happened. This group of wisecracking westerners is silent. There is ample opportunity to whoop and holler at every improbable ploy, but it is churchly quiet. We have reproduced enough of the theatrical qualities that this is no longer television where conversation is an ordinary part of the viewing experience. For the moment, at least, we are at the cinema. It doesn't last long. Perhaps it was Karen, mindful of her responsibilities to her guests, who brought us back by asking one of the children to get another bag of chips. At any rate, about a third of the way through the film it became all right to comment on the action.

Offhand comments are an ethnographer's stock and trade. They provide references to an otherwise unspoken understanding which develops in the engagement of symbolic material. These comments showed the group confirming the moves of the plot as the terminator hunted the woman—that vessel of the future—and as her flawed but human male attempted to effect her rescue. I heard "Oh, she gave it away" over a telephone conversation; "he's got it figured out" as we saw a pensive Schwarzenegger; and a prediction of "They're dead" at the before-the-mayhem phase of a massacre.

Interpretive Representation

With the procedures of interpretive representation, we move into the domain of analytic methods to answer the initial questions of "what, how, and why" of the field. Traditional and contemporary ethnographies, just as traditional and contemporary criticism or journalism, split on the issue of representation. For the traditionalist in any of these fields it is possible to represent "the other" in objective, value free description. Contemporary theorists, however, are ardent in their rejection, pointing out that objective writing is simply a practiced means of deception which deliberately masks the political efforts advanced.[7]

In every field experience, nonetheless, there are facts which are uncontested: this person was present or not; this conversation was held; these words were spoken in an interview. Such facts, alas, are banal. They have no meaning for the agents of their creation and the service in which they will be engaged in the ethnographic argument. The moment facts become useful, they are politicized; but they are still facts.

The result is that we talk about a "constructive empiricism" (van Fraassen, 1980), which is, first of all, responsible for preserving the facts of the case, even when those facts are intractable to the interpretation the researcher wishes to advance. But constructive empiricism also acknowledges that for those facts to be meaningful, *some* interpretation (as opposed to *their* or *the* interpretation) must be fashioned. The explicit recognition of the constructive accomplishments of interpretation is the reflexive mark of contemporary qualitative research.

> Equally important is what I did not hear. I heard no feminist complaints. The woman is a strong character but she is unquestionably saving "mankind" by doing the work of men. Her strength is in her womanly duty. I heard no concerns about the violence and graphic blood spattered gore. I made no comment about it either, but sat there with that detached view that scientists are supposed to have while they watch their civilization go down the toilet.

> Other comments, however, did fashion the critical sequence by which I could come to understand at some level the engagement of the film. The hero and the heroine have momentarily escaped the terminator. They have a respite of several hours and a bed before them. And, well, this is war after all. At this point, Lisa, the elder, says "Oh no, here's that scene." Sarah, the younger, answers, "Oh no, this is the part that I don't like." With that she buried her head in her arms.

> The scene offers some nudity, most of which I missed trying to watch what the girls were going to do, and the simulation of very missionary sex. Lisa turned her body slightly away from the scene but in effect "toughed" it out watching the whole time. Sarah kept her head down. "That's right Sarah," someone said for the pleasure of the adults but also in

---

[7]They would, for example, point to my seemingly harmless use of the words *traditional* and *contemporary* to distinguish objectivist and hermeneutic approaches. These are obviously nominations which do particular work in the creating and branding of positions.

confirmation of what we all "knew" to be right, "you don't want to be watching that kind of stuff." As the movie returned to mutilation and killing, several in the audience reported to Sarah that it was now safe to watch.

That sequence struck me, disturbed me, has made exquisite sense to me—unfortunately in many different ways. In my first analysis, I focused on the fact that the violence, the crushing, ripping and tearing, the utter destruction of the human body in so many different ways was no more to the audience than a plot device and a graphic diversion. It had no power. Not because we were desensitized to it. This filmic violence was turned a minor pleasure. It had no power because we knew it was a movie.

But sex in an audience of the American mountain west? In this masculine west, we find an unrelenting power of the naked torso, the bare breast. I shared these comments with one of my colleagues who told me of finding some explicit videos in his son's room. Being the good journalist, he, of course, watched them. He did not like them. They offered images he could still recall and they repulsed him. We came to the conclusion that the tension between a sexual economy and a prudish morality had suppressed the explicit representations of good sex, adventurous, fun-loving sex between partners who may be actually married to one another. While not experts, my colleagues and I could think of no cinematic or video examples. What we were left with were infidelities, stolen moments, mindless performance, sleaze and on to the deeper depth of degradation. These are the images available to schoolboy and journalist alike.

Referential Analysis

Qualitative research is *not* a descriptive method. It is not prior to something else. Qualitative research arguments can certainly end in claims which are primarily descriptive—what philosophers of science would call claims of existence or "ontological" claims, but that is not the only direction such arguments can take. They are equally adept at making claims of how things happen ("praxeological claims") or why they happen (epistemological claims).

All such claims rise out of the methods of referential analysis. *Referential analysis* itself refers to the characteristic of qualitative research to be referenced to two intersecting domains: the domain of mundane practice—which provides the research site—and the domain of theory and argument—from which claims can be advanced. There are no positivist boundaries to these domains: The researcher becomes suffused in each, and in the argument; information passes seamlessly between them.

There is, however, a shifting priority. For example, two Austrian students were interested in what gay men and straight women might say about homosexuality given the chance to talk separately to a man and a woman previously known to them as gay and straight respectively. Though we can certainly see the contours of a generalized, human science background assumption field, there is no specific theory being advanced in this interest.

Once the interviews were conducted, however, they began to make sense when the students brought the terms and structures of a theory of community to bear. While this analysis is going on at this writing, a first cut suggests that gay men and straight women from the Austrian middle class describe boundaries and members of the gay community in very different ways.

The shift in priorities can be seen fairly clearly here. In the field stage, the priority was to provide as broad an opportunity for comment as the researchers were able. There were no prepared questions. Researchers attempted to simply keep the conversation going by using active listening and passive prompting. There were no questions on community; respondents did not use terms like *boundaries* or *community members*.

What was reported, however, could be appropriated into a set of claims about the character of communities seen from inside and out as well as those about the Austrian, middle class gay community. At that moment of appropriation, what was said was taken from its priority as a sentence in a conversation and moved to its priority as a textual warrant.[8] And, of course, all of the arguments about the legitimacy of that appropriation came along with it.

I was still struggling with the conclusion of this interpretive line when Brad and Karen's family met mine for a Sunday brunch. I was chatting to Karen and Sarah about this write up, this description of our audience. Karen remarked that she felt it important that her children be introduced to a variety of images in the home so as not to be taken by surprise by them elsewhere.

In talking with Sarah I learned that she and Lisa had seen the film several times before; both knew it sequence by sequence. Sarah's comment came back to me—"this is the part that I don't like." It slowly dawned on me that hers was a rehearsed performance. Hers was not an involuntary recoil from images too strong to stand, but the knowledgeable recreation of what it is to be a proper schoolgirl. It was the embodiment of the woman-to-be as spectacle and spectator.

The story of Sarah illustrates three major principles which come into play in any understanding of audiences. First, most encounters with symbolic material are part of some larger social action—they are the named engagements of watching television, going to the movies, reading a book, looking at the signs along the road, or participating in a psychology experiment. The rules governing the encounter are the rules of the larger social action in which the material becomes embedded. Second, symbolic material—the general term these days is "texts"—stand as a resource for action and not as an agent of effects. And, third, the texts of our lives—the movies, television programs, novels and tabloids—are interpreted in the uses we have for them in the lives we are able to create within the master identities we are given.

There is, of course, a much larger argument to be developed around these conclusions. The effort of this larger argument is to work against the conception of the media as the source of our social ills, to force the recognition that it is the social inequities—which we produce and which privilege us—which create the conditions of unhealthy lives.

The audiences for our media are not faceless aggregates defined only by their exposure to this or that unit of industry production and to be understood only in categories of age, race, caste, and the like. They are the Brads and Karens, Sarahs and Lisas, as well as the gang members and street punks of this now global village engaged in the kindnesses and cruelties of everyday life. In their daily performances, they are artful co-conspirators in an on-going system of reality construction in which the material and the mediated are

---

[8]Similarly, a check mark on a page is appropriated as an answer to an item in a questionnaire.

made sensible. It is this conspiracy, in which we are all implicated, which crafts a society of the elevated and oppressed. We are not victims of our media although media can be used to victimize some and reward others. Culpability is not in content but in human action.

Lives are lived and lost in the semiotic domain in the moment by moment, local, partial, and improvisational interpretations by which we understand the world. It is because the world must be interpreted in order to act within it that we are each empowered to work for the sensemaking strategies of our own good. There are no guarantees—the struggle for meaning is intense and immensely profitable. Each of us, scholar and scientist, critic and analyst, student and citizen is in the middle of that struggle, and it is a struggle full of doubt and uncertainty.

When we deny that uncertainty we may be moved to a dangerous surety of purpose. I believe a clear expression of that dangerous surety comes in the shrill rhetoric of the self-appointed who would seek to command the lives of others. The "watch-dog" groups and their house-broken scientists who demonize the different and who argue through carefully crafted experiments and surveys a pathology of effects for what is a condition of enforced subjugation. Such groups who declare "those people" (and we all recognize the coded racist meaning invoked) to be too weak to resist the blandishments of even sugared cereal and Barbi dolls much less the easy solutions of violence and sex. The primary effect of this level of meddlesome science is to deny the poor their pleasures. It is another act of containment and suppression to ensure that "those people" will not be like us

Critique

The place of the critical in qualitative research is both controversial and unconventional (Carbaugh, 1989/1990; Cushman, 1989/1990; Goodall, 1991). Most discussions of science, at this level, follow the age of enlightenment assumption of the separation of what is true and what is good. This is the notion of value-free science—a notion almost always marked as "not really possible" but then acted upon as if it were. Much of the practice of science would not see the section that immediately preceded this analysis as "scientific."

It is, however, the rejection of meaning realism and the acceptance of the subjectivity of analysis which opens the door to the critical in science (Taylor, 1987). When we abandon a belief in "brute sense data" and base our claims instead on the accomplishments of interpretation, we intermix what is right with what is true. This intermixing denies the scientist his or her innocence from the political outcomes of the practices of knowledge production (Jackson, 1989). Explanation and knowledge are no longer transcendental and propositional but rather rhetorical and actional. Our knowledge claims are platforms for action; our work to advance them pushes a program of action whether we acknowledge it or not.

The strong hermeneutic position in qualitative research (Rosaldo, 1993) holds researchers responsible for both the intended and unintended consequences of their research. Something is true because we create the conditions by which it can be held to be true. Each of us, therefore, is responsible for the claims we make.

CONCLUSIONS

Methods are always more than technique. They are emblematic of a set of epistemo-logical foundations which define the character of a scholar's life (Rose, 1990; Fowler & Hardesty, 1994). Those of us who are in the knowledge production business, as all the authors in this text are, live a privileged life.

Hermeneutic science calls on us to consider the instrumentality of our work and to repay the price of privilege by producing scholarship and supporting efforts that strive to make a meaningful difference in the lives of others (Harrison, 1991). That effort will lead us to the emancipatory struggle—a crucible of good intentions and corrective opposition—emancipation which is an on-going strategy (Sullivan, 1990).

So dedicated, our valid scholarship will produce the strategically engineered social action by which the occasions of opportunity, education, good housing and a secure life can be more than privilege.

REFERENCES

Anderson, J. A. (1987). *Communication research: Issues and methods*. New York: McGraw-Hill

Anderson, J. A. (1991). The social action of organizing: Knowledge, practice and morality. *Australian Journal of Communication, 18*, 1–18.

Anderson, J. A. (1992). On the ethics of research in a socially constructed reality. *Journal of Broadcasting and Electronic Media, 36*, 353–357.

Anderson, J. A. (in press). *Communication theory: Epistemological foundations*. New York: Guilford.

Anderson, J. A., & Goodall, H. L., Jr. (1994). Probing the body ethnographic: From an anatomy of inquiry to a poetics of expression. In F. L. Casmir (Ed.), *Building communication theories* (pp. 87–129). Hillsdale, NJ: Lawrence Erlbaum Associates.

Bakhtin, M. M. (1986). *Speech genres and other late essays* (V. M. McGee. Trans.). Austin: University of Texas Press.

Bellah, R., Madsen, R., Sullivan, W., Swindler, A., & Tipton, S. M. (1985). *Habits of the heart: Individualism and commitment in American life*. Berkeley: University of California Press.

Blaikie, N. W. H. (1993). *Approaches to social inquiry*. Cambridge, MA: Policy Press.

Bohman, J. (1991). *New philosophy of social science*. Cambridge, MA: MIT Press

Caputo, J. D. (1987). *Radical hermeneutics: Repetition, deconstruction and the hermeneutic project*. Bloomington: Indiana University Press.

Carbaugh, D. (1989–1990). The critical voice in ethnography of communication research. *Research on Language and Social Interaction, 23*, 261–282.

Chase, R. S., Anderson, J. A., & Larson, T. L. (1990, June). *Patterns of viewing and descriptions of use for broadcast television news*. Paper presented at the International Communication Association, Dublin.

Conquergood, D. (1991). Rethinking ethnography: Towards a critical cultural politics. *Communication Monographs, 58*, 179–194.

Cushman, D. P. (1989–1990). The role of critique in the ethnographic study of human communication practices. *Research on Language and Social Interaction, 23*, 243–250.

Denzin, N., & Lincoln, Y. (1994). *Handbook of qualitative research*. Newbury Park, CA: Sage

Erlandson, D. S., Harris, E. L., Skipper, B. L., & Allen, S. D. (1993). *Doing naturalistic inquiry: A guide to methods*. Newbury Park, CA: Sage.

Fowler, D. D., & Hardesty, D. L. (Eds.). (1994). *Others knowing others: Perspectives on ethnographic careers*. Washington, DC: Smithsonian Institute Press.

Glaser, B. G., & Strauss, A. (1967). *The discovery of grounded theory*. Chicago: Aldine.

Goffman, E. (1959). *The presentation of self in everyday life*. Garden City, NY: Doubleday.

Goodall, H. L., Jr. (1989). *Casing a promised land: The authbiography of an organizational detective as cultural ethnographer.* Carbondale: Southern Illinois University Press.

Goodall, H. L., Jr. (1991). Turning within the interpretive turn: Radical empiricism and a case for post-ethnography. *Text and Performance Quarterly, 11,* 153–169.

Habermas, J. (1984). *The theory of communicative action* (T. McCarthy, Trans.). Boston, MA: Beacon Press. (Original work published 1981)

Harding, S. (1986). *The science question in feminism.* Ithaca, NY: Cornell University Press.

Harrison, B. (1991). *Inconvenient fictions: Literature and the limits of theory.* New Haven, CT: Yale University Press.

Jackson, M. (1989). *Paths toward a clearing: Radical empiricism and ethnographic inquiry.* Bloomington, IN: Indiana University Press.

Lanigan, R. L. (1992). *The human science of communicology.* Pittsburgh, PA: Duquesne University Press.

Lindlof, T. (1994). *Qualitative communication research methods.* Newbury, Park, CA: Sage.

Lofland, J. (1975). *Doing social life.* New York: Wiley.

Madison, G. B. (1990). *The hermeneutics of postmodernity.* Bloomington: Indiana University Press.

Miller, D. L. (Ed.). *The individual and the social self: Unpublished work of George Herbert Mead.* Chicago: University of Chicago Press.

Newell, R. W. (1986). *Objectivity, empiricism and truth.* London: Routledge & Kegan Paul.

Parsons, T. (1937). *The structure of social action.* New York: McGraw-Hill.

Peirce, C. S. (1931). *Collected papers* (Vol. 1). Cambridge, MA: Harvard University Press.

Peirce, C. S. (1932). *Collected papers* (Vol. 2). Cambridge, MA: Harvard University Press.

Peirce, C. S. (1958). *Collected papers* (Vol. 8). Cambridge, MA: Harvard University Press.

Popper, K. R., & Eccles, J. C. (1977). *The self and its brain.* Berlin: Springer-Verlag.

Quine, W. V. O. (1980). *From a logical point of view* (2nd ed., rev.). Cambridge, MA: Harvard University Press.

Rosaldo, R. (1993). *Culture and truth.* Boston: Beacon Press.

Rose, D. (1990). *Living the ethnographic life.* Newbury Park, CA: Sage.

Roth, P. A. (1987). *Meaning and method in the social sciences: A case for methodological pluralism.* Ithaca, NY: Cornell University Press.

Schutz, A. (1965). The social world and the theory of social action. In D. Braybrooke (Ed.), *Philosophical problems of the social sciences* (pp. 53–67). New York: MacMillan.

Stacks, D. W., Hickson, M. L., & Hill, S. R. (1991). *Introduction to communication theory.* Fort Worth: Holt, Rinehart & Winston.

Sullivan, R. (1990). Marxism and the "subject" of anthropology. In M. Manganaro (Ed.), *Modernist anthropology* (pp. 243–265). Princeton, NJ: Princeton University Press.

Taylor, C. (1987). Interpretation and the sciences of man. In P. Rabinow & W. M. Sullivan (Eds.), *Interpretive social science: A second look* (pp. 33–81). Berkeley: University of California Press.

van Fraassen, B. C. (1980). *The scientific image.* Oxford: Clarendon Press.

Wagner, R. (1981). *The invention of culture.* Chicago: University of Chicago Press.

Weber, M. (1974). Subjectivity and determinism. In A. Giddens (Ed.), *Positivism and sociology* (pp. 23–31). London: Heinemann.

II

Mass Communication
Approaches and Concerns

5

Mass Communication Theory and Research: Concepts and Models

Bradley S. Greenberg
Michigan State University

Michael B. Salwen
University of Miami

Medieval Europeans knew, spoke, and thought about a universe within their immediate observation—a slice of land carved from the forests encompassing their villages. Few ever ventured beyond the timberland. They knew from occasional travelers that there were other villages beyond the woods. But, so little did they know of the other villages that the other villages might have well been distant planets.

The development of the printing press changed the medieval view of the world. The social consequences of the printing press were demonstrated in 1517 when Martin Luther published his 95 criticisms against the Church in Rome. He was not the first person to criticize the church. But, because his seditious writings were mass circulated, within months Europe was talking about Luther's defiant act. The Church, in kind, responded with its own attacks. Luther's criticisms ushered in the Protestant Reformation and "the first propaganda war" (Burke, 1985, p. 118).

The far-reaching and often unintended effects of Luther's mass communicated messages demonstrate the multifarious nature of mass communication. Suddenly, people know and think about a world beyond their observation. Although tempting, comparing the contemporary Third World village with the medieval village before the age of printing is unwarranted. As a result of the mass media—of radio and group television viewing—today's modern villagers "see" a pseudo-world beyond the forests. Some Third World leaders today view Western mass media in their countries as agents of media imperialism. Not only blatant propaganda, but even entertainment programs (e.g., "I Love Lucy") are thought to have the potential for undermining traditional cultures (Salwen, 1991). Indonesian President Sukarno, a 1960s Third World spokesperson, declared: "You may not think of a refrigerator as a revolutionary weapon. But if a peasant woman sees one on TV in her village square and realizes what it could do for her and her family, the germ of revolt is planted" (quoted in Manchester, 1993, p. 9).

This chapter reviews the development of theory and research in mass communication. The chapter concludes by proposing a scheme—a model of models—to help readers organize mass communication models. The chapter's main premise is that theory and research are inseparable. Without theory to guide the interpretation of data, research activity is mere data collection in a helter-skelter fashion. When such atheoretical data are quantitatively summarized, they are open to criticism as mere "number crunching." Likewise, empty theorizing and subjective interpretations without procedures to gather data open the researcher to what critics call "naval gazing," "mere speculation," or "armchair philosophy."

ESTABLISHING A BASE: METHODS AND THEORIES

Only in this century did researchers formalize broad "theories" about mass communication. The rise of daily newspapers with more than one million circulation and the introduction of electronic media fostered an interest in the effects of mass commmunication messages. Certain attributes appeared to distinguish mass communication from other modes of human communication: the diffusion of messages from a seemingly powerful, single source to a large, heterogeneous audience; the public nature of the messages; and the lack of (or delayed) feedback from receivers to the mass communication source.

Theoretical Development

After World War I, it appeared to some observers that clever politicians and governments had manipulated communication symbols in mass communication messages to bring the world to war. A crude "theory" of "propaganda" emerged in which mass media were seen as having a "hypodermic-needle" (or "bullet theory" or "theory of uniform effects") effect of direct, universal, and massive influences on malleable and impressionable audiences.

This notion of all-encompassing effects would have two primary limitations. First, wartime propaganda—whether during World War I or our more contemporary Gulf War—represents a relatively unique situation with few if any competing messages.

Anti-war propaganda is not common in the mass media of dictatorial nations or democracies; even in democracies those who oppose patriotic efforts are largely ignored by the mainstream media (Kellner, 1993). So the development of a model based on the lack of competitive messages cannot be generalized to more common situations.

A second assumption is that the receiving target (readers, listeners) is homogenous in composition and response. Yet there is no compelling evidence that audiences can be herded into a single media corral; indeed, contrary evidence suggests audiences are resistant to media messages.

Some media scholars argue that the hypodermic-needle "theory" never received serious scholarly attention; it was formulated years later for political and pedagogical reasons (Chaffee & Hochheimer, 1985; Sproule, 1989, 1990). Even if there never were a hypodermic-needle theory, the mass media would be—and still are—viewed by many as powerful instruments for communicators to convey persuasive messages to audiences. The assumption of massive and unmitigated media effects certainly influenced empirical mass communication research in the "effects" tradition. Lasswell (1927), for example, described how symbols could be manipulated through the mass media:

> A new and subtler instrument. . . .weld[s] thousands and even millions of human beings into one amalgamated mass of hate and will and hope. . . . The name of this new hammer and anvil of social solidarity is propaganda. . . . All the apparatus of diffused erudition popularizes the symbols and forms of pseudo-rational appeal; the wolf of propaganda does not hesitate to masquerade in the sheepskin. All the voluble men of the day—writers, reporters, editors, preachers, lecturers, teachers, politicians—are drawn into the service of propaganda to simplify a master voice. (p. 220)

Methodological Development

Starting in the 1920s, several modes of inquiry for studying mass communication were refined. One involved content analysis of media, defined by Berelson (1952) as "a research technique for the objective, systematic, and quantitative description of manifest content of communication" (p. 18). A popular form, "propaganda analysis," was pioneered by Lasswell (Rogers, 1994, pp. 203–243). The "Chicago School" of sociology, caught up in the progressive spirit of the era, did not shy away from advocating social causes and "do-goodism." Early Chicago School research displayed a methodological eclecticism that was "empirical but not very quantitative" (Rogers, 1994, p. 152). Chicago School researchers took advantage of their inner-city environs to conduct ethnographic studies of urban problems (Vidich & Lyman, 1993), while in Europe the Frankfurt Institute of Social Research applied neo-Marxist theory to critically analyze communication and culture (Bottomore, 1984).

Despite promising qualitative research developments, by the mid-1930s mass communication research in the United States was distinguished by "an aggressively empirical spirit" (Czitrom, 1982, p. 122). A confluence of factors accounted for quantitative empirical research's popularity. Among the factors was the development of measurement tools, such as the Likert scale and the formulations of systematic methods for gathering data.

In addition, statistical techniques for analyzing large set of data were introduced into the behavioral sciences. British mathematician Karl Pearson, for example, introduced the product–moment coefficient. Pearson, aware of the import of his discovery, declared that the product–moment coefficient "had the potential of introducing a major paradigm shift and revolutionizing the biological and social sciences" (quoted in Tankard, 1984, p. 66).1 Another statistical pioneer fascinated by quantitative analysis, Francis Galton, devised statistical measures of beauty, prayer, and boredom. Galton, however, serves to warn against the misuse of statistics; he applied statistical techniques to support the Eurocentric racial theories of the late 19th and early 20th centuries (Gould, 1981). Paralleling statistical advancements were technological improvements in computers that allowed researchers to analyze massive data sets (Lowery & DeFleur, 1988, p. 20; Nash, 1990). Meanwhile, within the media professions, the use of quantitative data became increasingly important for mass media "market research" (Hurwitz, 1988).

Newspapers relied on studies to learn about their readers. Developments in radio led to audience studies based on telephone coincidentals (e.g., "What are you listening to right now?"). This technique was later adapted into the first generation of television ratings. The financial resources of media industries to fund studies, and thereby have some say over the academic research agenda, encouraged investigation in the empirical tradition. Industry influence on the academic study of mass communication was evident in advertising (Hess, 1931; Link, 1938). As Scott (1921) noted: "[I]t can be stated, without fear of contradiction, that *no advertisement that defies the established laws of psychology can hope to be successful*[italics added]" (p. 2).

Despite research advances, empirical research faced a nagging problem. Conducting empirical research was expensive. Some researchers demonstrated an ability to obtain industry and government funding. But, many critics asked, at what price? Even Paul F. Lazarsfeld, who obtained substantial industry funding and was sometimes accused by critics for selling out to industry (Gitlin, 1978), was not oblivious to such dangers (Pasanella, 1994), and he warned: "[W]e academic people always have a certain sense of tightrope walking: at what point will the commercial partners find some necessary conclusion too hard to take and at what point will they shut us off from the indispensable sources of funding and data?" (Lazarsfeld, 1948, p. 116).

MASS COMMUNICATION GOES ITS OWN WAY

Many mass communication (and interpersonal communication as well) "founders" of the 1930s and 1940s were housed in sociology and psychology programs and did not call themselves communication scholars (Rogers, 1994). Lazarsfeld (1948), for example, was a sociologist who considered himself "a student of the mass media" (p. 115).

What mass communication needed was someone to champion its cause. This advocate was Wilbur Schramm (Dennis & Wartella, 1976; Rogers, 1994; Wartella, 1994), who sought to establish communication as a legitimate academic field with a firm grounding in the behavioral sciences. In a series of edited volumes from 1948 to 1972, Schramm brought together researchers from journalism, the behavioral sciences, and the mass communications industries. These volumes (especially Schramm, 1948,

---

1See Tankard (1984) for an account of the contributions of leading statisticians.

1954) trained future mass communication scholars, providing a firm research grounding for the emerging field. Although Schramm planted the seeds for a legitimate and independent field of study, it was many years before researchers viewed themselves as mass communication scholars setting an agenda for mass communication research.

Schramm did not originally distinguish mass communication from human communication. He hoped for a unified field of communication. But this contemporary separation was an inevitable result of parochial academic barriers (Reardon & Rogers, 1988). Rogers (1994, pp. 449–450) traces the human and mass communication dichotomy to 1950, when Schramm became the University of Illinois' dean of the Division of Communication, in charge "of every activity at the University of Illinois that was to be even remotely connected with communication" (p. 449). However, the rhetorically oriented Department of Speech decided not to join the division.

Academic Emergence

University journalism programs would have been the most logical place in academia for the emergence of the study of mass communication. But most journalism programs emphasized vocational training. Many were dominated by former journalists who held an antipathy for behavioral research. Even in the late 1950s, now prominent researchers (e.g., Westley, 1958a, 1958b) were able to publish articles in the flagship scholarly journal in journalism that portrayed the behavioral sciences as a novel approach. Most journalism faculty saw the social scientific study of mass communication "to have no practical value whatever, in part because few effects researchers bothered to expound on the implications of their studies for journalists, and also because many such researchers wrote the results of their studies in barely comprehensible language" (Weaver & Gray, 1980, p. 142).

This is not to say that applied journalism researchers, or those in advertising and public relations, did not contribute to mass communication theory during this formative era. Journalism professionals complained (and sometimes still complain) that journalism research is not geared to industry. Meanwhile, scholars from other academic disciplines claimed (and sometimes still complain) that journalism research is atheoretical and inappropriate for the academy. To deal with these two-pronged attacks, Sloan (1990) argued that journalism programs have become a mish-mash curriculum of skills training and scholarship:

> The result has been one of the most evident, peculiar features of journalism education. One might say it is schizophrenic. It is not known which way to go: Should it become primarily professional, or should it be a traditional academic discipline? Possessing a sense of inferiority to both professional journalism and academia, it has tried to prove itself to both. One inferiority complex is difficult enough to overcome, but two create a severe problem. (p. 4)

Perhaps as a result of journalism education's confused identity and unwillingness to be at the vanguard of mass communication theory and research during the 1940s, 1950s, and much of the 1960s, when the systematic study of mass communication blossomed, sociologists and other behavioral science researchers set the agenda for mass communication theory and research (Berelson, Lazarsfeld, & McPhee, 1954; Hovland, Lumsdaime, & Sheffield, 1949; Katz & Lazarsfeld, 1954; Lazarsfeld, Berelson, & Gaudet, 1944). Their "grand studies," guided by broad research questions, yielded unanticipated findings for the development of later models (e.g., the sleeper effect, two-step flow, opinion leaders, selective perception, reinforcement).[2] Much of this early research might appear unsophisticated today; they were based largely on breakdowns of media use and preferences by various demographic (i.e., socioeconomic status) groups. But their impact was enormous (Katz, 1987).

Not until the 1970s, when mass communication was an established area of study, did journalism researchers Maxwell McCombs and Donald Shaw (1972) offer the agenda-setting model. McCombs and Shaw's model hypothesized that the news media prioritized or set the agenda of issue concerns for the public. Agenda-setting was widely embraced by journalism scholars, and even entered common parlance among media professionals. Although the agenda-setting model was thoughtfully conceived, explicated, and provided valuable insights about the mass communication process, there were other reasons why the model was well-received. Agenda-setting was also important because it was the first popular "home-grown" mass communication model from self-declared journalism researchers (Tankard, 1990).

The quantitative tradition in mass communication has become dominant in the United States today, although there has been a renewed interest in qualitative research and the macro-level social effects (Potter, 1996). In 1983, a special issue of the *Journal of Communication* devoted to the "Ferment in the Field" brought together internationally prominent scholars to comment on the alleged upheaval in communication study. A number of critical scholars, who trace their roots to the Frankfurt Institute of Social Research, contributed to the "Ferment" issue. Many neo-Marxist, critical scholars attacked behavioral researchers, sometimes savagely, for failing to criticize mass communication industries.

Critical scholarship also has had an impact on mass communication thinking. It has stimulated interest in expanding inquiry beyond media effects on audiences—traditionally the main focus of mass communication—and looking at media production processes as well. Most behavioral researchers have not, however, responded to the critical scholars' harshest criticisms. Ithiel de Sola Pool (1983) was one of the few behavioral researchers in the "Ferment" issue to directly confront the charges from his critical colleagues. His criticisms were directed at a lack of coherent methods in critical research and, from his perspective, a reliance on speculation and academic cliches:

> So where is the ferment? There is, of course, a large and dull literature that claims to have overthrown empirical behavioral research. It condemns quantification and controlled observation as arid, naive, banal, and even reactionary and immoral. I chose not to digress into a debate about the morality of acquiring knowledge. The important point here is that,

---

[2]The sleeper effect posits (Hovland, et al., 1949; Hovland & Weiss, 1951) that over time receivers remember parts of the messages after forgetting the source. Two-step flow and the related concept of opinion leaders come from studies (Berelson, et al., 1954; Katz & Lazarsfeld, 1954; Lazarsfeld, et al., 1944) in which leaders in their areas of expertise gained information from the mass media that they filtered down to other people. Selective perception and reinforcement were implicit in Lazarsfeld's and Hovland's research. Selective perception maintains that people actively attend to and select messages that fit preconceptions. Reinforcement is conceived as an explanation for why people seek out messages that fit preconceptions.

if knowledge of the world is a good thing to have, there is no other way of acquiring it except by carefully and with well-designed controls. . . . But the scores of methodological and ideological essays about new approaches to the study of communications can hardly be honored by the term "ferment." There is a simple recipe for these essays: avoid measurement, add moral commitment, and throw in some of the following words: social system, capitalism, dependency, positivism, idealism, ideology, autonomy, paradigm, commercialism, consciousness, emancipation, cooption, critical, instrumental, techno-cratic, legitimation, praxiology, repressive, dialogue, hegemony, contradiction, problem-atic. (p. 260)

THE AGE OF MODELS

A good deal of mass communication research has been guided by so-called *models*, such as agenda-setting, spiral of silence, cultivation analysis, knowledge gap, and others discussed in Section II of this book. A good deal of mass communication research also consists of bodies of research such as violence, media ethics and so forth, as the other chapters attest. Westley (1958b) noted the trend toward "conceptual models" in mass communication as an effort to "stake out significant concepts in the field, to codify scattered findings of the past and weave them into a single conceptual framework which will help give direction and focus future work" (p. 313).

Models are shorthand attempts to capture the essence of a conceptual issue or question of interest. A model "seeks to show the main elements of any structure or process and the relationships between [and among] these elements" (McQuail & Windahl, 1993, p. 2). For example, Lasswell's (1948) cryptic model: "Who Says What in Which Channel to Whom with What Effect?" This simple model directs research attention to the source, the message, the channel, the receiver, and the outcome or consequences.

Although Lasswell's model draws attention to several key elements in the mass communication process, it does no more than describe general areas of study. It does not link elements together with any specificity, and there is no notion of an active "process." Still, it generated great interest. A dozen years after Lasswell, Berlo (1960) elaborated his own source–message–channel–receiver paradigm that became a stand-ard for the analysis of human communication processes for a decade.

Models are useful to the extent they:

1. specify relationships among concepts/variables. A useful model will generate conceptual hypotheses, indicating the nature and direction of linkages among the components;
2. are relatively simple to express verbally or visually;
3. characterize an active process;
4. stimulate research; and
5. are responsive to change and revision from research outcomes.

The hypodermic-needle model dominated until the 1940s. As discussed earlier, although there is some question whether such a model influenced scholarly research, anyone reading pre-World War II popular literature will see that it underlay much popular thinking about the mass media and their consequences. As one medical writer noted: "The story of mass media in America reads much like the case history of a public health menace" (Starker, 1989, p. 5).

In the war and postwar period, the introduction of quantitative, empirically-based research findings challenged the earlier exaggerated claims of unmitigated media effects. Only after Klapper summarized the newly accumulated research into an alternative model in 1960, resulting in the so-called "limited-effects" (or "minimal-effects") model, was the hypodermic-needle model rejected.

Klapper shifted attention from media messages to the role of audiences in the mass communication process. This was an important development, but one diminished by researchers who became overly enthused about the power of an "active" and even "obstinate" audience able to overcome media messages (Bauer, 1964). A failing of limited-effects research is found in a reliance on short-term experiments and surveys; it largely neglected how difficult it is to measure the effects of cumulative messages. Another limitation was a concern with affective and behavioral effects, rather than cognitive effects.

From the beginning, researchers were uncomfortable with the limited-effects notion that the mass media were relatively minor contributors to media effects. The limited-effects model contends that a variety of sociological and psychological factors mediate and reduce the effects of any mass communication message. Klapper argued that the major impact of the mass media was to reinforce existing opinions, rather than modify old ones—a position as extreme as the hypodermic-needle's had been in the opposite direction. Its influence was evident in research during this period. For example, a survey on *The American Voter* (Campbell, Converse, Miller, & Stokes, 1960) noted:

> [I]t is seldom wise to rely on even the most rigorous study of mass media for indications of the public's familiarity with any specific issue. In general, public officials and people involved in public relations tend to overestimate the impact that contemporary issues have on the public. They find it difficult to believe that the reams of newspaper copy and hours of television and radio time could be ignored by any normal person within the reach of these media. The fact seems to be, however, that human perceptions are highly selective, and unless it happens to be tuned to a particular wavelength, the message transmitted will be received only as noise. (p. 99)

The limited media effects model, like the bullet theory, is no longer popular. Today, the dominant general view is moderate media effects. Still, aspects of the limited-effects model endure. McGuire (1986) chided popular commentators and empirical scholars for adhering to the "myth of massive media impact" despite what he contends is substantial empirical evidence to the contrary:

> First, we are not arguing that no media effects have been found, but only that the demonstrated effects are not large. A formidable proportion of the published studies (and presumably and even higher proportion of the unpublished studies) have failed to show overall effects sizable enough to reach the conventionally accepted .05 level of statistical significance. Some respectable studies in several of the dozen impact areas reviewed below do have impacts significant at the .05 level, but even these tend to have very small effect sizes, accounting for no more than 2 or 3% of the variance in the dependent variables such as consumer purchases, voting behavior, and viewer aggression. (p. 177)

Such overarching, grand models as the hypodermic-needle theory and limited-effects are of little value to empirical researchers interested in designing specific studies. The 1960 to 1980 period produced a variety of small-scale models which specified sub-processes of social effects within mass communication (McQuail & Windahl, 1993). The small-scale models examined small slices of mass communication processes that led researachers to appreciate both the power and limitations of the mass media. If there is any dominant grand model today, however, it is a model of moderate media effects.

Popular models of moderate effects—such as agenda setting, knowledge gap, gatekeeping—pointed to regularities in mass communication effects and processes. These and other models are discussed at length in this section of the book. Advocates of moderate effects models accept the general processes of empirically-supported mass communication models, but also understand that they are by no means universal. They call for researchers to delineate the contingent conditions, locate the intervening variables, and specify the social contexts.

A MODEL OF MODELS

Several popular contemporary mass communication models receive in-depth treatments in succeeding chapters. Here we propose a scheme—a model of models—to help organize existing models and research. The scheme is useful for suggesting modified research paths. Our model is a broad classification-type model in the Lasswellian tradition for summarizing the plethora of mass communication models. It does not refer to any dynamic process.

Process-based research on mass communication phenomena can begin with a fairly linear collection of processes. After the processes are established, we can then speak of recursive or nonlinear features. The concepts are arrayed in a linear fashion in which they are likely to occur but, even here, we can graphically capture their potential for nonlinear or overlapping evolution as well. In trying to keep models relatively parsimonious, we limit our set of processes to four; each process, however, may constitute a separate model (see Fig. 5.1).

Processes of Selection

Of all the stimuli available to be reported, of all that is in gatekeepers' heads to be created, of all the entertainment story ideas that exist, how are a relatively small number of stimuli chosen for development? Typical gatekeeping studies begin in editorial

Selection
   Creation
      Dissemination
       Reception

FIG. 5.1.   Model processes.

offices, comparing material selected from the larger quantity that goes unused. Gatekeeping research in the selection process would encompass editorial and entertainment norms and decisions about what should be covered before any actual selection or rejection decision is made.

Determining the predilections, predispositions, interests, and biases of media decision makers is crucial in understanding decision making at the initial stage, before possible alternatives exist, and how ideas or events are developed into mass communication messages. This approach raises numerous questions: Do the decision makers have personal agendas? If so, do their personal agendas influence the selection process? Are they aware of the selection processes of other relevant media decision makers? If so, how does this awareness influence their selection process? How do they decode their environment? What are their reference points? . . . criteria? . . . standards?

One can also pose questions here regarding access. It has been said that reporters are only as good as their sources. Access to sources of information, events themselves, and ideas all become variables in the selection process. This approach provokes researchers to ask important questions: Whom do you know? Whom do you trust?

The 1990 Gulf War provided another generation of war correspondents with limited access to military sites, targets, and information sources (Greenberg & Gantz, 1993). The result was a media picture of the war that was carefully constructed by the military. Media decision makers can make their selections only from those issues, events, and ideas which are accessible.

Inherent in the selection process is the entity of the media system or institution. The institution consists of individuals in various work roles with professional and social norms. It is foolhardy to think that a single omnipotent gatekeeper makes these decisions. In some cases, there are layers of people who filter the offerings to the environment; story ideas go to editors who share them with senior editors, or producers, and so on. In other contexts, selection is a group process, (e.g., the designated creative advertising team for a new car will pool its impressions of the car's best features during the initial step in the advertising campaign proposal). And of course there are the mixes of individuals (the client) and groups (the ad team) and so forth.

In summary, then, the selection process links media institutions and systems with the world from which events, ideas, information, and other issues will be extracted for possible inclusion in that system's message pool.

Processes of Creation

Now the linkage shifts to encompass those media system components responsible for translating the events and ideas obtained from the selection process into sets of signs and symbols to be disseminated to receiving groups. That which has been decoded must now be encoded.

The composition of the creating unit is of interest. Is it an individual or a team? What are their respective abilities? How do they merge their talents and their disparate ideas about the event or story? To what extent are they compatible with each other? In other words, we have the same set of concerns about characteristics and predispositions of the communicators as we did when specifying their operating rules in the selection process. Here the questions apply to their encoding capabilities.

The creation process needs to identify the intentions of the communicating sources as well. If sources intend to inform rather than persuade, alternative message strategies will likely be chosen. Paralleling this should be an understanding of the motives which drive such individuals in their creative enterprises. One set of motivations relates to their understanding of the reward system accessible to them. For example, if two reporters assigned to the same story use different reference points, wherein one anticipates how his or her peers will respond to the story, and the second anchors his or her material in how the audience will respond, there emerges a basis for anticipating content differences in each message.

Content differences, examined through content analysis research, have long been the subject of mass communication research. These studies lie within the creation process as its end product, although many tend to be static investigations of available content. These studies sometimes infer motives and intentions rather than directly assess them. To avoid static, descriptive outcomes, researchers can consider trend analysis (if the content has been analyzed previously) and comparative analysis (looking across different media for the same kinds of content). Both approaches permit hypothesis testing.

Content analysis is perhaps the most common research method in mass communication. The substance of these analyses normally examines content for *topics, themes,* and *styles.*

Topical analyses provide the subsequent basis for agenda-setting research. Here, content analysis is a means to the end of understanding one component of media influence on the public. The purpose is to study how emphasized topics in the mass media encroach on the public's agenda. Media coverage of issues or individuals confers status (fame and infamy alike). Topics which are absent or less emphasized in the media are considered of less import to the public, although this conclusion is more often assumed than demonstrated.

Thematic analyses seek objective markers of how women and minorities are portrayed, how often violence is used to resolve conflict, or whether Middle Eastern combatants are given equal photo display. While topical analyses emphasize the presence and frequency of media content, thematic analyses focus on the directionality of that content.

Stylistic analyses, not as common as topical and thematic analyses, evolve from the grammar and structure of mass media messages. Forty or fifty ago, readability research was plentiful (Flesch, 1943, 1948). Readability studies determine the comprehensibility of written passages based on measures of verbal complexity, assessed with simple tools (e.g., sentence length and syllable counts). It is unfortunate that counterpart measures of listenability and viewability have not been developed. Today, formal features in television (e.g., zooming, panning) are examined for their potential and actual impact on viewers' enjoyment and understanding (Watt & Welch, 1983) and comprise a language referred to as *media literacy.* More structural assessments (e.g., order of presentation of information or arguments, the emphasis and placement of counterinformation) also fit within this creative process segment.

Topics, themes, and styles are the result of creative decisions made by individuals and small groups. They are dependent, in part, on the medium for which the messages are created. To this point, we have ignored media differences because the creative processes described are generic across all media. Their outputs, however, are media specific. So, creative process models are likely to require elements that account for media differences.

The context in which message creation processes occur also yields research considerations. For example, media creators often do their work in stressful contexts (e.g., the stress of deadlines and competitive pressure). How does stress impact on their product? Are there more errors? Does it take longer to encode? Is some amount of stress a positive motivator, while too much impedes the message creation process?

Processes of Dissemination

In practice, the concept of a dissemination process is not wholly separable from the process associated with receiving a message. It is also erroneous to assume that receivers will necessarily decode the messages as the senders intended. This separation of message dissemination and reception is an artificial and temporary separation that highlights approaches to the systematic and scientific study of mass communication. If not already apparent, all such separations are artificial, perhaps arbitrary; they are a convenient way to convey conceptions of a particular idea being studied at that time.

Dissemination processes link message producers and creators to their receivers via their messages. Gatekeepers then select from the flood of messages available to them; this is the traditional gatekeeping approach for determining how decisions are made and on what bases. As noted, this traditional gatekeeping model occurs after messages have already been created.

In part, dissemination is dependent on the media play given any event or idea. The two most popular dissemination models have dealt with the diffusion of news, almost entirely a media system configuration, and with the diffusion of innovations, in which the media have a central, but not exclusive, role. The former is interested in how rapidly breaking news disseminates among segments of the public, whereas the latter focuses on how rapidly new products, ideas, or services disseminate.

Diffusion of news research could begin in the newsroom with the decision-making process that determines how a story will be reported, when it will be released, and what sort of play it will be given. Diffusion of innovations' interest in the mass media focuses on the media's role in providing information about the innovation, in contrast with or in juxtaposition with the role of a source. Again, decisions about which media to use for disseminating, for how long, and with what anticipated effects are difficult to assess and have not received research attention.

Content analysis in the dissemination process focuses on what media play is given to a story, event, or idea. In a specific time frame, how frequently does it appear? How prominently is it featured? The diffusion of news research tradition often has chosen to examine crisis or catastrophe news events, in which almost all the major media (with any news component) interrupt their normal routine and transfer to an overwhelming examination of the happening, such as the unexpected death of a major figure. Given the unstable nature of crisis news events, it is also fair to examine the misinformation the media provide as the raw breaking news takes form over time before errors are corrected.

Processes of Reception

Linking the message to the receiver begins with selectivity processes. Of all the messages available to media audiences, with which ones are they familiar and unfamiliar? Awareness certainly precedes a certain amount of exposure. One may begin with acknowledging that there is a large business in making receivers familiar with messages. That business consists of making receivers aware that a media event will be available to attend. Whether the promotions are advertisements on ABC announcing new fall programs, or the stories and matrices in *TV Guide*, or the newspaper index at the bottom of the front page, they are designed to increase audience awareness as the first step toward increasing exposure. Their purpose is to cut into the selection process and cry out, "Try Me!"

Media use or the time and energy spent on the mass media is often measured by *exposure*. The issue of comparative time allocated to different media remains an enduring research concern. Is it fair to compare an hour of book reading with equal time spent watching television or reading a newspaper? Underlying the measure of media exposure is a concern with reception; it is assumed that media exposure and reception are positively correlated. While sheer time spent with media might be an operationally reliable measure, it is not a sufficient indicator of reception.

The process of selective exposure is receiving new scrutiny. Thanks to new media technologies, the public has more choices available than ever before. Rather than a half dozen off-air television stations, there are 40 to 80 cable television channels, plus another dozen offering pay-per-view, and a likely two dozen radio stations from which to select, if a portable tape deck isn't plugged into one's ears. Given a computer with a modem, tapping into one of several information data banks (is this mass communication?) offers several hundred information sources. What is the process of media choice-making, within available disposable time, which leads an individual to watch this, read that, or listen to something different? The range of strategies being used by receivers to cope with an overwhelming array of media options is a fertile, but largely uncultivated, area for research.

Exposure itself has often been mapped against what are called media *gratifications*—those needs and uses which prod individuals to choose a particular media activity, usually over others that are available at the same time. These motivating tendencies have been mapped for a wide variety of content—entertainment, news, game shows—to identify both underlying and content specific gratifications. Seeking gratifications from media experiences then can be linked to obtaining them; if what is sought is not fulfilled, what is the likelihood that one will return to that medium or that specific content for a second effort? Do some gratifications emanate from specific content and others from specific media, regardless of content offering? How much of our media exposure is gratifying in some way, or merely habitual?

Given selectivity in awareness and exposure, this phase in our model of models can also include assessments of selectivity in interpretation and recall. These follow logically from exposure. They also reverify the need to acknowledge that audiences may interpret the media systems output in terms of their own predispositions. Furthermore, audiences are likely to recall only that which are particularly outstanding and of special utility for them. This suggests that the relationship between what was initially identified in the selection process as a candidate for subsequent media creation and dissemination may bear little resemblance to the resultant message. Such a statement cuts across the modular processes being described, but is of sufficient import to highlight here.

At some point, model-making must cease and researchers commence to test the model and its components. One criterion for halting is when the model becomes overly complex. For that reason we end this effort at a model of models, by summarizing the elements to examine in the selection–creation–dissemination–reception criteria in the model of models in Table 5.1.

There is much more that researchers should examine in analyzing and critiquing mass communication models. Were we to continue our model of models, we might extend the reception process by discussing alternative potential effects one might highlight from mass media; alternatives to reinforcement effects might be one such effect. Because specification of such effects is likely to be contained within the hypotheses that link elements or concepts in each of these phases, we urge readers to continue with such speculation.

SUMMARY

In summary, contemporary study of mass communication is guided by popular models, often, but not exclusively, in the effects tradition. Given the time it takes for a model to produce a coherent body of research, it is difficult to predict whether major new widely-accepted models are on the horizon. This is not entirely a bad thing; a field that willy-nilly introduces and tosses out models the way that Detroit used to introduce new car models is a field unsure of its place.

There are some possible models on the horizon. The third-person effect, people's attributional beliefs that mass media messages affect other people but not themselves (Davison, 1983), is gaining credence as a popular model generating a paradigmatic body of empirical research (Gunther & Mundy, 1993; Perloff, 1993). Another, the drench hypothesis, focuses on whether television effects on viewers is the result of a relatively short-term intensive impact (drench) or incremental effects attributable to the repetition of messages and images over time (Greenberg, 1988; Reep & Dambrot, 1989).

In addition to an age of models, the field is to some extent in an age of normal research. Researchers are specifying the contingencies of popular models, rather than putting forward new ones. In short, the field of mass communication has wound down from an era of rapid growth and excitement during the 1930s to 1960s and established itself as a legitimate field of study forging new paths in understanding and delineating the mass communication processes.

TABLE 5.1
Selection–Creation–Dissemination–Reception Criteria

Selection	Creation	Dissemination	Reception
Decoding	Encoding	Gatekeeping	Decoding
Accessibility	Agenda-setting	Media emphasis	Gratifications
Selective choices	Channel choices	Institutional analysis	Selective responses
Gatekeeping	Motivations	News diffusion	Choice-making
Personal agendas	Message–content analysis	Cultivation analysis	Information-seeking
Biases and interests	Content manipulations		Effects analyses
Criteria and norms	Intentions		

REFERENCES

Bauer, R. A. (1964). The obstinate audience: The influence process from the point of view of social communication. *American Psychologist, 19,* 319–328.

Berelson, B. (1952). *Content analysis in communication research.* New York: Free Press.

Berelson, B. R., Lazarsfeld, P. F., & McPhee, W. N. (1954). *Voting: A study of opinion formation in a presidential campaign.* Chicago: University of Chicago Press.

Berlo, D. K. (1960). *The process of communication.* New York: Holt, Rinehart & Winston.

Bottomore, T. (1984). *The Frankfurt school.* Chichester, Sussex: E. Horwood.

Burke, J. (1985). *The day the universe changed.* Boston: Little, Brown.

Campbell, A., Converse, P. E., Miller, W., & Stokes, D. (1960). *The American voter.* New York: Wiley.

Chaffee, S. H., & Hochheimer, J. L. (1985). The beginnings of political communication research in the United States: Origins of the 'limited effects' model. In E.M. Rogers & F. Balle (Eds.), *The media revolution in America and Western Europe* (pp. 267–296). Norwood, NJ: Ablex.

Czitrom, D. J. (1982). *Media and the American mind: From Morse to McLuhan.* Chapel Hill, NC: University of North Carolina Press.

Davison, W. P. (1983). The third-person effect in communication. *Public Opinion Quarterly, 47,* 1–15.

Dennis, E., & Wartella, E. (Eds.). (1996). *American communication research: The remembered history.* Mahwah, NJ: Lawrence Erlbaum Associates.

Flesch, R. (1943). *Marks of a readable style: A study in adult education.* New York: Teachers College, Columbia University.

Flesch, R. (1948). A new readability yardstick. *Journal of Applied Psychology, 32,* 221–233.

Gitlen, T. (1978). Media sociology: The dominant paradigm. *Theory and Society, 6,* 205–253.

Gould, S. J. (1981). *The mismeasure of man.* New York: Norton.

Greenberg, B. S. (1988). Some uncommon television images and the drench hypothesis. In S. Oskamp (Ed.), *Television as a social issue* (pp. 88–102). Newbury Park, CA: Sage.

Greenberg, B. S., & Gantz, W. (Eds.). (1993). *Desert Storm and the mass media.* Cresskill, NJ: Hampton Press, Inc.

Gunther, A., & Mundy, P. (1993). Biased optimism and the third-person effect. *Journalism Quarterly, 70,* 355–372.

Hess, H. W. (1931). *Advertising: Its economics, philosophy and technique.* Philadelphia: Lippincott.

Hovland, C. I., Lumsdaime, A., & Sheffield, F. (1949). *Experiments in mass communication.* Princeton, NJ: Princeton University Press.

Hovland, C. I., & Weiss, W. (1951) The influence of source credibility on communication effectiveness. *Public Opinion Quarterly, 15,* 635–650.

Hurwitz, D. (1988). Market research and the study of the U.S. radio audience. *Communication, 10*(2), 223–242.

Katz, E. (1987). Communication research since Lazarsfeld. *Public Opinion Quarterly, 51,* S25–S45.

Katz, E., & Lazarsfeld, P. F. (1954). *Personal influence.* Glencoe, IL: The Free Press.

Kellner, D. (1993). The crisis in the Gulf and the lack of critical media discourse. In B. S. Greenberg & W. Gantz (Eds.), Desert Storm and the mass media (pp. 37–47). Cresskill, NJ: Hampton Press, Inc.

Klapper, J. (1960). *The effects of mass communication.* New York: The Free Press.

Lasswell, H. D. (1927). *Propaganda technique in the World War.* New York: Knopf.

Lasswell, H. D. (1948). The structure and function of communication in society. In L. Bryson (Ed.), *The communication of ideas* (pp. 117–130). Urbana, IL: University of Illinois Press.

Lazarsfeld, P. F. (1948). The role of criticism in the management of mass media. *Journalism Quarterly, 25,* 115–126.

Lazarsfeld, P. F., Berelson, B., & Gaudet, H. (1944). *The people's choice: How the voter makes up his mind in a presidential campaign.* New York: Columbia University Press.

Link, H. C. (1938). *The new psychology of selling and advertising.* New York: The Macmillan Company.

Lowery, S. A., & DeFleur, M. L. (1988). *Milestones in mass communication research* (2nd ed.). New York: Longman.

Manchester, W. (1993, October 25). A world lit only by change. *US News & World Report, 115,* 6–9.

McCombs, M. E., & Shaw, D. L. (1972). The agenda-setting function of the mass media. *Public Opinion Quarterly, 36,* 176–185.

McGuire, W. J. (1986): The myth of massive media impact: Savagings and salvagings. In G. Comstock (Ed.) *Public communication and behavior* (Vol. 1, pp. 175–257). San Diego, CA: Academic Press.

McQuail, D., & Windahl, S. (1993). *Communication models for the study of mass communication* (2nd ed.). London and New York: Longman.

Nash, S. G. (Ed.). (1990). *A history of scientific computing.* New York: ACM Press.

Pasanella, A. K. (1994). *The mind traveller: A guide to Paul F. Lazarsfeld's research papers.* New York: The Freedom Forum Media Studies Center.

Perloff, R. M. (1993). Third-person effect research 1983-1992: A review and synthesis. *International Journal of Public Opinion Research, 5,* 167–184.

Pool, I. de Sola. (1983). What ferment? A challenge for empirical research. *Journal of Communication, 33,* 258–261.

Potter, W. J. (1996). *An analysis of thinking and research about qualitative methods.* Mahwah, NJ: Lawrence Erlbaum Associates.

Reardon, K. K., & Rogers, E. M. (1988). Interpersonal versus mass communication: A false dichotomy? *Human Communication Research, 15,* 284–303.

Reep, D. C., & Dambrot, F. H. (1989). Effects of frequent television viewing on stereotypes: "Drip drip" or "drench." *Journalism Quarterly, 66,* 542–550, 556.

Rogers, E. M. (1994). *A history of communication study: A biographical approach.* New York: The Free Press.

Salwen, M. B. (1991). Cultural imperialism: A media effects approach. *Critical Studies in Mass Communication, 8,* 29–30.

Schramm, W. L. (Ed.). (1948). *Communications in modern society.* Urbana: University of Illinois Press.

Schramm, W. L. (Ed.). (1954). *The process and effects of mass communication.* Urbana: University of Illinois Press.

Scott, W. D. (1921). *The psychology of advertising.* New York: Dodd, Mead and Company.

Sloan, W. D. (1990). In search of itself: A history of journalism education. In W. D. Sloan (Ed.), *Makers of the media mind: Journalism educators and their ideas* (pp. 3–22). Hillsdale, NJ: Lawrence Erlbaum Associates.

Sproule, J. M. (1989). Progressive propaganda critics and the magic bullet myth. *Critical Studies in Mass Communication, 6,* 225–246.

Sproule, J. M. (1990). Propaganda and American ideological critique. In J.A. Anderson (Ed.), *Communication yearbook* (Vol. 14, pp. 211–238). Newbury Park, CA: Sage.

Starker, S. (1989). *Evil influences: Crusades against the mass media.* New Brunswick, NJ: Transaction Publishers.

Tankard, J. W., Jr. (1984). *The statistical pioneers.* Cambridge, MA: Schenkman Publishing.

Tankard, J. W., Jr. (1990). The theorists. In W. D. Sloan (Ed.), *Makers of the media mind: Journalism educators and their ideas* (pp. 229–286). Hillsdale, NJ: Lawrence Erlbaum Associates.

Vidich, A., & Lyman, S. M. (1994). Qualitative methods: Their history in sociology and anthropology. In N. K. Denzin & Y. S. Lincoln (Eds.), *Handbook of qualitative research* (pp. 23–59). Thousand Oaks, CA: Sage.

Wartella, E. (1994). Challenge to the profession. *Communication Education, 43,* 54–62.

Watt, J. H., & Welch, A. J. (1983). Effects of static and dynamic complexity on children's attention and recall of televised instruction. In J. Bryant & D. R. Anderson (Eds.), *Children's understanding of television* (pp. 69–102). New York: Academic Press.

Weaver, D. H., & Gray, R. G. (1980). Journalism and mass communication research in the United States: Past, present and future. In G. C. Wilhoit & H. de Bock (Eds.), *Mass communication review yearbook* (Vol. 1, pp. 124–155). Beverly Hills, CA: Sage.

Westley, B. H. (1958a). Journalism research and the scientific method: I. *Journalism Quarterly, 35,* 161–169.

Westley, B. H. (1958b). Journalism research and the scientific method: II. *Journalism Quarterly, 35,* 307–316.

6

Media Gatekeeping

Pamela J. Shoemaker
Syracuse University

One of the most enduring areas of research in mass communication is media gatekeeping—the process by which countless messages are reduced to the few we are offered in our daily newspapers and television news programs. Gatekeeping is such an essential part of the news gathering and dissemination process—because every potential news item cannot be gathered, and, from among those items gathered, they all cannot be disseminated—that it is often taken as a primitive or base part of news production, in the same way that writing is an assumed prerequisite for news production. Definition as a primitive process, however, can lead scholars to dismiss the gatekeeping process as uninteresting and something to be taken for granted.

Gatekeeping is not a primitive process and is not analogous to writing. Gatekeeping occurs as an antecedent to writing, and it feeds the many decisions involved in writing. What will we write about? What will we include or leave out? How will the topic be shaped? Gatekeeping also touches more of the news production and dissemination process than writing. It begins when potential news items are first conceived, discovered, and analyzed for news potential. From the news organization's standpoint, gatekeeping ends with the final selection and shaping of news items and their dissemination. Gatekeeping, therefore, is pervasive throughout the news production and dissemination process. It can be studied on many levels of analysis, with many different research methods.

ORIGIN OF THE CONCEPT

The basic idea of gatekeeping—that some selection of news items is necessary—has always been apparent. If there is space for only 5,000 newspaper column inches of news, then we must select from among the many stories available those that will be published; and, further, we must decide which portions of those stories will be published. A bucket can hold only so many walnuts—which are put in the bucket and which are left on the ground?

It was in theorizing about ways to change social norms that Kurt Lewin first coined the word *gatekeeping* (see: Shoemaker, 1991). The first pairing of the terms *gatekeeping* and *communication* came in Lewin's unfinished manuscript (published posthumously in 1947), "Frontiers in Group Dynamics: II. Channels of Group Life; Social Planning and Action Research" in the journal *Human Relations.* Lewin's "theory of channels and gate keepers" was elaborated in 1951 in *Field Theory in Social Science,* an edited collection of Lewin's work. He used the concept of "gate keeper" to illustrate how widespread social changes could be achieved in a community; his examples dealt primarily with how one could change a population's food habits. Lewin concluded that not everyone is equally important in making food selection choices, and he showed how influencing the person who orders or shops for food could change the food habits of the entire family.

Food, wrote Lewin, reaches the family table through "channels." One channel is the grocery store, and another might be the family garden. Figure 6.1 illustrates how Lewin thought food passed from these two channels to the dinner table. For example, in the grocery channel, food is discovered at the grocery store, purchased or not, and, if purchased, transported to the home. In the garden channel, decisions are made about what to plant, prune, and harvest. As fruits and vegetables grow, some will be eaten out of the garden by hungry children, some consumed by insects or disease, and others may die for lack of rain. Of the fruits and vegetables finally available to the household, only a subset will be harvested.

At this point, food from the grocery and garden channels merge, resulting in a whole new set of decisions. Should it be refrigerated or put in the pantry? Some food will rot in the refrigerator or languish in the deep recesses of the pantry. From among the usable food, the cook decides what to select for a given day—some items will be selected because they "go bad" if not eaten immediately. The cook also decides how to prepare and present the food to the family on the table. At every stage, a food item may be selected or rejected: Even if a potato is selected to be baked, it may be thrown away if rot is exposed when it is cut open.

The entrance to each channel or section of a channel is called a *gate.* Movement from one channel section to another is determined by human gatekeepers, or by a set of impartial rules (Lewin, 1951, p. 186).

A key to Lewin's theory was the understanding that positive and negative forces surround the gates. For example, if an expensive cut of meat is considered in the grocery store, the meat's cost is a negative force that tends to keep it from being selected and therefore not passing through the "meat selection gate"—*it's so expensive, how can I afford it?* If, however, the meat is purchased, its expense is transformed from a negative to a positive force once the meat passes through the gate—*it's so expensive, I must take care to transport, store, and prepare it carefully.* Because the forces surrounding a gate may differ, whether the item passes through it depends on the direction (positive or negative) and intensity of these forces. Since one channel may have multiple gates, there are many opportunities for an item to be rejected.

In Fig. 6.1, arrows show how forces facilitate or constrain the passage of items either within a channel section or on both sides of a gate. Forces are designated in italics; for example, fP,EF represents the force associated with the attractiveness of food within the section "buying," and it should facilitate the food's passage through the next gate into the "food on way to home" section.

Lewin believed that this theoretical framework could be generalized beyond the selection of food items. "This situation holds not only for food channels but also for the traveling of a news item through certain communication channels in a group, for movement of goods, and the social locomotion of individuals in many organizations" (Lewin, 1951, p. 187).

Although Lewin's terms *channel, section,* and *gate* imply physical structures, they are metaphors for a process through which some items pass on their way, step by step, from discovery to use. Sections correspond to events or states of being that occur in a channel. Gates are decision points. Gatekeepers determine both which items get into the channel and which pass from section to section. Gatekeepers may exercise their own preferences. They may act as representatives to carry out a set of preestablished policies.

EARLY STUDIES AND MODELS

David Manning White—Lewin's research assistant at the University of Iowa—was the first scholar to apply Lewin's channels and gatekeeper theory to a communication research project (1950). White said he "thought that the complex series of 'gates' a newspaper story went through from the actual criterion event to the finished story in a

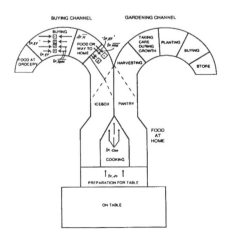

FIG. 6.1. Kurt Lewin's model of how food passes through channels on its way to the table. From *Field Theory in Social Science: Selected Theoretical Papers* (p. 175), by K. Lewin, 1951, New York: Harper. Copyright 1951 by Miriam Lewin. Reprinted with permission.

newspaper would make an interesting study" (Reese, Ballinger, & Shoemaker, 1993). His idea was to ask a small-city daily newspaper wire editor—whom he called "Mr. Gates"—to keep all copy that came into his office from three wire services during a one-week period in 1949. Mr. Gates also agreed to provide an explanation for why rejected stories (90% of the total received) were not used.

White (1950, p. 386) found that the selection decisions were "highly subjective." About one third of the articles coming across the wires were rejected on Mr. Gates' personal evaluation of the merits of the stories' content, particularly whether he believed them to be true. Other stories were rejected because of a lack of space or because similar stories had already run.

White's study stimulated communications researchers to look at selection decisions. Different reasons for selection decisions were found in other studies (e. g., Bass, 1969; Chibnall, 1977; Gandy, 1982; Gieber, 1956, 1964; Halloran, Elliott, & Murdock, 1970; McNelly, 1959). Gieber (1956, p. 432) concluded that the 16 newspaper telegraph editors he studied made decisions not based on their personal likes and dislikes, but rather because of a "strait jacket of mechanical details," such as "the number of news items available, their size and the pressures of time and mechanical production" (Gieber, 1964, p. 175). Gieber saw the wire editor as more passive than did White.

In 1957 a more theoretical model of gatekeeping was proposed by Westley and MacLean, based on Newcomb's (1953) ABX co-orientation model. Newcomb proposed the idea of *co-orientation*—two people (persons *A* and *B*) simultaneously orienting toward each other and an object (designated *X*)—as a way to study communication acts. Figure 6.2 shows how Westley and MacLean added the mass media (designated *C*) between the sender and the receiver. In this model, there are multiple events and story ideas (*X*s), some of which are discovered by sender *A* (in this model, a source) and then travel through the mass media (*C*) to receiver (*B*). Other events go

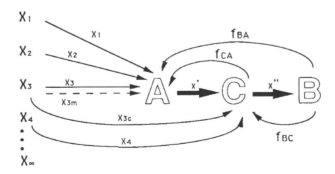

FIG. 6.2. Westley and MacLean's model of mass communication process, showing C as the gatekeeper. Reprinted by permission of the Association for Education in Journalism and Mass Communication from *Journalism Quarterly*, *34*, 31–38. Westely, B. H., MacLean, M. S., Jr., (1957).

directly to the media, bypassing sources. The introduction of the mass media *C* into Newcomb's model shows that not all messages that the source/sender *A* is aware of are transmitted to the receiver/audience (*B*). Some are unknown to the media; others are held by the media as unworthy of transmission. (*C*) represents the mass media gatekeepers, although sources/senders *A* can also perform a gatekeeping role.

Westley and MacLean's model and Gieber's study present very different views of the gatekeeping process than that originally described by White. White focussed on the decisions of one person, emphasizing personal and subjective aspects of the decision-making process. Gieber's study and the Westley and MacLean model, however, emphasized the gatekeeping aspect Lewin called *decision making according to a set of preestablished rules or policies*, the rules and policies are prescribed by representatives of an organization or social system applied more or less uniformly by those in the organization to make decisions.

In fact, Lewin's theory permits the study of gatekeeping on multiple levels of analysis; his examples include at least three levels. An individual can make personal decisions about what to buy at the market or cook on a given day, there are family routines or habits to take into account, and there are also societal and cultural forces at play. For example, certain foods are culturally unavailable within a given social system—insects are rarely eaten in some cultures but are prized as delicacies in others. Even if insects are culturally available as food, a particular family's eating habits may exclude insects from the shopping list. Or the individual shopper may make selections based on a personal preference that insects will be eaten only once a month.

The realization that gatekeeping can be studied on multiple levels of analysis allows for a richly elaborated concept. As shown by Shoemaker (1991; Shoemaker & Reese, 1991), gatekeeping in a communication context can be studied on at least five levels—individual, routines of communication work, organizational, social and institutional (extramedia), and societal. On the individual level, selection decisions are personal—*What do I like or dislike?* On the routines of work level, gatekeeping decisions are made according to a preestablished and generalized set of practices about how the work is to be done—*Is this newsworthy enough to be included in the day's television news program?* Such decisions cross media lines to the extent that media and communication workers share definitions of newsworthiness.

To continue, organizations have the power to hire and fire gatekeepers, thus ensuring that, if individuals have undesirable personal criteria for selection or if they apply selection rules (written or unwritten) improperly, they may be replaced with more acceptable candidates. On the organization level of analysis, we could also look at the gatekeeper's position within the organization as influencing the power that he or she has in making final selection decisions. Centrally located gatekeepers, such as newspaper publishers and television station managers, tend to have considerable power to develop organizational policies that greatly influence selection decisions (Hickey, 1966, 1968; Donohew, 1967).

Communication organizations also exist within an extramedia environment of social institutions that affect the gatekeeping process. There are many potential extramedia influences, such as sources, audiences and advertisers, markets and economic forces, government, interest groups, public relations efforts, and other media. Sources are often front-line gatekeepers, deciding to pass along some bits of information and not others;

perceived source accuracy is also a factor in selection decisions. Advertisers, in their quest for the most appropriate target audiences, exert direct and indirect influence on the mass media. Some newspapers, for example, have sought information about audience likes and dislikes to produce content that is attractive to the target audience, attracting more advertising dollars. Similarly, the success of a television program has long rested on its ratings—a measure of the number and type (through demographics and psychographics) of people watching the show. Shows with poor ratings are cancelled. Advertiser influence can also be indirect. Women's magazines, for example, traditionally have not run many stories about the harmful effects of smoking, presumably because the tobacco companies spend a lot of money on cigarette ads and ads for other companies that the tobacco conglomerates own (Kessler, 1989).

On the social system level of analysis, just as Lewin determined that some foods are not culturally available, events vary to the degree that they are culturally available as news items. Rape, for example, was rarely covered in newspapers 30 years ago but today is regular fare for mainstream news media. Culture—as well as other indicators of social significance, including political, military, and economic ties—also influence selection decisions, affecting the extent to which different parts of the world are covered. Media in the United States tend to give more coverage to European countries' events and issues than they do to those in Africa and South America. Even within the United States, the east and west coasts get more news coverage than does the American heartland.

METHODOLOGY

White's (1950) study used a content analysis research design that permitted White to compare stories included in the newspaper to those rejected. This remains a preferred gatekeeping method today; studying what does not become news is perhaps more revealing of the decision-making process than is studying only the news product. If we study only what is included in a television newscast, it is difficult to analyze what was left out and the process that led to the "in" and "out" decisions. For example, in her study of newspaper reporter sources, Seo (1988) found that individual source information is used in about the proportion that it is available. This puts a different light on the common finding (e.g., Gans, 1979; Sigal, 1973) that "official" sources are quoted far more than are individuals. It appears that there may be a lot more official sources available than there are individual sources, but to the extent that individual sources are available, they may be used.

Collection of all inputs, plus the designation of which are included and which excluded, is more important than studying only what is included. Content analysis of only selected items cannot determine what is being left out. For example, Scott and Gobetz (1990) did a content analysis of the amount of "soft news" coverage on the ABC, CBS, and NBC networks. They found that the amount of soft news increased between 1972 and 1987, but was this because there were more soft news events to cover? Or did journalists select an increasing percentage of soft news items? If journalists did select a greater proportion of soft news items, why should this be so? Because the journalists wanted more soft news? Or because journalists perceived that audiences wanted more soft news? Or were there other influences at work, such as a change over time in organizational routines? Such questions are vital in the study of gatekeeping. It is not sufficient to show changes in what is selected over time, or that one type of item is covered a lot at one time point. To more fully understand the gatekeeping process, the study of what is omitted is as important as studying what is selected.

Other recent study methods have included gatekeeper surveys (generally by mail, occasionally by telephone), in-person interviews (generally less structured than the usual survey instrument), observation of gatekeepers at work, and an occasional field experiment.

Surveys can inform us about psychological determinants of gatekeeping (e.g., Chang & Lee, 1992), such as preferences for one type of content over another or role conceptions. They can measure respondents' perceptions of forces working on the selection decision (e.g., space, time, directions from superiors). The problem with surveys is that respondents self-report their attitudes and preferences, speculate about what they would do under specified scenarios, and tell what they know (or think they know) about their colleagues and about how their organizations work. Such information may or may not provide valid measures of these forces and how they affect the gatekeeping process. The expression of an attitude does not always lead to attitude-consistent behavior. Survey data have less face validity than content analysis data when it comes to measuring whether specific news items are selected. Survey data do, however, provide insight into the respondents' own thought processes—processes that are invisible to the content analyst.

In-depth interviews with gatekeepers have also been conducted. For example, Berkowitz (1990) combined 4 weeks of observation of television news gatekeepers with interviews of 30 to more than 60 minutes in length about why specific decisions had been made. An unstructured interview format has the advantage of allowing respondents to take the discussion wherever they wish. This can be particularly helpful when interviewing gatekeepers about why they made specific selection decisions; the interview can be personally tailored to each gatekeeper. Personalization is also a disadvantage, however, because personalized interviews are generally not comparable; by definition there are no standardized questionnaires, thus lowering the study's external validity. Internal validity may be higher than in standardized surveys, however, because the causal chain between the selection decision and its antecedents can be traced in specific and detailed ways.

Gatekeeping studies using observational methods may suffer from the usual problem of reactivity, but this is generally lessened if the observational period is longer than a few days. In Berkowitz's (1990) study of television news gatekeepers, he devoted 2 weeks at the beginning of the study to "familiarization with the newsroom and the station's news process" (p. 57). Following this initial period, 4 weeks were spent observing gatekeepers at work, followed by 1 week devoted to personal interviews. This 7-week-long field period helped reduce the threat to internal validity due to reactivity, but it points to one of the disadvantages of observational research—it takes time to do it right. The longer the field period, the greater the external validity. The advantage of observation in studying gatekeeping is that the researcher sees real decisions being made in a real newsroom under realistic conditions and can observe some of the influences affecting the decisions, thus increasing external validity. Not all influences are observable, however, such as unwritten policies or socialization to newsroom routines. Combining observational data with interviews, however, can help the researcher more fully understand the gatekeeping process.

Experimental research in gatekeeping is unusual, but a field study by Hudson (1992) looked at how television news gatekeepers rated six staged versions of a murder story in which the violence levels were manipulated. The versions ranged from a story read by an anchor with no video to a version entailing a complete video of the murder occurring, subsequent shots of the body, pools of blood, and a close-up of the victim's face. All participants viewed six versions of the story and gave each a perceived acceptability level (PAL) of the violent material. Hudson then evaluated whether PAL scores varied for "participant" and "neutral" journalists, as measured by Johnstone, Slawski, and Bowman (1976).

The decision as to whether to use content analysis, surveys, personal interviews, observation, or experimental methods to study gatekeeping depends on the hypotheses being tested. It is clear, however, that the fullest understanding of gatekeeping will come from a multiple-method strategy.

CHANGES IN GATEKEEPING RESEARCH

Gatekeeping research has progressed from White's simple study of one gatekeeper's decisions to include or omit specific news stories to analyses of the process through which gatekeeping occurs. The expansion of gatekeeping studies to multiple levels of analysis has opened the door for the study of the most interesting of Lewin's concepts—the forces surrounding each gate. Most gatekeeping research routinely investigates the power that one or more forces have on whether a news item is permitted to pass through a gate. We are beginning to identify those forces that have the most impact on the selection of news items and whether the forces are positive or negative.

On the individual level of analysis, Chang and Lee's (1992) survey of a national sample of American newspaper editors looked at editors' attitudes toward selecting foreign news items and on the individual forces that affect gatekeeping. They found that these editor-gatekeepers preferred international stories that had some significant impact on American security and national interests. A key individual-level force affecting the decision was that editors with an "international perspective"—"liberal with foreign news interest and foreign language training" (p. 561)—were more likely to prefer stories about world events. The more professional journalism experience editors had, the less likely they were to select international stories. In this study the important forces around the gates were the characteristics of the gatekeepers themselves. Some forces were positively associated with news item selection (e.g., foreign language ability), but others were negatively related (e.g., years of journalism work experience).

Berkowitz's (1990, p. 66) television gatekeepers claimed to make selection decisions based on their "instincts" about what makes a good news program. In addition, Berkowitz found (see also Berkowitz, 1991, p. 246) that "news judgment" or "news values" influence gatekeeping. Whether this is an individual- or routines-level factor is debatable. Clearly, there are standard criteria for newsworthiness that are common across news organizations; however, the application of newsworthiness criteria may vary among individual gatekeepers.

Other routines-level forces include how much effort a news item takes to be transformed into a story, whether selection decisions are routinely made by individuals or groups of people (Berkowitz, 1990), and the desire for a "balanced" mix of stories (Stempel, 1985). McCombs and Becker (1979) suggest that whether a gatekeeper is assigned the work role of news manager (e.g., producer, assignment editor, news director) or information gatherer (e.g., reporter and anchor) is important in studying the gatekeeping process because people in the two types of jobs face different pressures (or *forces*). In using this role differentiation in a study of television gatekeepers, however, Berkowitz (1993) found that these work roles were not closely associated with selection of news items.

Organizational-level force research has included whether a radio station has a group affiliation (Riffe & Shaw, 1990); the number of gates a news item must pass through within the organization (Berkowitz, 1990); and resource constraints, such as number of staff, level of funding, and equipment availability (Berkowitz, 1991).

Extramedia force research has included the availability and capabilities of new technologies and the availability and quality of information subsidies, such as video releases (Berkowitz, 1991). Riffe and Shaw (1990) found that the size of the market positively influenced the amount of news that radio stations can carry.

A BRIEF STUDY PROPOSAL

An interesting gatekeeping study is an analysis of the forces that surround gates in the selection of news events. The following outlines one possible study in some detail to illustrate how theory and research can be integrated in a media gatekeeping study.

Introduction

The concept of forces is pivotal in gatekeeping research (Lewin, 1951). The identification of these forces and an assessment of their relative strengths and directions is important for new gatekeeping studies. This study uses two of the five levels of analysis identified by Shoemaker and Reese (1991)—the individual level and the routines level—to measure the strength and direction of forces working on each level and to assess at each level the relative importance of forces on the prominence with which events associated with the 1992 presidential election are published in a sample of American newspapers. Media critics have suggested that journalists' personal attitudes exert a powerful influence over media content. This study allows us to assess the influence of individual-level variables compared with that of variables from the routines level.

Theory

Lewin's (1951) concept of forces shows that influences on the publication of information about election events can be positive or negative and can vary in strength. On the individual level of analysis, Chang and Lee (1992) showed that editor-gatekeepers' personal interest in national security and national interests positively affected the extent to which they selected foreign news items. Conversely, the amount of professional experience editors had, the less likely they were to select international stories. On the routines level of analysis, Berkowitz (1990) showed that the extent to which an event fits the generally conceived concept of newsworthiness is positively related to its selection. McCombs and Becker (1979) also found that job roles could be influential in gatekeeping—news managers select different stories than do information gathers. On the organizational level of analysis, whether a radio station has a group affiliation or is independent has been found to impact selection (Riffe & Shaw, 1990). Berkowitz (1991) found that the resources of the organization (e.g., number of staff) influenced news item selection.

This study is interested in testing the following hypothesis: *Characteristics of an individual journalist-gatekeeper will affect how prominently an event is covered, even when journalistic routines are controlled* (although individual relationships among variables will also be of interest). If the hypothesis is supported, we can conclude that a gatekeeper's personal attitudes and characteristics influence the coverage of an event. Although journalistic routines may mediate personal influences, personal influences would still play a role in shaping media content.

The dependent variable is how prominently an event is covered in a newspaper. *Coverage prominence* includes both where the story is placed (with front pages of sections being more prominent than inside pages) and how long it is.

Independent variables are measured at both the individual and routines levels of analysis. Among the individual-level variables are: *political ideology,* the individual's personal assessment of how liberal or conservative her or his general political attitudes are; *journalistic experience*, the amount of time that an individual has been a newspaper journalist; and *voting*, whether the journalist votes in elections.

Routines-level independent variables include: *newsworthiness*, the extent to which an event meets the usual criteria for news (e.g., timeliness, proximity, importance, conflict, prominence, oddity); and, *balance of coverage,* editors' perceptions about whether stories concerning the major candidates in an election should be given equal amounts of space in a newspaper.

Method

The unit of analysis in this study is the news event. Events eligible for inclusion in the study will involve the 1992 presidential election between the dates of the Democratic and Republican conventions and election day. Fifty dates during the study period will be selected at random. Coders will look at *The New York Times* on each date and will determine the main event involving the U.S. presidential election. (As Reese & Danielian, 1989, showed, *The New York Times* sets the agenda for many other media, often picking up a story several days in advance of appearance in other media. *The New York Times* is not a perfect measure of the population of campaign events, but it probably covers more campaign events than most other newspapers.) Intercoder reliability checks will be performed on selection of the main event. The result will be a list of 50 campaign events to be used as a basis for the study of how these events are covered in another newspaper.

Dependent Variable.   To measure the dependent variable—the prominence with which an event is covered—coders will search a large daily newspaper, looking for the sampled events. The selection of a large daily newspaper is intended to maximize the probability that the event will be covered by a reporter at the newspaper rather than by relying solely on news service accounts. Only stories with a byline will be included to permit measurement of the individual-level independent variables. Coders will list all stories about each event that runs within one week after the event occurred. If more than one story about the event is present, the coders will be instructed on how to randomly select one of the stories for analysis. The full text of the sampled story will be retrieved. Intercoder reliability coefficients will be calculated for all content variables.

Prominence will be measured as an multiplicative index of the following variables:

Where the story about the event is placed in the newspaper: 3 = *covered on the first page of the first section of the newspaper,* 2 = *covered on the first page of another section of the newspaper,* 1 = *covered somewhere else in the newspaper,* 0 = *event is not covered.*

Amount of coverage: Number of words in the text. Events that are not covered will be assigned a score of zero.

Independent Variables. These will be grouped into two blocks, according to their level of analysis. Independent variables from the individual level will be measured by a mail survey. The author of each story will be mailed a questionnaire (or telephoned, if feasible) with the following variables:

Political ideology: Measured on a five-point scale: 1 = *very conservative,* 2 = *conservative,* 3 = *independent,* 4 = *liberal,* 5 = *very liberal.*

Number of years as a working journalist. Code to nearest whole year.

Whether the journalist voted for a presidential candidate in 1992. Dummy coded with 1 = *did vote for a presidential candidate.*

If an article has more than one author, only the first author will be interviewed.

Independent variables from the routines level will be measured by a mail survey to the political editors of the 100 largest daily newspapers. The following variables will be measured:

They will be given a brief description of each of the 50 events and asked to evaluate each according to its newsworthiness (4 = *exceptionally newsworthy,* 3 = *very newsworthy,* 2 = *moderately newsworthy,* 1 = *slightly newsworthy,* and 0 = *not at all newsworthy*).

They will be asked to evaluate the need for balanced coverage in a presidential election. "Newspapers ought to give about the same amount of coverage to all major presidential candidates on an issue or event like this." 5 = *strongly agree,* 4 = *agree,* 3 = *neutral,* 2 = *disagree,* 1 = *strongly disagree.*

Because we are interested in measuring journalistic routines rather than individual attitudes, scores on these two variables will be aggregated for each event across all political editors responding to the survey.

Analysis. Descriptive statistics will be provided for all variables in the study, and correlation coefficients will be provided for all variable pairs. The hypothesis will be tested via hierarchical regression analysis.

SUMMARY

The increasing convergence of news media industries make gatekeeping of continuing interest, particularly on the routines and organizational levels of analysis. If a newspaper and cable television company get together to provide a new form of news medium, do the routines of the newspaper or cable company prevail? Or is some new set of routines established? Likewise, when two organizations with different organizational cultures and structures collaborate on news production, how will their differing organizational characteristics impact on the selection and shaping of the news?

As we approach the 50th anniversary of gatekeeping, we need to think about new ways in which research can more fully elaborate the concept. Certainly, more research on the forces around gates needs to be done, and looking at gatekeeping as a concept on multiple levels of analysis is fruitful. But we should also operationalize aspects of gatekeeping other than mere selection. The way in which stories are shaped, timed, and presented is also part of the gatekeeping process, and such variables deserve to be included with selection in our arsenal of dependent variables. In addition, we should consider the ways in which these dependent variables may themselves interact to produce the final media content product.

REFERENCES

Bass, A. Z. (1969). Refining the "gatekeeper" concept: A UN radio case study. *Journalism Quarterly, 46,* 69–72.

Berkowitz, D. (1990). Refining the gatekeeping metaphor for local television news. *Journal of Broadcasting & Electronic Media, 34,* 55–68.

Berkowitz, D. (1991). Assessing forces in the selection of local television news. *Journal of Broadcasting & Electronic Media, 35,* 245–251.

Berkowitz, D. (1993). Work roles and news selection in local TV: Examining the business-journalism dialectic. *Journal of Broadcasting & Electronic Media, 37,* 67–81.

Chang, T. K., & Lee, J. W. (1992). Factors affecting gatekeepers' selection of foreign news: A national survey of newspaper editors. *Journalism Quarterly, 69,* 554–561.

Chibnall, S. (1977). *Law-and-order news: An analysis of crime reporting in the British press.* London: Tavistock.

Donohew, L. (1967). Newspaper gatekeepers and forces in the news channel. *Public Opinion Quarterly, 31,* 61–68.

Gandy, O. H., Jr. (1982). *Beyond agenda setting: Information subsidies and public policy.* Norwood, NJ: Ablex.

Gans, H. J. (1979). *Deciding what's news: A study of CBS Evening News, NBC Nightly News, Newsweek and Time.* New York: Pantheon Books.

Gieber, W. (1956). Across the desk: A study of 16 telegraph editors. *Journalism Quarterly, 33,* 423–432.

Gieber, W. (1964). News is what newspapermen make it. In L. A. Dexter & D. M. White (Eds.), *People, society and mass communication* (pp. 173–182). New York: Free Press.

Halloran, J. D., Elliott, P., & Murdock, G. (1970). *Demonstrations and communication: A case study.* Baltimore: Penguin.

Hickey, J. R. (1966). *The effects of information control on perceptions of centrality.* Unpublished doctoral dissertation, University of Wisconsin, Madison.

Hickey, J. R. (1968). The effects of information control on perceptions of centrality. *Journalism Quarterly, 45,* 49–54.

Hudson, T. J. (1992). Consonance in depiction of violent material in television news. *Journal of Broadcasting & Electronic Media, 36,* 411–425.

Johnstone, J. W. C., Slawski, E. J., & Bowman, W. W. (1976). *The news people.* Urbana: University of Illinois Press.

Kessler, L. (1989). Women's magazines' coverage of smoking related health hazards. *Journalism Quarterly, 66,* 316–322, 445.

Lewin, K. (1947). Frontiers in group dynamics II: Channels of group life; social planning and action research. *Human Relations, 1,* 143–153.

Lewin, K. (1951). *Field theory in social science: Selected theoretical papers.* New York: Harper.

McCombs, M. E., & Becker, L. B. (1979). *Using mass communication theory.* Englewood Cliffs, NJ: Prentice-Hall.

McNelly, J. T. (1959). Intermediary communicators in the international flow of news. *Journalism Quarterly, 36,* 23–26.

Newcomb, T. M. (1953). An approach to the study of communicative acts. *Psychological Review, 60,* 393–404.

Reese, S. D., Ballinger, J., & Shoemaker, P. J. (1993, August). *The roots of media sociology: Mr. Gates and social control in the newsroom.* Paper presented to the Communication Theory and Methodology Division, Association for Education in Journalism and Mass Communication, Kansas City.

Reese, S. D., & Danielian, L. M. (1989). Intermedia influence and the drug issue: Converging on cocaine. In P. J. Shoemaker (Ed.), *Communication campaigns about drugs: Government, media, and the public* (pp. 29–46). Hillsdale, NJ: Lawrence Erlbaum Associates.

Riffe, D., & Shaw, E. F. (1990). Ownership, operating, staffing and content characteristics of "news radio" stations. *Journalism Quarterly, 67,* 684–691.

Scott, D. K., & Gobetz, R. H. (1990, April). *Hard news/soft news content of the national broadcast networks.* Paper presented to the annual meeting of the Central States Communication Association, Detroit.

Seo, S. K. (1988, August). *Source-press relationship: Major characteristics of sources which influence selection of sources in news coverage.* Paper presented to the Newspaper Division, Association for Education in Journalism and Mass Communication, Portland, OR.

Shoemaker, P. J. (1991). *Gatekeeping.* Newbury Park, CA: Sage.

Shoemaker, P. J., & Reese, S. D. (1991). *Mediating the message: Theories of influences on mass media content.* New York: Longman.

Sigal, L. V. (1973). *Reporters and officials.* Lexington, MA: DC Heath.

Stempel, G. H. (1985). Gatekeeping: The mix of topics and the selection of stories. *Journalism Quarterly, 62,* 791–796.

Westley, B. H., & MacLean, M. S., Jr. (1957). A conceptual model for communications research. *Journalism Quarterly, 34,* 31–38.

White, D. M. (1950). The "gate keeper": A case study in the selection of news. *Journalism Quarterly, 27,* 383–390.

7

The Agenda-Setting Role
of Mass Communication

Maxwell McCombs
Tamara Bell
University of Texas at Austin

Too many events occur within a given day for the average American to personally attend to each one. News organizations, however, employ hundreds of people to observe those events and report what they see. Through the news media we learn which candidates are likely to win elections, which countries are likely to go to war, and which bills are likely to be approved by Congress. The media's daily reports alert us to the latest events and changes in the larger world beyond our reach. Consequently, most of our world is a second-hand reality created by the news organizations. There is no guarantee, however, that this reality accurately depicts our world.

The news media do not just passively transmit information, repeating verbatim the words of a public official or conveying exactly the incidents at an event. Nor do they select and reject the day's news in proportion to reality. Through their day-by-day selection and display of the news, editors and news directors focus attention and influence the public's perceptions of what are the most important issues of the day. Our attention is further focused—and our pictures of the world shaped and refined—by the way journalists frame their news stories.

This idea that the news media influence public perception of what are the important issues of the day has its roots in a classic 1922 book, *Public Opinion*. The author, American journalist and social commentator Walter Lippmann, titled his first chapter "The World Outside and the Pictures in Our Heads." It was Lippmann's thesis that the mass media, primarily newspapers and magazines in his day, create our pictures of the world. Lippmann understood, however, that the pictures provided by the press are often incomplete and distorted. After all, he consciously prefaced his book with Plato's allegory of prisoners in a cave who could see only the reflections of reality, never actual reality, on the wall before them. Yet, those reflections were their reality. Like the prisoners, we see only the reflections of reality in the news media. Yet, those reflections provide the basis for our pictures.

Not until 45 years later was the idea that the news media influence the "pictures in our heads" put to an empirical test (McCombs & Shaw, 1972). At that time, two researchers from the University of North Carolina wondered whether the topics selected by the news media to represent the "world outside" limited the kinds of events that people used to interpret that world. They also wondered if the public's perception of reality depended on which topics the news media covered and emphasized in their daily presentation of events.

Their research gave birth to a new mass communications theory, a theory which can be divided into two dimensions. The first dimension pertains to the transmission of issue or object salience from the media agenda to the public agenda. The second dimension pertains to the news media's role in framing those issues and objects in the public mind.

A FIRST TAKE ON LIPPMANN

During the 1968 presidential election, Maxwell McCombs and Donald Shaw (1972) conducted the first test of Lippmann's thesis in Chapel Hill, NC. The prevalent theory at that time, however, was that the mass media had only limited effects on the public (see chapter 5, this volume). Results from voting behavior studies in the 1940s indicated that exposure to campaign information had little influence on the public's voting intentions (Lazarsfeld, Berelson, & Gaudet, 1948; Berelson, Lazarsfeld, & McPhee, 1954). According to the limited effects model, voters relied on social groups and their predispositions to guide their voting decisions. The media only solidified and reinforced voters' preferences toward particular politicians. Joseph Klapper (1960) summarized this research in his often quoted conclusion that "mass communication *ordinarily* does not serve as a necessary and sufficient cause of audience effects, but rather functions among and through a nexus of mediating functions and influences" (p. 8).

In a challenge to the limited effects model, McCombs and Shaw tested the proposition that through their day-by-day selection and display of the news, the mass media influence public perception of what are the important issues of the day. In particular, they believed that a causal relationship existed between the media and the public—over time, the priority issues of the news media would become the priority issues of the public. The priorities of the news agenda are readily apparent to their audiences. In newspapers, cues include the size of the headline, the length of the story, and the page on which the story appears. Similar television cues include position of an item in the newscast and the length of the story. These cues assist the audience in prioritizing the small number of issues selected for attention in the daily news.

The dependent variable in the 1968 Chapel Hill study was *salience*, which refers to whether or not something is perceived as important or prominent. To operationalize this concept, McCombs and Shaw focused on one of public opinion's major outcroppings, the public's perception of the most important problem facing the country. Typically posed as an open-ended question, "What do you think is the most important problem facing this country today," it has been asked by the Gallup polling organization on a regular basis since the mid-1940s. The version that McCombs and Shaw asked undecided voters in the 1968 presidential election was, "What are you *most* concerned about these days? That is, regardless of what politicians say, what are the two or three *main* things which you think the government *should* concentrate on doing something about?" (p. 178). They then ranked the issues according to the percentage of voters naming each issue.

Subsequent research often has relied on similarly worded open-ended questions to measure salience (Erbring, Goldenberg, & Miller, 1980; Iyengar, 1979; Neuman, 1990; Yagade & Dozier, 1990). In one study, relating local newspaper coverage and public concern about community issues, Smith (1987) measured the public agenda by asking, "What do you think are our community's [Louisville and Jefferson County's] most important problems and needs?" This type of question has several advantages for measuring the salience of issues among the public. Because a number of polling organizations ask a similarly worded question about the importance of national problems, it is possible to combine sets of polls to address possible methodological weaknesses or limitations in coverage over time (Behr & Iyengar, 1985). Edelstein (1974) commended this approach because it allows respondents to define what problems are important to them rather than choosing from a list provided by the researcher.

Of course, the alternative approach, closed-end questions, offers other advantages. Presented with an open-ended question about the most important problem facing the country, most respondents name only a single issue. In other words, most analyses of the public agenda are based on single responses. Use of a closed-end question in which respondents are asked to rank or rate a series of issues provides a more detailed portrait of the public agenda. It also allows comparisons across the agenda on a variety of issues' importance. There are many ways to frame a question to determine issue salience.

The independent variable in the Chapel Hill study was news media content (i.e., media agenda). To test the agenda-setting hypothesis, McCombs and Shaw combined responses to their open-ended survey question with a content analysis of the nine major news sources used by Chapel Hill voters. The sources included television, newspapers, and news magazines. The open-ended survey question found five major issues of concern to Chapel Hill voters: foreign policy, law and order, fiscal policy, civil rights, and public welfare. The content analysis used these same five issue categories in its examination of the news coverage across three weeks of the fall presidential campaign. Just as the public agenda of issues had been rank-ordered according to the percentage of voters naming an issue, these same five issues were rank-ordered on the news agenda according to the percentage of news coverage on the issues falling into each category. There was a strong relationship (*rho* = +.967) between the public's and the media's agenda of issues. McCombs and Shaw named this transfer of salience from the media agenda to the public agenda the agenda-setting influence of mass communication.

Lippmann may have been the intellectual father of the agenda setting idea, yet he did not give the theory its name. Forty years after *Public Opinion*, the conceptualization of agenda setting was advanced by Bernard Cohen (1963) who wrote that "the press may not be successful much of the time in telling people what to think, but it is stunningly successful in telling its readers what to think about" (p. 13). Only a few years later was this theoretical notion named by McCombs and Shaw.

The value of the metaphor has been borne out historically. Rogers, Dearing, and Bregman (1993) found 223 publications that explicitly or implicitly concerned agenda setting from 1922 to 1992. The vast majority appeared after 1971, with the peak years of publication (1977, 1981, 1987, 1991) each producing 17 to 20 items. As they noted, "A research specialty evolves over time as a kind of family tree in which earlier studies influence later studies" (p. 74). McCombs and Shaw's 1972 article has been cited about 115 times, more than double the citations of the next closest study, in part because of the study's theoretical and methodological innovations (Rogers et al., 1993). In the article, for instance, McCombs and Shaw named the research specialty that was to emerge, and provided an empirical methodology for studying the agenda-setting process. This study mobilized a research tradition that closely has followed McCombs and Shaw's approach of combining news media content analyses with public opinion surveys.

In their initial study, McCombs and Shaw decided to examine an agenda of issues. However, since we rarely experience public affairs firsthand, we rely on the news media to construct the "pictures in our heads" about most aspects of public affairs—not just issues. Issues comprise only one part of our pictures, and they are only a third of the news coverage in most presidential campaigns. McCombs and Shaw might have chosen another agenda to examine. Perhaps they might have studied the agenda of political candidates, for the news media have a major voice in defining viable candidates for a party's nomination.

Many aspects of public affairs are worthy of examination, yet McCombs and Shaw chose issues because of the legacy of polling and democratic theory. Ascertaining how the public feels about the issues of the moment is the central activity of public opinion polling. Also, the fact that polls typically count all respondents equally bestows upon them a democratic character. Because polls permit quick and repeated assessments of public opinion, often enhancing the opportunities for citizen influence (Asher, 1992), it is believed that polls advance democracy by affording everyone a voice in their government.

The focus on issues also allowed McCombs and Shaw to refine two key points. First, they wanted to avoid the fallacy of "presumed effects," which occurs when only media content is studied. For example, we cannot assume that individuals watching televised graphic acts of violence will exhibit violent behavior. Only after testing television content and the public's reactions can we assert that a correlation exists (which it does). Secondly, McCombs and Shaw wanted to examine effects that result from the specific content of the media's messages. Previous media effects studies typically measured how frequently a respondent paid attention to the media. They did not attempt to link effects to specific media content. This study, however, sought to determine what the media were saying in their reports and how the public was responding. The goal was to link the content of the news agenda and the public agenda.

While the salience of issues on the news agenda and the public agenda is very much in the spirit of Lippmann, the Chapel Hill study design does not, strictly speaking, follow deductively. A content analysis of the media coupled with public opinion surveys provides only one approach to media influence on the pictures in our heads. McCombs and Shaw might have constructed a field, or a laboratory, experiment to determine the existence of agenda setting in mass communications. The fact that they chose to correlate the results of a content analysis and survey research does not preclude the use of other methods. However, the Chapel Hill design overwhelmingly set the methodological agenda for agenda-setting studies.

REPLICATION AND EXPANSION OF THE CHAPEL HILL STUDY

Examples of studies that have replicated and expanded this methodological approach are many.

• Funkhouser (1973) analyzed news coverage of the issues and public opinion about the most important problem facing the United States across an entire decade, the turbulent 1960s. He found considerable correspondence (+.78) between the media and public agendas. As a check on the spuriousness of the correlations, Funkhouser expanded his analysis to include statistical indicators of the reality behind these issues. In stark contrast to the prior correlation, there was little correspondence between statistical indictors of reality and trends across the 1960s in either news coverage or public opinion. The news media possess a power to create a picture of social reality whose saliences are at considerable variance with the "world outside."

• Shaw and McCombs (1977) conducted a large-scale panel study of the agenda-setting function of the news media. In addition to replicating the basic agenda-setting hypothesis, this study found that increasing media campaign exposure appears to raise voters' interest in politics, and it helps define salient features of the campaign; and that the influence of agenda setting on different categories of voters is a product of exposure, type of medium, political interest, need for orientation, and interpersonal communication.

• Palmgreen and Clarke (1977) examined whether differences existed in the media's agenda-setting role for local and national issues. The study, set in Toledo, Ohio, measured the public agenda by asking respondents the most important problem question. The media agenda was measured by content analyzing the Toledo *Blade*, the three national network newscasts, and local television news coverage. They found that the media's agenda-setting impact is weaker at the local level than at the national level. The researchers suggested that contingent conditions, such as interpersonal communications and personal observation, at the local level may have weakened the media's agenda-setting ability.

• Salwen (1988) replicated the basic related agenda-setting hypothesis with a particular focus on how long a set of issues must be in the news to have an optimal impact on the public agenda. His media and public agendas consisted of seven environmental issues. Initial evidence of significant agenda setting appeared after five to seven weeks of news coverage. The peak impact on the public agenda appeared after eight to 10 weeks of news coverage.

LONGITUDINAL STUDIES

Putting a different spin on previous agenda-setting research in which an entire agenda of issues is examined, some studies examined a specific issue (or issues) over a long period of time.

• Winter and Eyal (1981) discovered that the ebb and flow of national concern about civil rights from 1954 to 1976 mirrored the rise and fall of news coverage during those years. The percentage of Americans naming civil rights as the most important problem facing the country ranged from 0% to 52% in the 27 Gallup Polls conducted during those 23 years, a pattern that strongly reflects the news coverage in the 4 weeks immediately preceding each of those polls.

• In a study of the relationship between newspaper coverage and public concern about local issues, Smith (1987) used a series of 22 surveys conducted from 1974 through 1981 by the University of Louisville. The media agenda was ascertained by a content analysis of the *Louisville Times*. Agenda-setting effects were found for such local issues as crime and the environment. Of course, not all the issues covered in the news subsequently had high salience on the public agenda, leading to further questions regarding the "contingent conditions" that enhance or reduce agenda setting.

• Eaton (1989) examined media content from the three national network newscasts, five national newspapers, and three newsmagazines over 3½ years. He also used the Gallup Poll's most important problem question to measure the salience of 11 individual issues. All four hypotheses were confirmed: The amount of media content is positively correlated with issues the public says are most important to the nation; the correlation between media coverage and the issue importance varies by issue; recent coverage of an issue produces higher correlations with importance than earlier coverage; and correlations are greater when the media coverage leads measurement of importance rather than the reverse.

• Brosius and Kepplinger (1990) may have provided the ultimate set of evidence for the agenda-setting role of the news media. Comparison of the newscasts of the four major German television news programs for the entire year of 1986 with 53 weekly national opinion polls revealed significant agenda-setting effects for five issues: an adequate energy supply, East–West relations, European politics, environmental protection, and defense.

THE ACAPULCO TYPOLOGY

The generic design of the Chapel Hill study, a comparison of the media agenda with the public agenda, has been operationalized in four distinct variations. This typology of designs (McCombs, 1981), first presented at the International Communication

Association convention in Acapulco, Mexico, at the invitation of Everett Rogers, is often called the Acapulco typology.

- Type I compares the news coverage for a set of major issues to the *aggregate* public agenda. The original Chapel Hill study, plus studies by Funkhouser (1973) and Palmgreen and Clarke (1977), provide examples of Type I designs in the agenda-setting literature.
- Type II also examines the media agenda (defined in terms of a set of issues), but shifts the units of analysis for the public agenda from the aggregate population to the individual. That is, the rank-order of an agenda of issues is determined for *each individual*. McLeod, Becker, and Byrnes 1974 study is an example of a Type II design.
- Type III investigates the relationship between the media coverage of a single issue and its trend in public opinion over a period of time. An example of a Type III studies is that of Winter and Eyal (1981).
- Type IV examines the match between the media coverage of a single issue and the corresponding salience of that issue on an individual agenda. This type introduces laboratory experiments as a complement to field research. Iyengar and Kinder (1987), for instance, demonstrated agenda-setting effects repeatedly in a series of laboratory experiments. Participants viewed actual television broadcasts edited to enhance the salience of certain issues. The result was an increased level of concern for the manipulated issues compared to no changes for other public issues.

To date, only one study has undertaken the enormity of examining simultaneously all four types of the agenda-setting designs. In his analysis of Taiwan's first fully contested legislative election in more than 40 years, King (1994) found some evidence of agenda setting with all four designs. The strongest results emerged from a Type I analysis of the newspaper agenda.

This comprehensive panel study of the Taiwan legislative election also affords a parsimonious review and comparison of the research methodologies used in all four types of agenda setting research designs. King's Type I design largely parallels the original Chapel Hill study. Two versions of the public agenda were ascertained from an open-ended question that began, "In your opinion, what are the most important problems facing Taiwan today?" From the set of issues named, each respondent was then asked to identify the single most important problem facing Taiwan. Two public agendas were constructed from this two-part question, a *general agenda* of 13 issues based on the responses given to the first part of the question and a *priority agenda* of 12 issues singled out by respondents as the most important problem facing the country. In both cases agenda issues were rank ordered on the basis of the number of times each was mentioned. To measure the media agenda, the public agenda issue categories were used to organize a content analysis of three daily newspapers and the main news programs of three TV stations. Again, the issues were rank ordered on the basis of the number of news stories about each issue. As in the Chapel Hill study, a rank-order correlation was used to compare the various versions of the public agenda and the media agenda. In a Type I study the goal is to examine the agenda-setting influence of the news media on a community or nation by comparing the aggregate public agenda with the agendas of various news media serving that population.

King's Type I analysis also included a major innovation, use of the paired-comparisons scaling technique to construct an interval scale measure of the aggregate public agenda. Because the five issues selected by King for the paired-comparisons were determined on the basis of a pretest, they are identical with the top five issues on the priority version of the public agenda described previously. The data for this scaling technique are collected by presenting each respondent with a pair of issues and asking them to select the one issue regarded as more important to the country. All possible pairs of issues are judged by respondents, a total of 10 pairs in the case of five issues. As noted, the public agenda described by this scaling technique is an interval scale showing the distance between the issues as well as their rank order. This also produces an aggregate description of the agenda among the total population. Because it is based on responses to the entire set of issues, responses in which the issues are compared, this is a stronger measure of the public agenda than either the general public agenda or the priority public agenda. But in King's study it was limited to five issues because of the logistics of the data collection. (Adding a sixth issue to the set would have required the judging of 15 pairs; adding a seventh, 26 pairs.)

In contrast to the three versions of the public agenda just described, Type II studies emphasize individual differences. An issue agenda is constructed for each individual. Obviously, the items making up these individual agendas must be identical across all individuals. King used the paired-comparison data to create these individual agendas. By counting the number of times that each of the five issues was selected when compared with the other four, he determined the rank order of the five issues for each individual. In turn, the agenda-setting influence of the news media upon each individual was determined by comparing each individual issue agenda with the agendas of various news media. In this research design the media agendas are identical with those constructed for a Type I analysis. The result of these comparisons was a set of rank-order correlations for each individual or, in other words, a set of agenda setting scores for each individual ranging from -1 to +1. Not surprisingly, most of the correlations were quite low or even negative. People are not automations waiting to be programmed by the news media. Individual issues reflect the emphases of the news media, but, by and large, we do not reproduce the priorities of the news media in a rote fashion.

Both Type I and Type II studies use the metaphor of an agenda in a literal fashion. The agenda is a set of rank-ordered issues. In contrast, Type III and Type IV designs focus on a single issue, testing the hypothesis that variations in the salience of an issue on the public agenda reflect variations in the news coverage of that issue. A Type III study examines the agenda setting influence of news coverage *in a population*. A Type IV study examines the agenda setting influence of news coverage *on an individual*.

Most Type III studies compare the media agenda with the public agenda over extended time to provide a large number of comparison points. Because King studied an election, only a truncated version of the Type III analysis was possible. Using the issue of Taiwan–mainland China relations, King compared the salience of this issue at three points during the campaign with the news coverage pattern and found a considerable degree of correspondence. In the case of newspaper coverage, this agenda setting pattern also was replicated for another issue, the emergence of a democratic political system in Taiwan.

These same two issues were used for a Type IV analysis. In this research design the change in issue salience for an individual is compared to the variation in news coverage. Again, individual information comes from the paired-comparison data. For the first analysis, based on Taiwan–mainland China relations, the score for that issue in wave one (that is, the number of times this issue was selected over each of the other four issues as more important—a range of 0 to 4) was subtracted from the paired-comparison score in wave three. A similar analysis was conducted for the issue of the emergence of a democratic political system. In neither analysis was there substantial evidence of an agenda setting effect, in large measure because about half of the voters did not change during the five weeks of the election campaign. Although a small number did evidence agenda setting influence, just as in the Type II analysis, the more powerful effects of the news media are found in society taken as a whole. In sum, there are four distinct research designs for agenda setting research, designs that are based on the two key theoretical and methodological decisions that define the Acapulco typology.

FOUR PHASES OF AGENDA SETTING

The original Chapel Hill study and subsequent studies tested the basic agenda-setting hypothesis that news coverage patterns influence public perception of the important issues of the day. As early as the 1972 presidential election, Shaw and McCombs (1977) also examined a number of contingent conditions that might enhance or reduce the news media's agenda-setting influence. These conditions include the psychological concept of need for orientation, comparative roles of newspapers and television, and the fit of interpersonal communication in the mass communication process. They not only reconfirmed the original hypothesis, but also introduced a second phase in this research program, the exploration of contingent conditions. (It is important to note that in the history of agenda-setting research the appearance of a new phase does not supplant the previous phase[s]; rather, a new phase adds another domain to scholarly activity.)

The second phase merges traditional media effects research with the uses and gratifications approach. Research into the effects of mass communications typically has focused on the effects of media content on a mostly passive audience. The basic agenda-setting hypothesis—the media agenda affects the public agenda—is a product of this approach. Conversely, the uses and gratifications approach (see chapter 10, this volume) assumes that individuals are active mass communication participants who select certain media content to fulfill a particular need. Therefore, the second phase searches for psychological explanations for agenda setting. The original research question, "What are the effects of the media agenda on the public agenda?" becomes "Why do some voters expose themselves to certain mass media messages more than do other voters?"

McCombs and Weaver (1973) explored this question with their concept of need for orientation. This psychological concept asserts that people feel a need to be oriented to their environment, both the physical world and the cognitive world they operate in. In the absence of this familiarity with one's surroundings—the typical situation at the beginning of most political campaigns—an individual will strive to map these surroundings. This concept offers a psychological explanation for voter exposure to political communication in general, and for susceptibility to the agenda-setting influences of the news media in particular.

McCombs and Weaver developed a typology that depicts different levels of need for orientation by differing amounts of relevance and uncertainty. High relevance and high uncertainty result in a high need for orientation (Group I), while a high relevance and low uncertainty result in a moderate need for orientation (Group II). Regardless of degree of uncertainty, low relevance results in a low need for orientation (Group III). It has been predicted that individuals in Group I (high relevance and high uncertainty) will be more susceptible to agenda setting than those in the other two groups.

Using data from the 1972 Charlotte study, Weaver (1977) confirmed that, when relevance and uncertainty factors are measured in many ways, differing levels of need for orientation are related to the frequency of media use and to the strength of the agenda-setting effect. Scales measured relevance of politics to Charlotte voters and each respondent's degree of uncertainty about politics. Overwhelmingly, voters with high needs for orientation ranked highest on media use (79.8%). Those voters with moderate needs ranked second (62.5%), and voters with low needs ranked lowest on media use (47.4%). Additionally, need for orientation was positively related with agenda-setting effects of newspapers and television, although less strongly and less systematically than to frequency of media use.

From the Charlotte study, researchers also noted that the greatest constraints on the power of the news media to move issues onto the public agenda—and, for that matter, one of the greatest constraints on the power of direct personal experience to propel issues onto the public agenda—is the very limited capacity of that agenda. At any particular moment, the public agenda consists of no more than five to seven issues. Although the size of the public agenda was observed almost 20 years ago, only recently have the theoretical underpinnings of this assumption been more fully elaborated. Replicating the basic agenda-setting hypothesis, Zhu (1992) examined detailed analyses of public opinion on three issues—the federal budget deficit, the Gulf War, and the economic recession—finding that news coverage of the three issues influenced their salience among the public. But the salience of each was influenced by two other factors: the salience of the other two competing issues among the public and the salience of the news coverage for the other two competing issues. Zhu concluded that the public agenda is an agenda with a limited capacity, an agenda with the characteristics of a zero-sum game.

AN EXPANDED AGENDA

The news media play a key role in focusing public attention, and that role extends beyond setting an agenda of only public issues. During the 1976 presidential election, researchers expanded the domain of agenda-setting to include other key political elements—candidate images and voter interest in the campaign (Weaver, Graber, McCombs, & Eyal, 1981). Their results indicate that the news media enhanced the salience of politics among the participants. In particular, the data supported the agenda-setting theory as it relates to an expanded scope of agendas, such as the agenda of voter interest. Frequent use of television to follow politics during the primaries played a significant role in stimulating subsequent voter interest later in the election.

Other agendas include the political candidate agenda. Although mostly anecdotal, considerable literature exists supporting the view that the news media play a major role in defining who are the viable candidates for a party's nomination (i.e., Alger, 1989; Broder, 1987; Crouse, 1973; Germond & Witcover, 1989; Patterson, 1980). By January of 1992, political pundits had decided that Clinton was the front-runner in the race for the Democratic nomination. As journalist Ken Auletta (1993) wrote: "Before a vote was cast, and even though polls showed that more than half of all rank-and-file Democrats didn't even know who he was, Clinton was hailed on the covers of *Time*, the *New Republic*, and *New York* magazine" (p. 69).

In addition to expanding agendas beyond public issues, this third phase of agenda-setting research includes the explication of different kinds of agendas. Are the news media as successful in influencing the salience of issues on public policy agendas as they are in influencing the salience of issues on the public agendas? Conventional democratic theory states that the media impart information about policy matters to citizens, who, in turn, pressure officials to act on their concerns and priorities. But a different conclusion was reached by researchers at Northwestern University who studied the impact of investigative reporting on public opinion and policymaking. In *The Journalism of Outrage: Investigative Reporting and Agenda Building in America*, Protess et al. (1991) found that policymakers' responses to investigative stories often occur independently of any change in the public's agenda priorities. In fact, changes in policy priorities sometimes are arranged by journalists and policymakers without the public's assistance or knowledge. These conclusions are based on six case studies of media influence. Unlike most agenda-setting studies, Protess et al. used a quasi-experimental research design to explore public policy agendas. In each study, half of the randomly selected participants from the general public were designated as the treatment group, while the remainder constituted the control group. In addition to the public sample, most of the case studies assessed the impact of the investigative report on a sample of policymaking elites such as public officials and members of interest groups. Because of their contacts with investigative journalists in Chicago, the Northwestern team was able to employ before-after designs in their research.

Other research in phase three has extended the measurement of the public agenda. In an early study, McLeod, et al. (1974) examined agenda-setting effects by measuring three different public agendas. The first public agenda is defined as an intrapersonal, or individual, public agenda. The question asked in the Chapel Hill study ("What are you most concerned about these days?") and the question asked in most Gallup Poll surveys ("What is the most important problem facing this country?") are operational definitions of the intrapersonal agenda. They provide a psychological measurement of agenda-setting effects. However, it is possible to use a more behavioral measure by asking people what they talk about with family and friends. This yields a second public agenda—an interpersonal, or community, public agenda. The third public agenda, the perceived community public agenda, is present when people describe what others in the community regard as the most important issues.

Atwood, Sohn, and Sohn (1978) tested the second public agenda by asking, "To what extent does the newspaper set the agenda for community discussion?" Significant correlations were found between the content of the local daily newspaper and what people in the community report reading and talking about.

THE FOURTH PHASE

By the 1980s, a fourth phase of agenda-setting research transformed the news agenda from independent variable to dependent variable. The original research question, "Who sets the public agenda?" has been rephrased to ask, "Who sets the news agenda?" To answer this latter question, some researchers have concentrated on the work of journalists and editors as they operate as "gatekeepers," decision makers who control the flow of news.

In a study of how 24 Iowa daily newspapers used the Associated Press (AP), Gold and Simmons (1965) found an overall coefficient of concordance of +.915, indicating that local news agendas were strongly influenced by wire service reports. Although each local newspaper used only a small number of the wire stories available, their coverage reflected the same proportions for each category of news as did the wire reports. Another study examined 52 Ohio newspaper and television journalists whose duties include selecting wire stories. Whitney and Becker (1982) found a correlation ($r = .71$) between the number of items transmitted by the wire service and the number of stories selected from each category of news.

Other major or elite news organizations, such as *The New York Times* and *Washington Post*, also influence the play of topics on the news agenda. For example, public concern about drugs began to build after *The New York Times* "discovered" the drug problem in 1985. Reese and Danielian (1989) found that the *Times* took the lead in placing the cocaine story on the press agenda. The *Times'* influence was sustained by the drug-related deaths the next year of All-American basketball player Len Bias and professional football's Don Rogers. But those tragic events only sustained an agenda already in place among the news media. Illegal drugs appearing on the national agenda was a result of the intellectual discovery of the situation, not any response to external reality.

This intermedia influence can be found both among news organizations and individual newsworkers. Since journalists constantly cover an ambiguous social world, they rely heavily on each other for ideas and confirmation of their news judgments. Editors tend to question coverage that differs from other news sources, so journalists seek consistency and conformity in their reporting of events. This phenomenon, known as *pack journalism*, was most notably observed during the 1972 presidential campaign:

> What happened was that Johnny Apple of *The New York Times* sat in a corner and everyone peered over his shoulder to find out what he was writing. The AP guy was looking over one shoulder, the UPI guy over the other and CBS, NBC, ABC, and the Baltimore *Sun* were all crowding in behind. . . . He would sit down and write a lead, and they would go write leads. . . . Finally, at midnight, the guy announced that Muskie had 32 percent and McGovern had 26 percent, and Apple sat down to write his final story. He called it something like "a surprisingly strong showing for George McGovern." Everyone peered over his shoulder again and picked it up. It was on the front page of every major newspaper the next day. (Crouse, 1973, pp. 84–85)

Similar situations occur outside the parameter of a presidential campaign. Prichard (1987) described how a December 1982 story about a man attempting to blow up the Washington Monument was bumped from page 1A of *USA Today* until Dan Rather led with it on the "CBS Evening News." By appearing on a major network, the story had been given a "verification factor." Haws (1993) examined *The New York Times'* decision to identify William Kennedy Smith's alleged rape victim. The *Times* had identified Patricia Bowman in an article published on April 17, 1991. In the news story, the *Times* explained that it normally withheld the names of alleged sexual assault victims, but since NBC had identified Bowman the night before, it no longer felt responsible for protecting her privacy. The identification of Bowman was deemed legitimate by the *Times* because another news organization had previously named her.

News sources, such as the president and government agencies, also influence the media's agenda. A study of the public information offices of six state government agencies and the news content of the eight major dailies in Louisiana showed strong support for the agenda-setting theory. Using content analyses, interviews, and observations, Turk (1986) found that the news content reflected the agenda of the news releases provided by the government agencies. Another study compared the issues stressed in four State of Union addresses by three different presidents to the issues covered by the news media before and after the speeches. Each of the case studies by Wanta, Stephenson, Turk, & McCombs (1989) used a content analysis to determine the issues stressed by the presidents and the issues stressed by the media before and after the speeches. The data indicated that presidents Nixon and Reagan (during his first term) apparently influenced subsequent media coverage through their State of the Union addresses, while presidents Carter and Reagan (during his second term) were apparently influenced by prior media coverage.

Obviously, this fourth phase of agenda-setting research has many facets. A helpful way to remember the various elements of this phase is McCombs' (1992) metaphor of peeling the layers of an onion. The outermost layer is the array of sources routinely used by journalists to obtain news. Another layer is the diffusion of news stories, including angles as well as topics, among the news media themselves. The innermost layer consists of the professional core of journalism itself, those practices, values, and traditions into which every journalist is socialized, beginning with his or her college days and continuing through daily experiences on the job. These attitudes and behaviors are the ultimate filters shaping the nature of the news agenda. Although the onion metaphor outlines the different layers involved in this phase of research, a more detailed approach to these elements of agenda-setting theory was presented by Shoemaker and Reese (1991).

A SECOND TAKE ON LIPPMANN

Agenda setting research began 25 years ago with a simple hypothesis: News coverage influences our personal perceptions of what are the most important issues of the day. From that simple beginning, a vastly expanded portrait of public opinion has evolved. Considering the key term of this theoretical metaphor, the agenda, in abstract terms, the potential for moving beyond an agenda of issues to many new research questions becomes clear. In the original study and most of those that followed, both the media agenda and the public agenda consisted of a set of objects, public issues. However, public issues are not the only set of objects. Communication is a process. It can be about any set of objects—or even a single object—competing for attention.

There is another dimension to consider. Each of these objects has numerous attributes, and these attributes define another agenda. Just as objects vary in salience, so do the attributes of each object. Both the selection of objects for attention and the selection of attributes, that is frames for thinking about those objects, are powerful agenda setting roles. An important part of the news agenda and its daily set of objects are the perspectives that journalists and, subsequently, members of the public employ to think about each object. These perspectives draw attention to certain attributes and away from others.

How media *frames* impact the public agenda is the second dimension of agenda setting. The first dimension, of course, was the transmission of issue salience from the media agenda to the public agenda. Under the second dimension, research is examining the transmission of attribute salience. This research is about the role of the news media in the framing of issues and other objects in the public mind.

Gitlin (1980) introduced the concept of framing to mass communication studies in his classic examination of how an American television network trivialized a major student political movement during the 1960s. News coverage of any social movement can use a variety of framing strategies. The news can describe the scope of the social problem, critique alternative proposals for coping with the problem, or detail the tactical moves of activists and officials.

As defined by Entman (1993), *framing* essentially involves salience and selection. Noting the power of frames on the public, Entman wrote, "Frames call attention to some aspects of reality while obscuring other elements, which might lead audiences to have different reactions" (p. 55).

While exploring other avenues of agenda-setting research, many scholars have found evidence of frames in media content. In their 1976 presidential campaign study, Weaver et al. (1981) examined the images that voters held of presidential candidates. They found a high degree of correspondence between the agenda of attributes on the news agenda and the attributes salient in voters' minds. Benton and Frazier (1976) provided a detailed analysis of a single object on the public agenda, the economy, and probed two sets of attributes: the specific problems, causes, and proposed solutions associated with this general issue on the public agenda; and the pro and con rationales for economic solutions. Both of these agendas of attributes exerted significant influence on how the public viewed the economy. An examination of a complex environmental issue, the development of a large, man-made lake in central Indiana, revealed a level of correspondence between the picture in people's minds and the frames in local newspaper coverage of that issue (Cohen, 1975). All three studies used the classic Chapel Hill design, comparison of a media agenda measured by content analysis with a public agenda measured through survey research, but with a shift in focus from an agenda of objects to an agenda of attributes.

Another look at the data from Iyengar and Kinder (1987) indicated that not only was the agenda-setting hypothesis supported, but that there also was evidence of both framing and priming in the news media. *Priming* is a psychological process whereby media emphasis on particular issues not only increases the salience of those issues, but it activates in people's memories previously acquired information about those issues. That information is then used in forming opinions about persons, groups, or institutions linked to the issues. With this in mind, it is not surprising that participants exposed to a series of news stories on the inadequacies of American defense preparedness gave the president lower ratings on his performance in regard to defense than did those not exposed to those stories. But similar differences were found in evaluations of the president's overall performance, a considerable generalization from the specific information communicated to the audience. Under some circumstances, then, the news media's agenda can alter the standards that people use in evaluating their leaders.

The concepts of framing and priming can be linked to what George Gerbner and his collaborators (Gerbner, Gross, Morgan, & Signorelli, 1994) call *cultivation analysis*, named because of the belief that television violence cultivates feelings of victimization and other perceptions of social reality in viewers (see chapter 8, this volume). Framing and priming by the news media have consequences on the public. One consequence is that heavy viewers are more likely than light viewers to find the world a frightening place to live (Berger, 1989). Heavy viewers who witness crime and violence on television think that there is more crime and violence in society than is really present and therefore develop heightened fears of becoming a crime victim.

An emerging line of research into the consequences of media framing is the New Criticism. Traditional news criticism has centered on the content of the media's message, asking if it is accurate and balanced. The New Criticism examines the form and tone of media messages, the central characteristics of the media agenda as a genre, and the consequences of these characteristics for the public. Many critics contend that contemporary American journalism, especially national television, places a particularly aggressive and negative spin on certain types of news stories (i.e., Sabato, 1992; Hart, 1987). Not content to wait for the bad news, journalists actively pursue it. This is particularly evident during presidential campaigns. In an analysis of more than 10,000 print and television news stories of the 1960 to 1992 elections, Patterson (1993) concluded that the journalists' perspectives on politics dominate the news to a much greater degree than in the past with the effect that the news increasingly is negative in tone, embedded in controversy, told from a game-based scenario, and centered on the journalists more than the candidates.

Arguing that a steady diet of negative television news has influenced the public agenda, Robinson and Sheehan (1983) have cited the historical decline in the public's esteem for presidential contenders. Public attitudes toward both Democratic and Republican nominees for president have steadily declined since 1952. Since 1968, negative attitudes toward all candidates have equaled or exceeded positive attitudes. The media's reproachful tone also may be linked to a decline in public trust and respect for government institutions. Public opinion polls conducted by the University of Michigan's Institute for Social Research have shown a decrease in the respondents who trust the government to do the right thing, from 73% in 1958 to 44% in 1984. Similar responses have been expressed in the *Washington Post/ABC News* polls for 1985 through 1987. The proportion of people who trusted the government ranged between 38% and 44% (Sussman, 1988).

THE FUTURE

In generic terms, agenda setting analysis involves the comparison of two agendas and the exploration of the dynamics that account for the linkage between these agendas. In most of the research to date, the comparison has been between the media agenda and the public agenda. But there also are comparisons of various media agendas, of numerous political agendas with the media agenda, and a variety of agendas with policy agendas. Also found in the literature are advertising agendas and polling agendas. Furthermore, creative researchers have ranged far beyond the original domain, an agenda of issues, to consider a multitude of agenda objects and attributes, agenda items as varied as the facets of public issues and the tone of political reporting. This is the new frontier in agenda setting research.

In the next decade of agenda-setting research, innovative scholars will be exploring numerous dimensions of the news agenda. Probing beyond politics and government, a University of Texas project is exploring the role of the news media in the creation of public opinion and concern about crime. In 1993, the proportion of the American public naming crime as the most important problem facing the country jumped from 5% to 31%. However, crime statistics indicate that the number of households touched by crime has steadily declined. Therefore, scholars wonder what is the role of news coverage in the relationship between the public's perceived reality of crime and actual reality as measured by crime statistics.

This is just one contemporary instance of the usefulness of agenda-setting theory in expanding our understanding of the connections between the world outside and the pictures in our heads. Agenda-setting theory has opened many doors to reveal the power and ethical responsibility of the news media, and it continues to identify other intellectual doors.

REFERENCES

Alger, D. E. (1989). *The media and politics*. Englewood Cliffs, NJ: Prentice-Hall Inc.

Asher, H. (1992). *Polling and the public: What every citizen should know* (2nd ed.). Washington, DC: Congressional Quarterly.

Atwood, L. E., Sohn, A. B., & Sohn, H. (1978). Daily newspaper contributions to community discussion. *Journalism Quarterly, 55*, 570–576.

Auletta, K. (1993). On and off the bus: Lessons from campaign '92. *1-800-President* (pp. 63–89). New York: The Twentieth Century Fund Press.

Behr, R. L., & Iyengar, S. (1985). Television news, real-world cues, and changes in the public agenda. *Public Opinion Quarterly, 49*, 38–57.

Benton, M., & Frazier, P. J. (1976). The agenda setting function of the mass media at three levels of "information holding." *Communication Research, 3*, 261–274.

Berelson, B., Lazarsfeld, P., & McPhee, W. (1954). *Voting*. Chicago: University of Chicago Press.

Berger, G. (1989). *Violence and the media*. New York: Franklin Watts.

Broder, D. (1987). *Behind the front page: A candid look at how the news is made*. New York: Simon & Schuster.

Brosius, H. B., & Kepplinger, H. M. (1990). The agenda setting function of television news: static and dynamic views. *Communication Research, 17*, 183–211.

Cohen, B. (1963). *The press and foreign policy*. Princeton, NJ: Princeton University Press.

Cohen, D. (1975, August). *A report on a non-election agenda setting* study. Paper presented at the Association for Education in Journalism and Mass Communication, Ottawa, Canada.

Crouse, T. (1973). *The boys on the bus*. New York: Ballantine Books.

Eaton, H. (1989). Agenda-setting with bi-weekly data on content of three national media. *Journalism Quarterly, 66*, 942–948, 959.

Edelstein, A. (1974). *The uses of communication in decision-making: A comparative study of Yugoslavia and the United States*. New York: Praeger.

Entman, R. M. (1993). Framing: toward clarification of a fractured paradigm. *Journal of Communication, 43*, 51–58.

Erbring, L., Goldenberg, E. N., & Miller, A. H. (1980). Front-page news and real-world cues: a new look at agenda-setting by the media. *American Journal of Political Science, 24*, 16–49.

Funkhouser, G. R. (1973). The issues of the sixties: An exploratory study in the dynamics of public opinion. *Public Opinion Quarterly, 37*, 62–75.

Gerbner, G., Gross, L., Morgan, M., & Signorielli, N. (1994). Growing up with television: The cultivation perspective. In J. Bryant & D. Zillmann (Eds.), *Media effects: Advances in theory and research* (pp. 17–41). Hillsdale, NJ: Lawrence Erlbaum Associates.

Germond, J. W., & Witcover, J. (1989). *Whose broad stripes and bright stars: The trivial pursuit of the presidency 1988*. New York: Politics Today, Inc.

Gitlin, T. (1980). *The whole world is watching*. Berkeley, CA: University of California Press.

Gold, D., & Simmons, J. L. (1965). News selection patterns among Iowa dailies. *Public Opinion Quarterly, 29*, 425–430.

Hart, R. P. (1987). *The sound of leadership*. Chicago: University of Chicago Press.

Haws, D. (1993). A qualitative study: *The New York Times*, Patricia Bowman, and William Kennedy Smith. *Newspaper Research Journal, 14*, 137–145.

Iyengar, S. (1979). Television news and issue salience: A reexamination of the agenda-setting hypothesis. *American Politics Quarterly, 7*, 395–416.

Iyengar, S., & Kinder, D. R. (1987). *News that matters: Television and American opinion*. Chicago: University of Chicago Press.

Klapper, J. (1960). *The effects of mass communication*. New York: Free Press.

King, P. (1994). *Issue agendas in the 1992 Taiwan legislative election*. Unpublished doctoral dissertation. University of Texas at Austin.

Lazarsfeld, P., Berelson, B., & Gaudet, H. (1948). *The people's choice*. New York: Columbia University Press.

Lippmann, W. (1922). *Public opinion*. New York: Macmillan.

McCombs, M. E. (1981).The agenda-setting approach. In D. Nimmo & K. Sanders (Eds.), *Handbook of political communication* (pp. 121–140). Beverly Hills, CA: Sage Publications.

McCombs, M. E. (1992). Explorers and surveyors: expanding strategies for agenda-setting research. *Journalism Quarterly, 69*, 813–824.

McCombs, M. E., & Shaw, D. L. (1972). The agenda-setting function of mass media. *Public Opinion Quarterly, 36*, 176–187.

McCombs, M. E., & Weaver, D. H. (1973, May). *Voters' need for orientation and use of mass communication*. Paper presented at the International Communication Association, Montreal, Canada.

McLeod, J., Becker, L. B., & Byrnes, J. E. (1974). Another look at the agenda-setting function of the press. *Communication Research, 1*, 131–165.

Neuman, W. R. (1990). The threshold of public attention. *Public Opinion Quarterly, 54*, 159–176.

Palmgreen, P., & Clarke, P. (1977). Agenda-setting with local and national issues. *Communication Research, 4*, 435–452.

Patterson, T. E. (1980). *The mass media election: How Americans choose their president*. New York: Praeger.

Patterson, T. E. (1993). *Out of order*. New York: Knopf.

Prichard, P. (1987). The McPapering of America: An insider's candid account. *Washington Journalism Review*, 32–37.

Protess, D. L., Cook, F. L., Doppelt, J. C., Ettema, J. S., Gordon, M. T., Leff, D. R., & Miller, P. (1991). *The journalism of outrage: Investigative reporting and agenda building in america*. New York: Guilford.

Reese, S., & Danielian, L. (1989). Intermedia influence and the drug issue: Converging on cocaine. In P. Shoemaker (Ed.), *Communication campaigns about drugs* (pp. 29–46). Hillsdale, NJ: Lawrence Erlbaum Associates.

Robinson, M. J., & Sheehan, M. A. (1983). *Over the wire and on TV: CBS and UPI in campaign '80*. New York: Russell Sage Foundation.

Rogers, E. M., Dearing, J. W., & Bregman, D. (1993). The anatomy of agenda-setting research. *Journal of Communication, 43*, 68–84.

Sabato, L. J. (1992). Open season: How the news media cover presidential campaigns in the age of attack journalism. In M. D. McCubbins (Ed.), *Under the watchful eye: Managing presidential campaigns in the television era* (pp. 127–151). Washington, DC: Congressional Quarterly Inc.

Salwen, M. B. (1988). Effect of accumulation of coverage on issue salience in agenda setting. *Journalism Quarterly, 65*, 100–106, 130.

Shaw, D. L., & McCombs, M. E. (1977). *The emergence of American political issues: The agenda-setting function of the press*. St. Paul, MN: West Publishing Company.

Shoemaker, P. J., & Reese, S. D. (1991). *Mediating the message: Theories of influences on mass media content*. White Plains, NY: Longman.

Smith, K. (1987). Newspaper coverage and public concern about community issues. *Journalism Monographs, 101*.

Sussman, B. (1988). *What Americans really think and why our politicians pay no attention*. New York: Pantheon Books.

Turk, J. VanSlyke. (1986). Public relations' influence on the news. *Newspaper Research Journal, 7*, 15–27.

Wanta, W., Stephenson, M. A., Turk, J. VanSlyke, & McCombs, M. E. (1989). How president's state of union talk influenced news media agendas. *Journalism Quarterly, 66*, 537–541.

Weaver, D. H. (1977). Political issues and voters need for orientation. In D. L. Shaw & M. E. McCombs (Eds.), *The emergence of American political issues: The agenda-setting function of the press* (pp. 107–120). St. Paul, MN: West Publishing.

Weaver, D. H., Graber, D, McCombs, M. E., & Eyal, C. (1981). *Media agenda-setting in a presidential election: Issues, images, and interests*. New York: Praeger.

Whitney, C., & Becker, L. (1982). "Keeping the gates" for the gatekeepers: The effects of wire news, *Journalism Quarterly, 59*, 60–65.

Winter, J. P., & Eyal, C. H. (1981). Agenda-setting for the civil rights issue. *Public Opinion Quarterly. 45*, 376–383.

Yagade, A., & Dozier, D. M. (1990). The media agenda-setting effect of concrete versus abstract issues. *Journalism Quarterly, 67*, 3–10.

Zhu, J. (1992). Issue competition and attention distraction: A zero-sum theory of agenda setting. *Journalism Quarterly, 69*, 825–836.

8

Cultivation Analysis: Research and Practice

Nancy Signorielli
University of Delaware

Michael Morgan
University of Massachusetts

People around the world have been fascinated by television but concerned about its effects almost since the first show was broadcast. In this country, the popular press and the government keep asking "What is television doing to us?" "Is television somehow responsible for all the violence in our society?" Parents and teachers wonder whether television makes children more aggressive, or whether television helps or hinders learning. Critics of all political stripes complain about television's images of men and women, of the family, of politics, war, minorities, and a host of other issues. Students in both high school and college want to study the effects of the mass media but often look for simple, straightforward answers to their questions. Yet, as is true in so many areas of life and social research, the questions are complex and the answers are neither simple nor straightforward.

The Cultural Indicators project, founded by George Gerbner, provides a broad-based, empirical approach to answering some of these questions and to understanding the social consequences of growing up and living with television. The Cultural

Indicators paradigm involves a three-pronged research strategy (Gerbner, 1973). The first, called *institutional process analysis*, investigates how the flow of media messages is produced, managed, and distributed. The second, called *message system analysis*, has been used since 1967 to track the most stable, pervasive, and recurrent images in media content, in terms of the portrayal of violence, minorities, gender-roles, occupations, and so on. The third, called *cultivation analysis*, is the study of how exposure to the world of television contributes to viewers' conceptions about the real world. Cultivation analysis is the focus of this chapter.

Cultivation analysis is not concerned with the "impact" of any particular television program, genre, or episode. It is not concerned with formal aesthetic categories, style, artistic quality, issues of high versus low culture, or specific, selective "readings" or interpretations of media messages. Rather, cultivation researchers approach television as a *system* of messages, made up of aggregate and repetitive patterns of images and representations to which entire communities are exposed—and which they absorb—over long periods of time.

The concept of "story-telling" is central to the theory of cultivation. Gerbner contends that the basic difference between human beings and other species is that we live in a world that is created by the stories we tell (Gerbner, 1967). All living organisms exchange energy with their environments, and many creatures exchange information and change their behavior as a result of learning. But only humans *communicate* by the manipulation of complex symbol systems. Humans therefore uniquely live in a world experienced and constructed largely through many forms and modes of story-telling. We have neither personally nor directly experienced great portions of what we know or think we know; we "know" about many things based on the stories we hear and the stories we tell.

Television has transformed the cultural process of story-telling into a centralized, standardized, market-driven, advertiser-sponsored system. In earlier times, the stories of a culture were told face-to-face by members of a community, parents, teachers, or the clergy. Today television tells most of the stories to most of the people, most of the time. Therefore, the cultural process of story-telling is now in the hands of global commercial interests who have something to sell, and who in effect operate outside the reach of democratic decision-making.

BACKGROUND AND SCOPE

Like many landmark efforts in the history of communication research, the Cultural Indicators Project was launched as an independently funded enterprise in an applied context (Gerbner, 1969). The research began during the late 1960s—a time of national turmoil—after the assassinations of Martin Luther King and Bobby Kennedy and increased concern about the country's involvement in Vietnam. In 1968, The National Commission on the Causes and Prevention of Violence was formed to examine violence in society, including violence on television (Baker & Ball, 1969). Their charge was to examine the existing research relating to television's effects. The commission also funded one new study—a content analysis of violence in prime time programming under the direction of George Gerbner at the Annenberg School for Communication.

This earliest research of what was to become the Cultural Indicators Project documented the extent to which violence dominated dramatic television programming, described the nature of television violence, and established a baseline for long-term monitoring of the world of television (Gerbner, 1969).

Nationwide unrest continued, as did concerns about television's impact upon Americans. In 1969, even before the report of the National Commission on the Causes and Prevention of Violence was released, Congress appropriated one million dollars and set up the Surgeon General's Scientific Advisory Committee on Television and Social Behavior to continue research about television violence. All together, 23 projects, including Cultural Indicators, were funded. Cultural Indicators research focused primarily upon the content of prime-time and weekend–daytime network dramatic programming (Gerbner, 1972).

The cultivation analysis phase of the Cultural Indicators research paradigm was first implemented with a national probability survey of adults during the early 1970s in a study funded by the National Institute of Mental Health (NIMH; Gerbner & Gross, 1976). Cultivation research has continued, developed, and expanded ever since, in studies directed by the original investigators (with funding from numerous sources including NIMH, the American Medical Association, the Office of Telecommunications Policy, the Administration on Aging, the National Science Foundation, the Ad Hoc Committee on Religious Television Research, and other agencies), as well as studics undertaken by many other independent investigators in the United States and around the world.

Although the earliest efforts (and many published reports) focused primarily on the nature and functions of television violence, the Cultural Indicators project was broadly conceived from the outset. Violence was studied as a demonstration of the distribution of power in the world of television, with serious implications for the confirmation and perpetuation of minority status in the real world (Gerbner, Gross, Signorielli, Morgan, & Jackson-Beeck, 1979; Morgan 1983). For more than twenty years, cultivation research has explored a wide range of topics, issues, and concerns.

The Cultural Indicators research team has investigated, for example, the extent to which television viewing contributes to audience conceptions and actions in such realms as gender roles, age-role stereotypes, health, work, science, the family, educational achievement and aspirations, politics, and many other issues (Gerbner, Gross, Morgan, & Signorielli, 1980, 1981b, 1982, 1986, 1994; Gerbner, Gross, & Signorielli, & Morgan, 1980; Gerbner, Morgan, & Signorielli, 1982; Gerbner & Signorielli, 1979; Morgan, 1982, 1987; Morgan & Gross, 1982; Signorielli, 1982, 1987, 1989, 1991, 1993; Signorielli & Lears, 1992a, 1992b).

Cultivation research has been prominent and prolific. Overall, our bibliography of studies relating to Cultural Indicators lists over 120 studies published by the principal investigators (Gerbner, Gross, Morgan, and Signorielli) and their associates, along with over 130 additional replications, reviews, and critiques by independent researchers not associated with the original research team. Clearly, such a large body of work cannot be exhaustively reviewed here; in this chapter, wc discuss the general theoretical assumptions underlying the idea of cultivation, and describe the methodological procedures involved in the analysis.

TELEVISION IN SOCIETY:
THE THEORETICAL UNDERPINNINGS OF CULTIVATION

We are a mass mediated society. The mass media, especially television, play important roles in our daily lives. Television is the source of the most broadly shared images and messages in history, both in the United States and around the world. As the number of people who have always lived with television continues to grow, the medium is increasingly taken for granted as an appliance, a piece of furniture, a storyteller, a member of the family. Few can remember, or care to remember, what life was like before television.

Television sets, with their cable hookups and VCRs, are usually placed in prominent positions in our homes, whether in the family room, the living room, the kitchen, the bedroom, or all of the above. Furniture is arranged to provide the best sight lines to the TV, not to foster conversation. More and more homes have two or more sets and viewing may often be a solitary activity. For most viewers, expanded delivery systems such as cable, satellite, and VCRs signal even further penetration and integration of established viewing patterns into everyday life.

Television has thus become our nation's (and increasingly the world's) most common and constant learning environment. It both mirrors and leads society. It serves, however, first and foremost as our storyteller; it has become the wholesale distributor of images which form the mainstream of our popular culture. The world of television shows and tells us about life—people, places, striving, power, and fate. It presents the good and bad, the happy and sad, the powerful and the weak, and lets us know who or what is successful or a failure.

As with the functions of culture in general, the substance of the consciousness cultivated by television is broad, underlying global assumptions about the "facts" of life rather than specific attitudes and opinions. Nevertheless, television is only one of the many things that explain the world to us and our children. Television, however, is special because its socially constructed version of reality bombards all classes, groups, and ages with the same perspectives at the same time. More importantly, these images are presented primarily in the guise of entertainment, whether in sitcoms, drama, action-adventures, TV movies, news or information programs (as the lines between these formats continue to erode).

The views of the world embedded in television drama do not differ appreciably from images presented in other media, and its rules of the social hierarchy are not easily distinguishable from those imparted by other powerful agents of socialization. What makes television unique, however, is its ability to standardize, streamline, amplify, and share with virtually all members of society these common cultural norms.

Although television has a great deal in common with other media, it is different in some important ways. People spend far more time with television than with other media; more time is spent watching television than doing any other activity except working and sleeping. Most people under 45 began watching television before they could read or probably even speak. Unlike print media, television does not require literacy; unlike theatrical movies, television runs almost continuously and can be watched without leaving one's home; unlike radio, television can show as well as tell. Each of these characteristics is significant in and of itself; their combined force is unprecedented and overwhelming.

Television is different from other media in its centralized mass production and ritualistic use of a coherent set of images and messages produced to appeal to the entire population. Therefore, exposure to all television viewing rather than only specific genres or programs is what accounts for the historically new and distinct consequences of living with television—the cultivation of shared conceptions of reality among otherwise diverse publics.

THE MYTHS OF SELECTIVITY, DIVERSITY, AND CHOICE

The cultivation perspective does not deny or minimize the importance of specific programs, selective attention and perception, specifically targeted communications, individual and group differences, and research on effects defined in terms of short-run and individual attitude and behavior change. It just sees these as separate problems, generally irrelevant to the cultivation process. The point is that exclusive concentration on those aspects and terms of traditional effects research risks losing sight of what is most fundamental and significant about television as the common story-teller of our age.

When most people watch television the number and variety of viewing choices is limited by the fact that many programs designed for the same broad audience tend to be similar in their basic makeup and appeal and are often broadcast during the same time slots (Signorielli, 1986). Most programs are, by commercial necessity, designed to be watched by nearly everyone. Amount of viewing typically follows the style of life of the viewer and is relatively insensitive to specific programs. The audience is always the group available at a certain time of the day, the week, and the season, regardless of the programs. Most viewers watch by the clock and follow established routines rather than choose each program as they would choose a book, a movie or a magazine. Moreover, those who start by watching a specifically selected program often continue watching once their program is over. Series and fads come and go, yet for the past 15 to 20 years, viewing has stabilized at about seven hours a day for the average household and three hours a day for the average person (Nielsen, 1990).

Thus, the more people watch the less selective they can be. Most regular and heavy viewers watch more of everything. Researchers who attribute their findings to news viewing or preference for action programs, and so on, overlook the fact that people who watch more news or action programs typically watch more of all types of programs, and that, in any case, different genres of programs tend to manifest many of the same basic features. Moreover, stated preference for a specific genre does not necessarily mean that this is the only type of program watched, or that this genre will be selected every time it is available for viewing.

Of course, cable and especially VCRs have obviously and dramatically changed the home media environment. The family without a VCR is now the exception, especially when children are present. VCRs have contributed to the drop in audience share (and revenue) among the three major broadcasting networks (Lawrence, 1989), and have profoundly altered the marketing and distribution of films formerly found only in movie theatres. Likewise, cable's increased channel capacities, movie channels, and "pay-per-view" also appear to have changed the nature of home viewing.

On the surface, the VCR has undeniably changed the way television is perceived and used by the typical viewer. Through its time-shifting capabilities, VCRs allow viewers to watch broadcast and cable programming whenever and as often as they like. They may thus feel a new sense of power and control over their viewing fare, derived from the ability to freeze a frame, review a scene, zip through commercials (or zap them entirely), and so on. Moreover, through renting prerecorded cassettes, viewers may now believe they have an unprecedented range of choice in what they select to watch.

It may appear that cable and the VCR strongly challenge or even negate some assumptions of cultivation theory. Armed with a VCR, the viewer may be more selective than ever. Instead of being limited to whatever happens to be on the air, viewers can pick and choose what they want to record or rent from a vast range of alternatives. This scenario, however, assumes that the specific content seen by VCR users (especially heavy VCR users and those who are heavy television viewers in general) presents alternative world views, values, and stereotypes from most network-type programs. This assumption seems unlikely, especially because available evidence suggests that cable and VCRs serve mainly to intensify rather than undercut cultivation; most regular and heavy viewers use cable and VCRs to watch more of the most popular fare, and cultivation patterns are even more pronounced among those who use these "new" delivery systems more often (Morgan & Rothschild, 1983; Morgan & Shanahan, 1991; Morgan, Shanahan, & Harris, 1990).

This should not be too surprising. Given the tight links among the various industries involved in the production and distribution of media content, and the fact that all these sources are trying to attract the same overlapping, heterogeneous audiences, the most popular program materials will tend to present consistent and complementary messages. For example, in regard to violence, a recent comparison of cable and broadcast dramatic programming (Gerbner, 1993) found similar levels of violence overall. Specifically, although cable's children's programming had slightly lower levels of violence than children's programming on broadcast television, the cable's general programming was somewhat more violent than similar programs on broadcast television.

From an economic standpoint, the industry's programming practices are geared to reproduce what has already proven to be profitable (Gitlin, 1983). Hence, the reliance on spin-offs, formulaic script writing, and cable's as well as independent stations' use of recently syndicated programs or classic TV programs.

In short, what is most popular, by definition, tends to reflect—and cultivate—dominant cultural ideologies. Certainly, the VCR allows selective viewers to seek out specialized, often "fringe" material (Dobrow, 1990), but for most average to heavy viewers, most of the time, the VCR and cable are likely to be used to consume more of what they already watch.

Therefore, from the point of view of the cultivation of relatively stable and common images, what counts is the total pattern of programming to which entire communities are regularly exposed over long periods of time. The pattern of settings, casting, social typing, actions, and related outcomes cuts across most program types and viewing modes and defines the world of television—a world in which many viewers live so much of their lives that they cannot avoid absorbing or dealing with its recurrent patterns.

VARIATIONS IN CULTIVATION

Cultivation is not a unidirectional flow of influence from television to audience, but part of a continual, dynamic, ongoing process of interaction among messages and contexts. In some cases, those who watch more television (the heavy viewers) are more likely—in all or most subgroups—to give the "television answers." But, in many cases the patterns are more complex. Television viewing usually relates in different ways to different groups' life situations and world views.

Cultivation is both dependent on and a manifestation of the extent to which television's imagery dominates viewers' sources of information. For example, personal interaction makes a difference. Parental coviewing patterns and orientations towards television can either increase (Gross & Morgan, 1985) or decrease (Rothschild & Morgan, 1987) cultivation among adolescents; also, children who are more integrated into cohesive peer or family groups seem less likely to be influenced by television (Rothschild, 1984).

Direct experience also plays a role. The relationship between amount of viewing and fear of crime is strongest among those who live in high crime urban areas (a phenomenon called *resonance*, which in everyday reality and television provide a double dose of messages that resonate and amplify cultivation). Further, relationships between amount of viewing and the tendency to hold exaggerated perceptions of violence are more pronounced within those real-world demographic subgroups (minorities) whose fictional counterparts are more frequently victimized on television (Morgan, 1983).

There are a variety of factors and processes that produce systematic and theoretically meaningful variations in cultivation patterns. One process, however, stands out, both as an indicator of differential vulnerability and as a general, consistent pattern representing one of the most profound consequences of living with television: mainstreaming.

MAINSTREAMING

American culture consists of many diverse currents, some weak, some strong. Some flow in the same general directions, some at cross-currents. Yet there is a "dominant" set of cultural beliefs, values, and practices, in some ways at the core of all the other currents, and in some ways surrounding them. This dominant current is not simply the sum of all the crosscurrents and subcurrents; rather, it is the most general and stable (though not static) mainstream, representing the broadest and most common dimensions of shared meanings and assumptions. It is that which ultimately defines all the other crosscurrents and subcurrents. Because of its unique role in our society, we see television as the primary manifestation of our culture's mainstream.

The "mainstream" can thus be thought of as a relative commonality of outlooks and values that heavy exposure to the features and dynamics of the television world tends to cultivate. *Mainstreaming* means that heavy viewing may absorb or override differences in perspectives and behavior which ordinarily stem from other factors and influences. In other words, differences found in the responses of different groups of viewers, differences that usually are associated with the varied cultural, social, and political characteristics of these groups, are diminished or even absent from the responses of heavy viewers in these same groups.

As a process, mainstreaming represents the theoretical elaboration and empirical verification of the assertion that television cultivates common perspectives. It represents a relative homogenization, an absorption of divergent views, and a convergence of disparate viewers. Former and traditional distinctions (which flourished, in part, through the diversity provided by print culture) become blurred as successive generations and groups become enculturated into television's version of the world. Mainstreaming means that television viewing may reduce or override differences in perspectives and behavior which stem from other social, cultural, and demographic influences. (The notion of mainstreaming implies some special analytical strategies beyond those of "standard" cultivation analysis; these are described in the methodology.)

CRITICISMS OF CULTIVATION THEORY AND RESEARCH

Of all the theoretical perspectives relating to mass communication, that deriving from Cultural Indicators research has probably been one of the most heavily criticized. In the early 1970s the methodology and findings of the content (message system) analysis, particularly the examination of television violence, were the focus of a number of colloquies. Most of these stemmed from critiques by industry researchers and involved differences over definitions (what is violence? what is a violent act? how is violence unitized? and so on). They also addressed concerns over sample size, reliability, validity, and numerous related issues (Coffin & Tuchman, 1972–1973a, 1972–1973b; Eleey, Gerbner, & Signiorelli, 1972–1973a, 1972–1973b; Blank, 1977a, 1977b; Gerbner et al., 1977a; Gerbner et al., 1977b).

Soon after the first cultivation results were published (Gerbner & Gross, 1976), cultivation analysis became the focal point of the Cultural Indicators project. Although message system analysis continued to be conducted and reported each year, for whatever reasons, the industry's critiques abated until recently when again public concern about the level of violence on television has increased. The end of the 1970s, however, brought a period of intense debate over cultivation theory and research. It is not possible or appropriate to review all the arguments and counter-arguments here. See Doob and Macdonald (1979), Hughes (1980), Gerbner, Gross, Signiorelli, and Morgan (1980b, 1980c), Hirsch (1980a), Gerbner, Gross, Signiorelli, and Morgan (1981c), Hirsch (1980b, 1981a), Gerbner, Gross, Signiorelli, and Morgan (1981a), Hirsch (1981b), and Gerbner, Gross, Signiorelli, and Morgan (1981b)—preferably in that order—for a relatively complete account.

More recent criticisms (i.e., Potter, 1993) have been voiced about the justifications for television world answers, television viewing measures, selective viewing, small effect sizes, and again concern about the nature of the relationship. As this chapter is designed to explain and describe the nature of cultivation theory and how it relates to ongoing research, we have not chosen to address any of these criticisms in specific detail. Rather throughout this chapter is a discussion of each of these issues in relation to the theoretical underpinning of cultivation or how the studies are conducted.

CULTIVATION ANALYSIS METHODOLOGY

The methods and assumptions behind cultivation analysis are different from those traditionally employed in mass communication research. Again, research and debate on the impact of mass communication often focused on individual messages, programs, episodes, series, or genres and their ability to produce immediate change in audience attitudes and behaviors. Cultivation analysis is concerned with the more general and pervasive consequences of cumulative exposure to cultural media. Hence, cultivation research is not suited to an experimental paradigm (cf., Bryant, Carveth, & Brown, 1981). Although its underlying theoretical framework could be applied to any dominant form of communication, most cultivation analyses have focused on television because of the medium's uniquely repetitive and pervasive message characteristics and its dominance among other media.

In its simplest form, cultivation analysis tries to ascertain if those who spend more time watching television are more likely to perceive the real world in ways that reflect the most common and repetitive messages and lessons of the television world, compared to people who watch less television but are otherwise comparable in terms of important demographic characteristics.

People who regularly watch a great deal of television differ from those who watch less television in many ways. Although all social groups include both heavy and light viewers (relative to the group as a whole), there are overall differences between heavy and light viewers according to sex, income, education, occupation, race, time use, social isolation–integration, and a host of other demographic and social variables. But there are also differences in terms of the extent to which television dominates their sources of consciousness. Cultivation theory assumes that light viewers tend to be exposed to more varied and diverse information sources (both mediated and interpersonal), while heavy viewers, by definition, tend to rely more on television for their information.

The goal of cultivation analysis is to determine whether differences in the attitudes, beliefs, and actions of light and heavy viewers reflect differences in their viewing patterns and habits, independent of (or in interaction with) the social, cultural, and personal factors that differentiate light and heavy viewers. Thus, again, cultivation analysis attempts to document and analyze the independent contributions of television viewing to viewers' conceptions of social reality. The existing research reveals that we have come a long way towards this goal; at the same time, the more work that is done, the more complex the questions (and the answers) become (Signorielli & Morgan, 1990).

PROCEDURES USED IN CULTIVATION ANALYSIS

Cultivation analysis generally begins with identifying and assessing the most recurrent and stable patterns in television content, emphasizing the consistent images, portrayals, and values that cut across most program genres. This is accomplished either by conducting a content (message system) analysis or by examining existing content studies. This phase is extremely important in the research because hypotheses concerning television's contribution to viewers' conceptions about social reality cannot be formulated without reliable information on the most stable and repetitive images and portrayals presented. There are many critical discrepancies between "the world" and "the world as portrayed on television." The shape and contours of the television world rarely match "objective reality" (although they often do match dominant ideologies and values).

Findings from systematic analyses of television's content are then used to formulate questions about people's conceptions of social reality. Some of the questions are semiprojective, some use a forced-error format, and others simply measure beliefs, opinions, attitudes, or behaviors. The questions juxtapose answers reflecting the television world (developed from the findings of the content studies) with those more in line with reality. The questionnaires typically include questions relating to social reality as well as measures of television viewing and demographic variables such as age, gender, race, education, occupation, social class, and political orientation.

Using standard techniques of survey methodology, the questions are posed to samples (national probability, regional, convenience) of children, adolescents, or adults. Secondary analysis of large-scale national surveys (for example, the National Opinion Research Center's General Social Surveys, GSS) have often been used when they include questions which relate to identifiable aspects of the television world and also include measures of television viewing.

For example, one of the most examined aspects of television content is sex or gender role stereotyping. Study after study found that women are underrepresented and that most television characters are extremely gender-typed (Signorielli, 1985). Two cultivation analyses focusing upon gender roles examined children's responses to two sets of questions dealing with gender role attitudes and behaviors (Morgan, 1987; Signorielli & Lears, 1992a). The questions relating to gender role attitudes asked if certain chores (wash or dry the dishes, mow the lawn, take out the garbage, help with the cooking, clean the house, help with small repairs around the house, and make the bed) should be done by *boys only, girls only,* or *either girls or boys.* Responses to these questions were analyzed to indicate whether or not the answer reflected traditional gender role divisions of labor. The children's gender role behaviors were ascertained by asking which of these seven chores they did. In these studies the "television answer" was responding that only girls should do "girl chores" (wash or dry the dishes, help with the cooking, clean the house, make the bed) and that only boys should do the "boy chores" (mow the lawn, take out the garbage, help with small repairs around the house). In regard to the children's own behaviors, the "television answer" was indicating that they did those chores that were consistent with their gender.

Another study (Signorielli & Lears, 1992b) examined the relationship between television viewing and children's conceptions about nutrition. Content studies have consistently revealed that the world of television is very unhealthy (Gerbner, Gross, Morgan & Signorielli, 1981b), particularly in relation to eating habits. The children in this study were asked five questions related to poor eating habits:

1. How often do you eat sugared cereal for breakfast?
2. How often each week do you eat at a fast food restaurant (eg., McDonald's, Wendy's, Burger King, etc.)?

3. How often do you eat a snack each day?
4. How likely are you to eat chips, cookies, candy, cupcakes, or fruit candied snacks for snacks?
5. During the day, how likely are you to drink sugared fruit drinks, fruit punch, or soda when you are thirsty?

The "television answer" in this study was to respond that these behaviors occurred more frequently.

Both of these studies used questionnaires designed specifically to test cultivation-related hypotheses. Secondary analysis of existing data sets provides yet another very useful way to conduct cultivation analyses. Secondary analysis, however, is often limited by the types of questions, particularly the measures of television viewing, included in the original questionnaire. On the other hand, secondary analysis enables researchers who may be short on research funds to examine data from national probability samples or to look at the same set of questions over a longer period of time.

For example, a number of cultivation analyses focusing on the mean world syndrome have used data from the National Opinion Research Corporation's General Social Survey (GSS; see Signorielli, 1990). The GSS is a very well-respected, personal interview that has been conducted on a national probability sample since 1972. Many of the questions in the interview schedule are asked each time the survey is conducted while others are rotated and asked every other year, every couple of years or are asked of a subset of the sample each year. Television viewing was added to the GSS in 1976 and is now gathered on a subset of the sample or the entire sample each year. The questions relating to the mean world syndrome have been included in just about every GSS. These questions (TV answer italicized) include the following:

1. Would you say that most of the time people try to be helpful, or that they are mostly *just looking out for themselves*?
2. Do you think that most people would try *to take advantage of you* if they got a chance, or would they try to be fair?
3. Generally speaking, would you say that most people can be trusted or that *you can't be too careful in dealing with people*?

Cultivation analyses have also been conducted using other existing data sets. For example, Signorielli (1993) examined high school seniors' conceptions about work using questions included in the Monitoring the Future Survey, conducted annually by the Survey Research Center at the University of Michigan.

To simplify and facilitate the data analysis, many cultivation studies combine responses to questions about similar topics into additive indices, which are then tested for internal consistency using Cronbach's α. For example, the questions comprising the mean world syndrome are combined into an additive index (Signorielli, 1990). Similarly, Signorielli and Lears (1992a) combined the answers to questions about eating habits into the "poor eating habits" index. The higher the score on this index, the poorer the child's eating habits and the more reflective of eating habits in the television world.

Television viewing is usually assessed by asking how much time the respondent watches television on an average day. The best measures provide estimates of the number of hours the respondent watches each day. These data may be used in their original form (a ratio scale) or may be reduced to relative viewing categories (*light*, *medium*, and *heavy* viewing). Viewing, when so categorized, is seen in relative terms and the determination of what constitutes *light*, *medium*, and *heavy* viewing is decided on a sample-by-sample basis, using as close to a three-way split of hours of self-reported daily television viewing as possible. Although the more specific measures of hours of viewing each day facilitate some data analysis procedures, from a conceptual standpoint, what is important is that there are basic differences in viewing levels, not the actual or specific amount of viewing.

The substantive questions posed to respondents do not mention television, and the respondents' awareness of the source of their information is seen as irrelevant. The resulting relationships, if any, between amount of viewing and the tendency to respond to these questions in the terms of the dominant and repetitive facts, values, and ideologies of the world of television (again, other things held constant) illuminates television's contribution to viewers' conceptions of social reality.

Data analysis techniques consist of both simple and more complex procedures. The standard analysis may begin with simple crosstabulations between television viewing (using a three-way split of light, medium, and heavy viewing) and the answers to the substantive questions (categorized by the TV and non-TV answers). The difference between heavy and light viewers is reported as the cultivation differential (CD), whereas the strength and direction of the relationship is indicated by Γ.

Typically, correlational techniques are used to look at the relationship between television viewing and responses to the substantive question. Partial correlation techniques, in particular, examine the relationship between viewing and the substantive question while controlling for pertinent demographic data. Partial correlation coefficients help to isolate what may be spurious relationships. For example, Signorielli and Lears (1992b) calculated zero-, first-, and fifth-order partial correlations coefficients, controlling for gender, race, reading level, parents' educational level, and parent's occupational status.

Mainstreaming hypotheses are tested by conducting standard cultivation analysis involving the comparison of responses given by light, medium, and heavy viewers within specific demographic subgroups, usually defined by gender, age, race, education, social class, political orientation, religiosity, and so on. Usually, some subgroups show significant associations between amount of viewing and the attitude or belief at hand while others do not. In many cases, the overall pattern of differential subgroup associations fits the mainstreaming model; that is, the subgroups showing no association tend to give the "television answer" regardless of amount of viewing (i.e., they are "already in" the mainstream), while their counterparts only give this answer if they are heavy viewers.

In these cases, the light viewers of counterpart subgroups (e.g., younger versus older respondents, or those of lower versus higher social class, or liberals, versus conservative) tend to give sharply different responses, but the heavy viewers in these subgroups converge towards the mainstream (television) view. This suggests that background, demographic factors exert a strong (and predictable) influence on attitudes, but only among lighter viewers, and the impact of these factors is markedly reduced among heavy viewers. Therefore, many studies also use regression analyses and analyses of variance to examine statistical interactions between amount of viewing and demographic characteristics; these provide stringent tests of the extent to which apparent mainstreaming patterns reflect significant interactions of television viewing with other viewer characteristics. Also, a number of cultivation studies have employed structural equation models and path analyses, especially with longitudinal panel data, where the same respondents are studied at more than one point in time.

CONCLUSION

As in most studies of media effects, the observable empirical evidence of cultivation is likely to be modest in terms of its absolute size. Even light viewers may be watching up to seven hours of television a week; in most national surveys we find that a trivial, and demographically eclectic, handful (about 4 percent or less) say they do not watch at all. But, if we argue that the messages are stable, that the medium is virtually ubiquitous, and that it is accumulated exposure that counts, then it seems reasonable that almost everyone should be affected, regardless of how much they watch. Even light viewers may watch a substantial amount of television per week and in any case live in the same cultural environment as heavy viewers; what they do not get through the tube can be acquired indirectly from others who do watch more television. It is clear, then, that the cards are stacked against finding evidence of cultivation. Therefore, the discovery of a systematic pattern of even small but pervasive differences between light and heavy viewers may indicate far-reaching consequences.

Accordingly, we should not dismiss what appear to be small effects, because small effects may have profound consequences. For example, a slight but pervasive (e.g., generational) shift in the cultivation of common perspectives may alter the cultural climate and upset the balance of social and political decision making without necessarily changing observable behavior. A single percentage point difference in ratings is worth many millions of dollars in advertising revenue and, thus, may signal the success or demise of a program. It takes but a few degrees shift in the average global temperature to have an ice age or global warming. A range of 3% to 15% margins (typical of most differences between light and heavy viewers) in a large and otherwise stable field often signals a landslide, a market takeover, or an epidemic, and it certainly tips the scale of any closely balanced choice or decision.

In summary, the theory of cultivation is an attempt to understand and explain the dynamics of television as a distinctive feature of our age. It is not a substitute for, but a complement to, traditional approaches to media effects research concerned with processes more applicable to other media. Designed primarily for television and focusing on its pervasive and recurrent patterns of representation and viewing, cultivation analysis concentrates on the enduring and common consequences of growing up and living with television: the cultivation of stable, resistant, and widely shared assumptions, images, and conceptions reflecting the institutional characteristics and interests of the medium itself and the larger society. Television has become the common symbolic environment—and the true "melting pot" of the 20th century—that interacts with most of the things we think and do. Therefore, understanding its dynamics can help develop and maintain a sense of alternatives and dependence essential for self-direction and self-government in the television age.

REFERENCES

Baker, R. K., & Ball, S. J. (Ed.). (1969). *Violence in the media*. Staff report to the National Commission on the Causes and Prevention of Violence. Washington, DC: U.S. Government Printing Office.

Blank, D. M. (1977a). Final comments on the violence profile. *Journal of Broadcasting, 21*(3), 287–296.

Blank, D. M. (1977b). The Gerbner violence profile. *Journal of Broadcasting, 21*(3), 273–279.

Bryant, J., Carveth, R. A., & Brown, D. (1981). Television viewing and anxiety: An experimental examination. *Journal of Communication, 31*(1), 106–119.

Coffin, T. E., & Tuchman, S. (1972–1973a). A question of validity: Some comments on "apples, oranges, and the kitchen sink." *Journal of Broadcasting, 17*(1), 31–33.

Coffin, T. E., & Tuchman, S. (1972–1973b). Rating television programs for violence: A comparison of five surveys. *Journal of Broadcasting, 17*(1), 3–20.

Dobrow, J. A. (1990). Patterns of viewing and VCR use: Implications for cultivation analysis. N. Signorielli & M. Morgan (Eds.), *Cultivation analysis: New directions in media effects research* (pp. 71–84). Newbury Park, CA: Sage Publications.

Doob, A. N., & Macdonald, G. E. (1979). Television viewing and fear of victimization: Is the relationship causal? *Journal of Personality and Social Psychology, 37*(2), 170–179.

Eleey, M., Gerbner, G., & Signorielli (Tedesco), N. (1972–1973a). Apples, oranges, and the kitchen sink: An analysis and guide to the comparison of "violence ratings." *Journal of Broadcasting 21*(1), 21–31.

Eleey, M., Gerbner, G., & Signorielli (Tedesco), N. (1972–1973b). Validity indeed! *Journal of Broadcasting, 17*(1), 34–35.

Gerbner, G. (1967). Mass media and human communication theory. In F. E. X. Dance (Ed.), *Human communication theory: Original essays* (pp. 40–60). New York: Holt, Rinehart & Winston.

Gerbner, G. (1969). Dimensions of violence in television drama, in R. K. Baker & S. J. Ball (Eds.), *Violence in the media* (pp. 311–340). Staff report to the National Commission on the Causes and Prevention of Violence. Washington, DC: U.S. Government Printing Office.

Gerbner, G. (1972). Violence and television drama: Trends and symbolic functions, in G. A. Comstock & E. Rubinstein (Eds.), *Television and social behavior: Vol. 1, Content and control* (pp. 28–187). Washington, DC: U.S. Government Printing Office.

Gerbner, G. (1973). Cultural indicators: The third voice. In G. Gerbner, L. Gross & W. H. Melody (Eds.), *Communications, technology and social policy* (pp. 555–573). New York: Wiley.

Gerbner, G. (1993). *Violence in cable-originated television programs*. Unpublished manuscript, University of Pennsylvania.

Gerbner, G., & Gross, L. (1976). Living with television: The violence profile. *Journal of Communication, 26*(2), 173–199.

Gerbner, G., Gross, L., Eleey, M., Jackson-Beeck, M., Jeffries-Fox, S., & Signorielli, N. (1977a). The Gerbner violence profile: An analysis of the CBS report. *Journal of Broadcasting, 21*(3), 280–286.

Gerbner, G., Gross, L., Eleey, M., Jackson-Beeck, M., Jeffries-Fox, S., & Signorielli, N. (1977b). One more time: An analysis of the CBS "Final comments of the violence profile." *Journal of Broadcasting, 21*(3), 297–2303.

Gerbner, G., Gross, L., Morgan, M., & Signorielli, N. (1980, April). *Media and the family: Images and impact*. Paper for the National Research Forum on Family Issues, White House Conference on Families.

Gerbner, G., Gross, L., Morgan, M., & Signorielli, N. (1981a). Health and medicine on television. *New England Journal of Medicine, 305,* 901–904.

Gerbner, G., Gross, L., Morgan, M., & Signorielli, N. (1981b). Scientists on the TV screen. *Society, May/June,* 41–44.

Gerbner, G., Gross, L., Morgan, M., & Signorielli, N. (1982). Charting the mainstream: Television's contributions to political orientations. *Journal of Communication, 32*(2), 100–127.

Gerbner, G., Gross, L., Morgan, M., & Signorielli, N. (1986). Living with television: The dynamics of the cultivation process, in J. Bryant & D. Zillmann (Eds.), *Perspectives on Media Effects* (pp. 17–40). Hillsdale, NJ: Lawrence Erlbaum Associates.

Gerbner, G., Gross, L., Morgan, M., & Signorielli, N. (1994). Growing up with television: The cultivation perspective. In J. Bryant & D. Zillmann (Eds.), *Media effects* (pp. 17–41). Hillsdale, NJ: Lawrence Erlbaum Associates.

Gerbner, G., Gross, L., Signorielli, N., & Morgan, M. (1980a). Aging with television: Images on television drama and conceptions of social reality. *Journal of Communication, 30*(1), 37–47.

Gerbner, G., Gross, L., Signorielli, N., & Morgan, M. (1980b). The "mainstreaming" of America: Violence profile no. 11. *Journal of Communication, 39*(3), 10–29.

Gerbner, G., Gross, L., Signorielli, N., & Morgan, M. (1980c). Some additional comments on cultivation analysis. *Public Opinion Quarterly, 44*(3), 408–410.

Gerbner, G., Gross, L., Signorielli, N., & Morgan, M. (1981a). A curious journey into the scary world of Paul Hirsch. *Communication Research, 8*(1), 39–72).

Gerbner, G., Gross, L., Signorielli, N., & Morgan, M. (1981b). Final reply to Hirsch. *Communication Research, 8*(3), 259–280.

Gerbner, G., Gross, L., Signorielli, N., & Morgan, M. (1981c). On the limits of "the limits of advocacy research": Response to Hirsch. *Public Opinion Quarterly, 45*(1), 116–118.

Gerbner, G., Gross, L., Signorielli, N., Morgan, M., & Jackson-Beeck, M. (1979). The demonstration of power: Violence profile No. 10. *Journal of Communication, 29*(3), 177–196.

Gerbner, G., Morgan, M., & Signorielli, N. (1982). Programming health portrayals: What viewers see, say and do. In D. Pearl, L. Bouthilet, & J. Lazar (Eds.), *Television and behavior: Ten years of scientific progress and implications for the 80's: Volume 2, technical reviews* (pp. 291–307). Rockville, MD: National Institute of Mental Health.

Gerbner, G., & Signorielli, N. (1979). *Women and minorities in television drama, 1969–1978.* Philadelphia: The Annenberg School of Communications, University of Pennsylvania.

Gitlin, T. (1983). *Inside prime time.* New York: Pantheon.

Gross, L., & Morgan, M. (1985). Television and enculturation, in J. Dominick and J. Fletcher (Ed.), *Broadcasting research methods* (pp. 221–234). Boston: Allyn and Bacon.

Hirsch, P. (1980a). On Hughes' contribution: The limits of advocacy research. *Public Opinion Quarterly, 44*(3), 411–413.

Hirsch, P. (1980b). The "scary world" of the nonviewer and other anomalies: A reanalysis of Gerbner et al.'s findings of cultivation analysis. *Communication Research, 7*(4), 403–456.

Hirsch, P. (1981a). On not learning from one's own mistakes: A reanalysis of Gerbner et al.'s findings on cultivation analysis, part II. *Communication Research, 8*(1), 3–37.

Hirsch, P. (1981b). Distinguishing good speculation from bad theory: Rejoinder to Gerbner et al. *Communication Research, 8*(1), 73–95.

Hughes, M. (1980). The fruits of cultivation analysis: A re-examination of the effects of television watching on fear of victimization, alienation, and the approval of violence. *Public Opinion Quarterly, 44*(3), 287–302.

Lawrence, R. (1989). Television: The battle for attention. *Marketing and Media Decisions, 24*(2), 80–82.

Morgan, M. (1987). Television, sex role attitudes, and sex role behavior. *Journal of Early Adolescence, 7*(3), 269–282.

Morgan, M. (1983). Symbolic victimization and real world fear. *Human Communication Research, 9,* 146–157.

Morgan, M. (1982). Television and adolescent's sex-role stereotypes: A longitudinal study. *Journal of Personality and Social Psychology, 43*(5), 947–955.

Morgan, M., & Gross, L. (1982). Television and educational achievement and aspiration, in D. Pearl, L. Bouthilet, & J. Lazar (Eds.), *Television and behavior: Ten years of scientific progress and implications for the 80's, Volume II, Technical Reviews* (pp. 78–90). Rockville, MD: National Institute of Mental Health.

Morgan, M., & Rothschild, N. (1983). Impact of the new television technology: Cable TV, peers, and sex-role cultivation in the electronic environment. *Youth and Society, 15*, 33–50.

Morgan, M., & Shanahan, J. (1991). Do VCRs change the TV picture? VCRs and the cultivation process. *American Behavioral Scientist, 35*(2), 122–135.

Morgan, M., Shanahan, J., & Harris, C. (1990). VCRs and the effects of television: New diversity of more of the same? In J. Dobrow (Ed.), *Social and cultural aspects of VCR use* (pp. 107–123). Hillsdale, NJ: Lawrence Erlbaum Associates.

Nielsen, A. C. (1990). *Nielsen report on television*, New York: Nielsen Media Research.

Potter, W. J. (1993). Cultivation theory and research: A conceptual critique. *Human Communication Research, 19*(4), 564–601.

Rothschild, N. (1984). Small group affiliation as a mediating factor in the cultivation process. In G. Melischek, K. E. Rosengren, & J. Stappers (Eds.), *Cultural indicators: An international symposium* (pp. 377–387). Vienna: Verlag der Osterreichischen Akademie der Wissenschaften.

Rothschild, N., & Morgan, M. (1987). Cohesion and control: Adolescents' relationships with parents as mediators of television. *Journal of Early Adolescence, 7*(3), 299–314.

Signorielli, N. (1991). Adolescents and ambivalence towards marriage: A cultivation analysis. *Youth & Society, 23*(1), 121–149.

Signorielli, N. (1987). Drinking, sex, and violence on television: The Cultural Indicators perspective. *Journal of Drug Education, 17*(3), 245–261.

Signorielli, N. (1982). Marital status in TV drama: A case of reduced options. *Journal of Broadcasting, 26*(2), 585–597.

Signorielli, N. (1985). *Role portrayals and stereotyping on television: An annotated bibliography.* Westport, CT: Greenwood Press.

Signorielli, N. (1986). Selective television viewing: A limited possibility. *Journal of Communication, 36*(3), 64–75.

Signorielli, N. (1993). Television and adolescents' perceptions about work. *Youth & Society, 24*(3), 314–341.

Signorielli, N. (1989). Television and conceptions about sex-roles: Maintaining conventionality and the status quo. *Sex Roles, 21*(5/6),337–356.

Signorielli, N. (1990). Television's mean and dangerous world: A continuation of the Cultural Indicators perspective. In N. Signorielli & M. Morgan (Eds.), *Cultivation analysis: new directions in media effects research* (pp. 85–106). Newbury Park, CA: Sage Publications.

Signorielli, N., & Lears, M. (1992a). Children, television and conceptions about chores: Attitudes and behaviors. *Sex Roles, 27*(3/4), 157–172.

Signorielli, N., & Lears, M. (1992b). Television and children's conceptions of nutrition: Unhealthy messages. *Health Communication, 4*(4), 245–257.

Signorielli, N., & Morgan, M. (Eds.). (1990). *Cultivation analysis: New directions in media effects research.* Newbury Park, CA: Sage Publications.

9

Theories and Methods in Knowledge Gap Research Since 1970

Cecilie Gaziano
Research Solutions, Inc.

Emanuel Gaziano
Indiana University

In 1970, Tichenor, Donohue, and Olien published a programmatic study of the social structure of public affairs and science knowledge entitled "Mass media flow and differential growth in knowledge." By that time more than 20 years of mass communication effects research had implicitly demonstrated "the apparent failure of mass publicity to inform the public at large," with the particular finding that media campaigns tend to reach precisely those "least in need of it . . . [whereas] those missed were the ones the plan tried to reach" (1970, p. 161). They argued, however, that this outcome was no mere "failure" of an information campaign, but rather the product of the social structure of mass communication. Terming this effect the *knowledge gap*, they formulated a hypothesis, a set of assumptions, explanatory factors, and a pair of testable statements which could explain—and perhaps even help alleviate—this relative deprivation of knowledge between social strata.

The ensuing quarter-century has seen a proliferation of contending positions regarding the knowledge gap. These positions range from the continuing research program of Tichenor, Donohue, and Olien, and their students,[1] modifying the original hypothesis to proposals for alternate perspectives defined in opposition to the 1970 hypothesis (including some who question the idea of "gaps" altogether) and a wealth of empirical results both confirming and disconfirming the validity and usefulness of the knowledge gap hypothesis.

This chapter reviews and accounts for this theoretical diversity. It also examines the principal methods employed in knowledge gap research.[2] Outside of the inevitable misinterpretations, the different knowledge gap approaches are ultimately reducible to a set of fundamental conceptualizations of sociocultural phenomena. Therefore, a basic typology of theoretical perspectives and conceptual models is developed as a heuristic device through a careful exegesis of representative models in knowledge gap research.

Three competing conceptions of knowledge gap phenomena combine, in varying proportions, to comprise its theoretical dimension. A *social structural perspective* locates differential knowledge acquisition within the collectivity. A broad *symbolic interactionist perspective* accounts for the knowledge gap in terms of the situational needs and motivations of individual actors. And a *cybernetic model* conceives of knowledge deprivation in the terms of the design and functioning of information delivery systems. This typology of theories aids in the comprehension of disparate methods and empirical results.

Our intention is not to resolve differences, nor to provide synthesis, but rather to recognize and account for differing approaches which may clarify terms and facilitate conversation among researchers. Toward that end, we also hope to provide a usable vocabulary for discussing the theories and data of knowledge gap research, as well as an indication of those areas where fresh research efforts would be most profitable.

THE KNOWLEDGE GAP AS SOCIETAL NATURALISM

The knowledge gap hypothesis was conceived against the backdrop of practical and progressive social change—indeed, a normative or ethical dimension permeates research efforts oriented toward closing knowledge gaps. As formulated by Tichenor, Donohue, and Olien, the knowledge gap hypothesis rests upon a cumulative change model of social structure. This pragmatic model holds that an increase in knowledge leads to an "increased rate of acceptance of a pattern of behavior, a belief, a value, or an element of technology in a social system" (1970, p. 159). Further, this tends to occur within certain subsystems possessing patterns of behavior and values that closely correspond to those of the intended social change. People holding different values tend to accept such innovations at a relatively reduced rate. That diverse strata acquire knowledge at different rates due to varying values and behaviors is not problematic for

---

[1]Because one purpose of this chapter is to identify influences in knowledge gap research, it should be noted that the first author is a former student of Phillip J. Tichenor.

[2]The increasing application of knowledge gap research outside of the United States and in cross-cultural settings opens up a series of important issues which we will not treat here, although the topic deserves careful scrutiny.

collective perspectives which posit relatively differentiated, specialized, and interdependent aspects of society. In other words, the existence of specialized knowledge held by certain classes and not others—for example, a knowledge of automotive repair—does not indicate a knowledge gap of societal level significance. Gaps are particularly poignant, however, when certain types of knowledge are supposed to have universal value, but are not universally held. In the American context, these values include democratic participation in public affairs (cf, Schudson, 1983), as well as science knowledge or health care promotion. This normative view is also closely related to the modernization and development perspective in diffusion research (cf, Rogers, 1976, 1983).

The concept of normativity is one of a complex of themes expressed in the original hypothesis which may be summarized as *societal naturalism* (sometimes rendered *social realism*).[3] In essence, a societal naturalist perspective conceives of society as a naturally occurring supraindividual collective entity whose organizational qualities cannot be reduced to its individual parts (Levine, 1995). Such a view is well expressed in the original knowledge gap hypothesis: "As the infusion of mass media information into a social system increases, segments of the population with higher socioeconomic status tend to acquire this information at a faster rate than the lower status segments, so that the gap in knowledge between these segments tends to increase rather than decrease" (Tichenor et al., 1970, pp. 159–160).

The knowledge gap concerns systemic social relationships—that is, the relative differences in knowledge acquisition among strata—as well as the linkages among "the source, channel, and audience components of the communication subsystem" (Olien, Donohue, & Tichenor, 1983, p. 455). They draw heavily from structural functionalism, stratification theory, community studies, and conflict theory to cast knowledge gap phenomena into these properly collective terms.

The Tichenor–Donohue–Olien group refined their hypothesis with a set of assumptions: (a) education validly indicates socioeconomic status, (b) information flow may be characterized by irreversible linear or curvilinear trends, (c) no upper limit of information has been reached, and (d) public affairs and science news have a "more or less general appeal" and value (1970, p. 160). Of these, the first three are explicitly designed to facilitate operationalizing the hypothesis, while the fourth is a generalization based upon the expectations of democratic and egalitarian ideology.

Although each assumption has profound consequences for the character of knowledge gap research, the definition and measurement of knowledge deserves special consideration. Throughout their studies Tichenor et al. employ the terms *knowledge* and *information* interchangeably. Yet close analysis shows that each carries a different meaning. On the one hand, knowledge denotes certain socially-structured collective representations, including beliefs and values (regarding, for instance, prospects for the future, the well-being of the community), which constitute the worldviews of different strata (Tichenor, Rodenkirchen, Olien, & Donohue 1973, pp. 60–63; Tichenor et al., 1970, p. 162). On the other hand, they conceive of information as the qualitatively

---

[3]These terms and their parallels (individual voluntarism, atomic naturalism, collective voluntarism) form a framework for analyzing social theories developed by Levine (1995).

undifferentiated data of the "information delivery system" (Tichenor, Donohue, & Olien, 1980, p. 180), the product of its "feedback" and "distribution-control" (Olien Donohue, Tichenor, 1983, p. 457). This homogenized and rather mechanistic view of information constitutes a muted cybernetic dimension to the original knowledge gap hypothesis.[4] A cybernetic view of information within knowledge gap research has definite advantages, not the least of which is the way it can be unproblematically measured in survey research. Furthermore, information delivery and reception provide a way of specifying the mechanisms and details of knowledge gap phenomena.

A social realist perspective locates cause within system organization itself. Social structures are conceived "to operate in such a way as to maintain themselves in some stable state" (Udy, 1968, p. 493), through self regulatory adaptation and integration which tend to maintain equilibrium. In particular, structural functionalist views assume that a "social pattern is explained by the effects on consequences of the pattern" and excludes all explanations relying on psychological, historical, hereditary, and nonhuman environmental factors (Cancian, 1968, p. 30). Tichenor et al. specifically argued that the creation of "greater differentials in knowledge across society is itself a profound social effect" (1970, p. 170). They also noted that knowledge gaps may be considered structurally functional from two points of view: first, insofar as more highly educated persons really are at the vanguard of progressive social change and, second, in the sense that knowledge gaps serve to maintain power differentials of super- and subordination through information control (Tichenor et al., 1973).[5] In the course of maintaining existing elites, however, knowledge gaps may also increase tension within the social system, leading to further social problems (Tichenor et al., 1970). They maintain throughout their work that "social power is the basic issue in the knowledge gap phenomenon" (Olien et al., 1983, p. 458).

While arguing that gaps are structurally functional, the original hypothesis also accounts for the social roles of individuals and the mass media. The mass media function similarly to other social institutions, namely, by reinforcing or increasing existing inequalities (Tichenor et al., 1970). In particular, mass media are oriented toward the more educated and more powerful groups in society (Tichenor, Donohue, & Olien, 1980), and "systematically project definitions of issues which are conducive to the interest of established power groups" (Olien et al., 1983, p. 459). The forms and functions of the mass media are determined by social structural needs and not the needs of the media subsystem itself (p. 457). By the same token, people also play social roles. An individual's structural location increases or reduces "the likelihood that details or interpretations will ever reach [that individual] and make sense in his [or her] frame of reference" (Tichenor et al., 1980, p. 181). This is not a point about individual personalities. Although roles are played by individuals, they are structurally defined

---

[4]*Cybernetics* was a term introduced in the 1940s by Norbert Wiener who defined it as "the entire field of control and communication theory, whether in the machine or the animal" (quoted in Maron, 1968, p. 4). The cybernetic view is intellectually related to economic and maximization theories (game theory, rational choice theory, information theory) and stimulus–response behaviorism in general, and forms a variant of atomic naturalism (see Levine, 1995; see also chapter 15, this volume).

[5]This latter explanation was prefigured in Moore and Tumin's (1949) functionalist account of ignorance.

and are not the product of the "idiosyncratic behavior of persons playing roles at any given point in time" (p. 182). Nor, in this perspective, are knowledge gaps due merely to people's interests, because interest itself is a socially structured "collective concern" (Olien et al., 1983, p. 458). Finally, the specific knowledge or message content does not determine gap phenomena; the structure within which it and its interpretations are located do (Tichenor et al., 1980).

Beginning in 1973, Tichenor et al. shifted their focus from an abstract notion of social systems to a concrete, geographically grounded, idea of the community.[6] This approach allowed for a much greater specification of the relative significance of issues, community conflict levels, community characteristics such as pluralism and homogeneity, and greater attention to specific patterns of media coverage in a particular locale (Donohue, Tichenor, & Olien, 1975). Indeed, they found that knowledge gaps decrease for local issues under conditions of high significance, high community conflict, and homogeneity of population (Tichenor et al., 1973; Donohue et al., 1975; Tichenor et al., 1980). In these cases, high arousal and salience induce interpersonal rather than mass communication which, in a homogenous community requiring less selective self-exposure, causes knowledge gaps to narrow. The reverse situation obtains when salience and conflict are low (in, for instance, nonlocal issues) and when a community is more complex, differentiated, and pluralistic. Whether the analytic frame is the community, the social system, or the public, however, the original knowledge gap hypothesis calls for collective-level explanations common to a social realist perspective.

THE KNOWLEDGE GAP AS INDIVIDUAL VOLUNTARISM

In 1977, Ettema and Kline challenged the original knowledge gap hypothesis. Citing mixed empirical results, they argued that the original hypothesis "requires a fuller understanding of the causal forces acting to widen and narrow the gap," making it necessary to specify the "contingent conditions" of gap phenomena (1977, pp. 180–181). In the course of doing so, they shifted the underlying perspective from societal naturalism to individual voluntarism by refocusing on an individual-level account of subjectivity and agency, rather than a structural level account. They adopted a voluntarist or constructivist view of social reality, rather than a naturalist one.

In accordance with this shift, Ettema and Kline employed the concepts of symbolic interaction (although they did not use this term).[7] Broadly, *symbolic interaction* "refers to the process by which individuals relate to their own minds or the minds of others" in a way that takes account of "their own or their fellows' motives, needs, desires, means and ends, knowledge, and the like" (Swanson, 1968, p. 441). Symbolic interaction represents the instrumental activities of actors—attitudes, beliefs, motivation, perception, thought, and choice—relative to the conditions and resources of the *situation*. This view conceives of the individual as a minded entity, a self, that employs

---

[6]This orientation is closely related to the work of classical human ecologists such as Robert Park and his colleagues who were also interested in the role of the mass media and the functions of community conflict (e.g., Park 1938/1972).

[7]An interactionist perspective is collective, but it is often recast in individual terms, as Ettema and Kline (1977) did.

signs and symbols to construct identity and take on roles within a role system. Since symbolic interaction was formulated, in part as a response to social structural, or cultural, determinism (Swanson, 1968), it is a particularly apt choice for Ettema and Kline's challenge to Tichenor et al.'s work.

After dismissing structural explanations as inadequate and tautological, Ettema and Kline (1977) concluded that gap phenomena causal factors are of two types: audience-related factors such as communication skills, motivation, and media self-exposure, and message-related "ceiling effects."[8] Within the category of audience-related causes they further discern what they termed transsituational "deficit" explanations and "situation-specific" difference explanations, following the work of Cole and Bruner (1971). The former type of explanation holds that "a community under conditions of poverty. . .is a disorganized community, and this disorganization expresses itself in various forms as deficits" (Cole & Bruner, 1971, quoted in Ettema & Kline, 1977, p. 185). Ettema and Kline characterized the work of Tichenor et al. as a deficit interpretation of knowledge gap phenomena.[9] In particular, they focused on communication skills, the first contributory factor in the original formulation of the hypothesis, arguing that if communication skills deficits always obtain among lower socioeconomic status (SES) persons, then knowledge gaps will always widen and never close—thereby contradicting empirical evidence (p. 188).

As a viable alternative, Ettema and Kline (1977) offered a difference interpretation of knowledge gap phenomena. This interpretation maintains that "persons from different social strata or cultures manifest their abilities in different circumstances" (Cole & Bruner, 1971, quoted in Ettema & Kline, 1977, p. 187). Specifically, these circumstances occur when individuals are motivated to exercise their abilities or it is functional for individuals to do so. (Although they employ the same term, individual-level and collective-level functionalisms need to be sharply distinguished). These situation-specific differences imply that gaps will widen when lower SES persons are less motivated to acquire knowledge, and will narrow or fail to manifest themselves when motivation or personal need for such knowledge is high. Consequently, Ettema and Kline indicated that knowledge itself is not stratified, but that differences in personal motivation produce this effect—a "situation gap." Or, put another way, they portrayed the link between specific audiences (composed of aggregated individuals, not collectivities) and specific knowledges as the relevant phenomenon (cf., p. 189).

This hypothesis reformulation allows Ettema and Kline to recast factors such as salience and conflict in terms of individual-level motivation and needs. They further reinterpret factors such as selective self-exposure and retention of information, and interpersonal communication, as intervening variables linking motivation and personal

---

[8]We ignore the issue of ceiling effects here because they are of less interest in a general theoretical account and because the original hypothesis specifically excludes such effects from its scope.

[9]There is absolutely no warrant in the work of Tichenor et al. to argue or assume that they impute deficits in basic cognitive capacity to members of low SES groups (*contra* Ettema & Kline, 1977, p. 190, and Dervin, 1980, p. 77). A deficit explanation is not a logically possible cause of gap phenomena within a social realist perspective, unless one conceives of deficits as somehow socially structured. In this latter case, such deficits would have the explanatory status of a contributory factor, but not the essential cause of gap phenomena. The individualist perspective of Ettema and Kline, Dervin, and others has hindered recognition of this important point: They have committed what Lieberson calls "the fallacy of nonequivalence" (1984, p. 114)

functionality to the rate of knowledge acquisition (p. 191). An equally important modification of the original hypothesis is their constructivist view of knowledge itself. Where Tichenor et al. see one homogenous type of knowledge—public affairs data, news facts—Ettema and Kline recognize the possibility of qualitatively different types of knowledge when they write that "higher and lower SES persons...may well see the world in somewhat different ways" (p. 189). In other words, people may employ different cognitive schemata to interpret incoming information.

THE KNOWLEDGE GAP AS ATOMIC NATURALISM (CUM VOLUNTARISM)

Another perspective on knowledge gap phenomena amplifies aspects of each of the previous two, but combines them to produce something wholly different. In her work on sense-making and communication gaps, Brenda Dervin fused a cybernetic model of information delivery systems with certain insights from phenomenology to produce a mechanistic and ultra-individualist—yet situationally relative—account of gap phenomena. Heavily influenced by a library science model of information collection, storage, and retrieval, Dervin's perspective conflated all such systems together: libraries, catalogs, databases, and mass media are undifferentiated (Dervin, 1989; Dervin & Nilan, 1986).[10] These information sources, or "machines," are accessible through hardware such as telephones, televisions, radios, newspapers, computers, and VCRs (p. 229), which constitute the interface for the human user. Ultimately, Dervin seeks a reconceptualization of communication, broadly conceived, which privileges the user and provides design principles for humanizing information delivery systems. Dervin argued for an alternative reconceptualization in terms of categories derived from user-experience because, she claimed, traditional conceptions of knowledge gaps and information inequality are wholly illusory products of observer categories.

The central opposition in Dervin's work is that between traditional and alternative approaches to communication. In her account, all traditional models of mass communication subscribe to the deficit interpretation of gap phenomena. In this source–receiver model, gaps occur "because some people are less willing and able to take in information than others" (Dervin, 1980, p. 77). The focus of this research, she claimed, is on source–goals and objective information, both of which establish information standards which, if they are not met, "receivers are blamed [for] when they fail to get the message" (p. 85). "Those receivers who do not catch the message are then labeled as being in gap or inequity" (p. 93). However, Dervin argued that research since the mid-1970s suggests that the knowledge gap "is more idea than reality" (p. 79), and is really merely an artifact of traditional source–receiver model assumptions. Therefore, "any data available on the presence of inequities and gaps is nothing more than numeric myths created by the use of inappropriate assumptions about the nature of information seeking and use" (p. 81).

By contrast, Dervin (1989) sought to modify the "mechanistic, transmission-oriented, objectivity-oriented" traditional model in terms of "the inner worlds of users, where most of the important acts of communicating . . . are performed" (p. 217). Such

---

[10]Consequently, Dervin's arguments ranged throughout the "communication and information science fields" (1980, p. 74). However, we restrict our concern to those issues relevant to mass communication and knowledge gap phenomena in particular.

a view, also termed the *sense-making approach*, begins from the assumption that all individuals creatively construct meaning unique to their circumstances, within the bounds of "time, space, change, and physiology" (Dervin, 1980, p. 92, p. 102; 1989, p. 223). This position entails an ultra-individualistic relativism in the sense that all "persons subjectively perceive their world" differently from other persons (Stewart, 1978, quoted in Dervin 1980, p. 89). Society itself is merely the "product of past and present cognitive/behavioral events" in aggregated form (Dervin, 1989, p. 226). Therefore, she redefined information "as the answers respondents create . . . to their questions in situations they personally face" (Dervin, 1980, p. 95), or more generally, as "any stimulus that alters the cognitive structure of a receiver" (Paisley, 1980, quoted in Dervin & Nilan, 1986, p. 17). In this view, collective-level gaps disappear and are replaced by "the 'gaps' seen by receivers between the pictures they have in their heads and the sense they require to design movements for their lives" (Dervin & Nilan, 1980, p. 105). As in Ettema and Kline's perspective, individuals will inform themselves at the point of need, when their circumstances call for information and provide motivation (Dervin, 1980, p. 103). Consequently, information that is sent by sources who construct meaning differently from their receivers is less useful and relevant—hence the gaps that traditional researchers find (p. 94).[11] The solution to these sense-making gaps is to train information professionals—from librarians to journalists—to "empathize systematically" (Dervin, 1989, p. 224).

The following sections of this chapter briefly review support for the original knowledge gap hypothesis and provide a research example illustrating how a knowledge gap study in a collective realist perspective incorporates theory into its methods.

RESEARCH SUPPORT FOR KNOWLEDGE GAPS

The evidence for education-based knowledge gaps is overwhelming, as confirmed by examination of some 90 reports (Gaziano, 1983, 1995). Seldom do researchers report null findings or reverse gaps with lower SES groups possessing more knowledge than higher SES groups. The role of variations in mass media attention in fostering knowledge inequalities is much less clear, however. Only a fraction of studies vary media publicity; therefore, this issue requires much more research attention.

Under certain conditions gaps decrease or do not occur. Gaps may decline because topics are local or controversial, both of which tend to heighten public attention. In general, the more distant a topic is from respondents in geography and personal experience and the more knowledge depends on access to high-status channels and characteristics, the greater the likelihood that knowledge inequities will occur.

Both low and high media coverage paradoxically can contribute to reduced knowledge gaps (Tichenor, Rodenkirchen, Olien, & Donohue, 1973). High media attention, especially to controversial issues, tends to bring public discussion to a boil, dispersing communication throughout a community system, equalizing knowledge gaps in some

---

[11]Neither Dervin's nor Ettema and Kline's perspective recognizes the possibility of structural patterns which may be reproduced without the knowledge or consent of constituent actors. Such an exclusion becomes both theoretically and practically problematic in situations where individual actors may not be aware of very real information needs, for example, among members of a population at high risk for HIV infection (see Freimuth, 1990).

cases (Tichenor et al., 1980), and broadening them in others (Gaziano, 1984). On the other hand, decreasing levels of media publicity can lead to declining public interest in issues and narrowed knowledge differentials (Griffin, 1990). It is not unusual, however, to observe an awareness knowledge gap closing at the same time depth knowledge gaps are widening (Gaziano, 1983).

Electronic media use (e.g., broadcast, CNN, cable) by the less educated can help to reduce knowledge disparities (Tomita, 1989; Pan, Ostman, Moy, & Reynolds, 1994; Miyo, 1983), although this does not always occur (see Olien, Donohue, & Tichenor, 1990, for a discussion of the role of television in deepening knowledge gaps between metropolitan and non-metropolitan communities).

Community structural variations have been studied by few researchers besides Tichenor et al. (cf., Gaziano, 1988). Pearson (1993) studied rural, small urban, and Anchorage respondents in Alaska. Education increased with size and urban status of the communities and was related to media access and knowledge disparities. The Minnesota Heart Health Program (MHHP) studies showed that knowledge gaps are more likely to close in smaller, more homogeneous communities, as Tichenor et al. predicted (Viswanath, 1990; Viswanath, Finnegan, Hannan, & Luepker, 1991). Over time, knowledge gaps ebbed and flowed, and continual introduction of new knowledge into communities impeded development of ceiling effects.

Other Research Issues

Other major considerations affect knowledge gap research. Six major research issues are considered next.

Level of Analysis.   Aspiring knowledge gap researchers first have the task of choosing a major theoretical perspective from which to set the level of analysis. Researchers need to be aware of the theoretical assumptions of each area; the underlying dissimilarities among the three main perspectives partly account for inconsistent findings. Researchers studying knowledge gap phenomena often have borrowed concepts and variables from each of the dominant perspectives without realizing how each varies from the others in level of analysis (i.e., in terms of individuals, a community, a society). Even though the statement of the knowledge differential problem frequently is given in the collective terms of the classic knowledge gap hypothesis, research analysis of knowledge disparities has tended to be on an individual level rather than on a collective level.

Research Design.   Internal and external threats to validity are important considerations when designing knowledge gap research. One-shot case study designs allow little or no control over such threats (Campbell & Stanley, 1963). Among the best designs is the Solomon four-group design, combining both panel and cross-sectional samples over time, as used by Griffin (1990) and in the MHHP studies, although only data from cross-sections have been published from the MHHP so far (e.g., Finnegan, Viswanath, Hannan, Weisbrod, & Jacobs, 1989; Viswanath, 1990; Salmon, 1985). For more on threats to validity regarding communication campaigns, see Chaffee, Roser, and Flora (1989).

Motivation and Interest.   Findings are not consistent for interest, motivation, involvement, or related variables. One reason is that widely varying operational definitions have been employed. Refining measures and clarifying findings also remain a challenge. Anyone desiring to study these variables is encouraged to consider as broad a range of studies with these variables as possible. Some authors to consult include: Genova and Greenberg (1979); Gandy and El Waylly (1985); Griffin (1990); Salmon (1985); Viswanath (1990); Salmon, Wooten, Gentry, Cole, and Kroger (1994); Viswanath et al. (1991).

Factors Reinforcing Gaps.   Tichenor et al. (1970) described some reasons for reinforcement of knowledge inequalities. These included: (a) communication skills, (b) amount of stored prior knowledge of pertinent topics, (c) relevant social contact (activities, reference groups, interpersonal discussion), (d) selective exposure, acceptance and retention of information (which often are correlated with education), and (e) the nature of the mass media information-delivery subsystems. For examples of research on some of the first four issues, see McLeod and Perse (1994); Simmons and Garda (1982); Kleinnijenhuis (1991); and Pan (1990). For work concerning the fifth, see Donohue, Tichenor, and Olien (1987), Donohue, Tichenor, & Olien (1986), and Tichenor, Olien, and Donohue (1987). (See Gaziano, 1989, on social trends reinforcing knowledge gaps.)

Cultural Context.   The culture of the research setting influences results. Studies of farmers in developing countries are not directly comparable to studies in industrialized nations. The media or informal communication systems and social organization are often too different to make valid comparisons. Such considerations also should be kept in mind when comparing with "control" communities.

Elements of a Complete Research Report.   The minimum items to report in any research include: dates of research, location, sample size, completion rate, interview method, population, research design, biases, operational definitions of all variables, including knowledge gaps, and statistical tests used. Some reports are unclear on some of these elements or omit others altogether—leaving the reader without a complete means of evaluation or replication.

HOW THEORY TRANSLATES INTO RESEARCH

The first step in the transition to research is specifying the independent and dependent variables. Variation in mass media publicity is the independent variable (the presumed cause) in much knowledge gap research. If alterations in media attention are not studied, at least media use or a similar variable will provide a proxy for publicity. Knowledge gap is the dependent variable (the presumed effect). SES, derived from the subsystem of social stratification, is part of that variable (Fig. 9.1). Frequently, education has been used as an indicator of SES, but components such as income or occupation are sometimes substituted or combined with other SES variables to form an index. How the SES indicator was measured should always be reported specifically. Such measurements are not as standard in the research world as many would believe.

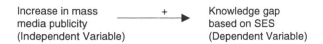

FIG. 9.1.   Primary relationships of variables in knowledge gap research.

Also, education sometimes has been measured as categorical but treated statistically as continuous, the results of which can be misleading (e.g., Hewes, 1978).

After the dependent variable is chosen, the next step is a theoretical definition of the concept, such as a dictionary definition). Then comes an operational definition of the concept (i.e., the way it will be measured in a questionnaire). Hage (1972) provided a fuller description of these concepts.

Here, *knowledge gap* is the abstract concept, and its theoretical definition is the degree of relationship between education and knowledge. Figure 9.2 shows how Frazier (1986) operationalized *knowledge gap*.

Usually, education has been measured as a nominal (categorical) variable or a continuous variable. As a nominal variable, it is usually divided into either two or three categories. When three categories are used, typical groups are those without high school diplomas (low education), high school graduates (medium education), and those with some college or more (high education). If there are only two groups, the break is usually less than college (low) and some college or more (high). When continuous measurement is desired, record the exact grade number. Additional numbers would capture work toward advanced degrees. Similarly, knowledge has been measured as two or three categories from low to high (nominal variable) or as a score (continuous variable).

The choice of measurement will depend upon the statistical test researchers wish to use for their hypotheses. Researchers will be less limited if they measure variables originally as continuous. Variables can be grouped later. Frequent operational definitions in the literature have included the following: Pearson product–moment correlations between education and knowledge (both measured as continuous); analysis of variance results (education as a nominal variable and knowledge as a continuous variable); regression results (knowledge as a continuous variable and education as either a nominal or continuous variable); and chi-square results (both knowledge and education as nominal variables and the relationship expressed by Cramer's V statistic). If measuring at more than one time, compare the size of the knowledge-education relationship at each time to determine whether or not the differential is increasing, decreasing, or unchanging.

Building upon Robert E. Park's (1940) distinction between *knowledge of* and *knowledge about*, which correspond roughly to awareness and depth knowledge, respectively, researchers usually have measured *awareness* of topics as any relevant item mentioned and *depth knowledge* as a score summing correct answers to a number of questions. One pitfall, however, is that attitudinal or behavioral measures can confound knowledge measures. This happens particularly with secondary analyses of data which come from studies designed for other purposes. Good research carefully notes how knowledge gap hypotheses are stated and how others have stated them; deviations from the original knowledge gap hypothesis are made clear to others, because deviations can inhibit comparability of findings across studies.

Abstract
Concept: Knowledge gap (dependent variable)

↓

Theoretical   Magnitude of differential among education groups on
Definition: knowledge of some issue

↓

Operational   From Frazier (1986): Differences in knowledge scores among
Definition   high, medium and low educational groups, by one-way analysis
                            of variance

FIG. 9.2.   Incorporating an abstract theoretical concept into research. Based on Hage (1972).

AN EXAMPLE

The progression from theory to methods can be demonstrated by a study embodying social realism elements conducted by Frazier (1986). She was concerned with the structure of public opinion within communities—relationships among social action, opinions, and knowledge, and their distribution within four communities along SES lines. Media dissemination of information was relevant in stirring up controversy, conflict, and public discussion.

This process varied by community and by issue, especially in one community where the fluoridation topic was more controversial than in the others. The other topic, public policy on requiring seat belts, was not controversial in any community. As Tichenor and his colleagues showed, conflict can be a central element in reducing knowledge gaps when talk about issues permeates most or all social strata. Frazier's issues are especially of interest because they were of community-wide importance and defined in both health and public affairs terms (technical knowledge and issue knowledge).

Focus on the Dependent Variable

Table 9.1 shows Frazier's theoretical and operational definitions of knowledge. Her complex measures provide a lot of information about the role of issue type in knowledge disparities. Statistical tests of her hypothesis were for differentials in knowledge scores among high, medium, and low education groups. Frazier's data show that knowledge gaps can be curvilinear, rather than linear. Further, medium education and high education groups can be more similar than medium and low education groups (Donohue, Olien, & Tichenor, 1990; Gaziano, 1984).

The knowledge gap hypothesis was supported for issue knowledge but not technical knowledge with regard to fluoridation, the high-conflict topic (Fig. 9.3). Significant fluoridation issue knowledge differentials occurred in three communities, but an issue knowledge gap was smaller and nonsignificant in the community (Brainerd, Minnesota) in which fluoridation was the most controversial. Further, all the communities had fluoridation misinformation gaps based on education, of which Brainerd's was the most pronounced. Small knowledge gaps developed for technical and issue knowledge of the seat belt issue, less publicized and less controversial, but communities did not show appreciable differences.

Other Research Considerations

Researchers often focus on the dependent variables of knowledge, attitude, and behavior (K–A–B). (Others could be studied, such as beliefs and values.) Examples of work incorporating both knowledge gap and behavior gap variables are Donohue et al. (1990), Frazier (1986), and Moore (1987). Frazier also examined SES-based opinion gaps.

Several scholars would integrate these three variables in research and theory (Chaffee & Roser, 1986; Hornik, 1989; Rogers, 1976). Rogers called this cluster of variables the *communication effects gap*. Scholars working within a social systems perspective would not be likely to use this term, however, as they perceive cause to be located in the social structure and would study the subsystems which deliver information and maintain power within a community or a society, for instance. Much more work remains to hone ideas about integration of knowledge, opinion, and behavior variables in theories of inequalities.

FUTURE RESEARCH STRATEGIES

This chapter has examined several theoretical orientations and other research decisions which can help scholars study knowledge differentials. Based on this examination, we propose three considerations for future research. First, it is of the utmost importance to identify and develop a coherent theoretical perspective—or set of perspectives—on the knowledge gap. The major dimensions of such identification include the location

TABLE 9.1

Theoretical and Operational Definitions of Knowledge

Theoretical definition of *technical knowledge:* "Level of knowledge of the effectiveness of fluorides and fluoridation for prevention of tooth decay and of the effectiveness of seat belts for preventing serious injuries in car accidents" (p. 115).

> Operational definition of *fluoridation technical knowledge:* Score 0 to 19 across 18 items of fluorides and fluoridation with one item weighted twice as much (concerning the one most effective way to prevent tooth decay).

> Operational definition of *technical knowledge of seat belt effectiveness:* Score 0 to 5 on four knowledge items on seat belt effectiveness (most effective way to prevent serious injuries in car accidents weighted more).

Theoretical definition of *issue knowledge:* "Level of knowledge of decision-making processes and socio-political issues associated with state laws requiring community water fluoridation and seat belt use" (p. 116).

> Operational definition of *fluoridation issue knowledge:* 0 to 32 across 14 items on fluoridation issue (certain issues weighted more).

> Operational definition of *seat belt issue knowledge:* 0 to 19 across 9 items on seat belt issue (the one most effective way weighted twice as much).

Note: From *Community Conflict and the Structure and Social Distribution of Public Opinion*, by P. J. Frazier, 1986, unpublished doctoral dissertation, University of Minnesota. Copyright P. J. Frazier. Reprinted with permission.

Hypothesis: "When an issue is controversial in a community, it is less likely that knowledge differentials will be observed according to age, education and social class levels" (p. 96). Partially supported; only education is discussed here.

Predicted relationships:

Under conditions of high controversy in a community:

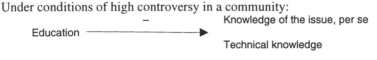

Frazier's findings:

Under conditions of high controversy in a community:

FIG. 9.3.   Hypothesis and findings (Frazier, 1986).

of subjectivity (and hence agency) at either the individual or collective levels, and the conceptualization of phenomena as either "naturally" occurring or socially "constructed." Clear theory reveals those places where additional work is required. Many theoretical realms are possible, including others not discussed here, but researchers should be clear about which they are using and why, compared with other perspectives. Differences in theoretical orientation, frequently related to levels of analysis, partly account for incongruent knowledge gap research results.

Second, theory must be translated into appropriate methods and thoroughly exploited. Ideally, studies within the first perspective would be carried out at more points in time, utilizing combinations of panel and cross-sectional designs. Those researchers interested in the construction of knowledge and the value of information should strongly consider such qualitative methods as clinical interviews, careful textual or semiotic analysis and, for an as yet undeveloped collective voluntarist approach, ethnographic methods.

Third, practical goals of knowledge gap research need to be carefully matched with underlying theory and methods. New variables are needed to increase the explanatory power of theories of knowledge inequalities. New variables could include values or behavior with respect to identifying potential change agents.

Finally, much discussion is needed on the issue of policy implications of knowledge differentials. Some knowledge gaps do not have serious consequences, but others, on such topics as AIDS and similar health issues, do. Many hard-to-eradicate knowledge differentials have long-term implications for social stability and ever-increasing social costs of differentials in general, to say nothing of the costs to the social segments lacking knowledge. If knowledge disparity reduction is a goal, focusing on changing social stratification—socially structured inequities—may be more fruitful than concentration on increasing information levels.

REFERENCES

Campbell, D. T., & Stanley, J. C. (1963). *Experimental and quasi-experimental designs for research.* Chicago: Rand McNally.

Cancian, F. M. (1968). Varieties of functional analysis. In D. L. Sills (Ed.), *International encyclopedia of the social sciences Volume 6* (pp. 29–43). New York: Macmillan.

Chaffee, S. H., & Roser, C. (1986). Involvement and the consistency of knowledge, attitudes, and behaviors. *Communication Research, 13*(3), 373–399.

Chaffee, S. H., Roser, C., & Flora, J. (1989). Estimating the magnitude of threats to validity of information campaign effects. In C. T. Salmon (Ed.), *Information campaigns: Balancing social values and social change* (pp. 285–301). Newbury Park, CA: Sage.

Cole, M., & Bruner, J. S. (1971). Cultural differences and influences about psychological process. *American Psychologist, 26*, 867–876.

Dervin, B. (1980). Communication gaps and inequities: Moving toward a reconceptualization. In B. Dervin & M. J. Voigt (Eds.), *Progress in communication sciences* (Vol. 2, pp. 73–112). Norwood, NJ: Ablex.

Dervin, B. (1989). Users as research inventions: How research categories perpetuate inequities. *Journal of Communication, 39, 216-232.*

Dervin, B., & Nilan, M. (1986). Information needs and uses. *Annual Review of Information Science and Technology, 21*, 3–33.

Donohue, G. A., Olien, C. N., & Tichenor, P. J. (1987). Media access and knowledge gaps. *Critical Studies in Mass Communication, 4*, 87–92.

Donohue, G. A., Olien, C. N., & Tichenor, P. J. (1990, May). *Knowledge gaps and smoking behavior.* Paper presented to American Association for Public Opinion Research, Lancaster, PA.

Donohue, G. A., Tichenor, P. J., & Olien, C. N. (1975). Mass media and the knowledge gap: A hypothesis reconsidered. *Communication Research, 2*, 3–23.

Donohue, G. A., Tichenor, P. J., & Olien, C. N. (1986). Metro daily pullback and knowledge gaps: Within and between communities. *Communication Research, 13*, 453–471.

Ettema, J. S., & Kline, F. G. (1977). Deficits, differences, and ceilings: Contingent conditions for understanding the knowledge gap. *Communication Research, 4*, 179–202.

Finnegan Jr, J. R., Viswanath, K., Hannan, P. J., Weisbrod, R., & Jacobs Jr., D. R. (1989). Message discrimination: A study of its use in a campaign research project. *Communication Research, 16,* 770–792.

Frazier, P. J. (1986). *Community conflict and the structure and social distribution of public opinion.* Unpublished doctoral dissertation, University of Minnesota.

Freimuth, V. S. (1990). The chronically uninformed: Closing the knowledge gap in health. In E. B. Ray & L. Donohew (Eds.), *Communication and health: Systems and applications* (pp. 171–186). Hillsdale, NJ: Lawrence Erlbaum Associates.

Gandy Jr., O. H., & El Waylly, M. (1985). The knowledge gap and foreign affairs: The Palestinian–Israeli conflict. *Journalism Quarterly, 62*, 777–783.

Gaziano, C. (1983). The knowledge gap: An analytical review of media effects. *Communication Research, 10*, 447–486.

Gaziano, C. (1984). Neighborhood newspapers, citizen groups and public affairs knowledge gaps. *Journalism Quarterly, 61*, 556–566, 599.

Gaziano, C. (1988). Community knowledge gaps. *Critical Studies in Mass Communication, 5*, 351–357.

Gaziano, C. (1989). Mass communication and class communication. *Mass Comm Review, 16*, 29–38.

Gaziano, C. (1995, May). *A twenty-five year review of knowledge gap research.* Paper presented to the American Association for Public Opinion Research, Fort Lauderdale, FL.

Genova, B. K. L., & Greenberg, B. S. (1979). Interests in news and the knowledge gap. *Public Opinion Quarterly, 43*, 79–91.

Griffin, R. J. (1990). Energy in the eighties: Education, communication, and the knowledge gap. *Journalism Quarterly, 67*, 554–566.

Hage, J. (1972). *Techniques and problems of theory construction in sociology* . New York: Wiley.

Hewes, D. (1978). "Levels of measurement" problem in communication research: A review, critique, and partial solution. *Communication Research 5*, 87–127.

Hornik, R. (1989). The knowledge-behavior gap in public information campaigns: A development communication view. In C. T. Salmon (Ed.), *Information campaigns: Balancing social values and social change* (pp. 113–138). Newbury Park, CA: Sage.

Kleinnijenhuis, J. (1991). Newspaper complexity and the knowledge gap. *European Journal of Communication, 6*, 499–522.

Levine, D. N. (1995). *Visions of the sociological tradition*. Chicago: University of Chicago Press.

Lieberson, S. (1984). *Making it count: The improvement of social research and theory*. Berkeley: University of California Press.

Maron, M. E. (1968). Cybernetics. In D. L. Sills (Ed.), *International encyclopedia of the social sciences*, (Vol. 4, pp. 3–6). New York: Macmillan.

McLeod, D. M., & Perse, E. M. (1994). Direct and indirect effects of socioeconomic status on public affairs knowledge. *Journalism Quarterly, 71*, 433–442.

Miyo, Y. (1983). The knowledge-gap hypothesis and media dependency. In R. N. Bostrom (Ed.), *Communication yearbook* (Vol. 7, pp. 626–650). Beverly Hills: Sage.

Moore, D. W. (1987). Political campaigns and the knowledge gap hypothesis. *Public Opinion Quarterly, 51*, 186–200.

Moore, W. E., & Tumin, M. M. (1949). Some social functions of ignorance. *American Sociological Review 14*, 787–795.

Olien, C. N., Donohue, G. A., & Tichenor, P. J. (1983). Structure, communication and social power: Evolution of the knowledge gap hypothesis. In E. Wartella, D.C. Whitney, & S. Windahl (Eds.), *Mass communication review yearbook* (pp. 455–461). Beverly Hills, CA: Sage.

Olien, C. N., Donohue, G. A., & Tichenor, P. J. (1990, November). *Media mix and the metro-nonmetro knowledge gap: Information deprivation in an information age?* Paper presented to Midwest Association for Public Opinion Research, Chicago, IL.

Pan, Z. (1990). *Inequalities in knowledge acquisition from mass media: Cross-generational changes and maintenance*. Unpublished doctoral dissertation, University of Wisconsin-Madison.

Pan, Z., Ostman, R. E., Moy, P., & Reynolds, P. (1994). News media exposure and its learning effects during the Persian Gulf War. *Journalism Quarterly, 71*, 7–19.

Park, R. E. (1940). News as a form of knowledge: A chapter in the sociology of knowledge. *American Journal of Sociology, 45*, 669–686.

Park, R. E. (1972). Reflections on communication and culture. In H. Elsner, Jr. (Ed.), *The crowd and the public and other essays* (pp. 98–116). Chicago: University of Chicago Press. (Original work published 1938).

Pearson, L. (1993). Desert Storm and the Tundra Telegraph: Information diffusion in a media-poor environment. In B. S. Greenberg & W. Gantz (Eds.), *Desert storm and the mass media* (pp. 182–196). Cresskill, NJ: Hampton Press.

Rogers, E. M. (1976). Communication and national development: The passing of the dominant paradigm. *Communication Research, 3*, 213–240.

Rogers, E. M. (1983). *Diffusion of innovations*. New York: Free Press.

Salmon, C. T. (1985). *The role of involvement in health-information acquisition and processing*. Unpublished doctoral dissertation, University of Minnesota.

Salmon, C., Wooten, K., Gentry, E., Cole, G., & Kroger, F. (1994, July). *AIDS knowledge gaps in the first decade of the epidemic*. Paper presented to the International Communication Association, Sydney, Australia.

Schudson, M. (1983). *The news media and the democratic process, a Wye Resource Paper*. New York: Aspen Institute for Humanistic Studies.

Simmons, R. E., & Garda, E. C. (1982). Dogmatism and the "knowledge gap" among Brazilian mass media users. *Gazette, 30*(2), 121–133.

Stewart, J. (1978). Foundations of dialogic communication. *Quarterly Journal of Speech, 64*, 183–201.

Swanson, G. E. (1968). Symbolic interaction. In D. L. Sills (Ed.), *International encyclopedia of the social sciences* (Vol. 7, pp. 441–445). New York: Macmillan.

Tichenor, P. J., Donohue, G. A., & Olien, C. N. (1970). Mass media flow and differential growth in knowledge. *Public Opinion Quarterly, 34*, 159–170.

Tichenor, P. J., Donohue, G. A., & Olien, C. N. (1980). Conflict and the knowledge gap. In P. J. Tichenor, G. A. Donohue, & C. N. Olien, *Community conflict and the press* (pp. 175–203). Beverly Hills, CA: Sage.

Tichenor, P. J., Olien, C. N., & Donohue, G. A. (1987). Effect of use of metro dailies on knowledge gap in small towns. *Journalism Quarterly, 64*, 329–336.

Tichenor, P. J., Rodenkirchen, J. M., Olien, C. N., & Donohue, G. A. (1973). Community issues, conflict, and public affairs knowledge. In P. Clarke (Ed.), *New models for mass communication research* (pp. 45–79). Beverly Hills, CA: Sage.

Tomita, M. R. (1989). *The role of cable television in providing information on world news: A test of the knowledge gap hypothesis (television)*. Unpublished doctoral dissertation, University of Minnesota.

Udy, S. H., Jr. (1968). Social structural analysis. In D. L. Sills (Ed.). *International encyclopedia of the social sciences* (Vol. 14, pp. 489–495). New York: Macmillan.

Viswanath, K. (1990). *Knowledge gap effects in a cardiovascular disease prevention campaign: A longitudinal study of two community pairs*. Unpublished doctoral dissertation, University of Minnesota.

Viswanath, K., Finnegan, J. R., Jr., Hannan, P. J., & Luepker, R. V. (1991). Health and knowledge gaps: Some lessons from the Minnesota Heart Health Program. *American Behavioral Scientist, 34*, 712–726.

10

Uses and Gratifications

J. D. Rayburn, II
Florida State University

After years of research on media "effects" yielded mixed and often disappointing findings, sociologists proposed an alternative model to account for how individuals used the media. Known as the *uses and gratifications approach*, this model viewed people's media consumption patterns as intended actions on the part of the viewers. And, while this assumption of an *active* audience in the mass communication process has been the center of much of the criticism of uses and gratifications, an impressive body of research supports the notion that individuals do make conscious choices about what they see and read in the media.

The uses and gratifications approach, however, has been criticized on several grounds. It was criticized for suffering from tautological shortcomings inherent in functional theories (Carey & Kreiling, 1974; Elliot, 1974), for being atheoretical (Elliot, 1974; Weiss, 1976; Swanson, 1977), and for beset by serious conceptual problems (Swanson, 1977). It was, in fact, Swanson who outlined four serious conceptual problems: a vague conceptual framework; a lack of precision in major concepts; a confused explanatory apparatus; and a failure to consider audiences' perceptions of media content.

In spite of these criticisms, researchers continued to conduct research using the uses and gratifications paradigm. In so doing, they have answered the criticisms—albeit not always to the satisfaction of the critics—and solidified the uses and gratifications approach as a major model for mass media research.

This chapter details the evolution of uses and gratifications. It follows not only the development of the approach but also integrates the different methodologies as the area has grown. In covering the approach's development, works are cited either because they represent pivotal thinking in the area or because they are examples of how a particular methodology was used to answer questions related to the uses and gratifications approach.

HISTORICAL ORIGINS

Early work in uses and gratifications centered around Laswell's (1948) findings on why people attend to the media. His research identified surveillance of the environment, correlation of events in the environment, and transmission of social heritage as the three functions of mass communication. These functions have served as the basis for most of the empirical investigations of gratifications relevant to seeking information in a variety of contexts. Wright's (1960) contribution of entertainment, as well as the notion of dysfunctions, completed the list. Almost all uses and gratifications research has implicitly adopted some conceptualizations which can be traced to these notions.

Early uses and gratifications research concentrated primarily on description and measurement of audience uses and motives of the media. Beginning in the 1940s, although not explicitly defined or guided by the uses and gratifications approach, researchers sought to detail and describe how audiences used different media. These early studies focused mostly on particular types of content (radio quiz programs, soap operas, and classical music, for example). Similar studies were the norm from the 1940s through the 1960s. After a surge of interest in the early 1950s (likely a result of the proliferation of television), uses and gratifications research waned until the late 1960s. The late 1960s found the convergence of political studies and the uses and gratifications approach in *Television in Politics* (Blumler & McQuail, 1969), the cornerstone study that merged the two schools.

Typological research is at the center of the uses and gratifications tradition, especially the early research. Its main purpose is to identify the types of motives for media consumption. These studies formed the bulk of uses and gratifications research prior to 1970, but continue to appear in current research as scholars begin to investigate, for example, cable use or the use of new technologies. Although these early studies were criticized as atheoretical, there was a need for typologies during this early stage of the research.

In the early days of uses and gratifications research, a common method of inquiry asked respondents to write essays about why they consumed particular media. Other common methods included interviews with audience members, either alone or in focus groups, or direct observation of individuals' behaviors during which the researcher inferred motivations presumed to intervene between media consumption and such antecedent variables as age, sex, and social location. In short, early methods tended to be largely qualitative.

Katz, Blumler, and Gurevitch (1973a) discussed the common features and main shortcomings of early uses and gratifications research. They evaluated the various typologies of audience participation reported to date while calling for a relevant theory of social and psychological needs relating to media use. Blumler and Katz (1974) noted in their landmark publication *The Uses of Mass Communications: Current Perspectives on Gratifications Research*, however, that the uses and gratifications approach was "well and truly launched on a third major phase of its development: a sort of coming of age" (p. 13).

One year before the publication of *Current Perspectives*, Katz, Gurevitch, and Haas (1973) published one of the more important articles of the day in uses and gratifications research. "On the Use of the Mass Media for Important Things" was important for two reasons. First, they were the first to compare gratifications across different media—their analysis of the uses of different media by Israelis during the Arab–Israeli War provided a mosaic of media use within a population; they also identified different uses for different media across this population. Second, Katz, et al. introduced multidimensional scaling to the approach. By using this measurement technique they demonstrated that audience members differentiated among five media on the basis of the perceived gratifications obtained.

With the publication of *Current Perspectives* in 1974, research in uses and gratifications profliferated. The introduction into academia of the mainframe computer made it possible to calculate in a few seconds what had previously taken hours. Researchers began to construct Likert-type scales about media use that had been summarized from focus groups, personal interviews, or observer inferences. These statements were then evaluated by respondents and submitted to data reduction procedures—factor analysis, multidimensional scaling, or cluster analysis. In a sense, this research was a continuation of early typological studies, but the speed with which a computer could calculate complex computations led to new typological studies. The data reduction techniques also contributed to the reliability and validity of early research.

In *Current Perspectives*, Katz, Blumler, and Gurevitch described the uses and gratifications approach as one concerned with "(1) the social and psychological origins of (2) needs, which generate (3) expectations of (4) the mass media or other sources, which lead to (5) differential patterns of media exposure (or engagement in other activities), resulting in (6) need gratifications and (7) other consequences, perhaps mostly unintended ones" (p. 20). This now classic precis has been the guiding model for uses and gratifications reseaarch for the last 20 years.

Whereas many (if not most) studies of uses and gratifications have focused on some aspect of television—news, program genres, and so forth—other media and media content have been the subject of study. Children's use of home VCRs (Cohen, Levy, & Golden, 1988), Jamaican radio call-in shows (Surlin, 1986), religious television (Abelman, 1986; Korpi & Kim, 1986; Pettersson, 1986), supermarket tabloid reading (Salwen & Anderson, 1984), the use of the telephone (O'Keefe & Sulanowsky, 1992), playing arcade video games (Selnow, 1984), the PTL Club (Abelman, 1989), magazine reading (Payne, Severn, & Dozier, 1988; Towers, 1987a), channel-changing with remote controls (Walker, 1989), and reading horoscopes (Weimann, 1982) are examples of the scope of uses and gratifications research.

Palmgreen (1984), in the best review of the approach to date, summarized uses and gratifications research in six main areas: (a) gratifications and media consumption, (b) social and psychological origins of gratifications (c) gratifications and media effects, (d) gratifications sought and obtained, (e) expectancy-value approaches to uses and gratifications, and (f) audience activity. Although "Uses and Gratifications: A Theoretical Perspective" is more than 10 years old, research in the area still falls into these six main divisions.

In 1985, Palmgreen, Wenner, and Rosengren created a generalized uses and gratifications paradigm which incorporated many important assumptions. These assumptions include:

(1) the audience is active, thus (2) much media use can be conceived as goal-directed, and (3) competing with other sources of need gratification, so that when (4) substantial audience initiative links needs to media choice, (5) media consumption can fulfill a wide range of gratifications although (6) media content alone cannot be used to predict patterns of gratifications accurately because (7) media characteristics structure the degree to which needs may be gratified at different times, and further because (8) gratifications obtained have their origins in media content, exposure in and of itself, and/or the social situation in which exposure takes place. (p. 14)

The Katz et al. (1974) model, along with Palmgreen et al.'s (1985) assumptions, set the parameters of gratifications research in the last 10 years. The remaining literature reviewed in this chapter will follow Palmgreen with updates on research published since 1984 with one modification: the expectancy-value approach. Recently some research employing this approach has incorporated an elaborated expectancy-value model known as the theory of reasoned action. Modification of the expectancy-value approach with reasoned action is addressed in the literature review.

Gratifications and Media Consumption

Research on the relationship between gratifications sought and obtained and media consumption falls into two main categories. One category focuses on typological studies of gratifications sought (GS) and gratifications obtained (GO), whereas the other category is comprised of studies investigating the association between GS and GO and exposure to some medium or content choice. Before 1970, most uses and gratifications studies were typological, even though new typologies for specific content continue to be published (e.g., Al-Amoudi, Heald, & Rayburn, 1993b; Garcia 1990; Payne et al. 1988). Becker (1979; McLeod & Becker, 1981) noted three techniques used: self-report techniques, observer inferences of motivations, and experimental manipulation.

The self-report has been the most widely used method of inquiry. Although not as frequently used, the observer inferences method and the experiment have also contributed to uses and gratifications research. Used primarily in early stages of research into a particular area of media content, these methods are still evident in the literature. Shaver (1983), for example, used focus groups to identify the various dimensions of gratifications sought and obtained from viewers of cable television when cable was first introduced into a local market. Lemish (1985) employed participant observation (55 hours) and interviewing to investigate soap opera viewing by college students.

Self-report techniques, however, comprise the major method of data collection. These techniques include respondent essays about reasons for media or content consumption, personal interviews, focus groups, and closed-ended Likert-type gratifications indices which are often derived from open-ended interviews. Likert indices are then subjected to some type of data reduction through factor analysis (e.g., Payne et al., 1988; Greenberg, 1974; Palmgreen, Wenner, & Rayburn, 1980; Rayburn & Palmgreen, 1981), but multidimensional scaling techniques and cluster analysis also appear in the literature (e.g., Katz, Gurevitch, & Haas, 1973; Levy, 1978; Perse & Courtright, 1993).

Other sophisticated empirical procedures have also been used to measure gratifications and media consumption.[1] Rubin and Rubin (1982), for example, used canonical correlation analysis (see also Rubin, Perse, & Powell, 1985, for a canonical correlation example) in investigating how gratifications sought are related to viewing specific types of programs. They found that seeking passive entertainment gratifications from television was related to total viewing and viewing of daytime serials and game shows. Viewing television news, documentaries, and talk shows, on the other hand, were related to seeking of informational-type gratifications. Palmgreen, Wenner, and Rayburn (1981) and Rayburn, Palmgreen, and Acker (1984) used discriminate analysis to classify viewers of network evening news programs and morning news programs respectively. Wenner (1983) used hierarchical regression to predict exposure to evening news and *60 Minutes,* and Palmgreen and Rayburn (1979) used multiple regression to predict exposure to public television. Hedinsson (1981) used structural equations (linear structural equation model for latent variables; LISREL)[2] in a study of television use among Swedish children. Al-Amoudi et al. (1993b) also used LISREL to predict television and newspaper consumption among Saudi Arabian professors.

A review of the literature reveals at least three dozen studies that show empirical associations between various sought and obtained gratifications measures, and media exposure, medium choice, and content choice (Abelman, 1987; Armstrong & Rubin, 1989; Becker, 1976; Becker & Fruit, 1982; Blood & Galloway, 1983; Blumler & McQuail, 1969; Cohen et al., 1988; Cowles, 1989; Davis & Woodall, 1982; Dabose, 1988; Furno-Lamude & Anderson, 1992; Greenberg, 1974; Hedinsson, 1981; Hur & Robinson, 1981; Kippax & Murray, 1980; Kline, Miller, & Morrison, 1974; McLeod & Becker, 1974; McLeod, Bybee, & Durall, 1982; McLeod, Durall, Ziemke, & Bybee, 1979; McQuail, 1979; Nordlund, 1978; Palmgreen & Rayburn, 1979, 1982; Palmgreen et al., 1981; Pathania, 1991; Payne et al., 1988; Peled & Katz, 1974; Rayburn et al., 1984; Rosengren & Windahl, 1972; Rubin, 1981, 1983; Rubin & Rubin, 1982; Towers, 1987b; Wenner, 1983; Zohoori, 1988). Review of these studies indicate a wide variety

---

[1]It is beyond the scope of this chapter to cover sophisticated statistical procedures. Readers interested in uses and gratifications research, however, should become familiar with the techniques mentioned. Good beginning points are Williams (1992) and by Kerlinger (1986).

[2]LISREL is a statistical package that provides "relatively unmixed, invariant and autonomous features of the mechanism that generates the observed variables" (Joreskog & Sorbom, 1989, p. 1). The structural models created "specif[ies] the phenomenon under study in terms of putative cause-and-effect variables and indicators. . .[that] go well beyond, conventional regression analysis and analysis of variance" (p. 1). The program provides researchers a means to simultaneously test the paths of recursive and nonrecursive theoretical models.

of gratification items have been used to predict numerous media consumption measures; while most concern television, some address radio, newspapers, magazines, and other media.

This body of research on media type and media content consumption, however, account for low to moderate correlations between gratification and consumption indices. These correlations do, however, fall in the range—and often exceed—those found in most media effects studies. In addition, studies from countries outside the United States offer support for the notion that mass media consumption is associated with gratifications sought and obtained, even though, as Bogart (1965) and others argue, habit and external constraints also affect media consumption.

Social and Psychological Origins

According to Blumler (1979), many media-related needs come from position and interaction within a social environment. Blumler identified three major social origins of media gratifications: normative influences; socially distributed life changes; and the subjective reaction of the individual to the social situation. Psychological factors, such as the need for cognitive consistency or variety seeking to escape from a state of boredom (McGuire, 1974) may also stimulate use of the media. In general, however, there has been very little examination of traditional psychological variables and their association with media gratifications.

Social origins of media consumption appear frequently in the literature. According to Palmgreen (1984), about half of these studies are exploratory in nature only (Becker & Fruit, 1982; Davis & Woodall, 1982; Greenberg, 1974; Hur & Robinson, 1981; Kippax & Murray, 1980; Lometti, Reeves, & Bybee, 1977; Lull, 1980; McQuail, 1979; Peled & Katz, 1974; Rubin, 1981; Rubin & Rubin, 1982), while the other half take a more theoretical approach (Blumler, 1979; Brown, Cramond, & Wilde, 1974; Hedinsson, 1981; Johnsson-Smaragdi, 1983; Johnstone, 1974; Nordlund, 1978; Palmgreen & Rayburn, 1979; Roe, 1983a, 1983b; Rosengren & Windahl, 1972; Rubin & Rubin, 1982; Weaver, 1978).

The exploratory studies report that a variety of gratifications sought and obtained have empirical relationships with age, education, gender, income, family communication patterns, length of residence, discussions with other people, and membership in organizations. Results of the more theoretically oriented studies examined relationships between potential for social interaction and parasocial interaction with the media; other studies found that the need for escape and social orientation intervened between social variables and media consumption.

In the last decade, a few studies concerning the social and psychological origins of gratifications have been published. Garramone (1984) examined different motivational models across the mass media for conducting political campaigns. Morgan (1984) conducted a secondary analysis of interview data and determined that heavy viewers were much more likely to describe their lives in negative terms (e.g., lonely, depressed) and much less likely to say their lives were active, meaningful, or fun than other viewers. Broihier (1985) investigated sensation seeking motives and their relationship to media use.

Windahl, Hojerback, and Hedinsson (1986) examined Swedish adolescents during a television strike. Family communication climate was found to be an important correlate of media dependency and affinity. Individuals in more socially oriented climates tended to feel more deprived than those in conceptually oriented settings. Donohew, Palmgreen, and Rayburn (1987) specifically examined how social and psychological factors interacted to produce different lifestyles and patterns of media use. They identified four lifestyle types whose members differed significantly on a broad range of variables including newspaper and news magazine readership, and gratifications sought from cable television. People with a high need for activation had lifestyles involving greater exposure to media sources of public affairs information than those with a lower need for activation and less cosmopolitan lifestyles.

Horna (1988), in examining the links between the conceptual position of needs and gratifications and leisure functions, found specific relationships between leisure and the uses and gratifications of mass media. Specifically, findings demonstrated that the majority of media audiences are seeking entertainment, relaxation, or escape; and, for most, leisure and mass media are practically synonymous.

Wilson (1990) found that, within the context of a viewer's life, the media content assumes different relevance according to the viewer's interests and needs. It is also linked to the social role of leisure and preparation of work. Viewers understand the roles through individual experiences and their own understanding of the world. Rubin (1993), investigating how locus of control affected communication motivation for interpersonal and mass media contexts, found that external locus of control individuals viewed communication to be less rewarding and less satisfying, tended to avoid communication, and were motivated to communicate more ritualistically.

According to Palmgreen (1984), two conclusions about the social origins of media gratifications are apparent. First, sufficient evidence is present to conclude that many uses of the mass media do appear to have their origins in societal structure and social process. Second, no general theoretical framework exists that links gratifications to their social origin, even though some limited progress in this area has been made (Blumler, 1979; Johnstone, 1974; Roe, 1983a). Recent results do, however, add to these conclusions. Studies subsequent to 1984 indicate, for example, that the roots of media use are far deeper than previously believed (cf., Donohew et al., 1987).

GRATIFICATIONS AND MEDIA EFFECTS

Twenty years ago, Katz et al. (1974) concluded that little empirical effort had been conducted examining the relationship between motives for media use and media effects. Blumler (1979) bemoaned the lack of published research on gratifications and media effects studies. Windahl (1981) also called for a merger of uses and gratifications with effects studies, proposing a "conseffects" model that examines the outcomes of media content and media use.

Palmgreen (1984) found 20 empirical studies that examined uses and media effects. Summarizing these studies, he concluded that audience gratifications sought and obtained were related to a wide variety of media effects including knowledge, dependency, attitudes, perceptions of social reality, agenda-setting, discussion, and politics.

Multivariate techniques such as hierarchical regression, canonical correlation, multiple classification analysis, and structural equation modeling (LISREL) were used to control for media exposure and other intervening variables, thereby mitigating the likelihood that spurious relationships influenced the studies.

Probably the most researched effect variable from the uses and gratifications perspective is *media dependency*. While conceptualized in various ways, it has been operationalized most often by examining the extent to which an individual would miss a particular medium if it were not available (i.e., Ball-Rokeach & DeFleur, 1976; deBock, 1980; Elliott, 1986; Greenberg, 1974; Lindlof, 1986; Rubin, 1981, 1983, 1986; Rubin & Rubin, 1982; Rubin & Windahl, 1982; Wenner, 1982; Windahl, Hedinsson, Hojerback, & Nord, 1983). Results of these studies indicate that dependency is related to the number and strength of motives for attending to the media; the more motivated (in terms of gratifications sought and obtained) people are, the more they perceive they generally become dependent on the media. Structural living conditions and motivational orientations do, however, modify these conclusions (Lindlof, 1986).

Blumler (1979) criticized the few uses and media effects studies that had been published to date for a lack of theoretical perspective. Hoping to stimulate more effects studies, Blumler offered three hypotheses: cognitive motivation will facilitate information gain; diversion and escape motivations will favor audience acceptance of perceptions of social situations in line with portrayals frequently found in entertainment materials; and personal identity motivations will promote reinforcement effects. Some evidence supporting the cognitive motivation hypothesis has been found (Atkin, Bowen, Nayman, & Sheinkoph 1973; Atkin & Heald, 1976; Garramone, 1983; McLeod & Becker, 1974, 1981; McLeod, Luetscher, & McDonald, 1980). Two of these studies (McLeod & Becker, 1981; Garramone, 1983) used experimental situations to investigate these hypotheses—a rarely used research method in uses and gratifications studies. Support for the diversion hypothesis, however, has not been obtained (Greenberg, 1974; Rubin, 1979, 1981, 1983), and no studies on the personal identity motivation hypothesis appear in the literature, even though partial and indirect evidence was found (Blumler & McQuail, 1969; McLeod & Becker, 1981).

A final question in the uses and gratifications media effects literature addresses interactive versus additive effects. Some studies (Becker, 1976; McLeod & Becker, 1974; McLeod, Brown, Durall, Ziemke, & Bybee, 1977; McLeod et al., 1980; Wenner, 1982, 1983) have supported the notion of additive effects while others (e.g., Blumler & McQuail, 1969; McLeod, Becker, & Byrnes, 1974) have found support for interactive effects. Palmgreen and Rayburn (1985), in testing the best model to predict media satisfaction using gratifications and expectancy-value indices, also found support for interactive effects. Most probably the situation and sets of variables will determine the best model; that is, how the researcher combines variables or questions in a given study.

Gratifications Sought and Obtained

Until the 1970s, research in uses and gratifications focused on gratifications sought while ignoring outcomes, or gratifications obtained. Greenberg (1974); Katz, Blumler, and Gurevitch (1973b), and Lometti, Reeves, & Bybee, (1977) were among the first to call for research into the relationships between gratifications sought (*GS*) and gratifications obtained (*GO*) in order to predict media consumption and media behavior.

Palmgreen and Rayburn (1982) first published a study investigating *GS* and *GO* using a discrepancy model to predict viewing of public television. The model, which takes into account the distinction for both explanatory and predictive purposes, is depicted in equation 1:

$$E\sum_{i=1}^{n} = \frac{|GS_i - GO_i|}{n} \tag{1}$$

where:

E = an exposure measure for some medium, program, content, type, and so on.;

GS = a measure of the extent to which *i*th gratification is sought;

GO = a measure of the extent to which the *i*th gratification is perceived to be obtained; and

n = the number of gratifications under consideration.

The model states that exposure (or consumption) is a function of the average absolute discrepancy between the gratifications which audience members are seeking and the extent to which they perceive they are obtaining these gratifications. The research asked respondents about gratifications sought from television in general, and those they said they obtained (or perceived they would obtain) from viewing public television. By focusing on television in general and public television specifically, the level of abstraction problem (discussed below) was mitigated. The model successfully predicted level of exposure to public television content among respondents who made their own decisions concerning what programs to watch, but did not predict exposure for those who let others make the viewing decision.

Publication of the public television study using *GS* and *GO* stimulated several subsequent studies using some model of *GS* and *GO* to predict media consumption (e.g., Levy & Windahl, 1984; McLeod & Becker, 1981; McLeod et al., 1982; Palmgreen et al., 1980, 1981; Rayburn & Palmgreen, 1984; Rayburn et al., 1984; Wenner, 1982, 1983). These studies all found moderately strong positive correlations (.40 to .60, accounting for 16 and 36% of the variance) between *GS* and *GO* of corresponding gratifications (e.g., *GS* from television news with *GO* of most watched TV newscast) whereas much lower correlations (.20 to .53) were observed between *GS* and noncorresponding *GO* (e.g., *GS* from television news with perceived *GO* from a nonwatched evening newscast). These findings, therefore, support a feedback model relating *GS* and *GO*.

The teleological criticism often levied at uses and gratifications research was once again raised with the publication of these studies. Research demonstrates, however, that gratifications sought are both conceptually and empirically separate from gratifications obtained. Whereas, for example, *GS* and *GO* generally share moderately high correlations, considerable variance between the two concepts is not shared. If, as critics would argue, *GS* and *GO* become one and the same, we would see correlations approaching +1.0 rather than those found throughout the literature. Palmgreen (Palmgreen et al., 1980, 1981; Palmgreen & Rayburn, 1982; Rayburn & Palmgreen, 1984) deals with this issue in detail and demonstrates that *GS* and *GO* are, in fact, conceptually and empirically separate.

A final issue in the *GS–GO* research deals with the level of abstraction at which variables are measured. Lometti et al. (1977) questioned whether *GS* and *GO* become equivalent over time through the process of learning what to expect from a given source and subsequently receiving it. Rayburn and Palmgreen (1984) argue against this notion, claiming that the media can satisfy the diverse needs of a heterogeneous audience:

> If audience needs are being met perfectly by media structures at a given point in time, how can we account for the willingness of large proportions of the media audience to embrace changes in that structure (e.g., the introduction of cable television)? To use another example, a person may read a particular newspaper because it is the only one available, but this does not imply that she is perfectly satisfied with that newspaper. Indeed she may be dissatisfied enough to drop her subscription if an alternative paper becomes available. (p. 542)

At least two studies have successfully measured *GS* and *GO* at the same level of abstraction (Levy & Windahl, 1984; Rayburn & Palmgreen, 1984). Both studies found *GS–GO* correlations around +.50, similar to the findings where *GS* and *GO* were measured at different levels of abstraction. Palmgreen (1984) argued that measurement of *GS* and *GO* at the same levels of abstraction is crucial to direct comparison of communication outcomes and what is sought from media.

Expectancy-Value and Reasoned Action

Most uses and gratifications studies have incorporated some notion of expectancy into their models. Katz et al. (1974), as well as others, allude to expectations from the media on the part of the consumer. The selection of content from media and other non-media alternatives to fulfill certain needs is a central tenant of expectations. As the study of uses and gratifications has matured, researchers have turned to established theories of expectancy to explain media consumption.

The first attempt to join uses and gratifications to expectancy theory is found in the writings of Galloway and Meek (1981) and Van Leuven (1981). Whereas both articles attempted to tie uses and gratifications with expectancy-value, certain shortcomings were evident (e.g., Palmgreen & Rayburn, 1982, for a complete discussion). In 1982, Palmgreen and Rayburn tied uses and gratifications more directly to expectancy-value theory.

Although there are many psychological theories that deal with expectations, perhaps the most widely known and accepted is Fishbein and Ajzen's (1975) expectancy-value theory. According to Fishbein and Ajzen, there are three kinds of beliefs. *Descriptive beliefs* result from direct observation of an object. *Informational beliefs* are formed by accepting information from an outside source that links certain objects and attributes. *Inferential beliefs* are beliefs about the characteristics of objects not yet directly observed, or that are not directly observable. These are often inferred on the basis of logic, personal theories of implicit personality, causal attributions and stereotyping. Further, expectancy-value theory views behavior, behavioral intention, or attitudes as a function of expectancy (or belief)—the perceived probability that an object possesses a particular attribute or that a behavior will have a particular consequence; and evaluation—the degree of affect, positive or negative, toward an attribute or behavioral outcome.

Using Fishbein and Ajzen's (1975) assumptions about beliefs and expectations, Palmgreen and Rayburn (1982) developed a model that expressed gratifications sought as a function of both beliefs and evaluations (equation 2):

$$GS_i = b_i e_i \qquad (2)$$

where GS_i = the ith gratification sought from some media object X; b_i = the belief (subjective probability) that X possesses some attribute or that a behavior related to X will have a particular outcome; and e_i = the affective evaluation of the particular attribute or outcome.

A parallel formulation that predicts a general orientation to seek various gratifications from a particular source is found in equation 3:

$$\sum_{i=1}^{n} = GS_i = \sum_{i=1}^{n} b_i e_i \qquad (3)$$

Both models successfully predicted gratifications sought from television news (Palmgreen & Rayburn, 1982). Rayburn and Palmgreen (1984) combined uses and gratifications with expectancy-value to produce an expectancy-value model of *GS* and *GO*. This model is shown in Fig. 10.1.

The model in Figure 10.1 is a process model that states that the products of beliefs and evaluations influence gratifications sought, which in turn influence media consumption. Consumption results in the perception of certain gratifications obtained, which then feed back to reinforce or alter perceptions of media attributes. The model further states that obtaining a particular attribute at a higher or lower level than expected will affect the belief about the level to which the medium contains that attribute, but should not affect the evaluation of whether that attribute is good or bad. The results of hierarchical regression and correlational analyses reported by Rayburn and Palmgreen (1984) support the model.

An attempt to replicate and expand the Rayburn and Palmgreen study was conducted by Al-Amoudi (1990) in Saudi Arabia. Al-Amoudi combined uses and gratifications, expectancy-value theory, and the theory of reasoned action to predict exposure to television and newspapers. Reasoned action (Fishbein & Ajzen, 1975) incorporates the notions of individuals' normative beliefs with their motivations to comply with these normative beliefs. The model appears in Fig. 10.2.

In a traditional culture such as Saudi Arabia, Al-Amoudi argued, the addition of reasoned action (normative beliefs and motivations to comply with norms) was warranted. The study obtained partial support for the Rayburn and Palmgreen model.

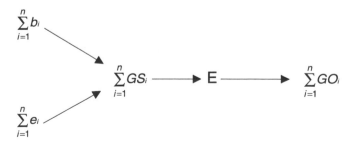

FIG. 10.1.   Expectancy-value model of *GS* and *GO*.

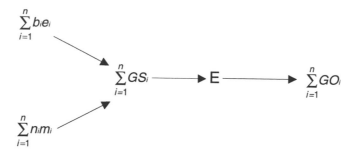

FIG. 10.2. Expectancy-value, reasoned action model of GS and GO.

It failed, however, to support media usage as an intervening variable between gratifications sought and gratifications obtained. Al-Amoudi also found differences between the use of Saudi newspapers and television. These differences are addressed by Al-Amoudi et al. (1993b) who used the LISREL program for structural equations modeling. This technique seems to be the "in vogue" technique throughout much of the contemporary communication literature, not without justification. LISREL, with its program improvements, provides researchers a means for simultaneous testing of paths in both recursive and non-recursive models. This technique promises to be of great value to the study of uses and gratifications where models with feedback loops are prevalent.

Finally, a limited amount of research using the expectancy-value approach has dealt with avoidance of media. Becker (1979) found that avoidance motivations are empirically distinct from gratifications. In general, *positive gratifications* are reasons for seeking media consumption whereas avoidances are *negative gratifications*, or reasons for avoiding media contact. Palmgreen (1984) describes a four-fold typology. Positive versus negative evaluations of an attribute are crosstabulated against belief or disbelief in the possession of an attribute. The typology of media motivations is thus classified as "positive approach, negative approach, seeking of alternatives, and true avoidance" (p. 39).

Active Audiences

One of the fundamental assumptions of the uses and gratifications approach has been that an "active" audience member makes conscious decisions about the consumption of media content. Although this assumption has been criticized by some (i.e., Elliot, 1974), gratifications researchers have generally treated it as an article of faith. Blumler (1979) lamented this assumption and called for its empirical investigation.

Levy and Windahl (1984) attempted to conceptualize activity. They produced a ninefold typology of audience activity using three levels of audience activity-selectivity, involvement, and use, and three levels of time-before, during, or after exposure. Unfortunately, their research only examined three of the activity types, but their findings indicate that measures of gratifications sought and obtained were related consistently and positively to all three measures of activity.

Other research has provided indirect evidence supporting the notion of an active audience. Katz et al. (1973b) demonstrated that audience members differentiate among five media on the basis of perceived gratifications obtained. Lometti et al. (1977) also found that audience members differentiated among six media and two interpersonal channels along three dimensions. Data also exist that demonstrate the ability of audiences to distinguish among different media on the basis of gratifications sought or obtained (Peled & Katz, 1974; Mendelsohn & O'Keefe, 1976; McLeod & Becker, 1981; Becker & Fruit, 1982). Other studies have controlled for type of medium by investigating the relationship of gratifications to content choice within a single medium (Rubin & Rubin, 1982), or by relating gratifications to choice of content within one medium (Nordlund, 1978; Palmgreen et al., 1981; Rayburn et al., 1984; Rubin, 1981, 1983).

AN EXAMPLE STUDY

While it would be naive to assume that *all* media consumption is purposive, certainly it is safe to assume that some consumption is purposive, especially consumption of interactive media. Interactive media are, by definition, intentionally consumed as an audience member must make conscious choices about which path to choose, for example, *Prodigy, CompuServe, America Online, GEnie,* and so forth.

Some studies within the last 10 years provide a background for a uses and gratifications study of interactive media. Heeter, D'Alessio, Greenberg, and McVoy (1983) examined channel selection data from subscribers to a Florida interactive cable system. Frequent channel changing at the half-hour, as well as during half-hour segments, indicate that cable viewers are highly active in the process of selecting programs. Similar evidence of activity is found in a study of video recorder use by Levy and Fink (1984). Barwise, Ehrenberg, and Goodhardt (1982) also found a marked degree of program loyalty from the examination of viewer diaries gathered from 18,000 viewers over a 3-year period. They concluded that the first stage of the viewing decision—whether to watch—was passive, but the second state—what to watch—was not so passive. Viewers, they concluded, do not just pick programs at random.

The new media of communication, particularly the interactive media (e.g., online services, CD-ROM, CD-I) are generating much interest on the part of media researchers. Among the questions being asked is, "How do we account for the multitude of choices available to the consumer?" The uses and gratifications approach, coupled with expectancy-value and reasoned action theories, provide a method to answer this question.

Research in this area is an example of a uses and gratifications study that could use a variety of methodological approaches—both quantitative and nonquantitative—to answer the question. James (1992) conducted a preliminary study of users of the *Prodigy* and *CompuServe* interactive online computer services. He asked respondents to write to him to describe their perceptions of uses and benefits of electronic bulletin boards and conducted a content analysis of the responses. He developed a series of reasons for why people use bulletin boards, what characteristics these users possess, and how using bulletin boards affected the use of other communication media.

Based on these findings, a quantitative study incorporating uses and gratifications items derived from James's findings, belief and evaluation statements (from expectancy-value theory), and normative expectations statements (from reasoned action theory) could be produced. Using a randomly selected sample from *Prodigy, CompuServe, America Online,* and *GEnie*, statements about gratifications sought and obtained could yield the dimensions of gratifications within service, and among services (as obtained through factor analysis). Similar procedures would reveal differences, if they exist, with respect to beliefs and evaluations of the various attributes of each service.

On a service-by-service basis, the model described by Al-Amoudi, Heald, and Rayburn (1993a) could be tested using multiple regression to predict choice of content within service, and choice between services if an individual used more than one. Depending on these findings, LISREL could provide further insight given the general non-recursive nature of the model. By following these procedures, then, the study would have incorporated content analysis (and possibly focus groups as a follow-up), factor analysis, multiple regression, path analysis, and structural equations using LISREL. This single study, then, would parallel both the content and methodological development of the uses and gratifications approach to media consumption.

SUMMARY

Since the early 1940s, uses and gratifications has matured into an accepted way to view media consumption. In the last 10 years, it has successfully integrated with other theories, permitting even more growth. This integration, coupled with advances in LISREL and increased microcomputer power, has positioned the apporach as a major area of theoretical study for new media and integrated communications technologies. For the near future, uses and gratifications offers a way to determine why, how, and for what reasons people choose to seek out and use media; the approach may be the most promising theoretical area for investigation of these new media theories.

REFERENCES

Abelman, R. (1987). Religious television uses and gratifications. *Journal of Broadcasting & Electronic Media, 31,* 293–307.

Abelman, R. (1989). "PTL" Club viewer uses and gratifications. *Communication Quarterly, 37,* 54–66.

Al-Amoudi, K. (1990). *Expectations, values, and norms as predictors of uses and gratifications of mass media in Saudi Arabia.* Unpublished doctoral dissertation, The Florida State University, Tallahassee.

Al-Amoudi, K., Heald, G., & Rayburn, J. (1993a, May). *Combining expectancy-value and uses and gratifications theory to predict Saudi Arabian television viewing and newspaper readership patterns: An exploratory analysis.* Paper presented at the meeting of the International Communication Association, Washington, DC.

Al-Amoudi, K., Heald, G., & Rayburn, J. (1993b, April). *Theoretic dimensions of media gratifications, beliefs, and normative expectations: An analysis of Saudi Arabian television viewing.* Paper presented at the meeting of the Broadcast Education Association, Las Vegas, NV.

Armstrong, C., & Rubin, A. (1989). Talk radio as interpersonal communication. *Journal of Communication, 39,* 84–94.

Atkin, C. K., Bowen, L., Nayman, O. B., & Sheinkopf, K. G. (1973). Quality versus quantity in televised political ads. *Public Opinion Quarterly, 37,* 209–224.

Atkin, C. K., & Heald, G. R. (1976). Effects of political advertising. *Public Opinion Quarterly, 40,* 216–28.

Ball-Rokeach, S. J., & DeFleur, M. L. (1976). A dependency model of mass media effects. *Communication Research, 64,* 359–372.

Barwise, T. P., Ehrenberg, A. S. C., & Goodhardt, G. J. (1982). Glued to the box? Patterns of TV repeat-viewing. *Journal of Communication, 32,* 22–29.

Becker, L. B. (1976). Two tests of media gratifications: Watergate and the 1974 election. *Journalism Quarterly, 53,* 28–33.

Becker, L. B. (1979). Measurement of gratifications. *Communication Research, 6,* 54–73.

Becker, L. B., & Fruit, J. W. (1982, May). *Understanding media selection from a uses and motives perspective.* Paper presented at the meeting of the International Communication Association, Boston, MA.

Blood, R. W., & Galloway, J. J. (1983, May). *Expectancy-value measures of audience uses and gratifications for media content.* Paper presented at the meeting of the International Communication Association, Dallas, TX.

Blumler, J. G. (1979). The role of theory in uses and gratifications studies. *Communication Research, 6,* 9–36.

Blumler, J.G,. & Katz, E. (1974). Foreword. In J.G. Blumler and E. Katz (Eds.), *The uses of mass communications: Current perspectives on gratifications research* (pp. 13–16). Beverly Hills, CA: Sage.

Blumler, J. G., & McQuail, D. (1969). *Television in politics.* Chicago: University of Chicago Press.

Bogart, L. (1965). The mass media and the blue-collar worker. In A. Bennett & W. Gomberg (Eds.), *The blue-collar world.* Englewood Cliffs, NJ: Prentice-Hall.

Broihier, M. (1985). The sensation seeking motive and media use. ERIC: ED 258 252.

Brown, J. R., Cramond, J. K., & Wilde, R. J. (1974). Displacement effects of television and child's functional orientation to the media. In J. G. Blumler & E. Katz (Eds.), *The uses of mass communications: Current perspectives on gratifications research* (pp. 93–112). Beverly Hills, CA: Sage.

Carey, J. W., & A. L. Kreiling (1974). Popular culture and uses and gratifications: Notes toward an accommodation. In J. G. Blumler & E. Katz (Eds.), *The uses of mass communications: Current perspectives on gratifications research* (pp. 225–248). Beverly Hills, CA: Sage.

Cohen, A., Levy, M., & Golden, K. (1988). Children's uses and gratifications of home VCRs: Evolution or revolution. *Communication Research, 15,* 772–780.

Cowles, D. (1989). Consumer perceptions of interactive media. *Journal of Broadcasting & Electronic Media, 33,* 83–89.

Davis, D. K., & Woodall, W. G. (1982, May). *Uses of television news: Gratification or edification.* Paper presented at the meeting of the International Communication Association, Boston, MA.

deBock, H. (1980). Gratification during a newspaper stride and a TV blackout. *Journalism Quarterly, 57,* 61–66, 78.

Dabose, J. (1988). Choices of new media and traditional channels in organizations. *Communication Research Reports, 5,* 131–139.

Donohew, L., Palmgreen, P., & Rayburn, J. (1987). Social and psychological origins of media use: A lifestyle analysis. *Journal of Broadcasting & Electronic Media, 31,* 255–278.

Elliott, P. (1974). Uses and gratifications research: A critique and a sociological alternative. In J. G. Blumler & E. Katz (Eds.), *The uses of mass communications: Current perspectives on gratifications research* (pp. 249–268). Beverly Hills, CA: Sage.

Elliott, W. (1986). Gratifications lost: The 1985 Philadelphia newspaper stride and media use. ERIC: ED 271 753.

Fishbein, M., & Ajzen, I. (1975). *Belief, attitude, intention, and behavior.* Reading, MA: Addison-Wesley.

Furno-Lamude, D., & Anderson, J. (1992), The uses and gratifications of rerun viewing. *Journalism Quarterly, 69,* 362–373.

Galloway, J. J., & Meek, F. L. (1981). Audience uses and gratifications: An expectancy model. *Communication Research, 8,* 435–450.

Garcia, M. (1990). Uses and gratifications and soap opera viewing: A study of the dimensions of gratifications sought and obtained. Unpublished master's thesis, The Florida State University, Tallahassee.

Garramone, G. M. (1983). Issue versus image orientation and effects of political advertising. *Communication Research, 10,* 59–76.

Garramone, G. M. (1984). Motivational models: Replication across media for political campaign conduct. *Journalism Quarterly, 15,* 537–541.

Greenberg, B. S. (1974). Gratifications of television viewing and their correlates for British children. In J. G. Blumler & E. Katz (Eds.), *The uses of mass communications: Current perspectives on gratifications research* (pp. 71–92). Beverly Hills, CA: Sage.

Hedinsson, E. (1981). *TV, family, and society: The social origins and effects of adolescents' TV use.* Stockholm: Almqvist & Wiksell.

Heeter, C., D'Alessio, D., Greenberg, B. S., & McVoy, D. S. (1983, May). *Cableviewing.* Paper presented at the meeting of the International Communication Association, Dallas, TX.

Horna, J. (1988). The mass media as leisure: A Western-Canadian case. *Society and Leisure, 11,* 283–301.

Hur, K., & Robinson, J. P. (1981). A uses and gratifications analysis of viewing of "Roots" in Britain. *Journalism Quarterly, 58,* 582–588.

James, M. (1992). An *exploratory study of the perceived benefits of electronic bulletin board use and their impact on other communication activities.* Unpublished doctoral dissertation, The Florida State University, Tallahassee.

Johnsson-Smaragdi, U. (1983). *TV use and social interaction in adolescence.* Stockholm: Almqvist & Wiksell.

Johnstone, J. W. C. (1974). Social integration and mass media use among adolescents: A case study. In J. G. Blumler & E. Katz (Eds.), *The uses of mass communications: Current perspectives on gratifications research* (pp. 35–47). Beverly Hills, CA: Sage.

Joreskog, K. G., & Sorbom, D. (1989). *LISREL 7: A guide to the program and applications* (2nd ed.). Chicago: SPSS.

Katz, E., Blumler, J. G., & Gurevitch, M. (1973a). Uses and gratifications research. *Public Opinion Quarterly, 37,* 509–523.

Katz, E., Blumler, J. G., & Gurevitch, M. (1973b, May). *Utilization of mass communication by the individual.* Paper presented at the Conference on Directions in Mass Communication Research, Arden House, NY.

Katz, E., Blumler, J. G., & Gurevitch, M. (1974). Utilization of mass communication by the individual. In J.G. Blumler & E. Katz (Eds.), *The uses of mass communications: Current perspectives on gratifications research* (pp. 19–32). Beverly Hills, CA: Sage.

Katz, E., Gurevitch, M., & Haas, H. (1973). On the use of the mass media for important things. *American Sociological Review, 38,* 164–181.

Kerlinger, F. N. (1986). *Foundations of behavioral research* (3rd ed.). New York: Holt, Rinehart & Winston.

Kippax, S., & Murray, J. P. (1980). Using the mass media: Need gratification and perceived utility. *Communication Research, 7,* 335–360.

Kline, F. G., Miller, P. V., & Morrison, A. J. (1974). Adolescents and family planning information: An exploration of audience needs and media effects. In J. G. Blumler & E. Katz (Eds.), *The uses of mass communications: Current perspectives on gratifications research* (pp. 113–136). Beverly Hills, CA: Sage.

Korpi, M., & Kim, K. (1986). The uses and effects of televangelism: A factorial model of support and contribution. *Journal for the Scientific Study of Religion, 25,* 410–423.

Lasswell, H. (1948). The structure and function of communications in society. In L. Bryson (Ed.), *The communication of ideas* (pp. 37–51) New York: Harper & Row.

Lemish, D. (1985). Soap opera viewing in college: A naturalistic inquiry. *Journal of Broadcasting & Electronic Media, 29,* 275–293.

Levy, M. R. (1978). The audience experience with television news. *Journalism Monographs, 55.*

Levy, M. R., & Fink, E. L. (1984). Home video recorders and the transcience of television broadcasts. *Journal of Communication, 34,* 56–71.

Levy, M. R., & Windahl, S. (1984). Audience activity and gratifications: A conceptual clarification and exploration. *Communication Research, 11,* 51–78.

Lindlof, T. (1986). Social and structural constraints on media use in incarceration. *Journal of Broadcasting & Electronic Media, 30,* 341–355.

Lometti, G. E., Reeves, B., & Bybee, C. R. (1977). Investigating the assumptions of uses and gratifications research. *Communication Research, 7,* 319–334.

Lull, J. (1980). The social uses of television. *Human Communication Research, 6,* 197–209.

McGuire, W. J. (1974). Psychological motives and communication gratification. In J. G. Blumler & E. Katz (Eds.), *The uses of mass communications: Current perspectives on gratifications research* (pp. 167–196). Beverly Hills, CA: Sage.

McLeod, J. M., & Becker, L. B. (1974). Testing the validity of gratification measures through political effects analysis. In J. G. Blumler and E. Katz (Eds.), *The uses of mass communications: Current perspectives on gratifications research* (pp. 137–164). Beverly Hills, CA: Sage.

McLeod, J. M., & Becker, L. B. (1981). The uses and gratifications approach. In D. D. Nimmo & K. R. Sanders (Eds.), *Handbook of political communication* (pp. 97–99). Beverly Hills, CA: Sage.

McLeod, J. M., Becker, L. B., & Byrnes, J. E. (1974). Another look at the agenda-setting function of the press. *Communication Research, 1,* 131–166.

McLeod, J. M., Brown, J. D., Becker, L. B., & Ziemke, D. A. (1977). Decline and fall at the White House: A longitudinal analysis of communication effects. *Communication Research, 4,* 3–22.

McLeod, J. M., Bybee, C. R., & Durall, J. A. (1982). Evaluating media performance by gratifications sought and received. *Journalism Quarterly, 59,* 3–12.

McLeod, J. M., Durall, J. A., Ziemke, D. A., & Bybee, C. R. (1979). Expanding the context of debate effects. In S. Kraus (Ed.), *The great debates 1976: Ford vs. Carter.* Bloomington: Indiana University Press.

McLeod, J. M., Luetscher, W. D., & McDonald, D. G. (1980, August). *Beyond mere exposure: Media orientations and their impact on political processes.* Paper presented at the meeting of the Association for Education in Journalism, Boston, MA.

McQuail, D (1979), The uses and gratification approach: Past, troubles, and future. *Massacommunicatie, 2,* 73–89.

Mendelsohn, H., & O'Keefe, G. J. (1976). *The people choose a president.* New York: Praeger.

Morgan, M. (1984). Heavy television viewing and perceived quality of life. *Journalism Quarterly, 61,* 499–504.

Nordlund, J. E. (1978). Media interaction. *Communication Research, 5,* 150–175.

O'Keefe, G., & Sulanowski, B. (1992, August). *More than just talk: Uses, gratifications, and the telephone.* Paper presented at the meeting of the Association for Education in Journalism and Mass Communication, Montreal, Canada.

Palmgreen, P. C. (1984). Uses and gratifications: A theoretical perspective. In R. N. Bostrom (Ed.), *Communication yearbook* (Vol. 8, pp. 20–55). Beverly Hills, CA: Sage.

Palmgreen, P. C., & Rayburn, J. D. (1979). Uses and gratifications and exposure to public television: A discrepancy approach. *Communication Research, 6,* 561–580.

Palmgreen, P. C., & Rayburn, J. D. (1982). Gratifications sought and media exposure: An expectancy-value model. *Communication Research, 9,* 561–580.

Palmgreen, P. C., & Rayburn, J. D. (1985). A comparison of gratification models of media satisfaction. *Communication Monographs, 52,* 334–346.

Palmgreen, P. C., Wenner, L. A., & Rayburn, J. D. (1980). Relations between gratifications sought and obtained: A study of television news. *Communication Research, 7,* 161–192.

Palmgreen, P. C., Wenner, L. A., & Rayburn, J. D. (1981). Gratification discrepancies and news program choice. *Communication Research, 8,* 451–478.

Palmgreen, P. C. Wenner, L. A., & Rosengren, K. E., (1985). Uses and gratifications research: The past ten years. In K. E. Rosengren, L. A. Wenner, & P. C. Palmgreen (Eds.), *Uses and gratifications research: Current perspectives* (pp. 11–37). Beverly Hills, CA: Sage.

Pathania, G. (1991, November). *Soc. Culture. Indian: Computer created community for Indian students and professionals.* Paper presented at the meeting of the Speech Communication Association, Atlanta, GA.

Payne, G., Severn, J., & Dozier, D. (1988). Uses and gratifications motives as indicators of magazine readership. *Journalism Quarterly, 65,* 909–915.

Peled, T., & Katz, E. (1974). Media functions in wartime: The Israel homefront in October 1973. In J. G. Blumler & E. Katz (Eds.), *The uses of mass communications: Current perspectives on gratifications research* (pp. 49–69). Beverly Hills, CA: Sage.

Perse, E., & Courtright, J. (1993). Normative images of communication media: Mass and interpersonal channels in the new media environment. *Human Communication Research, 19,* 485–503.

Pettersson, T. (1986). The audiences' uses and gratifications of TV worship services. *Journal for the Scientific Study of Religion, 25,* 391–409.

Rayburn, J. D., & Palmgreen, P. C. (1981, August). *Dimensions of gratifications sought and gratifications obtained: A study of "Good Morning America" and "Today."* Paper presented at the annual meeting of the Association for Education in Journalism, East Lansing, MI.

Rayburn, J. D., & Palmgreen, P. C. (1984). Merging uses and gratifications and expectancy-value theory. *Communication Research, 11,* 537–562.

Rayburn, J., Palmgreen, P., & Acker, T. (1984). Media gratifications and choosing a morning news program. *Journalism Quarterly, 61,* 149–156.

Roe, K. (1983a). *The influence of video technology in adolescence.* (Media Panel Report 27). Lund, Sweden: Vaxjo University College and Lund University.

Roe, K. (1983b). *Mass media and adolescent schooling: Conflict or co-existence?* Stockholm: Almqvist & Wiksell.

Rosengren, K. E., & Windahl, S. (1972). Mass media consumption as a functional alternative. In D. McQuail (Ed.), *Sociology of mass communications.* Harmondsworth: Penguin.

Rubin, A. M. (1979). Television use by children and adolescents. *Human Communication Research, 5,* 109–120.

Rubin, A. M. (1981). An examination of television viewing motivations. *Communication Research, 8,* 141–165.

Rubin, A. M. (1983). Television uses and gratifications: The interaction of viewing patterns and motivations. *Journal of Broadcasting, 27,* 37–51.

Rubin, A. M. (1993). The effect of locus of control on communication motivation, anxiety, and satisfaction. *Communication Quarterly, 41,* 161–172.

Rubin, A., Perse, E., & Powell, R. (1985). Loneliness, parasocial interaction, and local television news viewing. *Human Communication Research, 12,* 155–180.

Rubin, A. M., & Rubin, R. B. (1982). Older persons' TV viewing patterns and motivations. *Communication Research, 9,* 287–313.

Salwen, M. B., & Anderson, R. A. (1984). *The uses and gratifications of supermarket tabloid reading by different demographic groups.* East Lansing, MI: National Center for Research on Teacher Learning.

Selnow, G. (1984). *Some uses and gratifications of arcade video game playing.* ERIC: ED 248 840.

Shaver, J. L. (1983). *The uses of cable television.* Unpublished master's thesis, University of Kentucky, Lexington.

Swanson, D. L. (1977). The uses and misuses of uses and gratification. *Human Communication Research, 3,* 214–221.

Surlin, S. (1986). Jamaican call-in radio: A uses and gratifications analysis. *Journal of Broadcasting & Electronic Media, 30,* 459–466.

Towers, W. (1987a). *Adult readership of magazines and why they read.* ERIC: ED 284 282.

Towers, W. (1987b). Radio listenership and uses and gratifications: A replication. *Communication Research Reports, 4,* 57–64.

Van Leuven, J. (1981). Expectancy theory in media and message selection. *Communication Research, 8,* 425–434.

Walker, J. R. (1989). *The gratifications of grazing: Why flippers flip.* ERIC: ED 311 523.

Weaver, D. (1980). Audience need for orientation and media effects. *Communication Research, 7,* 361–376.

Weimann, G. (1982). The prophecy that never fails: On the uses and gratifications of horoscope reading. *Sociological Inquiry, 52,* 274–290.

Weiss, W. (1976). Review of "The uses of mass communications." *Public Opinion Quarterly, 40,* 132–133.

Wenner, L. A. (1982). Gratifications sought and obtained in program dependency: A study of network evening news programs and 60 Minutes. *Communication Research, 9,* 539–560.

Wenner, L. A. (1983, May). *Gratifications sought and obtained: Model specification and theoretical development.* Paper presented at the meeting of the International Communication Association, Dallas, TX.

Williams, F. (1992). *Reasoning with statistics* (4th ed.). New York: Holt, Rinehart & Winston.

Wilson, T. (1990). TV and the politics of caring. *Media Culture and Society, 12,* 125–137.

Windahl, S. (1981). Uses and gratifications at the crossroads. In G. C. Wilhoit & H. deBock (Eds.), *Mass communication review yearbook* (pp. 174–185). Beverly Hills, CA: Sage.

Windahl, S. Hedinsson, E., Hojerback, I., & Nord, E. (1983, May). *Perceived deprivation and alternate activities during a television strike.* Paper presented at the meeting of the International Communication Association, Dallas, TX.

Windahl, S., Hojerback, I., & Hedinsson, E. (1986). Adolescents without television: A study in media deprivation. *Journal of Broadcasting & Electronic Media, 30,* 47–63.

Wright, C. (1960). Functional analysis and mass communication. *Public Opinion Quarterly, 24,* 605–620.

Zohoori, A. (1988). A cross-cultural analysis of children's television use. *Journal of Broadcasting & Electronic Media, 32,* 105–113.

11

Spiral of Silence: Communication and Public Opinion as Social Control

Charles T. Salmon
Michigan State University

Carroll J. Glynn
Cornell University

Conceiving public opinion as unwritten law, or as an informal mechanism of social control is hardly new; indeed, one scholar (Noelle-Neumann, 1995) traced the notion back to antiquity and the writings of Pericles and the Old Testament. It can be found in the treatises of philosophers and scholars of many different eras and nations as well, including John Locke, James Bryce, Floyd Allport, Alexis de Tocqueville, Jacques Ellul, and others. For example, James Madison (1788/1961), writing in Federalist Paper No. 49, implicitly adopted this conceptualization:

> The strength of opinion in each individual, and its practical influence on his conduct, depends much on the number which he supposes to have entertained the same opinion. The reason of man, like man himself, is timid and cautious when left alone, and acquires firmness and confidence in proportion to the number with which it is associated. (p. 340)

In this century, sociologist W. Philips Davison (1958) drew on the notion of social control in his classic description of the public opinion process:

Therefore, [people] are likely to speak or act in one way if they anticipate approbation and to remain silent or act in another way if they anticipate hostility or indifference. . . . People who do not share the opinions expressed by the crowd's leaders are likely to remain silent, fearing the disapproval of those around them. This very silence isolates others who may be opposed, since they conclude that, with the exception of themselves, all those present share the same attitude. (p. 101)

The most elaborate development of this approach to public opinion, however, is found in the work of Elisabeth Noelle-Neumann, founder and director of the Public Opinion Research Center in Allensbach, Germany, and professor of communication research at the University of Mainz. To her, *public opinion* refers to "opinions on controversial issues that one can express in public without isolating oneself" (Noelle-Neumann, 1984, pp. 62–63), a conceptualization in which communication processes and effects figure prominently. Since publication of her work in English in the early 1970s, her model of the spiral of silence has attracted considerable scholarly attention, some in the form of attempts at social scientific tests and replication, others in the form of sometimes scathing criticism and commentary. The story of the scholarly evolution of the spiral of silence model is one of science inextricably intertwined with politics, personalities, and the long shadows of history.

The present chapter has three major goals.[1] First, it draws on several of Noelle-Neumann's important works (1973, 1974, 1977, 1979, 1980, 1984, 1985, 1991) to describe the model's components in terms of three major groupings of concepts and research. Second, it traces the early development of the model from its philosophical and historical origins in German society and outlines some of its contemporary applications. Third, it reviews major conceptual and methodological conundrums which have characterized the model throughout its brief existence and offers some avenues for future applications of the model.

THE SPIRAL OF SILENCE MODEL

Noelle-Neumann's model and resulting research branches may be summarized in terms of three categories: mass media and mass communication, the individual and interpersonal communication; and implications for public opinion, including contemporary applications.

Mass Media and Mass Communication

Noelle-Neumann ascribed a particular importance to the mass media's position in contemporary society. The media are, in her words, "ubiquitous" and "consonant." Indeed, it is difficult to conceive of a day without exposure to mass media in one form

---

[1]Sections of this essay are drawn from previously published works by Salmon and Moh (1992), especially pages 146–152, which review the generic spiral of silence process, and from Glynn, Ostman, and McDonald (1995).

or another, ranging from listening to a morning radio program, through reading a newspaper or magazine, to viewing television or a film in the evening. The inescapability of the media is potentially problematic, she argued, because media content tends to be remarkably consonant. That is, there is uncanny similarity of news and other media content that belies the liberal democratic ideal of diversity. The combination of a ubiquitous and consonant media system results in a largely monolithic "climate" that envelops most individuals in society, providing in the process a largely homogeneous depiction of social reality.

In large measure, our view of social reality is distorted because of the underlying ideology of the progenitors of media content. Producers of media content and journalists in particular, Noelle-Neumann (1973, 1980) argued, tend to be more liberal than the rest of society. In part, this liberalness is a function of shared journalistic norms and values that serve to reinforce the role of journalist as critic, as a foil to government and the powerful. Reflecting this underlying liberal orientation, she continued, media content tends to be liberal, as well. The product is a media environment, forged by liberal newsmakers, enveloping the individual in society and exposing him or her to a predominantly liberal depiction of society and the social good.[2] One of the most important functions of the media, to Noelle-Neumann, is their role as the predominant sources of cues regarding majority culture. Immersed in a ubiquitous and consonant media environment, individuals rely heavily on the media as a source of information about social roles, customs, and practices.

Noelle-Neumann claimed that this immersion in—and dependency on—the media environment induces powerful effects on individuals and that these effects occur as the result of an endless repetition of reinforcing messages and images. As a result, she argued, media effects cannot be studied validly under sterile, artificial laboratory conditions because such studies will necessarily underestimate the impact of a prolonged diet of monolithic media output emanating from a multiplicity of media sources (1973).

The Individual in a Social Setting

The second major strain of thought in the spiral of silence model deals with the linkage between macro- and microsocial levels of analysis. Drawing on the small-group conformity research of Solomon Asch and others (1970), Noelle-Neumann contended that individuals have an inborn fear of social isolation. To be alone, apart from, or at odds with "the crowd" is more than most individuals can endure. To wear an unpopular fashion or to express an idea that many consider old-fashioned or, worse, socially unacceptable is to risk incurring the wrath of others, a prospect that most find too unattractive to risk. As a result of this concern, individuals must constantly monitor the environment, searching for cues regarding which sentiments, ideas, knowledge, or

---

[2]As Salmon and Moh (1992, p. 156) noted, Noelle-Neumann's analysis of the consonant information environment forged by a liberal media is one of the most paradoxical aspects of the model. That is, if stripped of its criticism of media liberalism, the model is surprisingly compatible with the conclusions of critical theorists such as Edward Herman and Noam Chomsky (1988) and Todd Gitlin (1980), all of whom see the media environment as essentially ubiquitous and powerful, but forged by a conservative rather than liberal media.

fashions are shared by many or only by a few. Because of this fear, individuals draw on their "quasi-statistical organ" (in her later work, a quasi-statistical "sense," perhaps implying a shift from a biological to a social explanation; compare Noelle-Neumann, 1974, 1991) to gauge the nuances of culture and its dynamism. As noted, the mass media are seen as providing the bulk of the cues that serve to structure options for an individual's behavior.

An unstated assumption of this model, like most models of public opinion, is that individuals have opinions that they can and wish to articulate, a seemingly basic assumption that itself is contested (e.g., Bourdieu, 1979). Assuming this is the case, the individual is often confronted with a situation in which he or she must articulate that opinion in some social context; that is, private sentiment must become public. In this sense, Noelle-Neumann's use of the term *public* in *public opinion* is an adjective rather than a noun; it refers to an opinion that can be expressed publicly without fear of censure rather than the more typically American usage (as a noun) in which it refers to a group of individuals (Salmon & Kline, 1985).

Implications for Public Opinion

Static Version.   Given these presuppositions, there are two distinct implications for public opinion, one static and the other a dynamic process. In the case of the static outcome, if the individual perceives that his or her personal convictions are shared by the majority, he or she will be willing to express an opinion in public. On the other hand, if the perception is that the opinion represents a minority viewpoint, he or she will be reluctant to express the opinion publicly. There are thought to be two general exceptions to this outcome. First, if an individual perceives himself or herself to be in the minority but believes that his or her opinion is gaining ground—that it is viable, that it will be shared by the majority at some future point—the individual will be willing to express the opinion in public. Second, a few individuals who are apparently immune to social censure appear perennially willing to express unpopular opinions. These individuals, labeled *hardcores*, are thought to represent a relative small segment of the population (Noelle-Neumann, 1984, estimates about 15%).

Dynamic Version.   Unlike the static version, which can be tested with cross-sectional data, the dynamic version incorporates the element of time into the model and must be tested using longitudinal data. If relatively few people are willing to express an unpopular viewpoint, according to this version, it will slowly slip from the public consciousness because it has no vocal proponents. Over time, the majority faction will become increasingly confident and its view increasingly pervasive. The disproportionate frequencies of expression will eventually result in a silencing of the proponents of the minority viewpoint, and their sentiment will follow the paths of other unpopular, obsolete, or dated notions. Policy makers, who themselves monitor the information environment to gauge trends in opinion climates either out of a sense of obligation to constituents or as a matter of political survival, observe that one opinion frequently is expressed and another is not (Protess et al., 1991). This social perception becomes translated into policy, as only expressed opinion influences social change; silence is thought to have no impact.

HISTORICAL AND THEORETICAL ORIGINS

As suggested earlier, many of the constituent elements of the spiral of silence model were not newly conceived, but have been available in one form or another for centuries. Noelle-Neumann's creative contribution was to link notions of social control with mass media and interpersonal communication processes. When and how she originally did this is, like most aspects of the model, is a matter of some controversy. Leo Bogart (1991), a media and public opinion scholar, contended that the spiral of silence is "more of a footnote to the history of of Nazism than to the study of public opinion" (p. 49) because the model is rooted in the horrors of the World War II and, in particular, in Noelle-Neumann's first-hand experiences while a "propagandist for Nazism" writing for *Das Reich*.[3] Without question, the political conditions in Nazi Germany during the Holocaust provided an unusually vivid example of the dangers of publicly expressing opposition to a predominant political viewpoint. Indeed, in a totalitarian regime characterized by Gestapo ruthlessness and concentration camps, fear—of physical torture and death as well as milder forms of disapproval—undoubtedly was a prime motivator of social conduct, and silence a plausible means of defense.

As an ardent student of public opinion in the late 1930s, and as a journalist during the war who herself felt censured by the Nazi Party, Noelle-Neumann was certainly in a position to witness the process through which a minority faction is systematically intimidated into silence and concomitant political impotence. Nevertheless, Noelle-Neumann claimed that it was the 1965 election in the Federal Republic of Germany, rather than her first-hand experiences in Nazi Germany, which provided the inspiration for her elaborate model of communication and public opinion processes.

In that year, she found through her polling that, although the two competing political parties (the Christian Democrats and the Social Democrats) had equivalent levels of support over a 6-month period, expectations of who would win were far more dynamic, changing by some 18 percentage points over the same time period. As Noelle-Neumann (1984) wrote, "it was as though the measurements of how the electorate intended to vote and which party they expected to win had been taken on different planets" (p. 3).

Eventually the Christian Democrats won the election, leaving Noelle-Neumann (1984) with the challenge of interpreting these significant swings in voters' perceptions and preferences. Her explanation of this, under the "power" and "pressure" of public opinion was that "hundreds of thousands—no, actually millions of voters—had taken part in what was later called a 'last minute swing.' At the last minute, they had gone along with the crowd" (p. 2).

Differentiating this shift from the familiar bandwagon phenomenon, Noelle-Neumann turned to the writings of the German sociologist Ferdinand Tönnies, who is

---

[3]It is a matter of record that Noelle-Neumann studied and wrote several provocative articles on the topic of media and public opinion for *Das Reich* and the Frankfurter *Zeitung* during the war; however, she claims that she was ultimately fired from her jobs—effectively silenced as it were—for being anti-Nazi. Further, it is also the case that her dissertation contained what she described as "propaganda pieces," including passages explaining how this method could be useful to the Nazis. Her dissertation also used the term *Jew* regarding the writings of the American Walter Lippmann. Noelle-Neumann contended that these references were included only to appease the dictatorial censors and to conform to the prevailing regulations, both of which were essential if she was to be granted the opportunity to express her ideas publicly in a totalitarian state (Noelle-Neumann, 1992, p. 10)

perhaps best known for his notions of *gemeinschaft* and *gesellschaft* in his discussions of traditional and modern societies, respectively. To Tönnies (1922), public opinion represented a social force, an informal mechanism of social control: "Public opinion always claims to be authoritative. It demands consent or at least compels silence, or abstention from contradiction" (p. 138). Drawing on this conceptualization, Noelle-Neumann reasoned that "social conventions, customs and norms have always been included in the domain of public opinion. Public opinion imposes sanctions on individuals who offend against convention—a process of 'social control'" (Noelle-Neumann, 1973, p. 88; see also: Noelle-Neumann, 1995). It was the empirical observation of a changing electoral mood or political climate, and reliance on a conceptualization of public opinion as a form of social control, that served as the point of departure for what would turn out to be an ambitious and influential program of research.

Contemporary Applications of the Spiral-of-Silence Model

As a pollster and advisor to political parties in Germany, Noelle-Neumann counseled Christian Democrats' supporters to speak up in their everyday lives—to create and reinforce the impression that they are not afraid of expressing their views, thereby presumably implying to others that their viewpoint is winning.

Proponents of numerous social causes make similar use of the spiral of silence's principles in attempts to influence public opinion and public policy. The organization of rallies, demonstrations and marches is a common strategy employed by groups attempting to both demonstrate the magnitude of support for their issue position and to attract media coverage, the combination of which gives the appearance of confidence and burgeoning strength. Bumper stickers, political buttons, banners and other small media are integral components of such efforts; they legitimize—and thereby foster—the public expression of a particular viewpoint. The task for a group whose opinion is shared by a majority of citizens is clear: Engage in ongoing public communication in an attempt to reinforce the perception of confidence (i.e., that its opinion is—and will remain—the dominant one). Conversely, the task for a group whose opinion is not shared by the majority is equally clear: Use public communication in an attempt to give the impression that its (minority) opinion is either the dominant one or the one with substantial momentum, or to imply that the opposing opinion (i.e., the actual majority opinion) is not widely and confidently expressed in public (Salmon & Oshagan, 1990). In this sense, public expression of opinion constructs a psychological community of heretofore isolated individuals who now know that they are not alone in their opinion.

That the media play a crucial role in this struggle for control of perceptions should be readily apparent. An interesting illustration of this can be found in coverage of a 1989 pro-choice rally by two student newspapers at the University of Wisconsin-Madison. *The Daily Cardinal*, which had at the time the reputation of being the more liberal of the two papers, had as its front-page headlines, "We are the Majority" and "600,000 rally in Washington, D.C." The story began:

In a massive show of support for abortion and reproductive rights, as many as 600,000 people gathered in the nation's capital Sunday at a march sponsored by the National Organization for Women.

Confirmation for the numbers cited by organizers and the city police proved difficult, as local news stations conservatively estimated the attendance at one quarter of a million people.

On the very same day, *The Badger Herald*, which had the reputation of being the more conservative of the two papers, had as its headline on a page three story, "85,000 Pro-Choice Activists March in D.C." The story (Associated Press, 1989) noted that:

U.S. Park Police estimated the early crowd at 65,000 but said 20,000 other pro-abortion demonstrators were en route from nearby Robert F. Kennedy Stadium.

The interpretation is clear in both cases. The presentation of information in the liberal newspaper gave the impression of an historic gathering, a "massive show of support" for an issue position held by a "majority" of citizens. The presentation of information in the conservative newspaper, on the other hand, implicitly minimized the import of the event through its reporting of a significantly smaller crowd size, its relegation of the story to an interior page, and its marginalization of participants as "activists" and "pro-abortion demonstrators."

The social control aspects of public opinion can be observed in a variety of other situations, perhaps less dramatic but no less potent. For example, as recently as 20 years ago cigarette smokers confidently smoked in public places and assemblages, with little fear of censure from others. Indeed, it was more likely the case that an offended nonsmoker would feel qualms about speaking out in public to ask the smoker to refrain from engaging in his or her behavior. Today, the climate of opinion has shifted dramatically. Smokers constantly are subjected to majority pressure to conform. What political philosopher John Locke (1824/1985) spoke of as the "law of public opinion" actually has become codified as such: Public opinion, the informal mechanism of social control has, through a burgeoning social consensus, a virtually monolithic opinion climate and the concomitant inculcation of a dominant opinion, spiraled into regulation and law, the formal mechanisms of social control.

These examples imply that the spiral of silence process is not merely an artifact of totalitarian regimes, but potentially a condition of "free" societies as well.

CONCEPTUAL AND METHODOLOGICAL CONUNDRUMS

Though the model is intuitively seductive in its ability to explain situations such as those described above, it has not been as readily verifiable through traditional scientific hypothesis testing. It perhaps suffices to say that the entire spiral of silence model itself has never been subjected to a comprehensive empirical test, even by Noelle-Neumann herself, probably because it would be far too time consuming (perhaps spanning several decades) and expensive to undertake. Instead, researchers have tended to reduce the model into discrete, manageable fragments and tested hypotheses within those fragments.

Issues in Conceptualization

With few exceptions, researchers outside of Germany generally have not found much in the way of consistent empirical support for several of the model's pivotal assumptions and claims. Researchers, however, have found what might be characterized as a modest degree of reluctance, rather than a consuming fear, about publicly expressing a minority opinion on most issues. Indeed, it is very often the case that a plurality of those holding (or believing that they hold) the minority position are still willing to speak out, far more than the few hardcores that the model would predict. Partly as a result of such controversial empirical support for the model's contentions, there is no shortage of critiques, counter critiques, recommendations, and prescriptions (e.g., Csikszentmiha-lyi, 1991; Donsbach, 1988; Donsbach & Stevenson, 1984; Glynn & McLeod, 1985; Kennamer, 1990; McLeod, 1985; Merten, 1985; Moscovici, 1991; Noelle-Neumann, 1991; Noelle-Neumann, 1985; Price & Allen, 1990; Rusciano, 1989; Salmon & Kline, 1985). In this section, we review the more enduring points of contention.

Crossing International Boundaries.   The spiral-of-silence model had its origins in Germany, and took more than a decade before scholars in the United States began investigating its merits and weaknesses. Schulz and Schoenbach (1984) noted that the first direct data-based challenge to the model "...was offered by an American graduate student at the International Communication Association (ICA) conference in Boston," and asked "Why must we allow theories that dominate our discussion of media and politics to be tested by students in other cultures?" (p. 715). According to Schulz and Schoenbach (1984), the difference in research approaches between the two countries could be characterized as, on one side of the Atlantic, a rich lode of small-scale studies probing various aspects of the theory, and on the other side, " . . . either one large, multi-method study for a million marks or nothing at all" (p. 715).

This difference in research approaches, though interesting in and of itself, speaks to a larger question of whether the silencing phenomenon can be adequately observed and studied in cultures other than Germany. The issue of the model's ability to "cross national boundaries" has been debated in several essays, including those by Glynn and McLeod (1985) and Noelle-Neumann (1984, 1990), and remains one of its most problematic conceptual aspects.

As Glynn and McLeod (1984) note, Noelle-Neumann argues that certain aspects of German culture, such as differences in political campaigns or communication patterns, preclude absolute replication in other cultures. She adds that "the reality of the media in the Federal Republic of Germany and in English-speaking countries may be very different" (Noelle-Neumann, 1984, p. 68). The question remains, however, regarding what to do with the theory when it is applied in varied social settings. One approach is to consider these differences on an *ad hoc* basis and to adjust the theory for each new application. Thus, if media use is different between Germany and the United States, Noelle-Neumann (1984) suggests that "media effects should only be treated secondar-ily" (p. 68). A second approach, however, would be to take differences between cultures into account when developing the theory so the rationale that "this country is an exception" does not need to be invoked. This suggests that what is needed is a broader treatment of the spiral of silence where varied groups and cultures are treated as part of, rather than deviations from, the process.

We are quickly approaching the point at which such a broad integration may be possible, given that the model has been tested in such countries as Germany, the United States, Great Britain, Mexico, the Philippines, Taiwan, South Korea, China, and Japan (Salmon & Moh, 1992). The next step is to integrate results of these small-scale studies with more macro considerations of the nations, such as the degree of population homogeneity, government control of media, and conformity expected and tolerated in citizens, to truly make the spiral of silence an international model of communication and public opinion. One notion which in particular merits this type of analysis is that of *consonance* (i.e., that the media depict a relatively monolithic opinion environment), often a liberal one. Clearly, the degree of consonance achievable in a society is a function of economic and political controls on its media system, as well as various situational factors (Salmon & Moh, 1992). Further, consonance can occur at different levels of abstraction, ranging from explicit agreement on essential facts of a news story to implicit recognition of shared social norms and values.

Conformity as a Theoretical Base.   A second major conceptual issue which needs elaboration involves its grounding in the literature on conformity in small-group settings. Price and Allen (1990) claimed, for example, that Noelle-Neumann overstated the ubiquity of conformity and majority influence, adding that a majority of subjects in typical Asch-type group pressure experiments (about two thirds) in fact do not conform, even to a unanimous majority. Glynn and McLeod (1985) suggested that the Asch research is pertinent to the spiral of silence as a sort of "rough analogue" (p. 47).

There are some key differences between the Asch situation and the process described by Noelle-Neumann. First, the stimuli judged by the subjects in Asch's experiments were unambiguous, and subjects made definite judgments of their own prior to being subjected to group pressures. In the case of the spiral of silence, persons may have only weakly developed views or even no prior opinions when confronted with the opportunity or need to express an opinion. Second, in Asch's experiments, there was no interpersonal communication beyond the recording of majority opinion. In the spiral of silence, interpersonal communication plays a critical role because individuals are not subject to the confines of a laboratory situation. They may discuss the issue with friends and members of their family, and they may seek social reinforcement to anchor their opinion. Third, Asch's stimuli were generally administered at one time and effects studied soon thereafter. Noelle-Neumann, on the other hand, "gives considerable attention to the cumulative effects of opinion expressed (or not expressed) over relatively long periods of time" (Glynn & McLeod, 1985, p. 48). Fourth, Noelle-Neumann drew on Asch's work to justify her notion of fear of isolation, and yet holders of minority opinions may not be "isolated" whatsoever; indeed, in a nation of 250 million persons, a minority faction could include literally millions of people and, more importantly, members of primary and secondary groups who serve to reinforce the holding of that opinion (Salmon & Kline, 1985). To further complicate matters, research shows that members of minority groups may be more willing to speak out when they perceive that support for their viewpoint is declining (Price & Allen, 1990).

It would appear that there are enough differences between the spiral of silence model and conformity theory to beg consideration of an alternative theoretical base. However, aside from retentions of a better fit with the research of Muzafer Sherif (cf. Glynn &

McLeod, 1985), social identification and group conflict (cf. Price, 1989; Glynn, 1993), group attractiveness (Glynn & McLeod, 1985; Salmon & Kline, 1985), or with social influence theory (Price & Allen, 1990), little has been done to advance such theory development in this area. In fact, the predominat approach has been for researchers (ourselves included) to mention weaknesses of the theory and then proceed to test hypotheses based on the theory's original premises.

Issue Differences.   Although originally derived from the study of election campaigns, the spiral of silence model has been tested across a variety of issues, ranging from abortion (e.g., Bergen, 1986; Donsbach & Stevenson, 1984; Salmon & Neuwirth, 1990) to support for Radio Martí (Matera & Salwen, 1992), to English as the official language (Salwen, Lin, & Matera, 1994). Little systematic attention, however, has been paid to how the nature of the issue influences the dynamics of the spiral of silence process (Salmon & Kline, 1985). For example, Yeric and Todd (1989) offered a typology involving three major classes of issues. The first, *enduring*, remain in the public eye over a long period of time. Examples include defense spending, health, and gun control. The second, *emerging*, are relatively new to the public, but show potential for remaining in the public consciousness and hence becoming enduring. The third, *transitory*, do not remain in the public consciousness for very long, though they may emerge and re-emerge from time to time. Though a few studies have manipulated issue types in an attempt to study the influence of issues on opinion expression (e.g., Noelle-Neumann's research program across 20 years; Salmon & Oshagan, 1990), typologies such as the one described above could provide a useful conceptual foundation for augmenting the model's explanatory power. In such an undertaking, it would be important to add another dimension, that of opinion distribution. It is highly likely, for example, that an issue for which there is nearly equal support and opposition for some policy option might behave quite differently from one for which the levels of support and opposition are quite unequal.

METHODOLOGICAL CONSIDERATIONS

One of the singular strengths of the spiral of silence model is its use of highly innovative approaches to public opinion. To her credit, Noelle-Neumann provided a specified research methodology. Rather than offer a hypothetical study, it is worth examining Noelle-Neumann's own research to see how she integrated theory and research.

Designing the Classic Study.   As is the case for conventional approaches to public opinion research practiced in the United States by commercial pollsters, an interviewer will ask a respondent his or her opinion about some topic (e.g., raising children). For example, in surveys conducted by Noelle-Neumann's Allensbach Institute, women were asked whether spanking children was basically wrong or a necessary part of bringing up children. However, rather than an end, this question was merely the beginning in spiral of silence measurement, and was followed up by what has become regarded as the classic measure of public opinion for this approach:

Suppose you are faced with a five-hour train ride, and there is a person sitting in your compartment who thinks . . .

The ending of the question depended upon each respondent's personal opinion; that is, women

. . . were confronted with a fellow traveler who represented a point of view diametrically opposed to their own. The question was closed in uniform fashion with "Would you like to talk with this woman so as to get to know her point of view better, or wouldn't you think that worth your while?" (Noelle-Neumann, 1984, pp. 17–18)

Following the measurement phase, the analytic strategy involves comparing the willingness of supporters of spanking with that of opponents to enter into the dialogue with the fellow traveler. Hypothesis tests emanate directly from the central proposition of the spiral of silence model, namely that holders of the minority opinion will be less inclined to express their opinion in public than will holders of the majority opinion. Which faction is more confident, more willing to express a personal conviction, and hence more likely to subsequently have an influence on others' perceptions of the climate of opinion? These are the crucial research questions to be addressed in the spiral of silence approach, not merely the distribution of opposing opinions *per se*.

Adapting Measurement Approaches.   The approach described in the previous section may be modified in any number of creative ways. For example, an interviewer may show respondents (in-person interviews) a picture of an automobile with a flat tire and then ask:

Here is a picture of an automobile which has had its tire slashed. On the right rear window there is a sticker for a political party, but you can no longer read which party was on the sticker. But what is your guess: with which party's stickers do people run the greatest risk of having a tire slashed? (Noelle-Neumann, 1984, p. 54)

Or, an interviewer may use the following approach such as the following:

I would like to tell you about an incident which recently took place at a large public meeting on nuclear energy. There were two main speakers: One spoke in favor of nuclear energy and the other opposed it. One of the speakers was booed by the audience. Which one do you think was booed: the speaker supporting nuclear energy or the speaker opposing it?

Implicit in these measurement approaches seems to be the notion that opinion climates potentially engender quite nasty experiences (e.g., lengthy, uncomfortable train rides, slashed tires, hostile confrontations). Several of these measurement approaches also are peculiar to the setting in which they were first conceived; for example, discussions during five-hour train rides are far more common in Europe than in the United States if only because of the greater reliance on the train system in the former. As a result, spiral of silence tests in the United States have resorted to alternative measures to assess respondents' willingness to express their opinion publicly. These include willingness to participate in a demonstration; wear a pin or button in support of some cause; or be interviewed by a TV reporter with camera and microphone for airing on the TV newscast. As Salmon and Oshagan (1990, p. 163), noted, various measures of opinion expression are distinguishable in terms of the degree to which each form of expression is public; and the degree to which feedback will be immediate and perhaps unpleasant. For example, engaging in a discussion in a train compartment involves a limited public setting—two or three other people may hear your opinion—with immediate and direct feedback. In contrast, agreeing to express an opinion to a TV reporter involves a much greater public setting—an entire community or nation—but with delayed and perhaps indirect feedback. A significant research program could be developed to explore the role of cross-cultural and interpersonal factors in various forms of opinion expression as a way of investigating the spiral of silence phenomenon.

Analyzing Actual and Perceived Minority Status. Although Noelle-Neumann hypothesized that holders of the minority opinion are less likely than holders of the majority opinion to engage in the conversation, some attention should be paid to the distinction between actual versus perceived minority status (Salmon & Kline, 1985). That is, we know from the literature on pluralistic ignorance (e.g., Allport, 1924; Fields & Schuman, 1976; Miller & McFarland, 1987) that some individuals who are in the minority on some issue incorrectly believe themselves to be in the majority and vice versa. In her own research, Noelle-Neumann typically failed to analyze this distinction (an exception being Noelle-Neumann, 1973, p. 106); instead she merely compared the willingness to express an opinion among those actually in the majority and minority. At the same time, she recommended that researchers ask respondents "What do most people think" (about the issue) and "Which side is winning?" (Noelle-Neumann, 1989) as a way of gauging the respondents' perceptions of social environment dynamics. This is an area in particular in which spiral of silence analysis could greatly benefit from the infusion of ideas from other approaches to the study of individuals' perceptions of the social environment, such as pluralistic ignorance, false consensus, looking glass perception, impersonal impact, and the third-person effect (see Glynn et al., 1995, for a review).

A Caveat: The Suitability of Survey Research. Attention to such matters as question wording and analytic strategies inherently assumes the legitimacy of polling and survey research itself as a means of researching public opinion, an assumption which has been contested in several insightful and scathing critiques (e.g., Blumer, 1948; Bourdieu, 1979; Pollock, 1976). Certainly, the assumption that measuring public opinion can be done in the same manner as measuring intentions to vote or purchase toothpaste is conceptually naive. And the assumption that in a public opinion poll all opinions ought to be counted the same (i.e., have the same weight) is clearly rooted in some contrived, idealized notion of democracy rather than in democracy as it actually exists in its empirical form (see Salmon & Glasser, 1995, for an extended discussion of these issues). Though all survey approaches to the study of public opinion are inherently vulnerable to such criticisms, the spiral of silence is especially vulnerable for different reasons.

At the heart of the spiral of silence phenomenon is the idea that individuals holding a minority opinion will become reluctant to express that opinion publicly. As noted (Salmon & Moh, 1992), the survey interview is itself a communication setting in which a person is asked to express an opinion to a stranger. To the extent that the respondent is influenced by the perceived climate of opinion, he or she may be unwilling to participate in a survey on that topic much as the person on the train may be unwilling to participate in the discussion in the train compartment. At the very least, this may result in different response rates for holders of different opinions and thereby threaten the validity of the conclusions. The dynamics of the two situations are different in some important ways. On the train, the fellow traveler clearly expresses his or her opinion; in the research situation, the interviewer has been trained not to reveal his or her opinion on the issue in the hopes of minimizing social pressure on the respondent. Further, the respondent is treated as anonymous, and his or her opinions confidential in the hopes of maximizing the integrity of his or her response, something which may or may not happen on the train ride but is certainly not explicitly stated as such. Nevertheless, the intriguing possibility exists that the survey approach may be inherently unsuitable for studying the very phenomenon it was designed to study.

This potential paradox suggests the need for alternative and complementary methodologies to study the spiral of silence. In particular, experiments (Kennamer, 1990) and observational studies might provide important insights into the silencing process, as well as the opportunity to provide triangulation in an assessment of the validity of the survey approach. Two other methods—content analysis and interviews with journalists—have been employed to help in the interpretation of survey data on the silencing phenomenon (e.g., Noelle-Neumann, 1984), but only rarely and even then in a cursory fashion.

CONCLUSION

In its relatively brief lifespan to date, the spiral of silence model has engendered a rich legacy of research and commentary and infused the fields of public opinion and communication research with some needed conceptual and methodological vitality. If only by virtue of being one of the very few communication models studies which explicitly links mass and interpersonal communication processes, the spiral of silence has assumed an important place in the literature on communication processes and effects. Mass communication is seen as forging opinion climates, the perceptions of which in turn are said to influence individuals' willingness to engage in interpersonal communication about some topic. Less developed in the model is the mechanism of reverse causality, namely the manner in which individuals' willingness to engage in interpersonal communication exerts influence on mass media portrayals of the opinion climate. By using the metaphor of the downward spiral, which implies unidirectionality, Noelle-Neumann perhaps underestimated the power of minority factions to effect social change, to overcome majority sentiment, and reverse the spiraling process through judicious use of interpersonal and small-group communication processes. Or perhaps she overestimates the power of opinion climates in pluralistic societies. While the empirical evidence shows that some individuals are reluctant to express minority viewpoints in some settings on some topics with some people, the magnitude of the phenomenon is not nearly as pronounced as is implied in the Noelle-Neumann's claims and generalizations.

Nevertheless, the model clearly remains an interesting and controversial one, obviously for what it implies about the nature and vast powers of the mass media system, but perhaps more tellingly for its preoccupation with the potentially ominous consequences of commonplace conversations and expressions of opinion. Rather than a tool for crafting compromise and mutually acceptable resolutions to social conflicts, communication is depicted as a weapon capable of progressively bludgeoning weak opinion into obscurity. This dark side aspect of the spiral of silence cannot be understated. It is a central aspect of the controversy regarding the theory. To be sure, like all current models, the spiral of silence can be critized on theoretical and methodological grounds. But much of the criticism focuses on what the theory suggests about human nature, with human beings portrayed as weak and intiminated into silence, rather than vocal contributors to the democratic process and the marketplace of ideas.

REFERENCES

Allport, F. H. (1924). *Social psychology*. Boston: Houghton Mifflin.

Asch, S. E. (1970). Effects of group pressure upon the modification and distortion of judgments. In J. H. Campbell & H. Hepler (Eds.), *Dimensions in communication: Readings* (pp. 170–183). Belmont, CA: Wadsworth.

Associated Press (1989, April 10). 85,000 pro-choice activists march in D.C. *The Badger Herald* (Madison, WI), p. 3.

Bergen, L. (1986, May). *Testing the spiral of silence with opinions on abortion*. Paper presented at the annual meeting of the International Communication Association, Chicago, IL.

Blumer, H. (1948). Public opinion and public opinion polling. *American Sociological Review, 13*, 542–552.

Bogart, L. (1991). The pollster and the Nazis. *Commentary, 92*, 47–49.

Bourdieu, P. (1979). Public opinion does not exist. In A. Mattelart & S. Siegelaub (Eds.), *Communication and class struggle* (pp. 124–130). New York: International General.

Csikszentmihalyi, M. (1991). Reflections on the "spiral of silence." In J. A. Anderson (Ed.), *Communication yearbook 14* (pp. 288–297). Newbury Park, CA: Sage.

Davison, W. P. (1958). The public opinion process. *Public Opinion Quarterly, 65*, 299–306.

Donsbach, W. (1988). The challenge of the spiral-of-silence theory. *Communicare, 8,* 5–16.

Donsbach, W., & Stevenson, R. L. (1984, May). *Challenges problems and empirical evidence of the theory of the spiral of silence*. Paper presented at the annual meeting of the International Communication Association, San Francisco.

Fields, J., & Schuman, H. (1976). Public beliefs about the beliefs of the public. *Public Opinion Quarterly, 40*, 427–448.

Gitlin, T. (1980). *The whole world is watching: Mass media in the making and unmaking of the New Left*. Berkeley: University of California Press.

Glynn, C. J. (1993, August). *Public opinion and the normative opinion process*. Paper presented at the annual meeting of the Association for education in Journalism and Mass Communication, Kansas City, MO.

Glynn, C. J., & McLeod, J. M. (1985). Implications of the spiral of silence for communication and public opinion research. In K. R. Sanders, L. L. Kaid, & D. Nimmo (Eds.), *Political communication yearbook 1984* (pp. 43–65). Carbondale: Southern Illinois University Press.

Glynn, C. J., Ostman, R. E., & McDonald, D. G. (1995). Opinions, perceptions, and social reality. In T. L. Glasser & C. T. Salmon (Eds.) *Public opinion and the communication of consent* (pp. 249–277). New York: Guilford.

Herman, E. S., & Chomsky, N. (1988). *Manufacturing consent: The political economy of the mass media.* New York: Pantheon Books.

Kennamer, J.D . (1990). Self-serving bias in perceiving the opinions of others. *Communication Research, 17,* 393–404.

Locke, J. (1985). *The works of John Locke* (12th ed.). Frederic Ives Carpenter Memorial Collection. (Original work published 1824)

Madison, J. (1961). The Federalist No. 49. In J. E. Cooke (Ed.), *The Federalist* (pp. 338–347). Middletown, CT: Wesleyan University Press. (Original work published 1788)

Matera, F., & Salwen, M. B. (1992). Support for Radio Martí among Miami's Cubans and non-Cubans. *International Journal of Intercultural Relations, 16,* 135–144.

McLeod, J. M. (1985). An essay: Public opinion—Our social skin. *Journalism Quarterly, 62,* 649–653.

Merten, K. (1985). Some silence in the spiral of silence. In K. Sanders, L. L. Kaid, & D. Nimmo (Eds.), *Political communication yearbook 1984* (pp. 31–42). Carbondale: Southern Illinois University Press.

Miller, D. T., & McFarland, C. (1987). Pluralistic ignorance: When similarity is interpreted as dissimilarity. *Journal of Personality and Social Psychology, 53,* 298–305.

Moscovici, S. (1991). Silent majorities and loud minorities. In J. A. Anderson (Ed.), *Communication yearbook* (Vol. 14, pp. 298–308). Newbury Park, CA: Sage.

Noelle-Neumann, E. (1973). Return to the concept of powerful mass media. *Studies of Broadcasting, 9,* 67–112.

Noelle-Neumann, E. (1974). The spiral of silence: A theory of public opinion. *Journal of Communication, 24,* 43–51.

Noelle-Neumann, E. (1977). Turbulences in the climate of opinion: Methodological applications of the spiral of silence theory. *Public Opinion Quarterly, 41,* 143–158.

Noelle-Neumann, E. (1979). Public opinion and the classical tradition: A re-evaluation. *Public Opinion Quarterly, 43,* 143–156.

Noelle-Neumann, E. (1980). The public opinion research correspondent. *Public Opinion Quarterly, 44,* 585–597.

Noelle-Neumann, E. (1984) *The spiral of silence: Public opinion—Our social skin.* Chicago: University of Chicago Press.

Noelle-Neumann, E. (1985). The spiral of silence: A response. In D. Nimmo, L. L. Kaid, & K. Sanders (Eds.), *Political communication yearbook 1984* (pp. 66–94). Carbondale: Southern Illinois University Press.

Noelle-Neumann, E. (1989). Advances in spiral of silence research. *KEIO Communication Review, 10,* 3–34.

Noelle-Neumann, E. (1991). The theory of public opinion: The concept of the spiral of silence. In J. A. Anderson (Ed.), *Communication yearbook* (Vol. 14, pp. 256–287). Newbury Park: Sage.

Noelle-Neumann, E. (1992). Letter to the editor in response to Leo Bogart's "The pollster and the Nazis." *Commentary, 93,* 9–15.

Noelle-Neumann, E. (1995). Public opinion and rationality. In T. L. Glasser & C. T. Salmon (Eds.), *Public opinion and the communication of consent* (pp. 33–54). New York: Guilford.

Pollock, F. (1976). Empirical research into public opinion. In P. Connerton (Ed.), *Critical sociology* (pp. 225–236). New York: Penguin.

Price, V. (1989). Social identification and public opinion: Effects of communicating group conflict. *Public Opinion Quarterly, 53,* 197–224.

Price, V., & Allen, S. (1990). Opinion spirals, silent and otherwise: Applying small-group research to public opinion phenomena. *Communication Research 17,* 369–392.

Protess, D. L., Cook, F. L., Doppelt, J. C., Ettema, J. S., Gordon, M. T., Leff, D. R., & Miller, P. (1991). *The journalism of outrage: Investigative reporting and agenda building in America.* New York: Guilford.

Rusciano, R. L. (1989). *Isolation and paradox: Defining "the public" in modern political analysis.* New York: Greenwood Press.

Salmon, C. T., & Glasser, T. L. (1995). The politics of polling and the limits of consent. In T. L. Glasser & C. T. Salmon (Eds.), *Public opinion and the communication of consent* (pp. 437–458). New York: Guilford.

Salmon, C. T., & Kline, F. G. (1985). The spiral of silence ten years later: An examination and evaluation. In K. Sanders, L. L. Kaid, & D. Nimmo (Eds.), *Political communication yearbook 1984* (pp. 3–29). Carbondale: Southern Illinois University Press.

Salmon, C. T., & Moh, C. Y. (1992). The spiral of silence: Linking individual and society through communcation. In J. D. Kennamer (Ed.), *Public opinion, the press, and public policy* (pp. 145–161). Westport, CT: Praeger.

Salmon, C. T., & Neuwirth, K. (1990). Perceptions of opinion "climates" and willingness to discuss the issue of abortion. *Journalism Quarterly, 67,* 567–577.

Salmon, C. T., & Oshagan, H. (1990). Community size, perceptions of majority opinion and opinion expression. *Public Relations Research Annual, 2,* 157–171.

Salwen, M. B., Lin, C., & Matera, F. R. (1994). Willingness to discuss "official English:" A test of three communities. *Journalism Quarterly, 71,* 282–290.

Schulz, W., & Schoenbach, K. (1984). Book review of "Masenmedien und Wahlen" [Mass media and elections]. *Journalism Quarterly, 62,* 715.

Tönnies, F. (1922). *Kritik der offentlicher meinung* [Critique of public opinion]. Berlin: Springer.

Yeric, J. L., & Todd, J. R. (1989). *Public opinion, the visible politics* (2nd ed.). Itasca, IL: F. E. Peacock, Publishers.

12

International Communication

Robert L. Stevenson
University of North Carolina at Chapel Hill

As an area of study, international communication has no identifiable substance, body of theory, or specific research methods, only geography (Stevenson, 1992). This area of communication, perhaps more than others, is diverse and unorganized. Besides embracing anything "foreign," it includes all of the combinations of *cross*, *inter*, and *comparative* linked to *cultural*, *national*, and even *global* that surface in books, journal articles, and conference papers. The result is a set of confusing, ill-defined terms that do little to organize the area or guide its development. Is there anything that distinguishes international communication—other than geography?

DEFINITIONAL MATRIX

A simple, three-dimensional definitional matrix serves a good starting point for international communication. Some years ago, William Paisley (1984) proposed a two-dimensional matrix locating communication as a field of study within the behavioral sciences. He defined communication as one of the elementary behavior-defined disciplines such as cybernetics and systems analysis that served as elements of more general fields of study such as education (learning), economics (value), and political science (power). Communication was both one of the basic disciplines, incorporating cybernetics (self-regulating feedback) and systems analysis, as well as an element of the more general disciplines of education, political science, and economics.

Paisley's second dimension comprised disciplines defined by their units of analysis, ranging from atom and molecule (natural sciences) through cell and living subsystem (biological sciences) to individual, group, and culture (social sciences). A final category of particular interest to international communication could be the globe as a single unit. By combining the two, you define a specific behavior (such as communication) at a specific level (such as the individual). As a field, communication is studied mostly at the individual or small-group level in the United States, while in many other nations it is often studied at the economic and political levels.

At this point, communication is a behavior that incorporates some more basic behaviors (such as feedback and systems maintenance) and is itself part of more general behaviors (such as learning, value, and power). It is studied at levels ranging from the entire planet as a single system to individual molecules or atoms. As a social science, communication studies have focused on the individual and group with some outward exploration toward the single global system, as well as inward toward biological systems. At the broader levels, social science has produced few new ideas since Marxism, now discredited both as a theory of history and a basis of social organization. Some dramatic progress can be documented at the boundary between social and biological science. This is reflected in the growth of cognitive science, which seeks to understand the brain as a biological organ as a prelude to understanding the mind, and is consistent with the tradition in Western science of reducing disciplines to lower-order components.

To separate international communication from the more general field, a third dimension is needed that includes four distinct categories: foreign, comparative, international or intercultural,[1] and global. Foreign studies are single-country or single-culture studies, usually heavy on description and light on explanation. Comparison with other countries is usually implicit, if attempted at all. Comparative studies contrast the communication behavior of individuals or institutions within one culture or nation with equivalent behavior in another, usually with some national or cultural element to explain differences. International and intercultural studies examine the flow of information and influences from one nation or culture to another. Global studies consider the planet as a single, unified system.

The three dimensions form a cube whose sides define international communication in terms of (a) a focal variable that is some aspect of communication, (b) a unit of analysis that can range from the individual to the entire globe, and (c) the delineation of national or cultural boundaries that, in most studies, provide the basis of comparison or explanation.

METHODS

Is it possible to identify some areas of communication we can reasonably single out as *international* communication, although specific theories or even fragments of theory are in short supply? International communication is more an area of interest than an

---

[1]The difference between nation and culture is easy to define, but often difficult to deal with in practice. A nation is an independent political entity, usually identified by a flag, airline, and seat at the United Nations. A culture is a group of people who share values and behaviors derived from a common history.

area rich in theory, and one that, like other areas of interest, overlaps other disciplines. Our examination begins, however, with whether there are unusual or even unique research methods appropriate for its study. Does the international communication researcher need special tools—beyond sensitivity to other cultures—appropriate to any foreign expedition?

On the whole, no. The standards and methods of scholarly research do not stop at national borders. Despite occasional references to a different reality of non-Western cultures, the rules of probability and statistical logic are the same in every country. Within every facet of the field and every discipline, the researcher's bag of tools is the same: validity (am I measuring what I'm claiming to measure?), reliability (am I describing my methods so thoroughly that others can replicate them?), and adequacy of evidence (have I considered everything?). While associated with quantitative social science where these concerns are addressed explicitly, they also underlie claims to knowledge in all disciplines.

There is, however, a special question of research method that permeates much of the international communication literature. It is the difference between *research* and *polemic*. In the 1990s, polemic is closely linked to a mixture of scholarship and ideology called *critical research*.

Critical Research

The phrase *critical research* is identified with the phrase *Frankfurt School* (Bottomore, 1984). The School, technically the Institute of Social Research, was founded in Germany in 1923. Its focus was the dark side of industrial society and, while not always Marxist as understood now, research emphasized the themes found in Marx's critique of capitalism and exported them to sociology. Modern life was contrasted with both Marx's utopian vision of communism and with a romanticized landscape of the pre-industrial past.

Before World War II, many Frankfurt School researchers fled to the United States, where the Frankfurt School in exile met the Vienna School in exile (Delia, 1987). The two names most associated with the Vienna School were Paul Lazarsfeld and Karl Popper. Lazarsfeld, a sociologist, was to influence the development of communication research as an empirical field both in academia and the corporate world. Popper, who remained in Britain, is closely identified with positivism, a style of social science research modeled on the natural sciences, whose key elements are quantification, explicit attention to validity, reliability and weight of evidence (significance testing), and the "scientific" method (see chapters 1 and 5, this volume). Popper is identified with the idea that a statement can never be proven true because there are always possible alternative causes; a statement can only be proven false. This research approach goes back to Descartes: Build carefully from the simplest concepts, test everything, take nothing for granted. In practice, critical research relies more on deduction and definition, reflecting its roots in Hegelian philosophy. The key elements of positivism that are contrasted to critical research are an avoidance of anything that cannot be established empirically and an indirect testing of hypotheses by falsifying the reverse null hypothesis. The former excludes value judgments, the latter excludes many of the important questions of social and global media influence.

The question of the appropriate method for communication research—even a minimally adequate method—was confused in the debate between the Frankfurt and Vienna Schools after the war. Lazarsfeld (1941) contrasted an aloof, admittedly soft critical research probing the crucial links between the mass media and the power structure of society with what he called administrative research. Although claiming to be sympathetic to critical research, he presented it as mere speculation. *Administrative research* was the cautious conservatism of empirical positivism, an approach greeted enthusiastically by the media and derivative industries to advance commercial and political interests.

The differences Lazarsfeld described have been exaggerated to separate communication research, especially international communication research, into two hostile camps (Blumler, 1985; Rogers, 1985). On one side is critical research, often identified as the European approach, focusing on the use of communication to maintain political and economic power systems at the national or global level and disdainful of empirical data and the scholar's traditional aloofness from political activism. On the other, the American school focused on individuals, reliant on sophisticated (and sometimes inappropriate) data analysis to generate fragments of middle-range theories, unconcerned with broader issues of distribution of wealth and power.[2]

This has changed; the poles have reversed. Other countries have improved their access to computers and data-collection methods. In the United States, communication research is often caught up in the politics and rhetoric of social protest claiming oppression, suppression, and victimization. A good deal of current domestic academic rhetoric is imported from critical research's long-standing vocabulary. The literature of international communication now debates issues with terms such as *dependency*, *hegemony*, and *sovereignty*, as well as the more general trendy concepts associated with postmodern scholarship. Traditional research is out, critics claim; critical research is in, with all of its vocabulary, assumptions, and ideology ("Ferment in the Field," 1983; Levy & Gurevitch, 1993/1994).

Research Versus Polemic

Critics of international communication research often posit a dichotomy of critical versus administrative—or sometimes quantitative versus qualitative—methods. Within the area generally and certainly within the United States, the traditional methods, usually quantitative and almost always aloof and dispassionate, are in disrepute. To replace them, a style of committed research is proposed that rejects both traditions of impartiality and of caution in mixing scholarly research and partisan politics. This false dichotomy points toward a growing problem in communication research, and a specific problem of most international communication research. The problem is the growth of *polemic* (i.e., beginning with a conclusion and assembling data to support it, without regard to questions of reliability, validity, or adequacy of the evidence) in the guise of research.

---

[2]Middle-range theories are more restricted than high generality theories, which are more general and cultural in nature and low generality, which are more restricted in nature (see Stacks, Hickson, & Hill, 1991).

Research *begins* with a question or hypothesis; it is the outcome of research that is in doubt, although researchers often put forward logically derived hypotheses of their expectations. The evidence may be inadequate to support any conclusion, or it may contradict the expected outcome. There are circumstances when polemic is appropriate. Political campaigning, advertising, and one's defense in a criminal trial come to mind immediately. In these circumstances, we expect the best possible case to made. There is also an academic school—stronger in continental Europe than in the Anglo-American tradition—that values argument and rhetoric over evidence. A British observer described the 1970s international debate over "cultural imperialism" as a passage of the center of the field from "communication schools on the right bank of the Ohio River to the cafes on the left bank of the Seine" (Tunstall, 1982, p. 141). In similar fashion, the rise of critical research and its rhetoric in the United States reflects an embracing of the assumptions and vocabulary long a part of international communication.

A great deal of criticism of international communication research in the United States since 1970 is based on the assertion that it supports the existing order while claiming to be independent and value-free. However, the power of Western science in general is a product of the weight of evidence and logic that accompany claims of knowledge derived from it. The middle-range theories that communication can muster still rise or fall on the traditional criterion of empirical verification. The particular problem of international communication is that almost no research considers the variables assumed to account for the phenomenon in question. Part of the problem is a failure to develop appropriate hypotheses; part is a casual and sometimes deliberate disregard for the protections of reliability, validity, and adequacy of evidence.

Consider a hypothetical but typical international communication study submitted to a conference or journal. Its underlying premise is that media around the world support the status quo. A content analysis could be used to show that (a) coverage in *The New York Times* was more critical of the Tiananmen Square massacre than coverage in the *People's Daily* (because both papers reflect their governments' positions), or (b) coverage of Tiananmen Square was more negative than coverage of the abortive coup against President Gorbachev (because the United States opposed the Chinese government but supported Gorbachev), or (c) coverage of the coup against Gorbachev was greater than coverage of the coup against Jean-Bertrand Aristide in Haiti (because Gorbachev is White and European and Aristide is Black and from a developing country).

What is wrong with the study lies in several specifics and a couple of general problems unique to international communication. For one thing, if the hypothesis is that media systems universally maintain political hegemony, then the key variable is a constant, and no analysis is possible because there is no variance. Or if the hypothesis assumes no difference between the two newspapers, then the null hypothesis is predicted, which cannot be done logically. This is an assumption in the first example. However, if the study's purpose is to explain something about different media systems and the varied economic and political systems in which they function, then the basis of explanation of the difference is difficult at best and often dubious. The second example assumes that both events are equivalent, and that differences in coverage derive only from journalistic practice and political policies. The third example assumes that news coverage is determined by factors over which journalists have no control, some -*ism*, such as capitalism, imperialism, or racism. In each case, the assumption is less than persuasive at best, foolish at worst. In this hypothetical study and in most real studies, the explanatory variable is not explicit, not subjected to any real test, and not restrained by considerations of reliability, validity, or adequacy of evidence.

We learn to develop and test hypotheses in a manner such that A→B, or "if A, then B." If we can establish the presence of B, we conclude that it derives from A. This works only in a classical experiment, where the presence and absence of A is manipulated in controlled circumstances where alternatives to A are excluded. If there are multiple causes of B, then A may be sufficient but not necessary to cause B.

In the real world, where at best we can choose examples or circumstances that approximate experimental conditions—virtually the only kind of research possible in international communication where we cannot manipulate or otherwise control crucial factors—research is not so clearly cut. We need to be explicit about the explanation and at a minimum treat it as a hypothesis, not a given: "A→B because of C." The full hypothesis is: "If (A→ B because of C), then D." The testable hypothesis is D, and the first derivative should be the first basis of comparison: in the absence of C, A will not lead to B.

Looking at our three examples, where the explanation—implicit or explicit—is some economic or political aspect of the media system or the nation or culture in which it operates, the first test of the hypothesis is to compare media content with equivalent content in a country with a different media system. That may have been behind the intent in the first example above; in general, however, journalistic comparative studies fail to find the kinds of differences the hypotheses require and none that point to non-Western media systems that have overcome the difficulties that are the focus of most media criticism in the West.

In short, Western journalism has something in common with Churchill's definition of democracy: It is the worst in the world—except for all the others. Or, put another way, most of the failures, weaknesses, and excesses of Western mass media exist in other media systems—and are usually worse. Advanced capitalism, the universal explanation of critical analysis, fails as a general explanation of the state of global media and is not very useful as an explanation of the issues that occupy the center ground of international communication.

Critical studies should be in disrepute along with cultural studies, which it shares roots in Marxism, since Marx failed both as a historian and prophet. But both continue to flourish in academia, perhaps even becoming bolder as the few reality-checks of communism disappear. Among scholars who built their theories on Marxist polemic, only the historian Eugene D. Genovese (1994) questioned the link between theory and practice:

> Now, as everyone knows, in a noble effort to liberate the human race from violence and oppression we [communists] broke all records for mass slaughter, piling up tens of millions of corpses in less than three-quarters of a century. When the Asian figures are properly calculated, the aggregate to our credit may reach the seemingly incredible numbers widely claimed. Those who are big on multiculturalism might note that the great majority of our victims were nonwhite. (p. 371)

In the 1990s, polemic derived from Marxist critical analysis ought not to figure heavily in international communication, but it does. An overview of several substantive issues can highlight where research and polemic overlap and possibly separate real issues from rhetoric.

ISSUES

The international communication section of any relevant journal or conference program embraces an extraordinarily diverse set of substantive interests as well as research methods and ideological assumptions. The area is large enough that no single book offers a concise history of its past or road map to its future. However, three broad issues are now at its center and promise to stay there well into the next century.

National Development and Social Change

The assumption that mass media do have—or can have—direct mass effects is a temptation for those who are committed to rapid social change. The ranks of that group range from Lenin to the federal agricultural extension service in the United States. For five decades, the two represented opposite poles of a global effort to promote economic and social change in the Third World. The promise of communication as a magic multiplier of social change is now focused on the countries emerging from the wreckage of communism (Stevenson, 1988).

The main assumption of the traditional semitheory of communication in development, which is widely known as the *dominant paradigm*, derives mostly from the work of three international communication pioneers, with long-time influence from a fourth. One was W. Walt Rostow (1960), whose study of the rise of the industrial West emphasized the importance of the creation of a critical mass of resources (people, capital, information) to spark a curve of self-sustaining, accelerating growth. The second was Daniel Lerner (1958), whose research in the Middle East after World War II seemed to put mass media—particularly radio—at the center of a rapid movement toward modern (democratic) government. The third was Wilbur Schramm (1964), whose elegant synthesis of research around the world became a guide for a generation of Western and Third World scholars and development practitioners. A good candidate for expansion of this troika is Everett M. Rogers (1962), whose early work showed how the S-curve of adoption of innovations applied to Third World development.

Rogers later recanted his support for the dominant paradigm but, like many academics of the time, embraced an alternative approach that turned out to be worse (Rogers, 1976). While accepting that the Potemkin Village facade China showed to the outside world—"a miracle of modernization . . . a public health and family planning system that was envied by the richest nations . . . increasing equality . . . an enviable status for women" (pp. 129–130)—Rogers overlooked the darker side of a regime that was responsible, according to estimates in 1994, for the deaths of 40 to 80 million of its own citizens (Southerland, 1994a, 1994b). The other two examples of alternative development, Tanzania and Cuba, were less bloody but produced little more than bankrupt dictatorships dependent on Scandinavian foreign aid and—in the case of Cuba—a permanent exodus to southern Florida.

The failure of the dominant paradigm to lead the Third World to political stability and economic growth in the 1960s and 1970s was ascribed to several factors, ranging from the lack of fit between a Western theory and non-Western societies to the rigidity of many Third World governments that turned a revolution of rising expectations into a revolution of rising frustrations. The critical research explanation was a global theory of neoimperialism using communication and culture to maintain the West at the center of a global system and the Third World at the periphery in a state of dependence reminiscent of 19th century colonialism. The latter led to a call for a redistribution of global information resources known as the New World Information and Communication Order (NWICO) derived from a New World Economic Order (NWEO) and "authentic" Third World development based on disengagement from the global information system.

When the fury of the NWICO debate subsided about 1980, a new interest in communication and Third World development (or more broadly after the collapse of communism) emerged with a focus on telecommunication. The current debate is improved by a lower level of rhetoric but still hampered by a lack of empirical data and perhaps by the lack of any general pattern or theory applicable to the 200-plus countries claiming United Nations seats. If anything, the focus of comparison is between the old communist nations of Europe where the hope is that *glasnost* (political democracy) will lead to *perestroika* (economic growth) and the tigers of Asia that have emphasized economic growth while maintaining authoritarian control over the mass media. The question of how, or whether, communication can be mobilized to support economic, political, and social change is one of the puzzles to be sorted out in the next century.

Western Dominance

The competition between Asia and central Europe shares attention with another broad issue: Western dominance of all aspects of global communication, including news, popular culture, English as the global language, and communication technology (Hachten, 1992; Merrill, 1995). Western dominance spawned the global NWICO debate, giving birth to the phrase *cultural imperialism*, which became so debased by indiscriminate use that it now can mean virtually anything or nothing at all. Western dominance shows no sign of slowing—witness the invasion of fast food and other icons of pop culture in Eastern Europe—and is still the source of irritation and conflict. Concern in Canada and France over the United States' dominance of pop culture is evidence that the issue is more than anti-Western rhetoric.

Anglo-American dominance can be explained in part by a succession of successful British colonialism and unique postwar American global influence that paved the way for a self-sustaining global culture. Other factors include the size of the English-speaking market and its competitive, commercial base as well as the intrinsic appeal of an open culture promising life, liberty, and the pursuit of happiness and the possibility of fame and fortune.

The emergence of a global culture shaped and dominated by the West in general and especially the great English-speaking arc stretching from Sydney to London and on to New York and Hollywood, spawned a research agenda that will remain at the center of the field well into the next century. In addition to obvious questions of cause and effect, related issues include the role of Western media in the revolutions of 1989, the growing influence of journalism in international relations, and the still-unanswered questions of the role of communication in social change. One central and emotional question is the flow of news around a world more and more tightly bound into an Anglo-American global news system.

News Flow

Only the casual traveler from the United States—and to a lesser extent, other parts of the English-speaking world—can be unaware of the extraordinary circumstance he or she encounters in even the most remote parts of the world: newspapers, news magazines, radio and television news from home. The careful observer will also note familiar logos and credits in local media as well as a heavy dose of American coverage. People from no other region can travel the globe so surrounded by their own media environment.

As in other areas of modern communication, Anglo-American dominance of global news flow seems to grow simultaneously with a decline in traditional areas of international influence. The growth of global news systems, which communication technology makes possible, strengthens the Anglo-American imprint on the news. Even a partial listing of the major players in global news—CNN, BBC, AP, Reuters, Murdoch, Turner—reinforces the tourist's experience that news around the world is essentially Anglo-American (Negrine & Papathanassopoulos, 1990).

The trend toward globalization raises new and important questions for communication research. Beyond the obvious ones of dominance and Western or Anglo-American influence, there are new issues related to the rise of global media moguls, new definitions of wealth and sovereignty, and new problems for governments that want to control their national media.

A curious and often ignored element in the globalization issue is how much of it is non-American, even though it exudes a "Made in U.S.A." feel. For the United States, an important issue is the speed with which its popular culture industry is being sold to foreigners: Three of the "big five" Hollywood studios are owned by foreign corporations; the largest book publisher in the United States is Germany's Bertelsmann; and magazines are now a top prize for foreign investors. The rapid development of new multimedia technology, and the surprising appearance of a fully digital high-definition television standard, may return some of the leadership in communication hardware back to the United States just as its dominance in software is diffused to a new generation of entrepreneurs outside the country.

The trend toward multinational corporate production of news and entertainment material is reflected in the rise of regional (if not truly global) organizations in most parts of the world (Tunstall & Palmer, 1991). Some are relatively well known: Televisa in Mexico, Rede Globo in Brazil, Hachette and Hersant in France, Bertlesmann and Kirch in Germany, the late Robert Maxwell's media empire in Britain. In a few countries (e.g., Brazil and Italy) modern media moguls have used their visibility and money to become important political figures. Together, with their mostly Anglo-American global partners and competitors, they are shaping a new global culture that promises to change the nature and distribution of power as surely as Gutenberg's printing press did a half millennium ago.

Studying Foreign Images

Although there are plenty of studies that could be conducted in international communication, examining a major research project already conducted provides a better
example of the problems and promises of international communication research. A
large-scale study of foreign news in the late 1970s, possibly the most ambitious
collaborative research undertaking in international communication, illustrates both the
value of international cooperation in research and the pitfalls of working without
agreement on even the most basic elements of theory and method. One of the original
designers dismissed the final project as "a textbook example of how social science can
be misused for political purposes," whereas another major participant, originally
skeptical, concluded that "this study helps clear the air of the pseudo debate" (Nordenstreng, 1984, p. 137) about NWICO assertions that "probably never were true and are
certainly no longer true" (p. 141).

At the UNESCO General Conference in Nairobi in 1976—the flash point of the
NWICO debate—the Nordic countries introduced a resolution calling for a study of
"the image of foreign countries representing different social systems and developmental stages as portrayed by mass-circulated press in respective countries." The chairman
of the Section for Communication of the Finnish National Commission for UNESCO,
which originated the proposal, was Kaarle Nordenstreng, long-time president of the
left-leaning International Organization of Journalists (IOJ) and activist professor of
journalism at the University of Tampere. The proposal was approved and passed to the
International Association for Mass Communication Research (IAMCR), an academic
organization then located in Britain with status as a UNESCO nongovernmental
organization. A simple, conventional content analysis project was designed at the
University of Leicester where IAMCR's president, James D. Halloran, was head of the
Center for Mass Communication Research. After some collaboration on the design
from continental colleagues, Halloran invited IAMCR members to sign on. Richard
Cole, of the University of North Carolina, volunteered to represent the United States
but soon became dean of the School of Journalism and passed major responsibility to
Robert Stevenson, who enlisted cooperation from Donald L. Shaw.

As the project took shape, several curiosities and weaknesses were noted. The design
itself was cumbersome and unimaginative, exactly the narrow quantitative American
approach that Europeans, including Halloran, had frequently criticized. Each foreign
story, for example, was to be coded onto four 80-column computer cards and included,
among a long list of descriptive variables, a complicated measure of standardized
column-centimeters. The format was redesigned to fit on one card with several added
variables. Only the main news section of newspapers was to be included, and the
sample weeks excluded Sundays; the effect was to eliminate most of the information
critics claimed Western media failed to report.

It was clear that the world the project examined was almost entirely Western with
a handful of other countries with a Western research tradition, such as Malaysia,
Lebanon, and India. Africa was represented only by Nigeria, the Communist "Second
World" omitted the Soviet Union and China, and Latin America was missing completely. The project was then expanded in several directions. Indiana University
researchers offered to examine files of the major Western news agencies; the United
States Information Agency (USIA) agreed to collect media samples from a number of

missing countries and to underwrite the cost of coding. The sample was expanded to include Sundays and the entire newspaper. As a result, data were supplied on the global news agencies and media of 17 countries; 12 national teams contributed their own data.

At a meeting of participants in Paris after the data were collected, a committee was appointed to write a final report from sets of tables supplied by each team (Sreberny-Mohammadi, Nordenstreng, Stevenson, & Ugboajah, 1985). Meanwhile, the wide-ranging data were subjected to various analyses and collected in a book (Stevenson & Shaw, 1984). Data were also passed on to other researchers for further analysis, first on tape and later on personal computer disks.

The UNESCO report was mildly controversial from the beginning. Nordenstreng, the instigator of the project and member of the writing committee, wanted to exclude all of the non-U. S. data from the report because it was not "official." As a compromise, the UNESCO monograph contained all the data, but not a qualitative summary of these countries. Nordenstreng also objected when the World Press Freedom Committee, organized to defend Western media in the NWICO/NWiCO debate, and Freedom House cited early conference papers. The debate was carried to the *Journal of Communication*, which published a summary of the results and two opposing interpretations of them.

For Nordenstreng (1984), it was the familiar "hijacking" of critical research:

> [the original] idea called for the use of a delicate methodological instrument that would get at the qualitative sphere of image building, instead of just employing conventional categories of content analysis such as topic/types of news, countries/regions, etc. The final project was dominated by "vulgar" categories that capture ad hoc aspects of the media content, rather than a comprehensive image carried by the content. (p. 139)

Further, "perhaps the greatest contribution of this enterprise has been through a negative case—by demonstrating the scientific inadequacy and political risks involved in one-sided quantitative consideration of mass media content" (pp. 141–142).

On the other hand, I concluded that the project demonstrated that the NWICO's ideological rhetoric was misplaced: "First, many of the charges against the Western media and news services are without evidence to support them. Second, the lack of difference among media of very different political systems argues against the theory of cultural imperialism. And third, much of the rhetoric addresses outdated questions" (Stevenson, 1984, p. 137). Results clearly did not support Nordenstreng's critical theory conclusions, a factor in his effort to disown his own creation.

By the time the UNESCO monograph appeared, the United States, Britain, and Singapore were leaving UNESCO, and the NWICO debate had largely burned itself out. If anything, however, the collapse of communism produced not Hegel's "end of history" but an increasingly complex and uncharted world in which communication plays a more central role. There is plenty of work and opportunities for both independent and collaborative researchers in international communication.

SUMMARY

Even without clear theoretical or methodological boundaries, and even with the confusion of politics and academics, international communication is a growing area.

Researchers looking for new theoretical understanding, as well as those concerned with offering useful guidance to policy-makers, have a rich and largely unexplored terrain to explore. The world offers a fascinating and increasingly diverse array of cultures to serve as a laboratory for research in which individual and social differences are explained by national and cultural differences. In that quest, the same kinds of questions that have guided research and separated scholarship from polemic for generations are still useful.

What?   Good descriptive research is still needed, and the world offers more and more examples of interesting cultures and media systems. Of special interest are the "off-diagonal" systems that vary from the general pattern: small countries that sustain a vibrant indigenous culture, developing nations with independent media, successful marriage of Western influence and tradition. Of course, the researcher's traditional protections of reliability and validity of observation and adequacy of evidence are especially important when venturing outside of one's own environment.

Why?   Implicit in even descriptive research is some hint of explanation. If anything is needed in American academic research, it is a willingness to offer explanation of interesting or important phenomena and to subject hypotheses or conjectures to the glare of critical test. Anything in the definition of *international communication* offered above requires the researcher to address the question of *why* and assumes, in almost all cases, that the true definition lies somewhere in culture or nation.

So What?   Not all explanations are equal in value to practitioners or theory builders, and not all research questions carry implications that justify the drudgery that research entails. Some of the implications in the examples offered here and many of the implications of the published literature are vulnerable to the *so what?* question. Although harsh, it is better asked before one begins a research project than at the end.

Why Bother?   Too much international communication research fails both the *why?* and *so what?* questions, but even if a study can provide both explanation and implication, it may not address a very important question or add a very useful data point to the body of knowledge. The question of importance can be theoretical or pragmatic. Replicating an agenda-setting study or documenting American media influence in one more country is not likely to add to theory or offer useful guidance to policy makers.

Researchers can avoid the awkward silences that often follow these questions by thinking about them in advance. What will the presentation of results look like? If results are contrary to expectations, will it make any difference? Will the "suggestions for further research" be anything more than a summary of what I should have done in the first place? And, of course, *so what?* And, why even bother to conduct this research?

The clarity of hindsight is nearly perfect, but some of its revelations can be avoided with good advance planning. Any research project consumes enough time and energy and resources that we ought not to depend on serendipity and clever data analysis to avoid the awkward silences that often follow these four questions. Good ideas are rare in international communication research, but the area is important enough that the innovative and thoughtful researcher can find a productive research career and a guarantee of encounters with interesting people, places, and ideas.

REFERENCES

Bottomore, T. (1984). *The Frankfurt School*. London: Tavistock.

Blumler, J. (1985). European-American differences in communication research. In E. M. Rogers & F. Balle (Eds.), *The media revolution in America & western Europe* (pp. 185–199). Norwood, NJ: Ablex.

Delia, J. G. (1987). Communication research: A history. In C. R. Berger & S. H. Chaffee (Eds.), *Handbook of communication science* (pp. 2–98). Beverly Hills: Sage.

Ferment in the field [special section]. (1983). *Journal of Communication, 33.*

Genovese, E. D. (1994). The crimes of communism: What did you know and when did you know it? *Dissent, 41,* 371–376.

Hachten, W. (1992). *The world news prism; Changing media, clashing ideologies* (3rd ed.). Ames, IA: Iowa State University Press.

Lazarsfeld, P. F. (1941). Remarks on administrative and critical research. *Studies in Philosophy and Social Science, 9,* 2–16.

Lerner, D. (1958). *The passing of traditional society; modernizing the Middle East*. Glencoe, IL: Free Press.

Levy, M. R., & M. Gurevitch. (Eds.). (1994). *Defining media studies: Reflections on the future of the field*. New York: Oxford University Press. (Original work published 1993)

Merrill, J. C. (Ed.). (1995). *Global journalism: Survey of international communication* (3rd ed.). New York: Longman.

Negrine, R., & Papathanassopoulos, S. (1990). *The internationalization of television*. London: Pinter.

Nordenstreng, K. (1984). Bitter lessons. *Journal of Communication, 34,* 138–142.

Paisley, W. (1984). Communication in the communication sciences. In B. Dervin & M. J. Voigt (Eds.), *Progress in the communication sciences,* (Vol. 5, pp. 1–43). Norwood, NJ: Ablex.

Rogers, E. M. (1985). The empirical and critical schools of communication research. In E. M. Rogers & F. Balle (Eds.), *The media revolution in America & western Europe* (pp. 219–235). Norwood, NJ: Ablex.

Rogers, E. M. (1976). Communication and development: the passing of the dominant paradigm. In E. M. Rogers (Ed.), *Communication and development: Critical perspectives*. Beverly Hills, CA: Sage.

Rogers, E. M. (1962). *Diffusion of innovations*. New York: Free Press.

Rostow, W. W. (1960). *The stages of economic growth*. Cambridge: Cambridge University Press.

Schramm, W. (1964). *Mass media and national development: The rule of information in developing countries*. Stanford, CA: Stanford University Press.

Southerland, D. (1993, July 17). Uncounted millions: Mass death in Mao's China. *The Washington Post,* pp. A1, A22.

Southerland, D. (1993, July 18). Uncounted millions: Mass death in Mao's China. *The Washington Post,* pp. A1, A13.

Sreberny-Mohammadi, A., with Nordenstreng, K., Stevenson, R., & Ugboajah, F. (1985). *Foreign news in the media: International reporting in 29 countries*. Reports and Papers on Mass Communication No. 93. Paris: UNESCO.

Stacks, D. W., Hickson, M. L., & Hill, S. R. (1990). *An introduction to communication theory*. Fort Worth, TX: Holt, Rinehart & Winston.

Stevenson, R. L. (1992). Defining international communication as a field. *Journalism Quarterly, 69,* 543–553.

Stevenson, R. L. (1988). *Communication, development, and the third world: The global politics of information*. New York: Longman.

Stevenson, R. L. (1984). Pseudo debate. *Journal of Communication, 34,* 134–138.

Stevenson, R. L., & Shaw, D. L. (Eds.). (1984). *Foreign news and the new world information order*. Ames, IA: Iowa State University Press.

Tunstall, J. (1982). The media are still American: Anglo-American media in the world after the UNESCO MacBride report. In L. E. Atwood, S. J. Bullion, & S. M. Murphy (Eds.), *International perspectives on news* (pp. 133–145). Carbondale: Southern Illinois University Press.

Tunstall, J., & Palmer, M. (1991). *Media moguls*. London: Routledge. World of the news [special section]. (1984). *Journal of Communication, 34,* 121–142.

13

Violence and Sex in the Media

Jennings Bryant
Dolf Zillmann
University of Alabama

Perhaps no area of mass communication research has greater social implications than that on how violence and sex are portrayed in the media. This chapter examines both media violence and sexually explicit media fare as they affect the viewer. The chapter begins by looking at the role of violence in the media, reasons for that role, and the effect of violent media fare on individuals and on society. We then focus on the effects of sexually explicit media. The methods employed in conducting research in media sex and violence are then explored, and a sample study is provided.

MEDIA VIOLENCE

More research has been conducted on media violence than on any other media effects topic; some scholars estimate upwards of 3,000 studies (Huston et al., 1992). Gunter (1994) addressed the origins of the concern manifest in this robust research tradition:

> Concern about media violence has its roots in the unease that has historically been expressed whenever a new entertainment or communications medium that appeals to the

masses appears on the scene. Strong reactions were recorded on the appearance of popular romantic and adventure novels in the 19th century and were observed again in response to the growing popularity of motion pictures in the early part of the present century. (p. 163)

Similarly, in recent years, much public concern has been expressed about violence in television, video games, and newer communications media.

What is Violence?

Perhaps the first question that should be addressed is, "What is violence?" Three common definitions of *violence* are:

- "intentional physical harm to another individual. Excluded from this definition are accidental injury, so-called 'psychological' violence, and vandalism of property" (Harris, 1994, p. 186);
- "the overt expression of physical force (with or without a weapon, against self or other) compelling action against one's will on pain of being hurt and/or killed or threatened to be so victimized as part of the plot" (Gerbner, Gross, Morgan, & Signorielli, 1980, p. 11); and
- "hostile and intentional acts of one person against another through physical force" (NCTV Says Violence Up 16%, 1983, p. 63).

Obviously *media violence* is this kind of behavior depicted or presented in or on media.

Why Do Media Feature Violence?

Media programming includes a great deal of violence for several reasons. Violence embodies conflict, and conflict is the heart and soul of drama. Moreover, violence is a quick and easy way to solve problems; it is a convenient short-cut to more complex forms of conflict resolution. However, by far the most compelling reason for including violence is that producers, directors, writers, and editors believe that many audience members will not choose to watch, listen to, or read the media messages they offer if these messages do not contain fist fights, shootings, car crashes, and assorted other mayhem. Time after time, media message creators and providers rationalize heavy doses of gratuitous violence by saying, "we're only giving people what they want," or "they'll go elsewhere for entertainment if we don't stick in some violence" (e.g., Easton, 1993).

Despite numerous claims for the appeal of violence, empirical evidence to support such claims is quite sparse. Diener and colleagues (Diener & DeFour, 1978; Diener & Woody, 1981) found that viewers either exhibit no preferences or slight preferences for violent content when choosing media fare. On the other hand, Bryant and Musburger (1989) reported that child viewers rated a violent version of an animated television program significantly higher in enjoyment than humorous, action-packed, or control versions of the same program. Taken together, these investigations provide some limited evidence to substantiate the creative community's claims that the public likes media violence. But, in general, the appeal of violence does not seem to be nearly as strong as writers, producers, and editors would have us believe.

What Theories Help Explain the Effects of Media Violence?

To answer this question thoroughly, several categories of effects of media violence on individuals should be considered: behavioral, cognitive, and emotional.

Behavioral Theories.   Potential behavioral effects of media violence include: catharsis, disinhibition, imitation, and desensitization. *Catharsis* holds that vicariously participating in others' fictionalized hostility or aggression enables drama watchers, readers, or listeners to be purged of their anger and hostility and thereby become less aggressive. Although much of the general public and the media creative community believe strongly in the therapeutic benefits of catharsis, scientific evidence tends not to support this popular truism (e.g., Feshback, 1955, 1961; cf., Wells, 1973). Moreover, the few studies that would appear to support cathartic effects of media violence have been severely criticized on technical grounds (Berkowitz, 1993).

The idea of *disinhibition* is that watching, reading, or listening to media violence may serve to undermine learned social sanctions against using violence that usually inhibit aggressive behavior. This reduced inhibition from watching media violence enables people to legitimize using violence in real life, so they become more aggressive. At least a dozen experimental investigations have explored potential disinhibition effects of media violence, and all provided some support for this hypothesis (e.g., Berkowitz, 1964, 1965; Donnerstein, 1980; Malamuth, 1984). In general, disinhibition effects have been more pronounced when viewers of violence were already angry while they viewed or read violent media fare (Berkowitz, 1974).

Discussions of *imitation* of media violence typically are explained in terms of social learning theory, which proposes that humans "have evolved an advanced capacity for observational learning that enables them to expand their knowledge and skills on the basis of information conveyed by modeling influences" (Bandura, 1994, p. 66). Because the fictional characters of novels, television, motion pictures, and video games so often use violence to solve their problems, young viewers may learn that violent behavior is a useful and appropriate way of handling tough situations. A great number of investigations offered support for imitation effects.

In its most basic form, social learning theory explains how observers match the performances of models. For social learning of media violence to occur, four things must happen: The violent behavior of the actor must be seen, read, or listened to (attentional process); cognitive representations of the violent behavior must be retained (retention processes); the learner must have the potential to replicate the action (production processes); and the learner must have sufficient desire or will to perform the violent behavior that was witnessed (motivational processes; Bandura, 1979). The best-known early empirical examination of the modeling of violence were Bandura's Bobo doll studies (e.g., Bandura, 1965; Bandura, Ross, & Ross, 1963; Bandura & Walters, 1963). In a typical Bobo doll study, young children watched someone (either live or on film) behave aggressively toward a large inflatable doll designed to serve as a punching bag. The children were later placed in a playroom with a Bobo doll, and their behavior was observed. It was found that children frequently imitated violent behaviors of this type, whether the aggressive model was live or on film.

Recently, a great deal of attention has been paid to so-called desensitization effects of media violence. The desensitization hypothesis argues that repeated exposure to media violence causes a reduction in emotional responsiveness (i.e., habituation) to violence in fiction, news, and reality fare, which, in turn, leads to an increased acceptance of violence in real life. This notion has been widely touted to explain, for example, why onlookers failed to come to the aid of mugging victims—not even making an anonymous phone call to the police from the privacy of their homes. Few studies have sought to assess disinhibition effects directly. The limited research evidence available supports disinhibition effects (Gunter, 1994).

Cognitive Theories.   The study of media violence from a cognitive effects perspective refers to changes in people's beliefs, values, and attitudes that result from consuming violent media fare. In modern society, media increasingly provide vital information about life that may corroborate, contradict, or supplement learning that takes place from first-hand experience or information provided second-hand through interpersonal sources, including teachers. One area in which media appear to play an important role is in the public's perceptions about crime, especially violent crime. One theoretical perspective on media effects, cultivation analysis (see chapter 8, this volume), was utilized extensively to examine cognitive effects of heavy viewing of television's crime-laden action drama. Gerbner and associates (e.g., Gerbner, Gross, Morgan, & Signorielli, 1994) provided evidence that heavy exposure to television drama's overly violent world cultivates exaggerated perceptions of violence in viewers' own social reality.

Priming is another example of cognitive effects of television violence. Priming "essentially holds that when people witness, read, or hear of an event via the mass media, ideas having a similar meaning are activated in them for a short time afterwards, and . . . these thoughts in turn can activate other semantically related ideas and action tendencies" (Jo & Berkowitz, 1994, p. 45). Priming has been used to explain a number of cognitive effects from witnessing violence in the mass media, including the priming of aggressive thoughts that can cause alterations in the way people interpret the actions of others, changes in beliefs about the justification of the aggressive behaviors of others, and reductions in inhibitions about participating in aggressive behavior.

Emotional Theories.   Not all emotional effects of media violence are necessarily negative; in fact, many short-term emotional effects are essential to the enjoyment of drama, and their absence frequently leaves our entertainment experience flat. To make entertainment maximally enjoyable, we must laugh with the comic, suffer anxiety as the villain stalks the victim, experience elevated excitation at the suspense peak of the action drama, and "root, root, root for the home team" on the sportscast. All of these emotional effects are part of what we seek from entertainment, and many of them are precipitated by violence.

Because autonomic arousal in response to media depictions is largely nonspecific to particular emotions, however, it may have some unwanted behavioral consequences. Excitation transfer theory

> projects that, because of the comparatively slow decay of autonomic arousal (owing to humoral processes involved) and the individual's capacity to recognize stimulus changes and to select an appropriate response quasi-instantaneously (owing to speedy neural transmission), residues of excitation from a preceding affective reaction will *combine*

with excitation produced by subsequent affective stimulation and thereby cause an *overly intense* affective reaction to the subsequent stimulus. (Zillmann, 1991, p. 116)

It should be noted that the "residues of excitation" do not have to come from arousal to media violence (they can come from physical exertion, sexual arousal, feelings of annoyance, or a variety of other arousing sources), nor does excitation favor hostile, aggressive, or violent reactions (if prosocial responses are motivated, these responses are likely to be energized). However, if aggressive behavior has been instigated in the viewers and aggressive dispositions exist, residual arousal from media violence has been found to intensify motivated asocial feelings and destructive actions (e.g., Zillmann, 1971; cf. Zillmann, 1991).

In recent years, scholarly attention has been focused on another emotional effect of media violence: fright reactions in children. Cantor (1994) and associates have conducted programmatic research into what type of media violence frightens children, developmental differences in fright reactions, and strategies for preventing or reducing unwanted fear reactions. Their emphasis has been on *"immediate emotional response[s]* [italics added] that [are] typically of relatively short duration, but that may endure, on occasion, for several hours or days, or even longer" (Cantor, 1994, p. 214). This research takes on added importance because of recent trends in media programming for children that incorporate scary and horrific depictions, and because of the increased access of children to what has traditionally been considered programming for adults. Several interesting findings have been advanced by this research tradition, especially with regard to developmental differences in children's fear:

- "pre-school children . . . are more likely to be frightened by something that *looks* scary but is actually harmless than by something that looks attractive but is actually harmful; for older elementary school children. . . appearance carries much less weight, relative to the behavior or destructive potential of a character, animal, or object" (Cantor, 1994, pp. 231–232);
- "as children mature, they become more responsive to realistic, and less responsive to fantastic dangers depicted in the media" (Cantor, 1994, p. 233); and
- "as children mature, they become frightened by media depictions involving increasingly abstract concepts" (Cantor, 1994, p. 233).

We have briefly reviewed some of the behavioral, cognitive, and emotional effects of media violence. We would be remiss, however, if we failed to note that most of the impact of media violence is a product of cognitive, emotional, and behavioral elements combined. This very complexity is one circumstance that makes the effects of media violence so difficult to determine.

What are the Effects of Media Violence?

Perhaps the most reliable answer to this critical question comes from the results of macroanalyses of research on the effects of media violence, including (a) syntheses of longitudinal investigations of the effects of media violence, and (b) meta-analyses, which offer a method for integrating the results of different studies on the same topic so as to get a better understanding of the "big picture." Regarding the studies examining cumulative effects, Huesmann and Miller (1994) concluded: "The data available from longitudinal studies provide additional support for the hypothesis that television violence viewing leads to the development of aggressive behavior" (p. 181).

Andison (1977) conducted a meta-analysis of 31 laboratory experiments in media violence and concluded that, overall, viewing violence led to greater aggression than viewing control materials. Much later, Wood, Wong, and Chachere (1991) conducted a meta-analysis of 28 separate experiments in which the participants were free to display "natural aggression." The authors noted that media violence did tend to heighten the likelihood of aggressive behavior and added that "the mean effect of exposure to violent media on unconstrained aggression is in the small to moderate range, typical of social psychological predictors" (p. 379). Comstock and Paik (1991) macroanalyzed more than 185 different media violence investigations and concluded that the association between exposure to television violence and aggression is quite robust: "The data of the past decade and a half strengthens [sic] rather than weakens [*sic*] the case that television violence increases aggressive and anti-social behavior" (p. 54). Finally, Centerwall (1989, 1992) conducted epidemiological and population intervention studies of television violence, comparing homicide rates over a 30-year period (1945-1975) in the United States, Canada, and South Africa. The intervention on homicide rates was television set ownership. The results of this investigation were instrumental in the American Academy of Pediatrics' development of a policy statement urging parents to restrict their children's use of television to no more than two hours per day and to omit violent fare from their children's TV diet. Centerwall (1992) has not been timid in his condemnation of television violence. For example, his findings and recommendations published in *The Journal of the American Medical Association* categorically stated:

- "the epidemiological evidence indicates that if, hypothetically, television technology had never been developed, there would be 10,000 fewer homicides each year in the United States, 70,000 fewer rapes, and 700,000 fewer injurious assaults." (p. 3059)

And elsewhere:

- "Children's exposure to television and television violence should become part of the public health agenda, along with safety seats, bicycle helmets, immunizations and good nutrition." (p. 3063)

SEXUALLY EXPLICIT MEDIA FARE

Whereas the issue of media violence has received more sytematic research than any other area of media effects inquiry, Kinsey, Pomeroy, and Martin (1948) noted that human sexuality has received more thought, dicussion, and treatment than any other aspect of human behavior. Additionally, a variety of neuroendocrine and physiological connections are known to exist between sexual desire, arousal, and behavior, on the one hand, and aggressive actions, on the other (Zillmann, 1984). Sexual arousal is capable of enhancing aggression and, likewise, aggression-linked arousal is capable of intensifying sexual experience. This connection between sex and aggression gives added significance to the analysis of the effects of sexual material in the media.

It is little wonder then that numerous scholars have examined the effects of sexually explicit materials on readers, listeners, viewers, and users. It should be noted at the outset that sexually explicit communication is nothing new: Statuary featuring enlarged sexual organs dates back to 30,000 BC; human sexual intercourse was depicted in sandstone engravings from 7,000 BC; and explicit scenes of hetero- and homosexual activity were common in ancient Greece. So today's XXX adult videos, dedicated sex channels on premium cable tiers, pulp novels, slasher films, specialized magazines for those with exotic sexual fetishes, 1-900 hot hotlines, and sexually explicit computer games and bulletin boards (BBS) are but modern adaptations of a centuries-old tradition of sexually explicit material.

Then what is all the fuss about? Other than violations of moral sensibilities, which undoubtedly have accompanied the presentaion of sexual material in every generation, the modern-day uproar about sexual content in media has to do with easy access. "The principal reason for the apparent revival of concerns about unregulated poronography is simply the new technology" (Zillmann & Bryant, 1989, p. xii). Sexually explicit fare has gone public. It has become an affordable and readily available form of entertainment for all—children and adults alike. This has precipitated a revitalized interest in the impact of sexually explicit media content (e.g., Greenberg, 1994).

Whenever sex in media is discussed, definitions are almost mandatory. Terms such as *sexually explicit*, *erotic*, and *pornographic* have very different meanings for different people. In the 1986 *Final Report of the Surgeon General's Commission on Pornography*, five classes of pornographic materials were identified:

1. Sexually violent materials portray rape and other instances of physical harm to persons in a sexual context.
2. Nonviolent materials depicting degradation, domination, subordination, or humiliation constitute the largest class of commercially available materials. These generally portray women as "masochistic, subservient, and overresponsive to the male interest."
3. Nonviolent and nondegrading materials typically depict a couple having vaginal or oral intercourse with no indication of violence or coercion.
4. Nudity shows the naked human body with no obvious sexual behavior or intent.
5. Child pornography involves minors and, though illegal to produce in the United States, still circulates widely through foreign magazines and personal distribution (Harris, 1994, p. 248).

What Are the Effects of Viewing Sexually Explicit Materials?

The first effect is neither anti- or prosocial per se—it is sexual arousal. Viewing, reading, or listening to sexually explicit material causes elevated arousal in most people, whether the arousal is measured in self-reports, physiologically, or in direct genital measures, such as penile tumescence or vaginal engorgement. Contrary to what might be expected, the level of arousal is not accurately predicted by the degree of explicitness of the sexual materials. In fact, there are major individual differences in what arouses people sexually (e.g., Bancroft & Mathews, 1971).

Viewing or reading certain types of sexual materials has also been associated with cognitive effects—changes in perceptions, attitudes, and values, for example. One dimension of this is the cognitive component of disinhibition; that is, people's attitudes toward sex become less restricted after prolonged exposure to sexual fare. Evidence exists for other changes in attitudes and values after exposure to sexually explicit media as well. For example, prolonged exposure to sexually explicit messages was found to produce changes in sexual callousness, rape proclivity, moral values, family values, perception of normalcy in sexual behavior, attitudes toward censorship, general attitudes toward women, and many other cognitive effects (e.g., Zillmann, Bryant, & Huston, 1994).

A wide range of behavioral effects of using sexually explicit materials has been examined, including imitation, disinhibition, and criminal sexual behavior. In general, the evidence for imitation is anecdotal, because scientists are not willing—and often not permitted by university research regulations—to risk showing immature children sexually explicit materials to see if they can and will model the behavior they see. The *Final Report* and several other sources present a number of such anecdotes, ranging from an accidental suicide by hanging while reading and apparently imitating a "recipe" for autoerotic asphyxiation in *Hustler*, to reports of the forced bondage, rape, murder, and mutilation of an 8-year-old girl after her perpetrators read about and viewed photographs of bondage in *Penthouse*. Just how widespread such instances are has yet to be evaluated systematically (Harris, 1994).

As is the case with violence, disinhibition of sexual behavior is an issue with sexually explicit materials. This is especially critical because so many of the behaviors depicted in such materials are contrary to the prevalent norms about sexual behavior. Consider the case of rape. There is evidence that witnessing the brutal coercion of women into sexual intercourse enhanced college men's reporting that they might commit a rape if they were sure they would not get caught (Check & Guloien, 1989).

One of the behavioral effects areas where definitive research is likely never to be conducted involves sex crimes. Ethical and procedural constraints prohibit experimental research in this area. Scientists thus have resorted to procedures such as interviewing and developing clinical case studies of convicted sex criminals to determine the role of sexual materials in the etiology of such crimes, or they have studied archival evidence to determine the degree of association or correlation between changes in the availability of sexually explicit materials in a society and court records of crimes such as rape, exhibitionism, and child molestation. The results are more confusing than informative, and they may have generated more heat than light. For example, in Denmark and Japan, increases in the availability of sexually explicit materials were associated with decreases in the reporting of sex crimes. In Australia, the United States, and many other Western nations, the opposite pattern of association was found (*Final Report of the Surgeon General's Commission on Pornography*, 1986). At present, no firm conclusion can be drawn from this evidence. It would appear that cultural values, attitudes toward sex in a society, and many other conditions operate in concert in mediating the effects of sexual materials on sex crimes.

A large body of research has presented evidence for the effects of the consumption of sexual materials on aggression. Many of the complex arguments associated with this issue are beyond the scope of this chapter. Suffice it to report that several studies have demonstrated that prolonged use of nonviolent sexual materials is capable of facilitating aggression (e.g., Baron, 1979; cf., Zillmann, Bryant, Comisky, & Medoff, 1981). Other studies have yielded evidence that was interpreted as supporting the thesis that aggression increases only when material featuring sexual violence (e.g., rape scenes, or slasher films) is consumed (e.g., Linz, Donnerstein, & Penrod, 1984; Linz, Donnerstein, & Adams, 1989). Other research seems to suggest that the effects on aggression are more pronounced for consumption of sexual violence but exist to a lesser extent for nonviolent, sexually explicit fare (e.g., *Final Report of the Surgeon General's Commission on Pornography,* 1986; Lyons, Anderson, & Larson, 1994). Still other scholars argue that the keys to explaining these apparently conflicting findings are whether women or men depicted in the films, books, magazines, or videos are demeaned or dehumanized, whether the viewer becomes disgusted or sexually excited by what he or she sees or reads, and many other elements associated with media message features and individual differences in users (e.g., Malamuth, Check, & Briere, 1986; Sapolsky & Zillman, 1981; White, 1979). How and if these issues will ever be resolved satisfactorily remains unclear. In the interim, during which time we hope that clarifying research will be conducted, evidence from (a) a meta-analysis of 81 studies on the effects on aggression and other behavioral effects of viewing sexually explicit materials, and (b) a meta-analysis of 24 articles examining the effects of exposure to pornography on acceptance of rape myths urges user caution: *Caveat emptor*—using sexually explicit materials may be harmful to your psychological well-being and to that of others in society (Allen, Emmers, Gebhardt, & Giery, 1995; Lyons et al., 1994).

METHODS USED IN MEDIA VIOLENCE AND SEX RESEARCH

Scholars concerned with the effects of media sex and violence have asked such a range of research questions that it has been necessary to exploit the full repertoire of extant communication research methodologies to provide adequate answers. In fact, research into the effects of media sex and violence has produced several classic communication studies.

Content Analyses.   Since 1967, Gerbner and his associates (e.g., Gerbner et al., 1994) conducted a number of influential content analyses of media violence (among other variables of interest to their Cultural Indicators research program). Their "message system" analysis studies have tracked the nature and functions of television violence for portions of four decades, thereby providing invaluable indicators of various aspects of the evolution of television violence. No comparable longitudinal content analytic research tradition has been established for media sex; however, a recent review of content trends in media sex by Greenberg (1994) identified a dozen systematic content analyses of sex in media.

Laboratory Experiments.   If research into the effect of media violence would be assigned an archetype methodology, it would be the laboratory experiment. According to Geen (1994), there have been a vast number of laboratory experiments on the effects of televised violence on aggression. The most generally accepted conclusion from these investigations is that "observation of violence is often followed by increases in both physical and verbal aggression. This effect is most likely to occur when the viewer has been provoked in some way and is therefore relatively likely to aggress" (p. 152). Numerous designs and a wide range of experimental materials have been employed by researchers in investigating the effects of media violence. Although the designs and materials have varied dramatically, most have included violent media message versus nonviolent media message treatment conditions.

Lyons et al. (1994) included 81 experiments in their meta-analysis of the effects of sexually explicit fare; the majority of these studies were laboratory experiments. They concluded: "Although there are a number of methodological shortcomings in this literature, most are likely to lead to an underestimation of the causal effects of exposure to pornography. Despite this, the vast majority of studies demonstrates consistent short-term effects" (p. 305). Obviously lab studies have been central to our understanding of the effects of pornography as well as of media violence.

Whenever laboratory experiments are employed to help us better understand human communication behavior, criticisms are apt to be voiced. These criticisms include claims that laboratory environments are artificial, resulting in weak ecological validity; that the sort of dependent measures that can be employed in the lab are pale analogs of real-world antisocial manifestations of sex and violence (e.g., murder, rape); that most research participants in laboratory research tend to be college freshmen and sophomores selected by convenience sampling; that demand characteristics and experimenter expectations create invalid results; and the like. In truth, all of these criticisms are valid in some instances and do create undue limitations for some laboratory research. Nonetheless, a number of noteworthy lab studies have investigated the effects of media sex and violence, and when issues of media cause and effect are concerned, the alternatives typically are less credible, especially to policymakers. That is why laboratory experiments have proven to be so valuable in these research arenas.

Field Experiments.   In recent years, researchers have attempted to employ the rigors of experimental methodology while leaving the confines of the laboratory to conduct "field experiments." Regarding media violence, "these studies yielded consistent findings of a positive relationship between observation of televised violence and aggression" (Geen, 1994, p. 152). Similar findings of antisocial influences have been found from field experiments testing the effects of pornography (e.g., Zillmann & Bryant, 1989).

Longitudinal Studies.   With the growing realization that many media effects occur only after cumulative exposure to media messages, frequently over extended periods of time, longitudinal studies into the effects of media sex and violence have been conducted. In the area of television violence, research by Eron and his associates (e.g., Eron, Walder, & Lefkowitz, 1971; Lefkowitz, Eron, Walder, & Huesmann, 1977; Huesmann & Eron, 1986) revealed "a positive relationship between childhood television viewing and subsequent aggressiveness" (Geen, 1994, p. 153). Correspondingly, regarding prolonged consumption of pornography, longitudinal research by Zillmann and Bryant (e.g., 1982, 1986, 1988a, 1988b), Check (1985), Linz (1985), Weaver (1987), and others revealed social and psychological harm from exposure to pornography.

Surveys.   Scientific surveys have not played nearly as major a role in examining the effects of media sex and violence as they have in, say, attitude research. Nonetheless, surveys have been utilized productively in these areas. For example, Gerbner's cultivation analysis research has consistently used national surveys to determine public perceptions, anxiety, fear, and the like (e.g., Gerbner et al., 1994). Or, to cite just one example of such methodology applied to pornography research, an exemplary survey reported by the 1970 Presidential Commission on Obscenity and Pornography and conducted by Davis and Braught (1970) concluded, "One finds exposure to pornography is the strongest predictor of sexual deviance among the early age of exposure subjects" (p. 205).

Meta-Analyses.   The traditions of research on the effects of media sex and violence are sufficiently mature at this point to permit meta-analyses. In fact, in prior sections of this chapter entitled "What are the effects of media violence?" and "What are the effects of viewing sexually explicit materials?" meta-analyses were utilized to help define "the bottom line." Clearly, as research traditions in media sex and violence continue to develop, meta-analyses will become increasingly useful macro-analytic tools for developing accurate, sensitive profiles of media effects.

SAMPLE STUDY

We said that laboratory experiments are the archetype of investigations into the effects of explicitly sexual and explicitly violent media fare; therefore, our sample study should be a lab experiment. Let's be ambitious and tackle a complex media effects question: Which facilitates interpersonal aggression most dramatically: (a) explicitly sexual but nonviolent media fare, (b) explicitly violent but nonsexual media content, or (c) explicitly sexual *and* explicitly violent media programming?

If you review the earlier sections of this chapter, you will find that both sex and violence have been found to facilitate aggression. If we have reason to believe that the effects on aggressive behavior of viewing explicit sex and explicit violence are additive, we would hypothesize the consuming media presentations featuring both sex and violence would produce the most intense levels of interpersonal aggression.

If we choose to test this admittedly oversimplified hypothesis, we would be wise to include a control communication condition that features neither sexual nor violent content. This inclusion yields a communication condition independent variable with four treatment levels (sex, violence, sex plus violence, no sex/no violence control).

Based on prior research, we also anticipate that previously provoked research participants will be more likely to engage in aggressive behavior than their unprovoked peers, so we decide to include a second independent variable of motivation to aggress (provoked, unprovoked) and test a second hypothesis, that provoked individuals will be more aggressive than unprovoked ones.

The most efficient design we can use in our laboratory experiment is a 4 (treatment level) x 2 (motivation to aggress) factorial design. This design features four levels of the communication condition and two of motivation to aggress.

Our dependent measure of aggression is the level of intensity of noxious noise research participants choose to deliver to their opponent's ear (actually a confederate's ear) in the course of playing an electronic battleship game. In this game, the confederate's performance is a constant.

One of the keys to success in this investigation is the quality of the experimental materials employed for the communication variable. Because we are communication researchers who have unlimited access to the latest in digital multimedia production and editing facilities (dreaming's cheap!), we have created a 30-minute dramatic video presentation that varies only in a three-minute provocation segment. In the explicit violent version, the villain brutally batters a female hero-protagonist; in the explicit sex version, he seduces her to achieve his dastardly ends; in the explicit sex plus violence version, a brutal rape is employed to achieve the same ends; and in the control condition, the villain uses his brain and rhetorical prowess to momentarily outwit the hero. After the provocation sequence has ended, the hero regains control and brings the villain to justice.

At the end of the video, the research participant—who has either been provoked or unprovoked prior to viewing, according to the assigned motivation-to-aggress condition—participates in the battleship game. On six occasions during the game, the opponent misses the battleship by a prescribed distance. The cumulative intensity of noxious noise the research participant delivers as feedback to the opponent is the dependent measure of aggression.

The data will be analyzed by analysis of variance utilizing packaged statistical programs (e.g., SPSS, SAS). If research participants who see the televised rape (sex plus violence) use a significantly higher level of noxious noise than research participants in the other communication conditions, the first hypothesis will be supported. If those research participants who are provoked prior to viewing utilize higher levels of noxious noise than the unprovoked research participants, the second hypothesis will be supported. We will also pay considerable attention to potential interactions between communication condition and motivation to aggress, but such considerations are beyond the scope of the present investigation.

SUMMARY

This chapter examined the place of violence and sex in modern media presentations. It also considered the unintended social and psychological consequences these sensational elements can have. For both sex and violence, undesirable effects can occur for media consumers under some conditions. Some of the research methods that are typically utilized to examine the uses and effects of sex and violence and media were reviewed; and a sample hypothetical study that could be used to investigate the effects of sex and violence in media was presented. This brief treatment should lead you to want to learn more about this important area of media effects inquiry.

REFERENCES

Allen, M., Emmers, T., Gebhardt, L., & Giery, M. A. (1995). Exposure to pornography and acceptance of rape myths. *Journal of Communication, 45,* 5–26.

Andison, F. (1977). TV violence and viewer aggression: A cumulation of study results, 1956-1976. *Public Opinion Quarterly, 41,* 314–331.

Bancroft, L., & Mathews, A. (1971). Autonomic correlates of penile erection. *Journal of Psychosomatic Research, 15,* 159–167.

Bandura, A. (1965). Influence of models' reinforcement contingencies on the acquisition of imitative responses. *Journal of Personality and Social Psychology, 1,* 585–595.

Bandura, A. (1979). Psychological mechanisms of aggression. In M. vonCranach, K. Foppa, W. Lepeies, & D. Ploog (Eds.), *Human ethology: Claims and limits of a new discipline* (pp. 316–379). Cambridge: Cambridge University Press.

Bandura, A. (1994). Social cognitive theory of mass communication. In J. Bryant & D. Zillmann (Eds.), *Media effects: Advances in theory and research* (pp. 61–90). Hillsdale, NJ: Lawrence Erlbaum Associates.

Bandura, A., Ross, D., & Ross, S. A. (1963). Imitation of film-mediated aggressive models. *Journal of Abnormal and Social Psychology, 66,* 3–11.

Bandura, A., & Walters, R. H. (1963). *Social learning and personality development.* New York: Holt, Rinehart & Winston.

Baron, R. A. (1979). Heightened sexual arousal and physical aggression. *Journal of Research in Personality, 13,* 91–102.

Berkowitz, L. (1964). The effects of observing violence. *Scientific American, 210,* 35–41.

Berkowitz, L. (1965). Some aspects of observed aggression. *Journal of Personality and Social Psychology, 2,* 359–369.

Berkowitz, L. (1974). Some determinants of impulsive aggression: Role of mediated associations with reinforcements for aggression. *Psychological Review, 81,* 165–176.

Berkowitz, L. (1993). *Aggression: Its causes, consequences, and control.* Philadelphia: Temple University Press.

Bryant, J., & Musburger, R. (1989, April). *Children's enjoyment of action, violence, and humor in animated television programs.* Paper presented at the Annual Convention of the Broadcast Education Association, Las Vegas, NV.

Cantor, J. R. (1994). Fright reactions to mass media. In J. Bryant & D. Zillmann (Eds.), *Media effects: Advances in theory and research* (pp. 213–145). Hillsdale, NJ: Lawrence Erlbaum Associates.

Centerwall, B. S. (1989). Exposure to television as a cause of violence. In G. A. Comstock (Ed.), *Public communication and behavior* (Vol. 2, pp. 1–53). Orlando: Academic Press.

Centerwall, B. S. (1992). Television and violence: The scale of the problem and where to go from here. *Journal of the American Medical Association, 267,* 3059–3063.

Check, J. V. P. (1985). *The effects of violent and nonviolent pornography.* Ottawa: Department of Justice for Canada.

Check, J. V. P., & Guloien, T. H. (1989). Reported proclivity for coercive sex following repeated exposure to sexually violent pornography, nonviolent dehumanizing pornography, and erotica. In D. Zillmann & J. Bryant (Eds.), *Pornography: Research advances and policy considerations* (pp. 159–184). Hillsdale, NJ: Lawrence Erlbaum Associates.

Comstock, G. A., & Paik, H. (1991). The effects of television violence on aggressive behavior: A meta-analysis. In A. J. Reiss & J. A. Roth (Eds.), *A preliminary report to the National Research Council on the understanding and control of violent behavior* (pp. 41–54). Washington, DC: National Research Council.

Davis, K. E., & Braught, G. N. (1970). Exposure to pornography, character, and sexual deviance: A retrospective survey. *Technical report of the Commission on Obscenity and Pornography, Vol. 7.* Washington, DC: US Government Printing Office.

Diener, E., & DeFour, D. (1978). Does television violence enhance program popularity? *Journal of Research in Social Psychology, 36,* 334–341.

Diener, E., & Woody, W. (1981). TV violence and viewer liking. *Communication Research, 8,* 281–306.

Donnerstein, E. (1980). Aggressive erotica and violence against women. *Journal of Personality and Social Psychology, 39,* 269–277.

Easton, N. J. (1993, February 7). America's mean streak: It's cool to be cool. *Los Angeles Times Magazine*, 16–20, 43–44.

Eron, L. D., Walder, L. O., & Lefkowitz, M. M. (1971). *Learning of aggression in children*. Boston: Little, Brown.

Feshback, S. (1955). The drive-reducing function of fantasy behavior. *Journal of Abnormal and Social Psychology, 50*, 3–11.

Feshback, S. (1961). The stimulating versus cathartic effects of vicarious aggressive activity. *Journal of Abnormal and Social Psychology, 63*, 381–385.

Final Report of the Surgeon General's Commission on Pornography. (1986). Nashville: Rutledge Hill Press.

Geen, R. G. (1994). Television and aggression: Recent developments in research and theory. In D. Zillmann, J. Bryant, & A. C. Huston (Eds.), *Media, children, and the family: Social scientific, psychodynamic, and clinical perspectives* (pp. 151–162). Hillsdale, NJ: Lawrence Erlbaum Associates.

Gerbner, G., Gross, L., Morgan, M., & Signorielli, N. (1980). The "mainstreaming" of America: Violence Profile No. 11. *Journal of Communication, 30,* 10–29.

Gerbner, G., Gross, L., Morgan, M., & Signorielli, N. (1994). Growing up with television: The cultivation perspective. In J. Bryant & D. Zillmann (Eds.), *Media effects: Advances in theory and research* (pp. 17–41). Hillsdale, NJ: Lawrence Erlbaum Associates.

Greenberg, B. S. (1994). Content trends in media sex. In D. Zillmann, J. Bryant, & A. C. Huston (Eds.), *Media, children, and the family: Social scientific, psychodynamic, and clinical perspectives* (pp. 165–182). Hillsdale, NJ: Lawrence Erlbaum Associates.

Gunter, B. (1994). The question of media violence. In J. Bryant & D. Zillmann (Eds.), *Media effects: Advances in theory and research* (pp. 163–211). Hillsdale, NJ: Lawrence Erlbaum Associates.

Harris, R. J. (1994). The impact of sexually explicit media. In J. Bryant & D. Zillmann (Eds.), *Media effects: Advances in theory and research* (pp. 247–272). Hillsdale, NJ: Lawrence Erlbaum Associates.

Huesmann, L. R., & Eron, L. D. (1986). *Television and the aggressive child: A cross-national comparison.* Hillsdale, NJ: Lawrence Erlbaum Associates.

Huesmann, L. R., & Miller, L. S. (1994). Long-term effects of repeated exposure to media violence in childhood. In L. R. Huesmann (Ed.), *Aggressive behavior: Current perspectives* (pp. 153–186). New York: Plenum.

Huston, A. C., Donnerstein, E., Fairchild, H., Feshbach, N., Katz, P., Murray, J., Rubinstein, E., Wilcox, B., & Zuckerman, D. (1992). *Big world, small screen: The role of television in American society.* Lincoln: University of Nebraska Press.

Jo, E., & Berkowitz, L. (1994). A priming effect analysis of media influences: An update. In J. Bryant & D. Zillmann (Eds.), *Media effects: Advances in theory and research* (pp. 43–60). Hillsdale, NJ: Lawrence Erlbaum Associates.

Kinsey, A. C., Pomeroy, W. B., & Martin, C. E. (1948). *Sexual behavior in the human male.* Philadelphia: W. B. Saunders.

Lefkowitz, M. M., Eron, L. D., Walder, L. O., & Huesmann, L. R. (1977). *Growing up to be violent.* New York: Pergamon.

Linz, D. (1985). *Sexual violence in the media: Effects on male viewers and implications for society.* Unpublished doctoral dissertation, University of Wisconsin, Madison.

Linz, D., Donnerstein, E., & Adams, S. M. (1989). Physiological desensitization and judgments about female victims of violence. *Human Communication Research, 15*, 509–522.

Linz, D., Donnerstein, E., & Penrod, S. (1984). The effects of multiple exposures to filmed violence against women. *Journal of Communication, 34*, 130–147.

Lyons, J. S., Anderson, R. L., & Larson, D. B. (1994). A systematic review of the effects of aggressive and nonaggressive pornography. In D. Zillmann, J. Bryant, & A. C. Huston (Eds.), *Media, children, and the family: Social scientific, psychodynamic, and clinical perspectives* (pp. 271–310). Hillsdale, NJ: Lawrence Erlbaum Associates.

Malamuth, N. M. (1984). Aggression against women: Cultural and individual causes. In N. M. Malamuth & E. Donnerstein (Eds.), *Pornography and sexual aggression* (pp. 19–52). Orlando, FL: Academic Press.

Malamuth, N. M., Check, J. V. P., & Briere, J. (1986). Sexual arousal in response to aggression: Ideological, aggressive, and sexual correlates. *Journal of Personality and Social Psychology, 50*, 330–340.

NCTV says violence on TV up 16%. (1983, March). *Broadcasting, 63*.

Sapolsky, B. S., & Zillmann, D. (1981). The effect of soft-core and hard-core erotica on provoked and unprovoked hostile behavior. *Journal of Sex Research, 17*, 319–343.

Weaver, J. B. (1987). *Effects of portrayals of female sexuality and violence against women on perceptions of women*. Unpublished doctoral dissertation, Indiana University.

Wells, W. D. (1973). *Television and aggression: Replication of an experimental field study*. Unpublished manuscript, University of Chicago.

White, L. A. (1979). Erotica and aggression: The influence of sexual arousal, positive affect, and negative affect on aggressive behavior. *Journal of Personality and Social Psychology, 37*, 591–601.

Wood, W., Wong, F. Y., & Chachere, G. (1991). Effects of media violence on viewers' aggression in unconstrained social interaction. *Psychological Bulletin, 109*, 371–383.

Zillmann, D. (1971). Excitation transfer in communication-mediated aggressive behavior. *Journal of Experimental Social Psychology, 7*, 419–434.

Zillmann, D. (1984). *Connections between sex and aggression*. Hillsdale, NJ: Lawrence Erlbaum Associates.

Zillmann, D. (1991). Television viewing and physiological arousal. In J. Bryant & D. Zillmann (Eds.), *Responding to the screen: Reception and reaction processes* (pp. 103–133). Hillsdale, NJ: Lawrence Erlbaum Associates.

Zillmann, D., & Bryant, J. (1982). Pornography, sexual callousness, and the trivialization of rape. *Journal of Communication, 32*, 10–21.

Zillmann, D., & Bryant, J. (1986). Shifting preferences in pornography consumption. *Communication Research, 13*, 560–578.

Zillmann, D., & Bryant, J. (1988a). Effects of prolonged consumption of pornography on family values. *Journal of Family Issues, 9*, 518–544.

Zillmann, D., & Bryant, J. (1988b). Pornography's impact on sexual satisfaction. *Journal of Applied Social Psychology, 18*, 438–453.

Zillmann, D., & Bryant, J. (Eds.). (1989). *Pornography: Research advances and policy considerations*. Hillsdale, NJ: Lawrence Erlbaum Associates.

Zillmann, D., Bryant, J., Comisky, P. W., & Medoff, N. J. (1981). Excitation and hedonic valence in the effect of erotica on motivated intermale aggression. *European Journal of Social Psychology, 11*, 233–252.

Zillmann, D., Bryant, J., & Huston, A. C. (1994). *Media, children, and the family: Social scientific, psychodynamic, and clinical perspectives*. Hillsdale, NJ: Lawrence Erlbaum Associates.

14

Advertising

Esther Thorson
University of Missouri-Columbia

The scientific study of advertising is one of the oldest in communication, and one of the best developed both in terms of method and theory. An extensively used advertising textbook (Bovee & Ahrens, 1986) defines *advertising* as "the nonpersonal communication of information usually paid for and usually persuasive in nature about products, services, or ideas by identified sponsors through the various media" (p. 5).

A frequent confusion about the definition of advertising concerns its relationship to marketing. *Marketing* is a much broader term that includes everything an organization does to sell its products, services, or the company itself. This involves finding customers and figuring out what they want, developing products to satisfy those wants, and selling those products to customers. These three activities involve the subareas of product development, pricing, distribution, and promotion. Advertising, on the other hand, is a subcategory of promotion, which is defined as everything that is done to sell the product. Advertising refers only to the paid media aspects of selling.

But beyond its relation to marketing, what is advertising? Advertising involves information about a brand or idea. It often involves images, music, and stories. In the electronic media, it may be an interruption of ongoing processing of other materials such as news or entertainment. Often advertising is far less important to people than the material in which it is embedded.

These are generalizations about advertising, but it is important to go beyond them to create a taxonomy of advertising. In other words, we need an organizational scheme by which to categorize ads. Such a scheme is important for several reasons. First, we need a way to identify ads to develop rules for sampling them so that when we study "ads" we can generalize an ad to a specific population of ads. Second, if we need to manipulate ads to look at the impact of one or several effects, we must know that what we are studying is still advertising, not some other kind of message (Thorson, 1990). Unfortunately, there is no generally accepted advertising taxonomy. Many ways of categorizing ads have been suggested, but none are exhaustive or universally accepted.

One of the most basic ways to categorize commercials is in terms of what they are meant to sell. The most frequently occurring are product and service commercials. In advertising of this type, the focus is a product brand (e.g., Nike, Hanes) or a generic product (e.g., coffee, cheese) or a service (e.g., Sprint long distance service, Chemlawn).

A second category deals with public service commercials. These messages focus on information that is generally thought to improve lives or health. Designated driver ads, safe sex campaigns, and seat belt appeals are examples of public service ads.

A third category of ads involves issue advertising. Advertising of this type focuses on positions taken by corporations, individuals, or institutions on controversial issues. Examples include commercials by Gun Control, Inc., endorsing passage of a gun control law in Congress; antiabortion ads; or smokers' rights ads.

A fourth category is corporate ads, or those that tout the favorable qualities of companies themselves. IBM is the company that listens. G.E. brings good things to light.

And fifth, there are political commercials. These focus on reasons to vote for individuals running for political office, or they discuss issues appearing on the ballot.

Although there are many studies of each of these kinds of commercials, there are few studies that compare across the different kinds of advertising, and thus we know comparatively little about the structure or impact of ad type (Thorson & Coyle, 1994).

It is often said that advertising research is administrative; it is biased toward the creation of systems of social control to serve the status quo (e.g., Ewen, 1983). Although this claim was at least partially supported throughout the history of advertising research, the last twenty years have seen substantial movement toward understanding the role of advertising as it serves the consumer rather than the industry. Such research is particularly frequent in advertising and law studies (Cohen, 1978; Reich, 1979; Stewart & Martin, 1994; Zanot, 1985), economic studies of advertising (Albion & Farris, 1981; Arndt & Simon, 1983), and studies of the social impact of advertising (Leiss, Kline, & Sut, 1986; Pollay, 1986; Preston, 1975; Schudson, 1984; Stern, 1992). More recently, the consumer point of view has begun to appear in journals traditionally more administrative in nature (e.g., Richins, 1994; Thompson, Pollio, & Locander, 1994). Because of the limited length of this review, the concentration here is on the processing of advertising, rather than its social, legal, or economic aspects.

A BRIEF HISTORY OF RESEARCH ON ADVERTISING

The study of advertising has been influenced by a number of the social sciences, but the dominant influence has been psychology. The earliest models, which focused on the processes within the individual, were labeled *hierarchies of effect*. As early as 1898,

E. St. Elmo Lewis articulated a hierarchy model (see Preston, 1982). He suggested the critical steps in how an ad affected people included attention to the commercial, interest in the product, desire for the product, and some sort of action in response to the ad (e.g., purchase or the casting of a vote). Walter Dill Scott (1921) was another early proponent of using psychology to understand people and thereby how to sell them things or ideas. Although there is little overview material available on the history of advertising, a good beginning examination can be found in Fox (1984).

The hierarchy model re-emerged during the 1960s. Lavidge and Steiner (1961) suggested that the information consumers select from commercials travels through an ordered series of processing stages, focusing on psychological processes such as attention, comprehension, evaluation, intention to act, and acting. McGuire (1969) suggested that the effects hierarchy should include attention, comprehension, yielding to the conclusion, retention of the new information, and behavior (purchase). Although there are variations in the assumptions of the various hierarchy models (e.g., Preston, 1982; Preston & Thorson, 1984), most assume that failure at any of the steps of the hierarchy dictates no response to the advertising. Furthermore, hierarchy models rest on the assumption that attitudes and behaviors in response to advertising are developed consciously and rationally. The emphasis on rational, conscious responses to advertising developed early in advertising's history, and remained dominant well into the 1970s (e.g., Sandage, 1973; Shimp & Gresham, 1983).

The strength of hierarchy models is found in their concern with a whole family of responses stretching from exposure to a commercial to, eventually, an action response. The problem is that they are so broad that they are difficult to test. It is also difficult to determine when all the succeeding stages should occur; if all occurred immediately after an ad exposure, it is not clear what measures could be used to index them—or how one would tell which response came first.

In the 1970s, the dominant view of advertising focused on its impact on memory and attitudes. Memory, conceptualized as a rational and conscious process, perhaps emphasized an already-existing focus on people's rational, cognitive, and problem-solving orientations toward advertising. Similarly, attitudes were conceived as reason-based valenced orientations toward some object. Underlying most research during this time was the assumption that advertising persuaded people by offering them good, logical reasons to like an object or an idea and to respond positively to it.

One of the most influential models of commercial processing of this period was the Fishbein–Ajzen (Fishbein & Ajzen, 1975) multiattribute model. This attitude-based model suggested that a consumer's attitude toward any brand (or service) is determined by summing the consumer's evaluative response toward each individual product attribute (e_i), multiplied by a subjective estimate of the probability that the brand in question actually possesses attribute i (b_i). This relationship is represented by the equation:

$$A_o = b_i e_i \qquad (1)$$

where A_o is the attitude toward the object (the brand).

According to the model, an ad changes brand attitude either by changing a person's perception of the probability that a brand has some attribute, or by changing a person's evaluative beliefs about the attribute. In applications of the model, people were assumed to process ads by continually updating their attitudes toward brands. Although any information a consumer considers relevant can be included as a product attribute according to this model, researchers generally have limited their consideration to product attributes of a rational and intrinsic nature (e.g., price, performance, and availability).

At the same time the multiattribute model was dominant, there was also a focus on the influence of advertising on memory. Free recall or, as it is sometimes called, proven recall, was measured by asking viewers to list all the commercials they had seen during a particular television program. One of the most common measures was devised and implemented by the Burke Market Research Company. Their 24-hour recall measure involves calling viewers the day after a test commercial has been aired to determine how many of those who watched the program in which the commercial appeared could either freely recall it or recall it after being prompted with a product category or a brand name cue.

Whereas the advertising industry used memory as an index of the effectiveness of advertising, academics derived a variety of advertising memory theories. Srull (1983, 1984) developed a model of memory that related memory for ads to judgment about brands. He noted that judgments about brands are often uncorrelated with memory for information that the judgments are supposedly based upon. Srull's model explained this lack of correlation by suggesting that consumers store different information from ads depending upon whether they are motivated to make judgments at the time of exposure, or simply store the experience with the ad without making any immediate judgment. When judgments are made online, the correlation between memory for information and judgment is reduced, because when asked to make a judgment, people simply retrieve the judgment. But if judgments are made only later, when people are questioned and not when they are actually encountering the ad, then the judgment will have to be computed based on memory for the content of the ad, a process that makes it more likely that memory and judgment are correlated.

This conceptualization led to the distinction between retrieval and computational processes in response to advertising. Srull (1984) and his colleagues amassed an impressive body of reserach that supported just such a distinction. For example, when people are instructed to do online processing of print ads, the correlation between memory and judgments is low. Additionally, mood effects (making people happy or sad at the time of exposure to the ad) on judgments are low or nonexistent. But if people are instructed in such a way that online processing is unlikely, then memory and judgment are correlated, and mood effects from exposure affect the judgments themselves.

Since the early 1980s, however, the literature on advertising has come to concentrate on an entirely different conception of consumers and their reactions to advertising. The intellectual seed for this different conception was actually planted in the 1960s, when Krugman (1965) introduced the critical concept of *involvement*. For Krugman, involvement referred to how many cognitive connections a person made while processing media messages.

In its 30-year history, involvement has been argued to refer to many different concepts, some of which have been given different names. For example, some researchers characterize involvement as central rather than peripheral processing (Petty & Cacioppo, 1979), systematic rather than heuristic processing (Chaiken, 1980), or brand rather than non-brand-processing (Gardner, Mitchell, & Russo, 1985).

Regardless of concept variations, a critical feature of involvement is that it is effortful, conscious, intentional, and involves reasoning. It has become increasingly clear, however, that involved processing of advertising is not the normal state of affairs in the "real world." Consumers read magazines to find out about international affairs, or how to fish for bass; they read newspapers to find out what crimes were committed the previous night or to work the crossword puzzle; and they watch television to be entertained, or perhaps just to relax. Although the consumer occasionally desires—and is motivated to find and thoroughly process—the information in advertising, this is probably more the exception than the rule. This thinking led to several dominant models of advertising in the 1980s and 1990s, including conditioning, the Elaboration Likelihood Model, models about the role of attitude toward ads, emotion- or mood-based models, and models of attention to ads. These models are examined in detail in a later section.

SELECTION, CREATION, DISSEMINATION, AND RECEPTION OF ADS

Because advertising is so broad, a model is needed to provide an organizational scheme. To that end, Greenberg and Salwen's (chapter 5, this volume) "model of models" is employed. It includes three sociological processes: the selection, creation, and dissemination of ads. It also involves one psychological process: reception.

Selection

Although the concept of selection of news stories is intuitively appealing and represents an array of interesting research, the same concept applied to advertising is less clear. The closest translation to advertising asks which products, services, and ideas appear in advertising and which ones do not. Not much research has looked at this question. In terms of products, however, there is a clear emphasis upon brands—those products with names, identities, personalities, images, and so on. Starting around the beginning of the 20th century, marketers began to provide their products with brand names (Fox, 1984). It became clear that this was an excellent way to compete in an environment increasingly characterized by a surplus of goods, and, in fact, where many product brands were essentially identical to each other (i.e., were parity products). In this environment, it made good business sense to develop brand identities that would cause people to purchase one over another, develop brand loyalties, and be willing to pay a premium for certain brands. Of course, advertising developed to reflect this emphasis on brands. Today there is an area of advertising study concerned solely with the development, handling, and financial worth of brand images (Aaker & Biel, 1993).

There is also some analysis of political advertising. As the population has increased and mediated messages have become dominant over interpersonal political messages, massive use of political advertising has become the norm. Recently, extensive study has focused on the factors that lead to more use of political ads, what they contain, how they work, and media preferences for advertising (Tinkham & Weaver-Lariscy, 1990).

There is little study of what issues, either public service, corporate, or whatever appear in advertising. Such questions as the influence of the Advertising Council on selection of public service topics, how and when companies do corporate advertising and then what they say, and the influence of media organizations on what issue advertising manages are all interesting sociological questions about advertising.

Creation

What ads actually look like has been a major focus of advertising research in the last 40 years. Although ads can be easily distinguished by what they advertise (e.g., products, services, and public service or issue information), within these broad categories, ads can take an essentially infinite number of forms. In examining ad form, content analysis has played an important role, but often its purpose has focused on variations in *reception* as a function of what an ad looks like. Experimental presentation of ads has been heavily employed. Another important methodological tool has been secondary analysis of data indexing how well ads performed in either copy tests or the market as a function of their structure.

Early research concerning the creation of ads focused on a wide variety of independently defined ad attributes, often bearing no particular theoretical relationship to each other (Thorson, 1990). One of the earliest such studies was that of Haller (1972). He used experts to judge commercials on four dimensions: (a) the extent to which the visual elements aided the audio elements in getting the message across; (b) the stopping power of the message; (c) the clarity of the message; and (d) the extent to which the message spoke personally to the viewer. These dimensions, estimated by experts, were then used to predict consumer memory for 6 commercials for cigarettes, and accounted for about 20 percent of the variation in memory for the ads.

Haley, Richardson, and Baldwin (1985) generated 510 variables in 17 categories of nonverbal variables and found that 132 of the variables were significantly related to changes from previewing to postviewing persuasion measures of attitudinal responses to products advertised in 47 commercials. Categories of nonverbal variables measured in the study included voice characteristics, eye contact, distances between on-screen individuals, body motion, stance, and the use of gestures.

Using the largest sample of commercials ever examined in a single study of ad structures and their impact, Stewart and Furse (1985, 1986) defined 155 structural variables in 1,059 commercials. They then used the identified variables to predict the Research System Corporation's (ARS) three main commercial effect measures: recall, key message comprehension, and persuasion (i.e., the change from previewing attitude to postviewing attitude). After removing the differences associated with product category, they were able to account for 13 to 26 percent of the variance in commercial recall, 8 percent of the variance in key message comprehension, and 9 to 11 percent of the variance in persuasion. The descriptive variables used to categorize the commercials were divided into 11 categories: information content, brand/product identification, setting, visual and auditory devices, promises/appeals/propositions, tone/atmosphere, product comparisons, music and dancing, structure and format, characters, and timing and counting measures (e.g., length of the commercial or the number of times the brand name was shown).

A handful of the models of commercial structure were guided by theory about how people process messages. One example is the work of Thorson and her colleagues

(Thorson, 1983; Thorson & Rothschild, 1983; Thorson & Snyder, 1984) who used Kintsch and van Dijk's (1979) propositional text analysis model. Text analysis suggests that underlying all language comprehension are logically arranged idea units or propositions. The complexity and arrangement of the propositions is hypothesized to predict how well information will be remembered. Analysis of the propositional structure of samples of television commercials demonstrated that about 33 percent of the variance in both immediate and delayed recall of the content of commercials was indeed predictable from the propositional analyses.

Another way to categorize ads is by creating systems of responses that individuals might have to ads and then ask people to rate ads in terms of the responses they cause. Such "response profiles" can then be used to predict ad effects on memory, attitude change, or brand purchase. Again, as in classifications organized according to objective features of ads, some research has been theory-driven, but most has not.

Some important atheoretical approaches to classify variables include influential studies by Leavitt (1970), Schlinger (1979), McEwen and Leavitt (1976), and Puto and Wells (1984). Leavitt (1970) collected a list of 525 words used by consumers in focus groups to describe commercials. From this list, Leavitt selected words as a function of how often consumers had used them. Forty-five words were retained and found to load onto three commercial-descriptive factors: stimulating, personally relevant, and familiar. Schlinger (1979) developed a second consumer-based sytem. The Viewer Response Profile (VRP) was formed from an initial 600 descriptive statements gathered from consumer playback data and then reduced to 49 sentences about commercials. These sentences loaded on 7 factors: entertainment, confusion, relevant news, brand reinforcement, empathy, familiarity, and alienation.

Third, McEwen and Leavitt (1976) developed a list of 90 key executional elements, and asked judges to determine whether each one described or failed to describe each of 100 commercials. Analysis of the items yielded 12 factors: empathic product integration, integrated announcer, demonstration, pleasant liveliness, confusion, new product introduction, structured product story, problem solution, animation, unpleasant stimulation, persuasive stimulation, and attributes of the openings. Product demonstration and structured product story were positively related to recall of the commercials. Confusion and opening suspense were negatively related to recall.

Finally, in a more simplified approach, Puto and Wells (1984) suggested commercials are transformational, informational, or a blend of the two. Informational commercials discuss product attributes. Transformational commercials attempt to change the consumer's product experience ("This is not just hair coloring, it's a new and better you"). In a related approach, Wells (1987) suggested commercials are characterized as lectures, dramas, or mixtures of the two. A lecturer talks at the viewer, providing information. A drama draws the viewer into the screen by creating a play.

As noted, a handful of studies of response profiles to ads have been theory-based. For example, Leavitt (1968) developed a psycholinguistic analysis of viewer free recall protocols to characterize commercials. The primary measure in Leavitt's system was the number of related references made by viewers to parts of commercials. A related reference is a statement about relationships between any two objects, acts, or ideas in a commercial (e.g., "Solo cleans and softens"). Related references in viewer protocols predicted the order of recall strength for a number of commercials that Leavitt sampled.

In an extension of this work, McConville and Leavitt (1968) further divided related references into those with narrative emphasis only, product–narrative integration, and product–claim integration. They found that product narrative integration occurring in viewer protocols was the best predictor of recall of commercials. In a third related approach, Leavitt, Wadell, and Wells (1970) coded viewer protocols for personal product responses (i.e., viewer comments relating the product to favorable personal behavior) and demonstrated that it correlated well with both recall and eventual report of having purchased the product.

Recently, there has been less interest in categorizing ads and more interest in identifying ads in terms of the particular psychological impacts they have. An unusually active area has concerned emotional impact, and dozens of taxonomies of ad emotion have been suggested. One approach (Batra & Holbrook, 1987) used Plutchik's (1980) 8 emotional categories: joy, acceptance, fear, surprise, sadness, disgust, anger, and anticipation. Another approach, developed by Mehrabian and Russell (1974), employed a three-dimensional emotional system introduced by Osgood, Suci, and Tannenbaum (1957) that includes the dimensions of pleasure–displeasure, arousal–nonarousal, and domination–nondomination. Batra and Holbrook (1987) showed that all three of these emotional dimensions predicted people's liking for ads and advertised brands. Yet another approach (Edell & Burke, 1987) employed three feelings scales, including upbeat, negative, and warm. They found that all three kinds of feelings that people experienced in response to ads were predictive of how they evaluated ads, how much they liked ads, beliefs they had about the brands, and their attitudes toward the brands.

Dissemination

Dissemination has various important interpretations in the advertising literature. In general, it refers to the way ads move from creator to consumer. Often, this notion is considered a media issue. It involves questions such as, "What ads appear in what media and how often?" and is usually answered via content analyses. Another question concerns what happens to ads in the media in which they appear, "What influences whether an ad 'gets through' to a consumer?" and is usually studied via experiments and mathematical models of reach (the number of different consumers who receive an ad) and frequency (the average number of times people receive an ad). Leckenby and Rice's study (1986) is an example of this type of research.

Advertising media studies are extensive and well beyond the scope of this review, but two important areas of study should be mentioned. A first concerns media selection so that a marketer can maximize advertising dollars (e.g., Cannon, 1987; Rust & Eechambadi, 1989). A second concerns identifying the characteristics of the readers or audiences for various media (e.g., Cannon, 1988).

One of the most theoretically developed media studies areas concerns media context effects. This area looks at how the environment in which an ad is experienced influences its impact. The environment includes the medium (e.g., television versus magazines), program, and variables related to ad location within the break and the break within the program, and other ads present (Feltham & Arnold, 1994).

In one of the earliest studies, Kennedy (1971) hypothesized that suspense programs would create a high drive for closure and this would disrupt the processing of ads. Kennedy found that suspense program viewers had poorer recall of brand name in an embedded commercial, but were more positive in attitude toward it than were comedy program viewers. Soldow and Principe (1981) compared the impact of drama and comedy on ad processing, finding that viewers recalled brands and sales messages less well when the commercials were viewed in the drama, and, in contrast to Kennedy's results, viewers liked two of the commercials less well. Bryant and Comisky (1978) compared the impact of suspense within a single program, varying the degree of suspensefulness just before an ad. Recall was poorest when suspense was high and best when suspense was low. In another experiment, program response was operationalized in terms of mood (Kamins, Markes, & Skinner, 1991). The results indicated that upon viewing a happy commercial within the context of a happy program, the commercial was evaluated more favorably than if that same commercial was viewed during a sad program. Similarly a sad commercial was evaluated more favorably during a sad program than during a happy program.

To organize the various approaches and findings in this complex literature, Schumann and Thorson (1990) designed an intensity–affect model of program impact. This model posits that environments affect commercial processing only when the ratio of environment to program intensities of processing is low. According to the model, intensity of processing can be caused by a number of variables, with involvement being an important one. One of the model's most significant innovations is the examination of the competitive relations between ad environments and ads, and the prediction of the conditions under which context effects occurs. It also predicts that the influence of context on ads will differ as a function of whether memory or attitude is the dependent variable. Although the area remains complex, and the results often conflicting, most recent evidence suggests that, indeed, context operates differentially on memory and attitudinal responses to ads (e.g., Feltam & Arnold, 1994).

A second well-developed theoretical area of media studies concerns the influence of ad repetition—the frequency with which an ad is viewed. Berlyne (1970) was one of the first to find an inverted U-shaped relationship between liking a stimulus and exposure to it. Berlyne explained this relationship using two factors: (a) a reduction in uncertainty as a result of repeated exposure, and (b) habituation, tedium, or boredom after the stimulus has been processed enough so that no uncertainty or reason for curiosity remains.

The advertising version of this theory employs cognitive concepts to describe the underlying processes. During early ad exposure, when there is an opportunity for people to elaborate on messages, meaning support arguments are likely to be created because the message undoubtedly will emphasize them. But with more repetitions, boredom and inattention set in and people begin thinking about something else. Indeed, they may become irritated, and, as a result, create negative thoughts about the commercial or its brand, or counterargue the brand's attributes. Therefore, as repetitions increase, support arguments are believed to decrease, and counterarguments to increase, thus explaining a U-shaped function for attitude in response to commercial repetititions.

There are a number of studies that testify to the inadequacy of the U-shaped function describing repetition effects. In addition, there are data that question the cognitive approach to explaining the effect of repetition on attitude (Belch, 1982; Mitchell & Olson, 1981; Rethans, Swasy, & Marks, 1986; Stayman & Aaker, 1987). The literature indicates that many stimulus characteristics can mediate the pattern of wearout. Examples of mediating variables include execution style (grabber versus non-grabber ads, Ray & Sawyer, 1971); alternations in sequences of ads (Calder & Sternthal, 1980); commercial length (Rethans, Swasy, & Marks, 1986); emotional impact of the commercials (Batra & Ray, 1986a; Stayman & Aaker, 1987); the number of elements of information or complexity in the commercials (Cox & Cox, 1988); and variations in the structure of ads (Haugtvedt, Schumann, Schneier, & Warren, 1994). How repetition affects responses to advertising remains critically important for dissemination because of the industry mandate of high levels of repetition of ads, particularly in the broadcast media.

Reception

Probably the most developed area of advertising research concerns ad influence at the point of reception. As noted earlier, a number of models of reception have dominated research in the 1980s and 1990s. The oldest model was borrowed from psychologists, who defined an associative process called conditioning. The second is the Elaboration Likelihood Model (ELM) of persuasion, introduced to advertising by social psychologists, Petty and Cacioppo (1979). A third model focuses on the influence of attitude toward the ad. Given the intrinsic illogical nature of liking an ad leading to liking and purchasing a brand, this model clearly leaves behind a focus on rationality. A fourth model focuses on affective—emotional or mood—effects of advertising. Finally, there is a small but growing focus on the first step in the advertising hierarchy—attention to advertising. In addition, many studies have looked at several of the processes, in fact, the newest models of advertising talk about involvement, affect, attitude toward the ad, and sometimes even attention.

Conditioning Models of Advertising Reception.   One of the earliest presentations of data in support of a conditioning process was Rossiter and Percy's (1980) demonstration that an ad with high visual emphasis on a beer produced greater positive brand attitudes toward the beer. Mitchell (1983) showed that a brand connected with a picture for which there was strong positive affect also showed more positive brand attitudes. Gorn (1982) showed that people were more likely to select the color of a ballpoint pen that they had seen advertised with likeable than with unlikeable music. (Unfortunately, Kellaris & Cox, 1989, were unable to replicate Gorn's findings.) Most recently, Shimp and his colleagues (Stuart, Shimp, & Engle, 1987) showed that the direction and magnitude of attitude changes toward brands paired with emotion-eliciting visual stimuli were consistent with predictions from classical conditioning experiments. These manipulations included the influence of number of pairings, latent inhibition due to subject pre-exposure to the conditioned stimulus, and the fact that forward conditioning of attitudes was superior to backward conditioning.

The Elaboration Likelihood Model of Advertising Reception. The ELM was first articulated by Petty and Cacioppo (1979) and has undergone extensive metamorphoses in the ensuing years. The basic model suggests that attitudes are formed by two different routes. The *central route* focuses on message arguments, examining them for quality, and on the generation of thoughts (cognitive responses and evaluations) in reaction to them. This, the high involvement condition, occurs when the probability of thinking about or elaborating on the information in the ad is said to be high. Under many circumstances, however, consumer involvement is low. When it is, the *peripheral route* to processing advertising is taken. Consumers may simply associate positive or negative cues with the advertised brand, or they may infer things about the brand based on superficial analyses of cues in the commercial. There is little or no elaboration of the arguments.

Motivation, opportunity, and ability to process information are antecedent variables that determine whether central or peripheral processing occurs. Although the ELM is generally treated as a dichotomous-state model, wherein the consumer either processes an ad centrally or peripherally, Petty, Cacioppo, and Kasmer (1987) suggested that the involvement response is continuous and that blends of central and peripheral processing can occur (see Stiff, 1986, for a critique of the ELM, and Petty, Kasmer, Haugtvedt, & Cacioppo, 1987, for a response to that critique). There are a number of variations on the involvement models discussed here. These two-state variation models include: Batra and Ray's (1986b) motivation, ability, and opportunity to respond model; Burnkrant and Sawyer's (1983) information processing intensity model; Greenwald and Leavitt's (1984) involvement model; and Gardner et al.'s (1985) brand–nonbrand processing model.

Attitude Toward the Ad (A~ad~) Models of Advertising Reception. The basic concept in all of the A_{ad} research is that consumers' attitudes about commercials sometimes influence their attitudes toward brands and their intentions to purchase. Those who accept the concept of the reason-driven consumer may find objectionable the idea that people's feelings about ads could influence their attitudes toward brands. And unless one accepts the assumption that a brand's attributes include its advertising, A_{ad} models are inconsistent with the multiattribute models. Most A_{ad} models also include the concept of involvement. For example, it is often assumed that whenever the consumer operates with low-involvement processing, the cognitive processing necessary for thoughtful brand evaluation disappears, and the consumer takes heuristic shortcuts such as liking the brand if its ad is liked.

The A_{ad} models were introduced by Mitchell and Olson (1981) and Shimp (1981). Shimp suggested that liked ads create positive feelings or affect, and this affect is then transferred to the brand. Affect transference is often conceptualized as a classical conditioning process, although a simple association by contiguity explanation is more parsimonious. MacKenzie, Lutz, and Belch (1986) introduced the possibility that attitude toward the ad may affect brand attitude directly, via brand cognitions, or that attitude toward the ad may affect purchase intention without being mediated either by brand cognitions or brand attitudes. In general, there seems to be little question that A_{ad} influences consumer responses to brands, but the path(s) by which this occurs remain controversial.

A question asked more recently about A_{ad} (MacKenzie & Lutz, 1989) concerned the variables that precede and determine A_{ad}. The study showed that 70% of A_{ad}

variance was accounted for by advertiser and advertising attitude, advertiser credibility, ad perceptions, and ad credibility.

What has been particularly impressive about A_{ad} research is that A_{ad} effects on attitude toward the brand (A_{br}) are ubiquitous. Gardner (1985) summarized the studies that examined the effect of A_{ad} as consistently showing a significant effect on A_{br} when there was a nonbrand set. Only two studies that used brand sets showed mixed or limited effects of A_{ad}. For that reason Gardner (1985) specifically manipulated brand–nonbrand processing. Her results showed that A_{ad} effects were weaker under brand processing than under nonbrand processing, but were significant even under brand processing. MacKenzie et al. (1986) showed in two experiments with an unfamiliar brand of toothpaste that A_{ad} had dual effects. A_{ad} influenced A_{br} and self-reported cognitions about the brand. Homer (1990) recently demonstrated that for both television and print ads A_{ad} predicted attitude toward the brand under both brand and nonbrand processing instructions. These studies leave little doubt that the individual's response to the ad itself is a powerful predictor of ad impact.

Affective Models of Advertising Reception.   Human emotion has been difficult to define, even in psychology where its scientific study originated and was extensively researched. The four most common definitions of the concept include: a subjective experience that can be appraised and labeled, goal-directed behaviors like attack and flight, expressive behaviors (smiling, crying), and physiological arousal (Batra & Ray, 1986a). Psychologist Ross Buck (1985) suggests that these responses are all part of the emotional system, but they differ because they index occurrences at different levels of the emotional system.

Although there are many domains for defining emotion, most advertising researchers have relied upon appraisal processes. As noted, one of the most frequent approaches has involved attempts to identify all the words that people use to describe their emotional responses to advertising (Aaker, Stayman, & Vezina, 1987; Allen, Machleit, & Marine, 1987; Batra, 1984; Holbrook & Batra, 1987; Holbrook & Westwood, 1989). Some of these approaches start from psychological models of emotion and then ask which emotions are applicable to advertising. For example, Holbrook and Westwood (1989) hypothesized that Plutchik's (1980) taxonomy of 8 emotions (acceptance, disgust, fear, anger, joy, sadness, anticipation, and surprise) would exhaustively characterize advertising responses.

Other approaches have collected emotional terms from exhaustive reviews of the psychological literature and then tried to determine which were applicable to advertising responses. An example is Batra and Holbrook's (1987) list of 22 emotions (surprise, sadness, disgust, anger, shame, anxiety, affection, activation, confusion, attention, competence, helplessness, surgency (energy), skepticism, pride, serenity, tension, desire, faith, gratitude, purity, and involvement). Some approaches have been selective rather than exhaustive. Aaker, Stayman, and Hagerty (1986) concentrated on warmth, and Stayman and Aaker (1987) focused on warmth and irritation. Friestad and Thorson (1993) concentrated on positive, negative, neutral, and poignant feelings. In yet another approach, Stephens and Russo (1987) identified the emotions that the creators of commercials had intended them to elicit.

There are several models of how emotion operates as people watch commercials, most of them cognitive. For example, Batra and Ray (1986a) suggest that affective responses should be added to other cognitive response variables when analyzing what consumers say about commercials. They demonstrated that affective responses categorized as SEVA (surgency [energy], elation, vigor, activation), deactivation, social affection, and neutral would account for attitudes toward commercials and brands, even after the effects of other cognitive response variables (support and counterarguments, execution discounting, and bolstering) were removed. A popular conception of emotion is that it operates indirectly on brand attitudes via attitude toward the commercial (Edell & Burke, 1987; Gardner, 1985; MacKenzie et al., 1986). A competing theoretical notion is that emotion becomes associated via conditioning with other elements in the commercial, including memory for the whole commercial and attitude toward the brand. Srull (1983) suggested that when consumers are asked to evaluate brands as they process ads, moods induced by the ads affect brand attitudes via mood state associations.

Models of Attention to Advertising. A final area of theory and research about how commercials affect reception concerns the impact of attentional processes. The approaches are diverse. Certain areas of attitude theory suggest that distraction from the processing of commercials will reduce the accessing of relevant background information and thereby reduce counterarguing (Petty & Cacioppo, 1979). One test of the distraction hypothesis is to compress commercials so that they are presented at 20% to 60% faster speeds than normal. Moore, Hausknecht, and Thamodaran (1986) showed that brand attitudes for products in radio commercials with strong arguments were unaffected by compression, but brand attitude for commercials with weak arguments became increasingly positive as exposure rate increased. They concluded that distraction alters the cues that consumers use to form brand attitudes and hence changes attentional processing.

Another approach, limited capacity attention theory, explains the effects on reaction time to a secondary task of greater audio and video complexity in commercials and presence of the audio and video channels of commercials (Reeves, Thorson, & Schleuder, 1986). Reeves et al. suggest that changes in response time to a tone, light, or tactile stimulus presented while consumers are watching television can be used to understand which television commercial stimuli place additional demands on attentional processing. Further, they hypothesized that commercials are processed at a sensory level, where the modality of the secondary task, the degree of commercial compression, and momentary changes in audio and video complexity produce differentially slowed reaction times. Commercials are also processed at a meaning level, where global changes in audio and video complexity (e.g., more ideas per unit time or more edits and scene changes) and scene disordering differentially slow reaction times.

METHODOLOGICAL INNOVATIONS IN STUDIES OF AD PROCESSING

In addition to theoretical advances, advertising has also seen the development of some useful and interesting methodologies. It is important to emphasize that these methodological innovations are highly associated with progress on the theories already discussed.

The first area of methodological innovation involves physiological measures. Klebba (1985) provided an excellent review of four physiological methods and their application to advertising. Her review examined brain activity, electrodermal responses, pupil dilation, and voice analysis. Two additional measures—eye movement (Kroeber-Reil, 1984) and facial expressions (Weinberg & Konert, 1983)—have been addressed in the literature, but neither has received enough study to provide a good indication of their long-term usefulness.

Krugman (1971, 1977) introduced electroencephalogram (EEG) measures into the study of advertising. He suggested that print advertising was processed predominantly verbally and with higher involvement than television, which was alternatively processed impressionistically and with lower involvement. This led Krugman to suggest print advertising was predominantly left-hemispheric while television advertising was predominantly right-hemispheric. In subsequent years, there were numerous efforts to develop EEG measures in response to advertising (e.g., Olson & Ray, 1983; Rothschild, Hyon, Reeves, Thorson, Goldstein, 1988; Rust, Price, & Kumar, 1985).

Although EEG has traditionally been used to identify varying activities of the right and left hemisphere of the brain that might influence information processing, there are also hemispheric studies that do not use any physiological dependent variable at all. The basic assumption of this research is that the two brain hemispheres operate differently. The left brain processes sequentially, and logically, emphasizing the verbal and the analytical. The right brain emphasizes spatial and visual information, and is more holistic in its analysis.

One approach to the question of hemispheric lateralization is to give people paper and pencil tests to determine whether they are left or right dominated, or show some blend, and then to compare their processing of ads for interesting differences. Heckler and Childers (1986) used a lateralization test that produced mixed results. Right-dominated processors did show greater picture recall from print ads, but they also showed more copy recall. Integrated processors showed both more picture and more copy recall.

A second way to look at hemispheric differences, again testing the idea that visual material is more likely processed by the right hemisphere, was introduced by Janiszewski (1988). He asked subjects to read newspaper editorial material that was flanked either on the left or the right by a pictorial ad. This placement would encourage either the left or right hemisphere receiving the ad because it would be picked up by left or right peripheral vision while there was attentional centering on the article. In Experiment 1, Janiszewski showed that the pictorial ad was better liked when placed to the left of the article (which would mean the right hemiphere received it). In Experiment 2, Janiszewski showed that a pictorial ad was better liked when placed in the left visual field and that a verbal ad ("Coke is it!") was better liked when placed in the right visual field. This finding is consistent with the notion that the right hemisphere is likely affected by a visual stimulus, while the left hemisphere is more affected by a verbal stimulus. Janiszewski (1990) also showed that nonattended ad material presented to one hemisphere influenced processing of focally attended ad material. Recently he has shown mere exposure effects for ads explained by hemispheric processing theory as well (Janiszewski, 1993).

Heart rate responses differ in the duration of their changes (short changes are called *phasic* and longer lasting changes are dubbed *tonic*); direction (accelerations and decelerations), and the degree of acceleration or deceleration. It is now generally agreed that heart rate initially decelerates in response to uncertain or novel stimuli, and that these decelerations occur simultaneously with orienting responses. It is also clear that heart rate is responsive to emotional processing, although there is some controversy about how heart rate changes as a function of the valence and intensity of experienced emotion (Vrana, Spence, & Lang, 1988). Lang (1990) showed an orienting response pattern when events in commercials such as their onset, central object movement, and edits or cuts occur. This orienting pattern, however, was more intense (greater accelerations and decelerations) for emotional than neutral commercials. These results are encouraging, primarily because the collection of heart rate measures is much simpler than that of the other psychophysiological measures.

A second methodological innovation has focused on a new measure of memory. Traditional memory measures involve either recall or recognition, where consumers are aware of searching their memories. Implicit memory (Roediger, 1990), on the other hand, is indexed with apparently unrelated other tasks where ability to perform changes as a function of exposure to a previous stimulus, even though no reference is made to that stimulus. Examples of implicit memory tests are word or sentence completions and tachistoscopic identifications. Implicit memory studies (e.g., Duke & Carlson, in press) show that whether consumers are concentrating on learning from ads or are just reading through them, affects recall and recognition, but has no effect on completion of word fragments. It appears that implicit measures may indicate that a commercial has gained a minimum level of attention, even when explicit measures indicate the sensory data are not elaborated into information and attitudes. These results are consistent with Janiszewski's (1990, 1993) hemispheric processing theory. Use of attitudinal, explicit, and implicit memory measures may therefore allow further development of our understanding of the hierarchy of effects (e.g., Greenwald & Leavitt, 1984) where processing stages are conceptualized as occurring at levels varying from attention, to comprehension, to intention, and so on.

A FINAL COMMENT

Although so few pages can hardly do justice to the broad area of advertising, the research and theory reported here may suggest some leads about where to go to look for research of interest. It may also help introduce the student of communications to the idea that advertising contains a great deal of sophisticated theorizing and empirical methodological prowess that can be useful even to those only peripherally interested in the persuasive processes.

REFERENCES

Aaker, D. A., & Biel, A. L. (1993). *Brand equity & advertising: Advertising's role in building strong brands.* Hillsdale, NJ: Lawrence Erlbaum Associates.

Aaker, D. A., Stayman, D. M., & Hagerty, M. R. (1986). Warmth in advertising: Measurement, impact and sequence effects. *Journal of Consumer Research, 12*, 365–381.

Aaker, D. A., Stayman, D. M., & Vezina, R. (1987). Identifying feelings elicited by advertising. *Psychology & Marketing*, 5, 1–116.

Albion, M. S., & Farris, P. W. (1981). *The advertising controversy*. Boston: Auburn House.

Allen, C. T., Machleit, K. A., & Marine, S. S. (1987, October). *On assessing the emotionality of advertising via Izard's differential emotions scale*. Paper presented at the Association for Consumer Research, Boston, MA.

Arndt, J., & Simon, J. (1983). Advertising and economies of scale: Critical comments on the evidence. *Journal of Industrial Economics, 32*(2), 229–241.

Batra, R. (1984). Affective advertising: Role, processes and measurement. In R. A. Peterson, W. D. Hoyer, & W. R. Wilson (Eds.). *The role of affect in consumer behavior: Emerging theories and applications* (pp. 53–85). Lexington, MA: D. C. Health.

Batra, R., & Holbrook, M. B. (1987). Development of a set of scales to measure affective responses to advertising. *Journal of Consumer Research, 14*, 404–420.

Batra, R., & Ray, M. L. (1986a). Affective responses mediating acceptance of advertising. *Journal of Consumer Research, 13,* 234–249.

Batra, R., & Ray, M. L. (1986b). Situational effects of advertising repetition: The moderating influence of motivation, ability and opportunity to respond. *Journal of Consumer Research, 12,* 432–445.

Belch, G. E. (1982). The effects of television commercial repetition on cognitive response and message acceptance. *Journal of Consumer Research, 9*, 56–65.

Berlyne, D. E. (1970). Novelty, complexity and hedonic value. *Perception and Psychophysics, 8,* 279–280.

Bovee, C. L., & Arens, W. F. (1986). *Contemporary advertising*. Homewood, IL: Irwin.

Bryant, J., & Comisky, P. W. (1978). The effect of positioning a message within differentially cognitively involving portions of a television segment of recall of the message. *Human Communication Research, 5*, 63–75.

Buck, R. (1985). Prime theory: An integrated view of motivation and emotion. *Psychological Review, 92,* 389–413.

Burnkrant, R. E., & Sawyer, A. G. (1983). Effects of involvement and message content on information processing intensity. In R. J. Harris (Ed.), *Information processing research in advertising* (pp. 43–64). Hillsdale, NJ: Lawrence Erlbaum Associates.

Calder, B. J., & Sternthal, B. (1980). Television commercial wear-out: An information processing view. *Journal of Marketing Research, 17*, 173–186.

Cannon, H. M. (1987). Can national product-media indices be used to improve media selection efficiency in local market areas? *Journal of Advertising, 16*, 34–42.

Cannon, H. M. (1988). Evaluating the 'simulation' approach to media selection. *Journal of Advertising Research, 28*(1), 57–63.

Chaiken, S. (1980). Heuristic versus systematic information processing and the use of source versus message cues in persuasion. *Journal of Personality and Social Psychology, 39,* 752–756.

Cohen, D. (1978). Advertising and the First Amendment. *Journal of Marketing, 42*, 59–68.

Cox, D., & Cox, A. D. (1988). What does familiarity breed? Complexity as a moderator of repetition effects in advertisement evaluation. *Journal of Consumer Research, 15*, 111–116.

Duke, R., & Carlson, L. (in press). A conceptual approach to alternative memory measures for advertising effectiveness. *Journal of Current Issues and Research in Advertising*.

Edell, J. A., & Burke, M. C. (1987). The power of feelings in understanding advertising effects. *Journal of Consumer Research, 14*, 421–433.

Ewen, S. (1983). The implications of empiricism. *Journal of Communication, 33*, 219– 225.

Feltam, T. S., & Arnold, S. J. (1994). Program involvement and ad/program consistency as moderators of program context effects. *Journal of Consumer Psychology, 3*, 51–78.

Fishbein, M., & Ajzen, I. (1975). *Belief, attitude, intention and behavior: An introduction to theory and research*. Reading, MA: Addison Wesley.

Fox, S. (1984). *The mirror makers: A history of American advertising and its creators*. New York: Morrow.

Fox, S. (1984). *The mirror makers: A history of American advertising and its creators.* New York: Morrow.

Friestad, M., & Thorson, E. (1993). Remembering ads: The effects of encoding strategies, retrieval cues, and emotional response. *Journal of Consumer Psychology, 2,* 1–24.

Gardner, M. P. (1985). Does attitude toward the ad affect brand attitude under a brand evaluation set? *Journal of Marketing Research, 22,* 192–198.

Gardner, M., Mitchell, A., & Russo, J. E. (1985). Low involvement strategies for processing advertisements. *Journal of Advertising, 14,* 4–12.

Gorn, G. J. (1982). The effects of music in advertising on choice behavior: A classical conditioning approach. *Journal of Marketing, 46,* 94–101.

Greenwald, A. G., & Leavitt, C. (1984). Audience involvement in advertising: Four levels. *Journal of Consumer Research, 11,* 581–592.

Haley, R. I., Richardson, J., & Baldwin, B. M. (1985). The effects of nonverbal communications in television advertising. *Journal of Advertising Research, 24,* 11–18.

Haller, T. B. (1972). Predicting recall of TV commercials. *Journal of Advertising Research, 12,* 43–46.

Haugtvedt, C. P., Schumann, D. W., Schneier, W. L, & Warren, W. L. (1994). Advertising repetition and variation strategies: Implications for understanding attitude strength. *Journal of Consumer Research, 21,* 176–189.

Heckler, S. E., & Childers, T. (1987). Hemispheric lateralization: The relationship of processing orientation with judgment and recall measures for print advertising. In M. Wallendorf & P. Anderson, *Advances in consumer research* (Vol. 14, pp. 46–50) Provo, UT: Association for Consumer Research.

Holbrook, M. B. & Westwood, R. A. (1989). The role of emotion in advertising revisited: Testing a typology of emotional responses. In P. Cafferata & A. Tybout (Eds.), *Cognitive and affective responses to advertising* (pp. 353–372). Lexington, MA: Lexington Books.

Holbrook, M. B., & Batra, R. (1987). Assessing the role of emotions as mediators of consumer responses to advertising. *Journal of Consumer Research, 14,* 404–420.

Homer, P. M. (1990). The mediating role of attitude toward the ad: Some additional evidence. *Journal of Marketing Research, 27,* 78–88.

Janiszewski, C. (1988). Preconscious processing effects: The independence of attitude formation and conscious thought. *Journal of Consumer Research, 15,* 199–209.

Janiszewski, C. (1990). The influence of print advertisement organization on affect toward a brand name. *Journal of Consumer Research, 17,* 53–65.

Janiszewski, C. (1993). Preattentive mere exposure effects. *Journal of Consumer Research, 20,* 376–392.

Kamins, M. A., Markes, L. J., & Skinner, D. (1991). Television commercial evaluation in the context of program induced mood: Congruency versus consistency effects. *Journal of Advertising, 20,* 1–14.

Kellaris, J. J., & Cox, A. D. (1989). The effects of background music on advertising: A reassessment. *Journal of Consumer Research, 16,* 113–118.

Kennedy, J. R. (1971). How program environment affects TV commercials. *Journal of Consumer Research, 11,* 33–38.

Kintsch, W., & van Dijk, T. A. (1978). Toward a model of text comprehension and production. *Psychological Review, 85,* 363–394.

Klebba, J. M. (1985). Physiological measures of research: A review of brain activity, electrodermal response, pupil dilation, and voice analysis methods and studies. In J. H. Leigh & C. R. Martin, Jr., (Eds.), *Current issues and research in advertising* (pp. 53–76). Ann Arbor, Graduate School of Business Administration, University of Michigan.

Kroeber-Riel, W. (1984). Effects of emotional pictorial elements in ads analyzed by means of eye movement monitoring. In T.C. Kinnear (Ed.), *Advances in consumer research* (Vol. 11, pp. 591–596). Provo, UT: Association for Consumer Research.

Krugman, H. E. (1965). The impact of television advertising: Learning without involvement. *Public Opinion Quarterly, 29,* 349–356.

Krugman, H. E. (1971). Brain wave measures of brain involvement. *Journal of Advertising Research, 11,* 3–9.

Krugman, H. E. (1977). Memory without recall, exposure without perception. *Journal of Advertising Research, 18,* 7–12.

Lang, A. (1990). Involuntary attention and physiological arousal evoked by structural features and emotional content in TV commercials. *Communication Research, 17*, 275–299.

Lavidge, R. J., & Steiner, G. A. (1961). A model for predictive measurement of advertising effectiveness. *Journal of Marketing, 25*, 59–62.

Leavitt, C. (1968). Response structure: A determinant of recall. *Journal of Advertising Research, 8*, 3–6.

Leavitt, C. (1970). A multidimensional set of rating scales for television commercials. *Journal of Applied Psychology, 54*, 427–429.

Leavitt, C., Wadell, C., & Wells, W. (1970). Improving day-after recall techniques. *Journal of Advertising Research, 10*, 13–17.

Leckenby, J. D., & Rice, M. D. (1986). The declining reach phenomenon in exposure distribution models, *Journal of Advertising, 15*, 13–20.

Leiss, W., Kline, S., & Sut, J. (1986). *Social communication in advertising*. New York: Methuen Publications.

MacKenzie, S. B., & Lutz, R. J. (1989). An empirical examination of the structural antecedents of attitude toward the ad in an advertising pretesting context. *Journal of Marketing, 53*, 48–65.

MacKenzie, S., Lutz, R. J., & Belch, G. E. (1986). The role of attitude toward the ad as a mediation of advertising effectiveness: A test of competing explanations. *Journal of Marketing Research, 23*, 130–143.

McConville, M. N., & Leavitt, C. (1968). Predicting product related recall from verbal response. *Proceedings of the American Psychological Association 76th Annual Convention*, 677–678.

McEwen, W. J., & Leavitt, C. (1976). A way to describe TV commercials. *Journal of Advertising Research, 16*, 35–39.

McGuire, W. J. (1969). An information-processing model of advertising effectiveness. In H. L. Davis & A. J. Silk (Eds.), *Behavioral and management science in marketing* (pp. 156–180). New York: Ronald Press.

Mehrabian, A., & Russell, J. A. (1974). *An approach to environmental psychology*. Cambridge, MA: MIT press.

Mitchell, A. A. (1983). The effects of visual and emotional advertising: An information-processing approach. In L. Percy & G. Woodside (Eds.), *Advertising and consumer psychology* (pp. 197–218). Lexington, MA: Lexington Press.

Mitchell, A. A., & Olson, J. C. (1981). Are product attribute beliefs the only mediator of advertising effects on brand attitudes? *Journal of Marketing Research, 18*, 318–332.

Moore, D. L., Hausknecht, D., & Thamodaran, K. (1987). Time compression, response opportunity, and persuasion. *Journal of Consumer Research, 13*, 85–99.

Osgood, C. E., Suci, G. J., & Tannenbaum, P. H. (1957). *The measurement of meaning*. Urbana: University of Illinois Press.

Olson, J., & Ray, W. (1983). *Brain wave responses to emotional versus attribute oriented television commercials*. (Working paper No. 83-108). Cambridge, MA: Marketing Science Institute.

Petty, R. E., & Cacioppo, J. T. (1979). Issue involvement can increase or decrease persuasion by enhancing message-relevant cognitive responses. *Journal of Personality and Social Psychology, 37*, 1915–1926.

Petty, R. E., Cacioppo, J. T., & Kasmer, J. A. (1987). The role of affect in the elaboration likelihood model of persuasion. In L. Donohew, H. Sypher, & E. T. Higgins (Eds.), *Communication, social cognition, and affect* (pp. 117–146). Hillsdale, NJ: Lawrence Erlbaum Associates.

Petty, R. E., Kasmer, J., Haugtvedt, C., & Cacioppo, J. T. (1987). Source and message factors in persuasion: A reply to Stiff's critique of the elaboration likelihood model. *Communication Monographs, 54*, 257–263.

Plutchik, R. (1980). *Emotion: A psychoevolutionary synthesis*. New York: Harper & Row.

Pollay, R. W. (1986). The distorted mirror: Reflections on the unintended consequences of advertising. *Journal of Marketing, 50*, 18–36.

Preston, I. L. (1975). *The great American blow-up: Puffery in advertising and selling*. Madison: University of Wisconsin Press.

Preston, I. (1982). The association model of the advertising communication process. *Journal of Advertising, 11*, 3–15.

Preston, I., & Thorson, E. (1984). The expanded association model: Keeping the hierarchy concept alive. *Journal of Advertising Research, 24*, 59–66.

Puto, C. P., & Wells, W. D. (1984). Informational and transformational advertising: The differential effects of time. In T. C. Kinnear (Ed.), *Advances in consumer research* (Vol. 11, pp. 638–643). Ann Arbor, MI: Association for Consumer Research.

Ray, M. L., & Sawyer, A. G. (1971). Repetition in media models: A laboratory technique. *Journal of Marketing Research, 8*, 20–29.

Reeves, B., Thorson, E., & Schleuder, J. (1986). Attention to television: Psychological theories and chronometric measures. In J. Bryant & D. Zillmann (Eds.), *Perspectives on media effects* (pp. 251–279). Hillsdale, NJ: Lawrence Erlbaum Associates.

Reich, R. B. (1979). Preventing deception in commercial speech. *New York University Law Review, 54*, 775–805.

Rethans, A. J., Swasy, T. L., & Marks, L. J. (1986). Effects of television commercial repetition, receiver knowledge, and commercial length: A test of the two-factor model. *Journal of Marketing Research, 23*, 50–61.

Richins, M. L. (1994). Valuing things: The public and private meanings of possessions. *Journal of Consumer Research, 21*, 504–521.

Roediger, H. L., III. (1990). Implicit memory: Retention without remembering. *American Psychologist, 45*, 1043–1056.

Rossiter, J. R., & Percy, L. (1980). Attitude change through visual imagery in advertising. *Journal of Advertising, 9*, 10–16.

Rothschild, M. L., Hyon, Y., Reeves, B., Thorson, E., & Goldstein, R. (1988). Hemispherically lateralized EEG as a response to television commercials. *Journal of Consumer Research, 15*, 185–198.

Rust, R. T., & Eechambadi, N. V. (1989). Scheduling netwok television programs: A heuristic audience flow approach to maximizing audience share. *Journal of Advertising, 1*, 9–14

Rust, R. T., Price, L. L., & Kumar, V. (1985). EEG responses to advertisements in print and broadcast media. (Working paper No. 85111). Cambridge, MA: Marketing Science Institute.

Sandage, C. (1973). Some institutional aspects of advertising. *Journal of Advertising, 1*, 9–14.

Schlinger, M. (1979). A profile of responses to commercials. *Journal of Advertising Research, 19*, 37–46.

Schudson, M. (1984). *Advertising, the uneasy persuasion.* New York: Basic Books.

Schumann, D. W., & Thorson, E. (1990). The influence of viewing context on commercial effectiveness: A selection-processing model. In J. H. Leigh & C. R. Martin (Eds.), *Current issues and research in advertising* (pp. 1–24). Ann Arbor: Graduate School of Business Administration, The University of Michigan.

Scott, W. D. (1921). *The psychology of advertising.* New York: Dodd, Mead & Company.

Shimp, T. A. (1981). Attitude toward the ad as a mediator of consumer brand choice. *Journal of Advertising, 10*, 9–15.

Shimp, T. A., & Gresham, L. G. (1983). A perspective on advertising literature. In J. H. Leigh & C. R. Martin, Jr., *Current issues and research in advertising* (pp. 39–76). Ann Arbor: Graduate School of Business Administration, University of Michigan.

Soldow, G., & Principe, V. (1981). Response to commercials as a function of program context. *Journal of Advertising Research, 21*, 59–65.

Srull, T. K. (1983). Affect and memory: The impact of affective reactions in advertising on the representation of product information in memory. In R. P. Bagozzi & A. M. Tybout (Eds.), *Advances in consumer research,* (Vol. 10, pp. 572–576). Ann Arbor: Association for Consumer Research.

Srull, T. K. (1984). The effects of subjective affective states on memory and judgement. In (Ed.) T. C. Kinnear, *Advances in consumer research* (Vol. 11, pp. 530–533). Provo, UT: Society for Consumer Research.

Stayman, D. M., & Aaker, D. A. (1987). *Repetition and affective responses: Differences in specific feeling responses and the mediating role of attitude toward the ad.* Unpublished manuscript, University of Texas.

Stephens, D. L., & Russo, J. E. (1987). *Predicting post-advertising attitudes.* Unpublished manuscript: University of Maryland, University Park.

Stern, B. (1992). Feminist literary theory and advertising research: A new "reading" of the text and the consumer. In J. H. Leigh & C. R. Martin, Jr., *Current issues and research in advertising* (pp. 9–24). Ann Arbor: Graduate School of Business Administration, University of Michigan.

Stewart, D. W., & Furse, D. H. (1985). Analysis of the impact of executive factors on advertising performance. *Journal of Advertising Research, 24*, 23–26.

Stewart, D. W., and Furse, D. H. (1986). *Effective television advertising*. Lexington, MA: Lexington Press.

Stewart, D. W., & Martin, I. M. (1994). Intended and unintended consequences of warning messages. *Journal of Public Policy & Marketing, 13*, 1–19.

Stiff, J. B. (1986). Cognitive processing of persuasive message cues: A meta-analytic review of the effects of supporting information on attitutedes. *Communication Monographs, 53,* 75–89.

Stuart, E., Shimp, T., & Engle, R. (1987). Classical conditioning of consumer attitudes: Four experiments in an advertising context. *Journal of Consumer Research, 14*, 334–349.

Thompson, C. J., Pollio, H. R., & Locander, W. B. (1994). The spoken and the unspoken: A hermeneutic approach to understanding the cultural viewpoints that underlie consumers' expressed meanings. *Journal of Consumer Research, 21, 432–452.*

Thorson, E. (1983). Propositional determinants of memory for television commercials. In J. H. Leigh & C. R. Martin (Eds.), *Current issues and research in advertising* (pp. 139–156). Ann Arbor: Graduate School of Business Administration, The University of Michigan.

Thorson, E. (1990). Consumer processing of advertising. In J. H. Leigh & C.R. Martin (Eds.), *Current issues and research in advertising* (pp. 197–230). Ann Arbor: Graduate School of Business Administration, The University of Michigan..

Thorson, E., & Coyle, J. (1994). The third person effect in three genres of commercials: Product and greening ads, and public service announcements. In K.W. King (Ed.), *Proceedings of the 1993 conference of the American Academy of Advertising* (pp. 103–111). School of Journalism, University of Georgia.

Thorson, E., & Rothschild, M. L. (1983). Using a text comprehension analysis to compare recall and recogntiion of TV commercials. In L. Percy & A. G. Woodside (Eds.), *Advertising and consumer psychology* (pp. 287–301). Lexington, MA: Lexington Books.

Thorson, E., & Snyder, R. (1984). Viewer recall of television commercials: Prediction from the propositional structure of commercial scripts. *Journal of Marketing Research, 21*, 127–136.

Tinkham, S. F., & Weaver-Lariscy, R. A. (1990). Advertising message strategy in U.S. Congressional campaigns: Its impact on election outcome. In J. H. Leigh & C. R. Martin, Jr. (Eds.), *Current issues and research in advertising* (pp. 207–226). Ann Arbor: Graduate School of Business Administration, University of Michigan.

Vrana, S. R., Spence, E. L., & Lang, P. J. (1989). *The startle probe response: A direct measure of emotion?* Unpublished manuscript, Department of Clinical and Health Psychology, University of Florida, Gainesville.

Weinberg, P., & Konert, F. J. (1983). Emotional facial expressions in advertising. In T. C. Kinnear (Eds.), *Advances in consumer research* (Vol. 11, pp. 607–611). Provo, UT: Association for Consumer Research.

Wells, W. (1987, October). *Lectures and dramas*. Paper presented at the Association for Consumer Research, Boston.

Zanot, E. J. (1985). Unseen but effective advertising regulation: The clearance process. *Journal of Advertising, 14,* 44–51.

III

Human Communication
Approaches and Concerns

15

Human Communication Theory and Research: Traditions and Models

James C. McCroskey
Virginia P. Richmond
West Virginia University

The study of human communication has a long and distinguished history. We can safely say that, since humankind first acquired the ability to communicate through verbal and nonverbal symbols and norms, people have "studied" communication. Indeed, one advantage we hold over other animals is the ability to communicate abstractions such as time, place, and space as though each was a concrete object. Thus, since the beginning of our time, we have studied human communication—albeit unscientifically at first, but through more formal systems as we came to better understand both the role of communication in society and its role in daily activity. The importance of the study of human communication is found in its inclusion in educational programs since the first formal schooling systems were developed over 5,000 years ago.

In order to understand how human communication is studied today, it is important to appreciate how we got to where we are now. We will not, however, attempt to provide a complete discussion of the history communication scholarship here. Rather, we will focus on the more important developments and time periods which have impacted on the contemporary study of human communication. Our goal is to foster an understanding of how what was done in the past influences what we do today, and most likely will influence what we do in the future.

The importance of communication in human society has been recognized for thousands of years, far longer than we can demonstrate through recorded history. The oldest essay ever discovered, written about 3000 B.C., consists of advice on how to speak effectively. This essay was inscribed on a fragment of parchment addressed to Kagemni, the eldest son of the Pharaoh Huni. Similarly, the oldest extant book is a treatise on effective communication. The *Precepts* was composed in Egypt about 2675 B.C. by Ptah-Hotep and written for the guidance of the Pharaoh's son. While these works are significant because they establish that the study of human communication is older than any other area of current academic interest, the actual contribution to current communication theory was minimal.

The study of human communication today can be divided into two major classifications—rhetorical and relational (Shepherd, 1992). The rhetorical communication approach focuses primarily on the study of influence. The function of rhetorical communication is to get others to do what you want or need them to do and/or think the way you want or need them to think—to persuade them. The relational approach, on the other hand, examines communication from a transactional or coorientational perspective. That is, two (or more) people coordinate their communication to reach a shared perspective satisfactory to all. Of paramount concern is the relationship between the two people and the perceived well-being of the "other."

These two divergent orientations represent the dominant orientations of western (individualistic) and eastern (collectivistic) cultures. At their extremes, the western (rhetorical) orientation would sacrifice relationships to accomplish influence and the eastern (relational) orientation would sacrifice the achievement of influence to protect relationships. It is not pragmatic, however, to conceive of these two approaches to the study of human communication as polar opposites. Rather, they represent differences in emphasis. Both are interested in accomplishing objectives and maintaining good relationships through communication. Each, however, emphasizse one objective over the other.

We will examine the influence of both of these orientations toward the study of human communication. Since the impact of the rhetorical tradition has been the strongest and longest (McCroskey, 1968, 1993), we consider it first.

THE RHETORICAL TRADITION

The rhetorical tradition begins some 2,500 years after Kagemni's early writing, during the 5th century B.C., at Syracuse, in Sicily. When a democratic regime was established in Syracuse after the overthrow of the tyrant Thrasybulus, its citizens flooded the courts to recover property that had been confiscated during his reign. The "art of rhetoric" that Corax developed was intended to help ordinary people prove their claims in court. Although Corax and his student, Tisias, are also generally credited with the authorship of a manual on public speaking, the work is no longer extant. Although we are not certain of its contents, scholars suggest that it included two items significant to the development of rhetorical theory. The first was a theory of how arguments should be developed from probabilities, a theory more thoroughly developed by Aristotle a century later. Corax and Tisias are also credited with first developing the concept of message organization, what we today call an introduction, a body, and a conclusion.

In Athens, during the 5th century B.C., there was a large group of itinerant teachers, known as *sophists,* who established small schools and charged students for attending their lectures on rhetoric, literature, science, and philosophy. Many of these teachers became quite wealthy through their efforts. Protagoras of Abdara, sometimes called the "Father of Debate," was one of the first and most important sophists. His teachings contended that there were two sides to every proposition (a *dialectic*) and that speakers should be able to argue either side of the proposition equally well. This view, commonly accepted by today's teachers of argumentation and debate, provides the foundation in the U.S. for communication in today's legal and legislative systems, the very basis of democratic government itself.

Aristotle's *Rhetoric*

Aristotle, in the 3rd century B.C., is generally considered the foremost theorist in the history of the study of human communication from the rhetorical perspective. His *Rhetoric,* written in about 330 B.C., is the most influential work on the topic. It consists of three books, one primarily concerned with the speaker, another concerned with the audience, and the third with the speech itself.

Book I discusses the distinction between rhetorical communication and dialectical communication (the process of inquiry). Aristotle criticized his contemporaries for dwelling upon irrelevant matters in their rhetorical theories rather than concentrating on proofs—particularly enthymemes—or arguments from probabilities. He defined *rhetoric* as "the faculty of discovering in a particular case what are the available means of persuasion." To Aristotle, the means of persuasion were primarily *ethos* (the nature of the source), *pathos* (the emotions of the audience), and *logos* (the nature of the message presented by the source). He focused his concern on three types of speaking: deliberative (speaking in the legislature), forensic (speaking in the law court), and epideictic (speaking in a ceremonial situation). He was concerned with formal public speaking settings and did not address what we would call today "everyday" or "interpersonal" communication.

Within his overall theory of rhetoric, Aristotle included three critical elements. The first was that effective rhetoric is based on argumentation, and that all arguments must be based on *probabilities.* Aristotle held that absolute, verifiable truth is unobtainable in most instances. Therefore, persuasion must be based on what an audience believes to be true. Whereas his teacher, Plato, found this to be a defect in rhetoric and condemned it, Aristotle perceived it simply as a fact, and not a moral issue.

The second essential element in his approach was a conception of the rhetorical communicator's basic task was to *adapt to the audience.* Aristotle believed that you could not persuade a person unless you knew what was likely to persuade that individual. That is, he believed that a knowledge of what we now call "psychology" was essential to effective communication.

These two elements, probability and psychology, led to the third important element in his theory: rhetoric's basic "amorality." Aristotle viewed rhetoric as a tool, one which could be used by anyone—by a good person or a bad one, by a person seeking worthy ends or by one seeking unworthy ends. At the same time, he argued that rhetoric was a self-regulating art. By that he meant the person who is unethical, or who advocates evil, is less likely to be successful than the moral person advocating something good. As justification, he claimed that good and right, by their very nature, are more powerful persuasive tools than their opposites. While acknowledging that evil might win out in the short-run, Aristotle believed that evil would ultimately fail unless people arguing on behalf of good were incompetent rhetorical communicators.

During the Roman period, the 1st century A.D., Aristotle's work was known and writers such as Cicero and Quintilian (often called the "greatest orator" and "greatest teacher," respectively) wrote works within the general perspective of his work, although they were not always in agreement Aristotle's ideas. In general, the Roman period applied the rhetorical theory of the ancient Greeks, and helped to spread its use across the ancient world. Like the Roman period, there was not a great amount of writing on rhetoric in the Middle Ages. During the renaissance, however, more attention was directed toward rhetoric and, although Aristotle's works were known to the scholars of the time, most of their writings centered on matters of style rather than the concerns Aristotle had advanced.

During the 18th century writers such as George Campbell and Richard Whately in England resurrected the Aristotelian perspective toward communication and advanced it with their own theories. In the United States, Professor John Quincy Adams (the same John Quincy Adams to later become President of the United States), who held the chair of rhetoric at Harvard University, presented a series of lectures which set forth for the first time in America a thoroughly classical view of rhetoric. This view was extended in the early 20th century by the early writers, such as James Winans, in what became the field of "Speech."

American Rhetorical Study

The first professional organization of people concerned with the study of human communication, now known as the Eastern Communication Association, was formed in 1909 by a group of teachers of public speaking housed mainly in departments of English at eastern colleges and universities. Five years later, many of these same people joined with people from other parts of the United States to form what is now known as the Speech Communication Association, a national professional association that was then primarily composed of teachers of public speaking.

The people in these associations were primarily concerned (then and now) with developing greater understanding of how human communication works and how people can be taught to be more effective communicators. Because the political and social systems in American society in the first half of this century were very similar to those of Greece in the time of Aristotle, the Aristotelian rhetorical tradition was an excellent fit to the needs of the scholars of that era. The Aristotlian tradition soon became solidly entrenched as the dominant paradigm for the study of human communication.

During the first half of the 20th century the study of human communication expanded rapidly into what has come to be known as the "Speech" tradition. Academic departments of speech were founded in most major colleges and universities across the United States, particularly in the large midwestern institutions. The primary emphasis in these programs was the teaching of public speaking and the study of human communication in the Aristotelian rhetorical tradition. Most programs sponsored debating teams, *á la* Protagoras, and attempts to generate new knowledge about effective rhetoric were centered primarily on rhetorical *criticism* of the addresses of effective, or usually at least famous, public orators.

Although the rhetorical tradition held sway for the most part, departments of Speech expanded their attention to include many other aspects of oral communication. Theater and oral reading, voice and diction, speech pathology and audiology, radio and television broadcasting, and film classes all become common. By the middle of the 20th century many of these new offerings had grown into full-blown programs. Many of these speciality areas began leaving the Speech departments and forming academic units of their own. Theater and oral reading often joined other fine arts programs. Speech pathology and audiology, often accompanied by voice and diction, usually formed their own unit or joined other allied health programs. Broadcasting frequently joined with journalism, and print-oriented programs in public relations and advertising, to form Mass Communication programs. Sometimes film studies joined this group as well.

In many cases, departments which began with their focus on public speaking and the rhetorical tradition diversified extensively and split into several academic units. They then came full circle back to the study of public speaking and the rhetorical tradition. These programs continue to have a strong focus on public presentations, argumentation, and persuasion. Whereas, as we discuss more fully later, most of these programs have made major changes in their curricula (and their names) in the last half of the twentieth century, most continue to include a strong emphasis on work that follows the rhetorical tradition.

Perspectives on the Rhetorical Tradition

In order to understand the nature of the rhetorical approach to the study of human communication, it is useful to gain perspective on the culture in which it originated and where it still thrives. From today's perspective the cultures of ancient Greece and Rome had many positive and many negative characteristics. Despite their interest in philosophy, religion, and the arts and their commitment to a form of democracy, they were harsh cultures. Life expectancies were short, and life was very hard for most people.

These were slave-owning societies in which a slave could be killed or severely punished for even slight offenses against their masters. There was one dominant culture and the rulers of that culture were highly ethnocentric. People of other races and cultures were seen as inferior beings whose lives and well-being were of little value. Women were considered men's property and often treated only slightly better than the slaves. The men of the dominant race and ethnic group totally ruled society. The society was both racist and sexist, and these views were seldom challenged. For all, master and slave, that was just the way it was. From most people's perspectives, these were *not* the good old days.

The legislative and legal systems of these societies were devoted to the maintenance of the ruling class. It was important that the members of that class could resolve disputes and engage in coordinated action to maintain their power and control over the society. Understanding how to communicate effectively within this small ruling group was critical to one who wished to protect one's own interests or attain higher leadership status. Communication, then, was seen as a strategic tool—one to be used by those in power. The perspective was source-oriented—how a speaker could get an audience to do what he wanted them to do. Communication in the courts and in the legislature was primarily concerned with public speaking, and the effective orator was a much respected and powerful person.

Although we sometimes do not like to acknowledge it, this description of ancient Greece and Rome can be applied to the early Western culture, including the United States and many other societies of the 17th through 19th century. Like many other societies, we were a slave-owning society, one in which women, too, were seen as possessions of men. Our legislative and legal systems were modeled on Greco-Roman, Judeo-Christian, Anglo-European tradition. The rhetorical orientation of the Speech Tradition was tailor-made for this society.

The mass communication tradition, like the speech tradition, sprouted from roots in the rhetorical orientation. The predecessors of many of the people working in mass communication today were in departments of journalism and advertising, as well as in speech. Since the beginnings of the study of mass communication focused on public presentation and mass influence, the rhetorical orientation also fit the needs of these early scholars.

THE RELATIONAL TRADITION

The relational tradition is at least as old, and possibly older, than the rhetorical tradition. However, no serious attention was devoted to this orientation in the United States until the latter half of the 20th century. The foundations of the relational orientation stem from ancient Confucian philosophy. Hence, this orientation is most commonly associated with Eastern thought.

While individualism, competition, and straightforward communication are highly valued in most western societies, eastern societies have higher values for congeniality, cooperation, and indirect communication which will protect the "face" of the people interacting. Maintaining valued relationships is generally seen as more important than exerting influence and control over others.

The existence of approaches to communication other than the rhetorical approach was recognized by some scholars in the United States prior the mid-20th century. However, serious attention to the relational orientation did not begin until the 1950s and 1960s. Influential writers such as Robert Oliver (1962) attempted to get the field to pay more attention to the role of culture in communication and how different cultures viewed communication in other parts of the world.

Transitioning to the Relational

A new professional association for communication scholars was founded in 1950, the National Society for the Study of Communication, now known as the International Communication Association. This group was comprised of individuals disillusioned with studying communication exclusively from the rhetorical perspective. Some were general semanticists, others were primarily concerned with communication in organizations, and others in yet more applied communication settings. In the 1960s and 1970s this association attracted many scholars who were interested in interpersonal communication or the effects of mass media, particularly those who wished to study communication employing quantitative or experimental research methodologies.

The social-scientific movement was very important for the development of the study of human communication as it currently exists. Prior to the onset of this movement, most scholarship in this area employed critical or rationalistic approaches. These approaches were seen as appropriate for the study of essentially monological, one-way communication. Their focus was on the message and context as objects of study. As this one-way, hypodermic-needle approach to understanding communication came under increasing criticism, both the target of research and the methodologies for research came into question.

The social scientific approach to studying human communication had been employed by some since early in the 20th century. However, it was not until the post World War II era that the scientific method became the method of choice for a substantial number of communication scholars. It was natural that a different scholarly method would be applied to the same kinds of questions previously asked (how to persuade effectively) and to new questions. This, indeed, was the case. In the 1960s much of the social scientific research focused on the effects of sources and messages in producing persuasive effects. So much so that, when the early books on interpersonal communication were written, there was very little social scientific research which could be cited in them. By the mid-1970s, however, it was possible to base a book on human communication almost entirely on the social scientific research (McCroskey & Wheeless, 1976).

By the time NSSC became ICA and reached its 25th anniversary, sizeable groups of scholars had formed scholarly interest areas representing organizational communication, interpersonal communication, information systems, mass communication, intercultural communication, instructional communication, health communication, and political communication. Most of these groups also included people from both the rhetorical and the relational traditions.

The quarter-century between 1950 and 1975 represented revolutionary change both in the culture of the United States and in the way people chose to study human communication. The post-World War II and Korean War eras saw dramatic increases in the enrollments of women and members of ethnic and racial minorities in American colleges and universities. Higher education no longer was the domain only of the elite, male, White ruling class.

The civil rights movement of the early 1960s was followed by the women's rights movement of the later 1960s and 1970s. The way people saw themselves relating to others began to change. There were enormous enrollment increases in colleges and universities when the "baby boomers" reaching college age, which was exacerbated by rapid acceptance of the goals of the civil rights and women's rights movements.

These new students had different needs and arrived with different perspectives than those of their predecessors. Because colleges were no longer solely focused on educating "tomorrow's leaders," people began to question the extreme emphasis on teaching public speaking over all other types of communication. Classes in small group communication, and research in this area, greatly increased.

A Truly Relational Perspective

A call for more practical and realistic communication courses was heard. The response by the early 1970s was the initiation of new courses with the term "interpersonal" in their titles. Because little research from a relational perspective had been done by that time, the early courses tended to focus on rhetorical and psychological approaches to interpersonal communication. The early texts tended to focus on either humanistic (Giffin & Patton, 1971) or social scientific (McCroskey, Larson, & Knapp, 1971) orientations. A true relational perspective did not appear until later (Knapp, 1984).

Because *speech* was a term used to identify the traditional rhetorical orientation of the people who studied human communication, and the field was changing, people sought ways to change the identity of their field. While public speaking was no longer the sole, or even most important, focus of the field, people outside the field were generally unaware of this fact. At first, it seemed sufficient to simply add "communication" to the names of departments and associations. Soon it became clear that this change was not enough to make outsiders aware that a major change had been made. Thus, by the mid-1990s the term *speech* had been dropped from the names of almost all scholarly journals in the field, from the names of all the regional and many of the state professional associations, and from the names of most of the departments at major universities. The names generally were changed to "Communication" or "Communication Studies," but some were renamed "Human Communication," "Interpersonal Communication," or "Communication Sciences," although the latter could be confused with some names used by groups concerned with speech pathology and audiology.

HUMAN COMMUNICATION TODAY

The study of human communication today is more diversified than ever before in its history. This diversity is reflected in both what is studied and the way that one goes about studying it.

Both the rhetorical and the relational traditions are alive and well and reflected in the the the chapters that follow. Each chapter outlines current thinking in either what could pass for a subfield (persuasion, intercultural communication, organizational communication), or a topic area (credibility, nonverbal communication) which has been and continues to be a focus of attention for numerous scholars, or an approach that some prefer to take in their study of human communication (cultural, feminist).

Because these chapters speak to the way these subfields, areas, or approaches are examined today, there is no need to go into detail here. Within the limitations of a book this size, it is not possible to fully introduce all of the areas within the human communication side of the field. Thus, we simply mention a few that are important but for which no chapter is included here.

The individual differences approach is one which has been employed by some scholars for the past half century and continues to draw major attention today. This approach looks at how people consistently differ from one another in their communication orientations and behaviors. Sometimes this approach is referred to as the personality approach (McCroskey & Daly, 1987).

Scholars studying human communication from this approach investigate how different people have different traits or orientations which result in them communicating differently than other people and responding to others' communication differently as well. Two of the major topics within this area are concerns with people's general willingness to communicate with others and the fear or anxiety that people experience when confronted with communication (Daly & McCroskey, 1984).

With the rapid advances in social biology which indicate that personality has a firm genetic base, this area is one in which we can expect major advances in the next two decades. The possibility exists that through genetic engineering we will even be able to alter individual's patterns of communication behavior which are found dysfunctional in society. Whether we will want to do this, however, is another question.

From the beginning of professional associations in the communication field, a significant number of the members have had a major concern with teaching. Originally that interest was centered on how to teach people to be better communicators. In recent years, this interest in instruction has expanded to a concern with the role of communication in the instructional process generally, not just in teaching communication (McCroskey, 1992). Considerable research in this area (Richmond & McCroskey, 1992) has pointed toward a central position for the study of communication to improve instruction in all disciplines.

Another applied area of communication study is an expansion of the basic interpersonal area. It is the study of communication within the family (Pearson, 1989). Recent research has been able to track the impact of communication between parents and children into the relationships that the younger generation have years later with their significant others. It would appear that understanding the communicative relationships within the family may be key to understanding other relationships people have.

An area which has received considerable attention in recent years is the role of gender in communication (Pearson, 1985). Although research focusing on the impact of biological sex differences on communication has generally found little impact, research on culturally based gender roles has indicated a very large impact. This is an area in which cross-cultural study is particularly useful, for we have learned that gender communication roles are so socialized into people that they are unlikely to recognize they are behaving according to a norm unless they see that there are different norms in other cultures.

A comparatively new approach to the study of communication is the developmental approach (Nussbaum, 1989). This approach examines how communication orientations and behaviors are likely to change during the individual's life span. Of particular interest has been the impact of aging on communication (Nussbaum, Thompson, & Robinson, 1989).

SUMMARY

Although steeped in tradition, the general trend of scholarship in the human communication side of the field of communication is toward more sophisticated theoretical development. It continues to develop more diverse subareas within each larger area of the field, while grounding itself in research methodologies useful for the specific concerns in the study of communication (rather than borrowed from other fields). Its approach is also increasingly concerned with applied communication research. The study of human communication today is undertaken in a vibrant and forward looking environment, building on firm traditions but diversifying to confront new realities.

REFERENCES

Daly, J. A., & McCroskey, J. C. (1984). *Avoiding communication: Shyness, reticence, and communication apprehension.* Beverly Hills, CA: Sage.

Giffin, K., & Patton, B. R. (1971). *Fundamentals of interpersonal communication.* New York: Harper & Row.

Knapp, M. L. (1984). *Interpersonal communication and human relationships.* Boston, MA: Allyn & Bacon.

McCroskey, J. C. (1968). *An introduction to rhetorical communication.* Englewood Cliffs, NJ: Prentice-Hall.

McCroskey, J. C. (1992). *An introduction to communication in the classroom.* Edina, MN: Burgess International Group.

McCroskey, J. C. (1993). *An introduction to rhetorical communication* (6th ed.). Englewood Cliffs, NJ: Prentice-Hall.

McCroskey, J. C., & Daly, J. A. (1987) *Personality and interpersonal communication.* Newbury Park, CA: Sage.

McCroskey, J. C., Larson, C. E., & Knapp, M. L. (1971). *An introduction to interpersonal communication.* Englewood Cliffs, NJ: Prentice-Hall.

McCroskey, J. C., & Wheeless, L. R. (1976). *Introduction to human communication.* Boston, MA: Allyn & Bacon.

Nussbaum, J. F. (1989). *Life-span communication: Normative processes.* Hillsdale, NJ: Lawrence Erlbaum Associates.

Nussbaum, J. F., Thompson, T., & Robinson, J. D. (1989). *Communication and aging.* New York: Harper & Row.

Oliver, R. T. (1962). *Culture and communication: The problem of penetrating national boundaries.* Springfield, IL: National Textbook Company.

Pearson, J. C. (1985). *Gender and communication.* Dubuque, IA: William C. Brown.

Pearson, J. C. (1989). *Communication in the family: Seeking satisfaction in changing times.* New York: Harper & Row.

Richmond, V. P., & McCroskey, J. C. (1992). *Power in the classroom: Communication, control and concern.* Hillsdale, NJ: Lawrence Erlbaum Associates.

Shepherd, G. J. (1992). Communication as influence: Definitional exclusion. *Communication Studies, 43,* 203–219.

16

The Rhetorician's Quest

Walter R. Fisher
Stephen D. O'Leary
University of Southern California

Earlier chapters in this book provide a good grasp of theory and its uses. Theory consists of constructs that purport to explain or account for phenomena—in our case, for the experience of human communication. Theory guides inquiry, in such activities as observation, description, and prediction. Through this work, theory leads to knowledge or understanding, and, on occasion, to new or modified theory. In addition, theory can be used to evaluate not only procedures and standards of inquiry, but also the conduct of human communication itself.

How does the rhetorical theorist theorize or philosophize? Answering this question is this chapter's primary aim. Through a series of examples, we will detail various modes of thinking by which the rhetorician pursues knowledge or understanding of human communication processes and practices. Before getting to these ways of thinking, several general matters require attention, including clarifying the distinctions between theorizing and philosophizing, and between knowledge and understanding. Also considered are some relationships between rhetorical and social scientific theorizing, and the factors involved in the genesis and shaping of theory.

KNOWLEDGE, UNDERSTANDING, THEORIZING,
AND PHILOSOPHIZING

As for the distinctions between knowledge and understanding, while knowledge is commonly considered ideas that are generalizable and predictive, understanding is often considered ideas that explain phenomena and provide meaningful, useful comprehension of acts, deeds, and events. Theory is a particular aspect of both—knowledge and understanding. Philosophy is a larger set of constructs which would account for both—knowledge and understanding. "Cognitive dissonance" is a theory, which, when applied in research, may produce knowledge. Carl Hempel's "theory" of covering law (1965), however, is larger; it is a *metatheory*, reflecting a philosophy of what constitutes knowledge, how it should be pursued, and how it is applicable to any "scientific" theory. Although these distinctions are not absolute, as will be indicated, it is important to recognize them, because they are widely held and can be useful.

RELATIONSHIPS AMONG COMMUNICATION THEORISTS

One way the distinctions do not serve well is in trying to draw absolute differences between the theorizing of rhetoricians and other communication theorists. A popular notion is that rhetoricians are "rationalists" and other communication theorists are empiricists; rhetoricians think in "armchairs" or live in libraries, while other communication theorists think in "laboratories." Evidence abounds that this characterization is grossly distorted, including the range and extent of current qualitative research and the gamut of philosophical positions arrayed in Richard Cherwitz's book, *Rhetoric and Philosophy* (1990). In this collection of essays, rhetoricians explored the relationships between rhetorical theory and realism, relativism, critical rationalism, idealism, materialism, existentialism, and pragmatism; there is also an essay on "rhetoric after deconstruction." Of these essays, the ones most pertinent to the dubious distinctions drawn between rhetorical theorists and other communication theorists are those on materialism and realism. Indeed, the strongest defense of "objectivity" in recent communication literature appears in a series of studies conducted by Cherwitz and Hikins, much of which is summarized in their book, *Communication and Knowledge: An Investigation in Rhetorical Epistemology* (1986).

This is not to say that there are no differences among rhetorical theorists and other communication theorists. Where most rhetoricians and some communication theorists differ from their colleagues is over whether or not one believes in and tries to pursue what Paul Ricouer referred to as the "science of praxis" (1991, p. 199). Those who chase this dream insist on theories that provide explanations entailing linear causation, reasoning from the existence of antecedents to a conclusion of consequences following from them. Rhetorical theorists, by and large, along with many others in the social sciences and humanities, are more than willing to accept explanations that assume teleological causation, reasoning from a comprehensive construct to an interpretation of particular acts, deeds, or events. Such explanations (or interpretations) dispel what is "confused, fragmentary . . . cloudy . . . [or] strange, mystifying, puzzling, [and] contradictory . . . ," according to Charles Taylor (1977, p. 103). Take, for instance, the concept of *culture* as it is applied in organizational communication research. The concept accounts for much, but does not predict anything. Like other theoretical constructs, it is a useful generalization insofar as it aids understanding and is fruitful in guiding inquiry. No generalization, however derived, is beyond contradiction or further qualification. This is one reason why new theories are always emerging; the search for better explanations is constant.

Another way to get at the similarities and differences among communication scholars is to consider their typical lines of inquiry, the questions they pursue, and the research they conduct to answer them. Table 16.1 facilitates this consideration (note the quotation marks around the headings). Several features are to be observed in this representation. First, each item in each column indicates a way of producing or constituting knowledge or understanding. Second, human communication cannot be appreciated fully without each of these avenues being pursued. Third, *the two categories are not discrete.* One cannot do empirical research, that is, deal directly with data, without concepts to work with, however elementary they may be. And one cannot develop useful concepts without due regard for data. Whatever else rhetorical theory–philosophy and communication theory may be, they are practical and pragmatic. They concern the world of lived experience. Their value is commensurate with their contribution to understanding and performing well here, now, and for the future. What ultimately separates some rhetorical and communication theorists from some others is, as noted earlier, whether or not they subscribe to "scientism," and the clearest evidence of this subscription is what they predicate as data in their theory and research, and what they demand as an adequate explanation.

THE GENESIS AND SHAPING OF THEORY

The question at this point is: How do theories/philosophies arise, and what ideas or conditions shape them? The answer to the first part of this question goes as follows: theories and philosophies arise whenever a well-informed mind becomes dissatisfied

TABLE 16.1

Ways of Producing Knowledge and Understanding

"Empirical"	*"Conceptual"*
Laboratory experiment	Definitions (analytic synthetic operational)
Field experiment	Models theories philosophy
Survey	Determinations of "data" (arguments appeals ideas images interacts behaviors etc.)
Content Analysis	
Ethnographic studies	Evaluative standards (logical ethical aesthetic)
History	

with conventional wisdom. They are born out of wonder and curiosity, out of a passion to understand, to improve understanding and conduct. They are nurtured by knowledge, intelligence, imagination, and insight—a commodity that does not occur in a vacuum. Theories and philosophies, although they begin with critique, cannot rest content with showing the faults and flaws of conventional wisdom; they must go on to articulate a better way of thinking that produces a better way of acting. The answer to this first part would not be complete if we were to ignore two other motivations in producing theory: ego and the desire to publish rather than perish. Needless to say, neither is sufficient to account for good theory. Indeed, one colleague maintains that there is only one requirement to formulate good theory—smart parents.

Earlier we noted differences between theory and philosophy, but maintained that the differences were not absolute. In fact, theories presuppose philosophical ideas: ontological assumptions about reality; epistemological concepts of knowledge, logic, and reason; axiological stances regarding ethical ideas of the good, the desirable, and the obligatory (and their opposites); and psychological beliefs about the nature of the human use/abuse of whatever means of communication by which one or more people can be related, including but not restricted to language, signs, and symbols. Theories are also affected by political considerations, including existing governmental realities and ideal conceptualizations. Theories, or the philosophy on which they are based, are constrained or accelerated by technology, ranging from oral means and opportunities for communication, to written systems of expression, to the various forms of electronic media that dominate current communication practices. All of these influences can be accounted for through one line of inquiry or another; the one element that evades clear understanding is genius, and this, too, is a factor in the formulation of theory. We will refer to each of these factors in theory building, except genius, as we detail the various modes of thinking that shape the process.

CREATING THEORIES/PHILOSOPHIES OF RHETORIC

What is rhetoric? What is its role in communication? In education? How does it interpret the communication act? One more clarification is needed before we proceed—the meanings of *rhetoric*.

Meanings of *Rhetoric*

The most familiar use of the word "rhetoric" is its common application as a pejorative label, signifying discourse that is untruthful, perhaps unethical, and certainly self-serving. In this signification, "rhetoric" is synonymous with deceit, distortion, or language used to create a biased impression or image of someone or some act, deed, or event. In its most condemnatory usage, it denotes unreality, as in "All they do is give us rhetoric; what we need now is talk about reality." The irony (or ignorance) in this usage is that it is itself rhetorical, a use of language to convey persuasive ideas. One may condemn rhetoric, use it in a condemnatory way, but one cannot escape it. To accuse one of being "rhetorical" is, in effect, accusing one of dishonesty. The important point to note is that *rhetoric pertains to all pragmatic, persuasive discourse, honest and dishonest.* Because pragmatic, persuasive discourse has the power to move people to concerted action, it is both feared and prized. It reveals human beings in the full range of their capacities for ignoble and noble words and deeds. Thus, whereas most people are accustomed to think of rhetoric as talk that they oppose to action, the rhetorician is trained to think of "talk"—or any form of communication—as a *kind* of "action" that needs to be studied on its own terms.

Because rhetorical competence (when it accords with one's own conception of truth and justice) is highly prized, it has played a prominent role in the education of citizens throughout the history of Western culture. Indeed, along with grammar and logic, it formed the original liberal arts. Each of these arts provided precepts and principles for fashioning ideas and information from all avenues of learning. Grammar taught clear and correct expression; logic instructed in the ways of sound thinking; and rhetoric offered procedures of invention, arrangement, style, memory, and delivery of subject matter. Rhetoric's offerings in this vein are evident today, especially in courses in speech and written composition. In this capacity, *rhetoric serves as a significant pedagogical art.*

In earlier times, especially in Europe, rhetorical pedagogy often focused on teaching the manifold features of style: the figures of speech, usually divided into schemes (unusual or extraordinary patterns of language and sentence structure, such as alliteration) and tropes (uses of words to signify something other than their lexical meaning, such as metaphor or hyperbole). Rhetoricians in the Renaissance devoted much energy to compiling and cataloguing these stylistic devices; the rhetorical handbooks from this era often list hundreds of terms with obscure Greek and Latin names for seemingly simple concepts, such as anaphora (repetition of a word or phrase at the beginning of successive sentences or clauses) or oxymoron (yoking together two opposite concepts in the same phrase, as in "painful pleasure" or "cruel kindness"), which students were expected to memorize. Because of this historically important aspect of rhetorical pedagogy, many people to this day tend to reduce rhetoric to the study of these flowery figures. This reduction is a mistake that distorts the rich history of rhetorical theory and teaching. Yet it is also worth noting that the rhetorical figures catalogued by generations of scholars should not be seen only as devices for embellishment or adornment of a preexistent message; figures of speech such as metaphor are also constitutive of thought, since we cannot form or communicate our ideas without them.

"Rhetoric" refers not only to discursive practices and pedagogy, it also specifies a category—a genre—of communication, a way of interpreting communication, and a theory or philosophy of communication. *As a genre, rhetoric names that form of communication which is argumentative or persuasive*—in contrast with such forms as exposition, narrative, drama, and so forth. Kenneth Burke's philosophy of rhetoric, which holds that rhetoric is the symbolic function of inducement—where there is persuasion, there is rhetoric—radically re-alters these distinctions, making it possible to think seriously about the rhetoric of architecture, film, fiction, ritual, and any other symbolic expression that relates human beings. It is from this stance that *rhetoric becomes a significant mode of interpretation.*

Long before Burke, rhetorical theory and composition informed the practices of dramatists, poets, musicians, and artists in Greece, Rome, the Renaissance, and today, thinking across the disciplines. A particularly impressive program that reflects the impact of using rhetoric as a mode of interpretation is the Iowa "Rhetoric of Inquiry Project." In the publication inaugurating its beginning conference, *The Rhetoric of the Human Sciences* (1987), there are essays on the rhetoric of mathematics, science, anthropology, psychology, economics, history, literature, law, political science, feminism, and theology. The common thread that runs through these essays is their attention to the way knowledge within and across fields and disciplines is formed through communication practices. For example, Donald McCloskey, one of the leading figures of the Iowa project, showed in his *The Rhetoric of Economics* (1985) that progress in theory-building, even in an avowedly empirical and quantitative discipline, depends on the ability to formulate persuasive arguments that employ the full range of human linguistic resources—not just scientific data presented in graphs and tables, but also through style, arrangement, metaphor, and analogy.

A more recent contribution to rhetoric as a mode of interpretation is that of Richard Lanham, who has employed rhetorical thought to examine the computer as an intrinsically rhetorical device. In *The Electronic Word: Democracy, Technology, and the Arts* (1993), he claims that computers encourage a mode of consciousness he calls "toggling"—the ability to switch back and forth between viewing a text or communicative act as an artificial construction, on the one hand, and seeing through the text to the reality that it represents, on the other. Through the ages, rhetorical training has sensitized audiences to be attuned not only to the communicator's intended meaning, but also to the linguistic and symbolic devices used to convey meaning. According to Lanham, the dynamic, interactive qualities of digital text place rhetorical modes of interpretation once again into the center of our culture, forcing us to recognize the artificiality of all self-consciously crafted communicative acts. Whereas some might find this insight unsettling, he celebrates it as a revival of rhetoric, with the potential to restore vitality to education, the arts, and democratic practice, claiming that "electronic expression has come not to destroy Western arts and letters, but to fulfill them" (1993, p. xiii).

Finally, there is *rhetoric as theory or philosophy,* which attempts to account for all of the above: rhetoric as discursive practice, pedagogy, form of communication, and mode of interpretation. The difference between rhetorical theory and rhetorical philosophy, as suggested earlier, is that theory advances explanations of particular features of rhetorical processes or practices, such as ideology, culture, or episteme (as will be shown later); philosophy proposes conceptions that explain the creation, composition, adaptation, presentation, and reception of rhetorical events and experiences—from an encompassing set of ideas concerning the nature of human beings, political systems, relevant technology, and the relationships among the various arts and disciplines. Such philosophical enterprises can be found in several of the works we discuss later, including Plato, Aristotle, George Campbell, and Kenneth Burke.

The abiding question that has animated the rhetorician's quest since its origins in ancient Greece is this, "How and in what ways do humans constitute themselves, others, and the world through the use and abuse of communicative instruments (words, signs, symbols, gestures, rituals, etc.)?" Answers to this question have been various, some particular, others comprehensive, some theoretical, others philosophical. There are almost as many theoretical and philosophical conceptions of rhetoric as there are significant theoretical and philosophical works. These varying conceptions reflect shifting philosopical presuppositions, political conditions, and technology, but the question persists.

BUILDING RHETORICAL THEORY OR PHILOSOPHY

The next task is to detail the principal ways in which different theorists and philosophers have pursued the quest-seeking knowledge and understanding of things rhetorical.

The Beginnings

The most appropriate way to begin is at the beginning, over 2,500 years ago in ancient Greece. (Theorizing about communication did not begin in the 1940s and 1950s with the Hovland, Janis, and Kelly, 1953, studies.) Rhetorical theory began, as the traditional story goes,when courts were established to settle disputes over property rights, a situation in which relevant documents had been destroyed. Thus, it was necessary for the disputants to "invent" persuasive arguments based on probabilities. For instance, a rich man has no need to claim property which is not his own. I am a rich man; the property is rightfully mine. A poor man cannot be expected to win a case against a rich man unless his cause is just. I am a poor man; my cause is just; the property is rightfully mine. The effort to classify, to note the various structures of the argument presented before the courts, was the beginning of rhetoric as a serious intellectual line of inquiry. The initial move was to lay the grounds for theory (i.e., grounded theory) by establishing a grammar or terminology that would identify key elements in a communicative process. The first step was description: cataloging and categorizing the strategic moves. The second step was to explain or account for them. A third step was to consider their consequences (social, political, and pedagogical). Another step is to consider the enterprise in regard to related arts and disciplines.

Building from "Grounds"

Three features of grounded theory are noteworthy here. First, it is descriptive but explanatory only in a limited way, and, of course, it is not predictive of human conduct. It is, in effect, but a first step. Second, naming or renaming the elements in a communication process is critical to theory building, it affects explanation and may signal the advent of a "new" theory or philosophy. For instance, it is one thing to use the terminology of Aristotle—ethos, pathos, and logos—and quite another to use the language of Burke—signs of consubstantiation, modes of identification. These different terms denote, among other things, different psychological presuppositions: Aristotle, a "rationalistic" definition of humans, and Burke, a Freudian conception of humans. Third, grounded theory is alive and well in the late 20th century.

Although Roderick P. Hart's *Verbal Style and the Presidency: A Computer-Based Analysis* (1984) is presented as "rhetorical history," it can be considered a superb example of the process of establishing grounds for theory. More than 400 speeches from Truman to Reagan were analyzed by computer using a program called "Diction." Actually, 800 messages were scanned, for indications of activity, optimism, certainty, and realism, also embellishment, self-reference, variety, familiarity, human interest, complexity, and symbolism. The result was an impressive, persuasive characterization of each of the presidents studied, and a second book, *The Sound of Leadership* (1987), which continued the empirical approach of *Verbal Style*. Hart did not offer his works in a theoretical fashion, but the data are there, and his generalizations provide useful explanations of presidential speechmaking.

Building from Observations of Practice

Because rhetoric, as discursive practice, became so vital to the life of ancient Greece through education as well as legal, political, and public address, it drew the attention of Plato, Aristotle, and Isocrates (rhetoric's "greatest teacher" of the age). Each took a different approach to rhetoric. Isocrates' approach may be called practical pheno-menological (as contrasted with philosophical [Husserlian] phenomenological). In an implied complaint against the kind of philosophy practiced in Plato's academy, he designated his work "practical philosophy." The keystone of Iscocrates' approach was the observations made in this passage (which became central to the rise and influence of humane studies):

> We ought, therefore, to think of the art of discourse just as we think of all the other arts, and not to form opposite judgments about similar things, nor show ourselves intolerant toward that power which, of all the faculties which belong to the nature of man, is the source of most of our blessings. For in the other powers which we possess . . . we are in no respect superior to other living creatures; . . . but because there has been implanted in us the power to persuade each other and to make clear to each other whatever we desire, not only have we escaped the life of wild beasts, but we have come together and founded cities and made laws and invented arts; and, generally speaking, there is no institution devised by man which the power of speech has not helped us to establish. For this it is which has laid down laws concerning things just and unjust, and things honorable and base; and if it were not for these ordinances we should not be able to live with one another. It is by this also that we confute the bad and extol the good. Through this we educate the ignorant and appraise the wise; for the power to speak well is taken as the surest index of a sound understanding, and discourse which is true and lawful and just is the outward image of a good and faithful soul. With this faculty we both contend against others on matters which are open to dispute and seek light for ourselves on things which are unknown. . . . [W]e shall find that none of the things which are done with intelligence take place without the help of speech, but that in all our actions as well as in all our thoughts speech is our guide, and is most employed by those who have the most wisdom. (1928, pp. 327–329)

The question is, "How did Isocrates know these things to be true?" The answer is that he observed everyday life. He did not try to look above, into, or below it. His approach was not eclectic, as is the wont of many contemporary textbook writers. He did not borrow precepts from humanists and empiricists (such as they were in his time). He devised his techniques of teaching rhetoric to accord with his foundational percep-tion of human speech performance and what he saw as pragmatic, effective experience to achieve excellence in advancing the highest ideals of Athenian society.

Although his celebrated essay "The Rhetorical Situation" (1968) reflects Aristote-lian realism, Lloyd F. Bitzer's approach to building rhetorical theory is like that of

Isocrates. By analyzing the nature of the occasions that give rise to rhetorical discourse, he is able to specify their constituents: exigence, audience, and constraints. How does he know that these are the constituents? Because they are there, not only for he to see them, but for anyone else who will look carefully. Later, we cite a work that uses Bitzer's observations, using metaphor as the beginning point.

Building by "Borrowing"

Because we have made reference to "borrowing" in a way that may seem pejorative, we need to say that "borrowing" is a legitimate way to build theory. Earlier use of the word only implies that there is something dubious about texts that employ distinctions based on 18th-century faculty psychology—to inform, to convince, to persuade—without awareness that they philosophically imply that humans are really two kinds of beings, rational and irrational (moved by desire, suggestion, impressions, and so forth). There is also the complication of introducing models of communication implying that humans are some sort of machine. Our complaint is not that these views have nothing to offer to communication studies; it is when they are indiscriminately put together that we demur.

The sort of borrowing that makes sense is that which adopts conceptions from related disciplines across the academy that further our ability to explain communicative practices in a philosophical and consistent manner. The practices are quite familiar to communication theorists as they borrow extensively from social psychological models and constructs such as cognitive dissonance, compliance, gaming theories, and attitudes, beliefs, and values. Prime examples in rhetorical theory are ideology, culture, and episteme. To worry about borrowing such ideas, to fear co-optation by other disciplines, is to hold to the misconception that knowledge/understanding is compartmentalized along departmental lines. Recent examples of theory-building through "borrowing" include Michael McGee's "The Ideograph: A Link between Rhetoric and Ideology" (1980), Thomas B. Farrell's *Norms of Rhetorical Culture* (1993), and Raymie E. McKerrow's "Critical Rhetoric: Theory and Practice" (1984). Each of these works is a significant contribution to rhetorical theory; none, however, represent a philosophy of rhetoric. On the other hand, each of them, respectively, is founded on a philosophical position: materialism, Aristotelianism, and postmodern (Foucaltian) thought.

Building from Observations of Ideal Reality

Plato's approach to rhetoric is philosophical through and through. This does not mean it is irrelevant to the "real world", only that it is based on philosophical presuppositions, most importantly Plato's metaphysical notions of ultimate reality. Whereas almost all other thinkers who write about rhetoric ground their works on ideas directly related to the phenomenological world, Plato thought in terms of the *noumenal* world, a world where truth, good, justice, and such existed eternally, fixed, and universal. Insofar as his philosophy derived its conceptions from this way of thinking, it can be called an ontological approach.

From this way of viewing the phenomenological world, rhetoric, which is always a matter of acting in the phenomenological, contingent, and quotidian world, had to be seen as not only deficient ethically, intellectually, and as a pedagogical art, but also as dangerous. The only salvation for rhetoric was for it to be informed by dialectical knowledge, that is, by philosopher kings. At the end of his dialogue *Phaedrus* (trans. 1961), Plato outlines what was called a "true" rhetoric. He demanded that the rhetorician *know* what he or she was talking about, the nature of the soul of the body politic, and the various uses of language which would implant a sense of sobriety and justice in the audience. Such a conception follows his idea of what a true art is. It must be like medicine: It should have a conception of the good (health), know the nature of the physical body, and apply the appropriate remedies by which the body could be restored or maintained in good health. There is a sense in which Plato outlined the first "science" of rhetoric and communication. It should also be noted how this conception was consonant with his ideal conception of the political state as imagined in the *Republic*.

Plato's modern day counterpart in rhetorical theory is Richard Weaver, who was, until his death, an intellectual leader of conservative thought in America. He began his best known work in rhetoric, *The Ethics of Rhetoric* (1953), with an essay titled "The *Phaedrus* and the Nature of Rhetoric." There, he writes: "There is . . . no true rhetoric without dialectic, for the dialectic provides that basis of 'high speculation about nature' without which rhetoric in the narrower sense has nothing to work upon" (1953, p. 17). He also wrote that "rhetoric at its truest seeks to perfect humans by showing them better versions of themselves, links in that chain extending up toward the ideal, which only the intellect can apprehend and only the soul have affection for" (1953, p. 25). Weaver was perhaps most closely identified with the view that "language is sermonic" (1963/1970), always moving closer toward or farther away from truth and justice.

Building from Observations of Contingent Reality

Where Plato and Weaver were convinced of an ultimate reality, Aristotle and Burke were convinced, at least in regard to the nature and functions of rhetoric, that the phenomenal world is "real," however differently they perceived it. On the presupposition that rationality distinguished humans from all other animals, Aristotle conceived rhetoric as the capacity (shared to some extent by all humans) for observing the available means of persuasion in a given case; the means of persuasion as proofs, demonstrations that were logical, ethical, and emotional; and the aim or end of rhetorical discourse as influencing human judgment. His "method" for observing the nature and functions of rhetoric (as with his study of the other subjects which came within the purview of his philosophy) was an intellective, intuitive, inductive process. For example, in determining the kinds of rhetorical discourse, he looked to where discursive practices occurred, saw that the key places of civic judgment were the assembly, the courtroom, and the agora where speeches of praise and blame were presented. He examined the addresses in each of these forums entelechially—that is, to see what they were when they became what they were, not individually, but as a class. From this examination, he concluded that deliberative speeches concerned the future and employed the topics of expediency and inexpediency regarding war and peace, exports and imports, ways and means, and national defense; forensic speeches concerned the past and employed the topics of accusation and defense, justice and injustice; and epideictic (ceremonial) speeches concerned the present, employing the topics of praise and censure, honor and dishonor. These determinations, it should be noted, were philosophical (analytical), not purely descriptive.

Contrary to Plato, Aristotle held that rhetoric was a useful art, because persons could be informed about the materials that composed their speeches, and precepts and principles could be systematically organized to teach students so that they could improve their capacity for observing appropriate persuasive proof for different situations. He also held that rhetoric had its own "logic," an epistemology attuned to reasoned probabilities which represented the only possible foundation for making civic decisions where absolute or scientific knowledge was unavailable. He also disagreed with Plato's view of the relationship of rhetoric and ethics, maintaining that while rhetoric did teach an ability to argue opposite conclusions, it was "absurd to hold that a man ought to be ashamed of being unable to defend himself with the limbs, but not of being unable to defend himself with speech and reason, when the use of rational speech is more distinctive of a human being than the use of his limbs." Aristotle has often been held to the idea that rhetoric is amoral. In fact, he wrote: "What makes a man a 'sophist' is not his faculty, but his moral purpose." Most important here, however, is his admonition: "We must not make people believe what is wrong" (Aristotle, 1954, 23–24). The significance of these views, at this point, is that they show critical differences between Aristotle's and Plato's positions on rhetoric; they also show how different philosophical presuppositions lead to these differences. Where Plato's philosophy is consonant with his conception of an ideal republic, Aristotle's philosophy is consonant with Athenian democracy, and, in many ways, with our own.

So far we have presented theorists and philosophers in such a way as to give the impression that their thinking follows some linear and systematic movement from presuppositions to precepts and principles, from sudden insights to elaborated constructs. Theory-building rarely, if ever, happens according to these happy, snappy procedures. We also may have suggested that it is always revolutionary rather than evolutionary, when the reverse is most often the case. We bring up these matters at this time because we are about to characterize the thinking of one of the most creative writers ever to grace the panoply of rhetorical philosophers: Kenneth Burke. We will juxtapose his position to Aristotle's, because he acknowledged his indebtedness to the Stagirite's philosophy (even though his own philosophy is based on different political and psychological presuppositions), because it facilitates clarification without too much distortion, and because comparison of their thinking on rhetoric vividly demonstrates how different origins leads to different offerings. This last point may be better put this way: we can see what a difference real differences can make in knowledge and understanding, what justifies claiming that something "new" has been generated—like a rhetorical theory.

Earlier we noted that the introduction of a "new" grammar is a sign that a new theory or philosophy is present. This is certainly the case in regard to Burke's opus, which features a major book entitled *A Grammar of Motives* (1945). Only after this work appeared was his next major book, *A Rhetoric of Motives* (1955), written and published. Burke agreed with Aristotle that human relations, including rhetorical transactions, were of the contingent, quotidian world. But where Aristotle held that what distinguished humans from other animals was their rationality, Burke's "Definition of Man" (1968) claimed that the propensity to the use and abuse of symbols was the essential distinguishing characteristic of human nature. Burke also claimed that rhetorical experience found its end or aim not in judgment (as Aristotle had it) but in identification; that proofs were not the instruments of rhetoric, but signs of consubstantiation; and that the function of rhetoric was not persuasion, but inducement. Where Aristotle's rhetoric grew out of epistemological presuppositions, Burke's emanated from onto-logical presuppositions. Aristotle's rhetoric served the Athenian democracy; Burke's rhetoric was intended to serve a socialistic community (understanding that socialism is used here with a small *s*). Aristotle got his ideas about rhetoric from an entelechial analysis of rhetorical practices; Burke got his, once he made it explicit in the *Grammar*, from what he called the "pentad," which was, interestingly, an analog of Aristotle's ten categories for determining the nature of things. Burke's questions of what kind of actor was performing, what kind of scene provided the context for the act, what kind of purpose animated the performance, what kind of action named the performance, and what kind of agency was employed in the performance was designed to reveal the motive inherent in any human relations. In other words, Burke was interested in how humans use and abuse symbols in attempts to move them to share conceptions of the identity of others in community, and the world itself. Like Aristotle, Burke advanced a normative philosophy of rhetoric. Aristotle formulated conceptions which would elevate knowledge, reason, and rational judgment; Burke's aim is revealed in his motto, "Ad bellum purificandum" ("Toward the purification of war"). The "purification" idea is basic to Burke's philosophy and criticism; it can be succinctly summarized as "if we must have conflict, let it be verbal conflict." Both were realists of a sort—Aristotle being a "logical realist," and Burke a "linguistic realist," somewhat in the same vein as Hans-Georg Gadamer. Contrasting the views of Aristotle and Burke in this way stresses differences; however, it is more the case that Burke simply expands and subsumes Aristotle's thought.

Building Theory by Analogy

One of the obvious conclusions to be drawn from this analysis of Aristotle and Burke is that different defintions of humanity inevitably lead to different philosophies of rhetoric. However, it is also true that one can build and use theories without such a radical, revolutionary move. This can be seen in theories generated through analogy. Analogy plays a significant role in all sorts of thinking (indicating similarites and differences which lead to significant new constructs), but what we are pointing to here is not just any sort of analogy or piecemeal borrowing. Our interest is in the large-scale relating of two phenom-ena. Particularly useful examples can be found in the works of Stephen Toulmin (1958) and Chaïm Perelman with L. Olbrechts-Tyteca (1969). These authors reconstruct argu-mentation theory to accord with a jurisprudential model. There are important differences in their thinking, but on this point, they are as one: their work is informed throughout by an extended analogy between jurisprudence and ordinary practical communication.

Toulmin's theory began with a critique of formal logic, in regard especially to ethical argument. His interest has been in reasoning per se. Perelman and Olbrechts-Tyteca's philosophy, which held that rhetoric should be the study of discursive means by which people are brought to adherence, is also concerned with reasoning, but in terms of the relationship between arguer and audience. Where Toulmin offers a schematic for laying out the anatomy of a line of argument, Perelman and Olbrechts-Tyteca delineate the structures of practical reasoning and propose a way to determine better argument by its ability to persuade the most demanding audience that one might imagine. Toulmin's measure of an argument is its ability to withstand appropriate criticism. Again, it is important to note that these speculations about reason are not just "armchair" productions, they are serious attempts to better understand how arguments naturally appear and can be assessed in the real world.

Building Theory Through Metaphor

Closely related to the use of analogy in building theory is the use of metaphor. Beginning with a biological metaphor: that communicative processes and practices affect the life of ideas in the minds of people, Fisher (1970) proposed a reconstruction of rhetorical genre. Instead of a category system based on judgments rendered in different sites of civic address, or a system based on 18th-century faculty psychology, a scheme was advanced that noted categories in which discourse functions to give life or acceptance to certain ideas (affirmation); to revitalize the life or acceptance of ideas (reaffirmation); to restore the health of ideas (purification); to undermine ideas (subversion). Later, another type of discourse was identified, which attempts not only to undermine ideas but to put into question any idea that insists things can be better (evisceration).

This example of theorizing not only shows how metaphor can be generative, it also demonstrates how theories can build on one another. Earlier, we outlined Bitzer's (1968) work on the constitutents of rhetorical situation, which are constant from one situation to another. Fisher's motive view of communication agrees that there are situations that are rhetorical, but insists there are different kinds of rhetorical situations which may be better understood by employing Burke's concept of motives as names for situations. For example, reaffirmation not only names the overall motive of Lincoln at Gettysburg, to revitalize the cause of the war, it also reveals that the scene, agency, purpose, and act were consonant with this motive; that is, the scene (the state of mind of the audience: Why are we fighting?), the form and content of the address (which formed an archetypal pattern of rebirth), the purpose (to revivify the principle on which the war was fought), and the act itself were all elements of a reaffirmation. That the motive view of communication has not altered the approach of composition textbook writers since its appearance in 1970 is testimony, perhaps, to the truism that old habits of thinking die hard, that new ideas are painful to contemplate and hard work to implement—inertia is a powerful restraint on change.

Building from Naturalistic Observations of Reality

One final approach to building a philosophy of rhetoric should be recognized. George Campbell's *Philosophy of Rhetoric* (Bitzer, 1963) is, he maintains in his introduction, founded on a tolerable sketch of the human mind and the radical principles on which it operates (1963, p. xliii). His understanding of these principles came from several sources: Humean and Lockean thought, "common sense philosophy," and, importantly, faculty psychology and David Hartley's associationism. Eighteenth-century philosophers attempted to understand the workings of the human mind by viewing mental operations as a function of the various capacities or "faculties." Reflecting this view, Campbell categorized the types and purposes of discourse with reference to the faculties that they sought to engage in the minds of audiences: to inform (the understanding), to convince (the intellect), to persuade (the will), to please (the imagination). There is much more to his philosophy of rhetoric than this, but Campbell's use of faculty psychology is sufficient to show how rigorously applied presuppositions may lead to necessary conclusions about communication.

There is no contemporary counterpart to Campbell's *Philosophy*, although several scholars have seen a relationship between his work and Burke's. Another whose work has been related to Campbell's is that of I. A. Richards, titled, like Campbell's, *The Philosophy of Rhetoric* (Bitzer, 1936/1963). Their works are actually quite different. Although each wanted to accommodate the best scientific thinking of his age, Campbell was concerned with the nature and functions of all sorts of discourse; Richards, strongly influenced by positivist thought, was concerned with "the study of misunderstanding and its remedies" (1936, p. 5). Campbell's and Richards' works each demonstrate how rhetorical theory is always being reformulated in response to major advances in other fields and disciplines. It is not difficult to imagine that if research in artificial intelligence, particularly schema theory, advances beyond its present state, someone will come forward to reconceptualize rhetoric on this new foundation.

From Theory to Philosophy

There is one more mode of theory or philosophy building that must be recounted before this survey is completed. It shows how theory construction begins with critique, leads to refinement, and, after reflection, results in a philosophical position. In 1963, Karl Wallace argued that the substance of rhetoric is "good reasons" (1963, pp. 239–249). In the process he proposed a conception of good reasons. Wayne Booth, in 1974, wrote a book entitled *Modern Dogma and the Rhetoric of Assent*, in which he advanced his own notion of good reasons. In 1978, Fisher critiqued the conceptions of Wallace and Booth, and formulated another definition of good reasons, one that subsumed those of Wallace and Booth. It should be noted that "subsumption" is often the mode of the progression of ideas in the social sciences and humanities, rather than by "accretion," as in the natural sciences.

Six years after Fisher wrote "Toward a Logic of Good Reasons" (1978), during which time he elaborated the idea in several articles, tested it in classes, read much more, and reflected, he came up with the proposal of the narrative paradigm (1984, pp. 1–22). The idea progressed through several more publications and eventuated in his book *Human Communication as Narration: Toward a Philosophy of Reason, Value, and Action* (1987). At this point, theory evolved into philosophy. The move that enabled this development was specifically questioning what one must assume in order to accept the construct of good reasons that had been advanced. The answer was: one had to see human beings as *homo narrans*, storytellers. Here again, "subsumption" was at work. The "new" idea did not deny Aristotle's notion of the rational capacity of human beings, or Burke's concept of humans as symbol using/abusing animals; it incorporated both. What may be worth remarking here is, that in order to build theory, one does not need to destroy what has gone before. The fact of the matter is that new theory or philosophy does not arise without context and predecessors who "built" the foundation for a continual rebuilding.

CONCLUSION

We have covered much ground in this chapter, making distinctions between knowledge and understanding, theorizing and philosophizing; relating the work of various communication theorists; identifying the major ways used in generating theories and philosophies: phenomenological, grounded research, borrowing, assuming ultimate reality, assuming contingent reality (epistemologically and ontologically), analogy, metaphor, naturalistic presuppositions, and evolutionary processes. A crucial conclusion that may be drawn from this is that the first—and last—test of a theory or philosophy is how well it accounts for the lived experience that it purports to explain. In the presence of an explanation that "fails" this test, the invitation or the demand of the theorist/philosopher is to formulate a better explanation.

Twenty years ago, this invitation was recognized and productively accepted by a number of feminist scholars, who argued that traditional histories and theories of rhetoric have failed to adequately represent and explain the communicative experience of women (see chapter 31, this volume). The essay that appeared to mark this acceptance and energized the work of others was Karlyn Kohrs Campbell's "The Rhetoric of Women's Liberation: An Oxymoron" (1973). The initial move among feminist scholars was to remedy the neglect of women in historical-critical studies. Much progress has been made in discovering and providing significant texts for public address studies (Campbell, 1989; Cooper, 1892/1988; Martin, 1987). Most recently, feminists have more directly concerned themselves with rhetorical theory. Karen E. Altman, for instance, argues that the traditional conception of rhetorical knowledge is gender biased, that "the 'body of knowledge' is a myopic metaphor. A more farsighted one is 'bodies of knowledge'" (Altman, 1992, p. 487). And Carol Blair critiques the traditional modes of organizing rhetorical theories according to influence or systems. She proposes, alternatively, a "critical history" approach, one that focuses on "text, particularity, change, and criticism," and which is always open to new ideas (1992, p. 418.) As yet, no explicit, elaborated feminist rhetorical theory has appeared—but the invitation remains open.

At this point, we are charged by the editors to speculate on future trends. We are tempted to say that what we have covered indicates that the fascination with how and in what ways humans create and recreate one another, their communities, and the world, continues unabated, indeed it has accelerated in recent years. One of the causes of the resurgence of interest in rhetoric has to do with the ongoing struggle between modern and postmodern thought. A key question in this struggle is whether or not there can be any sort of knowledge that can assure belief or human action. Rhetoric's reply, historically, is yes. In his essay "An Anthropological Approach to the Contemporary Significance of Rhetoric," Hans Blumenberg (1987) wrote of the role of rhetoric in guiding human choice in situations where evidence is incomplete, arguing that "The axiom of all rhetoric is the principle of insufficient reason." Yet, as Blumenberg noted, it is important to remember that acting out of necessity on insufficient evidence does not imply a rejection of rationality:

[T]he principle of insufficient reason is not to be confused with a demand that we forgo reasons. . . . One has to be cautious about making accusations of irrationality in situations where endless, infinitely extensive procedures have to be excluded; in the realm of reasoning about practical activities in life, it can be more rational to accept something on insufficient grounds than to insist on a procedure modeled on that of science, and it *is* more rational to do this than to disguise decisions that have already been made in arguments that are scientific in form. . . . In the realm in which the principle of insufficient reason holds, there are rational decision rules that do not resemble science. (1987, pp. 447–448)

The rhetorician's task is to identify, and occasionally help to reformulate, the rational decision rules that guide communication and judgment in the groups, cultures, and societies that we study. In a world without foundations—God, logic, science, language, history, and so forth—rhetorical theory and philosophy provides guidance for reconstructing reason, reinserting ethics and practical wisdom into the fabric of private and public life, and restoring a meaningful, useful conception of the public and its culture. A major prospect for future inquiry would be to pursue modes of communication that can ameliorate the conflicts arising out of religious, tribal, ethnic, gender, and economic class differences which appear to have replaced the foundations that served to ground authority for belief and action in centuries past. These differences act as anchors for self-identity and worldviews that must be transcended if conflicts are to be resolved peacefully. What rhetorical strategies and tactics can do this? That is a question eminently worth working on for the foreseeable future.

By connecting past and present writers throughout this chapter, we strove to reveal the heritage of rhetorical thinking, to indicate where it is and where it appears to be going. But then, one cannot predict the future, one can only anticipate and fashion adaptations influenced by new practices, theory, and technology. There is, of course, still the matter of genius.

SUGGESTED READINGS

Bizzell, P., & Herzberg, B. (Eds.). (1990). *The rhetorical tradition: Readings from classical times to the present.* Boston: St. Martin's Press. An anthology of works from the traditional rhetorical canon that ranges from the Sophists to contemporary literary criticism, with excellent connecting chapters that provide historical biographies, discussions of the significance of the anthologized texts, and comprehensive references. Very useful for both beginning and advanced students.

Blackman, M. (Ed.). (1987). *Rhetoric: Essays on invention and discovery.* Woodbridge, CT: Ox Bow Press. Of special import is McKeon's essay among others in this volume.

Bryant, D. C. (1953). Rhetoric: Its function and scope. *Quarterly Journal of Speech 39,* 401–424. A seminal discussion of the nature of rhetoric by an influential early scholar in the field of speech communication. Bryant assigns a four-fold status to rhetoric: as an instrumental discipline concerned with pragmatic communication managment, as a literary study concerned with style and semantics, as a philosophical study concerned with methods of investigation and inquiry, and as a social and political study of the influences of language in society. His definition of the function of rhetoric as that of "adjusting ideas to people and people to ideas" (p. 413) has become a commonplace.

Conley, T. (1990). *Rhetoric in the European tradition.* New York: Longman. A thoughtful overview of the history of rhetorical theory that devotes attention to aspects of the tradition (such as Byzantine rhetoric) neglected in most other survey works. Conley distinguishes four basic types or models of rhetoric:

dialectical, problematical, controversial, and operational. Though it gives too little space to contemporary rhetorics, Conley's expert discussion of classical and medieval theory makes this work well worth reading.

Corbett, E. P. J. (1990). *Classical rhetoric for the modern student* (3rd ed.). New York: Oxford. An excellent adaptation of classical rhetorical theory. Although intended as a textbook in English and composition, its perspective is broad enough to be useful to communication scholars; the book includes lengthy applications of rhetorical concepts to a wide variety of literary and political texts. Corbett's discussion of figures of speech is comprehensive and useful, especially given the usual dryness of most treatments of this topic.

Howell, W. S. (1956). *Logic and rhetoric in England, 1500–1700.* The authoritative study of rhetoric in the English Renaissance.

Ijseeling, S. (1976). *Rhetoric and philosophy in conflict: An historical survey.* The Hague: Martinus Nijhoff. This work is a thematic history of the conflict between rhetoric and philosophy that extends from the ancient Greeks and Romans, through the church fathers of late antiquity and the medieval period, to the Italian humanists, to early modern philosophers such as Descartes, Kant, and Nietzche, and finally to Freud and Heidegger. Ijseeling takes the perspective that "whoever embarks upon reflection on language necessarily confronts the problems of rhetoric" (p. 4).

Kennedy, G. (1963). *The art of persuasion in Greece.* Princeton, NJ: Princeton University Press. The three books by Kennedy (one of the great classical scholars of the rhetorical tradition) listed here provide exhaustive and fascinating accounts of the development of rhetorical thought. Required reading for students of the history of rhetoric and philosophy.

Kennedy, G. (1972). *The art of persuasion in the Roman world.* Princeton: Princeton University Press.

Kennedy, G. (1980). *Classical rhetoric and its Christian and secular tradition from ancient to modern times.* Chapel Hill: University of North Carolina Press.

Murphy, J. J. (1974). *Rhetoric in the middle ages: A history of rhetorical theory from St. Augustine to the Renaissance.* Berkeley: University of California Press. A comprehensive survey of medieval rhetoric that links its development to social, cultural, and religious trends.

Ong, W. J. (1988). *Orality and literacy: The technologizing of the word.* London: Routledge. A thought-provoking study of the relationship of technology and rhetorical theory that ought to be of immense utility to all communication scholars. This book provides the best introduction to Ong's theory of the evolution of communicative cultures as constituted by oral, written, printed, and electronic media.

Vickers, B. (1988). *In defence of rhetoric.* Oxord: Clarendon Press of Oxford University Press. A polemical history that serves as a useful corrective to the abuses of rhetoric from Plato to modern literary theory. Vickers details the impact of rhetorical theory on a number of other arts, including music, painting, and literature.

REFERENCES

Altman, K. E. (1992). Bodies of knowledge. *Quarterly Journal of Speech, 78,* 483–489.

Aristotle. (1954). *Rhetoric.* (W. R. Roberts, Trans.). New York: Modern Library.

Bitzer, L. (1963). *The philosophy of rhetoric.* Carbondale, IL: Southern Illinois University Press. (Original work published 1936).

Bitzer, L. F. (1968). The rhetorical situation. *Philosophy and Rhetoric, 1,* 1–14.

Blair, C. (1992). Contested histories of rhetoric: The politics of preservation, progress, and change. *Quarterly Journal of Speech, 78,* 403–428.

Blumenberg, H. (1987). An anthropological approach to the contemporary significance of rhetoric. R. M. Wallace (Trans.). In K. Baynes, J. Bohman, & T. McCarthy (Eds.), *After philosophy: End or transformation?* (pp. 429–458). Cambridge, MA: MIT Press.

Booth, W. (1974). *Modern dogma and the rhetoric of assent.* Chicago: University of Chicago Press.

Burke, K. (1945). *A grammar of motives.* New York: Prentice-Hall.

Burke, K. (1955). *A rhetoric of motives.* New York: George Braziller.

Burke, K. (1968). Definition of man. In *Language as symbolic action: Essays on life, literature, and method* (pp. 3–24). Berkeley: University of California Press.

Campbell, K. K. (1973). The rhetoric of women's liberation: An oxymoron. *Quarterly Journal of Speech, 59,* 74–86.

Campbell, K. K. (Ed.). (1989). *Man cannot speak for her: A critical study of early feminist rhetoric* (2 Vols.). New York: Greenwood Press.

Cherwitz, R. A. (Ed.). (1990). *Rhetoric and philosophy.* Hillsdale, NJ: Lawrence Erlbaum Associates.

Cherwitz, R. A., & Hikins, J. W. (1986). *Communication and knowledge: An investigation in rhetorical epistemology.* Columbia: University of South Carolina Press.

Cooper, A. J. (1988). *A voice from the South.* New York: Oxford University Press. (Original work published 1892)

Farrell, T. B. (1993). *Norms of rhetorical culture.* New Haven, CT: Yale University Press.

Fisher, W. R. (1970). A motive view of communication. *Quarterly Journal of Speech, 56,* 131–39.

Fisher, W. R. (1978). Toward a logic of good reasons. *Quarterly Journal of Speech, 64,* 376–84.

Fisher, W. R. (1984). Narration as a human communication paradigm. *Communication Monographs, 51,* 1–22.

Fisher, W. R. (1987). *Human communication as narration: Toward a philosophy of reason, value, and action.* Columbia: University of South Carolina Press.

Hart, R. P. (1984). *Verbal style and the presidency: A computer-based analysis.* Orlando, FL: Academic Press.

Hart, R. P. (1987). *The sound of leadership: Presidential communication in the modern age.* Chicago: University of Chicago Press.

Hempel, C. G. (1965). *Aspects of scientific explanation and other essays in the philosophy of science.* New York: Free Press.

Hovland, C. I., Janis, I. L., & Kelly, M. M. (1953). *Communication and persuasion.* New Haven, CT: Yale University Press.

Isocrates. (1928). Antidosis. In G. Norlin, (Ed. and Trans.), *Isocrates* (Vol. 2, pp. 185–365). New York: G.P. Putnam.

Lanham, R. (1993). *The electronic word: Democracy, technology, and the arts.* Chicago: University of Chicago Press.

Martin, T. P. (1987). *The sound of our own voices: Women's study clubs, 1860–1910.* Boston: Beacon Press.

McCloskey, D. (1985). *The rhetoric of economics.* Madison: University of Wisconsin Press.

McGee, M. C. (1980). The "ideograph": A link between rhetoric and ideology. *Quarterly Journal of Speech, 66,* 1–16.

McKerrow, R. E. (1984). Critical rhetoric: Theory and practice. *Communication Monographs, 56,* 91–111.

Perelman, C., & Olbrechts-Tyteca, L. (1969). *The new rhetoric: A treatise on argumentation.* J. Wilkinson & P. Weaver (Trans.). Notre Dame: University of Notre Dame Press.

Plato. (1961). Phaedrus. R. Hackforth (Trans.). In E. Hamilton & H. Cairns (Eds.), *Plato: The collected dialogues.* Princeton: Princeton University Press.

Richards, I. A. (1936). *The philosophy of rhetoric.* New York: Oxford University Press.

Ricouer, P. (1991). *From text to action: Essays in hermeneutics* (K. Blamey & J. B. Thompson, Trans.). Evanston, IL: Northwestern University Press.

Taylor, C. (1977). Interpretation and the sciences of man. In F. R. Dallmayr & T. M. McCarthy (Eds.), *Understanding and social inquiry* (pp. 101–131). Notre Dame/London: University of Notre Dame Press.

Toulmin, S. (1958). *The uses of argument.* Cambridge, England: Cambridge University Press.

Weaver, R. M. (1953). *The ethics of rhetoric.* Chicago: Henry Regnery Company.

Weaver, R. M. (1970). Language is sermonic. In R. L. Johannesen, R. Strickland, & R. T. Eubanks (Eds.), *Language is sermonic: Richard M. Weaver on the nature of rhetoric.* Baton Rouge: Louisiana State University Press. (Original work published 1963)

Wallace, K. (1963). The substance of rhetoric: Good reasons. *Quarterly Journal of Speech, 49,* 239–249.

17

Persuasion

Michael D. Miller
Timothy R. Levine
University of Hawaii at Manoa

Implicitly or explicitly, persuasion underlies much of mass and human communication theory and research. Persuasion is a special case of the larger study of social influence. Social influence may be defined as creating, changing, or reinforcing the attitudes, beliefs, or behaviors of another person. Persuasion involves an intentional communicative act that excludes force (i.e., coercion). At a minimum a successful persuasive attempt generates some type of cognitive, affective, or behavioral modification in the target. In the following discussion we begin by defining several important terms and types of persuasion research, examine different research paradigms, explore the variables that influence persuasive strategies, and offer a sample study.

DEFINITIONAL ISSUES

The concepts of *attitude*, *belief*, and *behavior* are inextricably linked to persuasion. *Attitudes* are evaluative tendencies regarding some feature of the environment and can typically be phrased in terms of like and dislike or favor and disfavor (see Eagly & Chaiken, 1993). *Beliefs* are assessments that something is or is not the case. Thus, beliefs are expressed as true–false or exist–does-not-exist. For example, "I like the Miami Dolphins" expresses my attitude toward the team, while "I think the Dolphins will go to the playoffs next year" expresses a belief. *Behavior* refers to observable actions. If, as a result of my beliefs, I bet on the Dolphins making the playoffs, I engaged in a behavior.

The extent to which attitudes predict behaviors has long been controversial, and many have claimed that attitudes are, at best, only modest predictors of behaviors (LaPiere, 1934; Wicker, 1969). A recent meta-analysis (a statistical study that seeks to objectively evaluate research in a given area through statistical procedures that summarize the results reported in several studies on a common metric, Stacks & Hocking, 1992) by Kim and Hunter (1993), however, demonstrates that so long as the attitude is relevant to the behavior observed, attitudes are highly correlated with behaviors (r = .86) when taking measurement problems into account.

TYPES OF PERSUASION RESEARCH

Research on persuasion can be divided into three categories. First, research has focused on the pragmatic issue of isolating those factors that enhance or inhibit persuasion. These factors can be further divided into three broad groups: source effects, message effects, and recipient characteristics. The second category involves explaining why persuasive messages are persuasive. Several theories of persuasion attempt to address this issue. Finally, researchers have investigated the selection or generation of persuasive messages. Much of this final type of research has been done under the label of compliance-gaining.

Factors Affecting Persuasion

Source effects refers to perceptions of sources that make them more or less influential. Aristotle's *ethos*, now more commonly referred to as source credibility, refers to perceived believability. The persuasive advantage held by credible sources has long been recognized (e.g., Hovland & Weiss, 1951). Perceived competence (or expertise) and trustworthiness are commonly recognized as contributing to perceptions of source credibility, although others have argued for additional dimensions of source credibility (e.g., Berlo, Lemert & Mertz, 1969; McCroskey & Young, 1981; Self, chapter 27, this volume).

Other source effects include social power (e.g., French & Raven, 1959), authority (e.g., Milgram, 1974), attractiveness (e.g., Chaiken, 1979), liking (e.g., Ragan, 1971) and demographic (e.g., Cantor, Alfonso & Zillmann, 1976) and attitudinal similarity (e.g., Woodside & Davenport, 1974). Generally speaking, we are more likely to be persuaded by sources we perceive to be powerful, in authority, attractive, likable, or similar to us than by sources we perceive as not possessing these traits.

Characteristics of messages such as discrepancy, language intensity, message sidedness, and the quality and quantity of evidence provided also influence persuasiveness. *Discrepancy* refers to the distance between a target's existing attitude and the position advocated by a message (see Aronson, Turner, & Carlsmith, 1963). *Language intensity* refers to the degree to which the language used deviates from neutrality. Language intensity can be manipulated through the use of adverbial qualifiers ("That is a pretty good/good/excellent idea") or through the use of metaphors, especially those that have violent or sexual content ("The Contract with America would rape the working class while providing welfare for the rich"). As is the case with many message variables, language intensity interacts with other variables (such as prior attitude toward the topic, characteristics of the source, and receiver expectations) in persuasive situations (c.f., Burgoon, Jones, & Stewart, 1975; Miller & Burgoon, 1979)

Message sidedness refers to whether one side or both sides of an issue are presented. Research indicates that two-sided messages are more persuasive so long as the opposing side is explicitly refuted (Jackson & Allen, 1987). Providing evidence is most effective when the targets are involved in the issue (Stiff, 1986; see also Reinard, 1988; Reynolds & Burgoon, 1983, for reviews of this literature).

Research has also examined the effectiveness of specific *message types and persuasive strategies*, especially fear appeals (e.g., Boster & Mongeau, 1984; Witte, 1992). Other examples of specific strategies which have been investigated include altercasting (Weinstein & Deutchberger, 1963), foot-in-the-door (Freedman & Fraser, 1966), door-in-the-face (Cialdini, et al., 1975), low-ball (Cialdini, Cacioppo, Bassett, & Miller, 1978), moral obligations (Schmitt, 1964), and that's-not-all (Burger, 1986).

Often the intent of the persuader is to *prevent* the message recipients from changing their attitudes if they are subsequently exposed to a persuasive message. When prevention of message acceptance is the case, refutational message strategies were found to be effective under certain conditions (e.g., Pfau, Kenski, Nitz, & Sorenson, J., 1990; Pfau, Van Bockern, & Kang, 1992)

The persuasive impact of messages also depends upon the *recipient* of the message. Mere exposure to (Zajonc, 1968; see: Bornstein, 1989, for review) or mere thought (Tesser, 1978) about issues or things can produce attitude change. Also, the recipient's gender (Eagly, 1983), intelligence (Rhodes & Wood, 1992), and personality traits, including self-esteem (Rhodes & Wood, 1992) and argumentativeness (Levine & Badger, 1993), appear to influence persuasion.

THEORIES OF PERSUASION

A number of theories have been advanced to explain how, when, and why people are persuaded. Although no one theory can entirely explain persuasion, each is useful in understanding some aspect of persuasion.

Behavioristic learning theories represent one approach to explaining persuasion. Applications of classical, operant, and vicarious conditioning may result in persuasion (e.g., Staats & Staats, 1958; see Miller, Burgoon, & Burgoon, 1984; Eagly & Chaiken, 1993). Others argued that people are motivated to maintain consistency. Heider's (1946) balance theory and Festinger's (1957) theory of cognitive dissonance are examples of consistency theories. In addition to being one of the family of consistency theories, dissonance theory is noteworthy for placing an emphasis on counterattitudinal advocacy. In the traditional persuasion paradigm, the persuader is the primary source of persuasive messages (Miller & Burgoon, 1973). The persuader generates and transmits a persuasive message to the persuasive target. In counterattitudinal situations, the persuasive target is induced to become the primary symbolizing agent (Miller & Burgoon, 1973). That is, the persuasive target generates a message advocating a position different from the one he or she privately holds. Under certain conditions, this active encoding approach has been found to be an extremely effective persuasive strategy.

Self-perception (Bem, 1967) was originally advanced as an alternative to dissonance theory. Bem argued that under certain conditions people infer their attitudes from observing their own behaviors. Thus, we "discover" our own attitudes in much the same way we would make attributions about the attitudes of another person—we make inferences based on observed behavior. Research suggests that self-perception best explains proattitudinal effects, while dissonance theory explains counterattitudinal effects (Fazio, Zanna, & Cooper, 1977).

Another theory originally advanced as an alternative to dissonance is self-presentation. Self-presentation comes from the symbolic interactionist perspective. Although this approach has received more attention in psychology than in the communication discipline, it offers intriguing explanations and hypotheses concerning persuasion and a variety of interpersonal outcomes (see: Leary & Kowalski, 1990, for a review)

Social judgment theory (Sherif, Sherif, & Nebergall, 1965; see Granberg, 1982, for review) assumes that people perceive persuasive messages in much the same way they make judgments about physical stimuli. This theory predicts a nonlinear relationship between discrepancy and attitude change where the optimal degree of discrepancy is a function of the target's ego involvement with the topic.

The cognitive response approach (Petty, Ostrom, & Brock, 1981) and the theory of reasoned action (Fishbein & Ajzen, 1975) assume that targets of persuasive messages actively evaluate those messages, whereas research on heuristics (Cialdini, 1993; Tversky & Kahneman, 1974) assumes that persuasion is a result of mindless decision rules. The elaboration likelihood model (ELM; Petty & Cacioppo, 1986) attempts to integrate these approaches by arguing that all persuasion can be viewed along a continuum defined by cognitive effort. The ELM, however, has proven controversial on several grounds, including its controversial conceptualization of argument quality and failure to specify which of several "peripheral" routes to persuasion might be used (e.g., Eagly & Chaiken, 1993; Stiff, 1986). The systematic-heuristic model has been advanced as an alternative to ELM (Chaiken, 1987).

Message Selection and Generation

Most traditional persuasion research is based on the experimental manipulation of an experimenter's preestablished and pretested message on an audience. However, a program of research arose based not on persuasive exposure, but instead on the selection or generation of message strategies used in influencing others. Based on Marwell and Schmitt's (1967) classic study of the typology of compliance-gaining message strategies, Miller, Boster, Roloff, and Seibold's (1977) research on compliance-gaining message selection has stimulated a good deal of research. Most compliance-gaining research has sought to either identify and classify the types of messages individuals use to influence others (e.g., Cody, McLaughlin, & Jordan, 1980; Kearney, Plax, Richmond, &

McCroskey, 1985) or determine the situational (e.g., Dillard & Burgoon, 1985; Miller et al., 1977; Miller, 1982) and individual difference variables (e.g., Boster & Levine, 1988) that influence compliance-gaining message selection or generation. Reviews of this literature are provided by Seibold, Cantrill, and Meyers (1986) and Wheeless, Barraclough, and Stewart (1983). Unfortunately few conclusions can be drawn from compliance-gaining research. To date, methodological debates (e.g., Boster, Stiff, & Reynolds, 1985; Burleson et al., 1986; Wiseman & Schenck-Hamlin, 1981) have been a dominant feature of this literature.

RESEARCH METHODS IN THE STUDY OF PERSUASION

As with any research, the design, procedure, and analysis of persuasion studies are dictated by the questions one poses and the hypotheses one tests. Perhaps the most basic methodological issue to be addressed is whether an experimental or a nonexperimental design will be used.[1] As we noted earlier, a great deal of persuasion research seeks to identify specific source, message, or receiver factors which enhance or inhibit persuasive effectiveness. This focus on the identification of specific causal variables in persuasion makes experimental research particularly useful. While there are exceptions, classic studies of both source and message effects on persuasion and attitude change have relied heavily on experimental methods (e.g., Aronson et al., 1963; Hovland & Weiss, 1951).

Experimental Research

Why the reliance on experimental methods? Experimental designs allow the researcher the *control* necessary to precisely specify and manipulate the source or message characteristics he or she is interested in comparing. Suppose a researcher interested in the persuasive effects of fear appeals develops hypotheses suggesting that the claimed likelihood of occurrence of some frightening event will be related to compliance with the message. The researcher might then construct a prototype persuasive message which suggests this frightening event will occur unless the receiver complies with some requested behavior. By using this message as a template, and varying only the probability of occurrence of the frightening event, the researcher creates experimental messages which differ *only* in the characteristic of interest.

The experimenter manipulates or controls levels of the independent variable, possibly including a "control" group or groups that do not receive any manipulation. Research participants are then randomly assigned to experimental conditions. Random assignment ensures that "any" participant might be assigned to "any" experimental or control condition; it helps ensure that any results are effects of the variables of interest and not things brought to the study by the participant. After exposure to the experimental messages, measurements of compliance (the dependant variable) are made and compared across different experimental "conditions."

---

[1]Much of the commentary on design issues in this chapter draws heavily from the work of Donald Campbell and his associates (Campbell & Stanley, 1966; Cook & Campbell, 1979).

Taken together, the consistency of procedures across experimental conditions, the random assignment of participants to conditions, and the strict control of the stimuli (in this case the variations of the persuasive message) help ensure the internal validity of the experiment (*internal validity* refers to whether a stimulus—manpulation of the independent variable—had a known effect in the study being conducted). To the researcher conducting experimental research in persuasion, the most important and fundamental question is, "Were the observed differences in the dependant variables due to variations in the manipulated independent variables?" In the example above, "Were variations in compliance due to variations in the claimed likelihood of occurrence of the frightening event?" A well designed and executed experiment allows us to answer "yes" to these questions with a high degree of confidence. The experiment allows us to study the causal relationships between variables, but does so in often very unnatural settings (i.e., the laboratory). As such, it may suffer from problems of *external validity,* a question of the extent to which the results can be generalized to other settings and populations.

Nonexperimental Research

While research on the effects of source and message variables lends itself to the manipulation inherent in experimental studies, the question of how receiver characteristics are related to persuasion is often examined via *nonexperimental* investigations. Although receiver characteristics (gender, sex role, intelligence, age, aggressiveness, or other individual difference variables) generally cannot be manipulated or randomly assigned in experimental studies, they can be measured. Thus, the most basic approach to the study of these receiver variables has been to measure the characteristic of interest in a collection of people who are then exposed to some type of persuasive stimulus. Responses to the message are then compared. For example, we expose women and men (or older and younger, cognitively simply and cognitively complex participants) to the same persuasive message and compare their responses. Differences in responses are attributed to differences on the previously identified and measured independent variable.

Clearly, the internal validity of research of this type is more suspect than that of a true experiment. In an experiment, we take steps, including randomization and random assignment, to insure that our experimental groups differ *only* as a result of planned exposure to the persuasive message (or other independent variable under the experimenter's control). Thus, differences in the outcome measures are attributable to differences in the manipulated independent variable. In an investigation of receiver variables, we begin with groups we know are *already* different on at least one characteristic and then expose them to the same persuasive stimulus. Differences apparent in outcome variables are attributed to the pre-existing differences in the measured receiver variable. For example, if men and women are exposed to the same persuasive message and evidence different degrees of attitude change, the researcher might attribute those differential responses to the measured independent variable of gender. However, reasonable alternative explanations for the results might be that men and women differed on some factor in addition to biological sex (sex role or interest or knowledge in the topic, for example) which might be the true explanation of the differences in attitude change.

Quasi-experimental Research

Many persuasion studies have both manipulated and measured independent variables. These types of studies are referred to as *quasi-experimental* designs. Quasi-experimental designs have actively manipulated experimental variables, but rather than using random assignment, also rely on comparisons made across groups created via at least one measured independent variable as in nonexperimental research discussed earlier (Cook & Campbell, 1979). Although quasi-experimental research has been used in many areas of persuasion, many studies on personality and persuasibility provide clear examples of quasi-experimental designs (see, for example, several studies reported in Hovland & Janis, 1959). The sample persuasion study we discuss later in this chapter is an example of a quasi-experiment.

ATTITUDE MEASUREMENT

Another important decision in conducting research in persuasion is the nature of the dependent variable. The majority of persuasion research in the past has used self-reports of attitudes as the dependent variable. Without a doubt one reason for the popularity of self-report measures is the apparent ease of administration. Theoretical questions about the nature of attitudes and the related issues of their valid and reliable measurement has generated a number of different approaches and techniques of attitude measurement. Probably the most common techniques of self-report measurement of attitudes involve the use of semantic-differential scales, developed by Osgood, Suci, and Tannenbaum (1957). The semantic differential scale consists of a series of items bounded by "bipolar" terms, usually separated by seven equal spaces that participants use to evaluate an attitude or belief statement. One advantage of the semantic differential is that the same scales can be used to measure attitudes toward a variety of different topics. Since the different attitudes are measured similarly, direct comparisons are possible.

Another reason for the popularity of self-report measures of attitudes is the assumption (either explicitly or implicitly) that cognitive variables, including those generally considered to be components of attitudes, serve as "causes" or antecedents of subsequent behaviors. Although the nature of the attitude–behavior relationship was proven controversial (see Kim & Hunter, 1993, for a review), assuming that cognitive or affective restructuring precedes behavioral change has provided at least an implicit justification for the use of self-report measures of attitudes as the dependent variables in persuasion studies.

Responding to findings of frequent weak relationships between attitudes and subsequent behavior, Fishbein and associates (e.g., Fishbein & Ajzen, 1974) utilized measures of behavioral intentions. As a part of this approach to measurement, participants are asked how they *intend* to behave in situations relevant to the attitude being measured. Not surprisingly the measurement of behavioral intentions increases correspondence between self-reports of attitude and subsequent behavior.

A number of affective indicators of attitudes have also been utilized. A sampling of these approaches include galvanic skin response (GSR), pupillary response, and facial electromyographic activity (Himmelfarb, 1993).

Another alternative is to simply measure the overt behavior itself without resorting to measures of attitude (or relying on this observation of behavior as an indicator of related attitudes). This is not always as simple as it might seem. Problems include isolating the behavior or set of behaviors of interest, selecting which behavior or behavioral array is theoretically most relevant, and operationalizing the behavioral observations.

Ultimately, the dependent variables and their operationalizations must reflect the theoretic or pragmatic interests of the researcher. What would be the most appropriate variable in, for example, a study of political persuasion? The conspicuously simple answer is voting behavior. In many cases this might also be the correct answer. However, depending on the interest and theoretic rationale of the researcher, affect toward the candidates, knowledge and beliefs about the candidates, or voting intentions might be as or more appropriate dependent variables. Even in research guided primarily by pragmatic concerns, such as that being conducted on behalf of a political candidate, attitudes, beliefs, or behavioral intentions might be the most appropriate measures of interest.

A SAMPLE STUDY OF ARGUMENTATIVENESS AND RESISTANCE TO PERSUASION

Research on resistance to persuasion has primarily focused on two distinct domains. First, some researchers have examined the effects of messages intended to instill resistance. Much of this research is based upon McGuire's inoculation construct (Papageorgis & McGuire, 1961). In the inoculation paradigm, participants are exposed to a message which both motivates them to counterargue future persuasive attacks and provides refutational content to assist them in this process.

Recent applications of inoculation in resistance to political attack messages (Pfau et al., 1990) and smoking initiation among adolescents (Pfau et al., 1992) have documented the effectiveness of this technique.

Second, other researchers examined characteristics of message receivers which make them more susceptible or resistant to persuasive appeals. For example, research has explored the effects of gender (e.g., Eagly, 1983), self-esteem (e.g., Rhodes & Wood, 1992), and propensity to counterargue (e.g., Stacks & Burgoon, 1981) on persuasibility. This research suggests that some individuals may be naturally more resistant to persuasion than others.

One individual difference that should have implications for resistance to persuasion is argumentativeness. Drawing upon the work of Infante and his colleagues on argumentativeness (e.g., Infante, 1981; Infante & Rancer, 1982) and the cognitive response approach to persuasion (e.g., Greenwald, 1968; Petty, Ostrom, & Brock, 1981), it is reasonable to advance argumentativeness as an important recipient factor influencing persuasion. Kazoleas (1993) found that highly argumentative individuals were more difficult to persuade, but Levine and Badger (1993) found that high argumentatives were more easily persuaded.

Explicating Argumentativeness

The proposed sample study looks at persuasibility as a function of an individual's level of argumentativeness and his or her initial agreement with a message. It is argued that the conflicting results obtained in previous research might be a result of an argumentativeness by message agreement interaction. To explain why this should be the case, the cognitive response approach to persuasion, argumentativeness, and two recent studies must be discussed.

The cognitive response approach to persuasion is predicated on the view that the persuasive effect of an externally produced message is attributable to the thoughts generated by exposure to the message (Petty & Cacioppo, 1981). That is, recipient thoughts or cognitive responses "mediate" and explain message effectiveness. To the extent that a message generates promessage thoughts on the part of the receiver, the receiver will be swayed to the position advocated by the message. If, on the other hand, a message generates unfavorable thoughts (i.e., is counterargued), then less persuasion will result. Extensive counterarguing can result in attitude change opposite to message recommendations (i.e., a boomerang effect). From this perspective, any variable that systematically affects the nature of cognitive responses should systematically affect persuasion. *Argumentativeness* should be one such variable (Kazoleas, 1993; Levine & Badger, 1993).

Argumentativeness is a personality trait that reflects an individual's inherent tendency to approach or avoid arguments. *Argumentativeness* is conceptualized as a generally stable trait which predisposes the individual in communication situations to advocate positions on controversial issues and to attack the positions other people take on these issues (Infante & Rancer, 1982).

High trait argumentatives are thought to differ from their less argumentative counterparts in several ways. For example, arguing is associated with more learning, less egocentric thinking, more accurate social perspective-taking, more creativity, and better problem-solving and decision making (Johnson & Johnson, 1979). Better arguing skills are also directly related to leadership skills (Schultz, 1982).

Another way high and low argumentatives differ is in how they process messages. High trait argumentatives, by definition, tend to refute others' ideas (Infante & Rancer, 1982). The refutation of others' arguments has both cognitive and behavioral elements. In order to effectively dispute another's position on an issue, one must first identify weakness in the other's argument and generate counterpoints. Such refutational thoughts are labeled counterarguments in the persuasion literature (Petty & Cacioppo, 1981).

Two recent studies hypothesized that due to high argumentatives' proclivity toward counterargumentation, highly argumentative individuals should be more difficult to persuade than their less argumentative counterparts (Kazoleas, 1993; Levine & Badger, 1993). Kazoleas's results were consistent with this hypothesis, but Levine and Badger found the opposite. Highly argumentive subjects in the Levine and Badger study showed significantly more attitude change than their less argumentative cohorts.

Important differences in the messages used in these two studies may explain these conflicting results. Kazoleas (1993) exposed participants to three persuasive advertisements. These messages encouraged moderation in drinking, opposing the clean air act, and avoiding exposure to the sun. Levine and Badger's (1993) study used persuasive speeches given in public speaking classes. The topics of the speeches were chosen by participants' classmates.

Suppose that highly argumentative individuals generate more cognitive responses, but, counter to Kazoleas's (1993) and Levine and Badger's (1993) reasoning, do not always generate more negative ones. Specifically, although such individuals should generate more counterarguments when faced with an objectionable message, they may generate more promessage thoughts when faced with an acceptable message. Such reasoning may explain the conflicting findings. Highly argumentive individuals may be more or less resistant to persuasion depending on a certain set of conditions.

Unfortunately, neither Kazoleas's (1993) nor Levine & Badger's (1993) designs allowed for a direct test of this reasoning. The information that is available, however, seems consistent with this speculation. In the Kazoleas study, the mean attitude scores suggest few subjects favored the positions advocated. Also, the largest effects were found for the topic (anti-clean air act) with which the subjects least agreed. That is, the more the subjects disagreed with the message, the more resistant the argumentative subjects.

In the Levine and Badger (1993) study, sources were allowed to select their own topics, and they seemed to pick topics they favored. Examination of initial favorability scores showed that most of these subjects favored most topics. Thus, participants in the Levine and Badger study may have heard only pro-attitudinal persuasive presentations.

Thus, there is reason to expect that the relationship between argumentativeness and resistance to persuasion is moderated by initial agreement with the message. Based on this reasoning, one might propose that the predicted effect of argumentativeness instilling resistance to persuasion is valid for positions that targets would not readily endorse. Alternatively, one might predict an effect like that obtained in the Levine and Badger (1993) study for pro-attitudinal messages. Argumentativeness should lead to less resistance to pro-attitudinal messages. This reasoning allows us to posit that:

H_1: Initial agreement with a persuasive message will moderate the effects of argumentativeness on resistance to persuasion such that:

> H_{1a}: For counter-attitudinal messages, low-trait argumentatives will report more attitude change in the direction of the message recommendations than high-trait argumentativeness, but

> H_{1b}: For pro-attitudinal messages, high-trait argumentatives will report more attitude change in the direction of the message recommendations than low-trait argumentatives.

Method

In order to test our hypothesis, we would need to expose high-and low-argumentative subjects to pro- and counterattitudinal messages. This would produce 4 experimental conditions. Comparing the degree of attitude change in the different conditions would allow for a test of our hypothesis that intial agreement moderates resistance to persuasion and our subhypotheses of specific effects.

Participants

Participants in this study would be selected on the basis of a pretest. This pretest would assess their argumentativeness, as well as their opinions on a variety of potentially controversial issues.

Pretest

At the beginning of the semester, each participant would be asked to complete a questionnaire containing the 20 item Argumentativeness Scale (Infante & Rancer, 1982) and an opinion survey. By comparing their responses to the argumentativeness scale with the group median, each participant could be classified into one of two equal-size groups: high in argumentativeness or low in argumentativeness.

The opinion survey would contain a variety of topics, and three sets of items for each topic. These sets of items would assess the participants' positions on each topic, knowledge of the topics, and views of the topics' importancd. The first set of items would be a measure of initial attitudes. The latter two sets of items, intended as measures of prior knowledge and issue involvement, respectively, would be included for control purposes.

For the experiment, the topic with the most variance in initial attitude (i.e., most controversial) would be utilized. Participants who were neutral on the topic would be excluded from the study. For the purpose of illustration, suppose we chose the topic of legal abortion. Some participants would be pro-life, whereas others would be pro-choice. Since we are interested in pro- and counterattitudinal messages, participants who were neutral or undecided would be excluded from the study.

Procedure and Measurement

Selected participants (either high or low in argumentativeness, who were either pro-choice or pro-life) would be randomly assigned to experimental conditions in which they would listen to a speech that would be either pro-choice or pro-life in nature. This procedure would create both pro-attitudinal messages (pro-choice participants listening to pro-choice messages, and pro-life participants listening to pro-life messages) and counterattitudinal messages (pro-choice participants listening to pro-life messages, and pro-life participants listening to pro-choice messages). Since participants are either high or low in argumentativeness, this creates four quasi-experimental conditions: High argumentatives exposed to a pro-attitudinal message, high argumentatives exposed to a counterattitudinal messages; low argumentatives exposed to a pro-attitudinal message and low argumentatives exposed to a counter-attitudinal message.

Immediately following the persuasive speech, experimental participants would complete the opinion survey a second time. The responses to the initial attitude items would be subtracted from the post-speech attitude measures for the topic. This would served as the dependent measure.

Results

The data could be analyzed via 2 x 2 analysis of variance with argumentativeness (high and low) and message-attitude agreement (pro-attitudinal and counter-attitudinal) as the independent variables, and attitude change as the dependent variable. If the hypothesized interaction was found, the data would be consistent with our hypothesis.

Research Methods Revisited

The design used in this hypothetical experiment is an example of a quasi-experimental design. It has one measured independent variable (argumentativeness). Assignment to the high and low trait argumentativeness conditions is clearly not random. Assignment decisions would be made on the basis of responses to the measured variable of trait argumentativeness. Our other independent variable, pro-attitudinal versus counterattitudinal messages is manipulated, but we have to recognize that its manipulation is based indirectly on measures of prior agreement and disagreement.

Now consider the validity of our hypothetical study. Earlier in this chapter we noted how characteristics of design influence on the internal validity of persuasion research. An additional concern might be the generalizability of the findings (external validity). For example, our study uses only one experimental topic (legalized abortion) and one message for each message-agreement condition. This raises concerns about the degree to which the results can be generalized to other topics or to other messages on the same topic (Jackson & Jacobs, 1983). This might be especially problematic if a topic like abortion were used, since people are so polarized on the issue.

Another concern is the way in which the experimental conditions are created. The pro-attitudinal condition is comprised of both pro-life participants (listening to a pro-life message) and pro-choice participants (listening to a pro-choice message). By collapsing these two groups into one experimental condition, we have implicitly assumed the two subgroups are equivalent. Whether this is the case is actually an empirical question. If the subgroups are not significantly different on the dependent measure, our decision to combine them is defensible. Otherwise, an alternative analysis to diagnose the nature and effects of nonequivalence would be appropriate.

Rather than presenting a perfect hypothetical study, one which the experimenter has complete control and unlimited resources, we have tried to present a doable study which exemplifies some of the issues, problems and even pitfalls often experienced by persuasion researchers. Our study certainly would not provide an unequivocal and complete answer to the problem. It should, however, contribute to our knowledge on how argumentativeness is related to resistance to persuasion

SUMMARY

In much the same way, this chapter as a whole offers only a superficial and incomplete overview of persuasion research. We hope, however, it provides some important information on what we know about persuasion and how persuasion research is conducted. We note by way of concluding that persuasion is a type of social influence that can take many forms. Those forms often dictate the types of methodological decisions made. Persuasion research is also guided by a number of theoretical perspectives, each offering a different methodological perspective to its study.

REFERENCES

Aronson, E., Turner, J. A., & Carlsmith, J. M. (1963). Communicator credibility and communication discrepancy as determinants of opinion change. *Journal of Abnormal and Social Psychology, 67,* 177–181.

Bem, D. J. (1967). Self-perception: An alternative interpretation of cognitive dissonance phenomena. *Psychological Review, 74*, 183–200.

Berlo, D. K., Lemert, J. B., & Mertz, R. J. (1969). Dimensions for evaluating the acceptability of message sources. *Public Opinion Quarterly, 33*, 563–576.

Bornstein, R. F. (1989). Exposure and affect: Overview and meta-analysis of research. *Psychological Bulletin, 106*, 265–289.

Boster, F. J., & Levine, T. R. (1988). Individual differences and compliance-gaining message selection: The effects of verbal aggressiveness, argumentativeness, dogmatism, and negativism. *Communication Research Reports, 5*, 114–119.

Boster, F. J., & Mongeau, P. (1984). Fear-arousing persuasive messages. In R.N. Bostrom (Ed.), *Communication yearbook* (Vol. 8, pp. 330–375). Beverly Hills, CA: Sage.

Boster, F. J., Stiff, J. B., & Reynolds, R. A. (1985). Do persons respond differently to inductively-derived and deductively-derived lists of compliance-gaining message strategies? A reply to Wiseman and Schenck-Hamlin. *Western Journal of Speech Communication, 49*, 177–187.

Burger, J. M. (1986). Increasing compliance by improving the deal: The that's-not-all technique. *Journal of Personality and Social Psychology, 51*, 277–283.

Burgoon, M., Jones, S. B., & Stewart, D. (1975). Toward a message-centered theory of persuasion: Three empirical investigations of language intensity. *Human Communication Research, 1*, 240–256.

Burleson, B. R., Wilson, S. R., Waltman, M. S., Goering, E. M., Ely, T. K., & Whaley, R. B. (1986). Item desirability effects in compliance-gaining research: Seven studies documenting artifacts in the strategy selection procedure. *Human Communication Research, 14*, 129–486.

Campbell, D. T., & Stanley, J. C. (1966). *Experimental and quasi-experimental designs for research.* Chicago: Rand McNally.

Cantor, J. R., Alfonso, H., & Zillmann, D. (1976). The persuasive effectiveness of the peer appeal and a communicator's first-hand experience. *Communication Research, 3*, 293–310.

Chaiken, S. (1979). Communicator physical attractiveness and persuasion. *Journal of Personality and Social Psychology, 37*, 1387–1397.

Chaiken, S. (1987). The heuristic model of persuasion. In M. P. Zanna, J. M. Olson, & C.P Herman (Eds.), *Social influence: The Ontario symposium* (Vol. 5, pp. 3–40). Hillsdale, NJ: Lawrence Erlbaum Associates.

Cialdini, R. B. (1993). *Influence: Science and practice.* Glenview, IL: Scott, Foreman & Co.

Cialdini, R. B., Cacioppo, J. T., Bassett, R., & Miller, J. A. (1978). Low-ball procedure for producing compliance: Commitment then cost. *Journal of Personality and Social Psychology, 36*, 463–476.

Cialdini, R. B., Vincent, J. E., Lewis, S. K., Catalan, J., Wheeler, D., & Darby, B. L. (1975). Reciprocal concessions procedure for inducing compliance: The door-in-the-face technique. *Journal of Personality and Social Psychology, 31*, 206–215.

Cook, T. D., & Campbell, D. T. (1979). *Quasi-experimentation: Design & analysis issues for field settings.* Boston, MA: Houghton Mifflin.

Cody, M. J., McLaughlin, M. L., & Jordan,W. J. (1980). A multidimensional scaling of three sets of compliance-gaining strategies. *Communication Quarterly, 28*, 34–46.

Dillard, J. P., & Burgoon, M. (1985). Situational influences on the selection of compliance-gaining messages: Two tests of the predictive utility of the Cody-McLaughlin typology. *Communication Monographs, 52*, 289–318.

Eagly, A. H. (1983). Gender and social influence. *American Psychologist, 34,* 971–981.

Eagly, A. H., & Chaiken, S. (1993). *The psychology of attitudes.* Fort Worth, TX: Harcourt Brace Jovanovich.

Fazio, R. H., Zanna, M. P., & Cooper, J. (1977). Dissonance and self-perception: An integrative view of each theory's proper domain of application. *Journal of Experimental Social Psychology, 13*, 464–479.

Festinger, L. (1957). *A theory of cognitive dissonance.* Evanston, IL: Row, Peterson.

Fishbein, M., & Ajzen, I. (1975). *Belief, attitude, intention, and behavior: An introduction to theory and research.* Reading, MA: Addison-Wesley.

Freedman, J. L., & Fraser, S. C. (1966). Compliance without pressure: The foot-in-the-door technique. *Journal of Personality and Social Psychology, 4*, 195–203.

French, J. R., & Raven, B. (1959). The bases of social power. In D. Cartwright (Ed.), *Studies in social power* (pp. 150–167). Ann Arbor, MI: University of Michigan Press.

Granberg, D. (1982). Social judgment theory. In M. Burgoon (Ed.), *Communication yearbook* (Vol. 6, pp. 304–329). Beverly Hills, CA: Sage.

Greenwald, A. G. (1968). Cognitive learning, cognitive response to persuasion, and attitude change. In A. G. Greenwald, T. C. Brock, & T. M. Ostrom (Eds.), *Psychological foundations of attitudes* (pp. 147–170). New York: Academic Press.

Heider, F. (1946). Attitudes and cognitive organization. *Journal of Psychology, 21,* 107–112.

Himmelfarb, S. (1993). The measurement of attitudes, in A. H. Eagly & S. Chaiken, *The psychology of attitudes* (pp. 23–87). Fort Worth: Harcourt Brace Jovanovich.

Hovland, C. I., & Janis, I. L. (Eds.), (1959). *Personality and persuasibility.* New Haven: Yale University Press.

Hovland, C. I., & Weiss, W. (1951). The influence of source credibility on communication effectiveness. *Public Opinion Quarterly, 15,* 635–650.

Infante, D. A. (1981). Trait argumentativeness as a predictor of communicative behavior in situations requiring argument. *Central States Speech Journal, 32,* 265–272.

Infante, D. A. (1985). Inducing women to be argumentative: Source credibility effects. *Journal of Applied Communication Research, 13,* 33–44.

Infante, D. A., & Rancer, A. S. (1982). A conceptualization and measure of argumentativeness. *Journal of Personality Assessment, 46,* 72–80.

Jackson, S., & Allen, M. (1987, May). *Meta-analysis of the effects of one-sided and two-sided argumentation.* Paper presented at the annual meeting of the International Communication Association, Montreal.

Jackson, S., & Jacobs, S. (1983) Generalizing about messages: Suggestions for the design and analysis of expeiments. *Human Communication Research, 9,* 169–181.

Johnson, D. W., & Johnson, R. T. (1979). Conflict in the classroom: Controversy and learning. *Review of Educational Research, 49,* 51–70.

Kazoleas, D. (1993). The impact of argumentativeness on resistance to persuasion. *Human Communication Research, 20,* 118–137.

Kearney, P., Plax, T. G., Richmond, V. P., & McCroskey, J. C. (1985). Power in the classroom III: Teacher communication techniques and messages. *Communication Education, 34,* 19–28.

Kim, M. S., & Hunter, J. E. (1993). Attitude-behavior relations: A meta-analysis of attitudinal relevance and topic. *Journal of Communication, 43,* 101–142.

LaPiere, M. A. (1934). Attitudes vs. actions. *Social Forces, 13,* 230–237.

Leary, M. R., & Kowalski, R. M. (1990). Impression management: A literature review and two component model. *Psychological Bulletin, 107,* 34–48.

Levine, T. R., & Badger, E. E. (1993). Argumentativeness and resistance to persuasion. *Communication Reports, 6,* 71–77.

Marwell, G. M., & Schmitt, D. R. (1967). Dimensions of compliance-gaining behavior: An empirical analysis. *Sociometry, 30,* 350–328.

McCroskey, J. C., & Young, T. J. (1981). Ethos and credibility: The construct and its measurement after three decades. *Central States Speech Journal, 32,* 24–34.

Milgram, S. (1974). *Obedience to authority.* New York: Harper.

Miller, G. R., Boster, F. J., Roloff, M. E., & Seibold, D. R. (1977). Compliance-gaining message strategies: A typology and some findings concerning the effects of situational differences. *Communication Monographs, 44,* 37–51.

Miller, G. R., & Burgoon, M. (1973). *New techniques of persuasion.* New York: Harper & Row.

Miller, G. R., Burgoon, M., & Burgoon, J. K. (1984). The functions of human communication in changing attitudes and gaining compliance. In C. C. Arnold & J. W. Bowers (Eds.), *Handbook of rhetorical and communication theory* (pp. 400–474). Boston, MA: Allyn & Bacon.

Miller, M. D. (1982). Friendship, power, and the language of compliance-gaining. *Journal of Language and Social Psychology, 1,* 111–121.

Miller, M. D., & Burgoon, M. (1979). The relationship between violations of expectations and the induction of resistance to persuasion. *Human Communication Research, 5*, 301–313.

Osgood, C. E., Suci, G. J., & Tannenbaum, P. H. (1957). *The measurement of meaning.* Urbana: University of Illinois Press.

Papageorgis, D., & McGuire, W. J. (1961). The generality of immunity to persuasion produced by pre-exposure to weakened counterarguments. *Journal of Abnormal and Social Psychology, 62*, 475–481.

Petty, R. E., & Cacioppo, J. T. (1981). *Attitudes and persuasion: Classic and contemporary approaches.* Dubuque, IA: William C. Brown.

Petty, R. E., & Cacioppo, J. T. (1986). The elaboration likelihood model of persuasion. In L. Berkowitz (Ed.), *Advances in experimental social psychology* (Vol. 19, pp. 123–205). San Diego, CA: Academic Press.

Petty, R. E., Ostrom, T. M., & Brock, T. C. (1981). *Cognitive responses in persuasion.* Hillsdale, NJ: Lawrence Erlbaum Associates.

Petty, R. E., Ostrom, T. M., & Brock, T. C. (1981). Historical foundations of the cognitive response approach to attitudes and persuasion. In R. E. Petty, T. M. Ostrom, & T. C. Brock (Eds.), *Cognitive responses in persuasion* (pp. 5–29). Hillsdale, NJ: Lawrence Erlbaum Associates.

Pfau, M., Kenski, H. C., Nitz, M., & Sorenson, J. (1990). Efficacy of inoculation strategies in promoting resistance to political attack messages: Application to direct mail. *Communication Monographs, 57*, 25–43.

Pfau, M., Van Bockern, S., & Kang, J. G. (1992). Use of inoculation to promote resistance to smoking initiation among adolescents. *Communication Monographs, 59*, 213–230.

Ragan, D. T. (1971). Effects of a favor and liking on compliance. *Journal of Experimental Social Psychology, 7*, 627–639.

Reinard, J. C. (1988). The empirical study of the persuasive effects of evidence: The status after fifty years of research. *Human Communication Research, 15*, 3–59.

Reynolds, R. A., & Burgoon, M. (1983). Belief processing, reasoning, and evidence. In R. N. Bostrom (Ed.), *Communication yearbook* (Vol. 7, pp 83–104). Beverly Hills, CA: Sage.

Rhodes, N., & Wood, W. (1992). Self-esteem and intelligence affect influenceability: The mediating role of message reception. *Psychological Bulletin, 111*, 156–171.

Schmitt, D. R. (1964). The invocation of moral obligation. *Sociometry, 27*, 299–310.

Schultz, B. (1982). Argumentativeness: Its effect in group decision-making and its role in leadership perception. *Communication Quarterly, 30*, 368–375.

Seibold, D. R., Cantrill, J. G., & Meyers, R. A. (1986). Communication and interpersonal influence. In M. L. Knapp & G. R. Miller (Eds.), *Handbook of interpersonal communication* (pp. 551–614). Beverly Hills, CA: Sage.

Sherif, C. W., Sherif, M., & Nebergall, R. E. (1965). *Attitude and attitude change: The social judgment-involvement approach.* Philadelphia, PA: W. B. Saunders.

Staats, A. W., & Staats, C. K. (1958). Attitudes established by classical conditioning. *Journal of Abnormal and Social Psychology, 57*, 37–40.

Stacks, D. W., & Burgoon, J. K. (1981). The role of nonverbal behaviors as distractors in resistance to persuasion in interpersonal contexts. *Central States Speech Journal, 32*, 61–73.

Stacks, D. W., & Hocking, J. E. (1992). *Essentials of communication research.* New York: HarperCollins.

Stiff, J. B. (1986). Cognitive processing of persuasive message cues: A meta-analytic review of the effects of supporting information on attitudes. *Communication Monographs, 53*, 75–89.

Tesser, A. (1978). Self-generated attitude change. In L. Berkowitz (Ed.), *Advances in experimental social psychology, 11*, 289–338.

Tversky, A., & Kahneman, D. (1974). Judgment under uncertainty: Heuristics and biases. *Science, 185*, 1124–1131.

Weinstein, E. A., & Deutchberger, P. (1963). Some dimensions of altercasting. *Sociometry, 26*, 454–466.

Wheeless, L. R., Barraclough, R., & Stewart, R. (1983). Compliance-gaining and power in persuasion. In R. N. Bostrum (Ed.), *Communication yearbook* (Vol. 7, pp. 105–143). Beverly Hills, CA: Sage.

Wicker, A. W. (1969). Attitude versus actions: The relationship of verbal and overt behavioral responses to attitude objects. *Journal of Social Issues, 25,* 41–78.

Wiseman, R. L., & Schenck-Hamlin, W. (1981). A Multidimensional scaling validation of an inductively-derived set of compliance-gaining strategies. *Communication Monographs, 48,* 251–270.

Witte, K. (1992). Putting the fear back into fear appeals: The extended parallel process model. *Communication Monographs, 59,* 329–349.

Woodside, A. G., & Davenport, J. W., Jr. (1974). The effect of salesman similarity and expertise on consumer purchasing behavior. *Journal of Marketing Research, 11,* 198–202.

Zajonc, R. B. (1968). Attitudinal effects of mere exposure. *Journal of Personality and Social Psychology Monographs, 9* (No. 2, Part 2).

18

Interpersonal Communication

Charles R. Berger
University of California—Davis

During the 1950s and 1960s, the study of interpersonal communication was coterminous with the study of communication and social influence processes (Berger, 1977). Experimental studies of attitude change, inspired by the Yale group's work on communication and persuasion (Hovland & Janis, 1959; Hovland, Janis, & Kelley, 1953; Hovland et al., 1957; Hovland & Rosenberg, 1960; Sherif & Hovland, 1961) and by balance (Heider, 1958; Newcomb, 1953), congruity (Osgood, Suci, & Tannenbaum, 1957), dissonance (Brehm & Cohen, 1959; Festinger, 1957), reactance (Brehm, 1966), and social judgment theories (Sherif & Hovland, 1961; Sherif, Sherif, & Nebergall, 1965) were the order of the day. During this time, communication researchers of many stripes, including those interested in the effects of mass media, employed these theoretical frameworks to explore relationships between a variety of source and message variables on the one hand and persuasion on the other (Berger & Chaffee, 1988), and landmark reviews of the persuasion literature (McGuire, 1969, 1985) employed a communication effects framework to organize research findings. Although interpersonal communication researchers continue to be interested in the relationships between communication and social influence processes (Boster, in press; Burgoon,1995; Miller, 1987; O'Keefe, 1990; Petty & Cacioppo, 1981), the purview of interpersonal communication has become markedly more catholic since the 1960s.

Theory and research concerned with such topics as goal-directed strategic communication, interpersonal attraction, relationship development, nonverbal communication, marital and family communication, speech style and language attitudes, bargaining and negotiation, interpersonal conflict, language and discourse processing, small group communication, communication in social support networks, and technology-mediated social interaction has burgeoned since this earlier period.

Some of these research areas—nonverbal communication, persuasion, and small group communication—have achieved an identity of their own. Even today, however, they are subsumed under the general rubric of *interpersonal communication studies.* Even if they were to be excluded from the interpersonal communication domain, the great diversity of research topics within the field precludes exhaustive review of each and every topic area (for such reviews see Knapp & Miller, 1994). An in-depth review of even one of these topic areas would more than fill this chapter; therefore, after considering what it is we mean by the term *interpersonal communication*, a more general approach to the research area will be presented.

WHAT IS INTERPERSONAL COMMUNICATION?

A variety of approaches for defining interpersonal communication have emerged over the years. An early and pervasive approach asserted that interpersonal communication is face-to-face communication between two people (King, 1979; Smith & Williamson, 1977); face-to-face interaction involving from three to some relatively small number of people was defined as *small group communication.* Although this numerical distinction held sway for some time, Miller and Steinberg (1975), Berger and Bradac (1982), and Bochner (1984) questioned its utility. They argued that in contrast to the number of individuals involved in an interaction, a more useful defining attribute might be the kinds of knowledge people employ to make predictions about each other during their interactions.

Miller and Steinberg labeled interactions based primarily upon knowledge of cultural conventions noninterpersonal communication, since interactions depending upon the use of such conventions fail to individuate people; people are seen as interchangeable, not displaying unique individual identities. They argued that interpersonal communication occurs when knowledge of individuals' beliefs, attitudes, and personalities, or what they termed *psychological level information,* is used as the basis on which to communicate. When such information is employed, messages can be tailored to people as unique individuals rather than as members of ostensibly homogeneous cultural or sociological groupings based on such attributes as ethnicity, sex, and age. Within this perspective, both Berger and Bradac (1982) and Miller and Steinberg (1975) argued that interpersonal communication could occur in what are traditionally thought of as mass communication contexts. Public figures disclosing highly personal information on television, their addiction to drugs for example, engage in an act of interpersonal communication, even though they might be communicating with millions of people simultaneously.

Cappella (1987) objected to this knowledge-based approach on the grounds that people participating in the impersonal, role-defined relationships Miller and Steinberg (1975) labeled *noninterpersonal relationships* still employ communication to carry out their roles. He observed that many impersonal interactions are nevertheless very important in people's lives, for example those involving doctors and patients and teachers and students. To relegate such significant communication situations to the *noninterpersonal* category seemed undesirable to him. As an alternative to the knowledge-based approaches to defining interpersonal communication, Cappella proposed that at a minimum interpersonal communication occurs when it can be demonstrated that an individual's behaviors affect the probability of the other's subsequent behaviors in reference to an individual baseline rate of the behavior. When such behavioral influences are mutual (i.e., when people alter each other's behaviors) the preconditions for interpersonal communication have been met.

These two approaches to definition are not necessarily incompatible. If the *mutual influence postulate* is granted, and it is assumed that mutual influence is necessary for interpersonal communication to occur, it is still possible to ask whether variations in message content (verbal and nonverbal) that are exchanged between people influence their psychological states. Mutual influence may occur when an individual asks a store clerk for a pack of chewing gum or when the same individual requests a paramour's hand in marriage; however, the relationship consequences of these mutually influencing exchanges are radically different. Consequently, it is reasonable that interpersonal communication rests on a foundation of mutual influence, and, further, the degree to which the mutually influencing messages exchanged are personal or impersonal is both constitutive and diagnostic of the type of relationship people have with each other (Bell, Buerkel-Rothfuss, & Gore, 1987; Bell & Healey, 1992). One important implication of this perspective is that the concepts of interpersonal *communication* and interpersonal *relationship* are distinct. Interpersonal communication affects interpersonal relationships, and relationship states influence the communicative activity of those involved in them (Cappella, 1987).

INTERPERSONAL COMMUNICATION AND RELATIONSHIP DEVELOPMENT

Since the early 1970s, the study of interpersonal communication's role in relationship development has grown exponentially. Altman and Taylor's (1973) social penetration model, which explained the growth and decline of interpersonal relationships by recourse to principles derived from social exchange theories (Adams, 1964; Blau, 1964; Homans, 1961; Roloff, 1981; Thibaut & Kelley, 1959), played an important heuristic function in stimulating interest in the study of relationship development over time. In their view, relationships grow or become more intimate when perceived rewards of relationships outweigh perceived costs of remaining in them. When the reverse situation occurs, relationships tend to deteriorate. Although such theories of relationship development imply smooth trajectories of relationship development and decline (Knapp, 1978, 1984; Knapp & Vangelisti, 1992), others questioned the viability of this characterization (Altman, Vinsel, & Brown, 1981; Baxter, 1988, 1990; Baxter & Simon, 1993; Bochner, 1984; Montgomery, 1993; Rawlins, 1992), arguing that those involved in relationships frequently are pulled simultaneously by different dialectical forces. For instance, people may desire both a connection with their partners, as well as a measure of individual autonomy in that relationship. These so-called *dialectical polarities* appear similar to instances of approach–approach conflict (Berger, 1993a; Lewin, 1935), regardless of how they are labeled. These tensions produce significant discontinuities in relationship growth and deterioration processes, thus leading to highly variable rather than smooth developmental paths (Baxter, 1988, 1990, 1993).

Initial Interaction and Attraction

Much of the interest in relationship development grew out of early studies designed to answer the question, "Why are people attracted to each other?" A number of studies have examined how information gained in a relationship's first stages influences judgments of individuals' attractiveness. That perceived similarities with regard to attitudes, values, and other personal characteristics promote interpersonal attraction is a widely accepted proposition (Bryne, 1971; Duck, 1973; Newcomb, 1961), and similarity with respect to personal construct systems tends to promote relationship escalation to friendship (Duck, 1973). However, there is some question as to whether actual similarities between people—rather than perceived similarities—act to induce interpersonal attraction (Sunnafrank, 1991, 1992).

Much of the early research done to determine the antecedents of interpersonal attraction was experimental. Byrne (1971) advanced his *law of attraction*, asserting that interpersonal attraction is a linear function of the proportion of rewards that individuals provide each other. He argued that one reward source is perceived similarity. To test his hypothesis, he used the *bogus stranger* technique. This method requires people to fill out questionnaires indicating their opinions on a wide variety of issues. The questionnaires are collected and the researcher creates a second set of questionnaires, allegedly completed by another group, which vary in the degree to which they "match" those given by the original participants. In some cases, the bogus questionnaires agree with 80 to 90 percent of the original opinions expressed. Other questionnaires agree on only 50 percent of the issues, whereas still others on 10 to 20 percent of the issues. At some later date, each original participant is given a bogus questionnaire and asked to read through it. They are told that a stranger filled out the questionnaire, and, after reading the questionnaire, are asked to indicate the degree to which they would like the person who filled it out. Byrne's (1971) results are both consistent and impressive. Typically, those who receive questionnaires containing responses highly similar to their own are much more attracted to that person than are people who receive questionnaires containing proportionally fewer agreement responses. Thus, people are more highly attracted to those who demonstrate attitudes similar to their own.

Some have questioned the generality of Byrne's (1971) findings. For example, Rosenbaum (1986) suggested that attitude similarity does not lead to attraction because people expect others to hold views similar to their own. Because we expect strangers to be at least somewhat similar to us, and because we typically enter initial encounters with strangers holding somewhat positive attitudes toward them (Kellermann, 1984), finding that a stranger shares our attitudes should not necessarily make the person any more attractive. By contrast, and consistent with Byrne's claim, when attitude dissimilarity is displayed, individuals will be less attracted to the dissimilar person (Rosenbaum, 1986). Others (Sunnafrank, 1983, 1984, 1991, 1992; Sunnafrank & Miller, 1981) argued that when individuals are allowed to interact with each other, as opposed to reading attitude responses on questionnaires, the relationship between attitude similarity and interpersonal attraction is attenuated significantly. Unfortunately, some of the experiments conducted to test this hypotheses did not manipulate the *proportion* of attitude agreements across a number of diverse attitude issues.

Byrne's (1971) law of attraction stipulates that attraction is a linear function of the proportion of agreements across attitude issues as well as of the relative salience of the attitude issues themselves. A fair test has to allow for agreement or disagreement across a wide range of issues. Any adequate test in the context of ongoing interactions also would have to directly assess the effects of similar and dissimilar attitude disclosures during the interactions themselves, a procedure not employed by Sunnafrank (Cappella & Palmer 1990, 1992). Although a detailed discussion of these issues cannot be presented here, the relationships among attitude similarity, communication, and attraction are addressed elsewhere (Byrne, 1992; Cappella & Palmer, 1992; Duck & Barnes, 1992; Hatfield & Rapson, 1992; Sunnafrank, 1992).

One criticism of bogus stranger studies is that the research participants do not interact with anyone. The "stranger" is simply a collection of opinion responses on a questionnaire rather than an actual person (see Duck, 1988). The idea is that in actual interactions, verbal and nonverbal information beyond that related to opinions is exchanged and this information affects interpersonal attraction. Another criticism is that these studies provide only limited snapshots that fail to take into account developmental factors and trends beyond the first few minutes of interaction, although Newcomb's (1961) classic study of the acquaintance process featured a longitudinal panel design in which the same group of students was observed and interviewed on multiple occasions during the school year, and others have examined the development of interpersonal attraction over time (Clatterbuck, 1979; Van Lear & Trujillo, 1986). A third criticism is that people's relationship histories partially determine whether or not they will seek out particular others in the first place and, once they have, whether they will develop a relationship beyond the initial stages of acquaintance. Although in any given study random assignment of individuals to experimental groups controls the potentially confounding effects of relationship histories, it is these histories that may account for considerable variance in relationship development trends (i.e., Hazen & Shaver, 1987; Shaver & Brennan, 1992). Moreover, once in a close relationship, partners' histories may play a large role in determining the degree to which they are able to adapt to the inevitable changes that visit all social arrangements, including those involving close bonds, and thus maintain their relationship. Still other research has sought to determine the patterns of information exchanged during initial conversations between strangers (Berger, 1973, 1975; Berger & Douglas, 1981; Berger, Gardner, Clatterbuck, & Schulman, 1976; Berger, Gardner, Parks, Schulman, & Miller, 1976; Berger & Kellermann, 1983, 1989, 1994; Berger & Perkins, 1978, 1979; Douglas, 1987b, 1990, 1993; Gudykunst, 1983, 1985, 1988; Gudykunst, Chua, & Gray, 1987; Gudykunst & Hammer, 1987; Gudykunst & Nishida, 1984, 1986; Gudykunst, Nishida, & Chua, 1986; Gudykunst, Sodetani, & Sodona, 1987; Gudykunst, Yang, & Nishida, 1985; Kellermann & Berger, 1984). Much of this work has been conducted in connection with *uncertainty reduction theory* (URT) (Berger, 1979, 1987, 1988; Berger & Calabrese, 1975; Berger & Gudykunst, 1991).

URT suggests that patterns of information exchanged during initial interactions can be explained because strangers seek information to reduce their uncertainties about their conversational partners to devise more effective messages for reaching their interaction goals. A general finding emerging from URT research is that decreases in felt uncertainty are associated with increases in attraction toward others (Clatterbuck, 1979; Douglas, 1990; Gudykunst et al., 1985; Van Lear & Trujillo, 1986), although there are questions about the direction of causality involved in this relationship (Berger, 1987, 1988; Berger & Gudykunst, 1991). Other studies explored strategies used to acquire information from others (Baxter & Wilmot, 1984; Berger & Kellermann, 1983; Kellermann & Berger, 1984), and the strategies employed to thwart the information-seeking attempts of inquisitive others (Berger & Kellermann, 1989).

Confining relationship development study and factors that foster interpersonal attraction to initial interactions strangers may not result in a comprehensive under-standing of relationship growth and deterioration processes. It is the case, however, that people mark the beginnings of significant relationships with celebrations of anniversaries and similar special occasions. People involved in relationships that span several decades can recall first meetings; thus, in a psychological sense, the beginnings, as well as the endings, of important relationships are significant markers in psycho-logical time. Beyond the symbolic significance relationship beginnings, however, is the enduring question of whether is it possible, in principle, to forecast relationship trajectories given initial interaction, or whether individual, interpersonal, and broad social factors merge together in a chaotic stew, making such prediction virtually impossible. The practical implications of this question are important to those interested in reducing both marital strife and divorce rates by employing premarital counseling and other methods designed to identify relationships having significant potential for dissolution before any long-term commitments are made.

Interpersonal Conflict

Given dialectical tensions in relationships, the balance of rewards and costs in rela-tionships may shift in the direction of perceived inequities. Thus, interpersonal conflict is more likely as the degree of interdependence between individuals increases (Kelley, 1979; Kelley & Thibaut, 1978; Thibaut & Kelley, 1959). It is not surprising that those interested in the study of communication and relationships have focused considerable attention on the study of interpersonal conflict (see Roloff, 1987). Conflict is an inevitable feature of relationships, especially close ones. Research involving surveys of both couples and individuals has examined the typical attributions people make for conflicts in close relationships (Bradbury & Fincham, 1990; Harvey, Wells, & Alvarez, 1978; Kelley, 1979; Orvis, Kelley, & Butler, 1976; Sillars, 1981, 1985), and in instances of divorce (Goode, 1956).

Not surprisingly, these studies reveal that people tend to attribute the causes of their conflicts to stable, dispositional attributes of their partners such as their personality. Even when individuals are asked to focus on specific aversive partner behaviors, rather than partner personality dispositions, they insist on locating the causes of conflict of their partner's negative dispositions (Kelley, 1979). In addition, when individuals involved in unhappy marriages experience negative events in the relationships, they tend to attribute responsibility to global conditions in the relationship and to their partners' selfishly motivated and negative intentions. When positive events are experienced by unhappy couples, they tend to be attributed to transient, unstable causes residing in the specific situation rather than global tendencies of the partner (Bradbury & Fincham, 1990). These attributional tendencies make amelioration of conflict difficult; changing personality dispositions and malevolent intentions is presumably more difficult than altering specific, bothersome behaviors. Apparently, even when positive events occur in unhappy marriages, the causes of these events tend to be perceived as unstable and tied to the specific situation rather than judged as peoples' positive dispositions. Sillars (1981) has linked patterns of attribution with patterns of communication that are deployed when conflict occurs.

Others have observed ongoing interactions between couples to determine patterns of communication that typically occur during interpersonal conflict episodes (Gottman, 1979; Raush, Barry, Hertel, & Swain, 1974; Sillars & Wilmot, 1994). Typically, these studies have contrasted the communication patterns of couples whose marriages are in distress—usually defined as couples who are involved in marriage counseling—with couples whose marriages are nondistressed. One finding is that distressed married couples tend to display communication patterns that involve considerable cross-complaining; the complaint of one spouse is responded to immediately by a complaint from the other. In nondistressed marriages, such cross-complaining is less frequent (Gottman, 1979). Sillars and Wilmot (1994) have catalogued a number of differences in communication taking place between distressed and nondistressed married couples. In general, the patterns of conflict among married couples are highly variable and couples do not generally employ constructive communication strategies for dealing with conflict. Frequently, marital conflicts begin on a specific issue but then become more abstract and less focused, leading to an ever-growing list of complaints and countercomplaints.

As this brief survey shows, a considerable amount of the research conducted in relationship development was theoretically motivated. Theoretical frameworks related to attachment, attribution processes, social exchange, and uncertainty reduction have been invoked to explain why relationships develop or fail to develop and why relationships remain stable or deteriorate. Still, from the perspective of interpersonal communication research, much remains to be learned about communication processes' roles in developing relationships. For example, observing that specific patterns of conflict occur more frequently in particular types of marital relationships (Fitzpatrick, 1988; Sillars, Pike, Jones, & Redmon, 1983; Zietlow & Sillars, 1988) does not explain why these conflict patterns are more prevalent within different marital arrangements. Only theoretical elaboration beyond the findings themselves can provide explanation. Attention now turns to an area of inquiry within interpersonal communication that has not had the benefit of extensive theoretical elaboration.

STRATEGIC INTERPERSONAL COMMUNICATION

The strategic perspective on interpersonal communication includes the assumption that when individuals are involved in face-to-face encounters, they are usually pursuing one or more goals in the interaction. This approach to interpersonal communication seeks to identify the strategies individuals use to reach various goals and to understand the conditions under which various strategies are likely to be deployed during interactions. Initial interest was stimulated by research in the area of compliance-gaining behavior, or how individuals "get their way" in social situations (Clark, 1979; Falbo, 1977; Falbo & Peplau, 1980; Marwell & Schmitt, 1967; Miller, Boster, Roloff, & Seibold, 1977). These early studies were followed by an avalanche of compliance-gaining studies in the 1980s (i.e., Boster, in press; Cody, Canary, & Smith, 1994; Cody & McLaughlin, 1990; Dillard, 1990).

As the compliance-gaining research engine gained momentum during this period, researchers sought to identify strategies used to achieve goals other than behavioral compliance. Strategies for seeking affinity (Bell & Daly, 1984; Daly & Kreiser, 1994 Douglas, 1987a), comforting others (Burleson, 1990, 1994), acquiring social and personal information (Baxter & Wilmot, 1984; Berger & Kellermann, 1994), and embarrassing others (Petronio, Snider, & Bradford, 1992) were identified. Much of the research reported in this tradition relied on self-reports of strategy use or estimates of the likelihood of using strategies presented to research participants in list form; research methods about which Miller (1987) raised serious questions. Relatively few studies in this genre have reported observations of strategy deployment during on-going face-to-face encounters (see Berger & Kellermann, 1994, and Burleson, 1994, for some exceptions), an alternative approach strongly advocated by Miller (1987).

Unfortunately, this spate of research activity, aimed, as it was, at isolating various communication strategies, was not matched by the development of equally impressive theoretical frameworks for explaining strategy development and use (Berger, in press; Dillard, 1990; Greene, 1990). Consequently, after a decade's work, no research has contrasted competing theories for explaining any aspect of strategic communicative action. This is not surprising, since there are no well-formulated theoretical frameworks to contrast in the first place (Berger, 1994b; Boster, in press). Even more troubling is that within the domain of compliance-gaining research, the area in which most strategically oriented research has been reported, there is considerable doubt concerning the comparability of so-called compliance-gaining strategies from one study to the next. Thus, it is difficult, if not impossible, to accumulate evidence for strategy choices across studies (Kellermann & Cole, 1994), a problem that may plague research reported in other strategic communication domains as well.

This very brief history of strategic interpersonal communication serves to highlight a number of important issues concerning strategies for viable research programs that may yield long-term payoffs in both theoretical and practical terms. As Boster (in press) noted, after conducting over 100 studies of compliance-gaining behavior, students of the compliance-gaining process still cannot answer the basic question of what strategies work best in given situations. The inability to answer this elementary question is relatively easy to understand: compliance-gaining researchers never set out to answer the question of the relative effectiveness of various strategies; a choice that is difficult to fathom.

The preoccupation of compliance-gaining research from the beginning was to discover the relative likelihood that specific strategies would be used under varying sets of circumstances (Miller et al., 1977) rather than the relative effectiveness of strategies in ongoing interactions. Thus, even if the problem of comparing compliance-gaining strategies across studies could be solved (Kellermann & Cole, 1994), an even more fundamental question concerns the overall goal of the entire research enterprise. Apparently, a single, widely-read and cited study (Miller et al., 1977) set a research precedent that, in some ways, led subsequent researchers into an intellectual cul-de-sac where very important questions about interpersonal communication and compliance-gaining simply were not asked. Of course, Miller et al. (1977) did not intend this to be the case. As observed previously, some ten years after the study was published, Miller (1987) and Miller, Boster, Roloff, and Siebold (1987) lamented the fact that most subsequent compliance-gaining studies followed the individual self-report approach, rather than studying messages exchanged during actual compliance-gaining episodes. The lesson gleaned here is that an initial, highly influential and widely cited study may inadvertently narrow the range of research questions subsequently asked in ways that are dysfunctional for producing research and expanding knowledge.

Theorizing About Strategic Communication

A fully articulated theory of strategic communication cannot be presented here; however, a full-blown theory would consist of at least two large pieces, one individual and the other social. The individual piece would address such questions as: How are goals represented in human memory? How are goals formulated and activated? How are mental representations like plans or scripts retrieved to guide goal-directed action, including verbal and nonverbal communication? When people lack plans and scripts for attaining goals, how do they construct the mental representations necessary for guiding their actions? And, when people fail to attain their goals, how do they adapt plans and scripts to overcome various sources of failure? The theory's social part would deal with such questions as: How do individuals represent each other's mental plans and scripts so that they can anticipate each other's actions with reference to their goals? Under what conditions do individuals collaborate in the formation of goals and plans? When such collaboration takes place, how is coordination between interactants accomplished? How are goal and plan conflicts played out in the actions and counter-actions of those involved in the conflict? And, to what extent can regular patterns of social interaction be traced to the meshing of individuals' plan-driven action sequences versus spontaneous non-plan-driven responses to actions presented during the interaction?

There are at least two important things to note about these 10 questions. First, they are quite abstract. None of them refers to any specific social goal, such as affinity seeking, compliance-gaining, comforting, or social information gathering; all of the questions are relevant to any and all social goals. Second, all of the questions refer to processes of generating and deploying strategic communicative *action*. None ask what the specific strategies are for attaining various social goals. Answers to them would presumably provide a better understanding of how the human cognitive system guides strategic communicative action, and how social factors intersect with individual, cognitive factors to produce such action. There are, of course, many more questions that could be raised about the production of strategic communicative action (Greene, 1990). This list demonstrates how asking questions at higher levels of abstraction may lead to developing theoretical frameworks that explain strategic communicative action across a wide range of social goals and contexts, and how asking certain questions directs us to understanding strategic communication processes.

Extracting Order from Chaos: Testing the Hierarchy Principle

To provide an illustration of how even a modest theoretical shift might encourage the development of broader principles of strategic communication, the fifth individual question listed above, "When people fail to attain their goals, how do they adapt plans and scripts to overcome various sources of failure?" is addressed here. It is presented as a representative way to conduct research in interpersonal communication.

The *hierarchy principle* was derived from two fundamental postulates. First, cognitive plans that guide social actions are organized hierarchically with abstract actions located at the tops of plan hierarchies and more concrete actions at lower levels (Berger, 1993b, in press; Berger & Abrahams, 1993; Berger & diBattista, 1993; Berger & Knowlton, 1994). The assumption that plans are organized hierarchically is commonly made in the natural language processing literature (Carberry, 1990; Cohen, Morgan, & Pollack, 1990; Green, 1989; Levelt, 1989; Levinson, 1981; Lichtenstein & Brewer, 1980; Litman & Allen, 1987; Perrault & Allen, 1980; Schank & Abelson, 1977; Schmidt, 1976; Varonis & Gass, 1985; Wilensky, 1983), and there is considerable evidence to support this claim (Abbott & Black, 1986; Black & Bower, 1979, 1980; Bower, Black, & Turner, 1979; Cahill & Mitchell, 1987; Lichtenstein & Brewer, 1980; Seifert, Robertson, & Black, 1985). Message plans that subserve strategic communicative action might contain abstract act types such as *threaten* or *cooperate,* which could be realized concretely as verbal and nonverbal action in a number of different ways; that is, there are a many verbal and nonverbal actions that might be used to instantiate abstract actions in a social interaction episode.

The second fundamental postulate underlying the hierarchy principle is that individuals are loath to expend significant amounts of their time and scarce cognitive resources seeking and processing large amounts of information. It is commonly assumed that people tend to be "cognitive misers" (Fiske & Taylor, 1991), frequently taking shortcuts via heuristics to reduce the time and effort necessary to make judgments and arrive at decisions (Kahneman, Slovic, & Tversky, 1982; Nisbett & Ross, 1980). When viewed within the present context, the postulate suggests that, when people fail to reach desired goals and wish to pursue their goals, they tend to alter their message plans that are the least effortful to implement. An important corollary is the following: As desire to reach goals increases, people will be more likely to expend increasing amounts of effort altering their plans.

The hierarchy principle lies at the confluence of the two postulates. It asserts that, when people fail to reach desired goals but wish to achieve them, they tend to alter message plans at relatively low levels, rather than at abstract levels. This is because message plan modifications at abstract levels demand more cognitive effort and resources. Thus, for example, when attempting to coerce others by threats fails, we will most likely continue to employ an abstract threat and alter lower level behaviors in future influence attempts. This can be seen in parents' behavior toward noncompliant children. When children fail to comply with their parents' wishes, parents often simply repeat what was said, but in a louder voice, and perhaps a more assertive tone. Such nonverbal alterations are less effortful to implement than are those associated with either reorganizing the content of the message or switching to a completely different act type such as reward, although, as suggested previously, when desire to reach goals is relatively high, such high level message plan alterations are more likely to be made.

Evaluating the Hierarchy Principle: An Interpersonal Study

In an initial effort to assess the hierarchy principle's veracity, Berger and diBattista (1993) asked research participants to provide geographic directions to confederates who, unbeknownst to them, were instructed to indicate that they were unable to follow the initial rendition of the directions, thus forcing the direction-givers to provide a second rendition of the directions. In some conditions, confederates indicated that inability to follow the directions was due to their limited ability to understand English. In another condition, no specific reason was provided. Regardless of the locus of communication failure, direction-givers tended to increase their vocal amplitude while providing the second rendition of the directions, even though confederates never suggested that they might be hearing impaired. This finding was observed again in a follow-up study (Berger & diBattista, 1992).

Berger and diBattista (1993) also revealed that only about 4% of the direction-givers spontaneously altered their routes used in the second rendition of the directions. A similar proportion of participants provided different walk routes in a follow-up study (Berger & diBattista, 1992). When compared with increasing vocal amplitude, the strategy of altering the walk route contained in a set of geographic directions is considerably more cognitively taxing. In the former case, the direction-giver simply repeats the sequence of streets and turns, but in a louder voice. In the latter, thinking of alternative routes requires both time and cognitive effort. Consequently, the studies provide some support for the hierarchy principle; that is, a preference for easily implemented message plan alterations in the face of goal failure.

Although initially encouraging, it was desirable to directly assess the viability of one of the fundamental postulates underlying the hierarchy principle. Specifically, we conducted a series of studies to determine whether alterations of message plans at progressively higher levels of abstraction is, in fact, more demanding of scarce cognitive resources. By demonstrating this relationship, the preference for lower level message plan alterations observed in the prior two studies could be explained more completely. In four different experiments, two of which were conducted in a laboratory setting (Berger, 1993b; Berger & Abrahams, 1993) and two of which were conducted under field conditions (Berger, 1994a; Berger & Knowlton, 1994, Experiment 1), participants were asked to provide directions to a specific destination. After being provided directions, confederates indicated they had trouble following the directions. At this point, confederates provided direction-givers information indicating the level in the message plan hierarchy at which the understanding failure occurred. In the low-level condition, direction-givers were told that their initial directions were difficult to follow because they had spoken too quickly and were asked to provide the directions again but to speak more slowly. High level condition direction-givers were informed that their directions were difficult to understand because the route they used was too difficult to follow, and were asked to provide the directions again using a different route. In some of the experiments (Berger, 1993b; Berger & Abrahams, 1993), the design included an intermediate level condition in which direction-givers were told that their directions were difficult to follow because they included too few landmarks in them, and direction-givers provide a second set of directions which included more landmarks.

In all of the experiments, cognitive load was indexed by the amount of time it took direction-givers to begin the second rendition of their directions after confederate feedback. Response latencies have been used routinely to index cognitive load (Greene,

1984; Greene & Lindsey, 1989). In the field experiments (Berger, 1994a; Berger & Knowlton, 1994, Experiment 1), randomly selected pedestrians were approached on street corners at a specific intersection and asked for directions to a specific locale by a confederate. Yoked with each confederate was an observer who recorded the direction-givers' response latencies using a concealed stop watch.

Both the laboratory and field experiments yielded strong and consistent support for the cognitive load postulate. Specifically, individuals asked to provide an alternative route in the second rendition showed significantly longer response latencies, in the range of three to four times longer, than individuals asked to reduce their speech rate in their second rendition. Average response latencies for direction-givers in the intermediate level condition fell midway between the other two conditions. As implied by the hierarchy principle, this pattern of response latencies strongly suggests that abstract level message plan alterations demand increased utilization of scarce cognitive resources to be implemented.

To determine conditions that might ameliorate the increased cognitive loads demanded by high-level message plan alterations, Berger and Knowlton (1994, Experiment 2) had research participants prepare for the direction-giving task under different conditions. Within the iconicity treatment, half of the participants prepared highly iconic representations (maps) of the direction routes, while the remaining participants prepared low iconicity written directions. Within each condition, half of the participants prepared one set of directions or one map, and the other half prepared three sets of directions or three maps, depending upon their iconicity assignment. A fifth group engaged in no preparation before delivering directions.

After preparing directions, participants were placed in a situation in which they were asked to provide directions to a confederate. Participants who had prepared maps or written directions were not permitted to use their prepared directions while providing them to the confederate. As in the previous experiments, after the direction-givers completed the first rendition of their directions, confederates indicated difficulty following them, that the route provided in the first set of directions was unclear. They were asked to provide the directions again using a different route. Again, response latency was used as a measure of cognitive load.

Our theoretical expectation was that highly iconic representations (maps) would be more memorable than the less iconic written directions. Furthermore, those who prepared three sets of written directions or maps should have more readily available alternatives from which to choose when asked for an alternative route, compared to those who prepared only one set of directions or map. However, when iconicity and the number of representations are considered together, people who prepared a single, highly iconic representation should have the most difficulty generating an alternative route—they would be fixated on a single, highly salient memory representation. By contrast, people preparing three highly iconic representations should require the least time to generate an alternative route. Thus, it was predicted that those who prepared three maps would demonstrate the shortest response latencies, while those who prepared one map would manifest the longest latencies. Furthermore, it was surmised that the cognitive load levels of the no preparation control condition, as well as the load levels of the written condition, would fall between the two extremes. The response latency data comported very closely with the predicted pattern.

That's Nice, But What Does the Hierarchy Principle Buy Us?

There are at least three answers to this rather pointed question. First, the hierarchy principle not only enables one to predict the communicative moves that people are likely to make when they fail to reach goals in social interaction situations, it also tells us something about the interaction between social action and individual cognitive processes. Only by advancing and testing theoretical notions such as the hierarchy principle are the complex interactions between social action, including action expressed through verbal and nonverbal channels, and individual cognitive processes understood in any detail.

Second, theoretical moves such as the hierarchy principle serve to integrate the melange of seemingly disparate lines of research subsumed under the strategic interpersonal communication label. Presently, some members of the interpersonal communication research community tend to organize the study of strategic interpersonal communication on a goal-by-goal basis; that is, studies of affinity-seeking, comforting, compliance-gaining, social information gathering, and the like. When viewed in a broader theoretical context, this mode of organization is somewhat dysfunctional; this mind-set countervails against the development of broader theoretical principles that would transcend apparent differences to integrate strategic interpersonal communication research into a unified and coherent perspective.

Third, the practical implications of the hierarchy principle are considerable. In their everyday social commerce people experience goal failures. Not only are they misunderstood, but they fail to reach other desired end-states even when they are understood. Consequently, to ignore how people adapt to everyday goal failures is an egregious oversight. More importantly, however, is the fact that research strongly suggests that when people fail to reach communication goals and alter certain aspects of their message plans to increase the likelihood of success, the modifications implemented frequently are not particularly successful. Increasing one's level of vocal intensity to a noncompliant child while reiterating the same words, is neither a formula for inducing compliance nor for maintaining an amicable long-term relationship with the child. Yet, causal observation of parent–child interactions in public venues (e.g., supermarkets and department stores) reveals the pervasiveness of this less than optimal adaptation to goal failure. Again, the hierarchy principle not only provides an explanation for suboptimal adaptations, it suggests strategies that might disabuse parents of displaying undesirable patterns of communication. Conflict interactions involving people from any sociodemographic categories may manifest similar communication patterns; patterns that can be accounted for and remedied by application of the hierarchy principle. After all, from the individual's perspective, isn't *conflict* just another way of saying *goal failure*?

SOME CONCLUDING THOUGHTS

It is difficult to offer predictions about future directions for the strategic interpersonal communication research enterprise. Researchers can and do change their research agendas. This dynamic activity in the research marketplace makes predicting future research trajectories extremely chancy. By thinking of strategic interpersonal communication as a process, rather than a haphazard collection of goals, considerably more theoretically interesting and practically important research questions can be asked. Consequently, instead of asking what *strategies* people use to attain particular goals, we should ask questions concerning the *processes* responsible for the fabrication and deployment of strategies in general and how people adapt to strategic failure, regardless of the goal or goals they are pursuing. It is not that the former question should never be asked and answered, but answers to the latter questions tell us much more about how strategic communication works in social interactions.

Just as it is extremely difficult to predict future trends in strategic interpersonal communication research in particular, it is equally daunting to prognosticate about the trajectory of interpersonal communication studies in general. It is probably safe to say that the domain of interpersonal communication inquiry will continue to expand in terms of research topics, as it has since the 1960s. In addition, considerable interest has been shown in integrating some aspects of interpersonal and mass communication research (Berger & Chaffee, 1988; Reardon & Rogers, 1988; Wiemann, Hawkins, & Pingree, 1988). Certainly, those who approach the study of human communication from a cognitive perspective (Hewes & Planalp, 1987) find it relatively easy to endorse the view that media information and information provided during the course of face-to-face interactions ultimately is processed by similar cognitive structures and processes. Thus, for example, memory for television programs and memory for conversations should share some commonalties. From this cognitive perspective, then, until otherwise demonstrated, differences in inputs (media versus face-to-face) may make relatively little difference in terms of understanding how individuals process and act on information. These possibilities may lead to future blurring of the boundaries that currently demark the subfields of interpersonal and mass communication. The cognitive perspective also might serve as a force for integrating interpersonal and other traditional areas of communication. Furthermore, the introduction of new communication technologies could make the boundaries currently separating the various communication subfields somewhat permeable. Whatever future unfolds, it is important to remember that unless research conducted in any domain is undergirded by theory, the insights offered by the research are likely to be limited. Consequently, no matter what future research in the interpersonal communication is about, we can hope it will rest on the firm foundation of broader theoretical principles.

REFERENCES

Abbott, V. A., & Black, J. B. (1986). Goal-related inferences in comprehension. In J. A. Galambos, R. P. Abelson, & J. B. Black (Eds.), *Knowledge structures* (pp. 123–142). Hillsdale, NJ: Lawrence Erlbaum Associates.

Adams, J. S. (1964). Inequity in social exchange. In L. Berkowitz (Ed.), *Advances in experiemental social psychology* (Vol. 2, pp. 267–299). New York: Academic Press.

Altman, I., & Taylor, D. (1973). *Social penetration: The development of interpersonal relationships.* New York: Holt, Rinehart, & Wintson.

Altman, I., Vinsel, A., & Brown, B. (1981). Dialectic conceptions in social psychology. In L. Berkowitz (Ed.), *Advanced in experimental social psychology* (Vol. 14, pp. 107–160). New York: Academic Press.

Baxter, L. A. (1988). A dialectical perspective on communication strategies in relationship development. In S.W. Duck (Ed.), *Handbook of personal relationships* (pp. 257–273). Chichester, England: Wiley.

Baxter, L. A. (1990). Dialectical contradictions in relationship development. *Journal of Social and Personal Relationships, 7,* 69–88.

Baxter, L. A., & Simon, E. P. (1993). Relationship maintenance strategies and dialectical contradictions in personal relationships. *Journal of Social and Personal Relationships, 10,* 225–242.

Baxter, L. A., & Wilmot, W. W. (1984). "Secret tests:" Strategies for acquiring information about the state of the relationship. *Human Communication Research, 11,* 171–201.

Bell, R. A., Buerkel-Rothfuss, N. L., & Gore, K. E. (1987). "Did you bring the yarmulke for the cabbage patch kid?" Idiomatic communication of young lovers. *Human Communication Research, 14,* 47–67.

Bell, R. A., & Daly, J. A. (1984). The affinity-seeking function of communication. *Communication Monographs, 51,* 91–115.

Bell, R. A., & Healey, J. G. (1992). Idomatic communication and interpersonal solidarity in friends' relational cultures. *Human Communication Research, 18,* 307–335.

Berger, C. R. (1973, December). *The acquaintance process revisited: Explorations in intitial interaction.* Paper presented at the annual convention of the Speech Communication Association, New York, NY.

Berger, C. R. (1975). Proactive and retroactive attribution processes in interpersonal communication. *Human Communication Research, 2,* 33–50.

Berger, C. R. (1977). Interpersonal communication theory and research: An overview. In B.D. Ruben (Ed.), *Communication yearbook* (Vol. 1, pp. 217–243). New Brunswick, NJ: Transaction Press.

Berger, C. R. (1979). Beyond initial interaction: Uncertainty, understanding, and the development of interpersonal relationships. In H. Giles & R. St.Clair (Eds.), *Language and social psychology* (pp. 122–144). Oxford: Basil Blackwell.

Berger, C. R., (1987). Communicating under uncertainty. In M. E. Roloff & G. R. Miller (Eds.), *Interpersonal processes: New directions in communication research* (pp. 39–62). Newbury Park, CA: Sage Publications.

Berger, C. R. (1988). Uncertainty and information exchange in developing relationships. In S.W. Duck (Ed.), *Handbook of personal relationships* (pp. 239–255). Chichester: Wiley.

Berger, C. R. (1993a). Goals, plans, and mutual understanding in relationships. In S. Duck (Ed.), *Individuals in relationships* (pp. 30–59). Newbury Park, CA: Sage Publications.

Berger, C. R. (1993b, November). *Planning, plan adaptation and cognitive load: An assessment of the hierarchy hypothesis.* Paper presented at the annual convention of the Speech Communication Association, Miami, FL.

Berger, C. R. (1994a, November). *Communication failure, message plan adaptation, and cognitive load: Further assessment of the hierarchy principle.* Paper presented at the annual convention of the Speech Communication Association, New Orleans, LA.

Berger, C. R. (1994b). A plan-based approach to strategic communication. In D. E. Hewes (Ed.), *The cognitive bases of interpersonal communication* (pp. 450–507). Hillsdale, NJ: Lawrence Erlbaum Associates.

Berger, C. R. (in press). Power, dominance, and social interaction. In M. L. Knapp & G. R. Miller (Eds.), *Handbook of interpersonal communication* (2nd ed.). Newbury Park, CA: Sage Publications.

Berger, C. R., & Abrahams, M. F. (1993, May). *Altering communication plans in response to goal failure.* Paper presented at the annual convention of the International Communication Association, Washington, DC.

Berger, C. R., & Bradac, J. J. (1982). *Language and social knowledge: Uncertainty in interpersonal relations.* London: Edward Arnold.

Berger, C. R., & Calabrese, R. J. (1975). Some explorations in initial interaction and beyond: Toward a developmental theory of interpersonal communication. *Human Communication Research, 1,* 99–112.

Berger, C. R., & Chaffee, S. H. (1988). On bridging the communication gap. *Human Communication Research, 15,* 311–318.

Berger, C. R., & diBattista, P. (1992, October). *Adapting plans to failed communication goals.* Paper presented at the annual convention of the Speech Communication Association, Chicago.

Berger, C. R., & diBattista, P. (1993). Communication failure and plan adaptation: If at first you don't succeed, say it louder and slower. *Communication Monographs, 59,* 368–387.

Berger, C. R., & Douglas, W. (1981). Studies in interpersonal epistemology III: Anticipated interaction, self-monitoring, and observational context selection. *Communication Monographs, 48,* 183–196.

Berger, C. R., Gardner, R. R., Clatterbuck, G. W., & Schulman, L. S. (1976). Perceptions of information sequencing in relationship development. *Human Communication Research, 3,* 29–46.

Berger, C. R., Gardner, R. R., Parks, M. R., Schulman, L. S., & Miller, G. R. (1976). Interpersonal epistemology and interpersonal communication. In G. R. Miller (Ed.), *Explorations in interpersonal communication* (pp. 149–172). Newbury Park, CA: Sage Publications.

Berger, C. R., & Gudykunst, W. B. (1991). Uncertainty and communication. In B. Dervin (Ed.), *Progress in communication sciences* (Vo. 10, pp. 21–66). Norwood, NJ: Ablex.

Berger, C. R., & Kellermann, K. A. (1983). To ask or not to ask: Is that a question? In R. N. Bostrom (Ed.), *Communication yearbook* (Vol. 7, pp. 342–368). Newbury Park, CA: Sage Publications.

Berger, C. R., & Kellermann, K. (1989). Personal opacity and social information gathering: Explorations in strategic communication. *Communication Research, 16,* 314–351.

Berger, C. R., & Kellermann, K. (1994). Acquiring social information. In J. A. Daly & J. M. Wiemann (Eds.), *Strategic interpersonal communication* (pp. 1–31). Hillsdale, NJ: Lawrence Erlbaum Associates.

Berger, C. R., & Knowlton, S. H. (1994, July). *The hierarchy principle in strategic communication.* Paper presented at the annual convention of the International Communication Association, Sydney, Australia.

Berger, C. R., & Perkins, J. W. (1978). Studies in interpersonal epistemology I: Situational attributes in observational context selection. In B. D. Ruben (Ed.), *Communication yearbook* (Vol. 2, pp. 171–184). New Brunswick, NJ: Transaction Press.

Berger, C. R., & Perkins, J. W. (1979, November). *Studies in interpersonal epistemology II: Self-monitoring, involvement, facial affect, similarity and observational context selection.* Paper presented at the annual convention of the Speech Communication Association, San Antonio, TX.

Black, J. B., & Bower, G. H. (1979). Episodes as chunks in narrative memory. *Journal of Verbal Learning and Verbal Behavior, 18,* 309–318.

Black, J. B., & Bower, G. H. (1980). Story understanding as problem-solving. *Poetics, 9,* 223–250.

Blau, P. M. (1964). *Exchange and power in social life.* New York: Wiley.

Bochner, A. P. (1984). The functions of human communication in interpersonal bonding. In C. C. Arnold & J. W. Bowers (Eds.), *Handbook of rhetorical and communication theory* (pp. 544–621). Boston, MA: Allyn & Bacon.

Boster, F. (in press). Commentary on compliance-gaining message behavior research. In C. R. Berger & M. Burgoon (Eds.), *Communication and social influence processes.* East Lansing: Michigan State University Press.

Bower, G. H., Black, J. B., & Turner, T. J. (1979). Scripts in memory for text. *Cognitive Psychology, 11,* 177–220.

Bradbury, T. N., & Fincham, F. D. (1990). Attributions in marriage: Review and critique. *Psychological Bulletin, 107,* 3–33.

Brehm, J. W. (1966). *A theory of psychological reactance.* New York: Academic Press.

Brehm, J. W., & Cohen, A. R. (1959). *Explorations in cognitive dissonance.* New York: Wiley.

Burgoon, M. (1995). Language expectancy theory: Elaboration, explication, and extension. In C. R. Berger & M. Burgoon (Eds.), *Communication and social influence processes* (pp. 29–151). East Lansing, MI: Michigan State University Press.

Burleson, B. R. (1990). Comforting as everyday social support: Relational consequences of supportive behaviors. In S. Duck (Ed.), *Personal relationships and social support* (pp. 66–82). London: Sage Publications.

Burleson, B. R. (1994). Comforting messages: Features, functions, and outcomes. In J. A. Daly & J. W. Wiemann (Eds.), *Strategic interpersonal communication* (pp. 135–161). Hillsdale, NJ: Lawrence Erlbaum Associates.

Byrne, D. (1971). *The attraction paradigm.* New York: Academic Press.

Byrne, D. (1992). The transition from controlled laboratory experimentation to less controlled settings: Surprise! Additional variables are operative. *Communication Monographs, 59,* 190–198.

Cahill, A., & Mitchell, D. C. (1987). Plans and goals in story comprehension. In R. G. Reilly (Ed.), *Communication failure in dialogue and discourse* (pp. 257–268). New York; North-Holland.

Cappella, J. N. (1987). Interpersonal communication: Definitions and fundamental issues. In C. R. Berger & S. H. Chaffee (Eds.), *Handbook of communication science* (pp. 184–238). Newbury Park, CA: Sage.

Cappella, J. N., & Palmer, M. T. (1990). Attitude similarity, relational history, and attraction: The mediating effects of kinesic and vocal behaviors. *Communication Monographs, 57,* 161–183.

Cappella, J. N., & Palmer, M. T. (1992). The effect of partners' conversation on the association between attitude similarity and attraction. *Communication Monographs, 59,* 180–189.

Carberry, S. (1990). *Plan recognition in natural language dialogue.* Cambridge, MA: MIT Press.

Clark, R. A. (1979). The impact of self interest and desire for liking on the selection of communicative strategies. *Communication Monographs, 46,* 257–273.

Clatterbuck, G. W. (1979). Attributional confidence and uncertainty in initial interaction. *Human Communication Research, 5,* 147–157.

Cody, M. J., Canary, D. J., & Smith, S. W. (1994). Compliance-gaining goals: An inductive analysis of actors' goal types, strategies, and successes. In J. A. Daly & J. W. Wiemann (Eds.), *Strategic interpersonal communication* (pp. 33–90). Hillsdale, NJ: Lawrence Erlbaum Associates.

Cody, M. J., & McLaughlin, M. L. (1990). *Psychology of tactical communication.* London: Multilingual Matters.

Cohen, P. R., Morgan, J., & Pollack, M. E. (1990). *Intentions in communication.* Cambridge, MA: MIT Press.

Daly, J. A., & Kreiser, P. O. (1994). Affinity seeking. In J. A. Daly, & J. W. Wiemann (Eds.), *Strategic interpersonal communication* (pp. 109–134). Hillsdale, NJ: Lawrence Erlbaum Associates.

Dillard, J. P. (1990). A goal-driven model of interpersonal influence. In J. P. Dillard (Ed.), *Seeking compliance: The production of interpersonal influence messages* (pp. 41–56). Scottsdale, AZ: Gorsuch Scarisbrick.

Douglas, W. (1987a). Affinity-testing in initial interactions. *Journal of Social and Personal Relationships, 4,* 3–15.

Douglas, W. (1987b). Question-asking in same- and opposite-sex initial interactions: The effects of anticipated future interaction. *Human Communication Research, 14,* 230–245.

Douglas, W. (1990). Uncertainty, information seeking, and liking during initial interaction. *Western Journal of Speech Communication, 54,* 66–81.

Douglas, W. (1993). *Uncertainty reduction during acquaintanceship: A reexamination of the anticipated future interaction hypothesis.* Unpublished manuscript, School of Communication, University of Houston, Houston, TX.

Duck, S. W. (1973). *Personal relationships and personal constructs: A study of friendship formation.* Chichester, England: Wiley.

Duck, S. (1988). *Relating to others.* Chicago: Dorsey Press.

Duck, S., & Barnes, M. K. (1992). Disagreeing about agreement: Reconciling differences about similarity. *Communication Monographs, 59,* 199–208.

Falbo, T. (1977). Multidimensional scaling of power strategies. *Journal of Personality and Social Psychology, 35,* 537–547.

Falbo, T., & Peplau, L. A. (1980). Power strategies in intimate relationships. *Journal of Personality and Social Psychology, 38,* 618–628.

Festinger, L. (1957). *A theory of cognitive dissonance.* Stanford, CA: Stanford University Press.

Fiske, S., & Taylor, S. E. (1991). *Social cognition,* (2nd ed.). New York: McGraw-Hill.

Fitzpatrick, M. A. (1988). *Between husbands and wives: Communication in marriage.* Newbury Park, CA: Sage.

Goode, W. J. (1956). *After divorce.* Glencoe, IL: Free Press.

Gottman, J. M. (1979). *Marital interaction: Investigations.* New York: Academic Press.

Green, G. M. (1989). *Pragmatics and natural language understanding.* Hillsdale, NJ: Lawrence Erlbaum Associates.

Greene, J. O. (1984). Speech preparation processes and verbal fluency. *Human Communication Research, 11,* 61–84.

Greene, J. O. (1990). Tactical social action: Toward some strategies for theory. In M. J. Cody & M. L. McLaughlin (Eds.), *Psychology of tactical communication* (pp. 31–47). London: Multilingual Matters.

Greene, J. O., & Lindsey, A. E. (1989). Encoding processes in the production of multiple-goal messages. *Human Communication Research, 16,* 120–140.

Gudykunst, W. B. (1983). Uncertainty reduction and predictability of behavior in low- and high-context cultures. *Communication Quarterly, 31,* 49–55.

Gudykunst, W. B. (1985). A model of uncertainty reduction in intercultural encounters. *Journal of Language and Social Psychology, 4,* 79–98.

Gudykunst, W. B. (1988). Uncertainty and anxiety. In Y. Y. Kim & W. B. Gudykunst (Eds.), *Theories in intercultural communication* (pp. 123–156). Newbury Park, CA: Sage Publications.

Gudykunst, W. B., Chua, E., & Gray, A. (1987). Cultural dissimilarities and uncertainty reduction processes. In M. McLaughlin (Ed.), *Communication yearbook* (Vol. 10, pp. 456–469). Newbury Park, CA: Sage Publications.

Gudykunst, W. B., & Hammer, M. R. (1987). The effects of ethnicity, gender, and dyadic composition on uncertainty reduction in initial interactions. *Journal of Black Studies, 18,* 191–214.

Gudykunst, W. B., & Nishida, T. (1984). Individual and cultural influences on uncertainty reduction. *Communication Monographs, 51,* 23–36.

Gudykunst, W. B., & Nishida, T. (1986). Attributional confidence in low- and high- context cultures. *Human Communication Research, 12,* 525–549.

Gudykunst, W. B., Nishida, T., & Chua, E. (1986). Uncertainty reduction in Japanese-North American dyads. *Communication Research Reports, 3,* 39–46.

Gudykunst, W. B., Sodetani, L. L., & Sonoda, K. (1987). Uncertainty reduction in Japanese-American–Caucasian relationships in Hawaii. *Western Journal of Speech Communication, 51,* 256–278.

Gudykunst, W. B., Yang, S. M., & Nishida, T. (1985). A cross-cultural test of uncertainty reduction theory: Comparisons of acquaintance, friend, and dating relationships in Japan, Korea, and the United States. *Human Communication Research, 14,* 7–36.

Harvey, J. H., Wells, G. L., & Alvarez, M. D. (1978). Attribution in the context of conflict and separation in close relationships. In J. H. Harvey, W. Ickes, & R. F. Kidd (Eds.), *New directions in attribution research* (Vol. 2, pp. 235–360). Hillsdale, NJ: Lawrence Erlbaum Associates.

Hatfield, E., & Rapson, R. L. (1992). Similarity and attraction in close relationships. *Communication Monographs, 59,* 209–212.

Hazen, C., & Shaver, P. (1987). Similarity and attraction in close relationships. *Communication Monographs, 59,* 209-212.

Heider, F. (1958). *The psychology of interpersonal relations.* New York: Wiley.

Hewes, D. E., & Planalp, S. (1987). The individual's place in communication and science, In C. R. Berger & S. H. Chaffee (Eds.), *Handbook of communication science* (pp. 146–183). Newbury Park, CA: Sage.

Homans, G. C. (1961). *Social behavior: Its elementary forms.* New York: Harcourt Brace Jovanovich.

Hovland, C. I., & Janis, I. L. (Eds.). (1959). *Personality and persuasibility.* New Haven, CT: Yale University Press.

Hovland, C. I., Janis, I. L., & Kelley, H. H. (1953). *Communication and persuasion.* New Haven, CT: Yale University Press.

Hovland, C. I., Luchins, A. S., Mandell, W., Campbell, E. H., Brock, T. C., McGurie, W. J., Feierabend, R. L., & Anderson, N. H. (Eds.). (1957). The order of presentation in persuastion. New Haven, CT: Yale University Press.

Hovland, C. I., & Rosenberg, M. J. (Eds.). (1960). *Attitude organization and change.* New Haven, CT: Yale University Press.

Kahneman, D., Slovic, P., & Tversky, A. (1982). *Judgment under uncertainty: Heuristics and biases.* New York: Cambridge University Press.

Kellermann, K. A. (1984). The negativity effect and its implications for initial interaction. *Communication Monographs, 51,* 37–55.

Kellermann, K., & Berger, C. R. (1984). Affect and the acquisition of social information: Sit back, relax, and tell me about yourself. In R. N. Bostrom (Ed.), *Communication yearbook* (Vol. 8, pp. 412–445). Newbury Park, CA: Sage Publications.

Kellermann, K., & Cole, T. (1994). Classifying compliance gaining messages: Taxonomic disorder and strategic confusion. *Communication Theory, 4,* 3–60.

Kelley, H. H. (1979). *Personal relationships: Their structures and processes.* Hillsdale, NJ: Lawrence Erlbaum Associates.

Kelley, H. H., & Thibaut, J. W. (1978). *Interpersonal relations: A theory of interdependence.* New York: Wiley.

King, R. G. (1979). *Fundamentals of human communication.* New York: Macmillan.

Knapp, M. (1978). *Social intercourse: From greeting to good-bye.* Boston, MA: Allyn & Bacon.

Knapp, M. L. (1984). *Interpersonal communication and human relationships.* Boston, MA: Allyn & Bacon.

Knapp, M. L., & Miller, G. R. (Eds.). (1994). *Handbook of interpersonal communication* (2nd ed.). Newbury Park, CA: Sage Publications.

Knapp, M. L., & Vangelisti, A. L. (1992). *Interpersonal communication and human relationships* (2nd ed.). Boston: Allyn & Bacon.

Levelt, W. J. M. (1989). *Speaking: From intention to articulation.* Cambridge, MA: MIT Press.

Levinson, S. (1981). Some preobservations on the modeling of dialogue. *Discourse Processes, 4,* 93–116.

Lewin, K. *(1935).* *A dynamic theory of personality.* New York: McGraw-Hill.

Lichtenstein, E. H., & Brewer, W. F. (1980). Memory for goal directed events. *Cognitive Psychology, 12,* 412–445.

Litman, D., & Allen, J. (1987). A plan recognition model for subdialogues in conversation. *Cognitive Science, 11,* 163–200.

Marwell, G., & Schmitt, D. R. (1967). Dimensions of compliance-gaining behavior: An empirical analysis. *Sociometry, 30,* 350–364.

McGuire, W. J. (1969). The nature of attitudes and attitude change. In G. Lindzey & E. Aronson (Eds.), *Handbook of social psychology* (Vol. 3, 2nd ed., pp. 136–314). Reading, MA: Addison Wesley.

McGuire, W. J. (1985). Attitudes and attitude change. In G. Lindzey & E. Aronson (Eds.), *Handbook of social psychology* (Vol. 2, 3rd ed., pp. 233–346). Hillsdale, NJ: Lawrence Erlbaum Associates.

Miller, G. R. (1987). Persuasion. In C. R. Berger & S. H. Chaffee (Eds.), *Handbook of communication science* (pp. 446–481). Newbury Park, CA: Sage Publications.

Miller, G. R., Boster, F., Roloff, M., & Seibold, D. (1977). Compliance-gaining message strategies: A topology and some findings concerning effects of situational differences. *Communication Monographs, 44,* 37–51.

Miller, G. R., Boster, F., Roloff, M. E., & Seibold, D. (1987). MBRS rekindled: Some thoughts on compliance-gaining in interpersonal settings. In M. E. Roloff & G. R. Miller (Eds.), *Interpersonal processes: New directions in communication research* (pp. 89–116). Newbury Park, CA: Sage.

Miller, G. R., & Steinberg, M. (1975). *Between people: A new analysis of interpersonal communication.* Chicago, IL: Science Research Associates.

Montgomery, B. M. (1993). Relationship maintenance versus relationship change: A dialectical dilemma. *Journal of Social and Personal Relationships, 10,* 205–223.

Newcomb, T. M. (1953). An approach to the study of communicative acts. *Psychological Review, 60,* 393–404.

Newcomb, T. M. (1961). *The acquaintance process.* New York: Holt, Rinehart, & Winston.

Nisbett, R. E., & Ross, L. (1980). *Human inference: Strategies and shortcomings of social judgment.* Englewood Cliffs, NJ: Prentice-Hall.

O'Keefe, D. J. (1990). *Persuasion: Theory and research.* Newbury Park, CA: Sage Publications.

Orvis, B. R., Kelley, H. H., & Butler, D. (1976). Attributional conflict in young couples. In J. H. Harvey, W. J. Ickes, & R. F. Kidd (Eds.), *New directions in attribution research* (Vol. 1, pp. 353–386). Hillsdale, NJ: Lawrence Erlbaum Associates.

Osgood, C. E., Suci, G. J., & Tannenbaum, P. H. (1957). *The measurement of meaning.* Urbana, IL: University of Illinois Press.

Perrault, R., & Allen, J. (1980). A plan-based analysis of indirect speech acts. *American Journal of Computational Linguistics, 6,* 167–182.

Petronio, S., Snider, E., & Bradford, L. (1992, October). *Planning strategy for the embarrassment of friends: An application and test of Berger's planning theory.* Paper presented at the annual convention of the Speech Communication Association, Chicago, IL.

Petty, R. E., & Cacioppo, J. T. (1981). *Attitudes and persuasion: Classic and contemporary approaches.* Dubuque, IA: W. C. Brown.

Raush, H. L., Barry, W. A., Hertel, R. K., & Swain, M. A. (1974). *Communication and conflict in marriage.* San Francisco: Jossey-Bass.

Rawlins, W. K. (1992). *Friendship matters: Communication, dialectics, and the life course.* New York: Aldine de Gruyter.

Reardon, K. K., & Rogers, E. M. (1988). Interpersonal versus mass media communication: A false dichotomy. *Human Communication Research, 15,* 284–303.

Roloff, M. E. (1981). *Interpersonal communication: The social exchange approach.* Newbury Park, CA: Sage Publications.

Roloff, M. E. (1987). Communication and conflict. In C. R. Berger & S. H. Chaffee (Eds.), *Handbook of communication science* (pp. 484–534). Newbury Park, CA: Sage Publications.

Rosenbaum, M. E. (1986). The repulsion hypothesis: On the nondevelopment of relationships. *Journal of Personality and Social Psychology, 51,* 1156–1166.

Schank, R. C., & Abelson, R. P. (1977). *Scripts, plans, goals and understanding.* Hillsdale, NJ: Lawrence Erlbaum Associates.

Schmidt, C. F. (1976). Understanding human action: Recognizing the plans and motives of other persons. In J. S. Carroll, & J. W. Payne (Eds.), *Cognition and social behavior* (pp. 47–67). Hillsdale, NJ: Lawrence Erlbaum Associates.

Seifert, C. M., Robertson, S. P., & Black, J. B. (1985). Types of inferences generated during reading. *Journal of Memory and Language, 24,* 405–422.

Shaver, P. R., & Brennan, K. A. (1992). Attachment styles and the "big five" personality traits. *Personality and Social Psychology Bulletin, 18,* 536–545.

Sherif, M., & Hovland, C. I. (1961). *Social judgment: Assimilation and contrast effects in communication and attitude change.* New Haven, CT: Yale University Press.

Sherif, C. W., Sherif, M., & Nebergall, R. E. (1965). *Attitude and attitude change: The social judgment-involvement approach.* Philadelphia, PA: W. B. Saunders.

Sillars, A. L. (1981). Attributions and interpersonal conflict resolution. In J. H. Harvey, W. J. Ickes, & R. F. Kidd (Eds.), *New directions in attribution research* (Vol. 3, pp. 279–305). Hillsdale, NJ: Lawrence Erlbaum Associates.

Sillars, A. L. (1985). Interpersonal perception in relationships. In W.J. Ickes (Ed.), *Compatible and incompatible relationships* (pp. 227–305). New York: Springer-Verlag.

Sillars, A. L., Pike, G. R., Jones, T., & Redmon, K. (1983). Communication and conflict in marriage. In R. N. Bostrom (Ed.), *Communication yearbook* (Vol. 7, pp. 414–441). Newbury Park, CA: Sage.

Sillars, A. L., & Wilmot, W. W. (1994). Communication strategies in conflict and mediation. In J. A. Daly & J. W. Wiemann (Eds.), *Strategic interpersonal communication* (pp. 163–190). Hillsdale, NJ: Lawrence Erlbaum Associates.

Smith, D. R., & Williamson, L. K. (1977). *Interpersonal communication: Roles, rules, strategies and games.* Dubuque, IA: William C. Brown.

Sunnafrank, M. (1983). Attitude similarity and interpersonal attraction in communication processes: In pursuit of an ephemeral influence. *Communication Monographs, 50,* 273–284.

Sunnafrank, M. (1984). A communication-based perspective on attitude similarity and interpersonal attraction in early acquaintance. *Communication Monographs, 51,* 372–380.

Sunnafrank, M. (1991). Interpersonal attraction and attitude similarity: A communication-based assessment. In J. Anderson (Ed.), *Communication yearbook* (Vol. 14, pp. 451–483). Newbury Park, CA: Sage.

Sunnafrank, M. (1992). On debunking the attitude similarity myth. *Communication Monographs, 59,* 164–179.

Sunnafrank, M., & Miller, G. R. (1981). The role of initial conversations in determining attraction to similar and dissimilar strangers. *Human Communication Research, 8,* 16–25.

Thibaut, J. W., & Kelley, H. H. (1959). *The social psychology of groups.* New York: Wiley.

Van Lear, C. A., & Trujillo, N. (1986). On becoming acquainted: A longitudinal study of social judgment processes. *Journal of Social and Personal Relationships, 3,* 375–392.

Varonis, E. M., & Gass, S. M. (1985). Miscommunication in native/nonnative conversation. *Language in Society, 14,* 327–343.

Wiemann, J. M., Hawkins, R. P., & Pingree, S. (1988). Fragmentation in the field—and the movement toward integration in communication science. *Human Communication Research, 15,* 304–310.

Wilensky, R. (1983). *Planning and understanding: A computational approach to human reasoning.* Reading, MA: Addison-Wesley.

Zietlow, P. H., & Sillars, A. L. (1988). Life stage differences in communication during marital conflicts. *Journal of Social and Personal Relationships, 5,* 223–245.

19

Modeling Cultures:
Toward Grounded Paradigms

Eduardo Nieva
Mark Hickson, III
University of Alabama at Birmingham

Culture is not a ghost under the midday sun; it is always present in all human interactions. Human interaction does not come first and culture second. Neither culture nor human interaction can aspire to be behind one another. Interaction is made possible by the very stuff of culture: the signs[1] that we share. This chapter explores the mutual influence of communication and culture. As is noted, communication is pervasive in culture—and some cultural theorists go as far as to suggest that without communication, there is no culture. Culture serves a *modeling* function. What we "see"—interpret—in a culture is based on our expected model of what that culture should look like through the sharing of signs. In our discussion we will explore both theoretical and grounded (*capta*) models of culture. First, however, we must define what *culture* is from both sociological and anthropological approaches to communication.

---

[1]Contrary to some uses of the term, *sign* is here understood as a general concept comprising all forms of representations, natural and human. *Symbols* are a product of convention and have therefore been considered the main element of cultural exchange. Umiker-Sebeok (1977) and Singer (1984) wrote two excellent critiques leading to a semiotics of culture.

HISTORICAL PERSPECTIVES

Culture as a concept, and its relationship to communication has a long history, and there is a fervent revival of interest led by those who use such concepts as *intercultural*, *cross-cultural*, and *multicultural* study. Some writers trace the original research on culture to Herodotus in the 5th century B.C. and certainly to Tacitus in Western culture and Fa-hsien in the East (Reischauer & Fairbank, 1958). Noted anthropologist E. Adamson Hoebel (1966), however, disagreed, claiming that the early Greeks were interested only in the *ideal* political structure and social organization of other peoples. Hoebel did credit Tacitus with writing a tract on Germany—referring to it as "an early ethnography." Hoebel believed that one must trace the origins of ethnography to the *Enlightenment*, in the sense that time establishes a comparative point of view.

The Anthropological Track

For anthropologists, ethnography and the study of other cultures began with the French Jesuit Joseph-François Fafitau, who worked among the Iroquois and Hurons of western New York state in the 18th century (Hoebel, 1966). Another example of early research is Arthur Young, who published accounts of agricultural practices in Great Britain between 1771 and 1793 (Wax, 1971), forerunners of agricommunication studies and organizational communication studies in the United States.

These early anthropologists were also early pioneers in what was to become two tracks of theory and research formulated from two different directions. One, the anthropological track, which came foremost from the London School of Economics, was lead by Bronislaw Malinowski (Powdermaker, 1966), whose views were espoused by British and American anthropologists, including Hortense Powdermaker and Ruth Benedict (Fletcher, 1971). Malinowski, who had received a PhD in physics and mathematics from the University of Cracow, noted that there was "no such thing as 'theory-free' knowledge" (Fletcher, 1971, p. 689). He felt that social science was a basis for "social engineering," clearing the way for anthropologists to argue that social science is a way to ensure that history never repeats itself.

With Malinowski, we find an option for the historicist tenets haunting anthropological evolutionism. Malinowski's (1944) method requires that segments of a cultural whole not be displaced for they are part of institutional contexts that grant their sense. Malinowski was firm in that a subject matter must be created and methodology based on that subject matter. For him, everything was a matter of getting to generalizations, a goal, however, that could only be achieved via comparative studies of a rather narrow focus. His cultural "units of analysis" for study were *institutions*. In his functional theory, the analysis of institutions included studying the institution's charter—its purpose, its rules or norms, the material apparatus (capital), its activities, and its functions.

Functionalist assumptions were but the offsprings of a conception of society as organic cohesion that creates legitimate, valid, and effective possibilities for the individual—the social actor—and the social fabric. Culture analysis was hedged into precise social limits. In Malinowski's radical empiricism nothing is more imminent than culture; culture takes a context-bound form; and a culture is "only intelligible when it is placed within its *context of situation*" (Malinowski, 1923, p. 306). It was Ruth Benedict,

Malinowski's student, who developed the prototype cultural configuration study in her *Patterns of Culture* (Benedict, 1934). The American prototype is found in Powdermaker's (1966) study of blacks in Indianola, Mississippi.

The German-Sociological Track

The other track—in many ways similar to Malinowski's—is that utilized by German professors of economics and philosophers to better understand their underprivileged class. In 1890, Paul Göhre, "a student of theology, undertook what may have been the first systematic attempt at participant observation" (Wax, 1971, p. 27). Göhre pretended to be a factory apprentice, each night recording his observations. After reading some of Göhre's field research publications, German sociologist Max Weber collaborated with Göhre on a study of agricultural workers.

The German influence continued in the United States. Early in his career, University of Chicago philosopher William I. Thomas was strongly influenced by William Wundt's *Völkerpsychologie*. Although he never met Wundt, social philosopher George Herbert Mead also was influenced by Wundt, when Mead studied at the University of Leipzig (Miller, 1973, p. 88). Thus, both the philosophy and sociology departments at Chicago were to pursue study from the German track. Later, with Florian Znaniecki, Thomas completed the first major piece of ethnography in sociology (Coser, 1977).

Impact on Communication Theory and Research

Although both tracks use similar theoretical and methodological approaches, one will rarely find a single sociological fieldworker quoting the works of an anthropological ethnographer or vice versa. The impact of each on the field of communication, however, has been monumental. Even so, one rarely finds crosspollination. The sociological approach has been utilized primarily by communication researchers studying organizations, such as Linda Putnam, Michael Pacanowsky, Stanley Deetz, and H. Lloyd Goodall. The anthropological approach has been used by nonverbal communication researchers such as Edward T. Hall, Erving Goffman, and Judee Burgoon.

With this background, it is important for us to discuss terminology. Hoebel (1966) defined *culture* as "the integrated system of learned behavior patterns that are characteristic of members of a society and which are not the result of biological inheritance" (p. 5). Farb (1978) wrote:

> Although social scientists disagree about the exact definition of culture (one descriptive inventory totaled 164 items), they do agree about its general character. Culture is human-made; it includes ideas, values, and codes known to all members of the group; it is transmitted from generation to generation. A culture does not exist until it is shared with other human beings. It influences the way in which a person behaves toward others in the group and also the way that person expects others to behave. Culture represents a new stage in evolution: the ability to acquire, store, and exchange information and then to pass it on to the next generation, so that it will not have to be relearned from scratch. An individual human being thereby accumulates vastly more information than could be acquired by experience alone. (pp. 11, 14)

From this, there should be little question on the importance of communication to culture. For the anthropologically-oriented communication researcher, the conceptualization of culture as an arena for the exchange of signs is qualitatively fundamental.

TOWARD THE CONCEPT OF CULTURE

The symbolic essence of human interaction—its extrasomatic trace—allows us to conclude that there ought to be the study of "a distinct order of phenomena, organized upon principles of its own and behaving in terms of its own laws" (White, 1968, p. 547). More than just a defense of culture, White suggests the inversion of the traditional link between culture and communication. Communication is not an aftereffect of culture. Communication—as an exchange of symbols—constitutes cultural networks.

White's contentions run counter to Radcliffe-Brown's redefining anthropology as only social anthropology dealing with social systems composed of real relations. If so, the social systems create the interconnectedness of individuals. One provision must be added to Radcliffe-Brown's redefinition: that the observable object of social anthropology has nothing to do with psychological concerns over the minds of the social actors. Mental relations do not belong to social analysis. Social and psychological laws are rigidly distinct. Concerns with culture belong to psychology; therefore social anthropology has the obligation of avoiding any contact with culture. To deal with culture is to be tainted. Radcliffe-Brown (1948b) knew that he was placing a horrifying taboo over the concept of culture.

Radcliffe-Brown was also opting for a strictly empirical perspective. The object of study in social anthropology is life as such; its task is to describe social relations, offered as an organized whole. It was inevitable that Radcliffe-Brown (1949) would assault White's view of a science of culture, arguing the impossibility of studying culture without consideration of lived relations and modes of interaction between social actors and groups in a particular society. Interaction and contract associations come first, and they are out of pace with White's conception of culture that relies on mental structures organizing a culture. The real questions concerned the way in which interaction creates a stable system, recognizable as a definite object. How is society welded? How is social interaction obtained? Culture leads us astray from the *particularities* of social integration. There should be no doubt that group integration and its quest for stability is, from a sociological analysis, more important than mental traces. Radcliffe-Brown is adamant in stating that one perspective precludes the other. Emphasis on social structure is untenable with the notion of culture (Radcliffe-Brown, 1949). Culture is just an element of the structure functioning in social life.

THE END OF CULTURE?

On the footsteps of Radcliffe-Brown, a whole generation of British anthropologists came to repudiate the notion of culture. In fact, by the middle of the century, Malinowski's influence as the Grandmaster of anthropological thought had dwindled. Radcliffe-Brown presided over British anthropology and was responsible for the expulsion of whatever he considered unworthy and wrong. Thus, Stocking (1984, p.

176) described Radcliffe-Brown's ascendence as "galvanizing small groups by the direct verbal force of his authoritative intellect, he elicited, if not demanded discipleship."

A cleavage was then opened in anthropological theory. Kroeber and Parsons (1958) saw the problems that segregation of culture and society brought about, and tried to tone down the dispute as just a matter of perspective:

> Sociologists tend to see all cultural systems as a sort of outgrowth or spontaneous development, derivative from social systems. Anthropologists are more given to being holistic and therefore begin with total systems of culture, and then proceed to subsume social structure as merely a part of culture. (Kroeber & Parsons, 1958, p. 582)

The intellectual authority of Kroeber and Parsons—one in anthropology, the other in sociology—seemed to warrant a truce. But was it really just a matter of perspective? Would a truce hide a deeper issue and erase a whole theoretical matter that could not be merely called off?

Why did Radcliffe-Brown lay such emphasis over social interaction? For him, society was an organism, relating its individual members in concerted harmony. What the anthropologist sees are "acts of behavior of such individuals, including their acts of speech, and the material product of past actions" (Radcliffe-Brown, 1968, p. 190). We do not *observe* a culture. Anthropological study's real object is the complex network of actually existing relations, its *social structure*. We do not doubt that societies are weaved around human action; but the consequences of Radcliffe-Brown's militant empiricism led to an theoretical impoverishment.

However much Radcliffe-Brown tried to dismiss Malinowski's role in theoretical anthropology as "irresponsibility" (Radcliffe-Brown, 1968, p. 188), both held similar prejudices concerning primitive groups. Malinowski stated that the "savages" were driven by narrow pragmatic purposes. The upholding of pragmatic principles to explain linguistic utterances of a society totally ignorant of the pragmatic doctrine was seen as natural and unproblematic.[2] For Radcliffe-Brown (1948a): "In speech the Andamanese express themselves in short disconnected sentences or phrases" (p. 504). The nexus of sentences were incomplete; they were left to be understood. The ethnocentricity of both contentions was taken for granted. Thus, language and communication in primitive societies could never be real modes of cognition, just practical devices, ruled by incompleteness. Although Malinowski still used the term culture, Radcliffe-Brown was eager to do away with it. Why should anthropologists deal with abstractions such as culture if the primitives were not qualified for abstraction and higher thought?

CULTURE AND MODELS

Is culture less real than actual interaction? How could concrete action ever exist without the presentation of possibilities or models for actors? Can we say that functionalist analyses are free from an a priori model of social interaction? Facing a definite social

---

[2]Fortes (1953) pointed out that one of the influential sources in British anthropology was, among others, the pragmatic psychology of William James. Leach (1957) said something similar, tracing the influence of pragmatic doctrines of Malinowski to the state of the academic field of British anthropology around 1910, when he came from Poland to England.

setting, the functionalist interpreter, like any other analyst, had the initial task of observing details to be later integrated into a whole. Nonetheless, the functionalist interpreter depended on an even more abstract model of social interaction. The functionalist presumption is untenable. How could we assume in a timeless way that every observed singularity is working stably and constantly in the overall frame? With strictly empirical requirements in mind, it is easy to conclude that a stable social frame is an abstraction from the actual hubbub and indeterminacy of interaction. How then could a functionalist sincerely believe that he works without recourse to abstraction?

What do interpreters do when facing an intercultural contact? They start with the pinning down of social norms. Whatever the interpretative presumptions held, the beginning is the same. It starts with the collection of norms, as informed by interaction with the members of the specific group. Because a model is at work, the indeterminacy of behavior and consequences in a social situation is reduced.

The models presented consciously by the informers—by the ones with whom the interpreters interact—are no more than barren sets of rules. Such models are "very poor ones" (Lévi-Strauss, 1963c, p. 281). Nutini (1970) would say that "these conscious phenomena—structures or whatever we wish to call them—are not themselves models" (p. 84). In the face of this, theoreticians not influenced by Radcliffe-Brown, such as Schneider (1976), devote little attention to action. The real concern of cultural interpretation is the recognition of how cultures as systems are *organized*.

TOWARD A THEORY OF CULTURE MODELS

A theory of culture models should account for the empirical dimensions of social interaction but without falling into the traps of a naive empiricism. Radcliffe-Brown's arguments about observable social action simply do not apply. In fact, the idea that formal models are present in actual life frees us from the ethnocentric prejudices recognized in the works of both Malinowski and Radcliffe-Brown. Only a formal model avoids the interference of definite contents, inevitably present as echoes of whatever is foreign to the analyzed object. To imagine that the analysis of social facts could deal with a living community in its daily interaction, using the principles of natural science, as suggested by Radcliffe-Brown (1948b) is more than just to condemn the field as a pseudoscience. It also projects the categories of a specific intellectual product—coming from the interpreter's society—over the object, therefore deforming it.

An alternative model sees social life as ruled by relationships of order, following a formal, mathematical pattern, as Lévi-Strauss (1954) and Leach (1971c) perceived. But the mathematical influence could never be what Lévi-Strauss (1954) called "borrowed quantitative methods which, even in mathematics itself, are regarded as traditional and outmoded" (p. 585). We have to search for the answer elsewhere, in *qualitative* methods. Magnitudes and unqualified quantification are irrelevant for the understanding of culture. As Lévi-Strauss (1954) states, "I would say that we are less concerned with the theoretical consequences of a 10 per cent increase in the population of a country having 50 million inhabitants, than with the changes in structure occurring when a 'two-person household' becomes a 'three-person household'" (p. 586). The precise relationship within the model is altered, a symptom of change in the cultural model.

The cultural analysis models are not integrated by a mysterious inner essence, or an otherwise rigid order. What is at work is a relative degree of constancy. We do not find a timeless stability, just variations in the pattern generating a process isomorphic to the previous model configuration. The nature of such models is qualitative and cannot be reduced to products of quantitative formulas. They are not, therefore, a product of induction, inferred from straight observation.

In thinking of formal social models we have to produce basic morphologies that follow social orders in the same way that human languages are formal. A typology of models must be recognizable as formal substrata, underlying the observed variety of social life. Models are certainly modified and transformed in social interaction. Just to use a simile presented by Leach (1971c, p. 7), it is as though the model is drawn in a transparent rubber sheet, and then submitted to pulling here and there, following the pressures of individual interests of the social actors. The pattern is altered, but—paradoxically—remains the same. A group does not need to hold crystal-clear and unanimous notions about what it experiences. Nonetheless, there is something —networking—that binds the actors.

No model can be rigidly stable; social interaction makes change inevitable. But the model is there, both for the external interpreter who tries to produce it, and for the interacting members of the group. Models are not restricted to observation, they belong to an intellectual order other than raw data. "Models would be useless, if they did not tell us more, and differently, than the data" (Lévi-Strauss, 1960, p. 51). Interpreters create a model, not inductively, but deductively building it up; and they repeat themselves in societies without historical and geographical contact. There is reason to presume that social formations are reducible to basic morphologies. The number of models cannot be unlimited: "[H]uman societies, like individuals, never create absolutely, but merely choose certain combinations from an ideal repertoire that it should be possible to define" (Lévi-Strauss, 1973, p. 178).

We can group such models into sets, if they are to emerge from similar pattern formations. And also, in the same limited group, models can coexist and produce specific configurations responding to an individual society's identity.

Two Basic Morphologies

Models are global representations that are locally transfigured; they reduce the complexity of empirical data. Models are not generated from local and empirical observations, but are made to explain observable events. Lévi-Strauss (1963c, p. 277–323) noted that he and Radcliffe-Brown used the same term—*social structure*—for different objects. Radcliffe-Brown confused social structure with social relations. In a letter to Lévi-Strauss, he recognized their differences, admitting that by social structure, he meant concrete reality, whereas for Lévi-Strauss "social structure has nothing to do with reality, but with models that can be built up" (Tax, Eiseley, Rouse, & Vogelin, 1952, p. 109). Lévi-Strauss (1952) then counterargued that "models are reality, and I would say that they are the only reality" (p. 115).

The connection between models and reality does not come from a one-to-one correspondence with empirical data. If it were so, models would be nothing but descriptions of events. Models are hypothetical constructions about facts. They do not ask *how* a certain interactive pattern occurred; instead they embrace the *how* into the *why*. Models should provide answers for the reason *why* a certain act happened, actually happens, will happen, or else could have happened.

From Elements to Models

Two morphological elements are to be identified in any social configuration: individual elements and groups. Both may be organized into an all-encompassing category unifying individuals and subwholes of the major group. It is through the topological relation of these elements that we can qualify basic morphological models.

We will not search for answers in anthropological literature, but in mathematics, in topology, more specifically in René Thom's *Structural Stability and Morphogenesis* (1975). Still, we cannot proceed with the argument without mentioning that Lévi-Strauss (1963b) said something similar to Thom about basic morphologies, claiming the existence of "two major structure types." One type is based on *reciprocity*, he calls it the structure of communication. The other type, *structure of subordination*, is qualified as univocal and irreversible. Here, he is referring to an individualistic model—ruled by an unqualified universal reciprocity for each member of the group—and also to a hierarchical, holistic model.[3]

Thom's models differ slightly from Lévi-Strauss'. In Thom's models, communication does not qualify one model as opposed to another. The two basic social morphologies are sustained and created by communication, or in his own words, by "circulation of complexity, of information, through the social body" (Thom, 1975, p. 318).

One model is called the *military society*. The name is not precise, for it defines a totality through the use of a tag pertinent to a segment of existing societies. Military societies are ruled by subordination. Each individual element is defined by its position in the overall configuration, and the totality qualifies both the model and the relationships of elements with each other. Each individual's positions are mutually dependent; they ideally move in a progressive action, hierarchically materialized as the point of a cusp. The cusp is the supreme representation of the overall totality. The whole determines the behavior of its parts. The tendency is to keep the formation of the pattern; that is, when changes occur in the configuration, the subordination to the cuspid point is restored. Individuals do not exist as values in themselves, but as positions in a seemingly rigid pattern, with predominant stability. The patterns of actions are governed by the whole. The cusp is not an individual in itself, it represents the whole. Thom sees such models in flocks of birds, shoals, fishes and bee hives. Among humans, caste formations follow precisely such a model.

Thom calls the other model the *fluid society*. The typical example is "a cloud of mosquitoes" (Thom, 1975, p. 319). The movements in the swarm are oriented from the individual's point of view. The glimpse of other individuals in the swarm corrects

---

[3]Reciprocity and subordination between moities of the Bororos are the central categories used by Lévi-Strauss to analyze their social system, in which all members of a community are part of one of the social divisions that keep dual relationships of solidarity and hostility, mutually exclusive (Lévi-Strauss, 1944). Lévi-Strauss understood reciprocity as a general principle of sociability, identifiable in our exchange of presents during Christmas, among the Andamese, in the southern coast of Ghana, in the northwest Pacific coast, in Melanesia, in Polinesia, all over human societies. Reciprocity is a social institution that defines "by this fundamental process the transformation from nature to culture" (Lévi-Straus, 1969, p. 63).

the course and its constant possibility of disintegration. No totality governs the pattern, the pattern happens. Each individual is related to another, and all of them—through reciprocity—correct the possible discontinuities, as when clear legal definitions of rules respected by each individual bar disorder. Without such unspoken agreement, nonetheless present, the collective experience disintegrates into chaos. So that order can be fully working, there are limits to each individual member of the group. Rules underlie the behavior of all, and chaos is the price to pay for the distortion of rules; nothing would ever exist, no concerted action, no fluid morphology, just pathological outbursts. The group is separated from its individuals, but one sphere regulates the other.

Thus, there are two basic morphologies with two different orders. Each mode of ordering is an attractor. The disappearance of the attracting order changes the pattern. A combination of basic morphologies, not only in the overall pattern of the group but also in subregions of the pattern, should account for diverse social formations. Cultures in turn form basic morphologies, thus creating their own particularity. Models are essentially iconic, analogic, and preconventional; models *precede* cultures; cultures are themselves symbolic and a product of shared conventions.

From Models to Cultures

The notion of model brings with it important consequences to the definition of culture. First and foremost, it acquires the traces of a quasi-integrated systems. Models are comparable, and comparison reveals transformations of basic morphology. Examining actual social groups we can see morphologies at work in dazzling combinations. Models confer identity to groups, and also establish their differences. Keeping this in mind, we refer to Lévi-Strauss's redefinition of culture as a fragment of human life that "creates significant discontinuities in relation to the rest of humanity" (Lévi-Strauss, 1963c, p. 295).

Consciously or unconsciously, understanding the existence of basic morphologies, interpreter of a different culture choose models that reflect what is perceived through their own eyes—because interpreters are observing a culture different than their own. They then proceed in a deductive manner going from a model tentatively established to presently interpret the specific culture they are observing. Interpreters behave as detectives, working from hypotheses; and from them, deduct explanations.

ON INDIVIDUALISTIC MORPHOLOGY

In *Democracy in America,* Alexis de Tocqueville (1954) chose the basic morphology, fluid society, as explanatory of the United States. It is true that Tocqueville did not use the terminology, or the concept of basic morphologies, or even of fluid society, but he identified the democratic principle as underlying social interaction in America—a specific formative morphology.

Tocqueville then identifies the democratic principle—a political expression of a fluid morphology—ruling social interaction in all of the system. For him, individualistic morphology and its consequence had a profound effect on American life. Basic individualistic morphology is transformed into the general political principle of equality. Besides Tocqueville, Lévi-Strauss (1946) also observed that in America there is the ideology that "what is valuable for the part is equally valid for the whole" (p. 643). American life moves itself through a deep and ingrained desire for equal opportunities, and its form of homogeneity. Equality means a defense against the springing of distinctions.[4] The individualistic streak is countered by a common desire to conform to general norms that should "discipline the formless reactions of individuals in the name of a living collective ideal" (Lévi-Strauss, 1946, p. 645).

More than liberty is thus required as an ideological condition for individualism. Extreme liberty—in the hands of an individual or a subgroup—can be undesirable in its effect of creating distinctions and differentiations. Isolated members of the group should live as if they are autonomous beings who cannot be subordinated to any other member of the group or subgroup. Relations among members of the social set are reciprocal; rights become more visible than duties, for rights confer autonomy, and duties imply subordination. All individual members of the group must equally comply with the prescriptions of the legal framework looming above each individual. In an individualistic society, homogeneity is a form of curbing antisocial actions of an individual nature. The community is composed of equals; hierarchy is denied. But it could emerge under the perverse forms of class distinctions, social neglect and indifference to destitution, racial discrimination, and totalitarian oppression.[5]

So, it is from individualistic and democratic principles that the American legal system has regulated inheritance, forcing the social division of family property among the offsprings. Concentration of wealth is therefore reduced, bringing with it "a constant revolution in property" (Tocqueville, 1954, p. 51).

We can see the action of a basic morphology in different areas of social life. Individualism is everywhere. That is why the First Amendment to the American Constitution sanctifies freedom of the press and the universal right of free speech to access individual consciences. In America we see a distrust in theoretical speculation and uninterested knowledge; the educational system, for example, is made to achieve immediate results as a consequent demand that theories should be concerned with producing pragmatic and immediate solutions for daily life. All over the social fabric, civil and contractual rights should be extended to every individual member of the community. In personal terms, "fun," "pleasure," to be considered "a nice fellow"—a way of being cherished by the community as a singular and special individual—are especially prized in American life. Even in serious lectures, there should be room for a funny quip, a joke, in fact. Administrators in universities write memos signing their first name. And the President of the United States may even abbreviate his first name into the nickname used in his household. Theoretically at least, everyone has an equal right to pursue "happiness;" society is not a simple technique of reason, as Durkheim observed, but it is a technique of bringing happiness (Lévi-Strauss, 1946) and the kingdom to come. Happiness is avaliable at an outpost to be reached in the future. Power in America is attained through periodic elections and rotation of individuals in

---

[4]Sartre (1955) has a similar insight: Individualism in America always implies freedom to conform.
[5]For a penetrating study of some of those trends in individualistic society, see Dumont's (1986) interpretation of Nazi racist ideology.

political positions, coupled with restrictions to their unending permanence in office. The political system depends on the principle that individual votes are added up to decide what collective course of action should be taken. Political hierarchy is reached through the counting of individual votes. Economically, we have a market society in America, defended as a holy ground, being in fact an effect of the emergence of economy as an autonomous and dominant sphere in social life.

Karl Polanyi examines the market society, where the market is a self-regulating and isolated instance, following an invidualistic model. In an economic oriented society, economic activities are ends in themselves. Polanyi (1968, 1975) stressed that traditional societies differ from modern and individualistic social formations; economic practices in traditional societies are submitted to social relations, whereas—after industrialism—the economic sphere is disembedded from the social fabric, thus becoming a dominion regulating itself with autonomy and outside of social relations. Social relations are subjected to economic interests. The emancipation of the economic sphere warrants individual and private property. Communities have no right to limit or to interfere with property, unless it is illegally acquired. The community has the obligation of upholding property rights. It is not surprising, considering the overall action of cultures, that, in the other extreme of capitalistic society, even Marx himself, brooding about revolution, would conceive it as the takeover of the means of production, subverting the social relations of ownership, but still thinking in terms of property.

In such a society, individuals are ruled by the general law of the market. In fact, only the economic sphere provides general and universal laws: "The economic mode of thought naturally enjoys an ideological supremacy over the political in the liberal or capitalistic world thanks to its embodying a purer of more perfect form of individualism (Dumont, 1985, p. 256). Political and social rights express individualistic tenets. Human rights are not really universal principles; they are a product of a historical moment and could only make sense for societies sharing individualistic premises.

ON HIERARCHICAL MORPHOLOGY

Equality and hierarchy may be superficially considered opposed to each other. But if we consider one morphology in relation to another, we must agree that individualism and holism, equality and hierarchy, are mutually illuminated. Louis Dumont (1964, 1970a), for example, discusses the caste system in India, by taking into account its relationship to the Western tradition of individualism. For him, Hindu society teaches us the lessons of hierarchy.

We must approach Indian civilization with caution. To understand India in its own terms we have to see how the system of ideas and values proper to Indian society works. Through a generalized hierarchical order, Indian society creates a system in which one social element embraces the other, in a relationship of encompassing and encompassed (Dumont, 1967; Khare, 1971). It is wrong to project the categories of a individualistic morphology to such a different social configuration.

Castes are social hedges incomparable to practices such as American class distinction and racial segregation. Castes are not modes of apartheid. The Hindu caste system has at its core the idea that its four social categories—the four *varnas*—are not just distinguished and separated. They fit into an overall pattern. At the top of the social cusp, we find the Brahmans, or priests, and going down the social slope we find "below them the Kshatriya or warriors, and then the Vaishyas, in modern usage merely merchants, and finally the Shudras, the servants or have-nots" (Dumont, 1970a, p. 67). Besides the four social categories, Dumont also identifies a fifth category, composed of the Untouchables, which is outside of the classification. Brahmans and Untouchables are as opposed to one another as purity is to impurity, as high is to low. In fact, the term "caste" is taken from the Portuguese "casto," which means pure, chaste, clean. What is particular of the Indian caste system is not the separation of social segments, but the fact that social function unites the segments. How can we talk about oppression when what happens is social *unification* through function? Unification through function means cooperation between social sectors.

Each group is socially circumscribed but the different castes, the *jāti*, are defined mutually as part of a larger whole. The Indian caste system is ruled by a social morphology, deemed hierarchical and holistic, irreducible to a individualistic morphology. It is not like the "close status group" that we see in race relations in individualistic society, or even the relationship between nobility and common men in Western monarchies (Leach, 1969, p. 2). In fact, *caste* should be used only in reference to Indian society.

The Indian order of castes is a cultural system with restrictions placed on food, sex, and rituals. Order is maintained through ideas concerning purity of the members of the castes, and therefore through kinship ties that direct endogamous connections, creating binds that anchor "the Hindu to his place in society and curbs the desire to strike out on his own" (Yalman, 1969, p. 125). For all this, no sociology of the individual could ever explain the hierarchical system of India (Dumont, 1970b). The category of social interaction, made from the strict point of view of individuality, is too outlandish to explain the generation of hierarchy.

In that case, we would have to rely on the notion of culture. Culture is more useful than society. Culture permits us to identify a constellation of ideas powerful enough to act upon individuals; the basic idea of caste hierarchy is the cultural distinction between purity and pollution culminating hierarchically in the Brahman priests. Purity and pollution simultaneously segregate and "mark the conceptual integration of a whole" (Dumont, 1970a, p. 252). Ideas join—and not only separate—social segments in Indian society. Even political power was subordinated to this conceptually-defined hierarchy: "The priest, the Brahman, is high in status even when he is poor and materially dependent." In the oldest texts referring to the *varna* order, priesthood is set above; that is, it encompasses rulership; and "at the same time these 'twin forces' together encompass all the rest" (Dumont, 1967, p. 34). The Brahman consecrated the king's power. The dependence of political force and secular authority on the purer member of the hierarchy indicates that hierarchy does not stem from power. Power is generated by hierarchy.

Hierarchy must be seen in a complex light. It exists among the distinct caste segments of India. But, inside a segment, equality predominates: "All members of my sub-caste (*jāti*) are my kinsmen and, vice versa, all my kinsmen are members of my caste" (Leach, 1969, p. 9). Individualistic and reciprocal relationships are not necessarily banished from hierarchical morphologies. Extreme individuality in India is also collectively conceptualized.

Western societies, in their effort to define individualism as an autonomous value, separated economy from social ties. Wealth and poverty, abundance and famine are private destinies that do not concern the social whole. That mode of individualism indicates a separation from social life, whereas, in a complementary manner, the member of a Catholic monastic order surrenders his wealth to his superiors that will manage the worldly goods according to the order's social priorities. In India, the rule is obverse. The layman accepts the holistic order of the social world, but there are religious individuals that radically renounce the mundane sphere: "The renouncer has the world behind in order to devote himself to his own liberation. He submits to his chosen master, or he may even enter a monastic community, but essentially he depends upon no one but himself, he is alone" (Dumont, 1970b, p. 45). The renouncer—the *sannyasi*—is what Indian culture produces as an extreme mode of individuality.

If we compare morphological configurations, we can see both principles of reciprocity and hierarchy in a complex interaction. Individualism generates a consensual hierarchy produced by reciprocal principles. Hierarchical systems cannot do away completely with individuality and reciprocity.

Individualistic and Hierarchical Morphologies Side by Side

Leach (1970) renders another combination of individualistic and holistic morphologies when analyzing the political systems in the Kachin Hills at North-East Burma. He identifies the existence of two contiguous groups in the region, so different that it was common practice to categorize them as Shans as opposed to Kachins. The Shans were deemed stable; the Kachins were ruled by instability. But Leach observed that these neighbors were more intertwined than it was at first possible to perceive. It is true that Kachins and Shans have distinct profiles. Shans are a homogeneous group of valley dwellers that cultivate rice. Kachins are highlanders; neither are unified linguistically. Leach refused to consider the groups as tightly sealed from each other. The whole area appeared as more of an interactive network than unified separate totalities. The image that Leach (1970) presented is one of an ongoing process, under relentless change, "a large system in a flux" (p. 6).

If we look at the Shans in relation to the Kachins, we can pinpoint two radically opposed political systems. The Shans are class stratified, divided into segments of "aristocrats, commoners, and low caste" (Leach, 1970, p. 56). The Kachins present a political model that is democratic, a kind of "anarchic republicanism." The military fluid and models are now side by side. The two morphologies do not exclude one another. Besides the *gumlao* democratic ideology, the Kachins developed a third model, based on Shan autocracy, generating a *gumsa* system, considered a "compromise between gumlao and Shan ideals" (Leach, 1970, p. 9).

Leach then observes that subgroups in the Burmese area will either choose a fluid or a military morphology, or will have them both, creating an overall system in northeast Burma that includes both *gumsa* and *gumlao* ideologies. Let us take for instance the Dulengs, a group defined linguistically as Jinghpaw, living in an area east of Mali Hka (Irrawaddy) and north of Shang Hka (Nam Tisang). The Dulengs live according to the democratic ideology of the *gumlao*. On the other hand, the Tsasen, also linguistically Jinghpaw, at the northern and western areas of the Hukawng Valley, developed a system both *gumsa* and *gumlao*. And another group, the Gauri, are solely *gumsa* (Leach, 1970, pp. 57–58). Sociologically and politically, the morphologies are combined. Then, the *gumsas* are seen as snobs and tyrants by the *gumlaos*, and *gumlaos* are seen as inferiors by the *gumsas* (Leach, 1970). Each member of the group takes a position in relation to what was generated by the excluding morphologies. We can have a coexistence of both rank and equality, hierarchy and reciprocity, all along the Kachin area.

For borderline situations, where ambiguity rules, there are ritual procedures that reinforce and define social positions. Any ritual implies culture and communication. With this in mind, we have to redefine culture as a presentation of possibilities, as something other than merely a set of given rules unifying a social area. Culture provides ideas that interpret and conduct conflicts within the group. Contradictory social positions are not an abnormal trend. Considering the Kachin differences in dealing with their mythologies, Leach (1970) noted that there is no need for "internal consistency in the various traditions" (p. 268). Why then is stability presumed?

It may be that looking at a certain social unit from afar, we are prone to recognize regularities. But contradiction and dissonance too can be significant. Some critics (Berreman, 1971; Leach, 1971a; Leach, 1971b; Marriott, 1966) saw Dumont's description of Indian society as a frozen and timeless representation with no room for actual social shunting. In defending the constructing of general models, we note that it is within the overall frame that interaction happens—there are no guarantees that frames remain pristine and virginally intact.

The advantage of having a model consisting of constancies comes from its generality. In any case, the model is precarious, and interaction deforms it. But this does not remove the underlying morphologies. Berreman (1971) tells us that low caste natives did not refrain from laughing at his interpretation of Indian society, according to him very similar to Dumont's. The natives would then say: "You have been talking to Brahmins" (Berreman, 1971, p. 23). Their reaction should be understood as a call to consider the active and dynamic dimension of cultural interaction, not just a dismissal of underlying morphologies.

Contemporary Brazilian society also perceives a peculiar combination of fluid and more rigidly ordered morphologies. Roberto Da Matta (1979, 1985, 1991, 1993), perceives that Brazilians conceive their society through three social spaces in mutual and dual opposition: the *house*, the *street* and the *other world*. All actors in Brazilian life circulate from one symbolic area to another, in search of compensations—daily life and actual interaction shift between these areas. Each area implies different morality and behavior and disparate provinces of action and social meaning harboring a whole and complete conception of the social world—in some cases inconsistent to the point of exclusion.

The *house* is made of protective rules, reciprocally valid for all members of the household, but not universally held along the social fabric. The members of this social subunit are sheltered from threats coming from the outside world, from the world of the *street*. In Brazil, the *house* is classified as an essentially feminine space, whereas the *street* is predominantly male. The *street* shows the impersonal side of society, with abstract and cold laws. The *street* displays the ugly face of hierarchy. It is worlds away from the *house*. The *house* is ruled by affection and sentimentality; it is an affair of the heart (Da Matta, 1985).

Individualistic morphology is present in the house, and hierarchy prevails in the street. But they are not so clearly divided. An actor may try to soften the hardness of the street through personal acquaintances, from personal relations that are bound by the ruling pertaining to the *house* (Barbosa, 1992). At a moment like this, and in several others, such as shown in Da Matta's (1979, 1991) description and interpretation of a familiar experience in Brazilian life, the ritual of social distinction, where one person tries to intimidate the other, by asking "Do you know who you are talking to?" that the *house* and the *street* overlap. The social position of a social actor in the social hierarchy, or his personal relations to powerful individuals, is used to resolve conflicting situations. The rule of the *house* serves to organize relations with strangers, with people from the social sphere of the *street*.

House and *street* are not impervious social areas. The *house* has a particular mode of hierarchy, a symmetrical inversion of the *street*. Staying at home, the woman reigns as a sovereign. Her husband commonly addresses her as *patroa* (boss). This implies the acceptance of male ruled in the "outside world," where, under a veil of ignorance or of disregard, males may establish relationships with women other than their wives. In the Portuguese spoken in Brazil, the expression *mulher da rua* means literally *woman of the street*, referring to a prostitute.

It is also telling of Brazilian culture that it generally conceives the "other world" as being more than just a religious sphere. The *other world* complements the relationship between the *house* and the *street*. The social world's hassles and upsets pertain to the universe of either the *house* or the *street*. In the *other world* resignation and renunciation prevails. where there is no room for the competition of the *street;* the *other world* is also immune to the opposition we–them, so typical of the *house*. Facing a death that will redeem and undo the social wrongs of the outside world, Brazilians are finally and peacefully equal to each other.

THE SINGULARITY OF MEANING IN CULTURAL LIFE

Discussions about cultural unity or diversity are grounded in a wrong perspective. Cultures are unique. But they are nonetheless "the result of an endless play of combination and recombination, forever seeking to solve the same problems by manipulating the same fundamental elements" (Lévi-Strauss, 1963a, p. 10). Cultural theory leads us to the basic models that serve as general categories of social life. But morphologies are combined in such complexity that the models—in their basic form—recede to the background, and what we have to deal with is a unique creation of rules underlining actions unfolding for the interpreter.

Models are nothing but hypotheses about actual cultures. If particular cultures generate the contextual mold in which singular actions occur, then we must go beyond generality and search for the singularities offered in specific contexts. We cannot be satisfied with an understanding based on an "average" survey of actual social relations. Examining other cultures provides a dilemma. What represents those cultures? Can one informer provide us the clues to a ruling model? Would the situation differ if we had six informers? Could we survey all the actors living in the culture that we have the task of interpreting? Is it a matter of numbers? If so, must we conclude that mass societies are not subjected to cultural interpretations? Perhaps we are searching for solutions guided by misleading questions.

Models are not containers made from extrinsic data provided by social interaction. Models have a general nature, radically distinct from actual happenings in particular cultures. Singular experiences play an active role in relation to models; they may stem from the underlining model, or they may be at odds with it. For the cultural interpreter, models are light beams, pointing toward contexts. That is no guarantee that the interpreter is right to the point. In the case of error, the interpreter obviously has to alter the initial model. Singular experiences both regulate and falsify general models. Keep in mind that we can never have absolute and total knowledge about a culture. We can only hope to attain an efficient, but fallible interpretation that will be changed and corrected—by us or other interpreters—through interaction with the culture in question. Cultures suffer the process of change; so too do cultural researchers.

This conception is different from Geertz's (1973) notion of models. Here, there are two forms of modeling: *models of*, representing actual relations, and *models for*, providing specifications to obtain a definite state of things in the outside reality. Geertz sees models only in relation to actual and particular cases of reality. Models are not ruled by a one-to-one correspondence with external events; they indicate the elements providing precarious hypotheses about the culture to be interpreted. Models are directly related to the interpreter's effort in dealing with singular and actual cultures. Geertz's bias is to deprecate the generality of any interpretation; we cannot, however, do away with general models.

Models cannot provide thorough and complete understandings of cultural life. They are, nevertheless, the inevitable starting point. From them, we reach out for the understanding of singularities; the more singular and particular understanding we can have, so much the better. Cultural analysis moves from hypothetical guidelines provided by the identification of models to the interpretation of singular actions that weave actual cultural experiences.

FROM IDEAL MODELS TO EMPIRICAL MODELS

The models thus presented are based on theoretical understanding, a method which Weber referred to as an "ideal type" (cf. Gloud & Kolb, 1964). The task at hand is, then, for the researcher to generate a grounded model (Glasser & Strauss, 1967)—one based on some form of empirical data. A grounded model is generated for future researchers to utilize as an "ideal type" theoretical paradigm.

Once the ideal type is known, the researcher must collect *capta*. Laningan (1992) wrote:

> Fortunately, the return to the human science paradigm is refocusing attention on the performance and practice of persons communicating at the intrapersonal, interpersonal, group, and cultural levels of context for affective and conative meaning along with the traditional cognitive meaning orientation. The human scientist is "taking reality" (*capta*) as the valid source of evidence in research, rather than falling victim to the "Postmodern condition" of positivism in which the assumption of a "given reality" (*data*) indexes the subsequent representations of judgement ("making it operational"). (p. 2)

By using such information, the totality of *experience of otherness* becomes the basic element of substance. *Capta* are combined elements of the experiencer, the experiencing, and the experienced. Thus, the intrerpreter realizes that these elements must be constructed, constructing, and deconstructing, all at the same time. The experience is both an immediate and a reflecting process.

In this context, microlevel *capta* are used for constructing themes, which are, in turn, abstracted and explicated. The communication researcher must observe such instances as standing in line in a grocery store, cashing a check, and riding a bus to develop a theme of turn taking and interpersonal stress (Levine, 1989). Hickson (1977) found that among bus riders, these themes changed as a result of external forces (an energy crisis). *Capta* then must be collected over changing conditions to develop a wider sense of cultural thematic. In the genesis of what we call an "empirically derived model" of communication within a particular culture, the *capta* should be visualized as mobile, floating, and tentative to develop a more generalized macro-model of otherness.

By using the ideal type, theoretical model with its empirically derived paradigm, the researcher finds a comparison between a deductively constructed model and an inductively constructed paradigm. It is where these models intersect and overlap that we created a grounded model. Such a grounded model becomes a theoretical model for the next phase of the investigation. The ultimate goal for the communication researcher is to determine the consistency of social epoxy of the investigated group. At the same time, the researcher needs to determine his or her own biases, especially in regard to the making of assumptions taken from one's own culture.

As mentioned, characterization cannot be made solely based on numerical averaging, for such a construct is itself culturally biased. The essential types of questions that must be asked when studying culture include: What are the basic, underlying assumptions unique to this culture? In what ways are these assumptions similar or different from other cultures? What are the culture's notions of otherness? What are the culture's notions of communication (as social epoxy)? What subcultures affect the integration–diversity of the culture? Is there really a culture? Obviously, such questions must be further broken down to formulate microlevel questions and issues.

Grounded models may be utilized by the same researcher at a later date or utilized by another researcher for retesting. In this case, the researcher goes through the same cyclical process for developing a new grounded model.

SUMMARY

We attempeted first to indicate that communication is the social epoxy of a culture, composed of shared signs. We discuss a difference between communication studies, which are based upon such semiotic systems, and psychological studies, which are based on inferences derived from social behavior. Next, we discussed the development of theoretical models of culture, based upon patterns of semiotic usage. We discussed types of theoretical culture models. The first was the *military model*, a hierarchical system, grounded on mutual interdependence. Another model, the *fluid society* is more like a "cloud of mosquitoes," when only compliance with a list of rules prevents chaos.

From all of these studies, we have learned that culture is an affair of integration. For example, the former Yugoslavia was a society, but not much of a culture. It appears that only the political and military system prevented its entire breakup. There was no culture—no social epoxy—no group rationale for holding itself together.

How do we go about studying culture? First, we must understand and develop theoretical models. Second, we must generate empirical models based on *capta*. Such models are inductive as set apart from deductive theoretical paradigms. Finally, we compare and contrast the theoretical (ideal type) with its empirical (emergent, isomorphic) equivalent to create a grounded model. Such a model is grounded in both theory and research and forms the basis for a new theoretical model. Such a process allows for communication researchers to improve our understanding of culture for future students.

REFERENCES

Barbosa, L. (1992). *O jeitinho brasileiro: ou a arte de ser mais igual que os outros* [The Brazilian 'Jeitinho': Or the art of being more equal than others]. Rio de Janeiro: Campus.

Benedict, R. (1934). *Patterns of culture*. Boston: Houghton Mifflin.

Berreman, G. D. (1971). The Brahmannical view of caste. *Contributions to Indian sociology, 5,* 16–23.

Coser, L. A. (1977). *Masters of sociological thought: Ideas in historical and social context* (2nd ed.). New York: Harcourt Brace Jovanovich.

Da Matta, R. (1979). *Carnavais, malandros e heróis: Para uma sociologia do dilema brasileiro.* [Carnivals, rogues, and heroes: Toward a sociology of the Brazilian dilemma]. Rio de Janeiro: Zahar.

Da Matta, R. (1985). *A casa & a rua: espaço, cidadania, mulher e morte no Brasil* [The house & the street: Space citizenship, woman and death in Brazil]. São Paulo: Brasiliense.

Da Matta, R. (1991). *Carnivals, rogues and heroes: An interpretation of the Brazilian dilemma.* Notre Dame: Notre Dame University Press.

Da Matta, R. (1993). *Conta de mentiroso: Sete ensaios de antropologia brasileira* [Liar's counting: Seven essays on Brazilian anthropology]. Rio de Janeiro: Rocco.

Dumont, L. (1964). *La civilisation indienne et nous* [The Hindu civilization and us]. Paris: Armand Colin.

Dumont, L. (1967). Caste: A phenomenon of social structure or an aspect of Indian culture? In A. de Reuck & J. Knight (Eds.), *Caste and race: Comparative approaches* (pp. 28–38). Boston: Little, Brown.

Dumont, L. (1970a). *Homo hierarchicus: An essay on the caste system.* Chicago: The University of Chicago Press.

Dumont, L. (1970b). *Religion, politics and history in India: Collected papers in Indian sociology.* Paris and Hague: Mouton.

Dumont, L. (1985). The economic mode of thought in an anthropological perspective. In P. Klosowski, (Ed.), *Economics and philosophy* (pp. 253–261). Tubingen: J. C. Mohr.

Dumont, L. (1986). *Essays on individualism: Modern ideology in anthropological perspective.* Chicago & London: The University of Chicago Press.

Farb, P. (1978). *Humankind.* Boston, MA: Houghton Mifflin.

Fletcher, R. (1971). *The making of sociology: A study of sociological theory* (Vol. 2). New York: Scribner's.

Fortes, M. (1953). *Social anthropology in Cambridge since 1900.* Cambridge: Cambridge University Press.

Geertz, C. (1973). *The interpretation of cultures.* New York: Basic Books.

Glasser, B. G., & Strauss A. L. (1967). *The discovery of grounded theory: Strategies for qualitative research.* New York: Aldine/Atherton.

Gloud, J., & Kolb, W. L. (Eds.). (1964). *A dictionary of the social sciences.* New York: Free Press.

Hickson, M., III (1977). Communication in natural settings: Research tool for undergraduates. *Communication Quarterly, 25,* 23–28.

Hoebel, E. A. (1966). *Anthropology: The study of man* (3rd ed.). New York: McGraw-Hill.

Khare, R. S. (1971). "Encompassing and encompassed:" A deductive theory of caste system. *The Journal of Asian Studies, 30,* 859–868.

Kroeber, A. L. & Parsons, T. (1958). The concept of culture and social system. *American Review of Sociology, 23,* 582–583.

Lanigan, R. L. (1992). *The human science of communicology: A phenomenology of discourse in Foucault and Merleau-Ponty.* Pittsburgh, PA: Duquesne University Press.

Leach, E. (1957). The epistemological bacground of Malinowski's empiricism. In R. Firth (Ed.), *Man and culture: An evaluation of the work of Bronislaw Malinowski* (pp. 119–138). London: Routledge & Kegan Paul.

Leach, E. R. (Ed.). (1969). *Aspects of caste in South India, Ceylon and North-West Pakistan.* Cambridge: Cambridge University Pres.

Leach, E. R. (1970). *Political systems of Highland Burma.* London: The Athlone Press.

Leach, E. R. (1971a). "Esprit" in *Homo Hierarchicus. Contributions to Indian sociology, 5,* 13–16.

Leach, E. R. (1971b). Hierarchical man: Louis Dumont and his critics. *South Asian Review, 4/3,* 233–237.

Leach, E. R. (1971c). *Rethinking anthropology.* Cambridge: Cambridge. University Press.

Levine, R. (1983a, October). Pace of life. *Psychology Today.*

Lévi-Strauss, C. (1944). Reciprocity and hierarchy. *American Anthropologist, 46,* 266–268.

Lévi-Strauss, C. (1946). La technique du bonheur [The technique of happiness]. *Esprit, 127,* 643–652.

Lévi-Strauss, C. (1952). Problems of process: Results I. In S. Tax, L. C. Eiseley, I. Rouse, & C. V. Voeglin (Eds.), *An appraisal of anthropology today* (pp. 108–124). Chicago, IL: The University of Chicago Press.

Lévi-Strauss, C. (1954). The mathematics of man. *International Social Science Bulletin, 4,* 581–589.

Lévi-Strauss, C. (1960). On manipulated sociological models. *Bijdragen tot de Taal-, Land- en volkenkunde 116/1,* 45–54.

Lévi-Strauss, C. (1963a). The bear and the barber. *The Journal of the Royal Anthropological Institute of Great Britain, 93,* 1–11.

Lévi-Strauss, C. (1963b). Confrontations over myth. *New Left Review, 62,* 57–74.

Lévi-Strauss, C. (1963c). *Structural anthropology.* New York: Basic Books.

Lévi-Strauss, C. (1969). *The elementary structures of kinship.* Boston, MA. Deacon Press.

Lévi-Strauss, C. (1973). *Tristes tropiqucs.* New York: Atheneum.

Malinowski, B. (1923). The problem of meaning in primitive languages. In C. K. Ogden & I. A. Richards (Eds.), *The meaning of meaning* (pp. 296–336). New York: Harcourt, Brace.

Malinowski. B. (1944). *A scientific theory of culture and other essays.* New York: Oxford University Press.

Marriott, M. (1966). Review of *Homo hierarchicus*: Essai sur le système des castes. *American Anthropologist, 71,* 1166–1174.

Miller, D. L. (1973). *George Herbert Mead: Self, language, and the world.* Austin: University of Texas Press.

Nutini, H. G. (1970). Some considerations on the nature of social structure and model building: A critique of Lévi-Strauss and Edmund Leach. In G. N. Hayes & T. Hayes (Eds.), *Claude Lévi-Strauss: The anthropologist as a hero* (pp. 70–107). Cambridge, MA: MIT Press.

Polanyi, K. (1968). *Primitive, archaic, and modern economies,* G. Dalton (Ed.). Garden City, NY: Anchor Books/Doubleday.

Polanyi, K. (1975). *The great transformation.* New York: Octogon.

Powdermaker, H. (1966). *Stranger and friend: The way of an anthropologist.* New York: Norton.

Radcliffe-Brown, A. R. (1948a). *The Andaman islanders.* Glencoe, IL: The Free Press.

Radcliffe-Brown, A. R. (1948b). *A natural science of society.* Glencoe, IL: The Free Press.

Radcliffe-Brown, A. R. (1949). White's view of a science of culture. *American Anthropologist, 51,* 503–512.

Radcliffe-Brown, A. R. (1968). *Structure and function in primitive society.* New York: The Free Press.

Reischauer, E. O. & Fairbank, J. K. (1958). *East Asia: The greater tradition* (Vol. 1). Boston, MA: Houghton Mifflin.

Sartre, J. P. (1955). *Literary and philosophical essays.* New York: Collin Books.

Schneider, D. M. (1976). Notes toward a theory of culture. In K. H. Basso & H. A. Selby (Eds.), *Meaning in anthropology* (pp. 197–220). Albuquerque: University of New Mexico Press.

Singer, M. (1984). *Man's glassy essence: Explorations in semiotic anthropology*. Bloomington: Indiana University Press.

Stocking, Jr., G. W. (1984). Radcliffe-Brown and the British social anthropology. In G. W. Stocking Jr. (Ed.), *Functionalism historicized: Essays on British social anthropology, History of anthropology* (Vol. 2, pp. 139–196). Madison, WI: The University of Wisconsin Press.

Tax, S., Eiseley, L. C., Rouse, I. & Voeglin, C. F., (Eds.). (1952). *An appraisal of anthropology today.* Chicago, IL: The University of Chicago Press.

Thom, R. (1975). *Structural stability and morphogenesis: An outline of a general theory of models.* Reading, MA: W. A. Benjamin.

Tocqueville, A. de (1954). *Democracy in America* (Vol. 1). New York: Vintage Books.

Umiker-Sebeok, D. J. (1977). Semiotics of culture: Great Britain and North America. *Annual Review of Anthropology, 6*, 121–136.

Wax, R. H. (1971). *Doing fieldwork: Warnings and advice.* Chicago: The University of Chicago Press.

White, L. A. (1968). Culturology. *International Encyclopedia of the Social Sciences, 3*, 547–550.

Yalman, N. (1969). De Tocqueville in India: An essay on the caste system. *Man, 4*, 123–131.

20

Intercultural Communication

Thomas Steinfatt
Diane M. Christophel
University of Miami

The study of intercultural communication is important in any society or culture. This is especially true in the United States, which has made *intercultural openness* a central feature of its cultural persona. The United States is currently experiencing the greatest period of immigration in its history. Although the late 19th and early 20th centuries witnessed a greater proportional population increase due to immigration, the actual number of *legal* immigrants entering the United States since 1980 was greater than in any previous decade in history. When illegal immigration is factored in, the current period of immigration is unsurpassed in American history, yielding a nation whose cultural heritage is changing, and, as a corollary, its communication is changing as well.

COMMUNICATION

Following Langer (1942), we believe that communication in its most fundamental form is intrapersonal. Communication begins as an attempt by human beings to come to know their environment through symbols. This occurs through a gradual recognition by the child that symbols, objects, and ideas, and internal mental representations of them, can be related to each other in a meaningful fashion. To paraphrase Langer, children first use communication to bring objects into their minds, not into their hands. Once children learn that this is possible, symbol–object–mind relationships are possible. Only after such relationships are learned can communication evolve to a social stage where people recognize that others also make similar symbol–object–mind inferences, and that these related networks of inferences can be used to interact with others. At the social stage, communication can be used for social tasks, such as making requests or transmitting cultural information. In all stages of human development, communication involves the assignment of meaning by the individual to external stimuli, including symbolically encoded messages from other persons. Communication is inherently a meaning assignment process within the individual. Since meaning is assigned to messages based on the beliefs, attitudes, and values of the individual, and since persons from different cultures often have different beliefs, attitudes, and values, the normal human misunderstandings which occur in same-culture interactions are often magnified by the wider differences in cultural assumptions and belief systems inherent in crosscultural interactions.

CULTURE

Culture may be conceived, in its broadest sense, as the accumulated knowledge and beliefs of humanity. Thus defined, the fundamental nature of culture is phenomenological (that is, culture exists fundamentally in the hearts and minds of people). Culture can be passed on to other persons and future generations only through communication. Intercultural communication involves communication between people from different cultures, leading to several questions: What constitutes a "different" culture? Do intercultural differences necessarily involve different languages? Different ways of thinking? Different world views? Different beliefs, attitudes, and values?

INTERCULTURAL COMMUNICATION

While there is little disagreement that communication between a Karen hill tribesman in northern Thailand and an American college student involves intercultural differences, we might ask if communication between any two persons with different attitudes, beliefs, and values also involves intercultural differences. For example, while the value system espoused by a given corporation is commonly referred to as *corporate culture*, does that mean that communication between workers at IBM and Microsoft involves intercultural differences? Perhaps. Between someone at IBM and a farm worker? Possibly. To study such interactions from an intercultural perspective might raise different questions and produce different answers than those found in a more standard organizational communication analysis. But rather than attempt to give final answers, we prefer to discuss the central thrust of intercultural communication, as opposed to attempting to delineate intercultural communication's absolute boundaries.

The study of intercultural communication is the study of communication between people with different mind sets and ways of looking at and perceiving the world. Though commonly applied to communication between persons who are each embedded in a different cultural group, intercultural communication also has heuristic utility when applied to the examination of two persons, ostensibly from the same culture, gender, age, ethnic group, and socioeconomic status, whose assumptions about the nature of the world and ways of relating to it are sufficiently divergent to produce misunderstandings commonly found in intercultural analysis. *The central thrust of intercultural communication is in the analysis of meaning assignment in interactions between persons whose attitudes, beliefs, and values differ due to a corresponding difference in their cultural or cocultural backgrounds.*

Four themes emerge from the study of intercultural communication, all stemming from a desire to understand what is happening when persons with different cultural mind sets interact. One is the *social science approach* to communication, which seeks to identify variables that predict communication outcomes across multiple cross-cultural interactions. This approach seeks theories of intercultural communication by developing an abstract calculus of relationships between and among variables that are observable and measurable. A second theme involves a more *humanistic approach,* though it shares features of cultural anthropology. It seeks to understand the features of specific cultures that are relevant to intercultural interactions involving people from those cultures; it examines communication concerning cultural diversity and multiculturality. Third is *developmental communication,* grounded in the social sciences. Developmental communication assumes a need and a desire to alter certain elements in or related to another culture. It forms theories and guidelines concerning the most effective ways of bringing about intentional cultural change. The fourth theme concerns the *relativity of thought to language and culture.* Because communication occurs through cognitive processing, are Eastern and Western ways of thinking different? Does such a notion imply different cognitive structures or communication processes, or can the observations which lead people to infer a different way of thinking be explained through different content in beliefs, attitudes, and values?

The Social Science Tradition

The history of intercultural communication as an area is often ascribed to the 1959 publication of Edward T. Hall's *The Silent Language* (Condon, 1981; Dodd, 1982; Gudykunst, 1985b; Klopf, 1987; Samovar & Porter, 1972; Singer, 1987), in which he introduced the term "intercultural communication." Leeds-Hurwitz (1990) and Rogers (1994) credited the term to Hall's work in training American diplomats through the U.S. Foreign Service Institute in the decade following World War II as the beginning of intercultural research. This training work led to the publication of *The Silent Language*, initially a handbook for intercultural training. Selecting Hall as the genesis of intercultural communication is not a bad choice, but it has the potential for limiting what is and ought to be studied in intercultural communication.

Clearly, Hall's research led to a major body of social science oriented communication scholarship. Hall refocused the study of culture, as practiced by post-World War II anthropology, in a number of ways (see Leeds-Hurwitz, 1990). Most important, however, was a shift from anthropology's emphasis on monadic and dyadic studies of a single culture, or a comparison of two cultures, into what Gudykunst (1987) called *intercultural communication proper*, the study of generalizations about intercultural communication independent of reference to any specific culture.

Because Hall's focus was on training, he also concentrated on the specific features of culture that affected the interpersonal interactions his trainees would encounter: tone of voice, gestures, and the conceptions of time and space. He largely ignored those features not directly relevant to these interactions. This decision established him as one of the founders of intercultural communication, but relegated him to secondary status at best within the field of anthropology.

Hall's concept of intercultural communication as patterned, learned, and capable of being analyzed were compatible with social science notions in mass and interpersonal communication from the 1960s on. While much of the current research in *intercultural communication proper* is quantitative in nature, this orientation is not derived from Hall. As an anthropologist, Hall was both qualitative and applied; his focus was on training. Rather, attention to social science has come from communication researchers' quantitative training, many of whom became interested in expanding the study of interpersonal communication into intercultural areas.[1]

Social Science Theories and Research

Prior to the 1960s, studies of culture shock appearing in *Practical Anthropology*, and of prejudice and ethnic relations scattered throughout scholarly journals in sociology, psychology, and anthropology, formed the basis for early intercultural communication research in the social science tradition. As early as 1924, Park and Burgess (1924) and their Chicago School colleagues studied European immigrants' integration into American culture, recognizing the initial social processes of accommodation and assimilation (Rogers, 1994). Schatzman and Strauss (1955) provide one of the first studies of intracultural communication. Publication of Hall's *The Silent Language* (1959), was followed by *The Hidden Dimension* (1966), Smith's collection of articles in *Communication and Culture* (1966) and Harms' (1973) *Intercultural Communication*. These publications focused the attention of many students on the study of intercultural communication. Increasing interest in intercultural communication led to the beginning of the *International and Intercultural Communication Annual* in the mid-1970s, where much of the social science oriented research is found.[2]

One of the more influential lines of social science research was established by Gudykunst and his colleagues who focused on three general areas applied to intercultural communication: uncertainty reduction processes, relationship issues, and communication effectiveness. Two influential articles (Gudykunst, 1988; Gudykunst, Chua, & Gray, 1987) are central in the examination of cultural influence on communication in interpersonal relationships. Early research tested Berger and Calabrese's (1975) uncertainty reduction theory by exploring similarities and differences in initial

---

[1]Leeds-Hurwitz (1990) provided an extended analysis of the role of these factors.

[2]Asante, Newmark and Blake (1979) and Asante and Gudykunst (1989) provided a number of summary articles. Theories of intercultural communication are summarized in Gudykunst (1983a) and in Kim and Gudykunst (1988).

intracultural and intercultural encounters (Gudykunst, 1983c, 1985c; Gudykunst et al., 1987; Gudykunst & Nishida, 1984). Extension of the original model explored boundary conditions (Gudykunst, 1985a), attribution confidence in high- and low-context cultures (Gudykunst & Nishida, 1986a), influence of language (Gudykunst, Nishida, Koike, & Shiino, 1986), social identity (Gudykunst & Hammer, 1988), group membership (Gudykunst, Nishida, & Schmidt, 1989), and anxiety reduction (Gao & Gudykunst, 1990).

In 1980, Gudykunst and Halsall generated a series of axioms and propositions synthesizing diverse research findings in various disciplines applicable to intercultural relationships. Gudykunst (1983b), reviewing the concept of *stranger*, derived a descriptive typology of stranger–host relationships that included newly arrived, newcomer, sojourner, stranger, immigrants, intruder, middle-man minority, and the marginal person. Related research focused on ethnic identity and close friendship communication patterns (Ting-Toomey, 1981), perceived similarity and social penetration (Gudykunst, 1985a), patterns of discourse (Sudweeks, Gudykunst, Ting-Toomey & Nishida, 1990), insider and outsider perspectives (Gudykunst & Nishida, 1986b; Ting-Toomey, 1985), and self-consciousness and self-monitoring (Gudykunst, Yang, & Nishida, 1987).

Dimensions of intercultural communication effectiveness have been investigated that tested sojourners' culture perspectives (Gudykunst, Wiseman, & Hammer, 1977), participation in workshops (Gudykunst, 1979), decision-making style (Stewart, Gudykunst, Ting-Toomey, & Nishida, 1986), and ethnocentrism (Hall & Gudykunst, 1989). Kim (1988a) offered a broad-based perspective that synthesized various disciplinary viewpoints of adaptation—including anthropology, communication, psychology, sociology, and sociolinguistics. Regardless of a sojourner's motivation for being in a new culture, all people share common adaptation experiences. Accordingly, as strangers they must cope with high levels of uncertainty and unfamiliarity based on their ambivalent status in the host community. Labels such as acculturation, adjustment, assimilation, and integration emphasize different aspects of the adaptation experience. Adaptation theory assumes that individuals can and do adapt to this new, unfamiliar culture. Consequently, the focus is on *how* adaptation is accomplished from a General Systems perspective that regards individuals and their host environment as codeterminants engaged in communication activities. Adaptation theory proposes assumptions, axioms, and theorems that increase understanding of, and ability to make predictions of, cross-cultural adaptation.

The Humanistic Tradition and Research on Specific Cultures

As noted, not all intercultural communication research is quantitative. Qualitative research focuses on ethnography (to produce insightful descriptions leading to sensitizing concepts and models which allow people to perceive events embedded in a particular culture in new ways) as a methodology and a focus on single rather than multiple cultural analysis.

Ethnography. In opposition to the social science approach is ethnography. Although ethnography has always been a principal method of social and cultural anthropology, its use has rapidly increased as a method in social psychology and communication over the past decade (Vidich & Lyman, 1994). The increase in the use of ethnography is based on several criticisms of social science methodology. Specifically, ethnographic analysis holds that the structure required by social science in the research process emanates from the researcher's cultural assumptions, which limit the chances of finding much which does not fit these preconceived assumptions. A second criticism holds that generalizations from controlled to natural settings (i.e., experimental to field) are suspect. Third, ethnographic analysis holds that interviews must be combined with observations to understand cultural perspectives. Fourth, it suggests that quantification necessarily selects some aspects of what is being studied and ignores others, thus reifying and unduly increasing the importance of the selected, while ignoring the unselected. And, fifth, ethnographic analysis holds that quantitative analysis ignores the role of human interaction and human choice in a mechanistic analysis based only on the variables selected by the researcher.

Beginning with his 1960s work on Javanese religion, Geertz (1973, 1983, 1988) was one of ethnography's principal proponents. Wolcott (1994) provides a clear description of the use of ethnography in multiple settings, where researchers are especially interested in studying the ways in which people embedded in a culture make decisions. Gladwin (1989) discussed the use of "decision trees" in this process.

Hammersley (1992) discusses problems and possibilities with the ethnographic approach. Perhaps the most telling criticism is that ethnography depends on realism, the doctrine that there is a reality out there to study, and on constructivism, the notion that individuals construct their own social reality. Ethnographers suggest that they study observed and constructed reality through observation and interaction and then report what they have learned. The problem is that the story produced by such an approach is constructed from personal observations and interactions, a construction just as subject to the ethnographer's culture and biases as any social science account, probably more so. Not only do each of the five criticisms aimed at social science analysis by ethnography apply as a critique of ethnographic analysis, ethnographic analysis often denies such criticisms thus putting itself in a position of nonfalsifiability (Popper, 1968). An analysis which cannot be falsified is not a serious scholarly analysis.

Ethnography and social science are two different methods which can both provide insights into intercultural analysis. Students of intercultural communication should learn the strengths and weaknesses of both, and not waste time defending any one method as the only possible approach to a problem. Some intercultural analysis have combined the use of ethnographic methods with social science research (cf., Steinfatt, 1996).

Specific Cultures.   Another critique of research stemming from Hall's tradition considers the assumptions on which the tradition is based. Hall's notion that only truths applicable beyond the confines of a single culture or the interaction of two cultures should be sought, truths based on what was true of intercultural communication across many if not all cultures, was based on the practical need to have a generalized training program useful for all American diplomats regardless of their culture of destination. Specific cultures and their features were deemphasized *not because their differences were irrelevant*, but because of practical considerations about packaging the information to groups of trainees about to embark to various different locations and cultures.

This emphasis on generalizations, practical though its origins, fit with American social science at the time, seeking nomothetic lawlike generalizations and shunning idiosyncratic knowledge. It seemed logical at the time; one could hardly develop a separate and unique psychology or interpersonal communication theory for each person studied. While recognizing that each individual is unique, social science concentrated on the *generalizations* which may be made *across* individuals as the only practical way to produce knowledge predictive of communication behaviors. While the existence of millions of people precludes the possibility of studying them all, there are far fewer cultures than people; thus social science's nomothetic assumptions cannot be justified solely on the basis of *practicality* when applied to the study of intercultural communication. While few people may be interested in the esoterica of the communication and culture patterns of, say, John Jones of Kentucky in 1837, it is possible to study individual cultures and their specific dyadic interactions with other cultures in a meaningful fashion over time.

Pike (1966) made a similar distinction. Pike borrowed terminology from descriptive linguistics, *etic* and *emic*, from *phonetic* and *phonemic* to make the point. Phonetics, he argued, studies sound and symbol production as observed by others outside the person being studied. Phonemics examines meaning, which is inside the person. Etic approaches to intercultural communication examine cultures from the outside—so their commonalities may be determined. Emic approaches look at a single culture, often from the perspective of a person thinking, communicating, and behaving within that culture—so their idiosyncrasies may be determined. Similarly, Geertz (1973) distinguished *thick* from *thin* description, wherein thin description results from the outside observation of behaviors with little interpretation, and thick description includes the interpretation of the behavior from the point of view of the cultural actor. Kim (1988b) discussed the distinction in terms of positivistic versus humanistic approaches.

In intercultural communication, it may be the case that nomothetic generalizations may profitably exist hand in hand with idiosyncratic theories of specific cultures. In fact, the combination of both types of knowledge approaches is needed in any practical setting where nomothetic laws are to be applied. A strong knowledge of intercultural communication principals is, in and of itself, insufficient for dealing with practical problems which arise in communication between two specific cultures. Just as Hall's (1959) students complained that a knowledge of Navajo culture was of little help to an administrator about to join the diplomatic corps in Paris, specific cultural knowledge—together with knowledge of intercultural communication principals—is needed to make practical decisions in real situations.

A note of caution is in order. When discussing a culture and defining its important communication features, the job of *abstraction* involves searching for what is central within the culture and ignoring the peripheral. Yet central to any culture is cultural variation: the peripheral. Because we tend to conceptualize intercultural communication as communication between, say, the Vietnamese and American cultures, or Black and White cultures within American society, this conceptualization implies a unity of culture for Vietnamese, Americans, Whites, and Blacks. Nothing is further from the truth. To employ a statistical analogy, we may say that the *variation within a given culture is normally of the same order of magnitude as the variation between cultures.* The attitudes, beliefs, values, and social behavior of upper class members of two different cultures are often far more similar to each other than intraclass differences within either culture. Ethnic variations within a given culture can easily be greater than the average variation between that culture and another. *The variation within can be greater than the variation between.* Learning how a particular cultural group thinks and communicates does not guarantee that such findings will hold for a specific member of a cultural group, especially when the cultural interaction situation is factored in. At a minimum, if the social class and ethnicity of the specific individuals involved is not considered, knowledge of the culture alone is of little use in predicting interaction outcomes, though this is not always the case (e.g., Jones, 1979). Kim, (1986) examines some of these interethnic factors within American society.

It is unlikely that people unfamiliar with their own culture, except through their experience of living in it, will fully appreciate the differences between their culture and another. For example, Stewart and Bennett (1991) explicated American cultural assumptions concerning styles of thinking and perceiving, action, social relations, world view, and the self. An appreciation of the ways in which one's own culture differs and could differ from another culture allows for a deeper and less ethnocentric view of any cultural interaction.

Perspectives on various cultural aspects are presented by Andersen and Collins (1992) and Gonzalez, Houston, and Chen (1994). These essays are representative of a multicultural and cultural diversity approach to intercultural communication. Central to their concerns are the concepts of racism, sexism, prejudice, self concept, and power differences which enter into interethnic interactions.

Perhaps the single cross cultural interaction which has generated the most in-depth, book-length communication research concerning intercultural communication with its members is Japanese–American communication. Barnlund (1989), Goldman (1990, 1994), Gudykunst (1993), Gudykunst and Nishida (1994), and Sato (1992) each discuss Japanese–American Communication from different perspectives. Goldman (1990) and Sato (1992) focus on Japanese communicating with Americans, while Barnlund (1989), Goldman (1994), and Gudykunst and Nishida (1994) are oriented toward the American perspective in interacting with Japanese. Gudykunst (1993) contrasts the study of communication in Japan with that in the United States.

The Developmental Communication Tradition

The third area of intercultural communication involves interactions with the goal of imposing the practices of one culture on a second culture. Such interventions involve intercultural communication in two primary ways: the study of effective cross-cultural persuasion and persuasive campaigns and the ethical system concerning making the decision to intervene in another culture. Developmental communication is of major interest to governments and organizations that have a stake—economic, political, moral, or ideological—in the way another culture operates. Most developmental communication centers on effective methods of introducing new ways of doing things and spreading awareness and adoption of the new concept throughout the culture: the diffusion of innovations. Rogers (1962) summarized and codified most of the prior research on diffusion from research traditions as diverse as mass communication, education, and rural sociology, into a blueprint for introducing cultural change. Rogers and Shoemaker (1971) updated Rogers's conceptualization (1962), and Fischer (1974) and Frey (1974) presented related aspects of the problem. While innovations diffuse naturally from cross-cultural interactions, the central question of diffusion and development research concerns identifying manipulable predictor variables which affect the rates of adoption and discontinuance of an innovation. Characteristics of "innovators" and "early adopters" which lead to opinion leadership are studied and contrasted with those of "later adopters" and "laggards." Diffusion studies examine the characteristics of the innovation itself, its compatibility with local cultural norms, the role of change agents, types of decision making, and consequences of the decision to adopt.

The majority of the consequences are often unintended, unanticipated, and not infrequently negative. Such consequences lead to the consideration of the ethics for deciding when to intervene in another culture. Ethical systems range from the rampant ethnocentrism of colonialism to the hands-off position of extreme multiculturalists. The concern with ethics is related to the more general problem of the ethics of foreign policy. What are the characteristics of a situation which justify intervention? Who should be allowed to make such a decision? Does the receiving culture have the right of refusal? Does the source culture have a similar right? Neither extreme position is tenable because no culture nor cultural practice is an island unto itself. Nazi culture led to the Holocaust; the world should have intervened sooner and more forcibly. The same might be said of Soviet culture under Stalinism and Cambodian culture under Pol Pot. But some intervention decisions that seem obvious to Western morality in areas such as prostitution, female genital mutilation, the oppression of women, and the control of disease, can lead to cultural upheaval and untold human hardship as a result. The Chinese and other Asian nations argue, for instance, that human rights are an invention of Western culture and a further extension of discredited colonialist practices.

What ethical system can be proposed that is not based in the moral norms of any culture over another? The traditional answer of Western philosophy is to dismiss any notion of ethical relativity (e.g., Hatch, 1983), for without set moral standards any action can be justified. Is it possible to devise a *multicultural* morality that allows us to distinguish the legitimate moral claims of any culture from those that are specious? For if morality is relative, it is then nonexistent. Yet, if an ethical system does not take into account the fundamental conceptions and world view of all cultures in which it is to be applied, what claim can it make to being a legitimate universal absolute morality?

The Tradition of Relativity of Thought to Language and Culture

The fourth area of intercultural communication can be traced to Aristotle's speculations on whether doing philosophy while using Greek as a symbol system would make the knowledge discovered different if, say, Latin were the symbol system (Steinfatt, 1989). Aristotle's answer was that the language in use would not make a substantial difference in the final result—that any thought could be expressed equally well in any language.

This view held sway until the late 19th century, when Cassirer (1953) suggested that the language used to conduct philosophical analyses could influence the resultant knowledge. Cassirer's work was not widely accepted in philosophy, but a young Yale anthropologist, Edward Sapir, began to write and lecture on topics in linguistic anthropology in the late 1800s. Sapir (1921) suggested that thought was potentially relative to language. Prior to 1920 Benjamin Lee Whorf, an undergraduate student in engineering at MIT who was working his way through college as an inspector for an insurance company, began to study Hopi and Myan cultures. In the 1920s he lectured extensively on his thesis, developed independently of Sapir's ideas, that the language of thought influences its content. Never Sapir's student, he had heard of Sapir and attended one of Sapir's lectures at Yale late in that decade. From this simple meeting, rather than from any formal collaboration or association, was born what has come to be called the *Sapir–Whorf hypothesis*, that language structures thought. Mandell (1931) presents an early view of linguistic relativity; reviews of experimental research may be found in Gibson and McGarvy (1937), Woodworth (1938), Heidbreder (1948), Johnson (1950), Humphrey (1951), Vinacke (1951), Diebold (1965), and Steinfatt (1989).

Sapir (1921), Whorf (1956), and Cassirer (1953) are perhaps the best known advocates of the notion that language influences thought. They treated linguistic relativity as an interlanguage phenomenon, a process attributable to differences between languages.

Sapir and Whorf's thesis involves both "linguistic determinism" and "linguistic relativity." *Linguistic determinism* holds that language shapes thought, but allows that people who speak different languages could still have the same thoughts and think in similar ways. For example, a counterfactual conditional is very difficult to express in Chinese. But while the language makes such thoughts difficult to express, linguistic determinism suggests that such thoughts could occur in Chinese, although they would be difficult. *Linguistic relativity*, a more radical version of linguistic determinism, holds that different languages actually shape thought differently (Glucksberg & Danks, 1975). Linguistic relativity would argue that speakers of Chinese could not think in counter factual conditional terms and that thought processes in Chinese would have to follow the structure of the language.

As initially proposed, the *Weltanschauung*—world view—thesis of linguistic relativity was very general and thus almost impossible to test. Greenberg (1956), Lenneberg and Roberts (1956), Henle (1958), Fishman (1960), and Osgood and Sebeok (1965), and Slobin (1979) all have suggested different ways of organizing the hypothesis. Steinfatt (1989) proposed that three groups of independent variables—phonological, syntactical, or semantic—are possible causative sets in linguistic relativity as the basis for any proposed differences in thought. At least one variable from at least one of these sets must influence at least one dependent measure in one of three variable sets—the logic of thought itself, the structure of cognition and world-view, or perception and areas of cognition—in order for a linguistic relativity effect to be claimed. Beyond looking at differences between natural languages as a source of linguistic relativity effects, Steinfatt (1989) also suggested that substantial phonological, syntactical, or semantic differences in any natural language would have to be regarded as a potential source of linguistic relativity effects. Thus, dialects such as Black–American English, compound bilingualism, aphasics relearning a language, and the deaf, should provide examples of linguistic relativity effects if such effects actually occur, and not just the natural language differences proposed by Whorf and others. Additionally, Steinfatt suggested that knowledge of the methods by which language is acquired should provide insight into whether linguistic relativity effects are likely to exist.

INTERCULTURAL TRAINING

Just as Hall's perspective on intercultural communication emanated from his training perspective, each of the areas of intercultural communication offer knowledge useful in intercultural training. In addition to Foreign Service training, major current intercultural training areas are in cultural diversity, cultural sensitivity, and in student exchange and study abroad programs (Kohls, 1984; Mestenhauser, Marty, & Steglitz, 1988). Brislin and Yoshida (1994) discuss methods of assessment and evaluation of intercultural communication training programs. Applications of intercultural communication research useful in various training programs also may be found in Brislin (1990).

DOING INTERCULTURAL RESEARCH

How one studies intercultural communication depends on *why* it is being studied. Some scholars seek to build a theory of intercultural communication based on research grounded in the social sciences. Others seek to understand how people interpret behaviors and how the behaviors come to have meaning within a given culture. Governments and organizations are often concerned with introducing change into a particular culture to reduce a perceived evil, such as disease or lack of education. People who must work in multicultural or crosscultural settings, or who train others to do so, are concerned with providing practical advice for improving intercultural communication and easing the way of the trainee in the unfamiliar cultural setting. Others are concerned with the conflicts and misunderstandings which occur in cross-cultural and multicultural interactions. They seek to reduce prejudice and ethnocentrism and to promote peace and tranquility. Theory construction, cultural meaning, cultural change, practical advice to the sojourner, the reduction of prejudice and conflict between ethnic groups—these different goals of intercultural communication research lead to different research questions and different methods for answering them. No single method is always most appropriate in an intercultural setting; method is always dependent upon the question being asked. Intercultural research is also complicated by the potential for violation of cultural norms, and by the "Heisenberg effect" of potentially changing the object of study through the means used to study it.

A Sample Study

Intercultural communication does not occur in a vacuum. It occurs in real situations with real people who have goals, desires, and much to gain or lose from the way a series of interconnected human interactions progresses. The nomothetic laws generated by research are ultimately useful if they can be applied to specific social interactions within specific cultural or crosscultural settings. If they cannot be so applied, they remain just so much academic esoterica gathering dust on library shelves and computer hard drives.

One of the more interesting areas of intercultural communication is the struggle within immigrant families between parents and children, especially when a socially liberal society such as the United States is the culture of entry. An inherent conflict exists between the role expectations for children in the old country and those in America.

As one example, families in the Suni Muslim community in Miami often experience conflict between parents and children. Parents complain of lack of respect, lack of obedience, willful disregard for and even ignorance of the Koranic Law by their children. These are not the ways of the old country, and the parents are genuinely frightened of the unknown and the physical and moral dangers posed by the larger society.

But the children have teenage friends in junior high or high school who can go unescorted to the mall. This is seen by immigrant parents as both a dangerous temptation inviting immoral activity and far too much freedom to ones so young. The children want to go to the mall, to have fun, to be American. Such insolence can lead to punishments that would be regarded as physical abuse by American standards, and certainly by social workers. This introduces the threat of social or even governmental interference into the family's life. The parents may resort to real, verifiable threats to send their children back to the old country if they do not obey.

Male dominance introduces an added problem of husband–wife conflict, which would be accepted as normal in the old country. Some women see the need for control of the children in the old ways, in the face of the dangers posed by the existence of violence and street crime in American society, and also perceive the freedom and potential power granted by this freedom which is offered to both themselves and their children. But this freedom cannot be realized for the woman within the confines of a traditional marriage. The only way to achieve true freedom would be for the woman to leave her husband. But this would mean rejection by her extended family, which she cannot tolerate. She exists only within the nexus of the family. To let the children have their freedom while denying the same to herself seems intolerable. She may decide to sacrifice herself and side with the children allowing them some measure of freedom while denying freedom to herself. But usually she will decide to side with her husband. Once she does, she is more motivated to keep the children within the family fold and the old ways. For if they stray, the blame will fall on her. She may then lose everything she has in terms of status in the family and in relationship to her husband, in addition to losing her children. She may even suffer the social death sentence of divorce because she could not keep the family together, a sentence which she has sought to avoid at all costs.

A useful study might examine methods of managing such family conflicts in a way that keeps the family together, continues the Islamic beliefs and behaviors, yet allows small and gradual increases in freedom to all the participants. Such a study would require integrating elements of ethnography, social science research methods, and, ultimately, of the diffusion of innovations, in order to be put into practice study.

In any applied setting, little advice is likely to be acted on which does not conform to the norms and belief systems of the participants. Rogers (1995) lists the criteria for likelihood of adoption of cross cultural recommendations. The applied researcher in intercultural communication would be well advised to keep these recommendations in mind. The challenge is to determine a message strategy which both achieves goals and operates within the existing belief system under study.

A number of factors need to be considered in order to conduct the study. First, who is the client? If the study is applied, someone is paying for it, and for a reason. Second, what is the reason? What is the problem as the client sees it? Failure to understand the reasons and reasoning behind the drive for an applied study can be a major source of problems in conducting, completing, and reporting the results of the study.

Third, is the problem, as seen by the client, a reasonable problem which can be studied in a useful manner? How will other groups involved in the problem perceive the purpose of the research and the research enterprise itself? Will there be persons or groups attempting to block the research or failing to cooperate with it? What can be done to phrase or rephrase the purpose and the sponsorship of the research in such a way that all or most parties involved can perceive ownership of the project and the results? How can this project be conceived in such a way that its results could be acted on in a manner which will help both the client and all other groups involved to achieve their goals in some manner? If questions such as these are not addressed prior to the start of data gathering the likelihood of success of the project will be reduced considerably. While the client is paying the freight, the project will be worth its cost only if the people and groups involved have some reasonable probability of acting on its recommendations. This point must be explained to and impressed upon the client prior to agreeing to conduct the study. Unless everyone benefits, the client will not benefit, for the results will probably not be implemented.

Fourth, is there a way that theory-driven questions could be integrated into the study without detracting from it? Applied intercultural research can often be a vehicle for testing portions of intercultural communication theories.

Fifth, what needs to be known in order to conduct the study and achieve usable results, and what do we already know? Answering this question corresponds roughly to the literature review phase of typical academic research. In addition to conducting bibliographic searches for a literature review, a "walking around and looking and talking with people" phase is needed. If this pilot review of the people and situations to be studied is not conducted for at least a short time with a few people prior to the project, then at the end of the project the researchers are likely to find they have conducted a pilot review but with a large group of subjects and at considerable expense. The bibliographic review itself should include a search of the bibliographic databases available on the Internet. As of this writing, over 50 such databases are currently available through *Firstsearch*. Both applied and theoretical research efforts need to be informed by past research. This information then needs to be sorted for applicability to the research problem. The research can then be designed and conducted.

Assume that the client is the local Islamic Community Association. Assume further that the problem is phrased as one of how to keep families intact, with the children remaining faithful believers in Islam. The problem is translated to read that the level of overt conflict (Steinfatt & Miller, 1974) in the families needs to be reduced. The perceptions of the parents, the children, and the community at large need to be addressed. The researchers may need to attend local community functions, to talk with the people involved, and to talk privately with the children in addition to talking privately with the parents and elders. If the researchers are perceived by any of the groups as either on the "side" of one group, or as aloof and distant, the effort will likely fail. Focus groups conducted as a part of the socializing after an evening community meeting can be especially helpful in this regard. Locating children who have actually left their families and the religion to learn their perspectives can also be quite helful. Questionnaires and procedures giving the apparence of academic research may be more trouble than they are worth in applied efforts. Often the appearence of listening, combined with actual sensitive listening and note taking, can be far more revealing and effective than information produced through questionnaires, though it is usually difficult to convince editorial reviewers of this if later publication is desired. Interviews and focus groups with members of an Islamic group which is geographicly removed from the group of interest may provide additional insights and information. But different groups can often have strikingly different problems and no firm conclusions should be drawn from work with these additional Islamic groups. If privacy can be maintained, asking members of an Islamic group which is geographically distant about conclusions and proposed solutions prior to presenting them to the client group can produce useful insights.

A model useful in most such intercultural conflicts is one based on getting each of the groups to subscribe as strongly as possible to the norms of respect of the other's status position and views, and respectful acceptance of the other's right to exist and to differ to an extent within a predefined context. While everyone will agree with respect, and some will agree with acceptance, producing actual respect and actual acceptance through message strategies designed to reduce the conflict and tailored to each of the constituent groups is often the ultimate goal. The strategies themselves may be based on applications of theory to the results of the focus groups and interviews. The message strategies must be acceptable, workable, and must meet the goals of the client and the other groups involved. Any workable message strategy set will usually have a minimum of two levels. The first level will be the initial strategy, and the second, an analysis of the various fallback positions depending on the response of the other to the initial communication attempt. Small scale training of innovators might be part of the initial research proposal. Larger scale training proposals need to wait for the acceptance of the proposed solutions by the client and other groups involved. But without larger scale training, diffusion of the proposed solutions will be both less likely to occur and much slower in implimentation.

SUMMARY

Intercultural communication poses challenges and opportunities for communication scholars. As this chapter has noted, intercultural communication study offers many approaches for researchers to investigate. The desire of American industry, government, and universities to foster multicultural environments means that intercultural communication researchers have their work cut out for them. But the rewards are great. Intercultural communication offers the opportunity to increase our understanding of other peoples and cultures.

This chapter has reviewed the basic concepts and research to begin the study of intercultural communication. A sample study suggests a way to investigate the area, noting, however, the problems that still face researchers interested in communication from cultures other than their own.

REFERENCES

Andersen, M. L., & Collins, P. H. (1992). *Race, class, and gender.* Belmont, CA: Wadsworth.

Asante, M. K., & Gudykunst, W. B. (Eds.). (1989). *The handbook of international and intercultural communication.* Newbury Park: Sage.

Asante, M. K., Newmark, E., & Blake, C. A. (Eds.). (1979). *The handbook of intercultural communication.* Beverly Hills: Sage.

Barnlund, D. C. (1989). *Communicative styles of Japanese and Americans.* Belmont, CA: Wadsworth.

Berger, C., & Calabrese, R. (1975). Some explorations in initial interactions and beyond: Toward a developmental theory of interpersonal communication. *Human Communication Research, 1,* 99–112.

Brislin, R. (1990). *Applied cross-cultural psychology.* Newbury Park: Sage.

Brislin, R., & Yoshida, T. (1994). *Intercultural communication training: An introduction.* Thousand Oaks, CA: Sage.

Cassirer, E. (1953). *The philosophy of symbolic forms* (Vol. 1). *Language.* New Haven, CT: Yale University Press.

Condon, J. (1981). Values and ethics in communication across cultures: Some notes on the North American case. *Communication, 6,* 255–265.

Diebold, A. R. (1965). A survey of psycholinguistic research, 1954–1964. In C. E. Osgood & T. A. Sebeok (Eds.), *Psycholinguistics* (pp. 205–291). Bloomington: Indiana University Press.

Dodd, C. H. (1982). *Dynamics of intercultural communication.* Dubuque, IA: William C. Brown.

Fischer, J. L. (1974). Communication in primitive systems. In I. de Sola Pool, W. Schramm, F. W. Frey, N. Maccoby, & E. B. Parker (Eds.), *Handbook of communication* (pp. 313–336). Chicago: Rand McNally.

Fishman, J. A. (1960). A systematization of the Whorfian hypothesis. *Behavioral Science, 5,* 323–339.

Frey, F. W. (1974). Communication and development. In I. de Sola Pool, W. Schramm, F. W. Frey, N. Maccoby, & E. B. Parker (Eds.), *Handbook of communication* (pp. 337–461). Chicago: Rand McNally.

Gao, G., & Gudykunst, W. B. (1990). Uncertainty, anxiety, and adaptation. *International Journal of Intercultural Relations, 14,* 301–317.

Geertz, C. (1973). *The interpretation of cultures.* New York: Basic Books.

Geertz, C. (1983). *Local knowledge: Further essays in interpretive anthropology.* New York: Basic Books.

Geertz, C. (1988). *Works and lives: The anthropologist as author.* Stanford, CA: Stanford University Press.

Gibson, E. J., & McGarvy, H. R. (1937). Experimental studies of thought and reasoning. *Psychological Bulletin, 34,* 327–350.

Gladwin, C. H. (1989). *Ethnographic decision tree modeling.* Newbury Park, CA: Sage.

Glucksberg, S., & Danks, J. H. (1975). *Experimental psycholinguistics.* Hillsdale, NJ: Lawrence Erlbaum Associates.

Goldman, A. (1990). *For Japanese only: Intercultural communication with Americans.* Tokyo: Japan Times.

Goldman, A. (1994). *Doing business with the Japanese: A guide to successful communication, management, and diplomacy.* Albany, New York: State University of New York Press.

Gonzalez, A., Houston, M., & Chen, V. (1994). *Our voices: Essays in culture, ethnicity, and communication.* Los Angeles: Roxbury.

Greenberg, J. H. (1956). Concerning inferences from linguistic to nonlinguistic data. In H. Hoijer (Ed.), *Language in culture* (pp. 3–19). Chicago: University of Chicago Press.

Gudykunst, W. B. (1979). The effects of an intercultural communication workshop on cross-cultural attitudes and interaction. *Communication Education, 28,* 179–187.

Gudykunst, W. B. (1983a). *Intercultural communication theory. International and intercultural communication annual.* Beverly Hills, CA: Sage.

Gudykunst, W. B. (1983b). Toward a typology of stranger-host relationships. *International Journal of Intercultural Relations, 7,* 401–413.

Gudykunst, W. B. (1983c). Uncertainty reduction and predictability of behavior in low- and high-context cultures. *Communication Quarterly, 33,* 270–283.

Gudykunst, W. B. (1985a). The influence of cultural similarity, type of relationship, and self-monitoring on uncertainty reduction processes. *Communication Monographs, 52,* 203–217.

Gudykunst, W. B. (1985b). Intercultural communication: Current status and proposed directions. In B. Dervin & M. J. Voigt (Eds.), *Progress in communication sciences* (Vol. 6, pp. 1–46). Norwood, NJ: Ablex.

Gudykunst, W. B. (1985c). A model of uncertainty reduction in intercultural encounters. *Journal of Language and Social Psychology, 4,* 79–98.

Gudykunst, W. B. (1987). Cross-cultural comparisons. In C. R. Berger & S. H. Chaffee, (Eds.), *Handbook of communication science* (pp. 847–889). Beverly Hill, CA: Sage.

Gudykunst, W. B. (1988). Culture and the development of interpersonal relationships. In J. Anderson (Ed.), *Communication yearbook* (Vol. 12, pp. 315–354). Newbury Park, CA: Sage.

Gudykunst, W. B. (Ed.). (1993). *Communicating in Japan and in the United States.* Albany, NY: State University of New York Press.

Gudykunst, W. B., Chua, E., & Gray, A. (1987). Cultural dissimilarities and uncertainty reduction processes. In M. McLaughlin (Ed.), *Communication yearbook* (Vol. 10, pp. 456–569). Newbury Park, CA: Sage.

Gudykunst, W. B., & Hammer, M. (1988). The influence of social identity and intimacy of interethnic relationships on uncertainty reduction processes. *Human Communication Research, 14,* 569–601.

Gudykunst, W. B., & Nishida, T. (1984). Individual and cultural influences on uncertainty reduction. *Communication Monographs, 51,* 23–36.

Gudykunst, W. B., & Nishida, T. (1986a). Attributional confidence in low- and high-context cultures. *Human Communication Research, 12,* 525–549.

Gudykunst, W. B., & Nishida, T. (1986b). The influence of cultural variability on perceptions of communication behavior associated with relationship terms. *Human Communication Research, 13,* 147–166.

Gudykunst, W. B., & Nishida, T. (1994). *Bridging Japanese/North American differences.* Thousand Oaks, CA: Sage.

Gudykunst, W. B., Nishida, T., Koike, H., & Shiino, N. (1986). The influence of language on uncertainty reduction: An exploratory study of Japanese–Japanese and Japanese–North American interactions. In M. McLaughlin (Ed.), *Communication yearbook* (Vol. 9, pp. 555–575). Beverly Hills, CA: Sage.

Gudykunst, W. B., Nishida, T., & Schmidt, K. (1989). Cultural, relational, and personality influences on uncertainty reduction processes. *Western Journal of Speech Communication, 53,* 12–29.

Gudykunst, W. B., Wiseman, R., & Hammer, M. (1977). Determinants of a sojourner's attitudinal satisfaction. In B. Ruben (Ed.), *Communication yearbook* (Vol. 1, pp. 415–425). New Brunswick, NJ: Transaction.

Gudykunst, W. B., Yang, S. M., & Nishida, T. (1985). A cross-cultural test of uncertainty reduction theory: comparisons of acquaintance, friends, and dating relationships in Japan, Korea, and the United States. *Human Communication Research, 11,* 407–454.

Hall, E. T. (1959). *The silent language.* Garden City, NY: Doubleday.

Hall, E. T. (1966). *The hidden dimension,* Garden City, NY: Doubleday.

Hall, P. H., & Gudykunst, W. B. (1989). The relationship of perceived ethnocentrism in corporate cultures to the selection, training, and success of international employees. *International Journal of Intercultural Relations, 13,* 183–201.

Hammersley, M. (1992). *What's wrong with ethnography?* New York: Routledge.

Harms, L.S. (1973). *Intercultural communication.* New York: Harper & Row.

Hatch, E. (1983). *Culture and morality: The relativity of values in anthropology.* New York: Columbia University Press.

Heidbreder, E. (1948). Studying human thinking. In T. G. Andrews (Ed.), *Methods of psychology* (pp. 96–123). New York: Wiley.

Henle, P. (1958). Language, thought, and culture. In P. Henle (Ed.), *Language and culture* (pp. 1–24). Ann Arbor: University of Michigan Press.

Humphrey, G. (1951). *Thinking: An introduction to its experimental psychology.* New York: Wiley.

Johnson, D. M. (1950). Problem solving and symbolic processes. *Annual Review of Psychology, 1,* 297–310.

Jones, S. E. (1979). Integrating etic and emic approaches in the study of intercultural communication. In M. K. Asante, E. Newmark, & C. A. Blake (Eds.), *The handbook of intercultural communication* (pp. 57–74). Beverly Hills: Sage.

Kim, Y. Y. (1986). *Interethnic communication current research.* Newbury Park, CA: Sage.

Kim, Y. Y. (1988a). *Communication and cross-cultural adaptation.* Philadelphia: Multilingual Matters.

Kim, Y. Y. (1988b). On theorizing intercultural communication. In Y. Y. Kim & W. B. Gudykunst (Eds.), *International and intercultural communication annual* (Vol. 12, pp. 11–21). Newbury Park, CA: Sage.

Kim, Y. Y., & Gudykunst, W. B. (1988). *Theories in intercultural communication: International and intercultural communication annual* (Vol. 12). Newbury Park, CA: Sage.

Klopf, D. W. (1987). *Intercultural encounters: The fundamentals of intercultural communication.* Englewood, NJ: Morton.

Kohls, R. L. (1984). *Survival kit for living overseas.* Yarmouth, Maine: Intercultural Press.

Langer, S. K. (1942). *Philosophy in a new key.* Cambridge, MA: Harvard University Press.

Leeds-Hurwitz, W. (1990). Notes in the history of intercultural communication: The Foreign Service Institute and the mandate for intercultural training. *Quarterly Journal of Speech, 76,* 262–281.

Lenneberg, E., & Roberts, J. M. (1956). *The language of experience.* Baltimore: Indiana University Publication in Anthropology & Linguistics.

Mandell, S. (1931). The relation of language to thought. *Quarterly Journal of Speech, 17,* 522–531.

Mestenhauser, J. A., Marty, G., & Steglitz, I. (Eds.). (1988). *Culture, learning, and the disciplines: Theory and practice in cross-cultural orientation.* Washington, DC: National Association of Foreign Student Affairs.

Osgood, C. E., & Sebeok, T. A. (1965). *Psycholinguistics.* Bloomington: Indiana University Press.

Park, R. E., & Burgess, E. W. (1924). *Introduction to the science of sociology.* Chicago: University of Chicago Press.

Pike, K. L. Etic and emic standpoints for the description of behavior. (1966). A. G. Smith (Ed.), *Communication and Culture* (pp. 152–163). New York: Holt, Rinehart and Winston.

Popper, K. R. (1968). *The logic of scientific discovery* (3rd ed.). London: Hutchinson.

Rogers, E. M. (1962). *The diffusion of innovations.* New York: Free Press.

Rogers, E. M (1995). *Diffusion of innovations* (4th ed.). New York: Free Press.

Rogers, E. M. (1994). *A history of communication study: A biographical approach.* New York: Free Press.

Rogers, E. M. & Shoemaker, F. F. (1971). *Communication of innovations: A cross-cultural approach* (2nd ed.). New York: Free Press.

Samovar, L. A., & Porter, R. E. (1972, 1994). *Intercultural communication: A reader.* Belmont, CA: Wadsworth.

Sapir, E. (1921). *Language: An introduction to the study of speech.* New York: Harcourt, Brace, & World.

Sato, A. (1992). *Understanding Japanese communication.* Tokyo: Japan Times.

Schatzman, L., & Strauss, A. (1955). Social class and modes of communication. *American Journal of Sociology, 60,* 329–338.

Singer, M. R. (1987). *Intercultural communication: A perceptual approach.* Englewood Cliffs, NJ: Prentice-Hall.

Slobin, D. T. (1979). *Psycholinguistics.* Glenview, IL: Scott Foresman.

Smith, A. G. (Ed.). (1966). *Communication and culture.* New York: Holt.

Steinfatt, T. (1996). *The bar: A study of bars oriented toward Western foreigners in Thailand—Their barworkers, customers, management, and owners.* Unpublished manuscript, School of Communication, University of Miami.

Steinfatt, T., & Miller, G. R. (1974). Communication in game theoretic models of conflict. In G. R. Miller & H. W. Simons (Eds.), *Perspectives on communication in social conflict* (pp. 14–75). Englewood Cliffs, NJ: Prentice Hall.

Steinfatt, T. M. (1989). Linguistic relativity: Toward a broader view. In S. Ting-Toomey & F. Korzenny (Eds.), *Language, communication, and culture: Current directions* (pp. 35–75). Newbury Park, CA: Sage.

Stewart, E. C., & Bennett, M. J. (1991). *American cultural patterns: A cross-cultural perspective.* Yarmouth, ME: Intercultural.

Stewart, L. P., Gudykunst, W. B., Ting-Toomey, S., & Nishida, T. (1986). The effects of decision-making style on openness and satisfaction within Japanese organizations. *Communication Monographs, 53,* 236–251.

Sudweeks, S., Gudykunst, W. B., Ting-Toomey, S., & Nishida, T. (1990). Developmental themes in Japanese-North American interpersonal relationships. *International Journal of Intercultural Relations, 14*, 207–233.

Ting-Toomey, S. (1981). Ethnic identity and close friendship in Chinese-American college students. *International Journal of Intercultural Relations, 5*, 383–406.

Ting-Toomey, S. (1985). Toward a theory of conflict and culture. In W. Gudykunst, L. Stewart, & S. Ting-Toomey (Eds.), *Communication, culture, and organizational processes* (pp. 71–86). Beverly Hills, CA: Sage.

Vidich, A. J., & Lyman, S. M. (1994). Qualitative methods: Their history in sociology and anthropology. In N. K. Denzin & Y. S. Lincoln (Eds.), *Handbook of qualitative research* (pp. 23–59). Thousand Oaks, CA: Sage.

Vinacke, W. E. (1951). The investigation of concept formation. *Psychological Bulletin, 48*, 1–31.

Whorf, B. L. (1956). *Language, thought, and reality*. Cambridge, MA: MIT Press.

Wolcott, H. F. (1994). *Transforming qualitative data*. Thousand Oaks, CA: Sage.

Woodworth, R. S. (1938). *Experimental psychology*. New York: Holt.

21

Intrapersonal Communication

Blaine Goss
New Mexico State University

Widespread interest in intrapersonal communication—the study of how people process messages—began in the late 1960s and early 1970s, when speech departments updated their programs to include behavioral approaches to the study of communication. In those days, speech departments were a conglomeration of performance-oriented scholars coming from rhetorical traditions and speech scientists who were known as the speech and hearing faculty. Many such departments included broadcasting and, perhaps, theater arts as well. In short, if it had anything to do with oral communication, it was in the speech department. The addition of the psychological behavioral sciences offered another perspective to the study of speech.

Because the speech scientists were primarily interested in the productive and receptive skills of the communicator, they were the early intrapersonal communication scholars. Even if intervention was the speech and hearing department faculty's chief motive, clients were studied as language using speakers and listeners. Thus, early interest in intrapersonal communication focused on either listening behavior or some aspect of speech science (speech perception, language acquisition, audiology).

The professional associations also reflected a speech and hearing interest. For instance, the Speech Association of America (as it was known then) had a Speech Science Division composed primarily of speech and hearing scientists and clinicians.

John Black from Ohio State was a prominent member of the division. Early in the 1970s, the division changed its name to Speech & Language Sciences to accommodate the growing interest in language studies. Since that time the division has changed its name again (Language & Social Interaction) to open its arms to conversation studies as well. Intrapersonal communication scholars broke away from this renamed division and formed a new alliance within the Speech Communication Association called the Commission on Intrapersonal Processes and Social Cognition. Charles Roberts of East Tennessee State University was the torchbearer for this new group.

While the field of communication is dynamic and everchanging, we have not forgotten our basic roots. To this day, scholars such as Frank Dance (1967, 1993) preach the centrality of speech behavior in understanding human interaction. And, people such as Larry Barker (cf., Barker, Johnson, & Watson, 1991) staunchly maintain listening's critical role in communication.

Interest in intrapersonal communication has burgeoned to include behavioral research in mental images, the mind, thought, self-concepts, memory, slips of the tongue, inner speech, brain functions, imagined interactions, and other psychological or physiological processes (Johnson, 1993; Korba, 1989; Motley, Camden, & Baars, 1979; Roberts, Edwards, & Barker, 1987; Schedletsky, 1983; Stacks, Hickson, & Hill, 1991). Other topics include self-talk, meditation, inner voices, cognitive schema, and social cognition. All of these are testimony to ever-increasing eclectic interests in intrapersonal communication.

We have reached a point where the study of intrapersonal communication is far less focused than it was earlier. Today almost anything "cognitive" is fair game for intrapersonal communication study. Although it is clear that mental processes are interesting in themselves, we must be careful to study these cognitive elements in the context of human communication. In other words, if you have an interest in, say, brain functions you should focus your inquiry on those functions which directly affect how people speak and/or listen. In support of this view, *intrapersonal communication* is defined as the study of the cognitive processes that directly affect one's communicative behaviors. In essence, it is concerned with how people mentally *process* messages.

After taking a quick look at where these mental processes operate—the communication aspects of brain functions—we focus on message processing and human listening. Finally, a sample intrapersonal communication study be described.

THE BRAIN

The cerebral cortex serves as the center of mental processing. It is believed that the left side of the cerebral cortex is more sensitive to linguistic data while the right side is more "artistic." (Andersen, Garrison, & Andersen, 1979). Cognitive psychologist John Anderson pointed out that "the so-called language areas are localized in the left hemisphere...while the right hemisphere is more associated with perceptual and spatial processing" (p. 29). Following Gazzaniga (1985), Stacks et al. (1991) even argued for a modular model which partitions the brain into six parts, not just two. These modules work in coordination with one another to create a "balanced" normal person. For any input, any one module may or may not become involved in the processing of the input. If the modules work with equal influence, things go smoothly. If one module of the brain is too dominant, dysfunctional behaviors can result.

Interest in the brain is certainly spurred by the belief that human behavior is neurologically driven. Thus, we assume that differences in brain activity will result in differences in behavioral patterns. Some even go as far as claiming that females and males have different brains, which accounts for differences in their respective behavior patterns. Specifically, Moir and Jessel (1991) stated that "each sex has a mind of its own at birth" (p. 53). For those who doubt this proposition, they asserted that "virtually every professional scientist and researcher into the subject has concluded that the brains of men and women are different" (p. 9) and reviewed some of the communication differences found between girls and boys (i.e., girls learn to read more quickly than boys, girls learn to speak earlier than boys, girls have an advantage in listening skills) as evidence of brain differences.

Whereas it is difficult to refute the importance of the brain, there are many unanswered questions concerning how brain functions impact communicative behavior. What is important, however, is that the brain is specially equipped to coordinate the production and reception of speech. Few speech scientists question the fact that the cerebral cortex contains areas specially designed for hearing and for speaking. Thus, human beings are born with the capacity for speaking and listening. This means, of course, that human beings are message processors.

Message Processing

Observing neurological message processing requires special equipment and training. Most communication researchers do not have such equipment and training. Yet, we can still study message processing behaviorally. In short, we can test through behavioral observation how people react to particular messages. One way to do so is to focus on listening behavior.

Most people do not understand how listening works (Wolvin & Coakley, 1992, 1993). Furthermore, people give themselves "high marks" in listening skills (Goss, 1991; Hunt & Cusella, 1983). Given these two things it is no wonder that Hunt and Cusella's 1983 study of listening in organizations found that people do not get much feedback from others about their listening skills and lack the motivation to develop stronger listening abilities. In short, if you think that you are a good listener and if you are not getting messages from others that tell you that you have a problem, you conclude that you do not have a listening problem.

Cognitive Readiness. Listening is an active process that looks passive, as though the ears simply receive sounds and then listening occurs automatically. *Hearing* is largely physiological, whereas *listening* is largely psychological. Although listening and hearing work together, one does not cause the other. The reason for this is that listening is an active process of comprehension (Witkin, 1993) which requires cognitive readiness. Goss (1989) maintained that "listening requires that you (1) recognize speech, (2) be prepared to respond, and (3) be able to respond meaningfully" (p. 113). To listen accurately, then, listeners must have both speech competence and linguistic competence.

In order to process speech, you have to know what speech sounds like. The auditory world is full of sounds, and normal hearing people can be bombarded by the din. Somehow speech sounds must "stand out" in the mind of the listener. Fortunately, the speech center of the human brain distinguishes speech sounds from nonspeech sounds. But even nonspeech sounds are important in listening, particularly those sounds which are meaningful and have specific referents. A ringing doorbell, for instance, alerts the listener that someone is at the door. A ringing telephone beckons you to answer the phone. The shrill of a siren tells you an emergency vehicle is passing nearby. Thus, nonspeech sounds not classified as noise are listened to in ways similar to speech sounds.

A second issue of readiness deals with linguistic competence. Listeners must possess a sufficient reservoir of language knowledge to understand spoken language. This means they must have familiarity with the words and rules of the language. Evidence for a lack of linguistic competence comes when you are overhearing a conversation in a foreign language. Most observers of foreign language usage cannot tell when sentences begin and end, let alone know what the sounds (words) mean. Fortunately, our innate ability to recognize speech sounds from other sounds, combined with an understanding of the spoken language, gives us the tools to begin the listening process.

Listening: Signal Processing

At the onset, listening requires signal processing—segmenting the spoken sounds into recognizable units of language (Goss, 1982). Signal processing is the initial analysis stage of listening wherein the signal is scanned for its discernible parts. It is a partitioning chore designed to identify linguistic units such as phonemes, morphemes, words, phrases, and sentences. Much of signal processing seems automatic (Anderson, 1990). Thus, experienced speakers of a language do not seem to labor much over deciphering the signal. We readily recognize the words and expressions spoken to us. This facility is, however, more related to past experience than to the purity of the speech signal itself. In fact, speech (spoken language) presents three problems.

First, speech is not neatly segmented into words with clearly articulated boundaries. When people talk, they punctuate their speech with pauses, but these pauses can occur in the middle of words as well as in between words. If spoken language was clearly punctuated, the pauses would occur only between words, phrases, and sentences, not in the middle of them. As it is, pauses are sprinkled throughout spoken discourse. This makes signal processing more challenging. In short, it means being able to do swift vocabulary guessing when listening to everyday spoken language.

Second, the words we hear are often not the same as the words we read. There is a lack of correspondence between letters (alphabet) and phonemes (spoken language sounds); and there may be little correspondence in the number of letters it takes to spell a word compared to saying it. For example, take the word *school*. There are six letters in the word. Yet, when said aloud you have *skul*, four letters. In English, this problem is further compounded by the fact that some letters are not articulated. In addition, similar letters may be pronounced differently in different words. For example, the word night is said as *nit*, whereas the word knit is pronounced as *nit*. What happened to the *gh* in *night* or the *k* in *knit*? Why does the letter *i* sound different in night and knit?

The third confounding signal processing variable is variation among speakers. Even speakers of the same language do not articulate the language identically. Regional dialects and speaker accents change the way words are spoken. Individual speaker styles also come into play; some speak more rapidly than others, and we can differ in pitch and inflection patterns as well. In spite of all this variation, most listeners can make sense out of a variety of speakers once they are accustomed to the speaker's style. Given the wide variety of spoken language, it is truly amazing that listeners are able to switch gears so readily.

Listening: Literal Processing

Whereas signal processing is a matter of auditory perception, the next stage, literal processing, deals with message comprehension. In this phase meaning is assigned to the segmented message. The main question of literal processing is "What is the speaker talking about?" Answering this question requires language competence; listeners need sufficient memory for words and grammar to properly assign meaning to the incoming messages.

Forecasting and Focusing. People have better memories for meaningful information than meaningless information; such is the case with literal processing. To accomplish meaningful message processing, listeners rely on two strategies: forecasting and focusing on ideas. Forecasting refers to the process of rapidly predicting what a speaker is saying even before he or she says it. The spoken word comes to us in serial order (one-word-at-a-time). Unlike reading, wherein the reader can see at once whole words and sentences, listeners have to wait for the speaker to say words and sentences. Or do they? Data from Marslen-Wilson and Tyler (1980) disagrees. According to Marslen-Wilson and Tyler, rather than waiting, listeners think ahead and guess what is coming up (forecasting). This strategy is employed during signal processing and literal processing. Because most of us can think faster than we can talk, forecasting is inevitable.

The second strategy is focusing on ideas rather than on individual words. When focusing, listeners assume that utterances represent thoughts and ideas, and that words are used to encode ideas. Thus, a spoken message should have a point—concepts linked together into oral assertions. If this is true, people listen for meaningfully related concepts (Ellis & Beattie, 1986); thus the speaker's encoding competence plays a big part in the listener's decoding success.

Schema. How do listeners access their memories to understand speech? They depend on something called semantic memory. There are at least three theories (associations, propositions, and schema) which describe how semantic memory is organized. Fortunately, schema theory incorporates the strengths of both association theory and propositional theory. According to schema theory, meanings and concepts are organized in sets that include all that we know about something. In essence, a set (schema) represents all you can say about a given concept. There are two kinds of schemas: *event schemas* (e.g., driving to visit your mother for the holidays) and *concept schemas* (e.g., a college education). Thus, when someone is talking about "the good old college days," listeners can respond by refering to their personal schemas of their days in college. As Edwards and McDonald (1993) note, listeners recall information that fits their existing schema. Information that is inconsistent with the existing schema is not as readily recalled. Thus, with a topic like the "good old days" we are likely to remember the positive things more than the mundane.

During conversations, people sometimes think that others have schemata similar to theirs. Just because two people use similar words to refer to the topic at hand, does not mean that they think the same way. To wit, a "just settlement" in contract negotiations could elicit similar general schemas in all listeners, but the specific contents of the various schemata are likely to be different. Having similar words (designating the presence of particular schemas) does not mean having identical content in the schemata. Thus, people may misunderstand each other because they are talking about the same schema but with different contents. Listeners apply, then, their personal schema to understand what the speaker is talking about. In literal processing, schemas serve as the main conceptual bank accounts from which to draw understanding (Edwards & McDonald, 1993).

Listening: Reflective Processing

Once a message is processed for its "literal" meaning, reflective processing can take place. This stage of message processing goes beyond the initial assignment of meaning. It includes further thought, leading to inferences and additional feelings. This means that reflective processing will be governed by one's personal value system, inductive and deductive reasoning skills, prior learning, longstanding perceptual habits, and so forth. Such further thought causes listeners to rely more heavily on schemata than when literally processing messages. Whereas signal and literal processing can occur rapidly, reflective processing takes time. Reflective processing can swell into time-consuming "deep thought." Listeners, then, need to be selective in what they reflect on. This brings us to the role of response time in intrapersonal communication.

UNCERTAINTY AND RESPONSE TIME

Although we may not be able to directly observe the internal mental processes that affect human communication, we can observe their effects. Response time is one way to measure intrapersonal processes and their impact on daily communication. For instance, if the respondent is unfamiliar with a task, and if that task is somewhat difficult, we would expect longer response times. On the other hand, if a task is familiar and simple, one should be able to respond quickly. Whenever someone takes a long time to come up with a response to something, we believe that the delay is due to prolonged reflective processing, indicating uncertainty. Uncertainty can be caused by a number of factors, such as task difficulty, inadequate schemata, or unclear messages. Two things, however, cause unclear messages: ambiguity and vagueness.

Ambiguity.   Ambiguity occurs when a person is uncertain about which response to choose. Lexical ambiguity is a special case of ambiguity caused by words which can mean more than one thing. For instance, the word "bark" is ambiguous. It can refer to a sound that a dog makes or to the covering on a tree.

Although many English words have multiple meanings, everyday listening seems to proceed as though ambiguity is not present. As Foss and Hakes (1978) reminded us, "listeners are not aware of the potential ambiguity that lurks within many of the utterances they hear. They generally come up with only one conscious interpretation of the input, and in a vast majority of cases it is the appropriate one" (p. 121). Notice that Foss and Hakes make three points. People are unaware of lexical ambiguity. They proceed accordingly. And, they end up thinking of the "right" thing.

Why does this occur? The answer lies in the context, both situational and linguistic. In other words, many ideas are made clear by the context of the ongoing conversation. If we are trekking through the woods talking about the beauty of the forest, our minds will be focused more on the tree side of bark than on the dog side. In short, the social and communicative context narrows our focus so that we do not perceive any ambiguity.

Vagueness.   If the context cannot clarify the confusion, the problem may be one of vagueness. A word is vague when it is so general that it does not seem to apply to any one specific thing. "Materials" is vague. So is "item." They can refer to an array of things. "Middle-aged" is another vague term. When does middle-age begin? When does it end? In short, vague words are vague because the ideas they represent are vague. Whereas the sentence context seems to clear up ambiguity, it probably will not help clarify something that is by its very nature vague. The following is an experimental intrapersonal communication study designed to investigate the effects language clarity on human listening behavior. Specifically, it explores how long it takes listeners to respond to ambiguous nouns and vague nouns presented either alone or in the context of a sentence.

SAMPLE STUDY

Regardless of the cause, response uncertainty will lead to longer response times. In this way, response time can be a measure of the effects of unclear messages on the listener. The following sample study is designed to test this proposition.

Rationale

Ambiguity and vagueness present interesting dilemmas for the listener. MacKay (1966) found that when people were given ambiguous statements, they took longer to come up with plausible responses than when they were presented unambiguous ones. Furthermore, MacKay found that if an utterance had several ambiguities within it, people needed even more time to respond meaningfully. Ambiguity, then, slows down response time when the respondent notices the ambiguity. Conversely, when the sentence context clarifies the ambiguity, the ambiguity disappears, and the respondent reacts without delay.

Variables

If it is true that the context (particularly sentence context) helps disambiguate the speaker's intended meaning, then we would expect that people would be able to respond more quickly to ambiguous nouns when they appear in the context of a sentence than when appear by themselves. While this argument makes sense intuitively, this study is designed to directly test its veracity. To understand more fully how ambiguity works, the following study compares listener responses to ambiguous nouns compared to vague nouns.

The independent variables are: *noun clarity* (ambiguous or vague); *context* (presented in a sentence, or not); *overall listening ability* (score on the Goss Listening Test). The dependent variable is response time (number of seconds it takes the listener to provide a one-word association). An ambiguous noun is one in which there are at least two possible but unrelated meanings. The following nouns are ambiguous: club (organization or tool), degree (diploma or angle), stake (wager or stick), and, seal (animal or insignia). A vague word refers to something that has no clearly definable boundaries. In other words, a vague word is "fuzzy" in that it tends to be largely inclusive. The following nouns are considered vague: organism, asset, item, and instrument.

In order to properly test the influence of sentence context, the above nouns should be cast into a common set of sentences. Thus, the following sentence sets are proposed:

> The (club/organism) was hard.
> The (degree/asset) was attractive.
> The (stake/item) was strong.
> The (seal/instrument) was active.

Notice that the first noun in parentheses is ambiguous, while the second is vague.

Overall listening ability is measured by the 12-item listening test developed by Goss (1991). The test queries the participants' comprehension skills, observable listening behaviors, and memory for messages. The total score serves as the covariate in the statistical analysis.

Procedure.   Randomly selected participants are invited one-at-a-time into a private room and told that they will be participating in a word association game in which they are to say aloud the first one-word response that comes to their minds. Half of the participants will respond to the words presented alone, while the other half will respond to the words in their sentence contexts. Each participant will respond to 8 words (4 each of the ambiguous and vague nouns). Each item will be presented orally, and the participants are to respond orally. After completing the word association task, the participants will take the Goss Listening Test.

To control for order effects in the presentation of the target words, the target words and sentence contexts should be presented in random order across participants. To keep track of response time and response variation, all sessions will be audiotaped. The researcher can then focus on administering the stimulus materials while working with the participants. After the participants have left the room, the researcher will playback the audiotape, time each response, and write down the answers given by the participants.

Hypotheses.   Given the different cognitive demands which these variables should place on the listeners, the following hypotheses are offerred.

H1: There will be a significant difference in response times for nouns appearing alone compared to nouns appearing in sentences.

H2: Ambiguous nouns appearing in sentences will produce significantly shorter response times than the same nouns appearing alone.

H3: There will be no significant difference in response times to vague nouns presented in a sentence compared to presented alone.

Given that one's overall listening skills may affect the quickness of responses, the following hypothesis if offerred:

H4: Participants who score in the upper 25% of the listening test will have shorter response times in all conditions than will those who score in the lower 25% of the listening test.

Analysis of Data.   Appropriate statistical tests include an independent and repeated measures analysis of variance (ANOVA) to analyze the results. The context variable (alone vs. in sentence) will be the independent measure, while the nouns (ambiguous and vague) and their four replications (four different examples) will be the repeated measures. The participants score on the listening test will serve as a covariate in the ANOVA.

SUMMARY

Over the last half of the 20th century, scholarly interest in intrapersonal communication has been rich and lively. What began as a speech and hearing science has evolved into a more inclusive cognitive science. Intrapersonal communication is the study of how people process messages. This requires both psychological and physiological perspectives. The brain, along with the rest of the nervous system, serves as the processing conduit for messages. One way to observe mental processing is to study human listening behavior, which can occur at different depths. And, one of the key dependent variables in message processing research is response time. Response time can be an indicator of processing depth or task difficulty. Ambiguity and vagueness can cause cognitive difficulties resulting in longer response times from listeners. The sample study is offered as a way to continue the study of intrapersonal communication.

SUGGESTED READINGS

Many fine books are now available which synthesize current thinking and research in intrapersonal communication. Following a few are listed:

Ellis, A., & Beattie, G. (1986). *The psychology of language and communication.* New York: Guilford. This is a psychology textbook but organized around communication topics. If you didn't know that Ellis and Beattie were psychologists, you might think that they were communication researchers.

Goss, B. (1995). *The psychology of human communication* (2nd ed.). Prospect Heights, IL: Waveland Press. A well-accepted, easy to read treatment of intrapersonal processes that underlie human communication. Cognitive in orientation.

Stacks, D., Hickson, M., & Hill, S. R., (1991). *Introduction to communication theory.* Fort Worth, TX: Holt. This is a textbook that gives strong credence to the intrapersonal aspects of human communication. Its strength is that it builds a firm foundation for studying communication.

Roberts, C., Edwards, R., & Barker, L. (1987). *IntrapersonaL Communication Processes.* Scottsdale, AZ: Gorsuch Scarisbrick Publishers. Another easy to read book on intrapersonal communication. Combines scientific and nonscientific topics.

Vocate, D. R. (Ed.). (1994). *Intrapersonal communication: Different voices, different minds.* Hillsdale, NJ: Lawrence Erlbaum Associates. An easy-to-read collection of intrapersonal theory and method.

Wolvin, A., & Coakley, C. (Eds.). (1993). *Perspectives on listening.* Norwood, NJ: Ablex. This is a neat reader with 13 chapters written by different scholars, primarily in the speech communication field. The chapters synthesize many important areas of study.

REFERENCES

Andersen, P., Garrison, J., & Andersen, J. (1979). Implications of a neurophysiological approach for the study of nonverbal communication. *Human Communication Research, 6,* 74–89.

Anderson, J. (1990). *Cognitive psychology and its implications.* New York: Freeman.

Barker, L., Johnson, P., & Watson, K. (1991). The role of listening in managing interpersonal and group conflict. In D. Borisoff & M. Purdy (Eds.), *Listening in everyday life* (pp. 139–162). New York: University Press of America.

Dance, F. (1967). *Human communication theory: Original essays.* New York: Holt.

Dance, F. (1993). *Researching intrapersonal communication and social cognition.* Paper presented at Speech Communication Association convention, Miami Beach, FL.

Edwards, R. & McDonald, J. (1993). Schema theory and listening. In Wolvin, A. & Coakley, C. (Eds.), *Perspectives on listening* (pp. 60–77). Norwood, NJ: Ablex.

Ellis, A., & Beattie, G. (1986). *The psychology of language and communication.* New York: Guilford.

Foss, D., & Hakes, D. (1978). *Psycholinguistics: An introduction to the psychology of language.* Englewood Cliffs, NJ: Prentice-Hall.

Gazzaniga, M. (1985). *The social brain: Discovering the networks of the mind.* New York: Basic Books.

Goss, B. (1982). Listening as information processing. *Communication Quarterly, 30,* 304–307.

Goss, B. (1989). *The psychology of human communication.* Prospect Heights, IL: Waveland Press.

Goss, B. (1991). A test of conversational listening. *Communication Research Reports, 8,* 19–22.

Hunt, G., & Cusella, L. (1983). A field study of listening needs in organizations. *Communication Education, 32,* 393–401.

Johnson, J. (1993). Functions and processes of inner speech in listening. In A. Wolvin & C. Coakley (Eds.), *Perspectives on listening* (pp. 170–184). Norwood, NJ: Ablex.

Korba, R. (1989). The cognitive psychophysiology of inner speech. In C. Roberts & K. Watson (Eds.), *Intrapersonal communication processes: Original essays* (pp. 217–242). New Orleans: Spectra.

MacKay, D. (1966). To end ambiguous sentences. *Perception and Psychophysics. 1,* 426–436.

Marslen-Wilson, W. & Tyler, L. K. (1980). The temporal structure of spoken language understanding. *Cognition, 8,* 1–8.

Moir, A., & Jessel, D. (1991). *Brain sex: The real difference between men and women.* New York: Carol Publishing Group.

Motley, M., Camden, C., & Baars, B. (1979). Personality and situational influences upon verbal slips: A laboratory test of Freudian and prearticulatory editing hypotheses. *Human Communication Research, 5,* 195–202.

Roberts, C., Edwards, R., & Barker, L. (1987). *Intrapersonal communication processes: Original essays.* Scottsdale, AZ: Gorsuch Scarisbrick Publishers.

Schedletsky, L. (1983). Cerebral asymmetry for aspects of sentence processing: A replication and extension. *Communication Quarterly, 31,* 78–84.

Stacks, D., Hickson, M., & Hill, S. (1991). *Introduction to communication theory.* Fort Worth, TX: Holt.

Witkin, R. (1993). Human information processing. In A. Wolvin. & C. Coakley (Eds.), *Perspectives on listening* (pp. 23–59). Norwood, NJ: Ablex.

Wolvin, Andrew & Carolyn C. (1992). *Listening* (4th ed.). Dubuque, IA: William C. Brown.

Wolvin, A. & Coakley, C. (Eds.). (1993). *Perspectives on listening.* Norwood, NJ: Ablex.

22

Nonverbal Communication

Amy S. Ebesu
University of Hawaii

Judee K. Burgoon
University of Arizona

As the King and his suite neared Akasaka, the palace of the Emperor, a bugle announced their arrival. The Emperor Meiji of Japan stood alone in a room adjacent to the entrance of the palace. He was dressed in European military uniform and the crest of his coat was decorated with orders. As [King] Kalakaua left the carriage and entered the palace, he stepped up to the Emperor alone and extended his arm to shake hands. For the first time in Japanese history an Emperor exchanged handshakes with a foreign sovereign. (Ogawa, 1973, p. 91)

Instead of the traditional bow, this momentous meeting between two monarchs in 1881 began with a simple handshake, which served as a precursor to friendly international relations between Japan and Hawaii. More recently, two Middle Eastern leaders greeted each other, not with the usual formal handshake, but with an embrace, and this seemingly inconsequential greeting ritual signalled a turning point in the tenor of peace negotiations.

So, too, are the warp and weave of daily interactions fashioned from a thousand and one presumably insignificant nonverbal gestures. A gaze broken too soon, a forced smile, a flat voice, an unreturned phone call, a conversation conducted across the barrier of an executive desk—together such nonverbal strands form the fabric of our communicative world, defining our interpersonal relationships, declaring our personal identities, revealing our emotions, governing the flow of our social encounters, and reinforcing our attempts to influence others. Understanding human communication requires understanding the multiple nonverbal codes by which it is transacted and the communicative functions those codes accomplish.

THEORIZING ABOUT NONVERBAL COMMUNICATION

By nonverbal communication we mean behaviors that are *typically sent with intent, are used with regularity among members of a social community, are typically interpreted as intentional, and have consensually recognizable interpretations* (Burgoon, 1980, 1994; Burgoon, Buller, & Woodall, 1994). This message orientation approach to communication requires attending to the meanings associated with nonverbal behaviors and focusing on meanings that are tied to communication functions within a given speech community.

Theorizing about nonverbal communication has been complicated not only by its multimodal and multifunctional nature, but also because our knowledge emanates from disparate disciplines with differing assumptions and methodologies. This makes efforts to synthesize theories and principles from all these different sources a challenge. For example, ethologists, who are interested in nonverbal communication as a basis for comparing humans to other species, approach nonverbal displays as biologically grounded signals with evolutionary survival value. Their methods require meticulous observations of nonverbal behaviors in their natural environs. Anthropologists, who see nonverbal behavior as manifestations of culture, are interested in how nonverbal rituals and norms reveal something about human society. They may rely on informants—members of a given culture—to clarify the nonverbal rules, norms, and sanctions in a given culture, or they may rely on ethnographic observations. Psychologists may examine nonverbal cues for what they reveal about intrapsychic processes such as arousal, personality, or cognition formation and processing. Among the methods used are experimental manipulations of conditions that elicit nonverbal cues or manipulations of the cues themselves. Sociologists may examine nonverbal patterns as manifestations of social hierarchies or as means toward achieving group influence and may combine observational and experimental procedures with survey methodologies. Scholars studying families, social ills, psychiatric problems, medical interactions, legal proceedings, intercultural and international relations, political image-making, and mediated versus nonmediated channels, among others, bring additional distinctive perspectives and methods to the study of nonverbal communication. Out of all these perspectives have emerged numerous theories and models of human communication.

Obviously, no single chapter can begin to do justice to this cornucopia of nonverbal literature. We will therefore focus our attention here on a single communication function—relational communication and relationship management—and the theorizing and methods attending it. The reader interested in more broad-based reviews of nonverbal theories is directed to Burgoon (1994), Burgoon, Buller, and Woodall (1989), Cappella (1994), and Knapp and Hall (1992).

RELATIONAL COMMUNICATION AND RELATIONSHIP MANAGEMENT

Aside from emotional expression, perhaps no area has been so closely aligned with nonverbal communication as relational communication. Relational communication refers *to the messages people exchange that define the nature of their interpersonal relationship;* more specifically, how two people feel about one another, about their relationship, or about themselves within the context of the relationship. Relational communication undergirds all interpersonal relationships. As the coinage by which people "transact" their relationships, it purchases relational trajectories of greater or lesser intimacy, trust, interdependence, commitment, and satisfaction.

Studying relational communication requires acknowledging several important features of this major communicative function. First, relational communication focuses on the participant's perspective. This means that people's evaluations and self-images are tied to reactions to and influenced by feedback from particular others (Ellsworth & Ludwig, 1972). Second, relational communication is directed toward a specific target and not toward a generalized audience. Third, relational communication spotlights the interaction between two people, where the central unit of analysis is the *dyad.* Finally, relational communication concentrates on the meanings ascribed to the behaviors of others, rather than on the behaviors that cause certain outcomes.

Beginning with Watzlawick, Beavin, and Jackson's (1967) classic work, *Pragmatics of Human Communication,* relational communication has often been treated as synonymous with nonverbal communication. According to Watzlawick et al. all communication entails two levels, the *content* or report level (the ostensive topic of conversation) and the *relational* or command level (the definition of the interpersonal relationship which serves as a metacommunication about how to interpret the content level). In reality, not all nonverbal communication is relational, nor is all relational communication nonverbal (see Bavelas, 1990; Burgoon et al., 1994), but it is evident that there is a strong division of labor such that much relational "business" is handled by the nonverbal codes while the occasioned discourse is managed by the verbal code.

Relational Communication Dimensions

Traditional approaches to relational communication originally proposed two or three dimensions (e.g., dominance, affection, inclusion) underlying all relationships. For example, Millar and Rogers (1987) suggested that control, trust, and intimacy are three basic issues that are revealed in relational communication. *Control* refers to the process of interdependence and regulation of the relationship definition and direction. *Trust* deals with the process of predictability, obligation, and dependability. *Intimacy* refers to the process of reciprocal self-confirmation and the affective tone of the relationship.

Although an important starting point for analyzing relationships and relational messages, early perspectives underestimated the variety and richness of message themes that are present in interpersonal encounters. After reviewing ethological, anthropological, psychiatric, sociological, psychological, linguistic, and communication literature, Burgoon and Hale (1984) proposed that the *topoi* or themes of relational communication be expanded to twelve nonorthogonal dimensions. They included a superordinate theme of *intimacy* comprised of subthemes of affection–hostility, intensity of involvement (often equated with immediacy), inclusion–exclusion (elsewhere labeled as affiliation, empathy, rapport, or receptivity), trust, and depth-superficiality (elsewhere described as familiarity or degree of acquaintance). Additional themes they proposed were *dominance* (which equates with relational control), *emotional arousal* (often equated with activation), *composure* (often labeled as relaxation or nervousness), *similarity–dissimilarity, formality–informality,* and *task versus social orientation.* Subsequent empirical investigations (Burgoon, 1991; Burgoon & Dillman, 1995; Burgoon & Hale, 1987; Le Poire & Burgoon, 1994) indicated that these dimensions could be combined into fewer, interrelated message clusters. These clusters offer a convenient way to organize empirical findings regarding which behaviors convey relational meanings (for summaries, see Burgoon, 1982, 1991, 1994; Burgoon, Buller, Hale, & deTurck, 1984; Burgoon & Newton, 1991; Cappella, 1983; Coker & Burgoon, 1987; Exline & Fehr, 1978; Hendrick & Hendrick, 1992; Henley, 1977; Heslin & Alper, 1983; Jones & Yarbrough, 1985; Kramer, Alloway, & Pliner, 1975; Le Poire & Burgoon, 1994; Mehrabian, 1972, 1981; Palmer, 1989; Patterson, 1973, 1983; Scheflen, 1974; Siegman, 1978; Thayer, 1986).

Messages of Intimacy.   Intimacy appears to be phenomenologically experienced through nonverbal behaviors (Register & Henley, 1992). These intimacy behaviors include the use of touch to more private body regions, softer voices, postural openness, motor mimicry and mirroring (i.e., exhibiting the same behavior as another), wearing similar apparel and "identification symbols" (i.e., tie-signs), punctuality, monochronic use of time, and sharing territories and possessions. In large part, the experience of intimacy is closely tied to the expression of nonverbal involvement. Involvement itself is composed of five dimensions: (a) *immediacy* (e.g., proximity, direct body orientation, forward lean, postural openness, gaze, and touch that signal approach and inclusion), (b) *expressiveness* (e.g., facial, gestural, postural, and vocal displays of animation and activity), (c) *altercentrism* (e.g., kinesic and auditory cues that signal one is attentive to and oriented toward the other rather than self), (d) *conversational management* (e.g., self-synchrony, fluency, coordinated movement, interactional synchrony, and short response latencies that create a well-paced, smooth interaction), and (e) *social composure* (e.g., postural and vocal cues of relaxation or fewer adaptor behaviors; Coker & Burgoon, 1987).

It is important to note that the meaning of individual behaviors may be ambiguous because isolated behaviors often have multiple relational interpretations. However, appropriate interpretations are more readily apparent when combinations and patterns of behaviors are viewed. For example, when involvement is combined with positive affect (e.g., smiling, nodding, vocal pleasantness, and relaxed laughter), it creates a message of greater attraction, liking, trust, affiliation, depth, similarity, and rapport.

When involvement is accompanied by negative affect, it conveys a strong signal of hostility. On the other hand, the combination of noninvolvement and nonimmediacy cues connotes detachment or privacy.

Arousal and Composure. Research has found that emotional arousal and lack of composure are created through a variety of kinesic, vocalic, and proxemic cues. For instance, composure and relaxation are communicated by behaviors such as asymmetrical limb positions, less body tonus and tension, close proximity, smiling, greater kinesic expressiveness, and faster tempo. More research needs to examine whether or not both messages of composure and noncomposure can be intentionally manipulated by people.

Dominance. Dominance appears to be expressed by behaviors such as use or possession of larger, more private, and more luxuriously appointed spaces; greater access to other people's belongings, time, and territories; initiation of talk, conversational distance, and touch patterns; asymmetrical use of touch and spatial intrusion (giving more, receiving less); indirect body orientation and backward lean; less frequent but more direct eye gaze and staring; less smiling and facial pleasantness and more frowning and scowling; greater postural relaxation and asymmetry; more talk time; lower and more varied pitch; vocal cues of anger; use of vocal interruptions; and more rapid speaking pace and control of silence. From this list, it is clear that the expressiveness dimension of involvement is also associated with dominance. Submissiveness is created by gestures such as the head tilt and open palms and cues that are the opposite of those linked to dominance.

These various dominance behaviors may be categorized according to several underlying principles. For instance, the principle of threat is illustrated by behaviors that increase or highlight one's physical size (e.g., large territories, deeper pitch, erect posture, and a "firm" stance) or suggest danger (e.g., threat stares and threatening gestures). The principle of elevation, where higher is perceived as more dominant, may be achieved through behaviors that allow for surveillance of others. The principle of initiation and precedence suggests that individuals express their dominance by initiating conversation, spacing, touch, or interaction rhythms and topic switches. The principle of expectancy violations means that dominant individuals are likely to behave nonnormatively. They may engage in too much conversational proximity or distance and they may communicate in an extremely immediate or nonimmediate style. The principle of privileged access may be achieved by behaviors that intrude on other's space or time, use of gatekeepers that limit others' access to self, and possession of status symbols. The principle of activity relies on sending messages of confidence and authority through dynamic, expressive, and fast-paced actions (e.g., a rapid speaking rate). The principle of relaxation is conveyed through moderate postural and vocal relaxation because dominant people are freer to drop their guard and to deviate from norms of "proper" behavior. Finally, the principle of task performance cues may be adhered to by exhibiting behaviors indicative of status and task-related ability (see Berger, Rosenholtz, & Zelditch, 1980; Ridgeway, Berger, & Smith, 1985).

Formality and Task versus Social Orientation. Formality, which is highly related to a task orientation, is conveyed through decreased vocal expressiveness, increased resonance and precise articulation, postural tension or erectness, and greater distance. Additionally, the use of cues such as response latency, gaze, loudness, fluency, posture, gestures, and seating position are inferred as relating to task competence and confidence (Ridgeway et al., 1985). For example, a person expecting to exercise leadership typically sits at the head of a table, and individuals seated at the head of a table become more participative and influential.

Relationship Management

The preceding section identified numerous nonverbal messages associated with particular relational message themes expressed in a given interchange. One can also take a more macroscopic approach to relational communication by considering its role in longitudinal relationship development. Some research and theorizing has taken this approach, examining how nonverbal cues function in the initiation, maintenance, and dissolution of interpersonal relationships. Scholars have long recognized that nonverbal behaviors serve as good indicators of the state of the relationship and can facilitate or hinder the development of intimacy (e.g., Altman & Taylor's, 1973, social penetration theory and Knapp's, 1983, 1984, dimensions of communication in relationship development). Other researchers have examined the association between nonverbal cues and measures of the relationship state such as satisfaction, intimacy, and commitment.

Several exemplars illustrate the directions of this growing trend in research. Detailed analyses of courtship stages and rituals have distinguished courtship cues from flirting behaviors and have revealed that different nonverbal behaviors are connected with each courtship stage (e.g., Givens, 1978, 1983; Scheflen, 1965; Simpson, Gangestad, & Biek, 1993). Work on relationship stages and types has identified variations in nonverbal intimacy, play, privacy, and emotional expressivity across such diverse relationships as acquaintance, friend, romantic, superior–subordinate, parent–child, and doctor–patient (Baxter, 1992; Burgoon et al., 1989; Guerrero & Andersen, 1991; Planalp & Benson, 1992; Wagner & Smith, 1991). Other research on relationship phases has developed typologies of strategies and tactics, composed of verbal and nonverbal behaviors, used during relational escalation, maintenance, and deescalation (e.g., Cupach & Metts, 1986; Shea & Pearson, 1986; Tolhuizen, 1989). Studies of marital conflict have uncovered nonverbal profiles accompanying different conflict strategies and have shown that conflicts often take the form of reciprocal escalating spirals of nonverbal hostility with nonverbal expressions of affect playing a deciding factor in whether or not conflicts are resolved (e.g., Gottman, 1979; Gottman, Markman, & Notarius, 1977; Newton & Burgoon, 1990; Sillars, Coletti, Parry, & Rogers, 1982). Work on relational satisfaction has identified which conflict resolution strategies and relational message themes influence satisfaction in physician–patient and marital relationships (e.g., Burgoon et al., 1987; Kelley & Burgoon, 1991; Rusbult, Verette, Whitney, Slovik, & Lipkus, 1991). Research comparing satisfied and dissatisfied couples indicates that dissatisfied couples are prone to misinterpret each other's nonverbal signals; that people in less satisfying relationships decode their partners' negative behaviors as more intentional, stable, and controllable and their partners' positive behaviors as external, unstable, and specific, whereas people in more satisfying relationships decode negative cues neutrally and positive cues as internal, stable, and global (Kahn, 1970; Manusov, 1990; Noller, 1980; Noller & Ruzzene, 1991; Noller & Venardos, 1986). One important conclusion is that nonverbal behaviors play a significant role in the life of a relationship by revealing its level of intimacy and closeness, distinguishing different stages or types of relationships, and affecting relational trajectories and outcomes.

RESEARCH METHODS IN STUDYING NONVERBAL RELATIONAL COMMUNICATION

Our discussion of the findings in the area of nonverbal relational communication naturally brings us to consider the methods used to conduct nonverbal research on relational communication and relationship management. The methods selected affect the validity and generalizability of the conclusions that can be drawn.

A basic decision point is whether to employ an experimental or nonexperimental design and attendant measurement strategies. This is dictated by the questions and issues at stake. Often, relational communication issues require a longitudinal focus and the need to access highly private information. In such cases, researchers may incorporate nonexperimental diary and account methods. But such methodologies are fraught with the difficulties attending the use of self-report methods. For instance, respondents may be unable to provide information regarding microlevel nonverbal behaviors. It is unreasonable to expect that people are able to report all of their nonverbal behaviors (i.e., kinesics, vocalic, physical appearance, proxemic, artifactual, chronemic, and haptic cues) or that nonverbal communication occurs at a high level of awareness. Jones' (1991) examination of the problem of validity in questionnaire studies using Jourard's tactile body-accessibility scale is illustrative. It revealed that people's recall of touch behaviors was heavily influenced by expectations about which touches should have occurred; it did not match the amount of touch. This suggests that researchers must find other ways, besides exclusive reliance on self-report data, to investigate specific nonverbal behaviors, and they must have alternate means to record nonverbal behaviors without solely relying on actual participants as the primary informants.

However, if researchers are interested in the general nonverbal encoding and decoding abilities of people (e.g., to investigate what messages people intend to send, what messages people receive, and what messages people think were intentionally sent), then questionnaire measures may be a useful method of assessment. Researchers can use a number of standardized scales which have been developed to test these nonverbal skills. These scales range from self-report questionnaires to videotape tests. Sample measures include the Affective Communication Test (Friedman, Prince, Riggio, & DiMatteo, 1980), the Contextual and Affective Sensitivity Test (Trimboli & Walker, 1993), the Interpersonal Perception Test (Archer & Costanzo, 1988), the Perceived Encoding and Decoding Ability Scales (Zuckerman & Larrance, 1979), the Profile of Nonverbal Sensitivity (Rosenthal, Hall, DiMatteo, Rogers, & Archer, 1979), the Social Interpretations Test (Archer & Akert, 1977), and the Social Skills Inventory (Riggio, 1986).

More often than not, research on nonverbal behavior entails direct observation and coding of behavior. This may occur in nonexperimental or experimental settings. In the former case, one might ask couples to interact naturally about some topic or even to recreate a previous discussion. The kinds of interaction patterns that are exhibited are then observed and coded or rated (e.g., Burman, Margolin, & John, 1993). In the latter case, some interactants might experimentally alter some behaviors—perhaps becoming uninvolved and detached—to see the effects on partner behavior or interpretations (e.g., Guerrero, 1994). Or couples might be placed under different experimental conditions, such as conducting a joint task and discussing personal fears, and their behavior patterns compared across partners and conditions (e.g., Gottman, 1979). In yet other cases, respondents might view various experimentally controlled enactments of nonverbal behaviors and ascribe interpretations to them (e.g., Burgoon et al., 1984).

Although nonverbal behaviors may be observed live or "online," researchers interested in nonverbal cues often analyze a permanent record of the interaction. Nonverbal studies typically use audiotapes or videotapes, depending on the specific research questions, and the ease and availability of using particular recording devices. Once recorded, nonverbal behaviors are frequently coded by outside observers. This is in line with a message orientation approach. In addition, in the case of relational communication, participants may also report their perceptions. One consequence of conducting nonverbal research in this manner is the additional expenses—in time and money—associated with equipment costs, hiring coders, training coders, and altering the videotapes or audiotapes to aid in coding (e.g., content-filtering procedures). Another consequence is that interpretation of the nonverbal data may become more difficult as various perspectives are taken into account. In the case where both participants and outside observers judge the nonverbal behaviors recorded, there may be striking differences in their ratings. For example, various research programs comparing participant and trained observer perspectives showed that observers and participants share some commonalities in perceptions but also some notable discrepancies (e.g., Burgoon & Newton, 1991; Floyd & Markman, 1983; Rusbult et al., 1991; Street, Mulac, & Wiemann, 1988).

A final important consideration when conducting nonverbal research is unit of analysis. Will it consist of nonverbal measurement of single and concrete behaviors, where observation is usually event-based or time-based using small time intervals (microlevel) or nonverbal measurement of larger and more abstract behaviors, where observation is usually time-based using larger time intervals or event-based using larger events (macrolevel)? Burgoon and Baesler (1991) suggested that nonverbal researchers should: (a) assess the representational validity between the level of measurement and the nonverbal phenomena of conceptual interest, such that the unit of measurement is socially meaningful, (b) compare the reliability using different levels of measurement, (c) consider the concurrent validity between the micro and macro measures, and (d) measure the predictive power using micro and macro measurements when determining the appropriate measurement strategy for particular research questions.

A SAMPLE EXPERIMENT

To illustrate how nonverbal relational research might be conducted, we turn now to a sample experiment in a specific area of relational communication and management: the nonverbal aspects of relational conflict. As context, most of the research for the past 25 years has focused on the impact of the negative or positive affective tone of communication during interpersonal conflict and whether or not people engage in or avoid conflict interactions (Sillars & Weisberg, 1987). In general, work on affect during conflict revealed that couples who are unhappy or dissatisfied are more verbally and nonverbally negative during their conflict interactions (Gottman, 1979; Pike & Sillars, 1985). In regard to engagement, research results are less consistent. For example, sometimes satisfied couples confront conflict issues and other times they avoid discussing conflicts (Pike & Sillars, 1985; Rusbult, Drigotas, & Verette, 1994; Rusbult & Zembrodt, 1983; Ting-Toomey, 1983). Fitzpatrick (1988) suggested that the choice to engage in conflict interactions or avoid discussion of conflicts may be a function of a couple's marital type, which is based on the couple's relationship definitions. For example, couples labeled as a "traditional" marital type tended to avoid conflict whereas couples labeled as an "independent" marital type were more assertive and tended to engage in conflict.

A nonverbal study providing a useful extension of these lines of research would be to examine *both* positive–negative behaviors and engaging–avoidant behaviors during conflict interaction and how the combination of these two classes of behavior impact relationship satisfaction. In this sample study, we will consider positive–negative behaviors as those cues which exhibit positive–negative affect such as vocal pleasantness, smiling, nodding, and relaxed laughter and engaging–avoiding behaviors as cues indicative of involvement–noninvolvement. We might pose the following research question: What are the effects of positive affect and involvement during a conflict interaction on relationship satisfaction? We might also want to investigate couples who interact in ways that are counter to their relationship definition. We might expect that couples who believe in engaging in conflict directly and speaking one's mind would be less communicatively satisfied if they used an avoidant or noninvolved style of interaction. Similarly, we might expect that couples who tend to avoid conflicts might be less communicatively satisfied if they are confronted with a partner who engages in conflict and demonstrates high levels of involvement. Thus, we also might pose the following research question: Are traditional marital types who engage in more involvement during conflict less communicatively satisfied than traditionals who engage in less involvement? Likewise, are independent marital types who engage in less involvement during conflict less communicatively satisfied than independents who engage in more involvement?

To investigate these questions in our sample experiment, we need to consider several things. The sample—who will be in our sample, what criteria will we use to select participants, and how will we classify people into the traditional and independent marital types? Procedures—what will be our general procedures for conducting this study and what will be the procedure for eliciting conflict between participants? How will we record the conflict interaction? What nonverbal behaviors will be coded and who will code the nonverbal data? What measure(s) will be used to assess relationship satisfaction and communication satisfaction? What will be the instructions for the manipulation (e.g., what instructions will be given for being more or less involved)? How will we determine whether or not participants followed the instructions? How will we analyze the data?

Specifically, we could recruit marital couples who have been married for more than two years and have never sought marital counseling or therapy to participate in this research experiment. Participants might be asked to interact in a comfortable setting that approximates a living room environment (or even their own living room). They might complete the Kansas Marital Satisfaction Scale (Schumm, Nichols, Schectman, & Grigsby, 1983; Schumm, Scanlon, Crow, Green, & Buckler, 1983) to assess the level of relationship satisfaction and the Relational Dimensions Instrument to classify couples as traditional or independent (Fitzpatrick, 1988). Couples who are classified into other marital types beyond the two types used in this investigation would be excluded from the analyses. After completing the Relational Dimensions Instrument, the couples could individually list topics of their conflicts and rate those conflicts on a scale of major to minor importance and high salience to low salience to the relationship. Comparisons of these two lists of conflict topics should yield a single topic of moderate importance and salience to both partners. Couples then might be asked to reenact the most recent conflict on that topic and to provide background information, such as when and where the conflict took place. Couples could be separated so that one member of each couple might be given instructions and training on how to behave during the interaction (either using an involving or noninvolving style).

Once reunited, couples might engage in the reenactment of the conflict while being videotaped. Following the conflict interaction, couples could be separated to assess their level of communication satisfaction using an interpersonal communication satisfaction measure (Hecht, 1978). Couples could then review their videotapes and rate their own and their partner's nonverbal behaviors (i.e., the level of involvement and the positive–negative affect cues following consideration of micro- and macromeasurement issues). Two trained outside observers could also rate the same nonverbal behaviors for both partners. The outsider observers' assessment of involvement would determine whether or not participants followed instructions. Statistical analyses would address the correspondence between partners' behaviors and the links among behavior-patterns, couple type, couple satisfaction, and communication satisfaction.

CONCLUSION

Understanding nonverbal communication entails recognition that research and theorizing in this field is based on a diverse foundation of interests. In this chapter, we sampled the vast array of approaches and methods for studying nonverbal communication to better appreciate the richness and complexity of research in this area. We gave special attention to the communicative function of relational communication, demonstrating how nonverbal scholars have sought to understand relationships through people's nonverbal behavior. In addition, we examined important decision points for those interested in research methods used in the study of nonverbal communication. Finally, we discussed a specific sample experiment to demonstrate how one might conduct a study on the nonverbal aspects of relational conflicts.

Other areas likely to attract increasing research attention are significant nonverbal events in relationships that affect the direction of a relationship's development, infrequent nonverbal events, and expected but omitted nonverbal cues as relational statements. For instance, the first time you and a potential romantic partner hold hands may signal an escalation in the relationship, or the one time that you yell and slam your fist into the wall during a conflict may signal a downward trend in your relationship. The absence of a goodbye kiss may be more telling to a spouse about the intimacy of the marriage than any other cue present. Nonverbal behaviors that are rarely performed or intermittent behaviors are likely to receive more attention as researchers try to find ways of capturing or observing them. Also, descriptions of the frequency and duration of specific relational cues, their sequences and cycles over time, the interrelatedness among cues, and changes in relational meaning depending on their placement in the relational trajectory are choice areas of investigation. The previous overemphasis on single cue and static analyses will doubtless give way to analyzing the interplay among multiple cues, longitudinal patterns, and the impact of those patterns on relational outcomes such as commitment and satisfaction.

As we explore these areas of study, we must recognize that answers to our questions may come from a diverse set of literatures and a variety of scholarly fields. Integration of research and theorizing on nonverbal communication can only aid in our search to better understand our nonverbal communication. Nonverbal researchers have only begun to tap this rich area of study as they strive to fully depict the role of nonverbal communication in the process of relationship communication and management.

REFERENCES

Altman, I., & Taylor, D. A. (1973). *Social penetration: The development of interpersonal relationships.* New York: Holt, Rinehart & Winston.

Archer, D., & Akert, R. M. (1977). Words and everything else: Verbal and nonverbal cues in social interpretation. *Journal of Personality and Social Psychology, 35,* 443–449.

Archer, D., & Costanzo, M. (1988). *The interpersonal perception task.* Berkeley, CA: University of California Extension Media Center.

Bavelas, J. B. (1990). Behaving and communicating: A reply to Motley. *Western Journal of Speech Communication, 54,* 593–602.

Baxter, L. A. (1992). Forms and functions of intimate play in personal relationships. *Human Communication Research, 18,* 336–363.

Berger, J., Rosenholtz, S. J., & Zelditch, M., Jr. (1980). Status organizing processes. *Annual Review of Sociology, 6,* 479–508.

Burgoon, J. K. (1980). Nonverbal communication in the 1970s: An overview. In D. Nimmo (Ed.), *Communication yearbook* (Vol. 4, pp. 179–197). New Brunswick, NJ: Transaction Books.

Burgoon, J. K. (1982). Privacy and communication. In M. Burgoon (Ed.), *Communication yearbook* (Vol. 6, pp. 206–249). Newbury Park, CA: Sage.

Burgoon, J. K. (1991). Relational message interpretations of touch, conversational distance, and posture. *Journal of Nonverbal Behavior, 15,* 233–259.

Burgoon, J. K. (1994). Nonverbal signals. In M. L. Knapp & G. R. Miller (Eds.), *Handbook of interpersonal communication* (2nd ed., pp. 229–285). Thousand Oaks, CA: Sage.

Burgoon, J. K., & Baesler, E. J. (1991). Choosing between micro and macro nonverbal measurement: Application to selected vocalic and kinesic indices. *Journal of Nonverbal Behavior, 15,* 57–78.

Burgoon, J. K., Buller, D. B., Hale, J. L., & deTurck, M. A. (1984). Relational messages associated with nonverbal behaviors. *Human Communication Research, 10,* 351–378.

Burgoon, J. K., Buller, D. B., & Woodall, W. G. (1989). *Nonverbal communication: The unspoken dialogue.* New York: HarperCollins.

Burgoon, J. K., Buller, D. B., & Woodall, W. G. (1994). *Nonverbal Communication: The unspoken dialogue* (2nd ed.). New York: Harper Collins.

Burgoon, J. K., & Dillman, L. (1995). Gender, immediacy and nonverbal communication. In P. J. Kalbfleisch (Ed.), *Gender, power, and communication in human relationships* (pp. 63–81). Hillsdale, NJ: Lawrence Erlbaum Associates.

Burgoon, J. K., & Hale, J. L. (1984). The fundamental topoi of relational communication. *Communication Monographs*, *51*, 193–214.

Burgoon, J. K., & Hale, J. L. (1987). Validation and measurement of the fundamental themes of relational communication. *Communication Monographs*, *54*, 19–41.

Burgoon, J. K., & Newton, D. A. (1991). Applying a social meaning model to relational messages of conversational involvement: Comparing participant and observer perspectives. *Southern Communication Journal, 56*, 96–113.

Burgoon, J. K., Parrott, R., Le Poire, B., Kelley, D., Walther, J., & Perry, D. (1989). Privacy and communication: Maintaining and restoring privacy through communication. *Journal of Personal and Social Relationships*, *6*, 131–158.

Burgoon, J. K., Pfau, M., Parrott, R., Birk, T., Coker, R., & Burgoon, M. (1987). Relational communication, satisfaction, compliance-gaining strategies and compliance in communication between physicians and patients. *Communication Monographs*, *54*, 307–324.

Burman, B., Margolin, G., & John, R. S. (1993). America's angriest home videos: Behavioral contingencies observed in home reenactments of marital conflict. *Journal of Consulting and Clinical Psychology*, *61*, 28–39.

Cappella, J. N. (1983). Conversational involvement: Approaching and avoiding others. In J. M. Wiemann & R. P. Harrison (Eds.), *Nonverbal interaction* (pp. 113–148). Beverly Hills, CA: Sage.

Cappella, J. N. (1994). The management of conversational interaction in adults and infants. In M. L. Knapp & G. R. Miller (Eds.), *Handbook of interpersonal communication* (2nd ed., pp. 380–418). Thousand Oaks, CA: Sage.

Coker, D. A., & Burgoon, J. K. (1987). The nature of conversational involvement and nonverbal encoding patterns. *Human Communication Research, 13*, 463–494.

Cupach, W. R., & Metts, S. (1986). Accounts of relational dissolution. *Communication Monographs*, *53*, 311–334.

Ellsworth, P. C., & Ludwig, L. M. (1972). Visual behavior in social interaction. *Journal of Communication, 22*, 375–401.

Exline, R. V., & Fehr, B. J. (1978). Applications of semiosis to the study of visual interaction. In A. W. Siegman & S. Feldstein (Eds.), *Nonverbal behavior and communication* (pp. 117–157). Hillsdale, NJ: Lawrence Erlbaum Associates.

Fitzpatrick, M. A. (1988). *Between husbands and wives: Communication in marriage*. Newbury Park, CA: Sage.

Floyd, F. J., & Markman, H. J. (1983). Observational biases in spouse observation: Toward a cognitive/behavioral model of marriage. *Journal of Consulting and Clinical Psychology*, *51*, 450–457.

Friedman, H. S., Prince, L. M., Riggio, R. E., & DiMatteo, M. R. (1980). Understanding and assessing nonverbal expressiveness: The affective communication test. *Journal of Personality and Social Psychology*, *39*, 333–351.

Givens, D. B. (1978). The nonverbal basis of attraction: Flirtation, courtship, and seduction. *Psychiatry*, *41*, 346–359.

Givens, D. B. (1983). *Love signals*. New York: Crown.

Gottman, J. M. (1979). *Marital interaction: Experimental investigations*. New York: Academy Press.

Gottman, J. M., Markman, H., & Notarius, C. (1977). The topography of marital conflict: A sequential analysis of verbal and nonverbal behavior. *Journal of Marriage and the Family*, *39*, 461–477.

Guerrero, L. K. (1994). *An application of attachment theory to relational messages and nonverbal involvement behaviors in romantic relationships*. Unpublished doctoral dissertation. University of Arizona, Tucson.

Guerrero, L. K., & Andersen, P. A. (1991). The waxing and waning of relational intimacy: Touch as a function of relational stage, gender, and touch avoidance. *Journal of Social and Personal Relationships*, *8*, 147–165.

Hecht, M. L. (1978). The conceptualization and measurement of interpersonal communication satisfaction. *Human Communication Research*, *4*, 253–264.

Hendrick, S., & Hendrick, C. (1992). *Liking, loving, & relating* (2nd ed.). Pacific Grove, CA: Brooks/Cole.

Henley, N. M. (1977). *Body politics: Power, sex and nonverbal communication.* Englewood Cliffs, NJ: Prentice-Hall.

Heslin, R., & Alper, T. (1983). Touch: A bonding gesture. In J. M. Wiemann & R. P. Harrison (Eds.), *Nonverbal interaction* (pp. 47–75). Beverly Hills, CA: Sage.

Jones, S. E. (1991). Problems of validity in questionnaire studies of nonverbal behavior: Jourard's Tactile Body-Accessibility Scale. *Southern Communication Journal, 56,* 83–95.

Jones, S. E., & Yarbrough, A. E. (1985). A naturalistic study of the meanings of touch. *Communication Monographs, 52,* 19–56.

Kahn, M. (1970). Nonverbal communication and marital satisfaction. *Family Process, 9,* 449–456.

Kelley, D. L., & Burgoon, J. K. (1991). Understanding marital satisfaction and couple type as functions of relational expectations. *Human Communication Research, 18,* 40–69.

Knapp, M. L. (1983). Dyadic relationship development. In J. M. Wiemann & R. P. Harrison (Eds.), *Nonverbal interaction* (pp. 179–207). Beverly Hills, CA: Sage.

Knapp, M. L. (1984). The study of nonverbal behavior vis-a-vis human communication theory. In A. Wolfgang (Ed.), *Nonverbal behavior: Perspectives, applications, and intercultural insights* (pp. 15–40). Toronto, Canada: Hogrefe.

Knapp, M. L., & Hall, J. A. (1992). *Nonverbal communication in human interaction* (3rd ed.). Ft. Worth, TX: Holt, Rinehart & Winston.

Kramer, I., Alloway, T., & Pliner, P. (Eds.). (1975). *Nonverbal communication of aggression.* New York: Plenum.

Le Poire, B., & Burgoon, J. K. (1994). Two contrasting explanations of involvement violations: Expectancy violations theory versus discrepancy arousal theory. *Human Communication Research, 20,* 560–591.

Manusov, V. (1990). An application of attribution principles to nonverbal behaviors in romantic dyads. *Communication Monographs, 57,* 104–118.

Mehrabian, A. (1972). *Nonverbal communication.* Chicago: Aldine-Atherton.

Mehrabian, A. (1981). *Silent messages.* Belmont, CA: Wadsworth.

Millar, F. E., & Rogers, L. E. (1987). Relational dimensions of interpersonal dynamics. In M. E. Roloff & G. R. Miller (Eds.), *Interpersonal processes: New directions in communication research* (pp. 140–171). Newbury Park, CA: Sage.

Newton, D. A., & Burgoon, J. K. (1990). Nonverbal conflict behaviors: Functions, strategies, and tactics. In D. D. Cahn (Ed.), *Intimates in conflict* (pp. 77–104). Hillsdale, NJ: Lawrence Erlbaum Associates.

Noller, P. (1980). Misunderstanding in marital communication: A study of couples' nonverbal communication. *Journal of Personality and Social Psychology, 39,* 1135–1148.

Noller, P., & Ruzzene, M. (1991). Communication in marriage: The influence of affect and cognition. In G. J. Fletcher & F. D. Fincham (Eds.), *Cognition in close relationships* (pp. 203–233). Hillsdale, NJ: Lawrence Erlbaum Associates.

Noller, P., & Venardos, C. (1986). Communication awareness in married couples. *Journal of Social and Personal Relationships, 3,* 31–42.

Ogawa, D. M. (1973). *Jan ken po: The world of Hawaii's Japanese Americans.* Honolulu, HI: University of Hawaii Press.

Palmer, M. T. (1989). Controlling conversation: Turns, topics and interpersonal control. *Communication Monographs, 56,* 1–18.

Patterson, M. L. (1973). Compensation in nonverbal immediacy behaviors: A review. *Sociometry, 36,* 237–257.

Patterson, M. L. (1983). *Nonverbal behavior: A functional perspective.* New York: Springer Verlag.

Pike, G. R., & Sillars, A. L. (1985). Reciprocity of marital communication. *Journal of Social and Personal Relationships, 2,* 303–324.

Planalp, S., & Benson, A. (1992). Friends' and acquaintances' conversations I: Perceived differences. *Journal of Social and Personal Relationships, 9,* 483–506.

Register, L. M., & Henley, T. B. (1992). The phenomenology of intimacy. *Journal of Social and Personal Relationships, 9,* 467–481.

Ridgeway, C. L., Berger, J., & Smith, L. (1985). Nonverbal cues and status: An expectation states approach. *American Journal of Sociology, 90,* 955–978.

Riggio, R. E. (1986). Assessment of basic social skills. *Journal of Personality and Social Psychology, 51,* 649–660.

Rosenthal, R., Hall, J. A., DiMatteo, M. R., Rogers, P. L., & Archer, D. (1979). *Sensitivity to nonverbal communication: The PONS test.* Baltimore: John Hopkins University Press.

Rusbult, C. E., Drigotas, S. M., & Verette, J. (1994). The investment model: An interdependence analysis of commitment processes and relationship maintenance phenomena. In D. J. Canary & L. Stafford (Eds.), *Communication and relational maintenance* (pp. 115–139). San Diego, CA: Academic Press.

Rusbult, C. E., Verette, J., Whitney, G. A., Slovik, L. F., & Lipkus, I. (1991). Accommodation processes in close relationships: Theory and preliminary empirical evidence. *Journal of Personality and Social Psychology, 60,* 53–78.

Rusbult, C. E., & Zembrodt, I. M. (1983). Responses to dissatisfaction in romantic involvements: A multidimensional scaling analysis. *Journal of Experimental Social Psychology, 19,* 274–293.

Scheflen, A. E. (1965). Quasi-courtship behavior in psychotherapy. *Psychiatry, 28,* 245–257.

Scheflen, A. E. (1974). *How behavior means.* Garden City, NY: Doubleday.

Schumm, W. R., Nichols, C. W., Schectman, & Grigsby, C. C. (1983). Characteristics of responses to the Kansas Marital Satisfaction Scale by a sample of 84 married mothers. *Psychological Reports, 53,* 567–572.

Schumm, W. R., Scanlon, E. D., Crow, C. L., Green, G. M., & Buckler, D. L. (1983). Characteristics of the Kansas Marital Satisfaction Scale in a sample of 79 married couples. *Psychological Reports, 53,* 583–588.

Shea, B. C., & Pearson, J. C. (1986). The effects of relationship type, partner intent, and gender on the selection of relationship maintenance strategies. *Communication Monographs, 53,* 352–364.

Siegman, A. W. (1978). The telltale voice: Nonverbal messages of verbal communication. In A. W. Siegman & S. Feldstein (Eds.), *Nonverbal behavior and communication* (pp. 183–243). Hillsdale, NJ: Lawrence Erlbaum Associates.

Sillars, A. L., Coletti, S. F., Parry, D., & Rogers, M. A. (1982). Coding verbal conflict tactics: Nonverbal and perceptual correlates of the "avoidance-distributive-integrative" distinction. *Human Communication Research, 9,* 83–95.

Sillars, A. L., & Weisberg, J. (1987). Conflict as a social skill. In M. E. Roloff & G. R. Miller (Eds.), *Interpersonal processes: New directions in communication research* (pp. 140–171). Newbury Park, CA: Sage.

Simpson, J. A., Gangestad, S. W., & Biek, M. (1993). *Journal of Experimental Social Psychology, 29,* 434–461.

Street, R. L., Jr., Mulac, A., & Wiemann, J. M. (1988). Speech evaluation differences as a function of perspective (participant versus observer) and presentational medium. *Human Communication Research, 14,* 333–363.

Thayer, S. (Ed.). (1986). The psychology of touch [special issue]. *Journal of Nonverbal Behavior, 10.*

Ting-Toomey, S. (1983). An analysis of verbal communication patterns in high and low marital adjustment groups. *Human Communication Research, 9,* 306–319.

Trimboli, A., & Walker, M. (1993). The CAST test of nonverbal sensitivity. *Journal of Language and Social Psychology, 12,* 49–65.

Tolhuizen, J. H. (1989). Communication strategies for intensifying dating relationships: Identification, use and structure. *Journal of Social and Personal Relationships, 6,* 413–434.

Wagner, H. L, & Smith, J. (1991). Facial expression in the presence of friends and strangers. *Journal of Nonverbal Behavior, 15,* 201–214.

Watzlawick, P., Beavin, J. H., & Jackson, D. D. (1967). *Pragmatics of human communication: A study of interactional patterns, pathologies, and paradoxes.* New York: Norton.

Zuckerman, M., & Larrance, D. T. (1979). Individual differences in perceived encoding and decoding abilities. In R. Rosenthal (Ed.), *Skill in nonverbal communication: Individual differences* (pp. 171–203). Cambridge, MA: Oelgeschlager, Gunn, & Hain.

23

Small Group Communication

Randy Y. Hirokawa
University of Iowa

Abran J. Salazar
Texas A&M University

Larry Erbert
University of Iowa

Richard J. Ice
St. John's College

It is difficult to say precisely when the systematic study of small group communication began. Early interest in group communication dates at least to the pioneering work of sociologist Kurt Lewin (1947) on the influence of small group processes on members' attitudes and behaviors, as well as Robert Freed Bales's (1950) landmark research on group interaction analysis. In their comprehensive review of the small group communication literature, Dennis Gouran and colleagues (Gouran, Hirokawa, McGee, & Miller, 1994) identify the mid-1960s as the approximate starting point of group *communication* research. They note that "prior to 1965, a limited amount of scholarship about groups produced in communication would qualify as research . . . most writing about group processes did so from a pedagogical perspective" (p. 242).

In the three decades since the first published studies of group communication, research on and theorizing about small group communication emerged as major facets of the field of communication. This chapter provides a general overview of the group communication literature as it has emerged in the field of communication.

EARLY RESEARCH

In communication studies, the first published study of group *communication* is credited to Edwin Black (1955), who examined interaction sequences in decision-making discussions to determine the causes of breakdowns in group deliberation. It was not until the mid-1960s, however, that studies of group communication appeared regularly in communication journals. In 1964, Thomas Scheidel and Laura Crowell published a study of idea development in group discussions. Their investigation utilized the innovative interaction analysis method proposed by Bales (1950) to analyze the role of communication in idea development in group deliberation. This was followed by research examining feedback sequences (Scheidel & Crowell, 1966), communicative traits of leaders (Geier, 1967), and thematic development of ideas in group discussion (Berg, 1967).

Increased emphasis on the communicative aspects of small groups continued with the publication of landmark studies by Dennis Gouran (1969) and B. Aubrey Fisher (1970), who focused on the relationship between communication and consensus formation in decision-making groups—albeit from different perspectives. Gouran attempted to distinguish groups achieving consensus from those failing to achieve consensus on the basis of specific communication variables, whereas Fisher was concerned with discovering how consensus is reached during group discussion. In short, Gouran was interested in identifying the communication *predictors* of consensus formation, while Fisher was more interested in identifying the communication *sequences* that lead to consensus among group members. Dale Leathers (1969, 1970) also began a research program examining the relationship between communication variables and group decision-making, and problem-solving performance.

EMERGENT LINES OF RESEARCH

The study of small group communication hit its full stride in the 1970s. Between 1970 and 1978 alone, a total of 114 studies dealing with groups were published in communication journals (Cragan & Wright, 1980). That number increased by an additional 89 articles by 1990 (Cragan & Wright, 1990). In short, during the time that small group research in allied fields such as social psychology were dwindling (Steiner, 1974), research on group communication emerged as a major facet of communication studies scholarship.

Most small group communication research can be classified into five major lines of research: (a) effective teaching of group discussion skills, (b) the communicative aspects of group leadership, (c) effective group discussion methods, (d) characteristics of group interaction processes, and (e) the relationship between communication variables and group outcomes (Cragan & Wright, 1980, 1990).

This chapter overviews the five lines of investigation. Its intent is not to provide an exhaustive summary of the literature, but, rather, to paint in broad strokes the landscape that is called "group communication" research.

Discussion Pedagogy Research

One of the earliest lines of group communication research focused on teaching group communication and discussion skills. Among the various research studies published in this area were those by Bormann (1970), focusing on the best strategy for teaching group discussion skills; Shields and Kidd (1973), exploring the use of media and film to teach group problem-solving and decision-making skills; Knutson, Wheeless, and Divers (1977), investigating teachable group communication behaviors; Jurma and Froelich (1984), examining the advantages of providing immediate videotape feedback of group discussion performance; Schultz and Anderson (1984), presenting a peda-gogical model for teaching students how to argue more constructively and effectively in group conflict situations; and Phillips and Santoro (1989), investigating the effec-tiveness of computer-mediated communication systems (such as e-mail and modified electronic bulletin boards) to teach group discussion and problem-solving skills.

Leadership Research

In terms of sheer numbers of published articles, group leadership is probably the most studied aspect of small group communication (Cragan & Wright, 1980, 1990). Gouran's (1970) review of communication-oriented leadership research provides a useful framework for organizing and classifying research in this area. Gouran identified four major approaches to the study of group leadership: *trait, style, situational, and functional.*

Trait Approach.   Many of the early studies focused on the individual qualities (or personal characteristics) of leaders, and attempted to produce prescriptive lists of communication traits for effective leadership. The trait approach is exemplified by John Geier's (1967) study of emergent group leader communication traits. Geier was interested in identifying the personal attributes that distinguish emergent group leaders from other members of the group.

Studying 16 leaderless groups using a combination of three different research methods—observation of group interaction, interviews with group members, and analysis of diaries kept by group members—Geier found that group leaders emerge through a two-stage process. First, group members rejected certain individuals who aspire to the leadership position on the basis of particular "negative" communication attributes or traits. Specifically, groups rejected leadership candidates because they were "uninformed about the task," "nonparticipants," or "overly rigid." Second, group members selected among the remaining candidates on the basis of both positive and negative personal attributes. Those rejected in this second stage were eliminated because they were too "authoritarian" or engaged in "excessive verbalization" (e.g., talking too much). In contrast, the person who emerged as the leader was selected because of her or his demonstrated concern for the group and its members.

Subsequent studies used Geier's findings as a basis for further trait-oriented re-search. These investigations revealed several additional communication traits related to group leadership, including talkativeness (Morris & Hackman, 1969), argumenta-tiveness (Schultz, 1982), and humor (Smith & Powell, 1988).

Style Approach.   The style approach to group leadership research was also concerned with the personal characteristics of group leaders. However, unlike the trait approach, which examined the communication *predispositions* of leaders, the style approach focused on the *behaviors* displayed by leaders in the process of exercising leadership. This line of research can be traced back to Lewin.

In 1939, Lewin and two of his students, Ronald Lippett and Ralph White, conducted a landmark study (Lewin, Lippeth, & White, 1939) of the effects of leadership styles on various aspects of a group. The purpose of their study was to determine whether different leadership styles would affect the socioemotional and task output of a group. Four five-member groups comprised of 10-year-old boys were exposed to three different styles of leadership: a "democratic style," in which the leader explained the group's task and helped the group formulate policies and procedures to complete the project; an "autocratic" style, in which the leader determined all policies for the group and told members what to do and how to do it; and a "laissez-faire" style, in which the leader did nothing to facilitate the group's efforts to complete its task.

Lewin et al. found that the democratic leadership style led to greater member satisfaction than either the autocratic or laissez-faire styles; the democratic style led to greater group cohesiveness than either the autocratic or laissez-faire styles; and both the democratic and autocratic styles were associated with higher work output than the laissez-faire style. The researchers thus concluded that, overall, the democratic style of leadership is the best of the three styles examined.

Over the years, a number of researchers have extended Lewin et al.'s pioneering study in various directions. Many sought to obtain a clearer understanding of the specific communication behaviors (Sargent & Miller, 1971) and personality traits (Rosenfeld & Fowler, 1976; Rosenfeld & Plax, 1975; Yerby, 1975) associated with different styles of leadership. Researchers also tried to explain why different leadership styles contribute to differences in socioemotional and task outputs in groups (Downs & Pickett, 1977; Shaw, 1955; Wood, 1977). As a result, we now have sufficient empirical data to reconsider the idea that the democratic style of leadership is always the best.

Situational Approach.   The situational approach to group leadership research is based on the notion that people can assume positions of leadership only if their skills and abilities match the requirements of a particular group situation. If conditions change, and different requirements emerge, other group members may have to assume the position of group leader. According to this view, then, great leaders are not born; rather, they find themselves in circumstances particularly suited for their respective talents. For example, while Napoleon's military genius was particularly well-suited for 19th-century France, it would not be as suitable for 19th- or 20th-century India. Hence, although Napoleon is recognized as one of the great leaders of France, it is questionable whether he would have been as effective a leader of India as, say, Gandhi.

Hersey and Blanchard's (1982) research on effective leadership styles represents a good exemplar of the situation approach. The authors separate leadership behaviors into task and relationship dimensions. The degrees of task and relationship behaviors used by a leader are dependent upon the maturity level of the group (i.e., the degree of established norms, procedures, and ongoing history). Hersey and Blanchard identified four communicative styles that can be employed by group leaders depending upon the maturity level of the group. Immature groups that display high task requirements and low relational requirements are usually best led by a leader who tells the members what to do, while leaders of mature groups with low task and relational needs should *delegate*. Leaders in moderately mature groups with high task and relational needs use the *selling* strategy, while *participation* is used by leaders of moderately mature groups with high relational needs and low task needs.

Functional Approach.   The fourth major approach to group leadership research is the functional approach. This approach attempts to identify communicative behaviors that perform specific leadership duties or roles. Two functional approaches seem to dominate the literature: leadership as influencing and leadership as organizing.

Shaw (1981) defined *leadership* as a positive influence that assists a group in attaining its goal. Gouran (1982) further focused the influence perspective by identifying the primary leadership function as counteractive influence. That is, group leaders counteract negative influences that lead a group away from its goal. Thus, the leader is the group member who keeps the group on the goal path, enabling the group to reach its desired outcomes.

An innovative functional approach to the study of group leadership, initially advanced by Karl Weick (1978, 1979) and later elaborated by B. Aubrey Fisher (1985, 1986) and J. Kevin Barge (1989, 1992), focuses on leadership as a form of organizing. Weick (1978, 1979) argued that task groups must do their work in a complex environment characterized by varying degrees of informational equivocality (or uncertainty). He argues that this equivocality must be properly managed if the group is to complete its task in a satisfactory manner. Failure to do so, he claims, will often result in a group's inability to take appropriate action (performance paralysis). According to Weick, group leadership involves the management of complexity and equivocality facing the group. For example, the jury in the controversial O. J. Simpson double-murder trial was undoubtedly faced with a very complex case—one involving massive amounts of technical scientific and forensic data. It is quite understandable how the members of this jury could easily get overwhelmed by, and lost in, this sea of data to the point where they might be unable to unanimously reach a decision regarding guilt or innocence. If Weick is correct, then the jury's ability to reach a unanimous not guilty verdict depended on the ability of some individual (or individuals) to provide leadership by helping the group to simplify the complex information provided to its lowest denominator (i.e., the facts of the case most crucial to making a decision on the guilt or innocence of the defendant).

Barge (1992) recently identified organizing functions that group leaders use when attending to input information. His model breaks leadership into three processes: sense making, decision making, and performance. Leaders need to be able to make sense of the informational inputs through the use of networking, data-splitting, and dialectical thinking skills. Further, leaders must possess the ability to help the group decide what information to utilize in reaching decisions. Finally, leaders must be able to guide and assist the group in performing behaviors that are appropriate and effective for successful group outcomes.

Discussion Methods Research

A third major line of group communication research centers on the study of effective group discussion methods. Early research assessed the effectiveness of various discussion formats and procedures for facilitating group problem-solving and decision-making outcomes (Larson, 1971). Among the discussion techniques examined were *brainstorming* (Jablin, Seibold, & Sorenson, 1977; Jablin, Sorenson, & Seibold, 1978; Philipsen, Mulac, & Dietrich, 1979), *Delphi method* (Delbec, Van de Ven, & Gustafson, 1975), PERT (Applbaum & Anatol, 1971; Phillips, 1966), *reflective* thinking (Bayless, 1967; Brilhart & Jochem, 1964; Larson, 1969), and *T-groups* (Larson & Gratz, 1970).

The central concern of these early studies was to identify the most effective discussion procedures. The findings of these studies, bolstered by the results of more recent investigations (Burleson, Levine, & Samter, 1984; Comadena, 1984; Hiltz, Johnson, & Turoff, 1986; Hirokawa, 1985; Jablin, 1981; Jarboe, 1988), suggest strongly that the discussion procedures used by a group in problem-solving or decision-making are not necessarily a determinant to effective group performance. Hirokawa (1985), for example, compared four different discussion formats (reflective thinking, single question, ideal solution, and free discussion) and found no difference among them in terms of their association with high-quality decisions. Similarly, Jarboe (1988) compared the reflective thinking format to the nominal group technique to determine which better facilitated group decision-making. She found that the nominal group technique led to a greater number of ideas than the reflective thinking procedure, but that the two procedures did not differ in terms of the uniqueness or quality of the ideas it produced. Hiltz et al. (1986) compared computerized conferences and face-to-face discussion procedures. They found that both discussion formats produced equally good decisions, although group members found it more difficult to reach consensus in a computerized conference.

What appears to matter most is whether the use of such techniques or procedures enable the group to satisfy critical functions in the problem-solving or decision-making process (Gouran, 1982; Gouran & Hirokawa, 1986; Hirokawa, 1982, 1983, 1987; Janis & Mann, 1977). In particular, Hirokawa (1985) maintained that any group discussion procedure is likely to result in successful group decision-making if it enables the group to satisfy the following three functions: understand the nature of its problem thoroughly and accurately, consider a range of realistic and acceptable alternatives, and assess, both the positive and negative aspects of alternative choices. According to Cragan and Wright (1990), this neodiscussion perspective takes the stance that the type of discussion format employed by a group must fit the functional demands of the task presented to the group if it is to be effective in facilitating group performance.

Interaction Characteristics Research

A fourth major line of research, spanning nearly three decades of scholarship, focuses on the processual characteristics of group communication. Two related although discernable foci characterized this line of inquiry: studies examining the interactional structure of group discussion, and studies examining the developmental nature of group discussion.

Interactional Structure. In 1971, B. Aubrey Fisher and Leonard Hawes wrote an influential article (Fisher & Hawes, 1971) in which they argued, among other things, that the primary concern of small group communication scholars should be the study of repetitive sequences of communication acts, and how the sequences become patterned over time. This interactional focus prompted researchers to determine whether group discussion is characterized by discernible structure (or patterns) of communication acts. John Baird (1974), for example, compared the discussions of cooperative and competitive groups. He found evidence suggesting that certain patterns of interaction tend to occur in all group discussions (e.g., questions asking for information followed by statements providing information; statements initiating or developing an idea followed by questions asking for clarification or information). At the same time, Baird also discovered patterns of interaction occurred more frequently in either the cooperative or competitive discussions. Baird found, for example, that statements expressing agreement were followed by statements expressing disagreement far more often in the competitive than cooperative groups. This suggests that conflicts were more prevalent in the competitive groups.

Other investigations have likewise explored the interactional structure of groups. Gouran and Baird (1972) compared the interactional structure of task and non-task groups; Saine and Bock (1973) compared the interactional structure of high- and low-consensus groups; and Saine, Schulman, and Emerson (1974) examined the interactional structure of groups of varying sizes.

By and large, these various investigations support the notion that communication in groups consists of nonrandom acts that tend to display repetitive patterns of interaction. In other words, the utterances of group members tend to follow each other in predictable ways such that it is often possible to anticipate what a group member will say if we know what another has said previously.

Developmental Structure. The study of group interaction development traces its roots to the work of Bales in the 1950s. Bales (1950, 1953) theorized that a group must solve three problems—orientation (gaining a mutual understanding of the task), evaluation (forming mutual values for assessing optional courses of action), and control (reaching a consensus on the best course of action)—and solve them sequentially—in order to successfully perform its task. This proposition, known as the phase hypothesis of group discussion, became the guiding notion behind nearly three decades of research.

In 1951, Bales and Strodtbeck (1951) tested the phase hypothesis by dividing the discussions of groups into three equal time segments. They then compared the frequency of different communicative acts found in each of the time segments to determine whether the segments could be qualitatively distinguished on the basis of the relative frequency of different acts. They found that the first time segment often contained a greater proportion of utterances asking for, and providing, information than the second and third segments. In contrast, they found that the second time segment was generally characterized by a greater proportion of utterances asking for, and giving, opinions than either the first or third segments. Finally, the third segment was characterized by proportionately more utterances asking for, and giving, suggestions than the first or second segments. Bales and Strodtbeck interpreted these findings as supportive of the phase hypothesis and, in so doing, left a legacy for future researchers (Pavitt & Curtis, 1990, p. 231).

Laura Crowell and Thomas Scheidel were among the first group communication scholars to investigative the developmental nature of group discussion (Crowell & Scheidel, 1961; Scheidel & Crowell, 1964). Unlike Bales and Strodtbeck, however, Crowell and Scheidel adopted a more microlevel focus by restricting their analysis to the development of ideas within the group discussion process. Further, unlike Bales and Strodtbeck, who focused on both task and socioemotional acts, Crowell and Scheidel focused exclusively on task-relevant utterances. Finally, instead of partitioning the group discussion into time segments, Crowell and Scheidel examined the development of ideas through the entire discussion process.

Crowell and Scheidel's research provided evidence indicating that the sequential development of ideas in discussion resembled a "forward-moving spiral." That is, group members first demonstrated a "reaching out" process, where they initiated a new idea or extended an existing one, then attempted to "test" this new or modified idea by soliciting evaluation of it. If the group eventually agreed that the idea was a sound one, it became an anchor point for the discussion and the reach-test process was reinitiated from that point. If, however, the new or modified idea received negative evaluation, the group returned to a previous anchor point to reach-test in a different direction. In short, Crowell and Scheidel's spiral model of idea development posited that group members tend to cycle back to previous topics of discussion as they move forward in elaborating current ideas and notions.

In the 1970s, several group communication researchers followed Bales and Strodtbeck's lead in examining the developmental nature of group interaction. Fisher (1970), for instance, studied the developmental nature of group discussion leading to consensus group decisions. His research provided evidence suggesting that decision-making groups go through a four-phase process in reaching consensus. He labeled these stages *orientation, conflict, emergence,* and *reinforcement.* In the orientation phase, utterances asking for, and providing, clarification were at their peak; in the conflict phase, evaluative comments and comments expressing disagreements tended to dominate the discussion; in the emergence phase, disagreements dropped off dramatically and comments providing support for particular ideas increased in frequency; and in the reinforcement phase, comments providing support and reinforcement of ideas dominated the discussion. In short, Fisher's orientation phase was nearly identical to Bales and Strodtbeck's orientation phase; his conflict phase was similar to Bales and Strodtbeck's evaluation phase; and his emergence and reinforcement phases roughly coincided with Bales and Strodtbeck's control phase.

Other researchers (Cheseboro, Cragan, & McCullough, 1973; Ellis & Fisher, 1975; Mabry, 1975a, 1975b) utilized different sets of communication variables to investigate the developmental nature of group interaction in the tradition of Bales and Stroudtbeck's phase research. The findings of these descriptive studies formed the corpus of a theoretical model of group interaction development referred to as the "unitary sequence model" (Poole, 1981). In essence, the model embraced Bales' phase hypothesis and posited that all groups display the same phases (or stages) of discussion development as they move toward completion of their task.

Interestingly, while unitary sequence model advocates embrace the notions of universal phases and a universal sequence of phases, they do not necessarily agree on the precise labels for those stages of development, nor do they necessarily agree on the number or sequential order of those phases. This recognition prompted Marshall Scott Poole to propose an alternative model of group interaction development that, in his view, "provides a richer and more complete description of developmental processes in task groups" (Poole, 1983, p. 326). In a series of studies, Poole and his colleagues provided empirical evidence challenging the unitary sequence model's notion that all groups move through the same phases of development in the same sequential order (Poole, 1981, 1983; Poole & Roth, 1989a, 1989b). To the contrary, Poole's research revealed that groups will *not* necessarily proceed through the same phases of development in the same sequential order, because each group responds to existing contingencies and exigencies in unique ways. For example, Poole and Roth (1989b) studied 29 groups of different types making 47 different decisions. They found that 11 of the discussions conformed to the unitary sequence model in that they progressed linearly from an analysis of the problem to an attempt to find solutions. In 22 of the groups, however, the discussions tended to cycle back and forth (as many as 7 times in one group) from analysis of the problem to possible solutions. In the remaining 14 groups, the members did not analyze the problem and, instead, only discussed solutions.

On the basis of their research, Poole and his colleagues (Poole, 1983; Poole & Doelger, 1986; Poole & Roth, 1989a, 1989b) proposed a developmental theory of group interaction. This theory recognizes that group processes will vary according to phases or steps taken to arrive at decisions. Hence, the phases do not necessarily conform to the phases outlined in the unitary sequence model. In fact, Poole (1983) argued:

> The complex nature of group activity types and the extreme variability of phases and phasic sequences suggests that there is a much wider range of group activities than has formerly been assumed and reinforces the notion that traditional phases may be too restrictive. (p. 325)

Poole and his colleagues (Poole & Doelger, 1986; Poole & Roth, 1989b) subsequently outlined the features of the developmental theory of group interaction in order to empirically investigate and account for the variety of factors which influence the group communication processes associated with decision-making. While a full explanation of Poole's developmental theory is beyond the scope of this chapter, the essence of the theory suggests that task characteristics (e.g., novelty, goal clarity, time requirements) and group structural characteristics (e.g., conflict history, group size) influence the development of the decision in three ways: (a) the nature of the "path" (i.e., sequence of decision activities) that a group employs in reaching a decision, (b) the complexity of the path that the group employs in reaching a decision, and (c) the degree of disorganization during group interaction (p. 551). Suffice it to say that Poole's developmental theory of group interaction asserts that structural and task characteristics have a direct affect on group decision path properties, complexity and disorganization of group interaction processes, and functional activities (Poole & Roth, 1989b, p. 552).

Communication and Group Outcomes Research

The 1970s marked the beginning of a fifth major line of research, one that focused on the relationship between communication and various group outcome variables. Among the group outcomes that received attention from communication scholars were consensus and the quality of group decisions and solutions.

By far, the majority of research assessing the relationship between communication and group outcomes has concentrated on decision-making and problem-solving groups. Gouran (1969) was one of the first to examine the relationship between communication variables and group decision-making outcomes. He focused on identifying the relationship between communication characteristics and a group's ability of reach consensus (unanimous agreement). He found that the communication variable most closely related to consensus decision-making is *orientation*. That is, groups that reached consensus, as contrasted with those that did not, made more statements that attempted to clarify and familiarize members with the group task, goals, procedures, and the like. Gouran's initial findings stimulated a series of investigation focusing on the relationship between orientation and group consensus (e.g., Kline, 1972; Kline & Hullinger, 1973; Knutson, 1972; Knutson & Holdridge, 1975; Knutson & Kowitz, 1977).

At around the same time, Leathers (1972) was independently investigating the relationship between group communication and group performance. Specifically, he found that groups characterized by high quality communication also tended to make high quality decisions. That is, groups experiencing *good* feedback (e.g., high quality, positive, task-oriented when necessary and maintenance-oriented when necessary) also tended to make good decisions.

The 1970s, then, was the blossoming period of research on group communication and group outcomes. These studies paved the way for the bloom that would characterize research in the 1980s. They especially marked the beginning of research concerned with decision-making effectiveness.

Although the 1970s witnessed the emergence of a greater number of studies focusing on the relationship between communication and group outcomes, that research was criticized on several fronts. First, much of the research focused on groups which consisted of college students gathered together as a group for the short time it would take to study them in a laboratory setting. Relatively few studies were being conducted in the field allowing for the study of "real-world" groups (Becker, 1980). And second, group communication researchers were still proceeding in an unsystematic manner in examining the relationship between communication and group outcomes. The tendency was to focus on variables pertaining to the hot issues of the time without consideration of how those variables fit into a larger theoretical framework (Bormann,

1980). As a result, much of the findings were diverse and fragmented, making it difficult to integrate the different strains of research. Investigators were left with the task of trying to make sense of the research findings they were generating.

Primarily due to this second criticism, the 1980s saw the development of *theory*. Efforts were undertaken to develop theoretical statements assessing *why* communication should be related to group outcomes in the first place. This was especially true for the relationship between communication and decision quality. One of the most important theoretical developments of the 1980s was the formulation of the functional perspective (Gouran & Hirokawa, 1983).

Up until the 1980s, very little research was conducted within the communication discipline to determine the nature of the relationship between communication and group decision-making. What little research had been conducted took place in disciplines other than communication studies. As noted earlier, this work was largely influenced by the work of Bales and his colleagues. The typical approach was to utilize Bales' Interaction Process Analysis (IPA) categories to examine the frequency with which particular types of communication acts were produced by group members during group meetings. Then, the quality of the decision made by the group was assessed. If there was a correlation between the frequency with which particular types of communication acts occurred (as measured by the categories of the IPA system) and the quality of the group's decision, a relationship between communication and decision-making quality was assumed to exist.

Hirokawa (1982), however, pointed out that Bales' IPA system did not distinguish between task and nontask related communication. Hence, for example, the statements "where are the hamburgers?" and "did you get an estimate of the cost of the proposal?" would be assigned to the same IPA category of *asks questions*. Clearly, the latter question is more relevant to the group task than the former and, as such, is more likely to be related to group performance. Hirokawa thus reasoned that the use of Bales's IPA scheme (or any other set of communication categories) must somehow distinguish task-relevant from nonrelevant utterances.

It is with this criticism in mind that Gouran and Hirokawa (1983) and their colleagues (Hirokawa & Pace, 1983; Hirokawa & Scheerhorn, 1986) developed a functional perspective of communication and group decision-making. This theory is concerned with explicating the processes by which communication affects the quality of group decision-making outcomes. More specifically, Gouran and Hirokawa (1983) noted that the functional perspective is concerned with explaining how communication influences group performance by affecting the satisfaction of a group's particular task requirements. These "functional requisites" include assessment of the problematic situation, identification of goals, identification of viable choices, and evaluation of choices (Gouran & Hirokawa, 1983; Hirokawa & McLeod, 1993). Central to the functional perspective is the notion that communication can function in either a promotive or counteractive manner (Gouran & Hirokawa, 1986). That is, communication can promote or inhibit the effective facilitation of the four requisite functions.

On the basis of this theory, Hirokawa (1982, 1985) subsequently developed the Function-Oriented Interaction Category System (FOICS). This set of categories focuses entirely on the task-relevant group communication; that is, communication that attends to the functional requisites of the task in question. Using this new system, Hirokawa found that groups which displayed utterances that fulfilled the functional requisites of a group's task tended to arrive at higher quality decisions than those that did not (Hirokawa, 1988). Further, as suggested earlier, the order in which the requisites were fulfilled did not appear to make a difference, nor did the particular format used by the group in fulfilling those requisites appear to matter (Burleson et al., 1984). Rather, what appeared to make the greatest difference for group performance was the number of functional requisites satisfied by a group during the course of its deliberation (Hirokawa, 1985). In short, the functional perspective dominated research focusing on the relationship between communication and group decision-making performance in the 1980s.

On the basis of research through the 1980s, Hewes (1986) advanced an influential critique of the methodology group communication scholars, as well as scholars in other disciplines, had been using to gain an understanding of the relationship between communication and group decision-making performance. Hewes argued that part of the problem with research to date was that group communication had not been adequately measured. As a result, we were left with equivocal findings about the actual impact of communication on group performance. That critique was partially answered by Jarboe (1988), although many of the questions raised by Hewes still remained.

Whereas a considerable amount of group communication research focused on group performance, other outcome variables also received attention in the 1980s. Group consensus research had been a hot topic of research in the 1970s. It continued to receive attention in the 1980s as well. DeStephen (1983), for example, found that there were communication characteristics which differentiated high and low consensus groups. She, along with Hirokawa (DeStephen & Hirokawa, 1988), also developed an instrument to measure the degree of consensus in decision-making groups. Further, Canary, Brossman, and Seibold (1987) found that groups arriving at consensus tended to use a greater percentage of convergent arguments than groups that did not arrive at consensus. Beatty (1989), meanwhile, examined the effect of group members' "decision rule orientation" on consensus formation. He found that groups composed of members with similar criteria for making a decision among a set of alternatives (similar decision rule orientation), arrived at consensus decisions with greater frequency than groups whose members were dissimilar in their selection criteria.

Another group outcome examined by group communication researchers in the 1980s was polarization. Group polarization refers to the tendency for group members to be collectively more conservative or more risky in their decision choices then they were as individuals prior to deliberating as a group. Alderton and Frey (1983) identified argumentation as a key communication determinant of group polarization. They found that the greater the number of positive reactions by group members to minority arguments (that is, arguments representing the minority opinion in the group) was associated with decreased group polarization. Further, more negative reactions to minority arguments led to increased polarization. Besides Alderton and Frey, a other researchers also advanced the claim that examining group argumentation and its relationship to polarization would be a worthwhile endeavor (Boster, Fryrear, Mongeau, & Hunter, 1982; Boster, Mayer, Hunter, & Hale, 1980).

As group communication research entered the 1990s, it was again subject to criticism. This time the criticism focused squarely on the use of laboratory groups consisting of students brought together as a group for a short period of time (Putnam

& Stohl, 1990) and the lack of exciting theoretical developments (Poole, 1990). The former criticism was especially focused toward studies examining group outcomes; in particular, the relationship between group communication and decision performance (Stohl & Holmes, 1993).

Frey (1994b) further argued that the dominance of the positivistic paradigm in small group communication research had led to a focus on laboratory groups. This focus has, in turn, circumvented research on groups operating in the natural environment. As a result, group communication research, as a whole, has declined in quantity. This argument may be more strawman than substance, however, because group communication research has increased substantially since the first critiques of the early 1970s (Cragan & Wright, 1990; Gouran et al., 1994).

The critiques of past research have been well taken. While some studies are still being conducted in the laboratory (e.g., Salazar, Hirokawa, Propp, Julian, & Leatham, 1994), more group outcomes research in the 1990s has focused on field settings (e.g., Frey, 1994a; Hirokawa & Keyton, 1995; Hirokawa & Rost, 1992). There is little doubt that the study of group communication and its relationship to group outcomes in the 1990s and beyond will be reflexive (Gouran, Hirokawa, Julian, & Leatham, 1993) and cover more diverse groups and outcomes. Groups such as self-help groups, medical teams, organizational work groups, family groups, social support groups, as well as outcomes such as individual and group learning, skills acquisition, knowledge retention, and sociological functioning will no doubt be among the contexts and topics of research conducted in the 1990s and beyond. Such research can only enhance our knowledge of group communication and its effects on specific group outcomes.

CONTEMPORARY THEORIES

Although the early research in group communication attempted to offer advice to group participants, it failed to produce systematic theories of group communication. It tended to focus on the impact of particular variables without integrating these variables and processes into coherent theories that guided the research. Thus, group communication came under criticism for its lack of theory-building (Bormann, 1970, 1980; Becker, 1980; Cragan & Wright, 1980) and problematic research designs that lacked theoretical grounding, coding systems, and replication of findings (Hewes, 1985, 1986; Hirokawa, 1980; Poole, 1981; Poole & Folger, 1981).

Kuhn (1970) noted that when a field is faced with such criticism it produces a crisis that generates paradigm shifts that direct or redirect research and research questions. Indeed, group communication has begun to build on this traditional research and produce new paradigms of research and theories that will be discussed in the next section.

Earlier it was noted that traditional lines of research have generally suffered from a lack of solid theoretical grounding. Before concluding this chapter, we would be remiss if we did not briefly focus on some of the contemporary theories that have been advanced to remedy theoretical deficiencies in group communication research. In fact, throughout our discussion of the major lines of group communication research, we have already presented two contemporary theories of group communication: Poole's developmental theory of group interaction, and Gouran and Hirokawa's functional perspective. In this section we examine two additional theories that have influenced the direction of recent group communication research.

Structuration Theory

Scholars in small group communication have adapted Giddens' (1979) theory of structuration to explain processes of group interaction. Since groups must function within the context of larger organizational and social frameworks, they have been described as having systems properties (Poole, Seibold, & McPhee, 1986; Contractor & Seibold, 1993). Structuration theory is useful for understanding how people, as active agents, produce and reproduce the structures of social systems (Giddens, 1979, 1981). Part of the appeal of structuration theory is that structures, whether they be groups, organizations, or institutions, can be viewed as a dynamic process with characteristics of both stability and change (Poole & DeSanctis, 1992). A driving concern for group scholars is to map out the influence of structural characteristics, internal and external organizational processes, consistent patterns of interaction, and incremental and radical change within groups. Given the complexity of issues, it is reasonable to ask about the utility of such a theory for group interaction processes.

Although structuration theory is not yet extensively used in small group communication research, Poole and DeSanctis (1992) argued that communication processes occupy a fundamental position in structuration theory because interaction is central to structuring processes. As they put it:

> Communicative interaction is crucial (in the production and reproduction of structures) because local structures are produced and sustained through the development of intersubjective understandings and coordinated actions. Over longer time frames and repeated reproduction, the structures that evolve in local systems ultimately generalize into institutions. (p. 6)

They go on to suggest that small group interaction is an ideal place to examine the intricacies of structural reproduction.

Poole, Seibold, and McPhee (1986) asserted that studying group processes must take into account two tensions: tension between structural factors and individual action, and tension between stability and change. Structural features include such aspects as decision rules, communication networks, and norms. The dialectic between stability and change results from an established structure (that is, a structure "in place") versus the created and negotiated structure which is a product of member activities. Structuration theory attempts to integrate the individual and the social or the micro and the macro.

Symbolic Convergence Theory

Although symbolic convergence theory is intended as a universal theory of human communication, Bormann (1986) has argued that it can be usefully adapted to research in small group decision-making. Symbolic convergence theory involves a three-part structure that includes discovering the patterns and forms of communication that indicate the presence of group consciousness, describing how and why group consciousness changes, and explaining why people share in fantasies (Bormann, 1985; Cragan & Shields, 1992). *Fantasy*, as defined by Bormann (1985), "refers to the creative and imaginative shared interpretation of events that fulfills a group psychological or rhetorical need" (p. 130). When people share fantasies, their feelings as group participants begin to converge and the result is a form of communion, or empathic meeting of the minds.

Research generated by symbolic convergence theorists is considered to fall within a narrative, as opposed to a rational paradigm (Bormann, 1985, 1986). A narrative paradigm is more concerned with collecting interpretive data than quantitative data. Methods for narrative paradigm research include case studies, rhetorical analysis of group transcripts, and examination of member stories within groups (Bormann, 1986). Bormann (1986) has suggested that the sharing of group fantasies is a part of the decision making process in groups and argued that "only after the emergence of a shared consciousness (addressing zero history groups) will they be able to focus their full attention on the tasks at hand and move into a phase of real work" (p. 231).

Practical applications of symbolic convergence theory can be observed in work with teachers and consultants for improving communication in interpersonal relationships, families, and small groups (Cragan & Wright, 1990). Poole (1990) argued that the strength of symbolic convergence theory, aside from its rich promise to small group research, is that the perspective applies to both task and socioemotional group processes. To date, researchers investigating symbolic convergence theory have provided data about the narratives, stories, or fantasies people share with each other in group situations, and link these data sources to the outcome of group interaction. For the most part, this approach is more concerned with describing rhetorical processes than outlining the potential benefits of rational decision-making.

A SAMPLE STUDY

It should be clear at this point that, although impressive strides have been made in group communication research, many questions are left unanswered. Let us take one of these questions and briefly examine how one might go about obtaining an answer to it.

An important question that has yet to be satisfactorily answered by group communication researchers concerns a phenomenon identified by Collins and Guetzkow (1964) as the *assembly effect*. According to the authors:

> An assembly effect occurs when the group is able to achieve collectively something which could not have been achieved by any member working alone or by a combination of individual efforts. The assembly effect bonus is productivity which exceeds the potential of the most capable member and also exceeds the sum of the efforts of the group members working separately. (p. 58)

For many years now, small group scholars speculated that the group interaction process plays an important, if not central, role in determining the occurrence of the assembly effect. To date, however, little is known about the nature of that role. Clearly an answer to this important question would be beneficial to those of us in the business of helping groups reach, and exceed, their full potential.

How might one go about investigating the relationship between group communication and the assembly effect? To begin with, it is clear that we are unlikely to discover the precise nature of this relationship in one sweeping study. To the contrary, it is more likely that we would have to conduct a series of studies that collectively provide an answer to our general question. Hence, our first step would be to decide what an appropriate starting point should be.

If a relationship exists between group communication and the occurrence of the assembly effect, it is reasonable to expect the occurrence of the assembly effect to be associated with identifiable communication properties. Hence, we might begin our research program by investigating the following question: *Is the assembly effect associated with specific group communication behaviors?*

Having identified our research question, we would need to address a series of methodological concerns. The first methodological concern is how to obtain the groups we need for our study. Because the assembly effect presumably does not occur in all groups (indeed, many groups fail to live up to their potential), we would have to obtain a set of groups that displayed the phenomenon we were interested in studying. We call this set of groups our *experimental sample*. Additionally, we would also need to obtain a comparable sample of groups that were similar in every way, except that they failed to display an assembly effect. This latter set of groups would serve as our *control sample*.

How would we obtain these two samples? One approach would be to search for naturally occurring examples of groups that displayed the assembly effect, as well as groups that did not display such an effect. That, of course, could be very problematic for two reasons: First, such naturally occurring groups may not be readily available; and second, even if they were, we have no way of knowing where to find them. A far easier approach would be to place a number of groups in a laboratory setting conducive to the occurrence of the assembly effect, and then select those groups that displayed the outcome we were interested in studying.

How would we accomplish this? First, we would create a number of zero-history groups comprised of volunteers for our study. Next, we would have the members of each group work on a problem-solving task that had a verifiably correct answer. We would first have the group members work on the task individually, then as a group. A comparison of the individual and group solutions to the task would serve as the basis for identifying the assembly effect. Specifically, whenever the group's solution exceeded the solution of its best member, we would include that group in our sample of groups experiencing an assembly effect. The remaining groups (i.e., those that did not display an assembly effect) would constitute our control sample.

Having obtained a sample of groups experiencing an assembly effect, as well as a sample of control groups, we would then proceed to analyze the interactions of the groups in both samples. To do so, we would have to select an appropriate group interaction coding scheme. For the sake of this example, let us select Hirokawa's Function-Oriented Interaction Coding System scheme because of its clear focus on task-relevant interaction. This coding scheme possesses six basic categories:

1. *Orientation comments*: statements that (a) identify or clarify group goals, (b) comment on time and resource limitations, or (c) suggest how the group should organize and conduct its discussion.

2. *Problem analysis comments*: statements that (a) identify or clarify the nature of the problem, (b) identify or clarify symptoms or indications of the problem, or (c) identify or clarify the cause(s) of the problem.
3. *Criteria development comments*: statements that (a) identify or clarify preexisting evaluation standards, or (b) identify or clarify a quality or characteristic of a good solution.
4. *Solution development comments*: statements that (a) identify or clarify a possible solution or (b) modify, build on, or provide details for a possible solution.
5. *Positive evaluation comments*: statements that (a) identify or clarify a positive quality or characteristic of a proposed solution or (b) elaborate or substantiate (provide proof for) a positive quality or characteristic of a proposed solution.
6. *Negative evaluation comments*: statements that (a) identify or clarify a negative quality or characteristic of a proposed solution or (b) elaborate or substantiate a negative quality or characteristic of a proposed solution.

Having decided on an interaction coding scheme, we would need to train multiple observers to utilize the coding scheme to analyze the interactions of the groups in the experimental and control samples. Multiple coders (usually two or three) are necessary to establish the reliability of the interaction data we obtain. *Reliability* is a term we use to indicate the degree of agreement between any two or more observers. Reliability is important in observational research of this kind because the more agreement we find between multiple coders (assuming they have worked *independently* of each other), the more confident we are that they are observing and interpreting aspects of interaction in the same general ways.

Training coders is a relatively straightforward matter. First we familiarize them with the categories comprising our coding scheme. This involves providing them with a conceptual definition of each category (i.e., explaining what each category represents), as well as specific examples of utterances classifiable within each category. Once we have familiarized the coders with the coding scheme, we would have them practice using the coding scheme on interactions that are similar in nature to the interactions they would be coding in the experimental and control samples. After each practice session, we would calculate the degree of agreement among the coders, and help them resolve any disagreements that emerged during the practice sessions. Practice sessions would continue until the coders were able to achieve a level of agreement of at least 75% for three consecutive practice sessions. Once that level of reliability was achieved, the coders would be ready to code the interactions in the experimental and control samples.

After the coders independently coded all of the interactions in the experimental and control samples, we would calculate reliability estimates for each group's interaction. The reliability for each group's interaction would have to equal or exceed 75% in order to be subjected to further analysis. If it did not possess this minimal level of reliability, it would have to be recoded by the observers until the 75% criterion was reached.

Once all of the interactions of the groups in the experimental and control samples were analyzed with an acceptable level of reliability, we would submit the frequency data to any of a variety of statistical tests to determine if significant differences exist among the frequency of utterances in any of the six FOICS categories between the groups in the experimental and control conditions. The discovery of such differences would provide us with important information regarding the association between certain types of task-relevant communicative acts and the occurrence of the assembly effect.

CONCLUSION

In the last two decades, researchers have been calling for improvements in small group theory and research (cf., Cragan & Wright, 1980, 1990; Hirokawa & Gouran, 1989). In fact, Gouran (1985) noted that, although models for group processes are becoming more sophisticated, researchers have typically focused on group or member characteristics, outcome–interaction relationships, or group and member characteristics and outcome relationships. Research to date lacks a way for researchers to account for the interdependence of the complex issues which affect group interaction. As Gouran (1985) concluded, "Until... studies begin reflecting more thoughtfully on the ways in which all classes of variables affecting group processes are interconnected, the prospects for accumulating integratable knowledge will remain more a hope than a reality" (p. 108).

Recently, however, researchers are making greater strides toward addressing issues of integration. First, Hirokawa and Gouran (1989) argued that research has not adequately addressed how strategic facilitation in communication can help improve the problems which interfere with a group's ability to problem-solve or make effective decisions. Specifically, it is suggested that substantive, procedural, and relational issues should provide the cornerstone of improvement for research in facilitative communication. A central concern with substantive issues is whether individual members can improve group performance by recognizing and applying relevant criteria needed for a high quality decision. Procedural issues may become problematic in group interaction when members introduce unimportant information, become impatient, move through the agenda too quickly, restrict efforts to identify alternatives, and apply inconsistent criteria to alternatives. Finally, relational problems affect interaction in such matters as "pressure for uniformity and deviance, authority relations, status differences, and a variety of conflicts attributable to incompatibility of group and individual goals as well as members' roles" (p. 83).

Second, Hirokawa and McLeod (1993) argued that an integration of the developmental and functional perspectives is necessary for continued research in small group decision-making. The integrated model, which combines Poole and Roth's (1989b) sequential contingency model and Hirokawa's functional model, "suggests that the degree of congruence (or fit) between the nature of a group's decision-making communication, and context-generated problems it faces, has a direct influence on the quality of its decision-making performance" (Hirokawa & McLeod, 1993, p. 11). Other attempts at integrating diverse (or similar) perspectives is represented in work by Gouran (1988) and Hirokawa and Johnston (1989). In addition to the call for more appropriate theories in small group communication, researchers are increasingly attempting to improve current methodological approaches to the field.

REFERENCES

Alderton, S. M., & Frey, L. R. (1983) Effects of reactions to arguments on group outcomes: The case of group polarization. *Central States Speech Journal, 34*, 88–95.

Applbaum, R. L., & Anatol, K. (1971). PERT: A tool for communication research planning. *Journal of Communication, 21*, 368–380.

Bales, R. F. (1950). *Interaction process analysis.* Reading, MA: Addison-Wesley.

Bales, R. F. (1953). The equilibrium problem in small groups. In T. Parsons, R. F. Bales, & E. Shils (Eds.), *Working papers in the theory of action* (pp. 111–161). Glencoe, IL: Free Press.

Bales, R. F., & Strodtbeck, F. L. (1951). Phases in group problem-solving. *Journal of Abnormal and Social Psychology, 46*, 485–495.

Baird, J. E., Jr. (1974). A comparison of distributional and sequential structure in cooperative and competitive group discussion. *Speech Monographs, 41*, 226–232.

Barge, J. K. (1989). Leadership as medium: A leaderless group discussion model. *Communication Quarterly, 37*, 237–247.

Barge, J. K. (1992). Leadership as organizing. In R. S. Cathcart & L. A. Samovar (Eds.), *Small group communication: A reader* (pp. 477–491). William C. Brown.

Bayless, O. (1967). An alternate pattern for problem-solving discussion. *Journal of Communication, 17*, 188–198.

Beatty, M. J. (1989). Group members' decision rule orientations and consensus. *Human Communication Research, 16*, 279–296.

Becker, S. L. (1980). Directions of small group research for the 1980's. *Central States Speech Journal, 31*, 221–224.

Berg, D. M. (1967). A descriptive analysis of the distribution and duration of themes discussed by small task-oriented groups. *Speech Monographs, 34*, 172–175.

Black, E. B. (1955). Consideration of the rhetorical causes of breakdown in discussion. *Speech Monographs, 22*, 15–19.

Bormann, E. G. (1970). The paradox and promise of small group research. *Communication Monographs, 37*, 211–216.

Bormann, E. G. (1980). The paradox and promise of small group communication revisited. *Central States Speech Journal, 31*, 214–220.

Bormann, E. G. (1985). Symbolic convergence theory: A communication formulation. *Journal of Communication, 35*, 128–138.

Bormann, E. G. (1986). Symbolic convergence theory and communication in group decision-making. In R.Y. Hirokawa & M.S. Poole (Eds.), *Communication and group decision making* (pp. 219–236). Beverly Hills, CA: Sage.

Boster, F. J., Fryrear, J. E., Mongeau, P. A., & Hunter, J. E. (1982). An unequally speaking linear discrepency model: Implications for polarity shift. In M. Burgoon (Ed.), *Communication yearbook* (Vol. 6, pp. 395–418) . Beverly Hills, CA: Sage.

Boster, F. J., Mayer, M. E., Hunter, J. E., & Hale, G. E. (1980). Expanding the persuasive arguments explanation of the polarity shift: A linear discrepency model. In D. Nimmo (Ed.), *Communication yearbook*, (Vol. 4, pp. 165–176). Beverly Hills, CA: Sage.

Brilhart, J. K., & Jochem, L. M. (1964). Effects of different patterns on outcomes of problem-solving discussion. *Journal of Applied Psychology, 48*, 175–79.

Burleson, B. R., Levine, B. J., & Samter, W. (1984). Decision-making procedure and decision quality. *Human Communication Research, 10*, 557–574.

Canary, D. J., Brossman, B. G., & Seibold, D. R. (1987). Argument structures in decision-making groups. *Southern States Communication Journal, 53*, 18–37.

Cheseboro, J. W., Cragan, J. E., & McCullough, P. (1973). The small group techniques of the radical revolutionary: A synthetic study of consciousness raising. *Communication Monographs, 40*, 136–146.

Collins, B. E., & Guetzkow, H. (1964). *A social psychology of group processes for decision-making.* New York: Wiley.

Comadena, M. E. (1984). Brainstorming groups: Ambiguity tolerance, communication apprehension, task attarction, and individual productivity. *Small Group Behavior, 15,* 251–254.

Contractor, N. S., & Seibold, D. R. (1993). Theoretical frameworks for the study of structuring processes in group decision support systems. *Human Communication Research, 19,* 528–563.

Cragan, J. F., & Shields, D. C. (1992). The use of symbolic convergence theory in corporate strategic planning: A case study. *Journal of Applied Communication,* 20, 199–218.

Cragan, J. F., & Wright, D. W. (1980). Small group communication research of the 1970's: A synthesis and critique. *Central States Speech Journal, 31,* 197–213.

Cragan, J. F., & Wright, D. W. (1990). Small group communication research of the 1980's: A synthesis and critique. *Communication Studies, 41,* 212–236.

Crowell, L., & Scheidel, T. M. (1961). Categories for analysis of idea development in discussion groups. *Journal of Social Psychology, 54,* 155–168.

Delbecq, A. L., Van de Ven, A. H., & Gustafson, D. H. (1975). *Group techniques for program planning: A guide to nominal group and delphi process.* Glenview, IL: Scott, Foresman.

DeStephen, R. S. (1983). High and low consensus groups: A content and relational interaction analysis. *Small Group Behavior, 14,* 143–162.

DeStephen, R. S., & Hirokawa, R. Y. (1988). Small group consensus: Stability of group support of the decision, task process, and group relationship. *Small Group Behavior, 19,* 227–239.

Downs C. W., & Pickett, T. (1977). Analysis of the effects of nine leadership-group compatibility contingencies upon productivity and member satisfaction. *Communication Monographs, 44,* 220–230.

Ellis, D. G., & Fisher, B. A. (1975). Phases of conflict in small group development: A Markov analysis. *Human Communication Research, 1,* 195–212.

Fisher, B. A. (1970). Decision emergence: Phases in group decision-making. *Speech Monographs, 37,* 53–66.

Fisher, B. A. (1985). Leadership as medium: Treating complexity in group communication research. *Small Group Behavior, 16,* 167–196.

Fisher, B. A. (1986). Leadership: When does the difference make a difference? In R. Y. Hirokawa & M. S. Poole (Eds.), *Communication and group decision making* (pp. 197–215). Beverly Hills, CA: Sage.

Fisher, B.A., & Hawes, L. (1971). An interact system model: Generating a grounded theory of small groups. *Quarterly Journal of Speech, 57,* 444–453.

Frey, L. R. (1994a). *Group communication in context: Studies of natural groups.* Hillsdale, NJ: Lawrence Erlbaum Associates.

Frey, L. R. (1994b). The naturalistic paradigm: Studying small groups in the postmodern era. *Small Group Research, 25,* 551–577.

Geier, J. G. (1967). A trait approach to the study of leadership in small groups. *Journal of Communication, 17,* 316–323.

Giddens, A. (1979). *Central problems in social theory.* Los Angeles: University of California Press.

Giddens, A. (1981). *A contemporary critique of historical materialism.* Los Angeles: University of California Press.

Gouran, D. S. (1969). Variables related to consensus in group discussion of questions of policy. *Speech Monographs, 36,* 387–391.

Gouran, D. S. (1970). Conceptual and methodological approaches to the study of leadership. *Central States Speech Journal, 21,* 217–223.

Gouran, D. S. (1982). *Making decisions in groups: Choices and consequences.* Glenview, IL: Scott Foresman.

Gouran, D. S. (1985). The paradigm of unfulfilled promise: A critical examination of the history of research on small groups in speech communication. In T. W. Bensin (Ed.), *Speech Communication in the 20th Century* (pp. 90–108). Carbondale, IL: Southern Illinois University Press.

Gouran, D. S. (1988). Group decision-making: An approach to integrated research. In C. H. Tardy (Ed.), *A handbook for the study of human communication,* (pp. 247–268). Norwood, NJ: Ablex.

Gouran, D. S., & Baird, J. E., Jr. (1972). An analysis of distributional and sequential structure in problem-solving and informal group discussions. *Speech Monographs, 39,* 18–22.

Gouran, D. S., & Hirokawa, R. Y. (1983). The role of communication in decision-making groups: A functional perspective. In M. S. Mander (Ed.), *Communications in transition* (pp. 168–185). New York: Praeger.

Gouran, D. S., & Hirokawa, R. Y. (1986). Counteractive functions of communication in effective group decision-making. In R. Y. Hirokawa & M. S. Poole, (Eds.), *Communication and group decision making* (pp. 81–90). Beverly Hills, CA: Sage.

Gouran, D. S., Hirokawa, R. Y, Julian, K. M., & Leatham, G. B. (1993). The evolution and current status of the functional perspective on communication in decision-making and problem-solving groups: A critical analysis. In S. Deetz (Ed.), *Communication yearbook* (Vol. 16, pp. 573–600). Newbury Park, CA: Sage.

Gouran, D. S., Hirokawa, R. Y., McGee, M. C., & Miller, L. L. (1994). Communication in groups: Research trends and theoretical perspectives. In F. L. Casmir (Ed.), *Building communication theories: A socio/cultural approach* (pp. 241–268). Hillsdale, NJ: Lawrence Erlbaum Associates.

Hersey, P., & Blanchard, K. H. (1982). *Management of organizational behavior*. Englewood Cliffs, NJ: Prentice-Hill.

Hewes, D. E. (1985). Systematic biases in coded social interaction data. *Human Communication Research. 12*, 554–574.

Hewes, D. E. (1986). A socio-egocentric model of group decision-making. In R. Y. Hirokawa & M. S. Poole (Eds.), *Communication and group decision making* (pp. 265–291). Beverly Hills, CA: Sage.

Hiltz, S. R., Johnson, K., & Turoff, M. (1986). Experiments in group decision-making: Communication process and outcome in face-to-face versus computerized conferences. *Human Communication Research, 13*, 225–252.

Hirokawa, R. Y. (1980). A comparative analysis of communicative patterns within effective and ineffective decision-making groups. *Communication Monographs*, 47, 312–321.

Hirokawa, R. Y. (1982). Group communication and problem-solving effectiveness: A critical review of inconsistent findings. *Communication Quarterly, 30*, 134–141.

Hirokawa, R. Y. (1983). Group communication and problem-solving effectiveness: An investigation of procedural functions. *Western Journal of Speech Communication, 47*, 59–74.

Hirokawa, R. Y. (1985). Discussion procedures and decision performance. *Human Communication Research, 12*, 203–224.

Hirokawa, R. Y. (1987). Why informed groups make faulty decisions: An investigation of possible interaction-based explanations. *Small Group Behavior, 18*, 3–29.

Hirokawa, R. Y. (1988). Group communication and decision-making performance. *Human Communication Research, 14*, 487–515.

Hirokawa, R. Y., & Gouran, D. S. (1989). Facilitation of group communication: A critique of price resarch and agenda for future research. *Management Communication Quarterly, 3*, 71–92.

Hirokawa, R. Y., & Johnston, D. D. (1989). Toward a general theory of group decision making. *Small Group Behavior, 20*, 500–523.

Hirokawa, R. Y., & Keyton, J. (1995). Perceived facilitators and inhibitors of effectiveness in organizational work teams. *Management Communication Quarterly, 8*, 424–446.

Hirokawa, R. Y., & McLeod, P. L. (1993, November). *Communication, decision development, and decision quality in small groups: An integration of two approaches*. Paper presented at the annual meeting of the Speech Communication Association. Miami Beach, FL.

Hirokawa, R. Y., & Pace. R. C. (1983). A descriptive investigation of the possible communication based reasons for effective and ineffective decision-making. *Communication Monographs, 50*, 363–379.

Hirokawa. R. Y., & Rost, K. (1992). Effective group decision-making in organizations: A field test of the vigilant interaction theory. *Management Communication Quarterly, 5*, 267–288.

Hirokawa, R. Y., & Scheerhorn, D. R. (1986). Communication in faulty group decision-making. In R. Y. Hirokawa & M. S. Poole (Eds.), *Communication and group decision-making* (pp. 63–80). Beverly Hills, CA: Sage.

Jablin, F. M. (1981). Cultivating imagination: Factors that enhance and inhibit crativity in brainstormings groups. *Human Communication Research, 7*, 245–258.

Jablin, F. M., Seibold, D. R., & Sorenson, R. (1977). Potential inhibitory effects of group participation on brainstorming performance. *Central States Speech Journal, 28*, 113–121.

Jablin, F. M., Sorenson, R., & Seibold, D. R. (1978). Interpersonal perception and group brainstorming performance. *Communication Quarterly, 26,* 36–44.

Janis, I. L., & Mann, L. (1977). *Decision making: A psychological analysis of conflict, choice, and commitment.* New York: Free Press.

Jarboe, S. (1988). A comparison of input-output, process-output, and input-process-output models of small group problem-solving effectiveness. *Communication Monographs, 55,* 121–142.

Jurma, W. E., & Froelich, D. L. (1984). Effects of immediate instructor feedback on group discussion participants. *Central States Speech Journal, 35,* 178–186.

Kline, J. A. (1972). Orientation and group consensus. *Central States Speech Journal, 23,* 44–47.

Kline, J. A., & Hullinger, J. L. (1973). Redundancy, self-orientation, and group consensus. *Speech Monographs, 40,* 72–74.

Knutson, T. J. (1972). An experimental study of the effects of orientation behavior on small group consensus. *Speech Monographs, 39,* 159–165.

Knutson, T. J., & Holdridge, W. E. (1975). Orientation behavior, leadership, and consensus: A possible functional relationship. *Speech Monographs, 42,* 107–114.

Knutson, T. J., & Kowitz, A. C. (1977). Effects of information type and level of orientation on consensus achievement in substantive and affective small-group conflict. *Central States Speech Journal, 28,* 54–63.

Knutson, T. J., Wheeless, L. R., & Divers, L. (1977). Developing teachable small group communication behaviors. *Communication Education, 26,* 333–337.

Kuhn, T. S. (1970). *The structure of scientific revolutions* (2nd ed.). Chicago: University of Chicago Press.

Larson, C. E. (1969). Forms of analysis and small group problem-solving. *Speech Monographs, 36,* 452–455.

Larson, C. E. (1971). Speech communication research on small groups. *Speech Teacher, 20,* 89–107.

Larson, C. E., & Gratz, R. D. (1970). Problem-solving discussion training and T-group training: An experimental comparison. *Speech Teacher, 19,* 54–57.

Leathers, D. G. (1969). Process, disruption and measurement in small group communication. *Quarterly Journal of Speech, 55,* 287–300.

Leathers, D. G., (1970). The process effects of trust-destroying behavior in small groups. *Speech Monographs, 37,* 180–187.

Leathers, D. G. (1972). Quality of group communication as a determinant of group product. *Speech Monographs, 39,* 166–173.

Lewin, K. (1947). Frontiers in group dynamics. *Human Relations, 1,* 5–41.

Lewin, K., Lippitt, R., & White, R. K. (1939). Patterns of aggressive behavior in experimentally created "social climates." *Journal of Social Psychology, 10,* 217–299.

Mabry, E. A. (1975a). Exploratory analysis of a developmental model for task-oriented small groups. *Human Communication Research, 2,* 66–74.

Mabry, E. A. (1975b). An instrument for assessing content themes in group interaction. *Communication Monographs, 42,* 291–297.

Morris, C. G., & Hackman, J. R. (1969). Behavioral correlates of perceived leadership. *Journal of Personality and Social Psychology, 13,* 350–361.

Pavitt, C., & Curtis, E. (1990). *Small group discussion: A theoretical approach.* Scottsdale, AZ: Gorsuch Scarisbrick.

Phillips, G. M. (1966). *Communication and the small group.* Indianapolis: Bobbs-Merrill.

Phillips, G. M., & Santoro, G. M. (1989). Teaching group discussion via computer-mediated communication. *Communication Education, 38,* 151–161.

Philipsen, G., Mulac, A., & Dietrich, D. (1979). The effects of social interaction on group idea generation. *Communication Monographs, 46,* 119–125.

Poole, M. S. (1981). Decision development in small groups I: A comparison of two models. *Communication Monographs, 48,* 1–24.

Poole, M. S. (1983). Decision development in small groups III: A multiple sequence model of group decision development. *Communication Monographs, 50,* 321–341.

Poole, M. S. (1990). Do we have any theories of group communication? *Communication Studies, 41,* 237–247.

Poole, M. S., & DeSanctis, G. (1992). Microlevel structuration in computer-supported group decision making. *Human Communication Research, 19,* 5–49.

Poole, M. S., & Doelger, J. A. (1986). Developmental processes in group decision-making. In R. Y. Hirokawa & M. S. Poole (Eds.), *Communication and group decision making* (pp. 35–61). Beverly Hills, CA: Sage.

Poole, M. S., & Folger, J. P. (1981). A method for establishing the representational validity of interaction coding systems: Do they see what we see? *Human Communication Research, 8,* 26–42.

Poole, M. S., & Roth, J. (1989a). Decision development in small groups IV: A typology of group decision paths. *Human Communication Research, 15,* 323–356.

Poole, M. S., & Roth, J. (1989b). Decision development in small groups V: Test of a contingency model. *Human Communication Research, 15,* 549–589.

Poole, M. S., Seibold, D. R., & McPhee, R. D. (1986). A structurational approach to theory-building in group decision-making research. In R. Y. Hirokawa & M. S. Poole (Eds.), *Communication and group decision making* (pp. 237–264). Beverly Hills, CA: Sage.

Putnam, L. L., & Stohl, C. (1990). Bona fide groups: A reconceptualization of groups in context. *Communication Studies, 41,* 248–265.

Rosenfeld, L. B., & Fowler, G. D. (1976). Personality, sex and leadership style. *Communication Monographs, 43,* 320–324.

Rosenfeld, L. B., & Plax, T. G. (1975). Personality determinants of autocratic and democratic leadership. *Speech Monographs, 42,* 203–208.

Saine, T. J., & Bock, D. G. (1973). A comparison of the distributional and sequential structures of interaction in high and low consensus groups. *Central States Speech Journal, 24,* 125–130.

Saine, T. J., Schulman, L. S., & Emerson, L. C. (1974). The effects of group size on the structure of interaction in problem-solving groups. *Southern Speech Communication Journal, 39,* 333–345.

Salazar, A. J., Hirokawa, R. Y., Propp, K. M., Julian, K. M., & Leatham, G. B. (1994). In search of true causes: Examination of the effect of group potential and group interaction on decision performance. *Human Communication Research, 20,* 529–559.

Sargent, J. F., & Miller, G. R. (1971). Some differences in certain communication behaviors of autocratic and democratic leaders. *Journal of Communication, 21,* 233–252.

Scheidel, T. M., & Crowell, L. (1964). Idea development in small discussion groups. *Quarterly Journal of Speech, 50,* 140–145.

Scheidel, T. M., & Crowell, L. (1966). Feedback in group communication. *Quarterly Journal of Speech, 52,* 273–278.

Schultz, B. (1982). Argumentativeness: Its effect in group decision-making and its role in leadership perception. *Communication Quarterly, 30,* 368–475.

Schultz, B., & Anderson, J. (1984). Training inthe management of conflict: A communication theory perspective. *Small Group Behavior, 15,* 333–348.

Shaw, M. E. (1955). A comparison of two types of leadership in various communication nets. *Journal of Abnormal and Social Psychology, 50,* 127–134.

Shaw, M. E. (1981). *Group dynamics: The psychology of small group behavior.* New York: McGraw-Hill.

Shields, D. C., & Kidd, V. (1973). Teaching through popular film: A small group analysis of the "Poseidon Adventure." *The Speech Teacher, 22,* 201–207.

Smith, C.M., & Powell, L. (1988). The use of disparaging humor by group leaders. *Southern Speech Communication Journal, 53,* 279–292.

Steiner, I. D. (1974). Whatever happened to the group in social psychology? *Journal of Experimental Social Psychology, 10,* 94–108.

Stohl, C., & Holmes, M. E. (1993). A functional perspective for bona fide groups. In S. Deetz (Ed.), *Communication yearbook* (Vol. 16, pp. 601–614). Newbury Park, CA: Sage.

Weick, K. E. (1978). The spines of leaders. In M. McCall & M. Lomardo (Eds.), *Leadership: Where else can we go?* (pp. 37–61). Durham, NC: Duke University Press.

Weick, K. E. (1979). *The social psychology of organizing* (2nd ed.). Reading, MA: Addison-Wesley.

Wood, J. T. (1977). Leading in purposive discusions: A study of adaptive behavior. *Communication Monographs, 44,* 152–165.

Yerby, J. (1975). Attitude, task and sex composition as variables affecting female leadership in small problem-solving groups. *Speech Monographs, 42,* 160–168.

24

Organizational Communication

Brenda J. Allen
Philip K. Tompkins
University of Colorado

Stephen Busemeyer
Northwest Colorado Daily Press

Studies of organizational communication date to antiquity. The Egyptians, for example, wrote a series of manuals to guide aspiring bureaucrats (Redding & Tompkins, 1988). As an academic area, however, organizational communication is relatively new. From the time of its formal introduction in the 1950s, the area has "borrowed" heavily from numerous academic disciplines (e.g., industrial psychology, social psychology, organizational behavior, administrative science, contemporary rhetorical theory, sociology, anthropology, linguistics, political science, and the philosophy of science; Putnam & Cheney, 1985; Redding & Tompkins, 1988). Moreover, scholars from a variety of disciplines conduct research on organizational communication. Consequently, literature abounds on historical, theoretical, and methodological issues. Rather than exhausting relevant literature, this chapter discusses selected theoretical/conceptual frameworks and related research perspectives and examples.

ORGANIZATIONAL COMMUNICATION:
A DEFINITION AND BRIEF HISTORY[1]

Tompkins (1984) defined *organizational communication* as "the study of sending and receiving messages that create and maintain a system of consciously coordinated activities or forces of two or more persons" (pp. 662–663). This definition reflects an evolution in perspectives on communication and on organizations: communication is dynamic and interactive, not static and linear (as formerly conceived), and *organizations* are *systems* of *interacting individuals*, rather than entities or containers in which communication occurs. In essence, communication is a *processual* activity that *constitutes* the organization (see Barnard, 1938; Farace, Monge, & Russell, 1977; Hawes, 1974; Weick, 1969). According to scholars who adopt this constitutive viewpoint, organizational actors' activities are integrated through role coordination, interdependence, and interlocked behaviors (see, for example, Redding, 1972; Weick, 1979). Therefore, a primary task for organizational communication researchers is to observe the communication behaviors which constitute social collectivities (Bantz, 1989; Hawes, 1974).

Although organizational communication officially commenced as a specialized area of speech communication in the early 1950s (Putnam & Cheney, 1985), Tompkins (in press) marked the late 1920s as the preparatory stage of the field, when universities first began offering courses on business and professional speaking to train men and women to communicate effectively in the workplace. Thus, the area's conceptual foundation derives primarily from three sources: (a) traditional rhetorical theory (the study of formal, structured public discourse, with an emphasis on persuasion); (b) human relations "models" of informal, interpersonal interaction; and, (c) early versions of management-organization "prototheories" (Redding & Tompkins, 1988).

Since the area's inception, organizational communication researchers have striven to understand the means whereby an individual or organization could achieve *effectiveness* (Redding & Tompkins, 1988). However, the area is evolving from an emphasis on managerial concerns to an interest in everyday interactions among organizational actors. Furthermore, it has expanded its initial focus on trying to solve applied, pragmatic problems to include in-depth examinations of the complexities of social collectivities (e.g., organizational culture, power, and control). Accordingly, as discussed next, researchers have applied a variety of theoretical frameworks and methodologies to address a multiplicity of research questions.

THEORETICAL FRAMEWORKS AND RESEARCH ACTIVITIES

Among several writers who review theoretical and methodological developments in organizational communication, Redding and Tompkins (1988) offered a two-dimensional schema of dominant approaches to theory and research. First, they outlined three phases or frames of reference (formulary–prescriptive, empirical–prescriptive, and

---

[1]For extensive overviews, see Hay (1974), Porterfield (1974), Redding (1966), Richetto (1977), Tompkins (1967), Van Voorhis (1974).

applied–scientific) for conducting scholarly work between 1900 and 1970, noting that, to a certain extent, each perspective persists. Second, they outline three orientations (modernist, naturalist, and critical) to organizational communication studies.

During the *formulary–prescriptive* phase (1900–1940s), publications offered formulas, rules, or guidelines about how to be an effective communicator (written as well as oral). Major themes included a focus on one-way communication, a concern for successful communication, and an underlying assumption that managers were the most important employees.

In the second phase, the *empirical prescriptive* (1950s), researchers were concerned with helping managers or supervisors develop expertise in speaking, listening, and writing. During this phase, researchers became a bit more sophisticated by gathering in-depth information, often using case study methods. A few tested principles from the "human relations" paradigm which emerged from the landmark Hawthorne studies. From 1927 to 1932, investigators from Harvard University conducted a series of productivity studies (experiments and interviews) to ascertain the optimal level of lighting at the Hawthorne, Illinois, plant of a Western Electric Company (see Roethlisberger & Dickson, 1939). Findings revealed that, regardless of the level of lighting, worker productivity increased. The researchers surmised that employees had responded positively to the attention they had received while participating in the experiments. In addition, interviews and observations illuminated informal aspects of organizational life (e.g., group dynamics and interpersonal communication), and their role in worker productivity. These studies helped researchers and managers to realize that employees have social as well as economic needs. From this insight, the Human Relations Movement emerged, under the leadership of Elton Mayo at Harvard University.

Although prescription remained important during the third phase (*applied–scientific*, 1948–1970s), investigators presented themselves as neutral and objective. They employed traditional scientific methods associated with logical positivism and hypotheticodeductive designs (e.g., experiments, quasi-experiments, content-analytic studies, network analysis, and readability studies). Popular research topics included superior-subordinate relationships and organizational communication climate.

The second part of Redding and Tompkins' schema outlines three orientations to organizational communication studies: modernist, naturalistic, and critical. This classification resembles Habermas' (1971) three methods of inquiry (empirical-analytic, historical-hermeneutic, and critical) as well as Putnam and Cheney's (1983) reliance on those categories in a critical review of the area (see: Anderson, Greenberg & Salwen, and Stevenson, this volume, for more on critical theory). However, Redding and Tompkins claim that their categories emerge from *within* the study of organizational communication rather than from an external philosophical system. In addition, they offer their model to expand Putnam's (1983) dichotomy of functional-interpretive approaches (one of the first to delimit orientations in organizational communication research; see also Putnam, 1982).

Designed with the goal to predict or control, *modernist* (*empirical*) research stems from an epistemology of logical positivism. Investigators view objective reality as a given, and the measure that reality with psychometric techniques such as experiments, questionnaires, and rating scales. They view organizations as machines, and communication as management's tool. Their research questions typically address managerial concerns. They use computers to conduct "dispassionate analysis of an objective world" (Tompkins, in press, p. 20). Topics studied from this perspective include channel research (which assesses how information flows relative to organizational structure (i.e., upward, horizontally, and downward; see Putnam & Cheney, 1985); superior-subordinate communication (Jablin, 1979; Redding, 1972); and network analytic research (see, e.g., Roberts & O'Reilly, 1978; Rogers, 1962; and Rogers & Argawala-Rogers, 1976).

The International Communication Association (ICA) Audit² instantiates the modernist approach. It was designed to gather factual data about internal organizational communication and to establish a data bank from which researchers could compare communication systems. The communication audit consists of five measurement instruments (questionnaire, interviews, network analysis, communication experience analysis, and communication diary) that collect data on climate, networks, communication satisfaction, information flow, and media usage (see Goldhaber & Rogers, 1979; Odiorne, 1954; Putnam & Cheney, 1985).

Based upon an epistemology of language and other forms of symbolic action, *naturalistic* research strives to anticipate and interpret human communicative action (Tompkins & Cheney, 1983, p. 142). Naturalistic researchers construe reality as socially constructed, and they attempt to gain organizational insiders' (at *all* hierarchical levels) subjective understanding (*Verstehen*) of their lived experiences in organizations. They regard organizations as "social organisms," as opposed to machines, consisting of cultures and language communities. They believe that communication is constitutive of organization, and that order is negotiated through communication. Thus, they focus on how meaning is created and maintained in everyday interaction, and they interpret symbolic aspects of organizational life (e.g., myths, rites and rituals, metaphors, rules, norms, stories, values, fantasy themes, etc.) (see Bantz, 1983; Pacanowsky & O'Donnell-Trujillo, 1982).

Data-gathering activities include such methods as participant–observation, ethnography, in-depth interviews, focus groups, case studies, and document and artifact analysis. (Putnam & Pacanowsky, 1983). For instance, Smith and Eisenberg (1987) conducted intensive interviews with employees from various hierarchical levels at Disneyland about their everyday experiences on the job. Analysis of interview transcripts revealed two root metaphors that characterized organizational actors' sense of Disneyland: drama and family. (For additional research examples, see Bormann, Pratt, & Putnam, 1978; Hawes, 1976; Pacanowsky, 1991; Rosen, 1988; Sypher, 1990; Tompkins, 1977, 1978; Tompkins & Cheney, 1983; Trujillo, 1983).

Redding and Tompkins contend that the epistemological orientation of *critical* research is difficult to discern, but the assumptions of the approach are unavoidably positivistic. The goal is social change: to raise workers' consciousness or to emancipate them and to establish free and open communication situations (Deetz, 1982; Deetz & Kersten, 1983; Putnam, 1983; Redding & Tompkins, 1988). Critical researchers hope to provide "insight, critique, and education" (Deetz, 1992, pp. 345-346). Similar to naturalistic investigators, they study symbolic practices and meaning systems (Mumby,

---

²Since 1979, the ICA audit is not an ICA-sponsored activity; the instruments and procedures are now part of the public domain (Goldhaber, 1993).

1993b). However, they view organizations as instruments of oppression. They believe that controlling individuals in organizations engage in systematically distorted communication (see Habermas, 1979). Further, they posit that organizational reality partially reflects material interests and resources, and they conduct their studies from workers' perspectives.

Critical investigators do not favor any particular research method. Rather, they employ whatever procedures seem appropriate for exposing and explaining relationships between communicative practices and dimensions and structures of power and control in social collectivities (Clegg, 1975; Conrad, 1983; Deetz & Kersten, 1983; Mumby, 1993b). Studies conducted from this perspective reveal a developing interest in a *political* perspective on communication (DeWine & Daniels, 1993). For instance, Mumby (1987) studied the political use of narratives (i.e., storytelling) in an organization to document ways that the process of recounting stories helps to reify an organization's rule system (see also Conrad, 1988; Deetz, 1992; Mumby, 1988; Mumby & Stohl, 1991; Wendt, 1994).

After acknowledging a bias toward naturalistic and critical orientations to research, Redding and Tompkins (1988) asserted that *"all forms of inquiry* are vital to continued progress in the study of organizational communication" (p. 27). A literature review which applied Redding and Tompkins' categories to identify topics and orientations to studying organizational communication (between 1979–1989) indicates that the modernistic orientation dominates research published in communication journals (Wert-Gray, Center, Brashers, & Meyers, 1991) Although the naturalistic orientation exhibited growth between 1987 and 1989, few of the published studies applied the critical approach.[3]

As evidenced by an increase in published articles, textbooks, and convention papers, the field of organizational communication is rapidly growing and becoming more mature and refined. In a review of the field, Putnam and Cheney (1985) cite four "families" of study (information processing, political perspectives, cultural, and rhetorical perspectives) that indicate an expansion in theoretical and research approaches to studying organizational communication. To describe a hypothetical research project, the remainder of this chapter focuses on a program of study derived from the rhetorical perspective.

HYPOTHETICAL RESEARCH PROJECT

From an early interest in helping managers become effective to contemporary concern about empowering and emancipating workers, organizational communication scholars have studied control and decision making in organizations. The following hypothetical study addresses these enduring issues by applying one of only a few theoretical frameworks which arise from organizational communication.

Theoretical Framework and Literature Review

Tompkins and Cheney (1983, 1985) developed a rhetorically grounded research program that focuses on communication and unobtrusive organizational control. Based in part upon work by Burke (1969), Edwards (1981), and Simon (1976), their approach

---

[3]Also see Allen, Gotcher, and Seibert (1993) for a review of organizational communication research journal articles published between 1980 and 1991.

addresses ways that organizational actors are influenced and controlled through premises inculcated by management. In an historical model, Edwards (1981) demonstrated that owner-managers have moved from obtrusive to unobtrusive control methods in three stages: (a) "simple control," in which management openly exercises power over workers; (b) "technical control," in which control is embedded in machines and other physical apparatus of the workplace; and, (c) "bureaucratic control," wherein control is "embedded in the social relations of production" (Edwards, 1981, p. 161). To this classification, Tompkins and Cheney (1985) add "concertive" control: "a new and post-bureaucratic type of control—one that stresses teamwork and coordination in all stages of production" (p. 184). In the concertive organization, "the explicit rules and regulations are largely replaced by common understanding of values, objectives, and means of achievement, along with a deep appreciation for the organization's 'mission'" (p. 184).

Tompkins and Cheney also integrate Simon's (1976) discussion of decision-making and "bounded rationality" into their theory. When faced with a decision, humans can neither know all conceivable options, nor choose from among them (Simon, 1976). Moreover, Simon claims that humans cannot attend to the multiplicity of goals and values which surround them. Thus, decision-making processes are "bounded." Tompkins and Cheney accepted Simon's (1976) unit of analysis, the decision premise, and introduced the concept of enthymeme2 (i.e., the organization provides the premises the individual will use in making decisions). The organization inculcates premises through a variety of means, including in-house publications, training, orientation programs, or through incentives.

Acceptance of organizational premises influences *identification*, the extent to which an employee, when faced with a decision, will choose "the alternative that best promotes the perceived interests of that organization" (Tompkins & Cheney, 1985, p. 194; the concept is derived from Burke, 1937, 1969, 1973). Identification prompts organizational actors to attend to particular organizationally sanctioned values, facts, and goals, first by influencing which problems and alternatives they see. Tompkins and Cheney (1985) explained: "The organizational member is limited at the outset to alternatives tied to his/her identifications; other options will simply not come into view, and therefore will not be considered" (p. 194). Second, identification directs organizational actors' choices to particular alternatives. To measure an individual's level of identification with an organization, Cheney (1982) developed the Organizational Identification Questionnaire (OIQ), a 30-item instrument which contains items such as: "I have warm feelings toward *Organization X*."

The literature contains numerous research articles and essays about identification or concertive control (e.g., Barker, 1993a; Barker & Cheney, 1994; Barker & Tompkins, 1994; Bullis & Tompkins, 1989; Cheney, 1983a, 1983b; Cox, 1983, 1988; Kelly & Busemeyer, 1992; Pribble, 1990; Sewell & Wilkinson, 1992; Tompkins & Cheney, 1983; Tompkins, Fisher, Infante, & Tompkins, 1975). For instance, Tompkins and Cheney (1983) used account analysis to ask teaching assistants to justify or explain their decision making behaviors. They then compared the assistants' accounts with individual scores on the OIQ. The quantitative data (OIQ scores) tended to validate interview (accounts) data.

Cox (1983) designed a Black Identification Questionnaire based upon the OIQ. Cox found that although White staff members had higher organizational identification scores than Blacks. Blacks who identified most highly with their organizations tended to score highest on Black identification scores. In a later project, Cox (1988) reported gender-related differences in identification and communicator style among Black subjects. An analysis of house organs revealed several strategies aimed at increasing organizational identification among employees (Cheney, 1983b). The most common strategy was *common ground*, or pointing out shared interests between the organization and the individual employee. Pribble (1990) evaluated the ethical dimension of a Fortune 500 Company's formal (videotaped) orientation program. Pribble found that the organization attempted to evoke organizational identification by demonstrating shared values and the family metaphor. Bullis and Tompkins (1989) analyzed interview data to identify decision premises among rangers in the U.S. Forest Service. Another study assessed decision premises among employees in the newsroom of a metropolitan newspaper (Kelly & Busemeyer, 1992).

An ethnographic study of an electronics firm that was changing from traditional, bureaucratic control processes to self-directed work teams corroborated Tompkins and Cheney's (1985) conclusion that concertive control increases the total amount of control in the organizational system (Barker, 1993b). In essence, concertive control exhibited in work teams "tightened the iron cage of bureaucracy" (Barker, 1993b).

Further investigation (Barker & Tompkins, 1994) asked employees in the same electronics firm to complete the Organizational Identification Questionnaire (Cheney, 1982) to assess, in a comparative way, their level of identification with their teams and with the overall organization. Employees who had worked longer in the teams tended to identify more with their teams than with the organization, whereas newcomers to teams were not as highly identifying.

In sum, Tompkins and Cheney's work shows promise for addressing traditional topics (e.g., decision making, control, identification) as well as contemporary issues (e.g., work teams, mergers, ethics, and diversity), whereas further developing a theoretical framework which the field can claim for itself. To extend and augment this research program, a project is proposed to describe, interpret, and document control practices and attitudes among work team members in a manufacturing company which is implementing diversity initiatives by hiring more females and members of ethnic minority groups. Developed from modernist, naturalistic, and critical perspectives, the proposed research project will seek to answer the following research questions:

1. According to their own reports or accounts, what decision premises do team members use to accomplish work-related tasks?
2. According to their own reports, how do members of a work team learn decision premises?
3. Do team members report or exhibit varying preferences for decision premises according to individual differences (e.g., gender, race or ethnicity, age, tenure within the organization)?
4. Does identification (with the organization and/or with the team) vary according to individual differences among team members?
5. What decision premises are advocated by management?
6. How does management attempt to inculcate decision premises?

7. (a) Does a relationship exist between organizational actors' identification with the organization and the extent to which they are most likely to use decision strategies preferred by management?

(b) Does a relationship exist between team members identification with their team and the extent to which they are most likely to use decision premises and strategies preferred by management?

(c) Do relationships assessed in 7a and 7b vary across time?

8. Does a relationship exist between control and organizational identification?

Methodology

To answer these questions, a team of three researchers will conduct a longitudinal (one year), triangulated research project, using a purposive sample of five work teams (each team consists of 10–12 employees). The investigative team will consist of two females and one male, each with a different racial-ethnic background. Data will be collected via an array of methods, including quantitative procedures such as repeated administration (once every 4 months) of the OIQ and Tannenbaum's (1968) control graph scale, an instrument that asks respondents to indicate degrees of influence that they and other organizational members have. The control questionnaire includes separate items that elicit perceived degree of influence of organizational members from various hierarchical levels (e.g., managers, supervisors, workers). Mean influence scores for each level are plotted on control graphs, providing a visual representation of respondents' perceptions of the control hierarchy.

Researchers also will employ a variety of qualitative techniques, including: participant–observation, interviews, taped meetings, and document analysis. For instance, during one-on-one semistructured interviews, organizational actors will be asked to tell stories about decision-making experiences and to account for their own decision-making behaviors. Transcripts of videotaped meetings will be analyzed to assess reflexive comments related to decision-making processes (see Geist & Chandler, 1984; Harre & Secord, 1972).

Researchers will meet periodically with study participants to conduct member checks (i.e., to ask stakeholders to review researchers' descriptions, interpretations, and conclusions; see Lincoln & Guba, 1985). Furthermore, each investigator will record observations (at least once a week) in a reflexive journal (see Erlandson, Harris, Skipper, & Allen, 1993). The research team will meet at least once a month to discuss its observations, to adjust (where necessary) the research plan, and to draw tentative interpretations, and conclusions. Thus, data analysis will be ongoing, interactive, and self-reflexive.

Researchers will apply a variety of research analytical methods, including: inductive interpretation of interview transcripts (e.g., the constant comparative method, in which data are sorted into categories and labeled; see Glaser & Strauss, 1967), and statistical analysis of quantitative data (e.g., the OIQ, the control graph questionnaire, demographic information).

Implications

As outlined, the proposed project signifies several implications for advancing the study of organizational communication. It clearly would address the need to continue developing the area's own theory, by augmenting an established research program that originated in studies of organizational communication, of which there are few (see Redding, 1992). In addition, it would also serve as a prototype for triangulating research (using a variety of methods) from a tripartite (modernist, naturalistic, and critical) perspective. This project also would add to the slowly growing numbers of naturalistic and critical research studies. As a longitudinal endeavor, the proposed project responds to a recurring call to provide motion pictures rather than "snapshots" of organizational life. It also answers a general need to conduct research that helps to solve human interaction problems or dilemmas (e.g., DeWine & Daniels, 1993), and two related concerns: first, to explore decision-making behaviors *in actual organizations* (e.g., O'Reilly, Chatman, & Anderson, 1987), and second, to focus on *connectedness* and collaborative interaction among organizational actors (see Stohl, 1995).

By utilizing a heterogeneous research team, and by studying participants based upon facets of their identity other than their work roles, the study counters the penchant in organizational communication studies for taking a monocultural perspective on organizational life (see Allen, 1995). This seems particularly timely, given population projections which predict a highly racially diverse heterogeneous workforce by the year 2000 (Johnston & Packer, 1987). Finally, by actively involving organizational actors in the project (for instance, by soliciting their feedback on researchers' interpretations), this study would represent an effort to take a "dialogical approach that explicitly recognizes organization members as playing a role in the knowledge process" (Mumby, 1993a, p. 21).

CONCLUSION

During its first half-century of existence, organizational communication has undergone significant changes, even as it has continued to address the ancient question of how to communicate effectively. With a natural predictability that comes with a sound understanding of disciplinary archaeology, contemporary organizational communication scholars have responded (and will continue to respond) to many issues: an ongoing tension between consulting and research; accusations of being antitheoretical; a perceived lack of theoretical infrastructure and feminist critique (e.g., Marshall, 1993; Mumby, 1993a; and Rush & Grubb-Swetnam, chapter 31, this volume). In addition, the field is being called upon to address several new topics and issues, such as the concept of democracy in the workplace, new approaches to rhetoric in organizational analysis (e.g., Cheney, 1991); ethics; work, teams, and concertive control; communication technology and information processing (e.g., Fulk & Boyd, 1991); critical studies; and feminism (for a discussion of trends in organizational communication associated with these topics, see Tompkins, Wanca-Thibault, & Redding, in press; see also Kovacic, 1994, and Poole, 1994, for discussions about new perspectives on organizational communication).

Regardless of the fluctuations and trends in scholarly activities, people who study organizational communication must first understand that, unlike other areas of study—even in the field of communication—the subject matter will change as society changes. As society changes, organizations change, develop, adapt, realign, and search for new paradigms. Organizational communication, therefore, must be a flexible field. Any newfound truth will soon become mythology as organizations change with their environment.

This is not to say, however, that studying organizational communication is a wild goose chase. Scholars should continue the tradition of addressing practical issues, but they must also ask research questions which consider *all* members of social collectivities and be willing to uncover and illuminate nonrational, negative aspects of organizational life. They also must assess their own proclivity (as "experts") to speak for those whom they study. To accomplish these daunting tasks, organizational communication scholars may need a mirror as well as a microscope.

REFERENCES

Allen, B. J. (1995). "Diversity" and organizational communication. *Journal of Applied Communication, 23,* 143–155.

Allen, M. W., Gotcher, J. M., & Seibert, J. H. (1993). A decade of organizational communication research: Journal articles 1980–1991. In S. Deetz (Ed.), *Communication yearbook* (Vol. 16, pp. 252–330). Newbury Park, CA: Sage.

Bantz, C. R. (1983). Naturalistic research traditions. In L. L. Putnam & M. E. Pacanowsky (Eds.), *Communication and organizations: An interpretive approach* (pp. 55–73). Beverly Hills, CA: Sage.

Bantz, C. R. (1989). Organizing and the social psychology of organizing. *Communication Studies, 40,* 231–240.

Barnard, C. (1938). *The functions of the executive.* Cambridge, MA: Harvard University Press.

Barker, J. R. (1993a). Tightening the iron cage: Concertive control in self managing teams. *Administrative Science Quarterly, 38,* 408–437.

Barker, J. R. (1993b). *Unobtrusive control in the self managing organization and control practices during a period of organizational transformation.* Unpublished doctoral dissertation, University of Colorado, Boulder.

Barker, J. R., & Cheney, G. (1994). The concept and the practices of discipline in contemporary organizational life. *Communication Monographs, 61,* 19–43.

Barker, J. R., & Tompkins, P. K. (1994). Identification in the self managing organization: Characteristics of target and tenure. *Human Communication Research, 21,* 223–243.

Bormann, E. G., Pratt, J., & Putnam, L. L. (1978). Power, authority and sex: Male response to female leadership. *Communication Monographs, 45,* 119–155.

Bullis, C., & Tompkins P. K. (1989). The forest ranger revisited: A study of control practices and identification. *Communication Monographs, 56,* 287–306.

Burke, K. (1937). *Attitudes toward history.* New York: New Republic.

Burke, K. (1969). *A rhetoric of motives.* Berkeley: University of California Press.

Burke, K. (1973). The rhetorical situation. In L. Thayer (Ed.), *Communication: Ethical and moral issues* (pp. 263–275). London: Gordon & Breach.

Cheney, G. (1982). *Organizational identification as process and product: A field study.* Unpublished master's thesis, Purdue University, West Lafayette, IN.

Cheney, G. (1983a). The rhetoric of identification and the study of organizational communication. *Quarterly Journal of Speech, 69,* 143–158.

Cheney, G. (1983b). On the various and changing meanings of organizational membership: A field study of organizational identification. *Communication Monographs, 50,* 324–362.

Cheney, G. (1991). *Rhetoric in an organizational society: Managing multiple identities.* Columbia, SC: University of South Carolina Press.

Clegg, S. (1975). *The theory of power and organization.* London: Routledge & Kegan Paul.

Conrad, C. (1983). Organizational power: Faces and symbolic forms. In L. L. Putnam & M. E. Pacanowsky (Eds.), *Communication and organizations: An interpretive approach* (pp. 173–194). Newbury Park, CA: Sage.

Conrad, C. (1988). Work songs, hegemony and illusions of self. *Critical Studies in Mass Communication*, *5*, 179–201.

Cox, M. (1983). *The effectiveness of black identification and organizational identification on communication supportiveness*. Unpublished doctoral dissertation, Purdue University, West Lafayette, IN.

Cox, M. (1988). The impact of sex and black identification on evaluations of communicator style: Implications for organizational sense-making. In L. B. Nadler, M. K. Nadler, & W. R. Todd-Mancillas (Eds.), *Advances in gender and communication research* (pp. 317–348). Lanham, MD: University Press of America.

Deetz, S. (1982). Critical interpretive research in organizational communication. *Western Journal of Speech Communication*, *46*, 131–149.

Deetz, S. (1992). *Democracy in an age of corporate colonization*. Albany: State University of New York Press.

Deetz, S., & Kersten, A. (1983). Critical models of interpretive research. In L. L. Putnam & M. E. Pacanowsky (Eds.), *Communication and organizations: An interpretive approach* (pp. 147–172). Newbury Park, CA: Sage.

DeWine, S., & Daniels, T. (1993). Beyond the snapshot: Setting a research agenda in organizational communication. In S. Deetz (Ed.), *Communication yearbook* (Vol. 16, pp. 331–346). Newbury Park, CA: Sage.

Edwards, R. (1981). The social relations of production at the point of production. In M. ZeyFerrel & M. Aiken (Eds.), *Complex organizations: Critical perspectives* (pp. 156–182). Glenview, IL; Scott, Foresman.

Erlandson, D. S., Harris, E. L., Skipper, B. J., & Allen, S. (1993). *Doing naturalistic inquiry: A guide to methods*. Newbury Park, CA: Sage.

Farace, R. V., Monge, P. R., & Russell, H. M. (1977). *Communicating and organizing*. Reading, MA: Addison-Wesley.

Fulk, J., & Boyd, B. (1991). Emerging theories of communication in organizations. *Journal of Management 17*, 407–446.

Geist, P., & Chandler, T. (1984). Account analysis of influence in group decision making. *Communication Monographs*, *51*, 67–78.

Glaser, B. G., & Strauss, A. L. (1967). *The discovery of grounded theory*. Hawthorne, NY: Aldine.

Goldhaber, G. M. (1993). *Organizational communication* (6th ed.). Dubuque, IA: Brown & Benchmark.

Goldhaber, G. M., & Rogers, D. P. (1979). *Auditing organizational communication systems: The ICA communication audit*. Dubuque, Iowa: Kendall/Hunt.

Habermas, J. (1971). *Knowledge and human interests*. Boston, MA: Beacon Press.

Habermas, J. (1979). *Communication and the evolution of society*. Boston, MA: Beacon Press.

Harre, R., & Secord, P. F. (1972). *The explanation of social behavior*. Totawa, NJ: Littlefield, Adams.

Hawes, L. C. (1974). Social collectivities as communication: Perspectives in organizational behavior. *Quarterly Journal of Speech*, *60*, 497–502.

Hawes, L. C. (1976). How writing is used in talk: A study of communicative logic-in-use. *Quarterly Journal of Speech*, *62*, 350–360.

Hay, R. D. (1974). A brief history of internal organizational communication through the 1940s. *Journal of Business Communication*, *11*, 6–11.

Jablin, F. M. (1979). Superior-subordinate communication: The state of the art. *Psychological Bulletin*, *86*, 1201–1222.

Johnston, W. B., & Packer, A. H. (1987). *Workforce 2000: Work and workers for the 21st century*. Hudson Institute: Indianapolis, IN.

Kelly, L., & Busemeyer, S. (1992). *Unobtrusive control in organizations: A barrier to social change*. Paper presented at the Eastern Communication Association Convention, Portland, ME.

Kovacic, B. (1994). New perspectives on organizational communication. In B. Kovacic (Ed.), *New approaches to organizational communication* (pp. 1–37). Albany: State University of New York Press.

Lincoln, Y. S., & Guba, E. G. (1985). *Naturalistic inquiry*. Beverly Hills, CA: Sage.

Marshall, J. (1993). Viewing organizational communication from a feminist perspective: A critique and some offerings. In S. Deetz (Ed.), *Communication yearbook* (Vol. 16, pp. 122–143). Newbury Park, CA: Sage

Mumby, D. K. (1987). The political function of narrative in organizations. *Communication Monographs*, *54*, 113–127

Mumby, D. K. (1988). *Communication and power in organizations: Discourse, ideology, and domination*. Norwood, NJ: Ablex.

Mumby, D. K. (1993a). Critical organizational communication studies: The next ten years. *Communication Monographs*, *60*, 18–25.

Mumby, D. K. (1993b). *Narrative and social control: Critical perspectives*. Newbury Park, CA: Sage.

Mumby, D. K., & Stohl, C. (1991). Power and discourse in organizational studies: Absence and the dialect of control. *Discourse and Society*, *2*, 313–332.

Odiorne, G. (1954). An application of the communication audit. *Personnel Psychology*, *1*, 235–243.

O'Reilly, C. A., Chatman, J. A., & Anderson, J. C. (1987). Message flow and decision making. In F. M. Jablin, L. L. Putnam, K. H. Roberts, & L. W. Porter (Eds.), *Handbook of organizational communication: An interdisciplinary perspective* (pp. 600–623). Newbury Park, CA: Sage.

Pacanowsky, M. E. (1991). Communication in the empowering organization. In S. Deetz (Ed.), *Communication yearbook* (Vol. 11, pp. 356–379). Newbury Park, CA: Sage.

Pacanowsky, M. E., & O'Donnell-Trujillo, N. (1982). Communication and organizational cultures. *Western Journal of Speech Communication*, *46*, 115–130.

Poole, M. S. (1994). Afterword. In B. Kovacic (Ed.), *New approaches to organizational communication* (pp. 270–277). Albany: State University of New York Press.

Porterfield, C.D. (1974). Organizational communication: Developments from 1960 to the present. *Journal of Business Communication*, *11*, 18–24.

Pribble, P. T. (1990). Making an ethical commitment: A rhetorical case study of organizational socialization. *Communication Quarterly*, *38*, 255–267.

Putnam, L. L. (1982). Paradigms for organizational communication research: An overview and synthesis. *Western Journal of Speech Communication*, *46*, 192–206.

Putnam, L. L. (1983). The interpretive perspective: An alternative to functionalism. In L. L. Putnam & M. E. Pacanowsky (Eds.), *Communication and organizations: An interpretive approach* (pp. 31–54). Beverly Hills: Sage.

Putnam, L. L., & Cheney, G. (1983). A critical review of research traditions in organizational communication. In S. M. Mander (Ed.), *Communications in transition* (pp. 206–224). New York: Prager.

Putnam, L. L., & Cheney, G. (1985). Organizational communication: Historical development and future directions. In T. W. Benson (Ed.), *Speech communication in the 20th century*. Carbondale: Southern Illinois University Press.

Putnam, L. L., & Pacanowsky M. E. (Eds.). (1983). *Communication and organization: An interpretive approach*. Beverly Hills, CA: Sage.

Redding, W. C. (1972). *Communication within the organization: An interpretive review of theory and research*. New York: Industrial Communication Council.

Redding. W. C. (1992). Response to professor Berger's essay: Its meaning for organizational communication. *Communication Monographs*, *59*, 87–93.

Redding, W. C., & Tompkins, P. (1988). Organizational communication—past and present tenses. In G. Goldhaber & G. Barnett (Eds.), *Handbook of organizational communication* (pp. 5–33). Norwood, NJ: Ablex.

Richetto, G. M. (1977). Organizational communication theory and research: An overview. In B. D. Ruben (Ed.), *Communication yearbook* (Vol. 1, pp. 331–346). New Brunswick, NJ: International Communication Association/Transaction Books.

Roberts, K. H., & O'Reilly, C. A. (1978). Organizations as communication structures. *Human communication Research*, *4*, 283–293.

Roethlisberger, F. J., & Dickson, W. J. (1939). *Management and the worker*. Cambridge, MA: Harvard University Press.

Rogers, E. M. (1962). *Diffusion of innovations*. New York: Free Press.

Rogers, E., & Agarwala-Rogers, R. (1976). *Communication in organizations*. New York: The Free Press

Rosen, M. (1988). You asked for it: Christmas at the bosses' expense. *Journal of Management Studies*, *25*, 163–180.

Sewell, G., & Wilkinson, B. (1992). "Someone to watch over me:" Surveillance, discipline and the just-in-time labour process. *Sociology*, *26*, 271–289.

Simon, H. A. (1976). *Administrative behavior* (3rd ed.). New York; Free Press.

Smith, R. C., & Eisenberg, E. M. (1987). Conflict at Disneyland: A root-metaphor analysis. *Communication Monographs*, *54*, 367–380.

Stohl, C. (1995). *Organizational communication: Connectedness in action*. Thousand Oaks, CA: Sage.

Sypher, B. D. (1990). *Case studies in organizational communication*. New York: Guilford.

Tannenbaum, A. (1968). *Control in organizations*. New York: McGraw Hill.

Tompkins, P. K. (1967). Organizational communication: A state-of-the-art review. In G. Richetto (Ed.). *Conference on organizational communication*. Huntsville, AL: George C. Marshall Space Flight Center, NASA.

Tompkins, P. (1977). Management qua communication in rocket research and development. *Communication Monographs*, *4*, 1–26.

Tompkins, P. (1978). Organizational metamorphosis in space research and development. *Communication Monographs*, *45*, 110–118.

Tompkins, P. K. (1984). Functions of Communication in organizations. In C. Arnold & J. W. Bowers (Eds.), *Handbook of rhetorical and communication theory* (pp. 659–719). New York: Allyn & Bacon.

Tompkins, P. K. (in press). How to think and talk about organizational communication. In P. Byers (Ed.). *Organizational communication: Theory and behavior*. Boston, MA: Allyn & Bacon.

Tompkins, P. K., & Cheney, G. (1983). Account analysis of organizations: Decision making and identification. In L. L. Putnam & M.E. Pacanowsky (Eds.), *Communication and organization: An interpretative approach* (pp 123–146). Beverly Hills, CA: Sage

Tompkins, P. K., & Cheney G. (1985). Communication and unobtrusive control in contemporary organizations. In R. D. McPhee & P. K. Tompkins (Eds.), *Organizational communication: Traditional themes and new directions* (pp. 178–210). Beverly Hills, CA: Sage.

Tompkins, P. K., Fisher, J. Y., Infante, D. A., & Tompkins, E. L. (1975). Kenneth Burke and the inherent characteristics of formal organizations: A field study. *Speech Monographs*, *42*, 135–142.

Tompkins, P. K., Wanca-Thibault, M. A., & Redding, W. C. (1995). *The location of organizational communication in academic discourse*. Unpublished manuscript

Trujillo, N. (1983). "Performing" Mintzberg's roles: The nature of managerial communication. In L. Putnam & M. Pacanowsky (Eds.), *Communication and organization: An interpretive approach* (pp. 73–97). Beverly Hills: Sage.

van Voorhis, K. R. (1974). Organizational communication: Advances made during the period from WW II through the 1950s. *Journal of Business Communication*, *11*, 11–18.

Weick, K. E. (1969). *The social psychology of organizing*. Reading, MA: Addison-Wesley.

Weick, K. E. (1979). *The social psychology of organizing* (2nd ed.). Reading, MA: Addison-Wesley.

Wendt, R. (1994). Learning to "walk the talk:" A critical tale of micropolitics at a total quality university. *Management Communication Quarterly, 8*, 4–45.

Wert-Gray, S., Center, C., Brashers, D., & Meyers, R. (1991). Research topics and methodological orientations in organizational communication: A decade in review. *Communication Studies*, *42*, 141–154.

IV

Integrated Approaches
to Communication

25

Multichannel Leadership: Revisiting the False Dichotomy

Kathleen K. Reardon
Emmeline G. de Pillis
University of Southern California

In 1988, Reardon and Rogers called into question the historical divide between the studies of interpersonal and mass media communication. In an article in *Human Communication Research*, they set out to "challenge one of the most guarded constructions in the study of human communication: the separation between interpersonal and mass media communication" (p. 285). They proposed that the distinction between the two fields "has had detrimental effects on the progress of communication theory and research. What communication scholars had considered an obvious and natural division of our field is . . . a disunifying distortion with far reaching implications" (Reardon & Rogers, 1988, p. 285). The purpose of this chapter is to revisit the false dichotomy perspective of interpersonal versus mass communication in the context of the new technologies and organizational structures that are reshaping the workplace, particularly the virtual office.

THE DICHOTOMY

"Mass media was defined for decades as all means of transmitting messages, such as the press, radio, television, and so on, that enable one or a few individuals to reach an audience of many," whereas interpersonal communication was limited to "face to face interaction between two or a few people with opportunities for feedback" (Reardon & Rogers, 1988, p. 285). Traditionally, interpersonal communication has been distinguished from mass communication mainly on the basis of the following elements: *channel type*—interpersonal communication is usually defined as face-to-face, whereas mass communication is said to use technology such as television or print; *number of potential message recipients*; and *potential for feedback*—mass media communication is defined as having almost no potential for feedback.

The divide is so enduring that a study of five mass media journals and the three interpersonal communication journals found almost no cross-citations. Only 17 out of 1,010 citations in interpersonal journals referred to mass communications journals; only 7 out of 333 cites in mass communication journals referred to interpersonal communication journals (Paisley, 1984).

REASONS FOR THE DICHOTOMY

The boundary between the subdisciplines of interpersonal and mass communication has less to do with communication theory than with university history and politics, as the following overview describes.

History

In 1949, Shannon and Weaver developed a simple model of communication that was embraced by communication scholars. Their information theory model standardized the terminology of basic communication study, introducing such terms as feedback, noise, and receivers. Unfortunately, the model oversimplified communication, leading to a communication paradigm that was linear and unidirectional. Feedback and other dynamic aspects of the model were deemphasized and eventually dropped. Later research, especially in mass communication, focused on *effects* on receivers caused by sources sending messages through either interpersonal or mass media channels. The growing emphasis on effects provided no counterpoint to the division of the communication field into interpersonal and mass media sectors. Interpersonal communication research began to take its lead from psychology, social psychology, and linguistics; mass media research drew upon sociology and political science, with an emphasis on policy concerns and application.

University Politics

For the first half of this century, universities did not have departments of communication. Communication simply was not considered a discipline. Social scientists made brief forays into the study of communication, only to return to their own fields. Communication research was "one of the greatest crossroads where many pass but few tarry" (Schramm, 1959, p. 8). In the 1950s, a few universities—among them Illinois, Stanford, Minnesota, and Wisconsin—began to offer doctorates in communication. A few years later, David Berlo initiated a program of study at Michigan State University designed to attract scholars interested in defining and developing the field of communication.

By the mid-1960s, communication departments were forming in earnest—not as independent departments, but as additions to existing departments. Quite apart from historical rationale for the bifurcation of the communication field were practical concerns about where to place communication studies within the university. Journalism was a good candidate for absorbing mass media studies. Journalism needed the scientific legitimacy of the mass communication field, and the connection between journalism and mass media (conceptualized as print, radio, and television) seemed logical (Carey, 1979). Speech departments typically focused on interpersonal communication study—often over the objections of rhetoricians, who opposed the introduction of social science into their field (Bochner & Eisenberg, 1985). Because speech and journalism departments were founded at most American universities prior to the introduction of Shannon and Weaver's potentially unifying model in 1949, the subfields of interpersonal and mass media communication were already organizationally structured and perhaps destined to grow apart.

There are exceptions to the dichotomy. Persuasion theory, for example, has bridged the subdisciplines of interpersonal and mass communication. Cognitive dissonance, counterattitudinal advocacy, inoculation, and balance theory have been applied both to interpersonal and to mass media communication research (e.g., Reardon, 1981; Roloff & Miller, 1980). There have been volumes published which integrate the work of interpersonal and mass media scholars (e.g., Gumpert & Cathart, 1982; Hawkins, Weimann, & Pingree, 1988). Since Reardon and Rogers's call for dialogue between the interpersonal and mass media communication subdisciplines, articles have been published integrating interpersonal and mass media communication research. For example, Coleman's 1993 study of personal-level and social-level risk judgments compared the effects of interpersonal and mass media channels on these judgments; Neumann and Charlton (1989) examined the effects of mass media versus interpersonal communication on children.

Consequences of the Dichotomy

The false dichotomy between interpersonal and mass communication studies has significant implications for the study of communication as a whole. Communication theory currently lacks integration; with a few exceptions, such as those noted above, theoretical intersections between the two subareas are rare. Integration is necessary because a total communication process cannot be understood fully by only one of the two subareas. For example, processes such as innovation or socialization cannot be fully understood using only interpersonal or mass communication theories. Moreover, new forms of technologically enhanced communication cannot fit comfortably in one category or the other. Those who have studied new communication technologies such as video teleconferencing, electronic bulletin boards, and two-way cablevision have recognized that these technologies share certain characteristics with interpersonal communication and mass communication.

Ball-Rokeach and Reardon (1990) introduced the term *telelogic* to describe communication forms that are neither monologic (a term which describes mass communication and public speaking) nor dialogic (a term which denotes interpersonal communication). Telelogic communication involves alternating dialogue between or among people who may be geographically distant, and uses technologically enhanced forms of communication such as electronic mail (e-mail). This new form of communication has engendered the development of the virtual communities predicted by communications theorists. Beniger (1987) wrote of the "personalization of mass media and the growth of pseudo-community" (p. 3), and Ball-Rokeach and Reardon (1988) predicted that telelogic communication "may develop into a new way of organizing interpersonal life, especially for persons who cannot be in the same geographic area at the same time" (1988, p. 150). Already, virtual communities are developing their own cultures and norms. For example, internet relay chat (IRC) groups, which are generally recreational and based on members' mutual interests, have devised their own way of increasing channel richness.

> Without facial expressions, tone of voice, body language, clothing, shared physical environment, or any other contextual cues that signal the physical presence of participants in a social group, IRC participants use words alone to reconstruct contexts . . . adding imagined actions (such as "Howard smiles ironically" or "Howard takes offense and it looks like he's going to punch you in the nose") as metadescriptors to the running dialogue. (Rheingold, 1994, p. 177)

Unlike the informal "netiquette" that has evolved to govern recreational communication on the Internet, however, no consensus has evolved as to how to adapt organizational communication to new technologies.

Suboptimal use of a communication technology in an organizational setting can have serious consequences. Trevino, Daft, and Lengel (1990) cited the insurance company executive who decreed that all communication by managers be done via electronic mail. Although e-mail was convenient and efficient, managers began to complain that some important issues were not being resolved. The managers began holding meetings and making phone calls on the sly to make up for perceived deficiencies in the e-mail format. Trevino et al., also pointed to the use of teleconferencing in making the fatal decision to launch the space shuttle Challenger in 1986. The teleconferencing medium was not the sole culprit in this disaster, but the decision to substitute a teleconference for a face-to-face final launch meeting may have contributed to the tragedy. Many of the engineers did not want to proceed with the launch but could not adequately communicate their conviction in the teleconferencing format.

THE VIRTUAL OFFICE: A CASE IN POINT

Recent years have seen the emergence of a special type of virtual community—the virtual office. The virtual office is the real-life version of utopian visions like Callenback's (1975) *Ecotopia* where, for the sake of the environment, physical transportation has been all but replaced by electronic communication:

Feeling that they should transport their bodies only when it's a pleasure, they seldom travel "on business" in our manner. Instead, they tend to transact business by using their picturephones. These employ the same cables that provide television connections; the whole country, except for a few isolated rural spots, is wired with cable. (p. 38)

Virtual office is not a technology per se, but it exists by means of communication technology. A virtual office does not exist in physical space. It is not limited to workers who telecommute from home. A true virtual office lets its workers work productively anytime, anywhere so long as the organization's goal is reached and the work is done on time. One example of virtual office can be found at AT&T, which has equipped many sales representatives with portable computers and modems so that they submit almost all of their paperwork from the field. These employees have no physical office building. Their office is wherever they are, preferably at a customer site.

We are all familiar with the structural changes organizations are experiencing. Organizations are becoming leaner, flatter, more temporally and geographically flexible, and more team-oriented. Much of this change is facilitated by advances in technologically enhanced communication. The culmination of this structural change, coupled with technological advance, is the virtual office—a way of organizing, where a work team exists, even if that team does not share a physical space. A virtual office can use phone, fax, e-mail, videoconferencing, and any other low- or high-tech long-distance communication medium.

A look at the popular press reveals that companies such as AT&T, GM's Oldsmobile Division, Primetime Publicity and Media, Pick Systems, IBM, Ernst & Young, and Xerox are adopting some form of virtual office. In June, 1994, *Business Week* and *MicroAge* cosponsored a virtual office conference in New York. Despite this trend, however, few companies pause to map out the terrain in advance. The impact of telelogic communication in general, and virtual office in particular, is not fully understood in the organizational context, and at this point there are more questions than answers. What does it take for a virtual office setup to succeed? What happens to productivity and morale when coworkers rarely meet face to face? How does one motivate employees who are scattered around town, or around the world?

ORGANIZATIONAL IMPLICATIONS

One primary area impacted by the virtual office is leadership. Leadership in the age of virtual office requires a certain degree of adventurousness and, more than ever before, an ability to motivate people. Individuals in a virtual office assume control of their own assignments. This can be seen as complete empowerment, but at the same time there is a loss of the synergy and interaction that creates a sense of belonging. Cohesiveness is desired, yet independence is paramount. Leaders in a virtual office environment must rely less on positional authority and face-to-face supervising and more on long-distance relationship-building and negotiation.

The selection of leaders for the virtual office environment presents a challenge. In the virtual office, the power of positional authority is far less effective than the power of persuasion and influence. A leader in the virtual office needs to "replace a sense of belonging to a place with a sense of belonging to a community" (Handy, 1995, p. 48). Such a leader must lead effectively from a distance. How can these leaders be identified? What characteristics place one candidate on the road to success and another on a dead end?

To answer these questions, we can use the Leadership Style Inventory (LSI) developed by Alan Rowe, Kathleen Reardon, and Warren Bennis (1994; see Fig. 25.1). The LSI instrument has proven helpful in evaluating individual leadership potential. It is based on two factors: broad versus specific goals, and the type of persuasion the leader uses to motivate others toward those goals.

The four categories describe the basic characteristics of each style along with the manner in which persuasion is used to introduce change. It is not uncommon to display more than one dominant style. For example, entrepreneurs are typically a combination of inspirational and commander styles. The inspirational has the vision to see new opportunities or ideas, and tends to be creative. The commander is focused, and able to translate ideas into actions. In an environment rife with changing demands, the leader's flexibility in the formation and communication of goals influences the likelihood of his or her success. There is no single leader style suited to all organizations and job types. There are, however, styles better suited to the dramatic changes confronting most organizations and the new organizational structures such as the virtual office.

An effective leader in the virtual office must become adept at utilizing a variety of communication leadership styles. Flexibility is key. A virtual office team leader explained: "As a leader in a virtual office environment, if you are going to keep up with your team members, you must be more organized than in a traditional office. You also must possess better and more varied communication skills" (Reardon, Rowe, & Whiting, 1995, p. 3).

The virtual office leader cannot rely solely on the traditional corporate leadership style, which incorporates the commanding and logical quadrants of the LSI. In the virtual office, the motivation of employees cannot always be accomplished through commands, logical explanations, and relentless surveillance. An effective leader must inspire and support from afar. Leading from a distance requires a move away from exclusive reliance upon command and control, toward a flexibility of style that allows the leader, using the appropriate technology, to motivate in the most effective way possible. Our research indicates that entering MBA candidates tend to be predomi-

	Performance Emphasis	Transformation Emphasis
Complex (Broad Goals)	*Logical* Analyzes new directions Persuades by reasoning Uses incremental change	*Inspirational* Envisions new opportunities Believes in radical change
Concrete (Specific Goals)	*Commander* Focuses on results Persuades by directing Relies on rapid change	*Supportive* Facilitates work Persuades by involvement Prefers limited change

FIG. 25.1.   Leadership styles.

nantly logical–commanding (de Pillis, Reardon, &Whiting, 1995). If business schools do not provide training in style flexibility, these students—particularly male students, for whom the logical–commanding bias is more pronounced—will be at a disadvantage. They will find it difficult to lead under a virtual office format, where inspiring people and supporting their initiative from a distance is imperative.

MULTICHANNEL LEADERSHIP

In addition to possessing style flexibility, an effective leader in the virtual office environment must be adept at using different technologies as circumstances require—and there may be many technologies from which to choose. Selecting the appropriate medium in an organizational setting is not a straightforward matter of matching the characteristics of the medium to the task. In organizational communication, multiple goals and strategies are enacted simultaneously in a single communication event. For example, a communication with a coworker may serve the dual purpose of furthering an organizational objective and cementing a relationship (Contractor & Eisenberg, 1990). In addition, the connotations of a medium are not fixed or objective. A medium's meanings change depending upon social information and individual experience (Fulk, Steinfeld, Schmitz, & Power, 1987).

One employee might prefer to receive instructions from her supervisor via voice mail; to this employee, voice mail use means "I know I only have to tell you this once, because I recognize that you are competent and trustworthy. I won't nag you about this, and you can get back to me when you feel it is appropriate to do so." Another employee may feel that voice mail is cold and impersonal; to this employee, a voice mail message says "I won't make the effort to reach you in person, because to me you are not, in fact, a person. I will leave instructions for you, and you will do them. Beyond this, you are of no use or importance to me."

A supervisor might assign a crucial task to an employee via e-mail, assuming that a message in a written format carries more importance than a spoken conversation. The employee, however, may think of e-mail as an informal medium, attributing minimal urgency to an e-mail message, assuming that if an issue were really important, the manager would telephone him about it. Similarly, a video teleconference may be interpreted by some employees as a meeting where ideas are exchanged and work gets done. Other employees, however, may focus on the teleconference format's similarity to a television broadcast, and may approach the video teleconference as a performance. This was called the "Hollywood syndrome" (Johansen, Vallee, & Spangler, 1979, p. 55). The successful multichannel leader knows not only how to use the available technology but also how employees may interpret different media choices. Multichannel leadership techniques required in the virtual office tread all over the fictitious boundary between interpersonal and mass media communication.

SUMMARY

We have come a long way since Reardon and Rogers first wrote about the false dichotomy between interpersonal and mass media studies. Since the publication of their article, we have seen more integration and cross-pollination in the communication field. Nevertheless, the rapid progress of communication technology ensures that there remains much to be done. In the virtual office one may study interpersonal communication, mass media communication, high technology, virtual communities, and a host of other topics. The virtual office is more than the sum of these parts, however; it is all of these parts coexisting and interacting. Leadership in this new business environment requires both a capacity to inspire and support subordinates from a distance and an adeptness in selecting and utilizing communication technology. A meaningful understanding of this type of leadership can only be achieved if researchers and practitioners work to integrate the subfields of communication to a greater degree than we have ever achieved in the past.

REFERENCES

Ball-Rokeach, S., & Reardon, K. K. (1988). Monologue, dialogue and telelog: Comparing an emergent form of communication with traditional forms. In R. Hawkins, J. Wiemann, & S. Pingree (Eds.), *Advancing communication science: Merging mass and interpersonal processes* (pp. 135–161). Beverly Hills: Sage.

Beniger, J. R. (1987). Personalization of mass media and the growth of pseudo-community. *Communication Research, 14,* 3.

Bochner, A. P., & Eisenberg, E. M. (1985). Legitimizing speech communication: An examination of coherence and cohesion in the development of the discipline. In T. W. Benson (Ed.) *Speech communication in the 20th century* (pp. 299–321). Carbondale: Southern Illinois University Press.

Callenback, E. (1975). *Ecotopia.* Berkeley, CA: Banyan Tree Books.

Carey, J. (1979). Graduate education in mass communication. *Communication Education, 28,* 282–293.

Coleman, C. L. (1993). The influence of mass media and interpersonal communication on societal and personal risk judgments. *Communication Research, 20,* 611–628.

Contractor, N. S., & Eisenberg, E. M. (1990). Communication networks and new media in organizations. In J. Fulk & C. Steinfeld (Eds.), *Organizations and communication technology* (pp. 143–172). Newbury Park, CA: Sage.

de Pillis, E. Reardon, K., & Whiting, V. (1995). *The leadership style inventory and the four faces of leadership: Are women really different?* Unpublished manuscript, University of Southern California.

Fulk, J., Steinfeld, C. W., Schmitz, J., & Power, J. G. (1987). A social information processing model of media use in organizations. *Communication Research, 14,* 529–552.

Gumpert, G., & Cathart, R. (Eds.). (1982). *Inter/media: Interpersonal communication in a media world.* New York: Oxford University Press.

Handy, C. (1995, May–June). Trust and the virtual organization. *Harvard Business Review,* 40–50.

Hawkins, R. Wiemann, J., & Pingree, S. (Eds.). (1990). *Advancing communication science: Merging mass and interpersonal processes.* Newbury Park, CA: Sage.

Johansen, R. Vallee, J., & Spangler, K. (1979). *Electronic meetings: Technical alternatives and social choices.* Reading, MA: Addison-Wesley.

Neumann, K., & Charlton, M. (1989). Massen-und interpersonale kommunikation im alltag von kind und familie [Mass and interpersonal communication in everyday child family life: Results of the Freiburg longitudinal study of children's media reception]. *Kolner Zeitschrift fur Soziologie und Sozialpsychologie, 30,* 364 –378.

Paisley, W. (1984). Communication in the communication sciences. In B. Dervin & M. J. Voigt (Eds.), *Progress in the communication sciences,* (Vol. 5, pp.1–44). Norwood, NJ: Ablex.

Reardon, K. K. (1981). *Persuasion: Theory and context.* Beverly Hills, CA: Sage.

Reardon, K. K., & Rogers, E. M. (1988). Interpersonal versus mass media communication: A false dichotomy. *Human Communication Research, 15,* 284–303.

Reardon, K. K., Rowe, A., & Whiting, V. (1995). *Selecting the right leader for the virtual office.* Unpublished manuscript, University of Southern California.

Rheingold, H. (1994). *The virtual community.* Reading, MA: Addison Wesley.

Roloff, M. E., & Miller, G. R. (Eds.). (1980). *Persuasion: New directions in theory and research.* Beverly Hills, CA: Sage.

Rowe, A., Reardon, K., & Bennis, W. (1994). *The leadership style inventory.* Unpublished manuscript. University of Southern California, Los Angeles.

Schramm, W. (1959). Comments on the state of communication research. *Public Opinion Quarterly, 23,* 6–9.

Shannon, C. E. & Weaver, W. C. (1949). *The mathematical model of communication.* Urbana: University of Illinois Press.

Trevino, L. K., Daft, R. L., & Lengel, R. H. (1990). Understanding managers' media choices: A symbolic interactionist perspective. In J. Fulk & C. Steinfeld (Eds.), *Organizations and communication technology* (pp. 71–94). Newbury Park, CA: Sage.

26

Diffusion of Innovations

Everett M. Rogers
University of New Mexico

Arvind Singhal
Ohio University

What is diffusion? *Diffusion* is the process by which an innovation is communicated through certain channels over time among the members of a social system (Rogers, 1995). An *innovation* is an idea, practice, or object perceived as new by an individual or other unit of adoption. The diffusion process involves both mass media and interpersonal communication channels.

This chapter analyzes the research tradition of the diffusion of innovations, focusing on the origins of the diffusion paradigm, its methodological tenets, and its influence on communication research. We identify the distinctive aspects of diffusion research, detail the seminal Iowa hybrid seed corn study, explain the strengths and limitations of the dominant paradigm that guided diffusion study for several decades, and look into the future of diffusion research.

DISTINCTIVE ASPECTS OF DIFFUSION RESEARCH

Several distinctive aspects of the diffusion of innovations set it off from other specialized fields of communication study.

1. The study of the diffusion of innovations began during World War II, prior to the establishment of communication study in university schools and departments (Rogers, 1994). So diffusion research was well underway as a research activity before communication scholars entered this research front.

2. Although most observers agree that the diffusion of innovations is fundamentally a communication process, communication scholars constitute only one of the dozen research traditions presently advancing the diffusion field (along with geography, education, marketing, public health, rural sociology, agricultural economics, general economics, political science, and others). Other communication research areas such as persuasion and attitude change and mass communication effects also began prior to the institutionalization of communication study in university units (Rogers, 1994).

3. Diffusion research is also distinctive in that the communication messages of study are perceived as new by the individual receivers. This novelty necessarily means that an individual experiences a high degree of uncertainty in seeking information about, and deciding to adopt and implement, an innovation. In the sense of the newness of the message content, the diffusion of innovations is unlike any other communication study except the diffusion of news. Diffusion of news, however, studies the spread of news events, concentrating mainly on such matters as how we become aware of news. In contrast, research on the diffusion of innovations centers not only on awareness-knowledge, but also on attitude change, decision-making, and implementation of the innovation. The new ideas investigated by scholars of the diffusion of innovations are mainly technological innovations, so the behavior studied is quite different from that investigated in news diffusion studies. Obviously, however, both communication research areas involve a similar diffusion process, and both have been informed by the other (Rogers, 1995).

4. Diffusion research considers time as a variable to a much greater degree than do other fields of communication study. Time is involved in diffusion in (a) the *innovation–decision process*, the mental process through which an individual passes from first knowledge of a new idea, to adoption and confirmation of the innovation; (b) *innovativeness*, the degree to which an individual is relatively earlier in adopting new ideas than other members of a system; and (c) an innovation's *rate of adoption*, the relative speed with which an innovation is adopted by members of a system (Rogers, 1995).

5. The diffusion of innovations field emphasizes interpersonal communication networks more than any other type of communication research. From the first diffusion studies conducted about 50 years ago, the nature of diffusion was found to be essentially a social process involving interpersonal communication among similar individuals. A person evaluates a new idea and decides whether or not to adopt it on the basis of discussions with peers who have already adopted or rejected the innovation. The main function of mass media communication in the diffusion process is to create awareness-knowledge about the innovation. Study of the diffusion of innovations involves both mass communication and interpersonal communication, and thus spans the dichotomy that otherwise divides communication into two subdisciplines.

BACKGROUND OF DIFFUSION RESEARCH

The study of the diffusion of innovations in its present-day form can be traced from the theories and observations of Gabriel Tarde, a French sociologist and legal scholar. Tarde originated such key diffusion concepts as opinion leadership, the S-curve of diffusion, and the role of socioeconomic status in interpersonal diffusion, although he did not use such concepts by these names. Such theoretical ideas were set forth by Tarde (1903) in his book, *The Laws of Imitation.*

The intellectual leads suggested by Tarde were soon followed up by anthropologists, who began investigating the role of technological innovations in bringing about cultural change. Illustrative of these anthropological studies was Clark Wissler's (1923) analysis of the diffusion of the horse among the Plains Indians. As in other anthropological works, the emphasis was on the consequences of innovation. For example, Wissler (1923) showed that adding horses to their culture led the Plains Indians, who had lived in peaceful coexistence, into a state of almost continual warfare with neighboring tribes.

The basic research paradigm for the diffusion of innovations can be traced to Bryce Ryan and Neal C. Gross's classic 1943 study of the diffusion of hybrid seed corn among Iowa farmers. This investigation was grounded in previously conducted anthropological diffusion work, which Ryan had studied while earning his doctoral degree at Harvard University, prior to becoming a faculty member in rural sociology at Iowa State University, where Gross was a graduate student. We discuss the hybrid corn study in detail later in this chapter.

During the 1950s many diffusion studies were conducted, particularly by rural sociologists at land-grant universities in the midwestern United States. They were directly influenced by the Ryan and Gross investigation. As soon as communication study began to be institutionalized, this new breed of scholars became especially interested in the diffusion of news events, particularly through an influential study by Paul J. Deutschmann and Wayne A. Danielson (1960).

COMMUNICATION RESEARCH ON DIFFUSION

Deutschmann was somewhat typical of the new breed of communication scholars coming out of the recently founded schools of communication at American research universities. He had several years of experience as a newspaper reporter and editor, and then enrolled in the new PhD program in communication at Stanford University, led by Wilbur Schramm. He gained competence in quantitative methods, communication theory, and social psychology. Deutschmann became a friend and research collaborator with Danielson, his fellow doctoral student at Stanford, and an individual with a similar background of professional newspaper experience. Deutschmann's first faculty position was in the new Department of Communication at Michigan State University, where he headed the Communication Research Center.

Deutschmann was a brilliant and intense communication scholar. Everett Rogers remembers meeting him in 1959 when he visited the newly established Department of Communication at Michigan State University. Shortly after introductions, Deutschmann showed the S-shaped diffusion curves for the spread of the news events that he and Danielson were then studying. Compared to the diffusion curves for the agricultural innovations that Rogers was investigating, the news events spread much more rapidly (Fig. 26.1). As Deutschmann stated at the time, this was "damn fast diffusion" (personal communication). Thanks to Deutschmann and Danielson's (1960) article on the diffusion of news events, this research topic became popular among communication scholars. Work on this topic continues today.

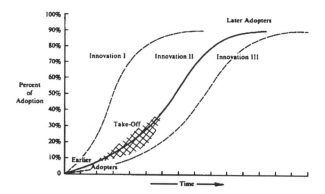

FIG. 26.1. S-shaped diffusion curves for three innovations. Compared to diffusion curves for technological innovation, news diffusion curves have a highly compressed time dimension, showing that news events spread very rapidly. Reprinted from *Diffusion of Innovations* (4th ed., p. 11) by E. M. Rogers, 1995, New York: Free Press. Copyright 1995 by E. M. Rogers. Reprinted with permission of the author.

In the early 1960s Deutschmann moved to San José, Costa Rica, where he directed a Latin American communication research center for Michigan State University. One of his first projects was conducted in collaboration with Dr. Orlando Fals Borda, a sociologist at the National University of Colombia in Bogotá. Fals Borda earned his doctorate in rural sociology at the University of Minnesota and was well-acquainted with diffusion research. For several years, he had been conducting a study in the Colombian village of Saució, a small Andean community of 71 farm households. Deutschmann and Fals Borda (1962) carried out a diffusion study in Saució, one of the first diffusion investigations in a developing nation. Soon there would be several hundred such diffusion studies, many conducted by communication scholars. The six agricultural innovations of study in Saució (such as chemical fertilizer, a new potato variety, and a pesticide) had been introduced in previous years by Fals Borda, who acted as an agricultural *change agent*—or one who introduced innovations to the public. The familiar S-shaped curve characterized the rate of adoption for each of these innovations in the Colombian village. Rather striking similarities were found between the diffusion process in this developing country village and the diffusion of agricultural innovations among commercial farmers that Rogers was then studying in Ohio (Deutschmann & Fals Borda, 1962).

Deutschmann's study with Fals Borda in Colombia stimulated interest among communication scholars in the diffusion of technological innovations. He attracted doctoral students to Michigan State University who were interested in diffusion research. When Deutschmann's life was cut short in 1962, Everett Rogers was hired as his replacement at Michigan State University to continue diffusion research in developing nations.

The number of diffusion studies completed by communication scholars expanded rapidly since 1960. By 1994, an estimated 454 diffusion publications by communication scholars were available, more than any other diffusion research tradition except rural sociology (with 825 diffusion publications) and marketing (with 569). Unlike rural sociologists, who are mainly concerned with agricultural innovations, or education diffusion scholars, who are interested in new educational innovations (for example, modern math or the multicultural curriculum), communication scholars investigate a wide range of different types of technological innovations. Communication scholars are interested in diffusion as a communication *process*, independent of the type of innovations that are diffused.

THE IOWA HYBRID SEED CORN STUDY

When Ryan arrived in Ames, Iowa, in 1938, he was intrigued with the scholarly question of noneconomic influences on economic behavior. This issue had become important to him during his doctoral studies in the Department of Sociology at Harvard University, where Robert K. Merton, a young faculty member who had recently completed his own dissertation research on the sociology of science, was Ryan's doctoral advisor. The Harvard doctoral program in sociology was relatively new, and somewhat interdisciplinary in nature. Students earning degrees in sociology were encouraged to take courses in economics, anthropology, and in social psychology. Professor Talcott Parsons, the intellectual leader of Harvard sociology, had been trained in economics in Europe and helped introduce the theories of Vilfredo Pareto to American sociology. This interdisciplinary intellectual background was good preparation for Ryan, the individual who, more than any other, was to formulate the paradigm for research on the diffusion of innovations.

Iowa State University was an agricultural college, and so Ryan decided to investigate the diffusion of hybrid seed corn. This innovation was a profoundly important new idea for Iowa farmers, leading to increased corn yields of about 20 percent per acre. Ryan received funding for his proposed study of the diffusion of hybrid seed from the Iowa Agricultural Experiment Station, Iowa State University's research and development organization, which had played an important role in developing hybrid seed. This important innovation had spread widely to Iowa farmers in previous years, but Iowa State administrators were concerned that such an obviously advantageous agricultural technology had required so many years (about a dozen) for widespread use. This type of frustration on the part of officials who cannot understand why a seemingly advantageous innovation is not adopted more immediately explains why many diffusion studies continue to be sponsored.

Ryan collaborated with several economics professors at Iowa State University in designing the hybrid corn study. As stated previously, Ryan was thoroughly familiar with the anthropological research on diffusion, and this work directly affected the design of the Iowa hybrid corn study. However Ryan proposed the seed corn study mainly as a survey relying on questionnaire-generated data, rather than using the ethnographic approaches of the previous anthropological research.

A newly arrived masters student at Iowa State, Neal C. Gross, was assigned as Ryan's research assistant. Ryan told Gross that if he would personally interview the several hundred farmers in the two Iowa communities of study, he could use the data for his master's thesis. Gross, who came from an urban background, was unfamiliar with the ways of Iowa farmers. Someone told Gross that farmers began work early in the morning, so he appeared at the farmstead of his first respondent at 4 am. Gross averaged 14 personal interviews per day during the summer of 1939, an enviable record by today's standards for survey research.

Ryan and Gross were specialists in rural sociology in the then Department of Economics and Sociology at Iowa State University (it was later to divide into departments of economics, sociology, and anthropology). Rural sociology was an applied branch of sociology, especially valued at Iowa State, which was a land-grant, agricultural university in a predominately farming state. Further, the rural sociology specialty was organizationally situated in the College of Agriculture, a unit dominated by administrators oriented to research, education, and extension service activities devoted to increasing farm production. Obviously, an investigation of the diffusion of hybrid seed corn in Iowa fit perfectly with this value on increasing agricultural production. Ryan's proposal was approved because it was expected to provide valuable insights about why farmers had been surprisingly slow to adopt an economically profitable innovation.

The choice of hybrid seed corn as the innovation of study in the Ryan and Gross investigation was to cast a long intellectual shadow over future generations of diffusion scholarship. Hybrid seed was an overwhelmingly beneficial innovation, boosting corn yields considerably. Given the sponsorship of the hybrid corn study, it is understandable that Ryan and Gross tended to assume that Iowa farmers ought to adopt the innovation, and that the rate of adoption should have been more rapid. This pro-innovation bias still characterizes most diffusion studies today. Ryan and Gross (1943) indicated their surprise that the diffusion of hybrid corn required 12 years to reach widespread diffusion, and that the average farmer needed seven years to progress from initial awareness of the innovation to full-scale adoption (indicated by planting all of the corn acreage on his farm in hybrid seed).

Stated another way, the hybrid corn study demonstrated just how difficult it was for most individuals to adopt an innovation. Hybrid corn had to be purchased from a seed corn company, at a price per bushel not trivial to Iowa farmers in the Depression years. Further, adopting the innovation meant that Iowa farmers no longer selected the more beautiful-appearing ears of corn for use as seed the following year. So the adoption of hybrid corn meant the unadoption of a previously existing practice, the visual selection of open-pollinated seed. Hybrid corn was one of the first of the new wave of scientifically based farm innovations that were to radically change the nature of Midwestern agriculture in the ensuing decades. In 1939, Iowa farmers were not accustomed to agricultural innovations that were later to flow from the land-grant universities like Iowa State and the U.S. Department of Agriculture.

Iowa State University was the perfect place for founding the paradigm for diffusion research in yet another sense: Ames was the principal point of importation for the introduction of statistical methods in America. These techniques for quantitative data analysis began among agricultural statisticians such as Sir Ronald Fisher and Karl Pearson in England. They were created to test hypotheses about the effects of fertilizers, new crop varieties, and livestock rations. Such statistical methods as analysis of variance and regression came to the United States in the early 1930s when Sir Ronald visited Iowa State University, where he helped establish the Statistical Laboratory. George Snedecor, leader of the Iowa State program in statistics, named the F statistic (for determining the significance of analyses of variance and regression) after Fisher. Snedecor popularized statistical methods for agricultural research in his book, *Statistical Methods* (1931). Iowa State's Statistical Laboratory went on to develop the area sampling methods widely used in survey research. Professors in the Department of Statistics, such as Paul G. Homemeyer, Ray J. Jessen, and Snedecor, served as informal consultants to Ryan in planning the hybrid corn study, and this pioneering diffusion investigation was designed as a highly quantitative analysis, utilizing statistical methods to test hypotheses. As noted earlier, this was a marked departure from anthropological ethnographic diffusion research.

In the late 1930s sociological research in the United States was moving toward quantification, away from the qualitative methods that had been pioneered by the Chicago School in the 1915 to 1935 era (Rogers, 1994). Sociologists thought that to become scientific was to pattern themselves after the biological and physical sciences, at least in their research methods. This move to quantification implied the use of individuals as units of response and as units of analysis, so that statistical methods, borrowed from agricultural-biological research, could be utilized in sociological studies.

Ryan and Gross's hybrid corn diffusion research expressed this sociological search for scientific respectability in its choice of methods. Data were gathered by personal interviews with all of the farmers in the two Iowa communities of Jefferson and Grand Junction (by coincidence, these communities were located within 30 miles of where Rogers grew up on a farm). Each farmer was regarded by the two rural sociologists as a decision-making unit for the adoption of hybrid corn.

The focus on individual farmers led to the greatest shortcoming of the hybrid corn investigation. Sociometric questions to measure the interpersonal network links among the Iowa farmers of study were not asked. This mistake is all the more puzzling given that diffusion is essentially a social process. While the mass media often create awareness-knowledge of an innovation, interpersonal communication with peers is necessary to persuade most individuals to adopt a new idea.

Ryan and Gross gathered data from a complete census of the farmers in Jefferson and Grand Junction, Iowa, an ideal sampling design for measuring network links and thus for determining peer influences on farmers' decisions to adopt the innovation. The farmer-respondents were asked about the sources and channels from which they first learned about hybrid corn (commercial seed dealers and salespeople were mentioned as most important) versus the sources and channels that convinced them to adopt (other farmers like neighbors and friends were reported as most important). So Ryan and Gross established the importance of social networks in diffusion, but failed to investigate them in an appropriate way.

THE DOMINANT PARADIGM FOR THE DIFFUSION OF INNOVATIONS

One can still detect the intellectual influence of the hybrid corn study on diffusion research, 53 years and some 5,000 publications later. More than any other diffusion investigation, the Ryan and Gross study formed the paradigm for later diffusion research. What were the essential elements of this diffusion paradigm?

1. The main dependent variable was *innovativeness*, defined as the degree to which an individual or other unit is relatively earlier to adopt than are others. For convenience in understanding diffusion research results, the continuous variable of innovativeness is often divided into adopter categories, such as innovators, early adopters, early majority, late majority, and laggards (Rogers, 1983). Ryan and Gross (1943) were the first to use adopter categories in their analysis (although they did not use these five categories by name).

2. When the cumulative number of farmers adopting hybrid corn was plotted over time, the distribution formed an S-shaped curve. When plotted on a frequency basis, the number of adopters over time formed a normal, bell-shaped curve (which later scholars utilized to divide the variable of innovativeness into the five adopter categories in a standard way).

3. The Iowa farmers' sources and channels of communication were found to differ at various stages in the innovation–decision process with the mass media more important at the awareness-knowledge stage and with interpersonal communication, especially from peers, more important at the persuasion stage. The notion of stages in the individual's innovation–decision process has been widely utilized by later diffusion scholars (Rogers, 1983).

The importance of the hybrid corn study in forming the paradigm for work on the diffusion of innovations is illustrated by Diane Crane's (1972) analysis of the invisible college of rural sociology diffusion researchers: 18 of the 30 most important scholarly innovations in the field were reported in the Ryan and Gross (1943) study. Each intellectual innovation consisted of the first time that either a dependent or an independent variable was used in an empirical study of diffusion. So the methods of study as well as what to look for in diffusion investigations were established by Ryan and Gross.

Because of World War II, the diffusion paradigm created by Ryan and Gross did not spread immediately among rural sociologists. A decade-long delay, until the mid-1950s, resulted from Gross' serving in the Navy while Ryan worked for a United Nations agency (he did not return to the faculty at Iowa State University after World War II). Two other Iowa State rural sociologists, George M. Beal and Joe M. Bohlen, popularized the diffusion paradigm, starting in 1954, and soon this approach to studying the diffusion of agricultural innovations was taken up by a widening circle of rural sociologists, especially at land-grant universities in the Midwestern states. By 1960, some 405 diffusion publications had appeared, with the largest number authored by rural sociologists. However, this diffusion research tradition soon ran out of intellectual gas, and thereafter fewer and fewer diffusion studies were conducted by rural sociologists.

SPREAD OF THE DIFFUSION PARADIGM

Meanwhile, the diffusion approach infected the other social sciences, and spread to other fields such as marketing, industrial engineering, and education. The key event in this wider acceptance was James S. Coleman, Elihu Katz, and Herbert Menzel's 1966 study of the diffusion of tetracycline, a new medical drug, among physicians. This investigation began when the director of marketing at the Pfizer drug company approached the three sociologists, then at Columbia University's Bureau of Applied Social Research, with a request to determine the effectiveness of Pfizer's tetracycline advertising in medical journals. This rather humdrum marketing question was converted into a particularly influential diffusion study by Coleman, Katz, and Mendel (1966).

They collected data via personal interviews with virtually all of the medical doctors in four small communities in Illinois. Prescription data were also collected from pharmacies, so they knew the date when each doctor first prescribed the new drug. This represented an important methodological improvement—observed actual adoption—over the usual diffusion investigation, which depended upon respondent accuracy in recalling the date at which an innovation was adopted. Further, Coleman et al. asked sociometric questions to determine the interpersonal network links among their sample. Interestingly, they were not aware of Ryan and Gross's hybrid seed corn study until after they had completed their data-gathering.

The rate of adoption of tetracycline followed an S-shaped curve, as had the rate of adoption for hybrid corn, although only 17 months elapsed before most doctors had adopted (compared to 12 years for the Iowa farmers adopting hybrid seed). The most innovative medical doctors were cosmopolite, making numerous out-of-town trips to medical specialty meetings. Similarly, the farmer-innovators in the hybrid corn study made numerous trips to Des Moines, the largest city in Iowa, located about 90 miles away. As with the Iowa farmers, mass media channels (such as articles in medical journals) were most important in creating awareness-knowledge, while interpersonal communication channels with peers were most important in persuading a doctor to try the medical innovation.

By far the most unique intellectual contribution of the medical drug study was the evidence that it provided of diffusion as a social process. For instance, Coleman et al. (1966) found that doctors who were linked in more interpersonal networks adopted the innovation more rapidly than did more isolated doctors. Even though tetracycline had been scientificly evaluated in numerous clinical trials, which were reported to the medical doctors of study in medical journals, and even though Pfizer salespeople gave them free samples, they evaluated the innovation mainly through the personal experiences of their fellow doctors. An early adopting doctor might tell his office partner, a social friend, or a golfing partner, "Look doctor, I prescribed tetracycline to several patients of mine last week and it acted like a miracle drug. Perhaps you should try it." Thus, the meaning of the medical innovation was socially constructed through interpersonal communication among peers. Since the Coleman et al. (1966) medical drug study, many other diffusion researches (i.e., Rogers & Kincaid, 1981; Anwal & Singhal, 1992) have gathered network data to better understand the social influences on individual's innovation-decisions.

The Bureau of Applied Social Research at Columbia University was a particularly prestigious center for social science research at the time of the drug study, and Coleman and Katz were soon to become much-admired scholars. The diffusion paradigm spread rapidly and was utilized by other sociologists. Publication of a general textbook about diffusion (Rogers, 1962) helped widen paradigm application in such fields as geography, economics, psychology, political science, and, as related previously, communication. In 1994, around 5,000 publications on the diffusion of innovations appeared (Rogers, 1995). The most important fields studying diffusion, as expressed in the number of diffusion publications published (in descending order) were rural sociology, marketing (and management), and communication.

RESEARCH METHODS FOR STUDYING DIFFUSION

Most diffusion researchers have followed the methodological path set forth by Ryan and Gross in the hybrid corn study. Data are mainly gathered by personal or telephone interviews from respondents who are asked to retrospect about their time of adoption, the sources or channels of communication that they used in the innovation-decision process, to report their network links with others, and other variables such as their personal and social characteristics. The individual is usually the unit of analysis, although in recent years a number of studies have been conducted in which an organization is the unit of analysis (Wildemuth, 1992; Zaltman, Duncan, & Holbek, 1973). Inadequate scholarly attention has been given to the consequences of technological innovations (only anthropologists have investigated such consequences in any significant way).

Alternative methods of data gathering have been little utilized, even as a means to supplement the predominant approach of survey data gathering and quantitative methodologies of data analysis. One wonders why ethnographic methods like in-depth interviews and observation have not been utilized more widely, especially in the organizational innovation studies—many of which are conducted by organizational communication scholars and by students of organizational behavior, both of whom increasingly utilize ethnographic methods. The dominant style of diffusion investigations is thus the quantitative analysis of data gathered by survey interview methods from large samples. The overall effect of these dominant research methods has been to emphasize an understanding of the diffusion process as the product of individual decisions and actions. Interpersonal influences on individuals in the diffusion process have been underemphasized because of the research methods used. Perhaps the approach to studying diffusion formulated by Ryan and Gross has become overly stereotyped.

However, in recent years, several communication scholars have investigated the critical mass and individual thresholds in the diffusion process, especially for the spread and adoption of interactive innovations such as electronic mail or fax in an organization or in some other system (Markus, 1987; Kramer, 1993). At a certain point in the diffusion process for any innovation, the rate of adoption begins to suddenly increase at an inordinate rate. This take-off in the rate of adoption creates the S-curve of diffusion (see Fig. 26.1).

For innovations that are essentially a means of interactive communication, however, such as the new communication technologies of fax and e-mail, a critical mass occurs when the diffusion process becomes self-sustaining. After the critical mass point, individuals in a system perceive that "everybody else" has adopted the interactive innovation. With each successive adopter of an interactive innovation, the new idea becomes more valuable not only for each future adopter, but also for each previous adopter.

For example, consider the first adopter of the telephone in the United States about 120 years ago. This innovation had zero utility to the first adopter. But when a second adoption occurred, the innovation became more valuable to both parties. And so it went until gradually there were so many adopters that an individual could assume that anyone he or she might wish to call would also have a telephone. Note that the first adopters of the telephone had a very low threshold of resistance to the innovation (they adopted when there was little actual benefit for doing so). Valente (1995) reanalyzed the Coleman et al. data in light of such concepts as the critical mass and individual thresholds, which he helped formulate and sharpen theoretically. Perhaps Allen (1983) said it all when he described the diffusion process for an interactive innovation as one in which "everyone is watching while being watched" (p. 270).

THE FUTURE OF DIFFUSION RESEARCH

Perhaps one might wonder why diffusion research has persevered for so many years, and why the number of diffusion publications continues to grow. Few other areas of communication research have such a lengthy history and represent such a tremendous scholarly outpouring. We suggest that the popularity of diffusion research is due to its practical importance and its applied nature. The agricultural officials at Iowa State University in the late 1930s who sponsored the hybrid corn study have contemporary counterparts in other organizations who are equally frustrated as to why their innovations are not adopted more rapidly; thus, diffusion studies continue to flourish.

Also, diffusion research promises to enhance our understanding of how social change occurs, a fundamental issue for all scholars of society. What is the role of technology in bringing about social change? One way to find out is through diffusion research, a microlevel type of study of the macrolevel issue of social change. Scholarly interest in new communication technologies by communication students has given a special boost to interest in diffusion research in recent years. There is no reason to expect that the scholarly popularity of diffusion research by communication (and other) scholars will decrease in the foreseeable future. Innovations continue to be generated and studied.

ANNOTATED BIBLIOGRAPHY

J. S. Coleman, E. Katz, & H. Menzel (1966). *Medical innovation: Diffusion of a medical drug among doctors*. Indianapolis, Bobbs-Merrill. One of the most influential diffusion studies in showing that the diffusion of an innovation is essentially a social process that occurs through interpersonal networks.

E. M. Rogers (1995). *Diffusion of innovations*. New York: Free Press. A comprehensive textbook that reviews the main investigations of diffusion and provides a general framework (which is an updated version of the Ryan and Gross paradigm).

B. Ryan & N. C. Gross (1943). The diffusion of hybrid seed corn in two Iowa communities. *Rural Sociology, 8*, 15–24. The most important diffusion study of all time, which set forth the paradigm for diffusion research.

REFERENCES

Allen, D. (1983). New telecommunication services: Network externalities and critical mass. *Telecommunications Policy, 12,* 257–271.

Anwal, M. A., & Singhal, A. (1992). The diffusion of the Grameen Bank in Bangladesh. *Knowledge, 14,* 7–28.

Coleman, J. S., Katz, E. & Menzel, H. (1966). *Medical innovation: Diffusion of a medical drug among doctors.* Indianapolis, Bobbs-Merrill.

Crane, D. (1972). *Invisible colleges.* Chicago: University of Chicago Press.

Deutschmann, P. J., & Danielson, W. A. (1960). Diffusion of knowledge of the major news story. *Journalism Quarterly, 37,* 345–355.

Deutschmann, P. J., & Fals Borda, O. (1962). *Communication and adoption patterns in an Andean village.* San José, Costa Rica: Programa Interamericano de Informacíon Popular.

Kramer, R. (1993). The policies of information: A study of the French Minitel System. In J. R. Schement & B. D. Ruben (Eds.), *Between communication and information* (pp. 453–586). New Brunswick, NJ: Transaction.

Markus, M. L. (1987). Toward a "critical mass" theory of intensive media: Universal access, interdependence, and diffusion. *Communication Research, 14,* 491–511.

Rogers, E. M. (1962). *Diffusion of innovations* (1st ed.). New York: Free Press.

Rogers, E. M. (1983). *Diffusion of innovations* (3rd ed.). New York: Free Press.

Rogers, E. M. (1994). *A history of communication study: A biographical approach.* New York: Free Press.

Rogers, E. M. (1995). *Diffusion of innovations* (4th ed.). New York: Free Press.

Rogers, E. M., & Kincaid, D. L. (1981). *Communication networks: A new paradigm for research.* New York: Free Press.

Ryan, B., & Gross, N. C. (1943). The diffusion of hybrid seed corn in two Iowa communities. *Rural Sociology, 8,* 15–24.

Snedecor, G. (1931). *Statistical methods.* Ames: Iowa State University Press.

Tarde, G. (1903). *The laws of imitation,* (E.C. Parsons, Trans.). New York: Holt.

Valente, T. W. (1995). *Network models of the diffusion of innovations.* Creskill, NJ: Hampton Press.

Wissler, C. (1923). *Man and culture.* New York: Thomas Y. Crowell.

Wildemuth, B. M. (1992). An empirically grounded model of the adoption of intellectual technologies. *Journal of the American Society for Information Sciences, 43,* 210–224.

Zaltman, G., Duncan, R., & Holbek, J. (1973). *Innovations and organizations.* New York: Wiley.

27

Credibility

Charles C. Self
Texas A&M University

Credibility is an intuitive concept. Each of us believes some sources of information more than others, some institutional sources of information more than others. Perhaps this is why scholarly examination of source credibility is among the oldest lines communication study, originating with the ancient Greeks (see McCroskey & Richmond, chapter 15, this volume). But its intuitive quality obscures its underlying complexity. The literature on credibility is plentiful, contradictory, and confused. It taps into core theories of rhetoric, persuasion, interpersonal communication, and mass communication. The concept of credibility is based on fundamental differences in the presupposition made by conflicting concepts of communication itself.

Credibility has been defined as believability, trust, perceived reliability, and dozens of other concepts and combinations of them (Burgoon, Burgoon, & Wilkinson, 1981; Greenberg & Roloff, 1974; Shaw, 1976). It has been defined in terms of the credulity of those trusting; the characteristics of the presenter, the presenting organization or medium, and the information or message offered; and the circumstances under which the message is being perceived. It also has been defined in terms of the recipient of the message, the characteristics of the social setting within which the communication takes place, and the underlying perceived dimensions of communication.

Beginning with Aristotle, communication scholars have explored the role of source credibility in persuasive messages. It was not until about 50 years ago, however, that communication scholars begain the scientific study of credibility—intrinsically tied to interpersonal and persuasion research. The focus of this chapter, however, moves away from rhetorical, interpersonal, and persuasive communication and integrates the construct to mass communication. To do so, however, requires an historical overview that briefly explores the origins, different approaches to defining the concept, and related research.

Recent controversy centered on studies of news report credibility and the mass media organizations that offer them. These studies, grounded in a variety of theoretical perspectives, produced conflicting findings (Whitney, 1985), driven by institutional interests within news organizations, by critics with a variety of political and social agendas (Dennis, 1986; Whitney, 1986), and by researchers representing a range of theoretical orientations (Delia, 1976; Stamm & Dube, 1994; Salmon, 1986). They used polling data, discourse data, and case study data (Self, 1988a).

A great deal of work has yet to be done to sort out the meaning of the construct. As such, it offers an excellent case study of the relationships among pretheoretical assumption, theory building, methodological approach, and research programs.

HISTORICAL DEVELOPMENT

The idea that some sources of information are more reliable than others is as old as discussions of rhetoric itself. Plato's famous description of the dialogue on rhetoric between Socrates and Phaedrus grapples with the issue.

Socrates and Phaedrus discuss the rhetorical skills taught by various sophist teachers. Socrates describes the skills advocated by the Sophists and used by their orators: "only the probabilities should be told either in accusation or defense, and that always in speaking, the orator should keep probability in view, and say good-bye to truth. And the observance of this principle throughout a speech furnishes the whole art" (Plato, 1952, p. 137). Socrates counters with his own view of true rhetoric: "the probability of which [the sophist] speaks was engendered in the minds of the many by the likeness of the truth, . . . he who knew the truth would always know best how to discover the resemblances of the truth" (p. 138). He objects to the notion that one should be driven by shaping the message to fit the predisposition of the audience, "unless a man estimates the various characters of his hearers and is able to divide all things into classes and to comprehend them under single ideas, he will never be a skillful rhetorician even within the limits of human power" (p. 138). The ontological assumption was that the better the speaker understood universal ideals of truth, the greater trust that individual would evoke in the audience, which would recognize the resemblances to truth offered by the speaker. According to Plato, credibility was engendered by a knowledge of truth.

If Plato delineated one pole of the concept of credibility of the source, Aristotle represented the other. "Rhetoric may be defined as the faculty of observing in any given case the available means of persuasion" (Aristotle, 1952, p. 595). He couched the concepts of credibility within a group of characteristics he referred to as the *ethos* of the communicator—the communicator's ability to inspire confidence and belief in what was being said. This group of characteristics was among three major modes of persuasion and was responsible for evoking trust among the hearers of a message.

> Persuasion is achieved by the speaker's personal character when the speech is so spoken as to make us think him credible. We believe good men more fully and more readily than others: this is true generally whatever the question is, and absolutely true where exact certainty is impossible and opinions are divided. This kind of persuasion, like the others, should be achieved by what the speaker says, not by what people think of his character before he begins to speak. It is not true, as some writers assume in their treatises on rhetoric, that the personal goodness revealed by the speaker contributes nothing to his power of persuasion; on the contrary, his character may almost be called the most effective means of persuasion he possesses. (p. 595)

Three major ideas behind source credibility are revealed in this debate. First, sources are credible because their message's rightness is perceived by the audience. Second, sources are credible because they rightly read how to reveal themselves to particular audiences. And, third, sources are perceived to be credible because of audience characteristics.

The concept of credibility reaches back to this great debate among the idealists and the realists over the nature of truth and rhetoric. Persuasion and credibility have been discussed in most of the theories of communication since Aristotle. These theories varied in how they deal with the issue but usually centered on source, audience, or message characteristics. The issue has been whether an audience's trust is won as a consequence of the knowledge of truth and, thus, the strength of the argument; the empirical observation of audience characteristics and the communicator's ability to match delivery and message to audience needs; or the situation of the audience members themselves—their credulity or persuasibility.

EARLY EMPIRICAL RESEARCH

Systematic *empirical* research in the modern sense has come only in the 20th century. Initially, this research was centered in what Harold Lasswell referred to as *administrative research* in the mass media. This research was driven by concern about the power of propaganda (Lasswell, Lerner & Speier, 1980) and by the need for the new broadcast media managers to demonstrate the power of their media. The desire to attract advertising dollars to radio from newspapers produced a series of studies through polling organizations, some inspired by Lasswell himself (c.f., Smith, 1969, especially pp. 42–89). The crucial ones included Roper, Gallup, National Opinion Research Center, and the Survey Research Center at the University of Michigan (Cantril, 1951). They attempted to determine which mass communication medium was "trusted" most for information and news. These studies were motivated by a desire to determine which medium or media were used by most individuals to get their news.

The studies began in the 1930s and have continued since.[1] The assumption of this research was that the medium itself was trusted. Grounded in what has been called the

---

[1]For a linear overview of the nature of these findings about credibility, see Erskine (1970–1971).

hypodermic-needle model of communication (see Lemert, 1981, and chapter 5, this volume, for a discussion of the approach's shortcomings), the research assumed that media had high levels of credibility among audiences to change attitudes, and that the crucial issue was which of the media were attended to most by audiences.

Initially, researchers found that newspapers were the most trusted source of information for news. In the late 1930s, they found that radio was the most trusted source. In the early 1950s, television assumed the role of most trusted source of information (Erskine, 1970–1971). These studies could not determine what caused one medium to be more trusted than another. For the most part, respondents were simply asked which source they trusted most on which issues.

Source Credibility Studies

It was, however, the need to develop support for the war effort in the 1940s that produced the first truly paradigmatic study of research examining why audiences believe a message from one communicator and not another.

Psychologist Carl Hovland and associates worked for the War Department in World War II and continued their experimental research at Yale University after the war. They studied how to persuade soldiers through war-time messages. Hovland and colleagues developed a message-learning approach based on what Hovland (1951) called "a strong predilection for stimulus-response learning-theory formulations and . . . an attempt is made to see how far the general principles of behavior theory can be extended into this field. . . . Attitudes are viewed as internalized anticipatory approach or avoidance tendencies toward objects, persons, or symbols" (p. 427). He thus accepted the Source–Message–Channel–Receiver (SMCR) model of communication advocated by a number of theorists interested in attitude change research in the first half of the 20th century (Rogers, 1994).

Hovland and colleagues defined *credibility* as "trustworthiness" and "expertise" (Hovland, Janis, & Kelley, 1953; Hovland &Weiss, 1951–1952), studying the credibility of mass communication messages by examining how individuals received such messages from "high credibility" sources. In order to measure the change in attitude evoked by a given message, Hovland controlled all variables but one in the communication chain from source to destination. This concept echoed Aristotle's argument that persuasion was based upon fitting the message to audience needs in the linear model of speaker–message–hearer.

Hovland and colleagues presented positive and negative messages from high credibility and low credibility sources to audiences and measured learning of information and changes in opinion. This study was followed up by measuring information retention by the same participants four months later. Hovland found that high credibility sources changed attitudes more than low credibility sources, but that information was learned about equally well from both source types. An unanticipated *sleeper effect* was found in the follow-up four months later. During that time, the source of the information was forgotten, but the information from both sources was retained; opinion shifted to about the same level of change for participants exposed to both types of sources (Hovland, Lumsdaine, & Sheffield, 1949; Hovland & Weiss, 1951–1952).

Hovland and colleagues drew a distinction among source credibility, message variables, and audience credulity in persuasion. They produced the first systematic knowledge about media credibility. Their research focused on the characteristics of audiences, messages, and communicators and explained why some messages are believed and some are not.

Variations on Three Themes

Following the work of Hovland and colleagues, a broad interest in the credibility of media sources of information developed. That research has centered on the three major possible reasons messages are credible: source (insititutional media, individual speakers, organizations as sources) characteristics, message characteristics, and audience characteristics and credulity.

Source Characteristics. Because credibility theories have applied value for mass media organizations (i.e., selling newspapers, increasing ratings), mass communication researchers have devoted inordinate attention to this *media* credibility; speech or human communication researchers have also spent considerable time examining the impact on *source* credibility (i.e., speaker, organization). Interest in media or source characteristics is seen in studies such as Shaw (1967), who found that increased reliance upon news sent by telegraph brought a sharp decline in stories judged to be "biased" about presidential campaigns in the 1880s. Baxter and Bittner (1974) found that among high school and college students of the "television generation," television was more credible than other media for all students, overriding previous findings of differences for sex and educational level. Brownlow (1992) found that baby-faced female speakers induced more agreement with their position when trust was questioned and mature-faced female speakers induced more attitude change when expertise was questioned.

Source characteristic research attempts to identify which information sources were believed or which characteristics of these sources lead to greater believability. A more recent approach has been to develop *dimensions* of characteristics thought to be related to credibility through advanced statistical techniques such as factor analysis or measurement techniques such as Q-Sort.[2] For example, McCroskey and colleagues (McCroskey, 1966; McCroskey & Jensen, 1975) employed three different instruments to measure credibility. One (McCroskey, 1966) employed a 42-item battery of statements with five-point answer sets in Likert-type format (*strongly agree, agree, neutral, disagree, strongly disagree*). The second employed 12 bipolar adjective semantic differential statements (McCroskey, 1966). Both revealed two dimensions of credibility: authoritativeness and character. The third used a 25 bipolar adjective semantic differential to measure source credibility (McCroskey & Jensen 1975). They found the

---

[2]Factor analysis is a *statistical technique* that seeks to identify dimensions or factors of scales that "group together" in "semantic space" whereby scale items or statements are created by a researcher and then given to respondents and then analyzed for their dimensionality. Q-Methodology (e.g., Q-Sort) is a *measurement technique* that takes a large number of potential scale items and asks respondents to sort them into piles (usually 11). The items are then analyzed and a scale is created using items from all or most groups. For more information on each, see Kerlinger (1986). Factor analysis has been conducted in media studies of source credibility. See, for example, Salwen (1987, 1992) and Mosier & Ahlgren (1981).

same two dimensions with this measure plus three more: sociability, composure, and extroversion. Sample items from each measure are presented in Table 27.1.

One of the most frequently used operational definitions for *media source credibility* comes out of the long series of Roper studies of differences in credibility of the news media (Roper, 1985). Those studies asked simply: "If you got conflicting or different reports of the same news story from radio, television, the magazines and the newspapers, which of the four versions would you be most inclined to believe—the one on radio or television or magazines or newspapers?" This question and others asked by Roper were aimed at discovering the *relative credibility* of different news media.

Carter and Greenberg (1965), skeptical of the Roper questions, believed them to be biased against newspapers. They altered the wording of two Roper questions and found that for general dependency, newspapers were indeed more credible. However, for belief when conflicting stories were reported, they found that even more of their respondents chose television over newspapers than had been reported by Roper.

Berlo, Lemert, and Mertz (1969) asked respondents to rate credibility across widely different types of sources. They identified three credibility factors or dimensions—safety, qualification, and dynamism. When media sources have been explored,

TABLE 27.1

Sample Credibility Scales

Sample Likert-Type Scale Items[a]

Authoritativeness Scales

    I respect this speaker's opinion on the topic.

    This speaker is not of very high intelligence.

    I have little confidence in this speaker.

    This speaker lacks information on the topic.

Character Scales

    I deplore this speaker's background.

    This speaker is basically honest.

    This speaker is a reputable person.

    The character of this speaker is good.

Semantic Differential Scale Adjective Pairs

Authoritativeness	*Character*
Reliable–Unreliable	Honest—Dishonest
Informed–Uninformed	Friendly–Unfriendly
Qualified–Unqualified	Pleasant–Unpleasant
Intelligent–Unintelligent	Unselfish–Selfish
Valuable–Worthless	Nice–Awful
Expert–Inexpert	Virtuous–Sinful

Note. [a]Responses: *strongly agree, agree, neutral, disagree, strongly disagree.*

similar results were obtained. Singletary (1976), for instance, generated 403 adjectives which described credible mass media sources. He asked 181 students to rate how consistent the words were with their understanding of the term *credibility*. His analysis yielded 41 different dimensions for mass media credibility, which he collapsed into 16 credibility categories and conducted a detailed analysis of six: knowledgeability, attraction, trustworthiness, articulation, hostility, and stability. Lee (1978) reported different dimensions of credibility for television and newspapers reporting national and international or state and local news. Whereas television was consistently seen as more credible, levels of credibility varied along the 45 scales of bipolar adjectives for both newspapers and television according to what types of stories were being reported. Factor analysis revealed different dimensions of credibility for each condition. Only the dimension, *intimacy,* surfaced for all conditions.

Another set of measures came out of the massive 1985 American Society of Newspaper Editors' study of credibility. Gaziano and McGrath (1986), asked 875 respondents to rate 16 bipolar semantic differential items. Their results yielded three factors, one of which was generated from 12 of the items that grouped together and that they labeled "credibility." The other two factors were labeled "social concerns" and "patriotic." The 12 credibility items were: *is fair or unfair; is biased or unbiased; tells the whole story or doesn't tell the whole story; is accurate or inaccurate; invades or respects people's privacy; does or does not watch after readers'/viewers' interests; is or is not concerned about the community's well-being; does or does not separate fact and opinion; can or cannot be trusted; is concerned about the public interest or is concerned about making profits, is factual or opinionated; has well-trained or poorly trained reporters.* The other four were: *cares or does not care what audience thinks; sensationalizes or does not sensationalize; is moral or immoral; is patriotic or unpatriotic.*) Respondent ratings for each of the 12 credibility factor items were then used to create an "index" of credibility.

Several attempts to validate or modify the Gaziano and McGrath scale were attempted. For example, Meyer (1988) produced two dimensions from the Gaziano–McGrath scales—one narrowly defined as *credibility* (believability); the other more broadly drawn to represent *affiliation with the community.* A further validation attempt was made by West (1994), who found the Meyer credibility scale to "validly and reliably measure credibility per se" (p. 164). He reported that the community affiliation scale was insufficiently reliable and that the Gaziano–McGrath scale appeared to measure more than one underlying credibility dimension.

Wanzenried and Powell (1993) employed the Leathers Personal Credibility Scale (Leathers, 1992), which posits three dimensions of credibility (competence, trustworthiness, and dynamism). Each dimension containing four sets of bipolar adjectives was used to measure the credibility of presidential candidates (see also Wanzenried, Smith-Howell, & Powell, 1992; Powell & Wanzenried, 1992).

These studies have attempted to elaborate on the basic concept of source characteristics associated with credibility. Instead of positing one or two characteristics, they attempted to identify underlying dimensions of perceived character that would promote confidence in these sources.

Message Characteristics.   Interest in message characteristics is seen in studies such as Anderson and Clevenger (1963), who suggested in their review of experimental research from 1921 to 1961 that message impact is related to source credibility. McCroskey (1969), in a series of experiments empirically testing the relationship of evidence and source credibility to persuasiveness in public speaking situations found that the credibility of evidence (high or low) used in a message alone did not persuade. When source credibility (high or low) was added as an intervening variable, however, persuasion occurred, but only when a source was *not* highly credible. Thus, we know that message credibility is important and more so when a source is not seen as highly credible. In a media credibility study, Slattery and Tiedge (1992) examined the effects on credibility of labeling staged video in television news stories and found that "labeling news video as staged is not in itself enough to bring about a change in the evaluation of news story credibility. . . [and] raise[s] the possibility that repeated use of labels identifying video as a dramatization or re-creation may raise questions about . . . authenticity" (p. 284).

Graber (1987) and Robinson (1987) conducted studies of the way respondents processed messages about presidential candidates in the 1984 election. Graber studied cues or spin in television pictures and Robinson examined cues or spin based on television's words or "what the journalists said about the candidates [sic] qualities as a leader." (p. 147). Graber found that television had more impact when character traits rather than issues were illustrated with pictures. Robinson found that televised words had little impact on public opinion regarding political candidates (in this case, presidential) at all.

One of the more promising lines of message research has been studies of *familiarity*. Boehm (1994) examined the affect on perceived validity of repeating statements several times to increase familiarity. He concluded that familiarity is the basis of judged validity. Further evidence about familiarity was found by Begg, Anas, and Farinacci (1992) who cued respondents about whether a source's messages were truthful. In a series of experiments, respondents heard statements from familiar sources and unfamiliar sources. In the early phases of the experiments, they were told which sources would be lying. The respondents then rated statements as either true or false in later experiments. Begg et al. found that familiarity increased the credibility of even false statements, even when respondents remembered that the statements were being made by a source who was lying.[3]

Audience Characteristics.   Interest in audience characteristics is seen in studies such as Greenberg (1966), Becker, Cobbey, and Sobowale (1978), and Lewis (1981). These studies attempted to trace the relationship between audience demographics and perceived media credibility. Others (Westley & Severin, 1964) attempted to develop an ideal type of audience likely to assign high credibility to a newspaper based upon demographic characteristics. Al-Makaty, Boyd, and Van Tubergen (1994) used Q-Methodology to discover types of Saudi men who found different media credible during the Gulf War. Recently, Wanta and Hu (1994) attempted to link uses and gratifications research (see chapter 10, this volume) with agenda setting (see chapter 7, this volume) to examine "how people use the news media, rather than how media

---

[3]For more on this line of research, see Bacon (1979), Begg, Armour & Kerr (1985), and Pratkanis, Greenwald, Leippe, & Baumgardner (1988).

affect people" (p. 91). To accomplish this, Wanta and Hu tested Meyer's (1988) credibility scales (believability and community affiliation) as predictors of media reliance, exposure, and, ultimately, agenda setting effects. The objective was to find out if audience perceptions of credibility predict media agenda setting effects. They found that credibility (defined as believability and community affiliation) leads to reliance on a medium and reliance leads to exposure. Exposure, in its turn, leads to agenda setting effects. In something of a surprise, they also found that perceived affiliation of the media also produces a statistically significant path coefficient with agenda-setting effects.

SOME RECENT MAJOR STUDIES

Recent research has focused with greater intensity on the dynamics underlying the active perceptions of the audience. This represents renewed interest in lines of thought that echoes back to the congruence (Osgood and Tannenbaum, 1954) and cognitive dissonance (Festinger, 1957) theories of the 1950s. Credibility, in this context, involves a variety of cognitive mediation theories such as the *constructivism* advocated by Delia and associates (Delia, 1976), the *social judgment–involvement approach* (Salmon, 1986), and the *cognitive processing approach* advocated by Stocking and Gross (1989).

Delia (1976) argued that a constructivist viewpoint sees credibility as consisting of "situational constructs." Salmon (1986) pointed out that the social judgment–involvement approach deals with highly involving attitudes regarded as components of self-concept or ego. Stocking and Gross (1989) argued that because journalists themselves see some sources as more credible than others, they engage in categorization processes that create cognitive biases. These category "filters" bias the cognitive processes by which stories are selected and facts are reported.

Applied to credibility, these theories explore the increased skepticism expressed by the public toward the media. As early as 1965, Sargent reported essential differences in how personal news sources (i.e., other people) were perceived compared to impersonal news sources. When she presented news stories variously attributed to individuals and organizations, she found significant differences in credibility evaluations by respondents rating story credibility for individuals and organizations. Newhagen and Nass (1989) argued that research requiring cross-media comparisons means that respondents employ different levels of analysis—that people compare judgments about the credibility of individuals to judgments about the credibility of organizations. They found evidence supporting this view in the massive 1985 American Society of Newspaper Editors' study. This body of research calls into question the validity of much of the cross-media comparative research.

Albert C. Gunther (1988, 1992), following on the work of social judgment theorists (Sherif & Hovland, 1961; Sherif, Sherif, & Nebergall, 1965), conceived that credibility was *relational*. He argued that "involvement" helps explain "a connection between an individual's personal involvement with issues or groups and distrust of media" (Gunther, 1992, p. 150; see also Johnson & Eagly, 1989; Salmon, 1986). Gunther suggested that "a person's involvement in situations, issues, or groups will show the greatest explanatory power" (p. 152). He offered four propositions underlying this approach:

- Media credibility is a receiver assessment, not a source characteristic.
- Audience demographics, proposed as predictors of trust in media, have little theoretical basis and little empirical support.
- Situational factors often outweigh a more general skeptical disposition as predictors of credibility judgments.
- Group involvement will stimulate biased processing, affecting evaluations of messages and sources.

Stamm and Dube (1994) joined Gunther in his critique of studies that define credibility as "a trait possessed by a source or a message; as inherent to the source or message. . . . The receiver's relationship to the content of the source's message must also be taken into account as something that makes a difference in credibility attributed to a source" (p. 105). They explored "other components" of attitude and their relationship to credibility.[4]

APPLIED RESEARCH

Gunther's (1992) findings grew out of a 1985 national data set collected under sponsorship by the American Society of Newspaper Editors. Credibility research represents one of those unusual areas of scholarly research that also has attracted a great deal of attention among communication industry owners and managers. Perhaps the reason for this interest has been the changing relationship of the mass media and their publics. In the 1960s, the role and place of news media came under scrutiny, along with a popular reexamination of many social institutions. What was called the *new journalism* of the 1960s challenged traditional concepts of the media's role among both young journalists and consumers. A new skepticism of all social institutions permeated views of the mass media.

Lionel Trilling (1965) attributed this skepticism of public institutions to a broad displacement of the "public" outside its social institutions. He suggested that it began with intellectuals in the 1930s and had a major impact among college students and the broader public in the 1960s, leading to a redefination of communication's role in society—to give journalists an independent and authentic voice distinct from that of their organizations (Leamer, 1972; Wolfe, 1972).

The skepticism of media grew during the Vietnam War era. The public was confused and frustrated by rapidly changing social and technological conditions, an unpopular war portrayed nightly on television, and an emotional bombardment caused by near-total and near-instant mass communication. A series of high profile reports blamed media coverage in part for social problems of the time. The Kerner Commission Report (National Advisory Commission on Civil Disorders, 1968), for example, concluded that the way the media handled coverage of the 1967 Detroit riots might have contributed to the violence.

---

[4]For more on the relational approach, see Vallone, Ross, and Lepper (1985) on perceptions of media bias among partisans on Mideast issues, or Perloff (1989) on the "Third Person Effect." Chaffee (1982) has also argued that credibility is situational or relational.

In 1971, the Nixon administration applied for and received a temporary restraining order blocking publication of the *Pentagon Papers*, claiming that national security would be endangered. Final clearance for publication was eventually granted by the U.S. Supreme Court. The prolonged series of revelations associated with Watergate, and subsequent Congressional hearings into illegal actions by Nixon Administration officials, were accompanied by bitter disputes about whether the revelations were damaging to the government. Investigative journalism and its direct role in power shifts in politics lead to the highest levels of public belief in news media ever recorded. But they also led to a counter-attack on media reports by officials in both political parties.[5] A series of media scandals were revealed during the 1970s. One prominent scandal was the finding by *The Washington Post* that one of its reporters, Janet Cooke, had fabricated information for a drug story that won a Pulitzer Prize (National News Council, 1981). In the 1980s, well organized attempts by the Reagan administration to manipulate the press also called into question the media's role in reporting public affairs (Hertsgaard, 1988).

Publications Challenging Media Credibility

A series of popular books and articles in news magazines about the credibility of the news media appeared in the late 1970s and early 1980s (e. g., Goldstein, 1985). Goldstein's book described the effects of political power struggles and a clash of ideas about the role communication should play in society, and described a "news credibility problem" for the mass media. This literature cited public opinion polls (Tillson, 1984), changing circulation and audience patterns, libel judgments (Hunsaker, 1979; Libel Defense Resource Center, 1985), and reader complaints (Griffith, 1983; Henry, 1983; Sanoff, 1981) in their arguments.

The publications created intense professional debate among journalists and lead to a series of credibility studies, this time centered on the credibility of the news media *themselves*. Gaziano (1988) has traced this concern from the early 1980s that lead to the perception of a credibility crisis and to a series of major studies by media organizations of public attitudes toward media credibility in 1985. The five most important of these studies were sponsored by The American Society of Newspaper Editors (ASNE; 1985), the Associated Press Managing Editors Association (APNE; 1985), the Gannett Center for Media Studies (Whitney, 1985), The Times-Mirror Company (Times-Mirror, 1986, 1987a, 1987b), and the *Los Angeles Times* media poll (Lewis Press, n. d.). Several other organizations also published studies about this time (i.e., APME, 1984; American Press Institute; API, 1984).

Gaziano and McGrath (1986), who handled the ASNE study, employed focus groups and polling techniques to collect data and sophisticated analytical techniques to examine the data. The Times-Mirror Company and Gallup conducted focus group studies, following up with polling data. Subsequent to collecting the polling data, they returned to their focus groups to help with the interpretation of the polling data. The Times-Mirror studies have become an ongoing longitudinal study in which portions of the original research are replicated to look for changes over time. The Gannett Center

[5]For a sampling of this argument, see Sigal (1973), Porter (1976), and Demac (1988).

study involved an extensive reanalysis of historical credibility studies, including a reanalysis of polling data accumulated over the years. The *Los Angeles Times* study was a national poll. The Associated Press Managing Editors study was an analysis of the discourse data among editors.

Gaziano (1988) summarized the consistencies among these findings as either in agreement or disagreement with each other. Findings that were generally agreed to over the studies included:

1. Media bias is among the public's greatest concerns.
2. Frequent complaints about too much bad news, overdramatization, and sensationalism.
3. That the media treat some groups too favorably, others not favorably enough.
4. The media are out of touch with concerns of average citizens, they treat ordinary people unfavorably.
5. The public supports news media coverage of government and public officials, believing that such scrutiny keeps officials in line.
6. The media tend to pull higher confidence ratings than other major social institutions.
7. Media critics come from opposite ends of the socioeconomic poles: best and least educated; most and least knowledgeable; highest and lowest income; most and least media use.

Disagreements in study results included:

1. Media accuracy.
2. The impact of national security issues.
3. Whether the media invade people's privacy.
4. How independent the media are.
5. Which media are most credible.

Some crucial findings from the ASNE study can be associated with perceptions of mass media credibility. On the positive side:

1. News men and women are overwhelmingly believed.
2. People like getting the news.
3. They think the watchdog role of the press is extremely important.

On the other hand:

1. Three-fourths of adults have some problems with the media's credibility in general.
2. One-sixth express frustrations with news media reporter treatment of victims, specific issues, or specific social institutions.
3. In general, as media sources, newspapers and television have similar credibility ratings.

In a separate study for ASNE in 1991, researcher Robert O. Wyatt observed that findings revealed a new right—"the right not to be offended" (p. 21). This finding was consistent with Rodney Smolla's study of the growth in numbers of libel suits. He argued that people now believe that whatever offends them personally should be restricted or prohibited; they believe they have a legal right to protect themselves from offense (Smolla, 1986).

The study commissioned by Times-Mirror and carried out by the Gallup Organization can be generalized three ways. First, if credibility is defined as believability, then there is no credibility crisis for the nation's news media. Second, the public appreciates the press far more than it approves of news media performance. And, finally, critics of the media are more critical than supporters are supportive.

Taken together, these five studies provide some interesting findings regarding the mass media's credibility in general, as well as specific dimensional findings. For example, on *trust*, audience members do not think journalists are very ethical, journalists do not care much about their readers or audiences. On *liking*, the better people know the press, the less they like and trust it and, the more readers identify with a particular media group, the less they like news organizations and journalists. The findings indicate that readers find journalists' professional standards alien to their own values; when issues involve rights of news organizations versus rights of government, the public usually sides with press; newspaper people are seen more positively than the newspaper organization.

The underlying assumption of this body of research is that the credibility perceived by audiences is tied to the characteristics of the medium itself. The research sought to identify those characteristics and behaviors of the media and its personnel that were creating the credibility problems with the public.

Shortcoming of Applied Studies

The five national studies have not been without substantial criticism. Some professional journalists pointed out contradictory findings in polling data even before these studies were undertaken (Greenberg & Roloff, 1974; McCombs & Washington, 1983; Tillson, 1984; Whitney, 1984). Others pointed out "contradictory findings" in the studies ("Inconsistency of surveys," 1985; Meyer, 1985; Rimmer & Weaver, 1987). The chairman of the APME credibility committee argued that credibility is best understood as a measure of whether the public *believes* in the press rather than whether it *believes* the press (Southerland, 1985).

Academic researchers, too, have challenged some data interpretations and questioned some of the methods employed. Meyer (1985), for example, challenged the interpretation of the data in an article published in *Presstime*, the major professional journal of the Newspaper Association of America. He argued that the data also could be interpreted as demonstrating *high* levels of credibility for news media (see also Rimmer & Weaver, 1987). Meyer (1988) also challenged the scaling technique used in the ASNE study. He demonstrated what he argues is a response set pattern generated by the structure of positive and negative scales, generating different factors (dimensions of credibility) using the same scales by simply altering their positive/negative structure.

Gaziano (1988) acknowledged and discussed this, arguing that the major studies results are "complementary," "congruent," and "consistent." "An additional source of perceived conflict in findings is the multitude of operational definitions of credibility used in these surveys. . . , as well as in previous research" (p. 269). She suggested that studies of an active audience should be supplemented by studies of journalists.

This raises fundamental conceptual questions about professionally sponsored research, and much of academic research as well. The professionally sponsored research depended on hypotheses based upon the limited effects model. The studies assumed that a number of perceived source or message characteristics can be revealed through polling techniques. These studies asked respondents to rate media credibility and specific media characteristics. For example, the ASNE study attempted to identify underlying dimensions of credibility by factor analyzing scaled responses to several operationalizations of possible source (news media) characteristics.

Two recurring problems in the academic literature are also apparent. First, credibility dimensions have not yet proved stable when the scales measuring them have been expanded or altered. Second, a great deal of evidence points to mediating constructs at work within active audiences (e.g., constructions, involvement, familiarity, cognitive processing).

Measurement also has been a problem in the research. Regarding the scales used to identify dimensions of credibility, the ASNE study used 16 statements, 12 of which clustered on a *credibility* dimension. Their factor loadings were used to create an additive index that would sum to a credibility score. Research, as discussed earlier, has shown that expanding or changing scales alters the numbers and types of factors or dimensions found. A study of the credibility literature and the professionally sponsored studies in the 1980s identified more than 100 such scaleable items in the credibility literature (Self, 1988a) which could be explained through five themes:

1. Insensitivity, arrogance, and generally bad behavior by journalists.
2. Inaccuracies, incompleteness and generally poor professional practices.
3. Disagreements over the kinds of news used and over news judgment.
4. Disagreements over proper press–government and press–social relationships.
5. Disagreements over the task of news in the lives of readers.

Self's study indicated the complaints were about how journalists behave, about the news reports themselves, and about the nature and role of news organizations in society. Each theme contained dozens of scaleable criticisms. The introduction of any of these additional items would likely alter the ASNE credibility index.

Mediating constructs also remain a problem. The five themes cited above imply that involvement constructs and active cognitive processing by readers and audiences are at work. The literature reviewed earlier indicates that cognitive schema or templates are likely to change individual responses in unpredictable ways, depending upon how the questions concerning credibility are asked and the degree (intensity and direction) of involvement in the issue or event being reported.

A SUGGESTED STUDY

This critique points to the significant potential for new research regarding mass media credibility. The ASNE study, and especially the Times-Mirror studies, revealed wide differences of opinion between readers and journalists about the news media's role and the task of the news report. The perceived task of the news report, for example, has been shown to predict which medium people will choose for their news (Self, 1988c).

Social judgment-involvement theory, constructivism, and cognitive processing theories all suggest that audiences make judgments about media credibility based on schemas or templates from prior experience with the issues and events reported. The literature suggests that journalists, too, make judgments on the basis of such schema (Stocking & Gross, 1989). A considerable body of literature suggests that public ideas about the task of the news report may itself be changing (Burgoon, Burgoon, & Atkin, 1982; Clark 1979). When concepts of the task of the news report change, they change what the news media are thought to do for their readers. Successful news organizations, however, are slower to adopt new ideas about the task of news than are their customers (Schudson, 1978).

Theories of the social construction of reality exemplified by Tuchman (1978) indicate that professional training and professional associations routinize (provide schema for) the journalist's thinking and behaviors just as surely as social involvement provides templates for ego involvement and cognitive processing by readers or viewers. Weaver and Wilhoit (1986) reported a high degree of professionalism among contemporary journalists when compared to the degree of professionalism in the past. This suggests a research question: *Have journalists and their publics developed different patterns of involvement—different epistemological communities—and thus different schema for task of news?*

Such a research question could be approached by a study of journalists and readers that permits them to self-report (a) degree of media involvement and (b) an assessment of the credibility of the news report.

Our hypothesis predicts that when *journalists and consumers share involvement patterns, credibility of the media would be high. When they do not, credibility of the media among both journalists and their consumers would be low.*

In conducting the research, samples could be drawn from several communities with competing news media. The study might proceed through three phases:

In the first phase, focus groups of readers and journalists would discuss issues, the media, and personal involvement with the issues and events affecting the community.

In the second phase, self-referent opinion statements drawn from the focus groups about involvement, issues, and credibility would be ranked by a small, structured sample of journalists and readers and analyzed using factor analysis through the Q-technique methodology (Stephenson, 1953). This would produce types of individuals who hold similar underlying schema about issue involvement and credibility. Some types might include journalists and readers; others only readers or only journalists (for examples of the use of Q-technique with credibility studies, see Self, 1988b, and Al-Makaty et al., 1994).

In the third phase, statements that best define the types of involvement and credibility types would be ranked using Likert-type scales by representative samples of media consumers and journalists. Each set of statements would be factor analyzed using Q-technique. The involvement types would be treated as independent variables. The credibility types would be treated as the dependent variable. The types would be examined to assess whether involvement types would predict credibility types.

The answer to Gaziano's question about why journalists perceive credibility to be a problem should be revealed in this study to be their epistemological isolation from involvement with their readers. Meyer's observation that the major studies in the 1980s contained both good news and bad should be shown in this study to result from common patterns of involvement between journalists and readers or divergent patterns of involvement.

CONCLUSION

This chapter has reviewed how changing concepts of communication change theories and research about a fundamental construct—credibility. The Greek philosophers Plato and Aristotle laid out the fundamental questions. They suggested that credibility might emanate from a confident knowledge of the truth or grow from a communicator's ability to read the needs of the audience.

Modern communication researchers began the systematic empirical study of the issue using the hypodermic-needle model. They have examined source and media characteristics, message characteristics and the familiarity of the message, and audience demographics and credulity.

As the research has proceeded, it has become clear that credibility is an exceedingly complex construct. Researchers have identified many dimensions of source characteristics. They found that not only manipulating messages changes their credibility, but repeating them or changing their position on a message alters the message's believability. They discovered that the audience hearing or viewing a message is extremely active in shaping its meaning based upon individual needs and experience.

The interest of politicians and media managers in credibility has driven large-scale media industry studies of credibility. Recent research suggests that media credibility research needs to take into account the active involvement of media users if they are to make sense of public perceptions of media credibility. New cultural and textual theories have yet to be brought to bear on this problem. This research should provide many more opportunities for fruitful study.

SUGGESTED READINGS

The following is an annotated list of some of the major studies of credibility.

American Society of Newspaper Editors. (1985). *Newspaper credibility: Building reader trust.* Washington DC: Author.—Seminal nationwide study of 1,600 adults completed by MORI Research Inc. examined a broad range of issues related to credibility finding that three-quarters of the public had some problem with the credibility of the media. The study is important methodologically, for its results, and for its widespread impact.

Erskine, H. G. (1970–1971). The polls: Opinion of the news media. *Public Opinion Quarterly, 34*, 630–634.—This is the most accessible summary of early polling data about media credibility by a wide range of polling organizations. The summary contains both direct questions about believability and broader questions related to trust.

Gunther, A. C. (1992). Biased press or biased public? Attitudes toward media coverage of social groups. *Public Opinion Quarterly, 56*, 147–167.—This study provides both a succinct review and an illustrative application of social judgment-involvement theory using the large data set from the ASNE study.

Hovland, C. I., & Weiss, W. (1951–1952). The influence of source credibility on communication effectiveness. *Public Opinion Quarterly, 15*, 635–650.—This replication contains the most succinct statement of the basic findings of the Hovland research team regarding credibility and the "sleeper effect." For greater detail, see Hovland et al., 1953.

McCroskey, J. C., & Jenson, T. A. (1975). Image of mass media news sources. *Journal of Broadcasting, 19*, 169–180. This study summarizes the early work by McCroskey and his colleagues in developing scales to measure underlying dimensions of perceived credibility of sources. They report three separate scales. The third one became a standard approach, both imitated and challenged, to measuring the construct.

Meyer, P. (1988). Defining and measuring credibility of newspapers: Developing an index. *Journalism Quarterly, 65*, 567–574.—This article reviews the problems associated with scales that attempt to measure dimensions of perceived credibility. It is particularly concerned with the scale used in the 1985 ASNE study and reports the instability of that scale when response set issues are taken into account. Meyer reports a paired down scale that has been used in other studies since.

Powell, F. C., & Wanzenried, J. W. (1992). An empirical test of the Leathers Personal Credibility Scale: Panel responses to the Clinton candidacy. *Perceptual and Motor Skills, 75*, 1255–1261.—This is another approach to measuring credibility using bipolar scales that has attracted considerable attention and use in measuring the credibility of political candidates.

Roper, B. (1985). *Public attitudes toward television and other media in a time of change*. New York: Television Information Office.—A summary of findings about attitudes toward the mass media that includes a full range of measures. It is not limited to issues of credibility.

Salmon, C. T. (1986). Perspectives on involvement in consumer and communication research. In B. Dervin & M. Voigt (Eds.), *Progress in communication sciences* (pp. 243–268). Norwood, NJ: Ablex.—An excellent overall review of the issues involved in social-judgment theory and cognitive processing. Salmon explores the conceptual evolution of the approach and some of the conflicting operationalizations used.

Times-Mirror Company. (1986). *The people and the press (Part I)* (1987a); *We're interested in what you think* (1987b); *The people and the press (Part III)*. Los Angeles: Times-Mirror.—The first three installments in an ongoing series of studies of public attitudes toward the press. The first was conducted by the Gallup organization for Times-Mirror in 1985. Its findings were interpreted in such a way as to appear to contradict some conclusions of the ASNE study.

Whitney, D. C. (1985). *The media and the people: Americans' experience with the news media: A fifty-year review*. Gannet Center for Media Studies. New York: Columbia University.—An extensive review of studies of media with an emphasis upon polling results. This was the third of five influential studies related to media credibility that had a strong impact on media practitioners in the mid-1980s.

REFERENCES

Al-Makaty, S. S., Boyd, D. A., & Van Turbergen, G. N. (1994). Source credibility during the Gulf War: A Q-study of rural and urban Saudi Arabian citizens. *Journalism Quarterly, 71*, 55–63.

American Press Institute. (1984). *The public perception of newspapers: Examining credibility*. Reston, VA: Author.

American Society of Newspaper Editors. (1985). *Newspaper credibility: Building reader trust*. Washington DC: Author.

American Society of Newspaper Editors. (1986). *Newspaper credibility: 206 practical approaches to heighten reader trust*. Washington, DC: Author.

Anderson, K. & Clevenger, T. (1963). A summary of experimental research in ethos. *Speech Monographs 30*, 77.

Aristotle. (1952). *The works of Aristotle II—Rhetoric*. (W. Rhys Robers, Trans.). Chicago: Encyclopedia Britannica.

Associated Press Managing Editors Association. (1984). *Credibility*. Miami: Author.

Associated Press Managing Editors Association. (1985). *Journalists and readers: Bridging the credibility gap.* San Francisco: Author.

Bacon, F. T. (1979). Credibility of repeated statements: Memory for trivia. *Journal of Experimental Psychology, 5,* 241–252.

Baxter, L. A., & Bittner, J. R. (1974). High school and college perceptions of media credibility. *Journalism Quarterly, 51,* 517–520.

Becker, L. B., Cobbey, R. E., & Sobowale, I. (1978). Public support for the press. *Journalism Quarterly, 55,* 421–430.

Begg, I. M., Anas, A., & Farinacci, S. (1992). Dissociation of processes in belief: Source recollection, statement familiarity, and the illusion of truth. *Journal of Experimental Psychology, 121,* 446–458.

Begg, I., Armour, V., & Kerr, T. (1985). On believing what we remember. *Canadian Journal of Behavioural Science, 17,* 199–214.

Berlo, D. K., Lemert, J. B., & Mertz, R. J. (1969). Dimensions for evaluating the acceptability of message sources. *Public Opinion Quarterly, 33,* 563–576.

Boehm, L. E. (1994). The validity effect: A search for mediating variables. *Personality and Social Psychology Bulletin, 20,* 285–293.

Booth-Butterfield, S., & Gotowski, C. (1993). Message modality and source credibility can interact to affect argument processing. *Communication Quarterly, 41,* 77–89.

Brownlow, S. (1992). Seeing is believing: Facial appearance, credibility, and attitude change. *Journal of Nonverbal Behavior, 16,* 101–115.

Burgoon, J. K., Burgoon, M., & Atkin, C. K. (1982, May). *What is news? Who decides? And how? A preliminary report.* Washington, DC: American Society of Newspaper Editors.

Burgoon, M., Burgoon, J., & Wilkinson, M. (1981). Newspaper image and evaluation. *Journalism Quarterly, 58,* 411–419, 433.

Carter, R. F., & Greenberg, B. S. (1965). Newspapers or television: Which do you believe? *Journalism Quarterly, 42,* 29–34.

Cantril, H. (1951). *Public opinion, 1935–1946.* Princeton: Princeton University Press.

Chaffee, S. H. (1982). Mass media and interpersonal channels: Competitive, convergent, or complementary? In G. Gumpert & R. Cathcart (Eds.), *Inter/Media: Interpersonal communication in a media world* (pp. 57–77). New York: Oxford University Press.

Clark, R. (1979). *Changing needs of changing readers.* Charlotte, NC: American Society of Newspaper Editors.

Delia, J. G. (1976). A Constructivist analysis of the concept of credibility. *Quarterly Journal of Speech, 62,* 361–375.

Demac, D. A. (1988) *Liberty denied: The current rise of censorship in America.* New York: PEN American Center.

Dennis, E. (1986, March 28). *The politics of media credibility.* Lecture delivered at Journalism Ethics Institute, Washington and Lee University, Lexington, VA.

Erskine, H. G. (1970–1971). The polls: Opinion of the news media. *Public Opinion Quarterly, 34,* 630–634.

Festinger, L. (1957). *A theory of cognitive dissonance.* Evanston, IL: Row Peterson.

Gaziano, C. (1988). How credible is the credibility crisis? *Journalism Quarterly, 65,* 267–278.

Gaziano, C., & McGrath, K. (1986). Measuring the concept of credibility. *Journalism Quarterly, 63,* 451–462.

Goldstein, T. (1985). *The news at any cost: How journalists compromise their ethics to shape the news.* New York: Simon & Schuster.

Graber, D. (1987). Kind pictures and harsh words. In K.L. Schlozman (Ed.), *Elections in America* (pp. 115–141). Boston: Allen & Unwin.

Greenberg, B. S. (1966). Media use and believability: Some multiple correlates. *Journalism Quarterly, 43,* 665–670, 737.

Greenberg, B. S., & Roloff, M. E. (1974). Mass media credibility: Research results and critical issues. *ANPA News Research Bulletin* (No. 6). Washington, DC: American Newspaper Publishers Association.

Griffith, T. (1983, May 9). Why readers mistrust newspapers. *Time,* p. 94.

Gunther, A. C. (1988). Attitude extremity and trust in media. *Journalism Quarterly, 65*, 279–287.

Gunther, A. C. (1992). Biased press or biased public? Attitudes toward media coverage of social groups. *Public Opinion Quarterly, 56*, 147–167.

Henry, W. A., III. (1983, December 12). Journalism under fire. *Time, 115*, 76–93.

Hertsgaard, M. (1988). *On bended knee: Press relations with Reagan.* New York: Farrar, Straus, Giroux.

Hovland, C. I. (1951). Changes in attitude through communication. *Journal of Abnormal and Social Psychology, 46*, 424–437.

Hovland, C. I., Janis, I. L., & Kelley, H. H. (1953). *Communication and persuasion.* New Haven, CT: Yale University Press.

Hovland, C. I., Lumsdaine, A. A., & Sheffield, F. D. (1949). *Experiments on mass communication.* Princeton, NJ: Princeton University Press.

Hovland, C.I., & Weiss, W. (1951–1952). The influence of source credibility on communication effectiveness. *Public Opinion Quarterly, 15*, 635–650.

Hunsaker, D. (1979). Freedom and responsibility in First Amendment theory: Defamation law and media credibility. *The Quarterly Journal of Speech, 65*, 23–35.

"Inconsistency of surveys" (1985, November 30), *Editor and Publisher,* 118.

Johnson, B. T., & Eagly, A. H. (1989). Effects of involvement on persuasion: A meta analysis. *Psychological Bulletin, 106*, 290–314.

Kerlinger, F. N. (1986). *Foundations of behavioral research* (3rd ed.). New York: Holt, Rinehart, & Winston.

Lasswell, H. D., Lerner, D., & Speier, H. (1980). *Propaganda and communication in world history: Vol. II Emergence of public opinion in the west.* Honolulu: University Press of Hawaii.

Leamer, L. (1972). *The paper revolutionaries.* New York: Simon & Schuster.

Leathers, D. G. (1992). *Successful nonverbal communications: Principles and applications.* New York: McMillan.

Lee. R. S. H. (1978). Credibility of newspaper and television news. *Journalism Quarterly, 55*, 282–287.

Lewis, I. A. (1981). *The media: Los Angeles Times Poll no. 46.* Los Angeles: Times-Mirror.

Lewis, I. A. (Director). (n. d.). *Los Angeles Times Poll no. 94.* Los Angeles: Times-Mirror.

Libel Defense Resource Center. (1985, June 30). *LDRC Bulletin* (No. 14, Summer).

McCombs, M. E., & Washington, L. (1983, February). Opinion surveys offer conflicting clues as to how public views press. *Presstime,* 4–9.

McCroskey, J. C. (1966). Scales for the measurement of ethos, *Speech Monographs, 33*, 65–72.

McCroskey, J. C. (1969). A survey of experimental research on the effects of evidence in persuasive communication. *Speech Monographs, 55,* 169–176.

McCroskey, J. C., & Jensen, T. A. (1975). Image of mass media news sources. *Journal of Broadcasting, 19*, 169–180.

Meyer, P. (1985, July). There's encouraging news about newspapers' credibility, and it's in a surprising location, *Presstime,* 26–27.

Meyer, P. (1988). Defining and measuring credibility of newspapers: Developing an index. *Journalism Quarterly, 65*, 567–574.

Mosier, N. R., & Ahlgren, A. (1981). Crediblity of precision journalism. *Journalism Quarterly, 58*, 375–381, 518.

National Advisory Commission on Civil Disorders. (1968). *Report.* New York: Bantam Books.

National News Council. (1981). *After "Jimmy's World:" Tightening up in editing.* New York: Author.

Newhagen, J., & Nass, C. (1989). Differential criteria for evaluating credibility of newspaper and television news. *Journalism Quarterly, 66*, 277–284.

Osgood, C. E., & Tannenbaum, P. (1954). Attitude change and the principle of congruity. In W. Schramm (Ed.), *Process and effects of mass communication* (pp. 251–260). Urbana: University of Illinois Press.

Perloff, R. M. (1989). Ego-involvement and the third person effect of televised news coverage. *Communication Research, 16,* 236–262.

Plato (1952). *The dialogues of Plato—Phaedrus.* (B. Jowett, Trans.) Chicago: Encyclopedia Britannica.

Porter, W. E. (1976) *Assault on the media: The Nixon years.* Ann Arbor: University of Michigan Press.

Powell, F. C., & Wanzenried, J. W. (1992). An empirical test of the Leathers Personal Credibility Scale: Panel responses to the Clinton candidacy. *Perceptual and Motor Skills. 75*, 1255–1261.

Pratkanis, A. R., Greenwald, A., Leippe, M. R., & Baumgardner, M. H. (1988). In search of reliable persuasion effects: The sleeper effect is dead. Long live the sleeper effect. *Journal of Personality & Social Psychology, 54*, 203–218.

Rimmer, T., & Weaver, D. (1987). Different questions, different answers? Media use and media credibility. *Journalism Quarterly, 64*, 28–36, 44.

Robinson, M. J. (1987). News media myths and realities: What network news did and didn't do in the 1984 general campaign. In K. L. Schlozman (Ed.), *Elections in America* (pp. 143–170). Boston: Allen & Unwin.

Rogers, E. M. (1994). *A history of communication study.* New York: The Free Press.

Roper, B. (1985) *Public attitudes toward television and other media in a time of change.* New York: Television Information Office.

Salmon, C. T. (1986). Perspectives on involvement in consumer and communication research. In B. Dervin & M. Voigt (Eds.), *Progress in Communication Sciences* (Vol. 7, pp. 243–268). Reading, MA: Ablex.

Salwen, M. B. (1987). Credibility of newspaper opinion polls: Source, source intent and precision. *Journalisim Quarterly, 64*, 813–819.

Salwen, M. B. (1992). The influence of source intent: Credibility of a news media health story. *World Communication, 21*, 63–68.

Sanoff, A. P. (1981, June 29). Uneasy press sets out to refurbish its image. *U.S. News and World Report, 91*, 71–72.

Sargent, L. (1965). The dimension of source credibility of television. *Journalism Quarterly, 42*, 35–42.

Schudson, M. (1978). *Discovering the news: A social history of American newspapers.* New York: Basic Books.

Self, C. C. (1988a). *An examination of themes and recommendations about the "news credibility issue."* Paper presented at the regional meeting of the newspaper division of The Association for Education in Journalism and Mass Communication, Tuscaloosa, AL.

Self, C. C. (1988b). A study of news credibility and task perception among journalists in the United States and England. *International Communication Bulletin, 23*, 16–24.

Self, C. C. (1988c). Task of news report as a predictor of choice of medium. *Journalism Quarterly, 65*, 119–125.

Shaw, D. L. (1967). News bias and the telegraph: A study of historical change. *Journalism Quarterly, 44*, 3–12.

Shaw, E. R. (1976). The popular meaning of media credibility. *ANPA News Research Bulletin* (No. 3). Washington, DC: American Newspaper Publishers Association.

Sherif, M., & Hovland, C. I. (1961). *Social judgment.* New Haven: Yale University Press.

Sherif, C. W., Sherif, M, & Nebergall, R. E. (1965). *Attitude and attitude change: The social judgment-involvement approach.* Philadelphia: W. B. Saunders.

Sigal, L. V. (1973). *Reporters and officials: The organization and politics of newsmaking.* Lexington, MA: D.C. Heath.

Singletary, M. (1976). Components of the credibility of a favorable news source. *Journalism Quarterly, 53*, 316–319.

Slattery, K., & Tiedge, J. T. (1992). The effect of labeling staged video on the credibility of TV news stories. *Journal of Broadcatsting & Electronic Media, 36*, 279–286.

Smith, B. L. (1969). The mystifying intellectual history of Harold D. Lasswell. In A. A. Rogow (Ed.), *Politics, personality, and social science in the twentieth century: Essays in honor of Harold D. Lasswell* (pp. 41–105). Chicago: University of Chicago Press.

Smolla, R. A. (1986). *Suing the press.* New York: Oxford University Press.

Southerland, B. (1985, December 5). Lecture to students in seminar in news credibility, University of Missouri, Columbia.

Stamm, K., & Dube, R. (1994). The relationship of attitudinal components to trust in media. *Communication Research, 21*, 105–123.

Stocking, S. H., & Gross, P. H. (1989). *How do journalists think? A proposal for the study of cognitive bias in newsmaking*. Indianapolis: ERIC Clearinghouse on Reading and Communication Skills.

Stephenson, W. (1953). *The study of behavior*. Chicago: University of Chicago Press.

Tillson, J. B. (1984). We're suffering declining confidence in all institutions. *Credibility* (pp. 31–32). Miami: Associated Press Managing Editors Association.

Times-Mirror Company. (1986). *The people and the press (Part I)*. Los Angeles: Author.

Times-Mirror Company. (1987a). *The people and the press (Part III)*. Los Angeles: Author.

Times-Mirror Company. (1987b). *We're interested in what you think. A sampling of a year's letters to the Chairman of Times-Mirror*. Los Angeles: Author.

Trilling, L. (1965). *Beyond culture: Essays on literature and learning*. New York: Harcourt, Brace, Jovanovich.

Tuchman, G. (1978). *Making news*. New York: The Free Press.

Vallone, R. P., Ross, L., & Lepper, M. R. (1985). The hostile media phenomenon: Biased perceptions and perceptions of media bias in coverage of the Beirut massacre. *Journal of Personality and Social Psychology, 49,* 577–585.

Wanta, W., & Hu, Y. (1994). The effects of credibility, reliance, and exposure on media agenda-setting: A path analysis model. *Journalism Quarterly, 71,* 90–98.

Wanzenried, J. W., Smith-Howell, D., & Powell, F. C. (1992). Source credibility and presidential campaigns: Governor Clinton and the allegation of marital infidelity. *Psychological Reports, 70,* 992–994.

Wanzenried, J. W., & Powell, F. C. (1993). Source credibility and dimensional stability: A test of the Leathers Personal Credibility Scale using perceptions of three presidential candidates. *Perceptual and Motor Skills, 77,* 403–406.

Weaver, D. H., & Wilhoit, G. C. (1986). *The American journalist*. Bloomington, IN: Indiana University Press.

West, M. D. (1994). Validating a scale for the measurement of credibility: A covariance structure modeling approach. *Journalism Quarterly, 71,* 158–168.

Westley, B. H., & Severin, W. J. (1964). Some correlates of media credibility. *Journalism Quarterly, 41,* 325–335.

Whitney, D. C. (1984, May). *Attitudes toward the news media: Three publics*. Paper presented to the American Association for Public Opinion Research. Lake Lawn Lodge, Delavan, WI.

Whitney, D. C. (1985). *The media and the people: Americans' experience with the news media: A fifty-year review*. New York: Columbia University, Gannett Center for Media Studies.

Whitney, D. (1986, April 8). *The news media and the public trust: The rise and fall of a public issue*. Remarks presented for the McGovern Distinguished Lecture in Journalism, University of Texas at Austin.

Wolfe, T. (1972). *The new nonfiction*. New York: Harper and Row.

28

Political Communication

Lynda Lee Kaid
University of Oklahoma

Political communication traces its roots to the earliest formal studies of communication. Classical studies from the time of Plato and Aristotle were interested in communication as it affected the political and legal institutions of the day. As a modern field of study, political communication, while incorporating this earlier focus, is an interdisciplinary field embracing concepts from communication, political science, journalism, sociology, psychology, history, and others. Unlike many of the traditional areas of study, political communication reflects communication theory, concern, and research from both mass and human approaches to commmunication.

Although propaganda studies (Doob, 1950) and early empirical voting behavior studies by sociologists (Lazarsfeld, Berelson, & Gaudet, 1944; Berelson, Lazarsfeld, & McPhee, 1954) can be labeled political communication studies, Nimmo and Sanders (1981) suggest in their seminal *Handbook of Political Communication* that political communication emerged as distinctly cross-disciplinary in the 1950s. Many definitions of *political communication* have been advanced, but none has gained universal acceptance. Perhaps the best is the simplest—Chaffee's (1975) offering that political communication is the "role of communication in the political process" (p. 15) suffices.

BACKGROUND AND DIMENSIONS OF THE DISCIPLINE

From an emerging concern in the 1950s, through the next decade, political communication evolved slowly. In the early 1970s, however, political communication as a discipline marked several milestones. University courses began to focus on political communication, publications were initiated,[1] and professional recognition quickly followed. Of particular significance was the 1973 founding of the International Communication Association's Political Communication Division. For nearly two decades, this organization served as the major scholarly division devoted to political communication. Recently, the American Political Science Association and the Speech Communication Association also established political communication sections.

During the 1970s and early 1980s, several important books, articles, and resource materials were published, providing researchers with the important background and conceptual information necessary to understand the roots and development of political communication. For instance, Dan Nimmo's *The Political Persuaders* (1970) was an important early text and research resource. The first five volumes of the International Communication Association's *Communication Yearbook* series contained useful bibliographic essays that helped define the area and guide researchers (Jackson-Beeck & Kraus, 1980; Larson & Wiegele, 1979; Mansfield & Weaver, 1982; Nimmo, 1977; Sanders & Kaid, 1978) and were supplemented by subsequent overviews (Johnston, 1990; Kaid & Sanders, 1985).

Bibliographic resources focusing on campaign communication were provided in two volumes that provided multidisciplinary citations (Kaid, Sanders, & Hirsch, 1974; Kaid & Wadsworth, 1984). The single best resource book remains the *Handbook of Political Communication*. Permeating all of these background materials is a preoccupation with political communication from a political campaign or public opinion influence perspective. In *New Directions in Political Communication*, Swanson and Nimmo (1990) acknowledged that "the field's center or mainstream continues to be devoted to studying the strategic uses of communication to influence public knowledge, beliefs, and action on political matters and to regard the political campaign as the paradigmatic instance of the subject" (p. 9). Calling attention to the broader interpretations of political communication, Swanson and Nimmo argued for a move beyond the voter persuasion paradigm.

In keeping with both the mainstream approaches to political communication and the broadening of the area in new directions, this chapter outlines the dominant approaches and theories that constitute political communication. It then addresses specific topics that have been the recent focus of particular research interest. In each case an effort is made to describe the primary research methods used to pursue each approach and topic.

APPROACHES, THEORIES, AND PERSPECTIVES

Four basic perspectives guide most political communication research: (a) rhetorical, critical, and interpretive approaches (see chapter 16, this volume), (b) effects research

---

[1]Of particular interest was *Political Communication Review*, sponsored by the Political Communication Division of the International Communication Association from 1975 through 1991. In 1993, this publication was incorporated, along with *Political Communication and Persuasion*, into a new journal, *Political Communication*, co-sponsored by the political communication divisions of the International Communication Association and the American Political Science Association.

(see chapter 4, this volume), (c) agenda-setting theory (see chapter 7, this volume), and (d) the uses and gratifications approach (see chapter 10, this volume). Each shares background theory and research methods with other research traditions.

Rhetorical, Critical, and Interpretive Approaches

Political communication research in the rhetorical (see chapter 16, this volume), critical, and interpretive vein focuses primarily on the source and message aspects of the political communication process. Researchers seek common themes in political messages, analyze the underlying motives of speakers, ferret out strategies and techniques of communication devices, analyze language characteristics and styles, and suggest ways of interpreting language and message variables. Critical theory analysts also fit into this category, although they concentrate more on underlying sociological, structural, and ideological aspects of messages and sources, rather than on individual analysis (Swanson & Nimmo, 1990).

Most researchers approaching political communication this way concentrate on a particular political message or series of messages. For instance, a mainstay of speech and rhetoric scholars for many years was the analysis of specific political speeches. The political speeches of great orators such as William Jennings Bryan (Sloan, 1965) and Winston Churchill (Underhill, 1966) made good subjects for analysis, as did later performances by John F. Kennedy, Martin Luther King, and the "great communicator," Ronald Reagan. Some of these analyses have been recently organized under the rubric of genre studies, grouping together the analyses of different types of political speeches into categories or genres. For instance, rhetoricians studied a speaking genre called the *apologia* in which the speaker attempts to apologize for some wrongdoing. Edward Kennedy's Chappaquiddick speech is an oft-cited example of this genre. Other researchers follow a simple descriptive or historical path, providing important background and factual information on a particular communication message(s).

It would be misleading to suggest that all such analyses share a common theoretical perspective; many different rhetorical and analytical underpinnings are at play. Such research, however, does share an interpretive philosophy and a humanistic, nonbehavioral approach. It is important to note that most current political communication studies in the rhetorical and interpretive mode have been concerned with modern communication messages, particularly those carried by the mass media. Such studies also proceed from a variety of perspectives.

A particularly interesting category is dramatistic analysis. Generally rooted in Kenneth Burke's analysis of the pentad, analysts interpret political events and messages in terms of dramatistic elements. The work of Nimmo and Combs (1983, 1990), in which they argue that many aspects of politics are experienced as mediated political reality emanates from this perspective.

Another popular interpretive perspective example is fantasy-theme analysis, advocated by Bormann (1972, 1973) as the way political messages take on meaning and "chain-out" among media audiences. Narrative analysis (Fisher, 1985; Bennett & Edelman, 1985) is another important example of this type of political communication research (see chapter 16, this volume).

The research methods used to study political communication from the rhetorical and critical perspective are generally qualitative. Some combine basic historical and factual reporting with descriptive and interpretive analysis. Researchers who use these methods are generally trained in rhetorical criticism or in the tenets of a particular approach, such as dramatistic analysis, which is then applied to the particular message(s) or political event(s) under examination. In some cases a quantitative methodology (e.g., content analysis) provides more conclusive and reliable evidence for descriptive findings.

Effects Research

While it is possible to argue that rhetorical and interpretive researchers are implicitly interested in the effects of messages, they offer no evidence beyond their own interpretations that such effects extend to wider publics. Research in the effects paradigm usually offers some type of behavioral or attitudinal evidence for the results attributed to messages. The modern dominance of social science and the behavioral research paradigm in communication should have made effects research important to political communication researchers. Whereas such interests underpinned early voting research, direct effects research was eschewed by many researchers because of a pervasive belief in the "minimal" or "limited effects" model that dominated intellectual thought during the 1960s and early 1970s (Klapper, 1960). Although Klapper's limited effects perspective was itself based on limited evidence, his findings about mass communication effects were widely extended and adopted. By the mid-1970s, however, researchers were discounting the minimal effects model and reasserting the usefulness of direct effects research (Chisman, 1976; Kaid & Sanders, 1978; Kraus & Davis, 1976).

Examples of direct effects political communication research have been more apparent in the 1980s and 1990s. A leading contributor to this perspective has been research on the effects of political advertising (Kaid, 1981). Research on the short- and long-term effects of political media messages on the formation of candidate images has also been important. Other types of direct effects research looked for more longitudinal effects of media and messages by focusing on political socialization (Atkin, 1975; Connell, 1987), the spiral of silence effect (Noelle-Neumann, 1974, 1977, 1984; see also chapter 11, this volume), or media exposure or attention (Reese & Miller, 1981). Modern effects researchers, however, are not simply blind repeaters of the mistakes of early "hypodermic needle" or "bullet theory" proponents; contemporary effects research acknowledges multiple causes and effects. They readily accept the notion that a given channel or message effect may be related to many intervening variables of source, situation, and receiver.

Effects researchers employ a variety of methods to seek answers to political communication outcomes. The most common methods are probably experiments and surveys. With experimental methods researchers can identify specific variable effects. For instance, Robinson (1976) was able to use experimental methods to establish that viewing the television documentary "The Selling of the Pentagon" affected viewer beliefs about the military system and, in combination with survey research results, was able to suggest that television viewing might create "political malaise." Survey research has been used to establish the effects of specific political events. For instance, surveys and polls taken after televised presidential debates have been used to provide evidence not only of "who won and who lost" but also about the types of effects such debates might have on viewer attitudes and beliefs about issues and candidate images. It is important, however, to note that while experiments establish causation, surveys cannot.

Agenda-Setting

Agenda-setting research might be considered a subcomponent of effects research, advocating a cognitive effect of the media. However, because it has been such an influential approach in political and mass communication research, it is considered separately. Agenda-setting research posits the notion, based on Cohen's (1963) assertion, that the media do not tell us what to *think*, but what to *think about*.

McCombs and Shaw (1972) first tested the agenda-setting principle during the 1968 presidential campaign and provided evidence that the agenda of issues communicated by the media became the agenda of issues salient to voters. This research and the subsequent efforts inspired by it (Protess & McCombs, 1991) rejuvenated media effects research, establishing that the media did, indeed, have significant effects and that it was possible to identify those effects and the contingent conditions related to them (McCombs, 1976; Weaver, 1987; see chapter 7, this volume for more details).

Agenda-setting is a good example of a research approach that combines different methodologies. Agenda-setting researchers typically use content analysis to measure the issue content of media messages (i.e., media issue agenda) and survey research to measure public issue agendas (i.e., the public issue agenda). These two agendas are then statistically correlated to reveal the level of association between the media issue agenda and the public issue agenda.

Uses and Gratifications

The contemporary uses and gratifications perspective received its major thrust and testing in the British political campaign settings of the 1960s (Blumler & McQuail, 1969). Although the intellectual roots of this model can be traced back decades earlier (McLeod & Becker, 1981), Blumler and his colleagues developed a method for identifying the reasons why audiences watched or avoided campaign programs on television. Early and subsequent research focused on an active audience. Unlike the passive audience myth of early direct effects research, uses and gratifications research posits that audience members have expectations about communication they receive, resulting in gratifications that are sought and received—or avoided (see Katz, Blumler, & Gurevitch, 1973, and chapter 10, this volume, for more on uses and gratifications).

In political communication, these ideas have been applied to suggest that different types of communication messages perform different types of functions for voters. For instance, voters might expect to use news media (Mendelsohn & O'Keefe, 1976) to serve a surveillance function (to keep up with what is happening in the campaign, to get to know more about the issues or candidates) or they might attend a campaign rally to participate in the campaign's excitement (Sanders & Kaid, 1981). Political communication researchers also have been interested in the interaction between effects and uses and gratifications, obtaining some support that a voter's expectations and gratifications can be related to the effects that result from a given communication message (McLeod & Becker, 1981). Survey methods provide the primary means of data-gathering for researchers who analyze political uses and gratifications. Researchers ask voters to report on their expectations and on the functions that various communication messages have performed for them.

SELECTED TOPICS IN POLITICAL COMMUNICATION

The discussion of major theoretical thrusts offers a hint of the topics that characterize political communication. Because political communication is broad and interdisciplinary, it is not possible to provide a comprehensive analysis or listing of topics. The areas discussed illustrate mainstream lines of research and methodologies.

Media Coverage of Political Campaigns and Events

How the mass media cover political campaigns and major political events is a dominant line of political communication inquiry and has been approached from many different perspectives. The overarching questions being asked here include: How are the media covering campaigns and events? What are the characteristics of such coverage? Is the coverage biased in any way? How does this coverage affect public perceptions of politics?

The first three questions are media content questions. They are generally answered by content analysis. Thus, researchers have investigated how the news media have covered political campaigns, concluding that for both newspapers and television the coverage is more focused on "horserace" journalism, concentrating on images over substantive issues (Graber, 1976; Lichter, Amundson, & Noyes, 1988; Patterson & McClure, 1976). Other studies concern questions pertaining to media bias in coverage (i.e., do the media exhibit favoritism in their selection and presentation of political candidates, issues, or events?). Here the results have been mixed and less certain: some researchers found political bias, while others find coverage differences more attributable to the structural characteristics of the media (Frank, 1973; Hofstetter, 1976).

The most prevalent criticism of this research vein has been that the categories used to analyze content do not fully tap the message content conveyed by newspaper and television stories about campaigns. Early criticisms were particularly valid in pointing to the lack of attention to nonverbal messages and the visual aspects of television coverage. Although efforts have been made to address these concerns, content analyses of media coverage still suffer from these problems.

Media coverage is one area of political communication where researchers have clearly stepped past the voter or campaign paradigm. Many researchers have examined media coverage of noncampaign, political events and public affairs happenings (Paletz & Entman, 1981), and even crisis events and coverage of policy issues. For example, Nimmo and Combs' analyses of crisis events and their detailing of mediated politics apply a dramatistic perspective to many noncampaign political events (Nimmo & Combs, 1983, 1985, 1990). Other researchers have considered the role of press coverage of the president in noncampaign times (Foote, 1990) and of Congress and the Supreme Court (see Johnston, 1990, for a review of additional media coverage areas, including cartoons and editorials, coverage of opinion polls, and international news flow).

While the overwhelming amount of research on news coverage has been devoted to analyses of content and its characteristics, and are thus primarily descriptive or interpretive in nature, some researchers employed survey and experimental methods to tie media coverage to public perceptions. Agenda-setting research is perhaps the best known example of the combination of media content analyses with public opinion surveys, establishing a crucial link between what the media cover and what people judge to be important. Chaffee, Zhao, and Leshner (1994) offered a helpful review of research linking media exposure to public campaign knowledge levels. A large body of research (primarily survey research) concerns the relationship between media use/exposure/attention/dependency and political attitudes, knowledge levels, evaluations of political leaders, and levels of political cynicism/efficacy/alienation. Iyengar, Peters, and Kinder (1982) demonstrated experimentally that television news can have an impact on political beliefs. Kaid, Downs, and Ragan (1990) used experimental methods to show that the 1988 encounter between President George Bush and Dan Rather on the *CBS Evening News* affected viewer images of both the politician and the news commentator. Neuman, Just, and Crigler (1992) employed a combination of experimental, survey, content analysis, and in-depth interview methods to examine media effects on political knowledge.

Political Debates

Because political debating with its expected interchange of competing ideas is often seen as the epitome of the democratic process, it has been popular with political communication researchers. While early rhetorical scholars analyzed the historic Lincoln–Douglas debates, modern researchers have concentrated on debates carried via electronic media. Since the first presidential debates in 1960 between Kennedy and Nixon, such encounters have fascinated political communication researchers. Sidney Kraus' *The Great Debates* (1962) remains a classic collection in political communication. It was not until the Federal Communication Commission reinterpreted the Equal Time Provision, however, that debates began to proliferate in the American political system.[2] In 1960 Congress voted to suspend the Equal Time Provision to allow the Kennedy-Nixon debates. Before the 1976 election, the FCC interpreted the Equal Time Provision to allow the media to cover debates as bona fide news events, thereby eliminating the need to open debates to every legally qualified candidate for the presidency.

Researchers examined political debates from multiple angles, including analyses of rhetorical arguments and styles, presentations of specific issues, candidate images conveyed, and effects on voter learning, image evaluations, and voting decisions. The

---

[2]Starting in 1976, there has been some form of presidential debate(s) in each presidential election. These televised spectacles are common in presidential primaries and in primary and general election campaigns at virtually every election level—even in local races.

best surveys of the research on political debates remain the classic summaries that followed the 1960 (Katz & Feldman, 1962) and 1976 (Sears & Chaffee, 1979) debates. Media coverage of debates have been approached from many methodological standpoints, most commonly rhetorical analysis, content analysis, experiments, and survey research.

Political Advertising

No area of political communication has achieved more prominence in recent years than the study of political advertising. Researchers in political communication recognize that political advertising, particularly on television, is the major form of communication between candidates and voters, constituting the overwhelming majority of campaign budgets in high-level races. Early research provided evidence that television ads were effective in overcoming selective exposure, influenced candidate images, conveyed issue information, had more effect on voter knowledge levels than did television news, and sometimes influenced voting behavior (Kaid, 1981).

A proliferation of content analysis studies in the 1980s and early 1990s demonstrated that political advertising more often contained issue information than image information (Joslyn, 1980; Kaid & Johnston, 1991; Kern, 1990) and that there were identifiable videostyles for candidate advertising (Wadsworth & Kaid, 1987; Kaid, Tedesco, Chanslor, & Roper, 1993). Several researchers provided important historical and descriptive analyses of political advertising (Diamond & Bates, 1984; Jamieson, 1992; West, 1993). Particularly useful is the series of descriptive and analytical accounts of presidential advertising by Patrick Devlin (1973–1974, 1977, 1981, 1987, 1989, 1993).

Great strides have also been made to experimentally identify specific effects from political television ads. Political television advertising research often more closely follows effects theories than do other avenues of political communication research. Thus, political advertising researchers have demonstrated the superiority of some types of ads over others (i.e., positive vs. negative ads, image vs. issue ads) and explicated the conditions under which televised ads may be successful in influencing candidate images, voter issue awareness, or vote likelihood (e.g., Kaid & Sanders, 1978; Kaid, Nimmo, & Sanders, 1986; Biocca, 1991; Kaid, Leland, & Whitney, 1992). Survey research has been less successful in obtaining definitive effects from political advertising exposure or attention (Chaffee et al., 1994).

Negative advertising is an increasingly salient topic in political advertising research. Content analysis has demonstrated that negative advertising comprised about one third of presidential ads between 1968 and 1988 (Kaid & Johnston, 1991) but reached new levels in 1992 when Clinton's rate of negative advertising reached the highest level ever in a presidential campaign—69 percent of Clinton ads were negative (Kaid, 1994). Negative advertising has received descriptive coverage as a genre by Johnston-Cartee and Copeland (1991) who outlined different types and strategies of negative advertising. Impressive experimental work spearheaded by Garramone also demonstrated that negative ads, although sometimes backfiring, can decrease an opponent's image evaluation, be offset by rebuttal ads, and are particularly effective when sponsored by a third party or independent group (Garramone, 1984, 1985; Roddy & Garramone, 1988). The increased use of negative political ads has also renewed interest in political advertising ethics and in the uses of technology to create potentially misleading and distorted ads (Kaid, 1991, 1993).

Relatively new to political advertising research are combined studies of media coverage and political advertising effects. As television advertising's campaign dominance has grown, news media have realized that they must cover the ads "as news" to capture the major streams of campaign dialogue. Consequently, the newspaper and television media have engaged in "ad watches" in which the news media attempt to analyze, interpret, and evaluate campaign advertising. Television news coverage of political ads has become an important aspect of political advertising (West, 1993), increasing dramatically between 1972 and 1988 (Kaid, Gobetz, Garner, Leland, & Scott, 1993). Such ad watches are now receiving attention from experimental researchers who have shown that the ad watches may effect how voters react to particular ads and candidates (Cappella & Jamieson, 1994; Pfau & Louden, 1994).

Political Rhetoric

Like news coverage, debates, and political advertising, studies of political speaking and language research generally revolve around either message analysis or effects analysis. Rhetorical critics often analyze the content of particular speakers or speeches (or public utterances in any form through any channel). They might examine collections of speeches on particular topics. For instance, Richard Nixon's resignation speech or Clinton's inaugural address might be analyzed, or speeches by a number of political leaders on civil rights issues or health care could be grouped together for analysis. Generally, this research utilizes rhetorical, critical, or interpretive perspectives, and a qualitative approach. However, some researchers have made interesting contributions by applying more quantitative or combinations of quantitative and qualitative methodologies. An outstanding example is the work of Roderick Hart, who developed a computerized content analysis system (DICTION) and applied it to presidential speeches beginning with Truman (Hart, 1984, 1985). Hart's research explicated the "verbal style" of the presidency. Analyses of political language and its implications take on other forms. Conversation analysis looked at political messages, and Murray Edelman's (1964, 1988) analyses of symbolic language in politics are landmarks.

Researchers concerned with measuring the effects of political speaking often conduct experimental or survey studies to determine whether a particular speech or set of speeches affect public opinion or actions. For instance, polling organizations often conduct surveys after a major presidential speech to see how it affected the president's approval ratings. Such studies may combine effects concerns with other theoretical perspectives. For instance, Sanders and Kaid (1981) employed a field experiment to measure changes in candidate image resulting from speeches of presidential primary candidates (effects) and how audiences used the candidate appearances to fulfill needs such as surveillance, vote guidance, and excitement (uses and gratifications).

New Research Directions and Methodologies

Political communication has grown dramatically in the past few decades. The theoretical perspectives and selected topics represent some of the major areas of inquiry that characterize the field. Many other topics are evolving. Great strides are being made in political communication study concerning interpersonal communication, group decision-making within political institutions, media and political ethics, pragmatic politics, and gender issues.

One of the most significant new directions in political communication is interest in cross-cultural research. Gurevitch and Blumler (1990), in calling for more such research, remarked that "the practices and ideologies of the American political communication industry are taking hold worldwide" (p. 311). Researchers have heeded the call and begun to broaden their perspectives, looking at the transference of political models and theories across political systems. For instance, agenda-setting has been applied to elections in Britain (Semetko, Blumler, Gurevitch, & Weaver, 1991) and Germany (Schoenbach & Semetko, 1992). A research team of French and American scholars applied multiple theoretical and methodological perspectives to compare the 1988 French and American presidential campaigns (Kaid, Gerstlé, & Sanders, 1991). Comparisons have been made of political advertising content similarities of in France, Germany, the United States, Italy, Israel, and Britain (Kaid & Holtz-Bacha, 1995). Hardt (1988) has called for recognition of cultural and critical theory concerns in such work. The evolution of new democratic systems in Eastern and Central Europe have made this even more important.

As new directions of political communication research develop, research methods and techniques are maturing and diversifying. Certainly traditional methodological approaches such as rhetorical/interpretive analysis, content analysis, survey research, and experimental methods remain the mainstays of political communication research. However, new technologies are being applied: Computer and video technology has made it possible to conduct experimental tests in which audience responses to political messages are measured every second, keyed to exact points in video message content; sophisticated focus group techniques have been developed for political message analysis; interactive media techniques are proliferating; and physiological measures are being applied in innovative ways.

There can be no doubt that communication, in all its forms and channels, plays a major role in how democratic systems are formed, in how they govern, and in how their publics respond. Political communication theory and research must therefore retain a preeminent place in communication study.

SAMPLE POLITICAL COMMUNICATION RESEARCH PROJECT

With interest in political advertising—particularly negative political advertising—at the forefront of political communication today, an interesting research project might measure the comparative effectiveness of negative and positive ads across different channels of communication (print, radio, and television media). A theoretical argument could be developed from the literature on effects of positive and negative ads (Biocca, 1991) and on channel variables (Cohen, 1976; McKinnon, Tedesco, & Kaid, 1993), resulting in a possible hypothesis that negative ads are more effective on television, and positive ads are more effective on radio. An experimental study could be designed using a 2 x 3 factorial design depticted in Fig. 28.1.

Advertisement

Medium	Positive	Negative
Print		
Radio		
Television		

FIG. 28.1.   2 x 3 factorial design.

Stimulus materials could be prepared in the form of political ads with similar content but altered to be positive or negative and to be presented via the print, radio, or television media. This would result in six political spots to serve as the stimulus materials for the experiment: negative spot in print, negative spot on radio, negative spot on television, positive spot in print, positive spot on radio, positive spot on television. Each could be produced either by adapting spots from real political campaigns, or the researcher could create the spots using realistic production techniques in a television studio or with computer-aided video technology. In either case, the candidate would be the same in each spot.

The researcher would then develop measurement techniques for the study, perhaps a series of measures to assess audience reactions or recall to the candidate in the spots to determine if issue or image information is learned, or an effect on vote likelihood. With the stimulus materials prepared and the measurement device or questionnaire constructed, the researcher would then need to recruit participants for the experiment. Once a participant pool has been identified, the researcher would randomly assign participants to each of the six cells in the experiment. Each cell would watch the spot appropriate for that cell and fill out the questionnaire developed to measure reactions.

Following data gathering, the researcher would analyze the data to determine if the hypotheses were supported. Two-way analysis of variance would be an appropriate technique here, allowing the researcher to determine if there are main effects (for medium and for ad type) and if there are interaction effects between medium and ad type. Depending on the outcome of the research project, the researcher might be able to advance the current level of knowledge about the effects of medium variables as well as positive and negative ads.

SUMMARY

Political communication is an interdisciplinary field of study that has grown substantially in the past few decades. The major theories and approaches to the subdiscipline of political communication include rhetorical/critical/interpretative work, effects research, agenda-setting theories, and uses and gratifications approaches. Among the most important topics currently considered by political communication researchers are media coverage of political campaigns and events, political debates, political advertising, and political rhetoric. Political communication researchers look at these topics from a wide variety of perspectives, ranging from qualitative methods that are critical and interpretive to quantitative methods such as content analysis, experimental design, and survey research.

REFERENCES

Atkin, C. (1975). Communication and political socialization. *Political Communication Review, 1*, 2–6

Bennett, W. L., & Edelman, M. (1985). Toward a new political narrative. *Journal of Communication, 35*, 156–171.

Berelson, B. R., Lazarsfeld, P. F., & McPhee, W. N. (1954). *Voting*. Chicago: University of Chicago Press.

Biocca, F., (Ed.). (1991). *Television and political advertising* (Vols. 1–2). Hillsdale, NJ: Lawrence Erlbaum Associates.

Blumler, J. G., & McQuail, D. (1969). *Television in politics*. Chicago, IL: University of Chicago Press.

Bormann, E. G. (1972). Fantasy and rhetorical vision: The rhetorical criticism of social reality. *Quarterly Journal of Speech, 58*, 396–407.

Bormann, E. G. (1973). The Eagleton affair: A fantasy theme analysis. *Quarterly Journal of Speech, 59*, 143–159.

Cappella, J. N., & Jamieson, K. H. (1994). Broadcast adwatch effects: A field experiment. *Communication Research, 21*, 342–365.

Chaffee, S. (Ed.). (1975). *Political communication*. Beverly Hills, CA: Sage Publications.

Chaffee, S. H., Zhao, X., & Leshner, G. (1994). Political knowledge and the campaign media in 1992. *Communication Research, 21*, 305–324.

Chisman, F. P. (1976). *Attitude psychology and the study of public opinion*. University Park, PA: Pennsylvania University Press.

Cohen, B. (1963). *The press and foreign policy*. Princeton, NJ: Princeton University Press.

Cohen, A. (1976). Radio vs. TV: The effect of the medium. *Journal of Communication, 26*, 29–35.

Connell, R. W. (1987). Why the political socialization paradigm failed and what should replace it. *International Political Science Review, 8*, 215–223.

Devlin, L. P. (1973–1974). Contrasts in presidential campaign commercials of 1972. *Journal of Broadcasting, 18*, 17–26.

Devlin, L. P. (1977). Contrasts in presidential campaign commercials of 1976. *Central States Speech Journal, 28*, 238–249.

Devlin, L. P. (1981). Reagan's and Carter's ad men review the 1980 television campaigns. *Communication Quarterly, 30*, 3–12.

Devlin, L. P. (1987). Contrasts in presidential campaign commercials of 1984. *Political Communication Review, 12*, 25–55.

Devlin, L. P. (1989). Contrasts in presidential campaign commercials of 1988. *American Behavioral Scientist, 32*, 384–414.

Devlin, L. P. (1993). Contrasts in presidential campaign commercials of 1992. *American Behavioral Scientist, 37*, 272–290.

Diamond, E., & Bates, S. (1988). *The spot* (Rev. ed.). Cambridge, MA: MIT Press.

Doob, L. W. (1950). Goebbels' principles of propaganda. *Public Opinion Quarterly, 14*, 419–442.

Edelman, M. (1964). *Symbolic uses of politics*. Urbana, IL: University of Illinois Press.

Edelman, M. (1988). *Constructing the political spectacle*. Chicago: University of Chicago Press.

Fisher, W. R. (1985). The narrative paradigm: In the beginning. *Journal of Communication, 35*, 74–89.

Foote, J. S. (1990). *Television access and political power*. New York: Praeger.

Frank, R. S. (1973). *Message dimensions of television news*. Lexington, MA: Lexington Books.

Garramone, G. M. (1984). Voter responses to negative political ads. *Journalism Quarterly, 61*, 250–259.

Garramone, G. M. (1985). Effects of negative political advertising: The roles of sponsor and rebuttal. *Journal of Broadcasting & Electronic Media, 29*, 147–159.

Graber, D. (1976). Press and television as opinion resources in presidential campaigns. *Public Opinion Quarterly, 40*, 285–303.

Gurevitch, M., & Blumler, J. G. (1990). Comparative research: The extending frontier. In D. Swanson & D. Nimmo (Eds.), *New directions in political communication* (pp. 305–325). Newbury Park, CA: Sage.

Hardt, H. (1988). Comparative media research: The world according to America. *Critical Studies in Mass Communication, 5*, 129–146.

Hart, R. P. (1984). . New York: Academic Press.

Hart, R. P. (1985). Systematic analysis of political discourse: The development of DICTION. In K. R. Sanders, L. L. Kaid, & D. Nimmo (Eds.), *Political communication yearbook 1984* (pp. 97–134). Carbondale: Southern Illinois University Press.

Hofstetter, C. R. (1976). *Bias in the news.* Columbus: Ohio State University Press.

Iyengar, S., Peters, M. D., & Kinder, D. R. (1982). Experimental demonstrations of the "not-so-minimal" consequences of television news programs. *American Political Science* Review, *76*, 848–858.

Jackson-Beeck, M., & Kraus, S. (1980). Political communication theory and research: An overview 1978–1979. In D. Nimmo (Ed.), *Communication yearbook* (Vol. 4, pp. 449–465). New Brunswick, NJ: Transaction Books.

Jamieson, K. H. (1992). *Packaging the presidency* (2nd ed.). New York: Oxford University Press.

Johnson-Cartee, K. S., & Copeland, G. A. (1991). Negative advertising: Coming of age. Hillsdale, NJ: Lawrence Erlbaum Associates.

Johnston, A. (1990). Trends in political communication: A selective review of research in the 1980s. In D. L. Swanson & D. Nimmo (Eds.), *New directions in political communication* (pp. 329–362). Newbury Park, CA: Sage Publications.

Joslyn, R. A. (1980). The content of political spot ads. *Journalism Quarterly, 57,* 92–98.

Kaid, L. L. (1981). Political advertising. In D. Nimmo & K. R. Sanders (Eds.), *Handbook of political communication* (pp. 249–271). Beverly Hills, CA: Sage.

Kaid, L. L. (1991). Ethical dimensions of political advertising. In R. Denton (Ed.), *Ethical dimensions of political communication* (pp. 145–169). New York: Praeger.

Kaid, L. L. (1993, May). *Ethics in televised political advertising: Guidelines for evaluation of technological distortions.* Paper presented at the International Communication Association Convention, Washington, DC.

Kaid, L. L. (1994). Political advertising in the 1992 campaign. In R. E. Denton (Ed.), *The 1992 presidential campaign: A communication perspective* (pp. 111–127). Westport, CT: Praeger.

Kaid, L. L., Downs, V. C., & Ragan S. (1990). Political argumentation and violations of audience expectations: An analysis of the Bush-Rather encounter. *Journal of Broadcasting & Electronic Media, 34,* 1–15.

Kaid, L. L., & Johnston, A. (1991). Negative versus positive television advertising in U.S. presidential campaigns. *Journal of Communication, 41,* 53–64.

Kaid, L. L., Gerstlé, J., & Sanders, K. R., (Eds.). (1991). *Mediated politics in two cultures.* New York: Praeger.

Kaid, L. L., Gobetz, R., Garner, J., Leland, C. M., & Scott, D. (1993). Television news and presidential campaigns: The legitimization of televised political advertising. *Social Science Quarterly, 74,* 274–285.

Kaid, L. L., & Holtz-Bacha. C. (Eds.). (1995). *Political advertising in Western democracies.* Newbury Park, CA: Sage.

Kaid, L. L., Leland, C. M., & Whitney, S. (1992). The impact of televised political ads: Evoking viewer responses in the 1988 presidential campaign. *The Southern Communication Journal, 57,* 285–295.

Kaid, L. L., Nimmo, D., & Sanders, K. R. (1986). *New perspectives on political advertising.* Carbondale: Southern Illinois University Press.

Kaid, L. L., & Sanders, K. R. (1978). Political television commercials: An experimental study of type and length. *Communication Research, 5,* 57–70.

Kaid, L. L., & Sanders, K. R. (1985). Survey of political communication theory and research. In K. R. Sanders, L. L. Kaid, & D. Nimmo (Eds.), *Political communication yearbook 1984* (pp. 283–308). Carbondale, IL: Southern Illinois University Press.

Kaid, L. L., Sanders, K. R., & Hirsch, R. O. (1974). *Political campaign communication: A bibliography and guide to the literature.* Metuchen, NJ: Scarecrow Press.

Kaid, L. L., Tedesco, J., Chanslor, M., & Roper, C. (1993). Clinton's videostyle: A study of the verbal, nonverbal, and video production techniques in campaign advertising. *Journal of Communication Studies, 12,* 11–20.

Kaid, L. L., & Wadsworth, A. (1984). *Political campaign communication: A bibliography and guide to the literature 1972–82.* Metuchen, NJ: Scarecrow Press.

Katz, E., Blumler, J. G., & Gurevitch, M. (1973). Uses and gratifications research. *Public Opinion Quarterly, 37*, 509–523.

Katz, E., & Feldman, J. (1962). The debates in light of research: A survey of surveys. In S. Kraus (Ed.), *The great debates* (pp. 173–223). Bloomington, IN: Indiana University Press.

Kern, M. (1989). *30-second politics*. New York: Praeger.

Klapper, J. (1960). *The effects of mass communication*. Glencoe, IL: Free Press.

Kraus, S. (Ed.), (1962). *The great debates*. Bloomington: Indiana University Press.

Kraus, S., & Davis, D. K. (1976). *The effects of mass communication on political behavior*. University Park, PA: Pennsylvania University Press.

Larson, C. U., & Wiegele, T. C. (1979). Political communication theory and research: An overview. In D. Nimmo (Ed.), *Communication yearbook* (Vol. 3, pp. 457–473). New Brunswick, NJ: Transaction Books.

Lazarsfeld, P. F., Berelson, B. R., & Gaudet, H. (1944). *The people's choice*. New York: Duell, Sloan and Pearce.

Lichter, S. R., Amundson, D., & Noyes, R. (1988). *The video campaign*. Washington, DC: American Enterprise Institute for Public Policy Research.

Mansfield, M. W., & Weaver, R. A. (1982). Political communication theory and research: An overview. In M. Burgoon, Ed., *Communication yearbook* (Vol. 5, pp. 605–625). New Brunswick, NJ: Transaction Books.

McCombs, M. E. (1976). Agenda setting research: A bibliographic essay. *Political Communication Review, 1*, 1–7.

McCombs, M. E., & Shaw, D. L. (1972). The agenda-setting function of the mass media. *Public Opinion Quarterly, 36*, 176–87.

McKinnon, L. M., Tedesco, J. C., & Kaid, L. L. (1993). The effects of presidential debates: Channel and commentary comparisons. *Argumentation and Advocacy, 30*, 1–14.

McLeod, J. M., & Becker, L. B. (1981). The uses and gratifications approach. In D. Nimmo & K. R. Sanders (Eds.), *Handbook of political communication* (pp. 67–99). Beverly Hills, CA: Sage.

Mendelsohn, H., & O'Keefe, G. J. (1976). *The people choose a president*. New York: Praeger.

Neuman, W. R., Just, M. R., & Crigler, A. M. (1992). *Common knowledge: News and the construction of political meaning*. Chicago: University of Chicago Press.

Nimmo, D. (1970). *The political persuaders*. Englewood Cliffs, NJ: Prentice Hall.

Nimmo, D. (1977). Political communication theory and research: An overview. In B. Ruben (Ed.), *Communication yearbook* (Vol. 1, pp. 441–452). New Brunswick, NJ: Transaction Books.

Nimmo, D., & Combs, J. E. (1983). *Mediated political realities*. New York: Longman.

Nimmo, D., & Combs, J. E. (1990). *Mediated political realities* (2nd ed.). New York: Longman.

Nimmo, D., & Combs, J. E. (1985). *Nightly horrors*. Knoxville: University of Tennessee Press.

Nimmo, D., & Sanders, K. R. (Eds.), (1981). *Handbook of political communication*. Beverly Hills, CA: Sage Publcations.

Noelle-Neumann, E. (1974). The spiral of silence. *Journal of Communication, 24*, 43–51.

Noelle-Neumann, E. (1977). Turbulences in the climate of opinion: Methodological applications of the spiral of silence theory. *Public Opinion Quarterly, 41*, 113–158.

Noelle-Neumann, E. (1984). *The spiral of silence: Our social skin*. Chicago: University of Chicago Press.

Paletz, D. L., & Entman, R. M. (1981). *Media-power-politics*. New York: Free Press.

Patterson, T., & McClure, R. (1976). *The unseeing eye*. New York: Putnam.

Pfau, M., & Louden, A. (1994). Effectiveness of adwatch formats in deflecting political attack ads. *Communication Research, 21*, 325–341.

Protess, D. L., & McCombs, M. (Eds.). (1991). *Agenda setting: Readings on media, opinion, and policy-making*. Hillsdale, NJ: Lawrence Erlbaum Associates.

Reese, S. D., & Miller, M. M. (1981). Political attitude holding and structure: The effects of newspaper and television news. *Communication Research, 8*, 167–188.

Robinson, M. J. (1976). Public affairs television and the growth of political malaise: The case of the "Selling of the Pentagon." *American Political Science Review, 70*, 409–432.

Roddy, B., & Garramone, G. M. (1988). Appeals and strategies of negative political advertising. *Journal of Broadcasting & Electronic Media, 32*, 415–427.

Sanders, K. R., & Kaid, L. L. (1978). Political communication theory and research: An overview 1976–1977. In B. Ruben (Ed.), *Communication yearbook* (Vol. 2, pp. 375–389). New Brunswick, NJ: Transaction Books.

Sanders, K. R., & Kaid, L. L. (1981). Political rallies. *Central States Speech Journal, 32,* 1–11.

Schoenbach, K., & Semetko, H. A. (1992). Agenda-setting, agenda reinforcing or agenda-deflating? A study of the 1990 German national election. *Journalism Quarterly, 69,* 837–846.

Sears, D. O., & Chaffee, S. H. (1979). The uses and effects of the 1976 debates: An overview of empirical studies. In S. Kraus (Ed.), *The great debates: Carter vs. Ford* (pp. 223–261). Bloomington: Indiana University Press, 1979.

Semetko, H. A., Blumler, J. G., Gurevitch, M., & Weaver, D. H. (1991). *The formation of campaign agendas: A comparative analysis of party and media roles in recent American and British elections.* Hillsdale, NJ: Lawrence Erlbaum Associates.

Sloan, J. H. (1965). "I have kept the faith:" William Jennings Bryan and the Democratic National Convention of 1904. *Southern Speech Communication Journal, 31,* 114–123.

Swanson, D. L., & Nimmo, D. (Eds.). (1990). *New directions in political communication.* Newbury Park, CA: Sage.

Underhill, W. R. (1966). Fulton's finest hour. *Quarterly Journal of Speech, 52,* 155–163.

Wadsworth, A., & Kaid, L. L. (1987, May). Incumbent and challenger styles in presidential advertising. Paper presented at the annual meeting of the International Communication Association, Montreal.

Weaver, D. (1987). Media agenda-setting and elections: Assumptions and implications. In D. Paletz (Ed.), *Political communication research* (pp. 176–193). Norwood, NJ: Ablex.

West, D. (1993). *Air wars.* Washington, DC: Congressional Quarterly Press.

29

Public Relations

Larissa A. Grunig
University of Maryland

If any area of communication integrates and applies communication theory and research, it is public relations. As an area of communication, public relations is relatively new, one nearly bereft of its own body of theoretical knowledge necessary to enhance its practice in the "real world." As such, research has been largely atheoretical, as a perusal of the *Body of Knowledge* (Public Relations Society of America, PRSA, 1988) establishes. The few theory-based public relations studies conducted have largely focussed on the process or effects of a single public relations program on individuals. Public relations, many would argue, is an applied field, dealing with the real world. Too often, public relations researchers fail to take into account the complex interplay of environment, organizational structure, corporate and societal culture, power, and the different approaches to public relations that are possible.

Examining public relations from this more comprehensive stance requires research methodologies that are equally comprehensive, unified, and global. This chapter's purpose is to acquaint readers with both a theory of public relations and a methodological approach appropriate for generating, testing, and developing such theory. Schneider[1] (aka L. Grunig, 1985a) began working on a general, integrative theory,

---

[1] L. A. Schneider, L. S. Grunig, and L. A. Grunig refer to the same researcher.

whose inception dates back at least a quarter-century. In the intervening years, the theory has been critiqued and refined. Based on a continuing body of research, L. Grunig and associates have developed a comparative research method that adds both substantive insights and credibility to the theory.

BUILDING A METHODOLOGY

Theorizing about methodology from this perspective of public relations research stems from the work of Lazarsfeld and Menzel (1969). They established a framework for research in the social sciences that offers special promise for studying public relations. They argued that the appropriate level of analysis is global—general and all-encompassing. At least until 1985, however, the slim body of knowledge in public relations had remained at the analytical level. At the analytical level, collective properties of organizations typically were determined by studying some property of their individuals—by aggregating data via group means, percentages, or correlations. Another possible level of analysis, according to Lazarsfeld and Menzel, is the structural or relational. At this level, properties of collectives are obtained by studying the relationship of each member to some or all of the others.

The global approach supersedes information about individual members or their interrelations. Because the notion of public relations goes beyond individuals to encompass the multiple interdependencies among and between collectives or publics, global analysis seems most appropriate. It suggests both a conceptual and a methodological approach that is broad and inclusive. However, according to Pavlik and Salmon (1983), public relations research is virtually barren at this highest, most conceptual level. J. Grunig (1984) agreed that the field needed a theory of the relationship between organizations and publics, which are higher level systems, and not a theory of the relationship among individuals. He further suggested that an entirely new theory was called for.

Development of such a theory using the global level of analysis began with Schneider's (1985b) doctoral dissertation. By looking beyond the individual and structural levels to the global, that study represented the first comprehensive attempt to use global analysis to construct the theoretical framework necessary for understanding the interaction between public relations practitioners and their organizations and environmental niches. It combined survey research, in-depth, personal interviews, observation, and analysis of organizational publications.

That triangulated, global approach proved to be a useful and interesting—albeit time-consuming, costly, and frustrating—way to study managed communication in organizations. It created a more multidimensional, comprehensive picture of public relations in diverse settings than any lower level analysis could. Perhaps more important, it helped set the stage for a more far-reaching international study a decade later. That research, *Excellence in Public Relations and Communication Management* (J. Grunig, 1992), is the most ambitious research project to date in public relations.

This chapter explains how the *Excellence* theory developed over time. Along the way, readers should come to understand the importance of situating their own research within an existing theoretical framework. Most research is what Kuhn (1970) called *normal science.* This refers to the day-to-day research of most scholars working within a paradigm. A guiding paradigm helps define what problems merit further study and the research methods appropriate for such study. In other words, few scholars set out to establish new paradigms or revolutionize the way in which research is done within their paradigm.

Choosing a topic, then, begins with an understanding of the existing paradigm. It continues with a consideration of the scholar's individual interest in solving one piece of the puzzle inherent in the paradigm. That piece should be a significant one. One's own curiosity is not enough to warrant spending several months or even years on a single study. Instead, interest or curiosity must be coupled with significance as a way of starting to repay the debt scholars owe the society that has supported our institutions of higher education.

Defining Public Relations

What, exactly, is public relations? The question is not trivial. Defining the concept is an important initial step in any research. Definitions set intellectual boundaries on the field to be investigated. It is often better to limit research and avoid the problem so cleverly described in Pencil's (1976) "Salt Passage Research." This tongue-in-cheek essay explores the antecedent conditions that give rise to the apparent regularity of salt being passed when someone says, "Please pass the salt." Every imaginable variable is considered—leading to a hodgepodge of hilarious yet seemingly randomly selected possible causes. Independent variables include others being present, time delay, source credibility, attitudinal consistency, dogmatism, phonemes, compliance, conformity, effects of payment, environmental cues, an interaction effect between substance and the shaker, trustworthiness, threats, exposure to mass media, motivation, and high demand characteristics in the situation. In his parody of social science research, Pencil (1976) concluded that "until our methods match the complexity of our phenomena, we are apt to be left with more questions than answers" (p. 35).

A good conceptual definition for public relations grows out of the *Excellence* research tradition. *Public relations* is the *management of communication between an organization and its publics. The key element is the notion of managed communication—whether it is called public relations, communication management*, or *organizational communication.* Included under this broad rubric are such narrow functional areas as employee communication, media relations, public affairs or government relations, financial relations, product publicity, and community relations.

Deliberately excluded from the definition is the concept of persuasion. This exclusion has been the basis for criticism of the theory. Heath (1993), for example, considered this a weakness of the *Excellence* project. He argued that minimizing the role of persuasive communication ignores the fact that companies can be "extremely successful in shaping the opinion fabric of society, such as AT&T's notorious campaign to legitimize regulated monopolies" (p. 2). His criticism was not unanticipated. It illustrates how scholars are influenced by the paradigm in which they operate. Schneider's background is in mass communication, sociology, and business management. Heath wrote from a rhetorical or speech communication perspective, wherein persuasion is central.[2] Thus, the researcher should set reasonable conceptual boundaries on the study, situating it in the theoretical literature that has come before.

Throughout the chapter, discussion of theory and method will be interwoven along with relevant criticisms of the theory and its operationalization. The chapter began with a description of the global method as it applies to public relations theory. It continues with an application of that method in Schneider's (1985b) dissertation and in the more recent *Excellence* project. The chapter concludes with a discussion of the advantages and disadvantages of this high-level analysis for public relations scholars.

LEVELS OF ANALYSIS

Of Lazarsfeld and Menzel's (1969) three levels of analysis, the global is the most general. Its findings are based not on information about individuals—such as public relations practitioners or their chief executive officers (CEOs)—or their interrelationships. Instead, it concentrates on global characteristics, which Pavlik and Salmon (1983) suggested might include the relationship between public information officers and the media. Such a relationship goes beyond the structural level to look for concepts that might be used to develop a theoretical framework necessary to understand that relationship.

The analytical level, which is the most specific of the three classes in the Lazarsfeld and Menzel schema, represents the more traditional approach to research in public relations. Analytical properties are ascertained by aggregating data typically collected in survey research—either using questionnaires or personal interviews. Interviewees or survey respondents may be either what Lazarsfeld and Menzel considered *individuals* or *members* of a collective or organization. This distinction is important in understanding their framework. "Individuals" can be members of the collective; "members" do not have to be individuals. For instance, individuals comprise the faculty and staff of a university. Many universities are the members of the National Association of Land Grant Colleges and Universities.

Pavlik and Salmon (1983) contended that most contemporary researchers operationalize *the public* as a simple aggregation of individuals—represented by this analytical level. They pointed out one major limitation in this conceptualization: "By aggregating the properties of individuals in order to describe a social grouping, or public, one overlooks the important properties which that public possesses as a unit, or as a whole" (p. 8).

The middle point in Lazarsfeld and Menzel's classification system is the structural, or relational. At this level, theory is developed by performing some operation on data about the relationship of each individual or member to some or all of the others in the collective. For example, sociometric—network—analysis in communication research may yield data on who talks with whom at the office, thus describing clusters of employees who interact with each other in certain identifiable ways. Studies of activism (e.g., L. Grunig, 1986) also employ the structural approach—looking for the impact of

---

[2] In his review of the *Excellence* book, Wright (1993) was somewhat critical of the lack of emphasis on rhetorical theory. At the same time, however, he pointed out that rhetorical theory was indeed covered in the text.

pressure groups rather than individuals on other groups—such as target organizations, the media, or governmental agencies.

The three analytical levels can be conceived as a continuum from the most specific (the analytical) to the most general (the global). According to Pavlik and Salmon (1983), the levels also represent an historical progression of public relations theory-building. The earliest studies, in what is still an immature area, typically were analytical. Only recently has the structural approach been used. Pavlik and Salmon acknowledged, however, that a handful of scholars has at least implied that global characteristics might be important for future studies of public relations.

Despite these calls for adopting global analysis, survey research alone has been the most popular method in public relations (Pavlik, 1987). Quantitative studies have been conducted (and funded), almost to the exclusion of qualitative methodology. This dichotomy between the qualitative and quantitative is somewhat crude, since scholars attempting global research face a range of possible approaches. In fact, commitment to the global dictates going beyond the quantitative alone. Even a man whom Kobland (1989) called the arch empiricist, Paul Lazarsfeld, acknowledged the importance of including phenomenological and contextual understanding along with the quantification of survey data.

According to Stempel and Westley (1981), communication researchers confront more and more information not readily quantifiable. This is certainly the case in research on organizations, whose complexity is almost overwhelming. Berger (1963) cited a second reason to adopt a mixed strategy of qualitative and quantitative methods: responsibility for studying human beings (in this case public relations practitioners in organizational settings) as live actors who improvise on their organizational stage rather than as prisoners of their own psyches or of the situation. Finally, Sanders (1982) suggested that a combination of qualitative and quantitative research provides for stronger analyses than would have been possible by collecting either type alone, especially in the study of organizations. She advocated collecting phenomenological information and quantitative data concurrently from the same organizational setting.[3] The next section of this chapter demonstrates this in two separate studies, conducted nearly a decade apart.

THE 1985 STUDY

In 1985, Schneider sought to develop a general systems theory of public relations, hoping it would lead to better management of the communication process by discovering how the practice of public relations varies with the environment and the structure of organizations. In Meehan's (1968) terms, she took an event she wanted to control (the internal and external public relations of organizations) and devised a structure homomorphic (analogous) to it. The theory that resulted should replace years of muddling through. The accuracy of her explanation is difficult to establish, but the methodology she employed should persuade scholars and practitioners of its acuity—Meehan's (1968) concept of *it ought to work*.

---

[3] For a solid synthesis of the literature on multiperspective methodology and its value to communication research, see Kobland (1989).

The overarching premise, her guiding hypothesis, was that the environment dictates the structure of the organization, which in turn has a mediating effect on its public relations activity. For an organization to maintain its equilibrium in any environment, it must depend in part on the boundary role of the public relations department.

Major structural dimensions include *scale*, conceptually defined as the repetitiveness of events (which typically correlates with size) and *complexity*, or technical sophistication. Juxtaposing these two variables into a typology developed by Hage and Hull (1981) produced four normative models. Traditional organizations have a low knowledge base and few employees. Mechanical organizations are large-scale, but low-complexity structures. Organic organizations are small in scale but high in complexity. Mixed mechanical and organic organizations are large-scale, high-complexity structures. One of the first steps in the research design was to place sample organizations into these four structural types, resulting in a total of 48 organizations: 12 that were craft, 12 organic, 12 mechanical, and 12 mixed.

Models of Public Relations

The first four research hypotheses related these types of organizations to J. Grunig's (1984) four models of public relations, predicting which model should predominate in each type of organization. To make sense of these hypotheses, a brief discussion of the models or typical approaches to public relations is in order.

The four models are press agentry or publicity, public information, two-way asymmetrical, and two-way symmetrical. The first two are one-way models that send information out from the organization to its publics. They both rely on the media for this dissemination, and they both ignore the potential value of doing any research. The first, *press agentry,* traces its roots to the ringmaster P.T. Barnum. In this model, truth is relatively unimportant. Promotional wizards embracing this model try to control or dominate their environment through advocacy or propaganda.

By contrast, public relations professionals who practice the *public information* model embrace the norms of the typical journalist. Thus, the information they generate is relatively objective—although they are hesitant to publicize anything about their organization that might put it in a "bad light." They see their role as "journalists in residence" for the organization. Ivy Lee, an early expert in public relations, is credited with developing this approach to providing factual information through a simple source-to-receiver model.

The two two-way models of public relations are considered more contemporary and far more sophisticated. They both rely on research, but for different purposes. In the *two-way asymmetrical,* or imbalanced, model, research helps determine the messages most likely to persuade the publics. The goal is advocacy for the organization's position. The communication model is source-to-receiver but with a feedback loop. Feedback allows the savvy practitioner to determine the attitudes of key publics or to gauge the effectiveness of his or her communicative efforts in persuading those publics. Edward L. Bernays, a pioneer practitioner and educator in the field, stressed the importance of this application of social science to public relations.

In the *two-way symmetrical,* or balanced, model of public relations, research helps to create mutual understanding between an organization and its publics. Both formative and evaluative research characterizes this model, but evaluation of understanding is more important than evaluation of attitudes. Although the two-way symmetrical model also builds on the work of Bernays and others, it is considered both the most ethical and the most effective model in contemporary practice. Practitioners following this approach go beyond dissemination of information and analysis of feedback to act as mediators or negotiators between the organization and it stakeholders.

In subsequent research, L. Grunig (1988, 1991, 1992) critiqued what had been considered the historical progression inherent in these models. She based her critique on two major arguments. First, all four models continue to be practiced today (the publicity model is the most common). Second, rather than being a linear process of development from the most primitive to the most sophisticated practice, public relations over the years seems to have been characterized more by ups and downs, suggesting that shifts in public relations practice may represent more of a curvilinear than linear pattern. That is, concurrent with the feminization of public relations, contemporary practice may reflect a return to what Rakow (1989) called "an ideology of cooperation and community" (p. 10).

Olasky (1987) also argued against the developmental nature first proposed for the models. Rather than adding to the feminist critique that public relations history has ignored the contribution of female practitioners over the years, Olasky suggested that *private* relations—characteristic of the 1800s—were symmetrical. Thus, in his view, the asymmetrical (whether one- or two-way) that marks contemporary practice actually is a step backward for public relations.

Finally, the models are susceptible to the criticism that can be made of any taxonomy. Twenty years ago, an anonymous reviewer objected to J. Grunig's (1976) initial attempt to classify behaviors as diverse as public relations activities into different types. The reviewer also doubted that the different types of behavior could be explained adequately. J. Grunig (Grunig & Grunig, 1992) countered that, although all models are false in the sense that they are simplified representations of reality, describing sets of values and patterns of behavior adds to our understanding of that reality.

These models continue to represent a major line of public relations inquiry. The models have been found to characterize public relations practice in a variety of organizations in the United States and abroad. Research conducted at the University of Maryland has found support for the models in Greece (Lyra, 1991), Taiwan (Huang, 1990), and southern India (Sriramesh, 1991). Practitioners in other countries have conducted research that discovered the models characterize public relations in France (Laufenburger, in press) and Slovenia (Gruban, Verčič, & Zavrl, 1994).

Hypotheses

Through this process of constant empirical investigation and refinement of the theory, J. Grunig (1984)—who first conceptualized the models of public relations—found that only the rare public relations department practices a pure form of any of his four approaches. Thus, the dissertation research qualified its expectations with the word *predominates*. Each hypothesis was based on an extensive body of relevant literature reviewed in the conceptualization section of the dissertation that preceded them. Hypotheses grow out of the theoretical literature, which in this study included journals of marketing, business management, speech communication, journalism, economics, cognitive and social psychology, feminist studies, philosophy, organizational sociology, and—of course—public relations. This comprehensive literature review may seem overly extensive.

Almost a decade later, one reviewer (Pratt, 1993) of the published conceptualization of the *Excellence* project wrote, "If the book has any limitation at all, it is the sheer breadth of the literature reviewed" (p. 10). Heath (1993), a second reviewer, considered this lengthy conceptualization "sometimes tedious" and the analysis of principles and research findings "repetitive" (p. 1). He pointed out, however, that this extensive discussion of key concepts would prove useful to communication directors who want to educate their senior management about the potential for excellent public relations. A third reviewer (Wright, 1993) justified the book's length—nearly 700 pages—by pointing out that "our turf includes more than most disciplines" (p. 12). Clearly, a literature review needs to be relevant and integrate and synthesize disparate bodies of knowledge. Consider the first four hypotheses (H_S) derived for testing from the literature review:

H1: The press agentry/publicity model of public relations predominates in traditional or craft organizations. Traditional organizations require little information from their clientele; as a result, simply publicizing the existence of the organization or the availability of its products should suffice.

H2: The public information model predominates in mechanical organizations. Mechanistic organizations, like the craft type, require little input from their external publics. Because they are large in scale, though, they do need to put forth a large volume of material about their products or services. As a result, the public information model—with its emphasis on dissemination of factual information—should predominate.

H3: The two-way symmetrical model predominates in organic organizations. Organic organizations, characterized by rapidly changing knowledge, must adapt to a dynamic environment. The two-way symmetrical model provides the necessary environmental scanning, interaction with publics, innovation, and flexibility.

H4: The two-way asymmetrical model predominates in mixed mechanical/organic organizations. Recall that the mixed type of organization incorporates aspects of both the organic and mechanical. As a result, both types of two-way public relations are required: asymmetrical and symmetrical. Based on a pilot study's findings, conducted a year before the actual research, the asymmetrical should prevail. Why? Pretesting the survey instrument found that disposing of a high volume of mixed products within the market context of large and moderately sized companies seemed to take precedence over anticipating the future needs of clients or customers.

The second group of 24 hypotheses related organizational type to size and importance of the public relations function. It resulted primarily from the literature of boundary spanning and of power. The last group of five hypotheses related organizational type to technology. Technology was the intervening variable in the study.

Research questions (RQs) rather than hypotheses were posed in the areas in which too little had been published to permit reasonable expectations. Researchers typically ask questions where existing literature is inadequate for predictions. The RQs asked how the four organizational types varied by structure, use of outside consultants, and budget of the public relations department. The questions also gauged the actual communication behavior of public relations practitioners as well as their job satisfaction, decision-making style, and demographic characteristics (such as age, years of experience, and gender). Finally, they asked how the relationship between the public relations department and advertising department, marketing department, and external constituencies varied by organizational type. Key external publics included mass media, government, community, stockholders, clients or customers, suppliers, competitors, and—especially important—activist groups.

Methodology

Because of the complexity of the research problem described above, qualitative methodology was employed for the bulk of data collection and analysis. The quantitative portion helped guard against subjective bias and perceptual data as reported by managers who participated in the study. Rather than delineating the quantitative and qualitative aspects of this research, though, consider the compelling case for their combined use.

Any adequate theory of communication is historical in a sense. It must be based on knowledge of what communication has been and how it has become what it is. For this reason, the four models of public relations developed by J. Grunig (1984) seemed like an appropriate beginning. This approach is differentiated from that of the historian, however, in that it is concerned not only with the explanation of past events but with contemporary phenomena as well. As a result, historical explanation was used as a part of the method, not as a subject, in the qualitative portion of the 1985 study.

As in Berlin's (1962) research, qualitative research was approached as a self-conscious attempt to restore the critical (and liberating) function to any intellectual investigation. The approach seems especially well suited to the social sciences since humans live by interpretations. They do not simply react to an event or to a message. Instead, they interpret the act or the contents of a message according to their schemata (Schneider, 1985b).

By having chosen the 48 cases appropriately, it is possible to make inferences at least as valuable as generalizations resulting from the quantitative portion of this study and tested statistically. According to Aydelotte (1971), such resulting inferences are merited as long as other researchers understand how the leap was made. Geertz (1973) described Gouldner's (1954) study of one factory as evidence of how even a single case study can expose the "world in a teacup." He credited Gouldner with using specifics of one bureaucratic organization to provide insight into corporate bureaucracy as a whole. Gouldner used the concrete to support broad cultural assertions and, in Geertz's opinion, he did so convincingly.

Although many historians do not consider generalization their goal (rather, it is understanding a particular event in a particular time or place or both), most would agree that some generalization is important in any form of explanation or even description. Christians and Carey (1981) called this *forthtelling*, or the prophetic element that comes with speaking the truth with insight and with conviction. Their assumption was that the researcher, or knower, is a part of what is known rather than independent of the action. By interviewing public relations managers at their desks in their offices, the researcher took advantage of the naturalistic observation and contextualization Christians and Carey recommended.

At the same time, this method has limitations. Two decades earlier, Madge (1965) had condemned such case studies as impressionistic and subjective. He also contended that observation itself modifies the situation being observed. Selltiz et al. (1965) cautioned that even this first step (in this case, developing profiles of 48 organizations) presupposes much prior knowledge. For this reason, almost all of the literature understood to be relevant to the study was reviewed before the data collection or even profile-building stages of this project.

Finally, replicating a study like this one would not be easy. However, by making the methods clear, additional work could be done by others investigating similar questions with the global level of analysis. Scrupulous detail when describing the method is especially important for the credibility of any qualitative research. Although scholars agree that the burden of replicating the study falls on the researcher who would do that replication, the researcher deserves a comprehensive blueprint of what was done in the original study.

One of the jobs of social science, then, is to better understand the meanings people use to guide their activities. Translated to the organizational setting, the question this study explored was how managers in an organization interpret external threats, instability, and technological change and by so doing, guide their public relations programs. This question taps into both the model of public relations practiced and the dominant role—manager or technician—of the practitioner.

This question was answered using a comparative research design—as recommended by Stinchcombe (1965)—to approach the global notion. The researcher used both long personal interviews with 96 public relations managers (two in each of the 48 organizations profiled) and an 8-page, self-administered questionnaire for each. During the interviews the office setting was observed for cues of stratification or obvious power differentials among the ranks. Media coverage of each of the organizations also was analyzed. As Pavlik and Salmon (1983) recommended, data were gathered on internal communiques such as company newsletters, annual reports, memoranda, brochures, direct mail pieces, organization charts, and public service announcements.

Such triangulation, or the combining of multiple data sources, should enhance validity (e.g., Denzin, 1970; Jick, 1979; Smith, 1975; Trend, 1978; Webb, Campbell, Schwartz, Sechrest, & Grove, 1981). Further, two types of triangulation were employed: between-method and within-method. The former involves using multiple methods (such as questionnaires, interviews, and content analyses) to observe a single variable (such as reliance on job descriptions). More specifically, organizational publications such as annual reports, organization charts, and in-house organs helped confirm the validity of the initial grouping of organizations typed by Hage and Hull. If the preliminary profile of a company deemed it mechanical, the annual report was scanned for indicators of large scale and repetitiveness of events. In the case of a presumed organic organization, evidence was sought of a shifting market and small-scale operation.

The latter, or within-method triangulation, involves using multiple variants within the same basic method. For example, the questionnaire included several items gauging professionalism, formalization, technology, and complexity. The survey instrument also included scales developed by J. Grunig (1984) to assess which of his four models predominates in each type of organization. The 27 items in the scales measured press agentry, public information, two-way asymmetrical, and two-way symmetrical models. The items were correlated with each other to find out which models tend to be practiced together within the same organization, since J. Grunig (1984) found that most organizations practice mixed models. The results then were juxtaposed with the four Hage–Hull types of organizations.

Interviewing two professionals within each organization, rather than a single manager, helped avoid idiosyncratic responses. According to Blau and Schoenherr (1971), objective attributes of the organization (factors such as size and educational background of the employees) could be answered adequately by any single member of the organization. Other researchers, such as J. Grunig (1976) and Hage and Aiken (1970), have administered questionnaires to more than one member of the organization and averaged their scores to characterize the organization. This technique is more appropriate when questions (such as values of the CEO or others in the dominant coalition and level of decision-making) involve subjectivity. Webb (1970) explained the value of such triangulation as follows:

> Every data-gathering class—interviews, questionnaires, observation, performance records, physical evidence—is potentially biased and has specific to it certain validity threats. Ideally, we should like to converge data from several data classes, as well as converge with multiple variants from within a single class. (p. 450)

In spite of the combined research method and the multiple measures used, one other methodological problem was anticipated: Were all forms of communication considered "public relations" in organizations measured? Most behaviors and characteristics associated with the organization and its external publics, however, were tapped.

Results

The press agentry model of public relations predominated. However, two-way asymmetrical communication also characterized the traditional organization. Mechanical organizations emphasized public information, with concomitant journalistic activities such as writing and editing (especially in-house publications). Organic organizations practiced two-way symmetrical communication more than did any other Hage–Hull type. They also emphasized internal communication. Mixed organizations practiced both models of two-way public relations. Practitioners in this type enjoyed the greatest autonomy, support, and value by top management. Together these findings provided limited support for the hypotheses. As a result, certain variables in the theory—such as models of public relations—have been retained as central to the theory while others—such as organizational structure, which showed significantly less power to explain the relationship among organizations, their communicative efforts, and their publics—have been reduced to a marginal role.

THE *EXCELLENCE* PROJECT

Our theoretical understanding of public relations has advanced exponentially since Schneider's (1985b) dissertation. In 1985, the International Association of Business Communicators (IABC) Research Foundation funded a $400,000 international study designed to answer two key questions: How does public relations contribute to organizational effectiveness and what is its contribution worth? To those two bottom-line queries the research team,[4] directed by James E. Grunig (also of the University of Maryland), added an important third question: What are the characteristics of public relations programs that actually do make an important contribution? In essence, the study tried to determine both the nature of *Excellence* in public relations and what such exemplary practice is worth. Taken together, the answers to the research questions should lead to a truly integrative theory of public relations—one that explaines the management of communication in all types of organizations and across cultural and societal boundaries.[5]

The research team was assembled to reflect the diversity of perspectives that would allow for a truly global analysis. For example, members came from both the academy and from the practice of public relations. Although all spoke English as a first language, one member was a British citizen who also had lived in Canada. This was important because we sampled organizations from the United States, the United Kingdom, and Canada. However, through exhaustive review of relevant literature (J. Grunig, 1992) and subsequent field work, we learned that certain principles we consider generic supersede geographical borders.

Initial data analysis (IABC, 1991) identified 12 general principles of *Excellence* in communication. They describe the ways in which public relations must be organized, managed, and conceptualized if it is to make the maximum contribution to organizational effectiveness. A brief discussion of these characteristics of *Excellence* and their concomitant effects follows. In essence, the excellent public relations department:

. . . *practices a judicious mix of the asymmetrical and symmetrical models of public relations.* Practitioners operate from what game theorists call *mixed motives.* They act as advocates both for their organization and for its strategic publics. Research is an integral part of their process, in large part because it helps practitioners understand those stakeholders.

. . . *is managed strategically.* That is, it communicates with the publics that provide the greatest threats and opportunities. In particular, it manages conflicts with stakeholders. This, in turn, results in increased autonomy for the organization because it helps avoid expensive government regulation, litigation, or pressure from dissatisfied employees or activist groups.

. . . *enjoys a direct reporting relationship to senior management.* It is integral to the management of the total organization. The head of public relations may not be a formal member of the dominant coalition or top policy-makers, but at least that person has the ear of the power elite.

. . . *is headed by a practitioner in the managerial rather than technical role.* *Excellence* in the technical tasks of public relations, such as writing and editing, is not

---

[4]Other team members were David M. Dozier, San Diego State University; William P. Ehling, retired, Syracuse University; Fred C. Repper, retired, Gulf States Utilities; Jon White, City University of London, and Larissa A. Grunig. Over the years, we have been assisted by more than a dozen capable, highly motivated graduate students.

[5]Verčič, L. Grunig, & J. Grunig (1996) have begun to address this concern in a chapter devoted to "generic principles" of public relations for a book on international communication. Ethics, they argue, is one of those overarching concepts that characterizes effective public relations wherever it is practiced.

enough to ensure effectiveness. The department must be directed by someone capable of serving at the highest levels of the organization.

   . . . requires expert practitioners, those who know how to manage the department strategically and symmetrically. Such expertise allows the head of public relations to function as a true professional, one who is empowered to act independently while still cooperating with his or her peers who head the other departments of the organization.

   . . . embraces a symmetrical world view or schema for public relations. Further, this value for collaboration with key publics is shared by the organization's top management. Members of the dominant coalition both expect and support the effort to devise win–win (rather than win–lose or zero-sum) solutions with strategic constituencies.

   . . . is separate from marketing (although in efforts such as product promotion they may function in a complementary fashion). Public relations addresses all of the organization's strategic publics, rather than focusing on the customer or client public.

   . . . is an integrated one, rather than being split among functions that may include community relations, government affairs, internal communication, and media relations. As a result of this integration, the department has the necessary flexibility to shifts its resources in response to changing conditions in its environment. It is not mired in pre-existing territories.

   . . . provides equal opportunities for men and women. Because of the rapid feminization of public relations, the department that discriminates against women will fail to capitalize on all its human resources. In a related point, the growing cultural diversity of both the work force and the environment means that the effective public relations department must be equally diverse.

   . . . has the support of top management. Further, the power elite values and even demands sophisticated, credible public relations rather than mere press agentry to deal with today's complex environment.

   . . . operates in an organizational culture that is more participative than authoritarian. The organization distributes power throughout—thus empowering the public relations staff to implement effective, two-way programs.

   . . . exists in an environment more characterized by dynamism and even hostility than by stability. We learned that activism actually pushes organizations toward *Excellence* as they try to cope with the expectations of their strategic constituencies. Such demands typically require greater sophistication in public relations than the simple one-way communication inherent in press agentry or public information. Thus public relations is valued because it helps the organization deal with social issues (but only if the head of public relations is empowered to play a role in strategic management). To some of the participants in our *Excellence* research, effective communication adds infinite value during times of crisis.

   How did we learn all this? After an exhaustive (666 page) literature search (J. Grunig, 1992), we surveyed almost 300 organizations selected to represent a variety of sizes, industries and cultures. Questionnaires came back to us from some 5,000 people in all—chief executive officers (or some other member of the dominant coalition), their top communicators (sometimes several in a single organization, if the public relations function was splintered rather than integrated); and about a dozen other employees of those organizations from outside of the public relations department. These employees provided insights into organizational culture and a reality check on how a given model of internal communication was meeting their information needs.

We had developed a set of three distinct questionnaires—one for top management, one for heads of public relations, and one for other employees. Questionnaires included a total of about 1,700 variables that measured what our literature review had suggested were the key attributes of excellence in communication. The statistical technique of factor analysis was central to our analysis of these survey data, allowing us to reduce the data into interpretable dimensions or groupings. The computer told us that a parsimonious set of about a dozen characteristics grouped together into a scale of excellence capable of measuring the kind of programs that make the greatest contribution to organizational goals.

In the second stage, we studied in greater depth two dozen organizations from the original sample of 283. We chose organizations from the top and the bottom of the *Excellence* scale. We spoke at length (usually in person, but sometimes over the telephone) with heads of public relations and others in the communication department. We also interviewed their CEOs or other members of the dominant coalition. We combined long interviews with a review of the survey data about each organization, media coverage of it, and its internal documents such as annual reports and employee newsletters. In most cases, we were participant observers as well.

How feasibile is such a study? Only with a group of researchers (the Excellence team had grown to 16 at this point) and adequate funding can such an ambitious study be undertaken, clearly indicating a need for more team-based public relations research.

Despite its extensive conceptualization, comparative methodology, and global analysis, even this study offers room for continued theoretical refinement and empirical observation. What's missing? The role of ethics or integrity, in particular, emerged as more significant than we had anticipated. In related points, reviewers of the *Excellence* theory suggested that the book should devote more attention to corporate social responsibility (Heath, 1993) and ethics and rhetorical theory (Wright, 1993).5 Thus we concluded our research with the traditional discussion of such areas for future investigation. It may be that research from the "normal science" tradition will explore any one finding of the *Excellence* project in greater detail.

Pavlik (1987), who summarized the extant scholarly research in our field in the late 1980s, determined that the general theory represented by the models of public relations, in particular, sets the stage for developing a useful paradigm for understanding the function of public relations in the organization. He concluded that "continued research is needed to enrich our basic understanding of all aspects of public relations and to help this field achieve full professional status" (p. 131).

In our own conclusions, we also discussed the limitations that are inherent in any research. Exploring the limitations is an exercise in academic honesty (and humility) that every scholar should take seriously. It does not necessarily mean that you "screwed up." Instead, it demonstrates that you are not naive to the fact that each method—including the global—has its own shortcomings.

EFFICACY OF THE GLOBAL APPROACH
TO RESEARCH IN PUBLIC RELATIONS

The methodology first employed in Schneider's (1985b) study is both unusual and efficacious for public relations research. It marked a major contribution, one perhaps equal to the study's findings. By combining survey research, interviews, observation, and analysis of publications, the individual level of analysis more typical of research in the field was superseded, as was the emerging structural or relational level. The research team working on the *Excellence* project adopted a similarly comparative and powerful methodology.

All of this comes with a price tag, of course. Triangulation increases the cost (of time and money) of data collection. Talking with two or more practitioners rather than a single representative of each organization at least doubles the fees of the interviewers or the time the investigator invests. Distributing questionnaires incurs costs for printing, typesetting, and mailing. Including multiple measures of variables on that questionnaire lengthens the survey instrument (and thus lessens the likelihood of cooperation on the part of potential respondents).

On top of these literal costs is the figurative price that researchers must pay when they are engaged in global analysis. One is the fact that few guidelines for interpreting data collected from multiple sources exist. Instead, researchers typically rely on ad hoc procedures for correlating their observations, interview and survey data, and analyses of organizational publications.

For example, interview data were analyzed in two main ways. First, responses were coded and entered into the computer. These coded responses were added to responses on questionnaires received from each interviewee. Second, interview transcripts helped explain the closed-ended responses indicated on the survey questionnaires. Verbatim remarks of interviewees taken from tape-recorded conversations appeared in the report of the study's findings where appropriate.

Also, cross-checking participants' responses with facts available in internal memoranda, newsletters, brochures, annual reports, organizational charts, and other related materials discounted or confirmed much of what was gleaned in the subjective portion of this combined research methodology. By assessing the quality of press releases, in particular, a second measure of the public relations practitioner's professionalism was obtained. The length, content, and structure of the releases also indicated the influence of top management on the workings of the public relations department. Finally, the sheer amount of material available was a measure of the extent of public relations activity in a given organization.

Most problematic was the area of *divergence* in several key variables. Although confidence in the validity of the findings was strengthened when data from different sources converged, divergence was often the result. Even so, though, contradictions were rarely irresolveable; divergence can be an opportunity for enriching the explanation of a phenomenon (Jick, 1979). For example, two measures of organizational type were used. The first was based on extensive contextualization of each organization. The second was quantitative, resulting from survey participants' answers to two key questions. Often, this determination differed from the qualitative one. Often, too, the respondents from a single organization disagreed on the characteristics used to define organizational type: complexity of knowledge and routinization (scale).

Usually, results using the two different measures were at least compatible. However, in a few instances the association between communication variables and type of organization differed in degree and even in direction using the two measures. This happened, for example, in determining the degree of job satisfaction in mixed mechanical and organic organizations, as well as in correlations between formalization and three of the four organizational types.

Because correlations tended to be larger when organizations were placed in their environmental niches qualitatively, the qualitative measure was deemed more valid. Still, findings must be interpreted in light of this limitation: The person with one watch knows what time it is; the person with two watches is never sure.

For global analysis in general, and the concomitant process of triangulation in particular, the strength of each source of data must correspond to the weakness of another (Jick, 1979). Thus Mandell and Bozeman (1983) called triangulation a *Jack Sprat tactic*. What depth interviews lack in objectivity, they make up for in richness of resulting data. Many scholars consider the personal interview to be the optimum way of gathering even survey data (Kerlinger, 1964). Its advantages include the trusting relationship created between interviewer and interviewee, the open-ended nature of questions, and the length of time spent in respondents' offices. What questionnaires lack in such richness, however, they typically make up for in objectivity and ease of analyzability. Standardized questionnaires—questionnaires used over a number of studies—permit reliable comparisons across large samples, helping researchers search for differences and similarities across studies.

SUMMARY

Questionnaires, publications, observation, and interviews all have been used to measure the internal and external public relations activities of different types of organizations—both in the 1985 dissertation and again in the *Excellence* project. They also tested for structural characteristics of scale and complexity, the intervening variable of technology, and other pertinent factors as identified in the review of the literature.

Each measure served as a check on each other. The survey instrument allowed for analysis of many variables within a reasonable length of time. The personal interviews fleshed out and explained many of the results. Publications helped to determine organizational type and to substantiate (or refute) findings from the survey. Computer analysis of all responses suggested the theoretical and operational linkages between the critical characteristics of organizations studied and the public relations techniques or models practiced there.

The theory developed in these two major studies allows practitioners not only to understand what traditionally has accounted for public relations programs but to forecast how such programs must change in response to dynamic environmental conditions. As such, they have helped fill a major gap in the understanding of public relations. The global level of analysis, occasionally mentioned in social science but rarely executed, helped create that understanding.

General Creighton W. Abrams (cited in Dickson, 1978) offered a piece of advice especially helpful to scholars who attempt a study of this magnitude: When eating an elephant take one bite at a time. The 1985 study is the first morsel of what is becoming a general theory of public relations as fully digested as many of the other theories in social science.

To date, entropy has us outnumbered. One important principle of Tinkertoys, also cited in Dickson (1978), is that if it can be understood, it's not finished yet. A second principle is that one should never do anything for the first time. Hopefully, this chapter helps short-cut the difficult yet rewarding process of research in the normal science of public relations.

REFERENCES

Aydelotte, W. O. (1971). *Qualifications in history*. Reading, MA: Addison-Wesley.

Berger, P. (1963). *Introduction to sociology: A humanistic perspective*. Garden City, NJ: Doubleday.

Berlin, I. (1962). Does political theory still exist? In P. Laslett & W. G. Runciman (Eds.), *Philosophy, politics, and society: Second series* (pp. 118–162). Oxford: Basil Blackwell.

Blau, P. M., & Schoenherr, R. A. (1971). *The structure of organizations*. New York: Basic Books.

Christians, C. G., & Carey, J. W. (1981). The logic and aims of qualitative research. In G. H. Stempel III & B. H. Westley (Eds.), *Research methods in mass communication* (pp. 342–362). Englewood Cliffs, NJ: Prentice-Hall.

Denzin, N. K. (1970). *The research act: A theoretical introduction to sociological methods*. Chicago: Aldine.

Dickson, P. (1978). *The official rules*. New York: Dell.

Geertz, C. (1973). *The interpretation of culture*. New York: Basic Books.

Gouldner, A. W. (1954). *Patterns of industrial bureaucracy*. New York: Free Press.

Gruban, B., Verčič, D., & Zavrl, F. (1994, January). Public relations in Slovenia. [special issue]. *pristop*.

Grunig, J. E. (1976). Organizations and public relations: Testing a communication theory. *Journalism Monographs, 46*.

Grunig, J. E. (1984). Organizations, environments, and models of public relations. *Public Relations Research and Education, 1*, 6–29.

Grunig, J. E. (Ed.). (1992). *Excellence in public relations and communication management*. Hillsdale, NJ: Lawrence Erlbaum Associates.

Grunig, J. E., & Grunig, L. A. (1992). Models of public relations and communications. In J. E. Grunig (Ed.), *Excellence in public relations and communication management* (pp. 285–325). Hillsdale, NJ: Lawrence Erlbaum Associates.

Grunig, L. A. (1988). A research agenda for women in public relations. *Public Relations Review, 14*, 48–57.

Grunig, L. A. (1991). Court-ordered relief from sex discrimination in the Foreign Service: Implications for women in development communication. *Public relations research annual* (Vol. 3, pp. 85–113).

Grunig, L. A. (1992). Toward the philosophy of public relations. In E. L. Toth & R. L. Heath (Eds.), *Rhetorical and critical approaches to public relations* (pp. 65–91). Hillsdale, NJ: Lawrence Erlbaum Associates.

Grunig, L. S. (1986, August). *Activism and organizational response: Contemporary cases of collective behavior*. Paper presented to the Public Relations Division, Association for Education in Journalism and Mass Communication. Norman, OK.

Hage, J., & Aiken, M. (1970). *Social change in complex organizations*. New York: Random House.

Hage, J., & Hull, F. (1981). *A typology of environmental niches based on knowledge, technology and scale: The implications for innovation and productivity*. (Working Paper 1). University Park: University of Maryland: Center for the Study of Innovation, Entrepreneurship and Organization Strategy.

Heath, R. (1993). A coherent research agenda. Review 1 in *Four reviews of excellence in public relations and communication management.* Reprinted from *Ragan Report* (pp. 1–3). Chicago: Ragan Communications.

Huang, Y. (1990). *Risk communication, models of public relations and anti-nuclear activism: A case study of a nuclear power plant in Taiwan.* Unpublished master's thesis, University of Maryland, College Park.

International Association of Business Communicators Research Foundation. (1991). *Initial data report and practical guide.* San Francisco: Author.

Jick, T. D. (1979). Mixing qualitative and quantitative methods: Triangulation in action. *Administrative Science Quarterly, 24,* 602–611.

Kerlinger, F. N. (1964). *Foundations of behavioral research.* New York: Holt, Rinehart & Winston.

Kobland, C. E. (1989, August). *Toward a synthesis of multiple methodologies.* Paper presented to the Communication Theory and Methodology Division, Association for Education in Journalism and Mass Communication, Washington, DC.

Kuhn, T. (1970). *The structure of scientific revolutions.* Chicago: University of Chicago Press.

Laufenburger, A. (1996). *Excellence in public relations in France.* Unpublished manuscript. Paris.

Lazarsfeld, P. F., & Menzel, H. (1969). On the relations between individual and collective properties. In A. Etzioni, (Ed.), *A sociological reader on complex organizations* (2nd ed., pp. 499–516). New York: Holt, Rinehart & Winston.

Lyra, A. (1991). *Public relations in Greece: Models, roles and gender.* Unpublished master's thesis, University of Maryland, College Park.

Madge, J. (1965). *The tools of social science.* New York: Anchor Books.

Mandell, M. B., & Bozeman, B. (1983). *Toward guidelines for conducting R&D on the guidance-system improvement approach.* Unpublished manuscript, Development Project Management Center, TAD/OICD/USDA, College Park, MD.

Meehan, E. J. (1968). *Explanation in social science: A system paradigm.* Homewood, IL: Dorsey.

Olasky, M. N. (1987). *Corporate public relations: A new historical perspective.* Hillsdale, NJ: Lawrence Erlbaum Associates.

Pavlik, J. V. (1987). *Public relations: What research tells us.* Newbury Park, CA: Sage.

Pavlik, J. V., & Salmon, C. T. (1983, August). *Theoretic approaches in public relations research.* Paper presented to the Public Relations Division, Association for Education in Journalism and Mass Communication, Corvallis, OR.

Pencil, M. (1976). Salt passage research: The state of the art. *Journal of Communication, 26*(4), 31–36.

Public Relations Society of America Task Force. (1988). Public Relations Body of Knowledge Task Force report. *Public Relations Review, 14,* 3–40.

Pratt, C. (1993). Indispensable tool. Review 3 in *Four reviews of excellence in public relations and communication management.* Reprinted from *Ragan Report* (pp. 8–11). Chicago: Ragan Communications.

Rakow, L. F. (1989, May). *From the feminization of public relations to the promise of feminism.* Paper presented to the Public Relations Interest Group, International Communication Association, San Francisco.

Sanders, P. (1982). Phenomenology: A new way of viewing organizational research. *Academy of Management Review, 7,* 353–360.

Schneider, L. A. (1985a). Implications of the concept of the schema for public relations. *Public Relations Research and Education, 2,* 36–47.

Schneider, L. A. (1985b). *Organizational structure, environmental niches, and public relations: The Hage-Hull typology of organizations as predictor of communication behavior.* Unpublished doctoral dissertation, University of Maryland, College Park.

Selltiz, C., Jahoda, M., Deutsch, M., & Cook, S. M. (1965). *Research methods in social relations.* New York: Holt, Rinehart & Winston.

Smith, H. W. (1975). *Strategies of social research: The methodological imagination.* Englewood Cliffs, NJ: Prentice-Hall.

Sriramesh, K. (1991). *The impact of societal culture on public relations: An ethnographic study of South Indian organizations.* Unpublished doctoral dissertation, University of Maryland, College Park.

Stempel, G. H., III, & Westley, B. H. (Eds.). (1981). *Research methods in mass communication.* Englewood Cliffs, NJ: Prentice-Hall.

Stinchcombe, A. L. (1965). Social structure and organizations. In J. G. March (Ed.), *Handbook of organization* (pp. 142–193). Chicago: Rand McNally.

Trend, M. (1978). On the reconciliation of quantitative and qualitative analysis. *Human Organization, 37,* 345–354.

Verčič, D., Grunig, L. A., & Grunig, J. E. (1996). In H. M. Culbertson & N. Chen (Eds.), *International public relations: A comparative analysi.* (pp. 31–65). Mahwah, NJ: Lawrence Erlbaum Associates.

Webb, E. J. (1970). Unconventionality, triangulation and inference. In N. K. Denzin (Ed.), *Sociological methods: A sourcebook* (pp. 34–43). Chicago: Aldine.

Webb, E. J., Campbell, D. T., Schwartz, R. D., Sechrest, L., & Grove, J. B. (1981). *Nonreactive measures in the social sciences* (2nd ed.). Boston: Houghton Mifflin.

Wright, D. (1993). Required reading. Review 4 in *Four Reviews of Excellence in Public Relations and Communication Management.* Reprinted from *Ragan Report* (pp. 12–13). Chicago: Ragan Communications.

30

Health Communication

Charles Atkin
Michigan State University

Alicia Marshall
Cornell University

Health communication, as a recognized area of study, is a relatively new but increasingly significant specialty that encompasses both mass and interpersonal communication (Rogers, 1994). It formally originated in the mid-1970s, when members of an International Communication Association interest group adopted the label *health communication* (Sharf, 1983), although the interdisciplinary marriage between health and communication was "certainly a common-law relationship" long before that (Finnegan, 1989, p. 9). To this day, health communication scholars have struggled to create an identity and carve out a niche uniquely their own.

This specialization has developed rapidly in response to growing pragmatic and policy interests, particularly in the public health agencies of the federal government and among private sector health care providers. Pressing needs to address alarming problems such as smoking, substance abuse, poor nutritional habits, and AIDS have given a strong impetus (and expanded funding) to the systematic study of health communication processes and effects. The area's popularity and legitimacy are evinced by rising membership in health communication divisions in both the International

Communication Association and the Speech Communication Association, the introduction of the *Health Communication* journal, and the explosion of health communication curricula across the country.

Health communication research has predominantly focused on the dissemination of
health-related information through the mass media and the role of interpersonal
relationships in individual health communication, particularly physician–patient communication and the effects of social support on health and illness. The common thread
weaving these diverse areas together is the emphasis on *health* as the desired outcome
of communication. Whether it be the investigation of patient-centered communication
behaviors exhibited by physicians on patient satisfaction or the examination of public
health campaign effectiveness on individuals engaging in safe sex, the ultimate goal
has been to identify effective communication strategies for improving the society's
overall health.

HISTORY

Although communication scholars have been applying their expertise to health promotion and disease prevention only in the last half of the 20th century, there have been
sporadic efforts to use communication to improve public health for more than 250
years. According to Paisley (1989), the history of American communication campaigns
has several notable examples involving health-related problems. The earliest case
occurred in 1721, when religious and political leader Cotton Mather utilized pamphlets
and speeches to successfully promote inoculation during Boston's serious smallpox
epidemic. In the 1800s, the social and health problems associated with alcohol misuse
resulted in the mobilization of a major movement lead by the Women's Christian
Temperance Union. With a deft combination of grassroot organizing, legislative
testimony, mass communication via newspapers and emerging magazines, and occasional confrontational incidents, charismatic leaders were able to promote antialcohol
reforms at both the societal and individual levels. Although the prohibitionists achieved
little direct impact in persuading drinkers to give up their vice, the temperance
movement eventually produced the ultimate form of environmental engineering: a
constitutional amendment banning the production and distribution of alcoholic beverages. As with many attempts to change unhealthy but pleasurable lifestyles, the effort
unraveled when many drinkers evaded the law and public opinion shifted.

At the turn of the century, muckraker reformers targeted a number of health-related
problems, such as impure food and inadequate health care for the poor. The print media
disseminated alarming stories that moved these issues higher on the public agenda, and
eventually local and federal government agencies were created to address the problems.

Theory and research played a minimal role in these early efforts, which occurred
prior to the ascendance of social science methodology and the discovery of communication principles. Campaign leaders and allied journalists relied on intuition and
conventional wisdom to formulate strategies and advocate solutions. In was not until
the mid-20th century that researchers began working in an uneasy tandem with
strategists and creative personnel to advance sophisticated campaign design and
implementation. The relationship has only recently evolved into a partnership with a

high degree of cooperation and mutual appreciation, particularly at the formative stage of campaign development. A critical turning point for the systematization of the health and communication relationship followed World War II, when the private medical sector and the public health sector began focusing on the behavioral aspects of health (Finnegan, 1989). As epidemiologists discovered connections between chronic diseases and culturally reinforced and induced behaviors, professionals and the public alike turned to the issues of prevention, particularly to identify strategies to effectively disseminate health-related information to the public. Critical communication processes such as persuasion and information dissemination were seen as playing a central role in an individual's health.

Neal (1962) was among the first to acknowledge the equally important role interpersonal communication played when he identified the communication between practitioners and patients as vital to study in the health field. The study of doctor–patient relationships emerged out of dissatisfaction among patients with the communication, or bedside manner, of their health care providers. Korsch and her colleagues were among the first to identify the effects of various communicative behaviors exhibited by physicians during the medical encounter on outcomes such as patient satisfaction and compliance (Korsch, Gozzi, & Francis, 1968). Their landmark findings of the importance of physician expression of positive affect, respect, friendliness, and empathy (Korsch, 1989) have stood the test of time in both academic and practitioner circles. As the study of the health–communication relationship in both public and private domains has matured, so too has the use of more sophisticated research methodology and theory development.

THEORY DEVELOPMENT

Communication as a discipline has come under fire for its limited and unsystematic theory development, particularly in the applied areas such as health communication. Berger (1991) observed that "there has been little evidence of theoretical activity by communication researchers within any of the particular contexts which define the field" (p. 102). He maintains that in identifying unique areas, such as health communication, it is implied that the communication phenomena occurring within these contexts are so distinctive that they merit their own context-specific theories.

Smith (1989) asserts that the uniqueness of the application context requires distinctive applied conceptualizations, and Sharf (1993) observed that "applied research can be complementary rather than antithetical to theory generation" (p. 39). For example, Rice and Atkin (1989) noted: "While health campaigns are typically viewed as merely applied communication research, the most effective campaigns carefully review and apply relevant theories; further, campaign results can be used to extend and improve theories about media effects and social change" (p. 9).

Health communication scholars have drawn upon a wide range of theoretical perspectives from communication, social psychology, and anthropology. A popular persuasion framework for guiding campaign efforts is McGuire's (1989) input–output model and classification of psychological theories. Communication variables such as source credibility and message organization constitute the laundry list of input factors, while the 12 output response steps proceed from exposure to post-behavioral consolidation. McGuire also discussed variants to the straightforward communication and persuasion model, including the peripheral route posited in the Elaboration Likelihood Model (Petty & Cacioppo, 1986) and reversal of certain sequences proposed in dissonance and self-perception theories.

Several theories and frameworks have been particularly popular among health communication researchers and practitioners. Social learning theory (Bandura, 1986) directs attention to the importance of modeling healthy behaviors and rewarding consequences. Bandura also emphasized self-efficacy of performance as a key factor in the success of health persuasion. The theory of reasoned action (Ajzen & Fishbein, 1980) focuses on the combination of the individual's belief expectancies about outcomes related to health practices and evaluation of those outcomes; it also accentuates the role of social norms in behavioral intentions. Classic persuasion theories, such as instrumental learning (Hovland, Janis, & Kelley, 1953), delineate critical input variables involving source characteristics, incentive appeals, and message repetition in producing information acquisition and attitude change. From the public health discipline, similar theoretical perspectives such as the health belief model and protection motivation theory have made significant contributions to the understanding of the persuasion process.

A complementary framework gaining wide acceptance is social marketing (Kotler & Roberto, 1989; Solomon, 1989). Based on the fundamental principle of exchange theory, social marketing applies practical techniques from commercial marketing such as packaging and positioning the health practice as an attractive product, minimizing the monetary (and social, psychological, and effort) costs, skillfully segmenting the audience according to demographic and risk profiles, and strategically mixing personal and media channels for promoting the product. The diffusion of innovation concept articulated by Rogers (1983) also helped to guide strategies of health campaign designers. Most recently, techniques of media advocacy were refined and applied in health campaign contexts (Wallack, Dorfman, Jernigan, & Themba, 1994).

Finally, scholars interested in the interpersonal aspects of health communication are embracing a broader range of theoretical approaches. For example, Sharf (1993) pointed to the merits of narrative theory to examine the discourse between health care providers and patients. Lupton (1994) called for the adoption of a more critical approach that allows for recognition and explicit examination of the inherent power differential and asymmetry of knowledge between health care providers and patients.

Features of Mediated and Interpersonal Channels

A remarkably diverse array of channels can be used for communicating health information to individuals. The primary medium of television disseminates messages in varied forms, such as public service announcements (PSAs), hard news items, feature stories, paid spots, talk show discussions, full-length educational programs, and entertainment program plot inserts. The other key mass media are radio (e.g., disk jockey commentary, PSA's), and newspapers and magazines (e.g., news, features, advice columns, editorials, ads, stuffer inserts). In addition, pamphlets and direct mail materials are distributed to individuals, films and slide shows are shown to groups, and posters and billboards are seen by passersby. Finally, interpersonal communication takes the form of interactions between patients and health care providers, contacts by health organization workers and volunteers, and informal discussions and support-giving among family members and friends. In assessing each option for channeling health messages, myriad advantages and disadvantages can be taken into consideration along these basic communicative dimensions:

- reach (proportion of community exposed to the message);
- specialization (targetability for reaching specific subgroups);
- intrusiveness (capability for overcoming selectivity and commanding attention);
- safeness (avoidance of risk of boomerang or irritation);
- participation (active receiver involvement while processing stimuli);
- meaning modalities (array of senses employed in conveying meaning);
- personalization (human relational nature of source-receiver interaction);
- decodability (mental effort required for processing stimulus);
- depth (channel capacity for conveying detailed and complex content);
- credibility (believability of material conveyed);
- agenda-setting (potency of channel for raising salience priority of issues);
- accessibility (ease of placing messages in channel);
- economy (low cost for producing and disseminating stimuli);
- efficiency (simplicity of arranging for production and dissemination).

There are substantial differences among channels on these dimensions, which can be illustrated by comparisons among three leading forms of communicating health information: Interpersonal communication is superior for specialization, intrusiveness, participation, modalities, credibility, and safeness; PSAs have greater reach, decodability, agenda potency, and efficiency; pamphlets are advantageous on accessibility, depth, and economy. Thus, there are distinct roles for various channels and modes; the optimum mix depends on the nature of the health topic, the target audience characteristics, and the communication objectives.

RESEARCH METHODS

Health communication researchers typically borrow standard methodological techniques from the mainstream social sciences rather than develop new methods. Aside from the Health Message Testing Service described in the next section, there are few unique research techniques created specifically with the health context. Despite a general acceptance and valuing of both quantitative and qualitative methodologies, the preponderance of health communication research to date has relied on quantitative approaches (Nussbaum, 1989).

The distinctive feature of health communication research is the way that certain methods have been applied to investigations. In particular, evaluation research approaches have been given greater emphasis in health-related studies than other domains of communication research. This section will describe the basic elements of health campaign evaluation methods. It will then briefly illustrate the application of other techniques such as experiments and doctor-patient interaction analysis.

Formative and Summative Evaluation

Evaluation research seeks to answer practical questions about the target audience for a health campaign via the collection of precampaign background information about receivers and the measurement of message effectiveness after dissemination (Atkin & Freimuth, 1989).

Formative research occurs both before campaigns are designed and during the development of messages. At the preproduction phase, evaluation data are useful in identifying target audience characteristics and predispositions, specifying the crucial intermediate response variables and behavioral outcomes, ascertaining channel exposure patterns, and determining receptivity to potential message components (Atkin & Freimuth, 1989). The primary research techniques are focus group discussions and formal surveys conducted with audience members.

For example, survey interviews with representative samples are typically used to segment the population along a number of dimensions defined in terms of demographic and psychographic characteristics, social role position, behavioral risk profile, beliefs and attitudes, and communication patterns. Ratings on a checklist of potential sources and arguments might also be measured. By contrast, focus group moderators elicit qualitative information to guide the development and refinement of message themes and appeals; the participants' in-depth comments yield insights into audience predispositions and provide feedback about substantive and stylistic message ideas that are under consideration.

The second phase of formative evaluation research focuses on message pretesting. Investigators solicit audience reactions to preliminary versions of message executions to determine which alternatives are most promising. This may involve either focus group comments following exposure to message components or rough executions, or systematic paper-and-pencil (or physiological) measures with larger samples of individuals. The purpose is to ascertain the amount of attention, extent of comprehension, degree of personal relevance, and level of persuasiveness. Strong and weak points are also identified, along with suggestions for improvements.

In the 1970s, two federal health agencies created the Health Message Testing Service, a standardized system to pretest radio and television spots (U.S. Department of Health and Human Services, 1989). It employed a "theater testing" approach, in which groups of about 25 respondents are exposed to several test messages embedded in entertainment programming in a manner that approximates real-life viewing or listening. Following exposure to the full tape, respondents answer a series of recall, comprehension, and learning items. After a repeat playing of each focal message at session's end, more elaborate responses are measured on scales such as believable, interesting, and pleasant. Theater testing also allows for use of electronic devices to record moment-by-moment evaluations of messages (Baggaley, 1988).

Because Health Message Testing Service data were systematically compiled over a large number of test spots, it was possible to develop norms and compare the scores of each new message along the response dimensions. Moreover, the cumulative data bank provided an opportunity to analyze the relationship between various message characteristics and the rating scores to isolate the most influential factors (Freimuth, 1985). Both types of formative research information are submitted to strategists and creative personnel, who incorporate this information into their campaign design. This provides a practical input for the operational implementation of relatively abstract theories, models, and principles in specific situations.

Summative research encompasses an array of techniques that are designed to ascertain the campaign outcomes. This form of post-campaign evaluation is prevalently practiced in the health domain because of the pragmatic results-oriented goals of health campaigns and the need for sponsor accountability due to high resource expenditure. Summative research is intended to answer questions about the size and characteristics of the audience reached, the influence of the campaign on attitudes and health behavior at individual and aggregate levels, and the isolation of causal processes. Investigators also seek to determine if any lack of effect is attributable to theory failure or program failure, in order to assess results and draw lessons for future efforts.

Flay and Cook (1989) describe three summative evaluation models employed. The superficial advertising model sensitively measures the early stages of audience response such as exposure, recall, and subjectively perceived effectiveness; sample surveys are most often used for this type of research. Second, the impact-monitoring model typically examines overt behavioral or aggregate societal outcomes, usually via secondary analyses of archival data. Finally, the experimental model focuses on large-scale tests of causal influences via controlled manipulation of treatments, typically at the community level; additional comparisons may be made between individuals with higher versus lower exposure to messages within experimental communities.

Other Interpersonal and Mass Communication Methods

Content analysis is one of the most widely used techniques in mass communication. Although systematic measurement of health-related message features does not permit inferences about the impact of the content, it does provide a basis for predicting likely effects as well as exploring the motives of media gatekeepers. For example, Wallack, Grube, Madden, and Breed (1990) measured the frequency of alcohol consumption depictions in television entertainment programming and the positive and negative outcomes associated with drinking. Freimuth, Greenberg, DeWitt, and Romano (1984) performed a content analysis of news stories about cancer. Warner (1987) examined both the number of cigarette ads carried in a set of magazines and the extent to which editorial content highlighted the health risks of smoking as a basis for speculating whether the advertisers exerted an influence on the editors' decisions.

Hundreds of laboratory experiments have been conducted to examine the impact of health messages. The most basic design is a simple after-only comparison between experimental and control groups. For example, Greenberg and Gantz (1989) showed randomly assigned sets of college students an entertaining educational television show about venereal disease called "VD Blues." Postviewing measures assessed the seriousness of the problem, knowledge levels, and conversational tabooness. Responses of nonexposed subjects provided a baseline for comparison. More sophisticated designs have been used to compare content manipulations featuring two or three versions of the same message (e.g., high versus medium versus low fear, or celebrity versus ordinary source), or factorial designs (e.g., level of fear by type of source).

Time series analyses have been computed with archival data collected on a regular basis. The federal government, for example, annually compiles the number of cigarettes sold in this country. Researchers have traced periodic fluctuations in sales and related these changes to variations in mass media messages about smoking. For example, sales dropped briefly in the early 1960s after extensive news publicity about cancer, declined again during the late 1960s when antismoking PSAs were prevalent, but rose in the 1970s when the PSAs went off the air and advertising dollars were rechanneled into targeted media such as women's magazines and billboards.

The most valid research method is the true field experiment, with a manipulated set of messages disseminated to randomly assigned treatment groups under naturalistic conditions. Although high cost seldom permits the application of this elaborate but rigorous technique, one notable example is the study of the impact of fear-oriented safety belt PSAs (Robertson, 1976). In a split-cable television system designed for testing commercial spots in a typical American community, six different belt-promotion PSAs were inserted during program breaks almost 1,000 times over a nine-month period in one grid of several thousand homes; a control set of comparable households did not see these spots. Actual use of safety belts was surreptitiously observed throughout the community for nine months following the campaign (vehicle license numbers were traced to households to determine the treatment condition of each driver). Differences in usage patterns between experimental and control groups enabled a precise assessment of campaign effects.

In the interpersonal domain of health communication, the vast majority of studies have relied on *interaction analysis* to systematically examine doctor–patient interaction. Korsch and her colleagues were the first to adapt Bales' (1950) Interaction Process Analysis scheme to categorize both physicians' and patients' statements (Korsch et al., 1968). Numerous other coding schemes have subsequently been developed relying on Bales' scheme as a foundation, most notably Roter's "Modified Interaction Process Analysis" (Roter, 1977). This has produced a plethora of studies that provide a numerical accounting of types of utterances present during typical medical encounters. Despite their descriptive utility and continued existence, such studies have faced criticism for their limited ability to definitively describe the complex process of physician-patient interaction (i.e., Wasserman & Inui, 1983). Smith (1989) is clear in his concern when he states "simply labeling acts, counting their frequencies, and running statistical manipulations have not proved very useful in communication studies generally and show no promise of being any more useful in health communication" (p. 22).

RESEARCH FINDINGS AND APPLICATIONS

Given the inherent applied nature of health communication, researchers are primarily interested in discovering which approaches work the best to provide useful advice to practitioners. Those practicing on the front lines, such as doctors, health agency officials, and PSA campaign designers, need to know what to say and how to say it. With respect to interpersonal health communication, the most fundamental application rests in the development and implementation of training programs for physicians (and patients) to improve the effectiveness of physician–patient interaction. Numerous professional medical associations, such as the American Board of Internal Medicine, have recently begun mandating communication or physician–patient relationship skills training programs. As a result, interdisciplinary teams across the country have begun to design and evaluate communication skills training programs, incorporating many of the early fundamental findings of researchers such as Korsch and her colleagues.

One example of such an evaluation is ongoing in the Department of Medicine at Michigan State University. A team of researchers and trainers (representing the communication, medicine, and psychiatry disciplines) is examining the efficacy of a four-week intensive communication skills training program required of all medicine residents. Using a biopsychosocial theoretical approach (Engel, 1980) as its foundation, the training program focuses on teaching the residents to use a variety of patient-centered interviewing and relationship development skills (Smith & Hoppe, 1990; Smith et al., 1991) during medical encounters with clinic and hospital patients. Smith and his colleagues have found significant relationships between the utilization of the desired communicative behaviors and factors such as residents' confidence in their ability to provide quality of care, patient satisfaction, and long term patient health status (Smith et al., 1991; Smith, Marshall, & Cohen-Cole, 1994). The implications suggest that fundamental communication skills are teachable in a medical education setting, and that these communicative behaviors significantly affect not only the relationship that develops between physician and patient, but perhaps patients overall health as well. Although long assumed, few programs are in existence that have successfully transformed these longstanding findings regarding the importance of physician-patient communication into functioning and effective training programs (Smith et al., 1994).

There are numerous practical implications of the plethora of public health campaigns research. The central questions examined in the theoretically based lab experiments and in the more applied pretesting research involve the relative effectiveness of health message appeals. For example, researchers are seeking to determine whether the public will be more effectively motivated by positive versus negative messages: promises of wellness or safety versus threats of illness or death. They are also examining which dimensions of persuasive incentives are most influential: physical health versus economic (e.g., saving money, losing a job) versus psychological (e.g., achievement, anxiety, regret, self-esteem) versus cognitive (consistency, ignorance, rationality) versus moral (e.g., propriety, guilt, fairness) versus social (e.g., acceptance, embarrassment, altruism, deviance). Furthermore, research is useful in isolating the most effective types of sources, evidence, organization of material, channels, and styles of presentation.

At a more macrolevel, summative evaluation research provides answers to questions about the overall impact of large-scale campaigns. Although it is difficult to isolate the relative contribution of various components of lengthy multifaceted efforts to disseminate health information (e.g., community-wide heart disease prevention campaign or national AIDS program), investigators attempt to ascertain the extent to which these comprehensive campaigns influence the knowledge, attitudes, and behaviors of the public. The following sections describe some of the key concepts that were investigated, present some principles that have been developed, and summarize the overall impact of health communication campaigns.

Guidelines for Designing Effective Health Messages

Based on the array of theoretical perspectives advanced by the academic community and the increasing body of lessons learned by practitioners, a basic set of principles for devising communication strategies has emerged in recent years (Atkin, 1994). The listing below provides a useful summary of some key conclusions from the research literature, beginning with substantive material in message development and proceeding to mechanical and stylistic presentational factors.

Selection of Incentive Appeals.   Messages should feature persuasive reasons for adopting the recommended behavior. In health campaigns, there has been an overreliance on fear appeals that threaten physical harm; these should be supplemented with positive arguments and with economic, social, or psychological incentives (e.g., rather than focusing on overdose death, antidrug messages should engender concerns about corporate drug-testing or portray a drug-free lifestyle as normal, healthy, and satisfying). It is preferable to use multiple rather than single appeals, within a typical length message, and particularly across a series of messages in a campaign.

Evidence.   In conveying an incentive appeal, it is usually more effective to provide dramatized case examples rather than statistical documentation supporting claims made in the message (e.g., the tragedy of a car crash victim or the triumph of person who has successfully quit smoking). In processing health information, audiences tend to be more responsive to depictions of other people's experiences rather than complex and often unimpressive facts and figures.

One-sided versus Two-sided Message Content.   A two-sided strategy that refutes, downplays, or concedes disadvantages of the target response is generally more influential. This strategy is superior when the drawbacks are familiar and the audience is resistant to change, as is the case with many health topics.

Source Featured in Message.   The source is the manifest messenger appearing in messages. Eight types of source presenters are used in health messages: celebrity (e.g., famous athlete, entertainer); public official (government leader, agency director); expert specialist (doctor, researcher); organization leader (hospital administrator, corporate executive); professional performer (standard spokesperson, attractive model, actor); average person (blue-collar male, middle class female); especially experienced person (victim, survivor, successful role model); and unique character (animated, anthropomorphic, costumed). The effectiveness of each type depends on topic and audience; the relative contribution of source credibility (expertise and trustworthiness), similarity, and likability vary according to the situation, so selection of the messengers should be guided by formative evaluation research.

Presentation of Target Response.   An explicit recommendation (or behavioral modeling) is generally more effective than the implicit approach; the advocated action should only be moderately discrepant with the initial position of the target audience.

Theme Line and Copy.   A health message should prominently and concisely present a statement that captures the main idea (or pose a question that provokes thought or further decoding). Messages should feature simplified vocabulary, short sentences, and low density of copy.

Arrangement of Message Elements.   The strongest copy points should be placed near the beginning of the message because attention often wanes for dull health topics. Refutation, diminution, or concession points should be located following the pro-arguments.

Audio and Visual Factors.   Carefully selected music typically produces positive reactions, and visualizations play a central role in attracting attention and facilitating processing. Messages should be technically sophisticated in terms of pacing, camera angles, colors, layout, and graphic devices.

Continuity Devices.   Each message should include an element that symbolizes the overall health campaign and provides a unifying common thread across various executions or across channels.

Style.   A serious rather than light approach is the safest strategy for delivering the substantive arguments, as long as the tone is not overly preachy. The rational style of presentation is most often advantageous, but emotional appeals may be needed to arouse drives.

Attractiveness and Vividness.   Entertaining styles generally enhance message impact; cleverness is an effective feature, but humor produces diverse responses and must be used carefully. Messages should use lively language, striking statements, fascinating facts, and vibrant visuals (and alluring alliteration).

Realism and Personalization.   Messages should depict situations and models that enable audiences to connect the material to own experiences.

Impact of Health Campaigns

In assessing health campaign effects, the key determinants are the degree of audience receptivity, the quality and quantity of messages, the dissemination channels, and the larger communication environment. Audiences are more readily influenced on certain topics and target responses (e.g., the designated driver to prevent drunk driving), while they are resistant in other cases (e.g., reducing excessive drinking). Some segments of the audience are much more receptive than others (e.g., casual versus hard core drug users, or children versus teenagers).

Quantitative potency of campaign stimuli is necessary but not sufficient for success. Both the total volume of messages and the prominence of message placement are crucial. Multiplicity of channels, appeals, and executions increases impact, providing there is some uniformity of elements across the various messages in a campaign.

Qualitative potency factors are also important, particularly the incentive appeals featured in the persuasive strategy. Incentives are needed to change attitudes and motivate action; both promises of rewards to be gained or threats of punishment are effective. Credibility plays a significant role in convincing people that the arguments are valid through the use of evidence and credible source presenters. Relevance is another quality that is essential in actively involving the audience and demonstrating how the target response and incentives are pertinent to their own situation. Attractive styles of presentation help attract audience attention, especially when subject matter is dull or distant topics and when quantity is limited.

Media channel effectiveness varies, depending on the target audience and the type of message. Televised PSA spots and newscast and newspaper publicity tend to be most influential, but other channels are effective in certain situations. Interpersonal communication usually augments the impact of media messages, especially via normative and personal influences on attitudes and practices.

The effects of health campaigns are often undermined by countermessages such as commercial advertising that glamorizes alcohol and tobacco, or entertainment programming that portrays the pleasures of sex or cocaine use. Occasionally, a consonant message environment will increase impact by reinforcing the campaign messages (e.g., ads for low-fat foods, entertainment depicting the designated driver, or news stories about AIDS deaths).

In conclusion, the overall magnitude of behavioral effects is modest in most campaigns; indeed, some health campaigns have been notably weak. The most successful campaigns (e.g., drugs, drunk driving, and smoking) involve receptive subaudiences, employ compelling rewards and punishments, and high quantities of message dissemination over a sustained period of time. Ineffective campaigns (e.g., safety belts, cancer, safe sex, and responsible drinking) tend to suffer from widespread audience resistance resulting from large immediate sacrifices relative to distant benefits; poor presentation of incentives; low prominence of message placement; lack of relevant message content; unattractive stylistic quality; and counteracting media environment.

MODEL STUDY: STANFORD HEART DISEASE PROGRAM

The leading cause of premature death in Western society is heart disease, and a significant portion of this health problem is due to lifestyle factors such as smoking, lack of exercise, high-fat diet, and chronic stress. Because these risk factors are partially preventable, communication researchers became interested in strategies for influencing the community environment and individual decisions that contribute to heart disease. The preeminent research program investigating this problem has been Stanford University's Three Community Study (TCS) and Five City Project (FCP). Combining expertise from the medical school and communication department, the Stanford program began in the early 1970s with a simple experimental design, a sophisticated theoretical conceptualization, and elaborate applied implementation.

Over the next two decades, it became the most influential and frequently cited health campaign in history; indeed, it is recognized by Rogers (1994) as the most significant turning point in the development of health communication. Moreover, the Stanford researchers have successfully blended theory and methods in a rigorous and sensitive manner. Thus, the heart disease program merits close examination as an exemplar in health communication research.

The program involves large-scale community-wide interventions featuring both mass media and interpersonal communication to change knowledge, attitudes, and risk-related practices. At the behavioral level, the campaigns sought to reduce intake of saturated fat, cholesterol, salt, and excessive calories; to eliminate tobacco use; to increase physical activity; and to promote blood pressure checks and adherence to hypertension control medication.

The original TCS successfully integrated theory into the design, implementation, and evaluation of the program. Combining various theoretical perspectives such as social learning, innovation diffusion, learning hierarchies, inoculation, social comparison, and reasoned action, the investigators created a Communication–Behavior–Change model (Farquhar, Maccoby, & Solomon, 1984). A large quantity and variety of messages were disseminated to the target audience of middle-age males in two middle-size communities. The messages included television and radio spots, newspaper columns, cookbooks, booklets, and bus cards. These materials were developed through formative evaluation at the preproduction and pretesting stages. The summative evaluation research featured a quasi-experimental design in three comparable sites: a media-only community, a second community where the same basic media campaign was supplemented by face-to-face communication, and a no-intervention control community. Randomly sampled respondents were repeatedly surveyed over three years.

The results showed that knowledge-gain impact occurred to a similar degree in both intervention communities, but that actual behavioral change was greater in the media-plus-interpersonal treatment site after the first year of the campaign. The key outcome measure was a heart disease risk score composed of plasma cholesterol, systolic blood pressure, and relative weight. After a second year of message dissemination, the sample in the media-only town caught up with those experiencing the more intensive intervention. The subsequent Five City Project sought to increase the exportability of the campaign by reducing the scope of the externally introduced intervention; the Stanford team relied more heavily on local community mobilization to sustain the campaign. A similar quasiexperimental design was used to isolate the effects of the communication effort over a far longer period, and more bottom-line outcomes such as morbidity and mortality were added to the study; significant reductions were demonstrated in treatment communities (Farquhar et al., 1990).

FUTURE DIRECTIONS

On the positive side, the health communication field can be currently characterized by a rapidly expanding research literature and increasingly sophisticated conceptual frameworks. However, researchers have a long way to go in advancing both theoretical knowledge and practical applications (Atkin & Arkin, 1990).

Perhaps the biggest criticism facing researchers engaged primarily in interpersonal health communication work is that the majority of studies have been conducted in a formal health care or medical setting; most investigations have been restricted to the relationship between physician and patient. Because Americans spend the majority of their time talking about health-related issues and learning health-related information in nonmedical settings, researchers should systematically examine health-related interactions between family members, friends, peers, and coworkers (Zook, 1994).

Rootman and Hershfield (1994) call on health communication researchers to expand their scope of investigation to recognize the critical role such settings play in the arena of health communication. Research should examine more closely the extent to which health-related communication activities are occurring in health care settings versus social or work-related settings. Moreover, investigators should extend this examination to encompass ultimate effects of these context-specific health communication messages on individual behavior.

Health communication researchers should continue in their efforts to identify effective mass and interpersonal communication strategies for motivating individuals to engage in desirable health behaviors. In particular, researchers should be encouraged to isolate potentially unique strategies necessary to motivate individuals that have been disenfranchised in society (e.g., the homeless, individuals living in poverty, individuals of color, members of the gay and lesbian communities).

Media-oriented scholars and practitioners should widen their focus beyond the personal level to encompass strategies designed to change societal-level environmental conditions within which individuals make health decisions. Wallack et al. (1990) pioneered the media advocacy approach for using mass communication to apply pressure for changes in policies that will promote public health goals.

Finally, despite health communication's applied focus and warnings voiced concerning the uniqueness of the context rather than phenomena, health communication researchers should generate theories about the nature and process of health communication. Only through such consideration and reflection will health communication scholars understand the inextricable link between communication and health.

KEY RESOURCE BOOKS

A large number of monographs, textbooks, and readers have been published primarily by scholars in the areas of mass communication, interpersonal communication, and public health. Briefly, there are many works that broadly deal with health communication: Atkin and Wallack (1990) examine the intersection of mass communication and public health; Backer, Rogers, and Sopony (1992) provided guidelines for designing health campaigns; Backer and Rogers (1993) described organizational aspects and case studies of campaign implementation; Egger, Donovan, and Spark (1993) presented principles and practices for health promotion via mass media; Frederiksen, Solomon and Brehony (1984) discussed social marketing approaches to health; Leathar, Hastings, O'Reilly, and Davies (1986) assembled papers dealing with the role of mass media in health education; Maibach and Parrott (1995) addressed theoretical and practical approaches to health message design; Ray and Donohue (1989) applied a unified framework integrating mass and interpersonal research on health communication; Ray (1993) covered a wide variety of interpersonally oriented topics and case studies; Rice and Atkin (1989) featured a number of health-related chapters in a general communication campaign book; Salmon (1989) examined the balance between social values and social change in information campaigns; and a manual published by the federal government (U.S. Department of Health and Human Services, 1989) presented useful guidance for health message design. In addition, Wallack et al. (1993) focused on the media advocacy approach to health promotion. There are two books dealing with the role of communication in drug abuse prevention (Donohew, Sypher & Bukoski, 1991; Shoemaker, 1989) and one emphasizing communication and AIDS prevention (Edgar, Fitzpatrick, & Freimuth, 1992).

REFERENCES

Ajzen, I., & Fishbein, M. (1980). *Understanding attitudes and predicting social behavior.* Englewood Cliffs, NJ: Prentice-Hall.

Atkin, C. (1994). Designing persuasive health messages. In L. Sechrest, T. Backer, & E. Rugers (Eds.), *Effective dissemination of clinical and health information* (pp. 99–110). Rockville, MD: U.S. Department of Health and Human Services.

Atkin, C., & Freimuth, V. (1989). Formative evaluation research in campaign design. In R. Rice & C. Atkin (Eds.), *Public communication campaigns* (pp. 131–150). Newbury Park, CA: Sage.

Atkin, C., & Arkin, E. (1990). Issues and initiatives in communicating health information to the public. In C. Atkin & L. Wallack (Eds.), *Mass communication and public health: Complexities and conflicts* (pp. 5–32). Newbury Park, CA: Sage.

Atkin, C., & Wallack, L. (1990). *Mass communication and public health: Complexities and conflicts.* Newbury Park, CA: Sage.

Backer, T., & Rogers, E. (1993). *Organizational aspects of health communication campaigns: What works?* Newbury Park, CA: Sage.

Backer, T., Rogers, E., & Sopony, P. (1992). *Designing health communication campaigns: What works?* Newbury Park, CA: Sage.

Baggaley, J. (1988). Perceived effectiveness of international AIDS campaigns. *Health Education Research, 3,* 7–17.

Bales, R. (1950). *Interaction analysis process.* Cambridge, MA: Addison-Wesley.

Bandura, A. (1986). *Social foundations of thought and action: A social cognitive theory.* Englewood Cliffs, NJ: Prentice-Hall.

Berger, C. (1991). Communication theories and other curios. *Communication Monographs, 58,* 101–113.

Donohew, L., Sypher, H., & Bukoski, W. (1991). *Persuasive communication and drug abuse prevention.* Hillsdale, NJ: Lawrence Erlbaum Associates.

Edgar, T., Fitzpatrick, M., & Freimuth, V. (1992). *AIDS: A communication perspective.* Hillsdale, NJ: Lawrence Erlbaum Associates.

Egger, G., Donovan, R., & Spark, R. (1993). *Health and the media: Principles and practices for health promotion.* Sydney: McGraw-Hill.

Engel, G. (1980). The clinical application of the biopsychosocial model. *American Journal of Psychiatry, 137,* 535–544.

Farquhar, J., Fortmann, S., Flora, J., Taylor, C., Haskell, W., & Williams, P. (1990). Effects of community-wide education on cardiovascular disease risk factors: Stanford Five-City Project. *Journal of the American Medical Association, 264,* 359–365.

Farquhar, J., Maccoby, N., & Solomon, D. (1984). Community applications of behavioral medicine. In E. Gentry (Ed.), *Handbook of behavioral medicine* (pp. 437–478). New York: Guilford.

Finnegan, J. (1989). Health and communication: Medical and public health influences on the research agenda. In E. Ray & L. Donohew (Eds.), *Communication and health: Systems and applications* (pp. 9–24). Hillsdale, NJ: Lawrence Erlbaum Associates.

Flay, B., & Cook, T. (1989). Three models for summative evaluation of prevention campaigns with a mass media component. In R. Rice & C. Atkin (Eds.), *Public communication campaigns* (pp. 175–196). Newbury Park, CA: Sage.

Frederiksen, L., Solomon, D., & Brehony, K. (1984). *Marketing health behavior: Principles, techniques, and applications.* New York: Plenum.

Freimuth, V. (1985). Developing the public service advertisement for nonprofit marketing. In R. Belk (Ed.), *Advances in nonprofit marketing* (pp. 55–95). Greenwich, CT: JAI.

Freimuth, V., Greenberg, R., DeWitt, J., & Romano, R. (1984). Covering cancer: Newspapers and the public interest. *Journal of Communication, 34*, 62–73.

Green, L., & Lewis, F. (1986). *Measurement and evaluation in health education and health promotion.* Palo Alto, CA: Mayfield.

Greenberg, B., & Gantz, W. (1989). Singing the VD blues. In R. Rice & C. Atkin (Eds.), *Public communication campaigns* (pp. 203–206). Newbury Park, CA: Sage.

Hovland, C., Janis, I., & Kelley, H. (1953). *Communication and persuasion.* New Haven, CT: Yale University Press.

Kotler, P., & Roberto, E. (1989). *Social marketing: Strategies for changing public behavior.* New York: The Free Press.

Korsch, B. (1989). Studying health communication: An agenda for the future. *Health Communication, 1,* 5–9.

Korsch, B., Gozzi, E., & Francis, V. (1968). Gaps in doctor–patient communication: Doctor–patient interaction and patient satisfaction. *Pediatrics, 42*, 855–871.

Kreps, G. (1989). Setting the agenda for health communication research and development: Scholarship that can make a difference. *Health Communication, 1,* 11–15.

Leathar, D., Hastings, G., O'Reilly, K., & Davies, J. (1986). *Health education and the media II.* Oxford: Pergamon.

Lupton, D. (1994). Toward the development of critical health communication praxis. *Health Communication, 6,* 55–67.

Maibach, E., & Parrott, R. (1995). *Designing health messages: Approaches from communication theory and public health practice.* Newbury Park, CA: Sage.

McGuire, W. (1989). Theoretical foundations of campaigns. In R. Rice & C. Atkin (Eds.), *Public communication campaigns* (pp. 43–66). Newbury Park, CA: Sage.

Neal, H. (1962). *Better communication for better health.* New York: Columbia University Press.

Nussbaum, J. (1989). Directions for research within health communication. *Health Communication, 1,* 35–40.

Paisley, W. (1989). Public communication campaigns: The American experience. In R. Rice & C. Atkin (Eds.), *Public communication campaigns* (pp. 15–38). Newbury Park, CA: Sage.

Petty, R., & Cacioppo, J. (1986). *Communication and persuasion: Central and peripheral routes to attitude change.* New York: Springer-Verlag.

Ray, E., and Donohew, L. (1989). *Communication and health: Systems and applications.* Hillsdale, NJ: Lawrence Erlbaum Associates.

Ray, E. (1993). *Case studies in health communication.* Hillsdale, NJ: Lawrence Erlbaum Associates.

Rice, R., & Atkin, C. (Eds.). (1989). *Public communication campaigns.* Newbury Park, CA: Sage.

Robertson, L. (1976). The great seat belt flop. *Journal of Communication, 26*, 41–46.

Rogers, E. (1983). *Diffusion of innovations* (3rd ed.). New York: Free Press.

Rogers, E. (1994). The field of health communication today. *American Behavioral Scientist, 38*, 208–214.

Rootman, I., & Hershfield, L. (1994). Health communication research: Broadening the scope. *Health Communication, 6,* 69–72.

Roter, D. (1977). Patient participation in the patient-provider interaction. *Health Education Monographs, 5,* 281–315.

Salmon, C. (1989). *Information campaigns: Balancing social values and social change.* Newbury Park, CA: Sage.

Sharf, B. (1983). Reading the vital signs: Research in health care communication. *Communication Monographs, 60,* 35–41.

Shoemaker, P. (1989). *Communication campaigns about drugs: Government, media, and the public.* Hillsdale, NJ: Lawrence Erlbaum Associates.

Smith, D. H. (1989). Studying health communication: An agenda for the future. *Health Communication, 1,* 17–27.

Smith, R. & Hoppe, R. (1991). The patient's story: Integrating the patient- and physician-centered approaches to interviewing. *Annals of Internal Medicine, 115*, 470–477.

Smith, R., Marshall, A., & Cohen-Cole, S. (1994). The efficacy of intensive biopsychosocial teaching programs for residents: A review of the literature and guidelines for teaching. *Journal of General Internal Medicine, 9*, 390–396.

Smith, R., Osborn, G., Hoppe, R., Lyles, J., Van Egeren, L., Henry, R., Sego, D., Alguire, P., & Stoffelmayr, B. (1991). Efficacy of a one-month training block in psychosocial medicine for residents: A controlled study. *Journal of General Internal Medicine, 6*, 535–543.

Solomon, D. (1989). A social marketing perspective on communication campaigns. In R. Rice., & C. Atkin (Eds.), *Public communication campaigns* (pp. 67–86). Newbury Park, CA: Sage.

U.S. Department of Health and Human Services. (1989). *Making health communication programs work.* Bethesda, MD: Office of Cancer Communications, National Cancer Institute.

Wallack, L., Dorfman, L., Jernigan, D., & Themba, M. (1993). *Media advocacy and public health.* Newbury Park, CA: Sage.

Wallack, L., Grube, J., Madden, P., & Breed, W. (1990). Portrayals of alcohol on prime-time television. *Journal of Studies on Alcohol, 51*, 428–441.

Warner, K. (1984). Cigarette advertising and media coverage of smoking and health. *New England Journal of Medicine, 312*, 384–388.

Wasserman, R., & Inui, T. (1983). Systematic analysis of clinician-patient interactions: A critique of recent approaches with suggestions for future research. *Medical Care, 21*, 279–293.

Zook, E. (1994). Embodied health and constitutive communication: Toward an authentic conceptualization of health communication. In S. Deetz (Ed.), *Communication yearbook* (Vol. 17, pp. 344–377). Thousand Oaks, CA: Sage.

31

Feminist Approaches

Ramona R. Rush
University of Kentucky

Autumn Grubb-Swetnam
Morehead State University

The thesis of this chapter is that the integration of theory and research, what this book is about, may have large parts of the scholarship missing, distorted, or coopted—and that it is our responsibility, all of us, as scholars to have the awareness, knowledge, and ethics to at least note, as in footnote, that this may be the case. Such a note, of course, is in reference to the limitations of the work in regard to validity, reliability, or generalizability. This chapter speaks to what Rush is calling here the "greening" of communication—the integration of theory and research as if "others," including women, mattered.[1]

---

[1]The original title was: "The 'Greening' of Communication: The Integration of Theory and Research as if 'Others,' Including Women, Mattered." E. F. Schumacher's classic contribution is acknowledged by paraphrasing the subtitle from *Small is Beautiful: Economics as if People Mattered.* (1973) New York: Harper & Row. We are appreciative of the time and efforts of graduate students Alyssa Eckman and Robin Crigler of the University of Kentucky for proofreading and providing comments. Also, University of North Carolina Communication professor Julia T. Wood provided comments throughout the manuscript that only a seasoned feminist researcher, and writer, could offer.

We have made a conscious decision, following the examples provided by Pam Creedon in *Women in Mass Communication* (1993, pp. 18–20) to use women's full names rather than initials, when possible, as a first mention in the text. Women's voices are silenced in ways that are covert and overt: In this small way, we want to indicate that we are trying our best to get out of that black hole of nonrecognition through gendered lack of acknowledgement.

We also try to point out that "others," or in this case, feminists, who undertake theory-building, the reworking of traditional methods or development of new methods of intellectual inquiry, do not necessarily set out to rebuke or discard existing theoretical and conceptual frameworks and methods of research. Rather, the primary purpose is to add to and enhance an academic discipline by contributing and establishing new, inclusive, and different perspectives and approaches; that is, the production of knowledge which is re-covered and dis-covered, perhaps leading to a covering law of, for example, communication.

Myths, philosophies, theories, and research have perpetuated male standpoints for some time. Marija Gimbutas (1989) and other archeomythologists[2] note that the repeated disturbances and incursions by the Kurgan people (who Gimbutas views as proto-Indo-European) put an end to Old European culture between 4300 and 2800 BC, changing it from gylanic to androcratic, and from matrilineal to patrilineal.[3] "The Aegean and Mediterannean region and western Europe escaped the process the longest. . . . Old European culture flourished in an enviably peaceful and creative civilization until 1500 BC, a thousand to 1500 years after central Europe had been thoroughly transformed" (p. xx). Gimbutas summarized, "We are still living under the sway of that aggressive male invasion and only beginning to discover our long alienation from our authentic European Heritage—gylanic, nonviolent, earth-centered culture" (p. xxi).

Attitudinal and behavioral adjustments take time, and the swing back to a gylanic culture, a social structure in which both sexes were equal, has begun. But that change will be difficult if particular areas of scholarship are silenced, ignored, or disregarded. The "greening" (see Griswold & Swenson, 1991) of communications—or the inclusion of all viewpoints—will only come about if communication students are *aware* that feminist scholarship is often conspicuous by its absence in curricula, in informal conversations, and in mainstream research papers and journals. They must care enough to have the courage and curiosity to ask, "Why?" or, "What is missing here? Why is this picture incomplete or distorted?"

To do so, students must not be put off or put out by the terms *feminist, feminist theory, feminist research,* or *women's issues,* and others used to describe particular perspectives and approaches. Reading or conducting research about how women and men "are portrayed in stereotypical ways that reflect and sustain socially endorsed views of gender" (Wood, 1994, p. 234) is not only interesting but necessary to an enlightened social scientist in a world where women and men are transforming gender

---

[2]Archeomythology, according to Gimbutas, is a field that includes archelolgy, comparative mythology, and folklore. It is a field that archeologists have yet to explore (1989, p. xviii).

[3]Gimbutas (1989, p. xx) used the term *gylanic* from Riana T. Eisler' book, *The Chalice and the Blade* (1987). Eisler proposed the term *gylany* (*gy-* from "woman," *an* from *andros*, "man," and the letter "*l*" between the two standing for the linking of both halves of humanity) for the social structure in which both sexes were equal.

roles. The mass media, for example, distort reality by underrepresenting women in ratios to white males by 3:1 in prime-time television and 2:1 in children's programming, or including men in newscast stories 10 times more often than women (Basow, 1992, p. 159; "Study Reports Sex Bias," 1989; Wood, 1994, p. 234).

WHO ARE FEMINISTS?: DEFINITIONAL DISTINCTIONS, BLURRINGS

Who is a feminist? It is not a difficult question to answer unless one cares to make it so. There is no single feminist ideology or character. In general, we can say that a *feminist* is a person who believes in equal rights for everyone, including women, and, when women are denied their rights, especially women.

Those rights include civil, political, educational, economic, social, and communication participation and equity. They also include relational values such as caring, loving, helping, and nurturing. In other words, a feminist believes that women, too, are human beings who should and expect to be treated that way. Feminist theory and research, then, advances and values the study of women and women's institutions separately, in comparison to, or inclusive with, those that have predominantly been of, for, and by men but generalized to all humans. It has been a male standpoint, a male norm to which women—the "others"—have been compared often *in absentia.*

How does research about women's issues differ from feminist research? Often, *the* distinction is one of description without the overlay of conceptual models or philosophy which attempts interpretation, explanation, or prediction of the phenomena under study. For researchers of women's issues in communication in the early 1970s, there was little preserved or shared information about the role and status of women in society, and few theories or methods to guide research. Women's theories had been around for a long time but were destroyed, silenced, distorted, or coopted. When Rush (1972, with Oukrop & Ernset) formulated the initial study about the role of women in journalism education, for example, she borrowed and used as a guide a questionnaire developed by women sociologists, not knowing how to ask questions about inequality and discrimination. At that time, who cared or thought about asking such questions?

In the mid-1980s when Rush and coeditor, Donna Allen, the founder of *Media Report to Women* and the Women's Institute for Freedom of the Press, were trying to bring together written voices for *Communications at the Crossroads: The Gender Gap Connection* (1989), feminist theories were in their formative stages, especially in communication. In the early 1990s, a female reviewer pointed to a need for more feminist theory in *Crossroads.* This statement indicates the tremendous progress made from those initial descriptive studies and beginning publications about women's issues in the late 1960s and early 1970s to the 1990s, when feminist theories and research were abundant enough to notice that they were largely conspicuous by their absence.

Nearly every book dealing with feminist research and theory defines *women, feminist, feminism,* and *gender.* Sheryl Bowen and Nancy Wyatt (1993)—and most other authors—suggested that there is no precise definition of *feminism* or *feminist* because by nature these concepts resist definitive statements (p. 2). Bowen and Wyatt noted that there are a number of statements that might ease the understanding, such as feminism is concerned with women's lives, theories about humans; the nature of knowledge; the way in which knowledge is generated and legitimated; the "canon" of traditional knowledge; and process and connection (pp. 2–6).

Perhaps the idea of feminism is best portrayed by *Ms.* Magazine's (1994) special anniversary issue and cover story collage of pictures of women with the title "Fifty Ways to be a Feminist." In the lead story—50 pictured women with short biographical sketches— *Ms.* noted:

> The beauty of this movement of ours is that it's so fluid—ever moving, evolving, growing. We are all changemakers seeking to make a better world. Every one of us is both leader and follower. There is so much good work being done. It seems only fitting that we celebrate the spirit of our movement in this twenty-second anniversary issue. On the following pages, you'll find a few old friends and others who may not be as familiar. We know that you know this doesn't even begin to scratch the surface here in the U.S. And then there are so many women the world over doing the work. If we devoted every page of every issue for the next 22 years to describing the many ways you are putting feminism into practice, we still wouldn't come close to covering it all. Here's to our movement! (p. 33).

For our purposes, *feminists* and *feminism* are terms that denote intellectual inquiry, praxis, and advocacy about women's issues.

The "Pennings" of Wild Women

As the 21st century approaches, hundreds upon thousands of feminist voices and writings have surfaced. The problem now goes beyond definitional and theoretical distinctions to the infrequency that such "wild women" writings appear in mainstream (malestream) publications, whether popular or scholarly. Feminist theories and research are often isolated, indeed segregated, in women's or alternative publications such as *Women's Studies in Communication* or *Z Magazine* and used primarily in women's studies courses or specialized courses having to do with the civil rights of particular groups, including women.

Indeed, as late as the early 1980s when Rush and Allen decided to write a book about women and communications, most publishers flatly stated that there was no market. To explore that notion in a more rigorous manner Rush and Allen sent a two-page book prospectus to 40 major publishing houses, including some affiliated with universities. Five editors were interested enough to seek an introductory chapter and book outline. Of the five, all but one were women, and one edited a women's series. One of the finest letters of rejection came from an associate editor of a major publishing house. She wrote:

> Thank you for giving me the opportunity to review the materials for *Communications at the Crossroads: The Gender Gap Connection*. While I remain enthusiastic about the idea of a volume that addresses these issues, I have several reservations about the proposal you sent me.

> The first is, quite frankly, that the tone is too activist for our current publishing program. While I am very sorry that I have to make such a statement, I feel it is best to be honest

with you from the start. *It would be impossible for me to get this proposal approved by our publications board* [italics added].

While I would be the first to deny that any research is value-free, there is a strong sentiment here that activist feminism is out of place in the social sciences when one is discussing research. Social science research can be applied to feminist issues and concerns (for example, we publish books dealing with policy issues that affect women), but our position is that feminist issues should not define the ways in which social science research is conducted, nor should activist positions determine the content of our books. While I personally disagree with this stand (and am doing my best to change it), I am nevertheless in the position of having to support it . . .

I hope that despite my negative reaction to the idea of ————————— publishing the collection my comments are helpful, and I would be happy to reconsider it if you are willing to take a less activist stand (in all honesty, I hope you won't!). . . .

Rush and Allen described this experience in *Crossroads'* preface, explaining that this was how women's voices were silenced, and how changing *that* was the revolution.

Studying entries for "women's/gender studies" in *Communication Abstracts* from 1983 to 1992, Kathryn Cirksena (in press) found a relatively small percentage increase over the 10-year period. Even in 1990, the year in which the largest number of entries was found, just 9% of *all* abstracts fell into the gender/women category. From 1991 to 1992, a decrease of 2% in the total number of entries was found. Cirksena pointed out that one factor artificially inflating the 1990 percentage was the inclusion that year of abstracts from three edited volumes of feminist communication scholarship: more than twenty of the one hundred thirty-six 1990 abstracts were chapters from those books. Cirksena wrote that:

> while some renditions of the development of communication studies in these years would attribute undue influence to feminist critiques and reworkings and others would hope to claim that feminist ideas have received increasingly wide discussion and use, the volume of work found in this analysis does not suggest that either is occurring. The pervasiveness of feminist re/formations of communication is not a claim that can be supported by this data.

Thus, even when feminist theory and research is conceived, researched, written, and published, getting it into the traditional academic curriculum through mainstream scholarship journals and books remains an obstacle. The traditional members of faculties and editorial boards of scholarly publications are conspicuous by their *presence*. As Dale Spender (1983) wrote, "while both sexes may have been making theories for as far back as we can trace, only one sex is seen as the theorists, one sex has its theories accepted as legitimate, only one sex owns the realm of theory" (p. 1).

Feminist theologian Elizabeth Dodson Gray wrote that *Patriarchy As a Conceptual Trap* (1982) "is to the thought world of the mind what the astronomers' black holes are to the universe. Once inside, there seems to be no way of getting out or seeing out. A conceptual trap is a way of thinking that is like a room which—once inside—you cannot image a world outside" (1982, p. 17).

Indeed, as Rush was working with a returning female doctoral student enrolled in an independent summmer study course to catch her up on several years of communication theory, special effort and time was taken for her to consult with professors who taught theory courses, all of whom were male, about what readings they recommended for inclusion. Her reading list reflected this consultation. It was not until a mid-course meeting that it was realized that she did not have one reading about feminist theory. Both professor and student were caught in that "black hole." This was all the more conspicuous since the student's dissertation topic concerned women at risk.

FEMINIST THEORY: A MULTISPLENDORED CHORUS

Feminist theory and research as a scholarship field is nearly beyond a summary chapter like this because women speak with many voices. There are, for example, lesbian feminists, environmental feminists, ecofeminists, postmodern feminists, third world feminists, womanists, and so on. And each group has its own standpoint perspective with various perspectives within that group.

Feminist Methods in Social Research author Shulamit Reinharz (1992) concludes that feminism is a perspective, not a method.[4] "The fact that there are multiple definitions of feminism means that there are multiple feminist perspectives on social research methods. One shared radical tenet underlying feminist research is that women's lives are important" (p. 241). Reinharz's concluding chapter offers a "meta-induction, i.e., an inductive definition of feminist methodology that arises from the collection of the previous chapters, just as each chapter offered an inductive analysis of a particular method" (p. 240). Using this approach, she identified ten themes:

1. Feminism is a perspective, not a research method.
2. Feminists use a multiplicity of research methods.
3. Feminist research involves an ongoing criticism of nonfeminist scholarship.
4. Feminist research is guided by feminist theory.
5. Feminist research may be transdisciplinary.
6. Feminist research aims to create social change.
7. Feminist research strives to represent human diversity.
8. Feminist research frequently includes the researcher as a person.
9. Feminist research frequently attempts to develop special relations with the people—studied (in interactive research).
10. Feminist research frequently defines a special relation with the reader. (p. 240)

Feminism, looked at as a philosophy of being, thinking, and knowing, is often conceptualized as a quilt with many different colors, textures, and patterns. Many writers, male and female, use the patchwork quilt symbolism to indicate the presence of many perspectives which fit under an umbrella framework, such as feminists of all persuasions fitting under a women's worldview perspective. These feminist quilt

---

[4]This was arrived at after delineating interview research, enthnography, survey research and other statistical research formats, experimental research, cross-cultural research, oral history, content analysis, case studies, action research, multiple methods research, all through chapter-length feminist prisms, including a chapter on original feminist research methods.

pieces are traditionally classified as liberal feminism, Marxist feminism, radical feminism, socialist feminism, existentialist feminism, psychoanalytic feminism, and cultural feminism. Each undertakes the explanation of women's oppression by focusing on different aspects of culture (i.e., laws, production, class, race, psychological development, and so on).

Karen Warren (1993) used the "boundaries of a quilt or collage" to describe what she calls *boundary conditions* of a feminist ethic. Warren writes that the boundaries "delimit the territory of the piece without dictating what the interior, the design, the actual pattern of the piece looks like. Because the actual design of the quilt emerges from the multiplicity of voices of women in a cross-cultural context, the design will change over time. It is not something static" (p. 331).

The feminist theory perspectives frequently used —the quilt designs we now often recognize—are briefly summarized here. For example, *liberal feminist theory* (e.g., Friedan, 1974; Rossi, 1792/1975; Wollstonecraft, 1975) is developed out of liberal political philosophy, arguing that through legal and political avenues of the mainstream, women can change laws and politics and therefore achieve gender justice. *Marxist feminists* (e.g., Holmstrom, 1982; Landes, 1977; Malos, 1980) focus on class division as the major factor in women's oppression, paying attention to the intersections between women's work and women's self perception. Their prescription for change centers on providing economic rewards for women's domestic production in the home.

Radical feminists (e.g., Daly, 1973, 1978; Frye, 1983; Hoagland, 1988) describe women's oppression as being grounded in reproduction, mothering, gender, and sexuality. They call for women to absent themselves emotionally and sexually from men so they may realize their full and whole selves as women. *Psychoanalytic feminists* (e.g., Belenky, Clinchy, Goldberger, & Tarule, 1986; Chodorow, 1978; Gilligan, 1993) theorize that women's nature is not biologically determined, but socially constructed. *Socialist feminism* (e.g., Jaggar, 1983; Young, 1980) combines Marxist, radical, and psychoanalytic feminist theories to study women's oppression, arguing that it is important to pay attention to both class and gender when studying women's oppression.

Recent feminist theorizing that combines many of the former mentioned theoretical frameworks includes postmodern, existential, women of color, and cultural feminists. Women of color (e.g., Anzaldua, 1990; Hill-Collins, 1990; hooks, 1984) and postmodern feminists (e.g., Radway, 1984; Theriot, 1990) have made visible the positive aspects of woman as "other." They argue the condition of otherness enables woman to stand back and criticize the norms, values, and practices that the dominant culture seeks to impose on everyone. These theorists, along with cultural feminists reveal that otherness, for all its associations with oppression and inferiority, is much more than an oppressed, inferior condition. Rather, it is a way of being, thinking, and speaking that allows for opennesss, plurality, diversity, and difference. In short, these more recent feminist theories offer an opportunity to explain the complexity and diversity of women's lives, not just the oppression they experience or the collusion in which they sometimes participate.

It should not escape the reader's attention that this chapter primarily reflects the work of white women, complete with attitudes, biases, and class and racial blindness forced by "White privilege." bell hooks (1994) spoke directly to this point in discussing Katie Riophe's *The Morning After*: "The book disturbs precisely because it erases the voices and thoughts of women of color" (p. 43). "Had she acknowledged the range of dissenting voices within feminism, the multi-dimensional critiques that already exist, the underlying premise of her book would have lost its bite" (p. 43). She explained:

> Visions of solidarity between women became more complex. Suddenly, neither the experiences of materially privileged groups of white females nor the category of "woman" (often used to refer to white women's experiences) could be evoked without some contestation, without white supremacy looming as the political ground of such assertions. These changes strengthened the power of feminist thought and feminist movement politically. They compelled feminist thinkers to problematize and theorize issues of solidarity, to recognize the interconnectedness of structures of domination . . . and build a more inclusive movement. That work now risks being undone and undermined by some of the current feminist writing by young white privileged women who strive to create a narrative of feminism (not a feminist movement) that denies race or class differences. (p. 42)

Crossroads was cited for being organized around the relation between gender and communications, rather than a multifaceted view of the individual that also includes at least culture, race, and class (Riano, 1994). This point is generally well taken, given the coeditors' standpoints at that time.[5] As Reinharz (1992) noted: "At first, the very act of discovering sexism in scholarship was revolutiontary. . . . It was radical simply to study women" (p. 11).

HISTORIES, HERSTORIES, MYTHSTORIES: THE COMMUNICATIONS QUILT

Contributions to the communication discipline by feminist thinking are extensive. Theories of feminism and feminist research have provided communication scholars insight about how the scientific model has figuratively and literally paled through comparison with other frameworks which indicate sexist, racist, homophobic, classist social projects (Harding, 1991). Through three decades of current feminist scholarship, we have learned that women's communication, along with minorities of both gender, have been "othered" or silenced in mainstream research. Gender theories and feminist research in communication have helped to reveal that we must be mindful in future research of actively refusing to continue the silencing, drawing out instead and making visible those who have been silenced, revealing their voices in social and historical context.

Lana Rakow (1986) argues that in the early stages of integrating feminism and communication, two major research foci predominated: sex differences and gender studies. Leslie Steeves (1988) delineated three approaches to feminist scholarship in

---

[5]It should be at least footnoted that the authors contributed informational perspectives to *Crossroads* not often found in early U.S. books on women and communications, such as women of color press; alternative communication for Latin American and Caribbean women; international groups, women, and media; international women's networks; women and Norwegian media.

speech, media, and literary studies in the United States: liberal, radical, and socialist. She explained that each branch of feminism makes different assumptions about the role of the media and the function of communication in society.[6]

Kathryn Carter and Carole Spitzack (1989) examined problematics of feminism and social science, theoretics of feminism and communication studies, and methods for studying women's communications. Their introductory comments about the difficulties faced by feminist scholars is as important reading now as it was in 1989.

Kathryn Cirksena and Lisa Cuklanz (1992) examined five feminist frameworks for communication studies—liberal feminism (reason and emotion), socialist-feminism (public and private), radical feminism (nature and culture), psychoanalytic feminism (subject and object), and cultural feminism (mind and body). They also looked at feminist critiques of communication research methods, as well as discussing whether the set of oppositional dualisms which are the central organizing principle for much of Western thought is necessary. They noted:

> In general, feminist approaches to history, literature, and communication focus on or emphasize three primary elements. First, they elucidate the constructed nature of knowledge, seeking to elaborate the ways in which knowledge depends on factors such as habit, language use, perspective, and personal experience. Second, feminist work argues that what has traditionally been considered the personal or private constitute valid areas for scholarship. Third, they point out and discuss perspective, both within text and audiences, and among scholars themselves. Feminist work in the humanities has most recently focused on the contingent nature of knowledge. The phrase "standpoint epistemology" has become a central notion in feminist work in these fields, because it refers to both the importance of perspective and experience to conceptions of truth and to the existence of differing concepts of knowledge for people of differing experiences. (p. 40)

Bowen and Wyatt (1993) edited a volume about feminist approaches that was envisioned as supplementary reading for any course in speech communication where "very few courses . . . incorporate either feminist readings or feminist principle or practices" (p. ix). They noted that:

> Feminism advocates interdisciplinary study by breaking down artificial barriers between areas of scholarship. We had to decide whether to live up to our principles by spanning boundaries and creating new areas for communication study based on feminist perspectives or whether we should limit ourselves in this initial effort to the critique of traditional areas of study within the relatively amorphous discipline called speech communication. Meeting as a group of authors, we decided that our primary goal was to reach the widest possible audience that could be achieved most easily by working within familiar areas of scholarship, providing critiques and correctives to the traditional scholarship that has historically excluded women's and minority concerns and perspectives. By detailing the distortions within traditional areas of our discipline, we could position ourselves to argue for new definitions and new connections among the disparate areas of our discipline. (p. vii)

---

[6]See Bowen & Wyatt (1993) for a distillation of Steeves' work.

Bowen and Wyatt's book explored the role of feminist scholarship in interpersonal, small group, organizational, mass communication, and intercultural communications as well as theatre studies and rhetorical criticism. Many of the feminist critiques in Bowen and Wyatt about traditional research groupings are briefly summarized in Rakow (1992):

> In media studies, feminist scholars have moved past initial work on women's images in content and women's employment in industries to more complex questions that make it impossible to separate study of the media from all other communication contexts. An interesting example is provided by Rosalind Coward's book, *Female Desires* (Coward 1985). Coward starts with how [White] women feel about themselves—their guilt, their pleasures, their obsessions, their contradictions—and connects these feelings to media content about fashion, beauty, the body, and the ideal home. Her work, while deficient because of its inattention to race, does show the way to understanding the interconnections of our personal lives and the ideology of media content. Cheris Kramarae's collection on technology and women's talk (Kramarae 1988) shows other interconnections previously invisible to those in the field. The organization of household, domestic, and office work involving technologies such as the washing machine, sewing machine, typewriter, and telephone have affected women's interactions with other women and their confinement to the private sphere or low-paying jobs. (p. 12)

Important and oft-used and -cited contributions to women in the mass media are included in Pam Creedon's (1989, 1993) work on the topic. She also edited an important variation of this theme concerning sports, the media, and women (1993). The current "mother of mass communication" is Margaret Gallagher's international account of *Unequal Opportunities: The Case of Women and the Media* (1981).

Liesbet van Zoonen (1994) contemplated using the typical liberal, radical, socialist feminism classifications in *Feminist Media Studies*, but was dissuaded because of the many *-isms* or standpoints emanating from current feminist literature. Instead, she begins by outlining her position on feminism (including gender and power) and cultural studies followed by identification of feminist themes in communication studies, such as stereotypes and socialization, pornography, and ideology. van Zoonen goes on to examine key questions posed by a gendered approach within communication and cultural studies, including theories of transmission, representation, construction and discourse; structures of media organization and production; interpreting media representation through content analysis and semiotics; contradictions of the gendered image as spectacle; new approaches to understanding the audience and the politics of media reception; the potential of feminist and interpretative research strategies.

In concluding van Zoonen noted that:

> It would be my assertion when assessing the relevance of (studying) media and popular culture for feminist concerns, that one should distinguish at least between the different struggles feminism is involved in. As a social movement it has the double edge of being an interest group lobbying and struggling for social and legal changes beneficial to women and of challenging cultural preoccupations and routines concerning femininity and gender. Undeniably, both struggles are political and inform each other, nevertheless, they

are of a different kind resulting in different interactions with the media and different requirements of media performance. (pp. 151–152)

Cirksena (in press) wrote that overview critiques of communication from a feminist perspective that attempt to define a feminist paradigm converge on the following five points: (a) communication studies should foreground and make explicit the inequitable power dimensions of gender relations in all human communication; (b) communication studies should "put women at the center" of research; (c) scholarship should not attempt to abstract gender from other aspects of identity, especially, but not be limited to identity based on race and class; (d) it should be "action-oriented"—part of the research should be linked to improving the status of women; and, (e) the "researched" (those people at the center of the investigation) should have some input into the framing of the issues and the research process.

Rush (in press) attempts a boundary-spanning, holistic approach. She suggested the following "10 Tenets of Deeper Communications" to transform theory and research:

1. A theory and its research will be ecologically based, inclusive and, thus, diverse.
2. A theory and its research will go beyond dualistic thinking and action.
3. A theory and its research must basically be concerned about human spirituality and sexuality—sometimes interchangeably, often interactively.
4. A theory and its research will be healing and liberatory.
5. A theory will employ realistic frameworks and will not be disregarded or discounted if it supports social action research.
6. A theory and its research will assess the traditional mass media, in their current corporate state, as demographic investigators and reporters of "who we are."
7. The alternative media will be included in a theory and its research as scenario servers for the strategic role they assume.
8. A theory and its research will emphasize peace, equality, and justice as dynamic growth forces through peace education and the processes of conflict resolution, especially mediation.
9. Envisionary media are possible when theory and research include both destructive and constructive roles and functions of communications.
10. A theory and its research will have a global civil society worldview with concern and respect for the integration of, through proactive and interactive communication and information with, its citizenry.

THE GREENING OF COMMUNICATION, AS IF ALL SPECIES MATTERED

A promising direction in the search to "integrate viewpoints, improve inclusivity, and promote solidarity" is *ecofeminism*. "Ecofeminists claim that environmental issues are feminist issues because it is women and children who are the first to suffer the consequences of injustice and environmental destruction" (Gaard & Gruen, 1993, p. 11). According to Gaard and Gruen, "ecofeminists believe that the current global crises are the result of the mutually reinforcing ideologies of racism, sexism, classism, imperialism, naturism, and speciesism" (p. 25). Ecofeminist theory is theory in process built on community-based knowing and valuing; the strength of this knowledge is dependent on the inclusivity, flexibility, and reflexivity of the community in which it is generated. Further, ecofeminist theory grows out of dialogue and focuses on reaching consensus (pp. 32-33). "Ecofeminists are developing a 'multi-systems' approach to understanding the interconnected forces that operate to oppress women and the natural world" (p. 25).

Karen Warren wrote that "What *all* ecofeminists agree about, then, is the way in which the *logic of domination* functioned historically within patriarchy to sustain and justify the twin dominations of women and nature" (p. 324). Further:

> Ecofeminists insist that the sort of logical of domination used to justify the domination of humans by gender, racial or ethnic, or class status is also used to justify the domination of nature. Because eliminating a logic of domination is part of a feminist critique—whether a critique of patriarchy, white supremacist culture, or imperialism—ecofeminists insist that *naturism* is properly viewed as an integral part of any feminist solidarity movement to end sexist oppression and the logic of domination which conceptually grounds it. . . . It is by clarifying this conceptual connection between systems of oppression that a movement to end sexist oppression—traditionally the special turf of feminist theory and practice—leads to a reconceiving of feminism *as a movement to end all forms of oppression.* (pp. 325–326)

And she continued later:

> Ecofeminism is quintessentially antinaturist. Its antinaturism consists in the rejection of any way of thinking about or acting toward nonhuman nature that reflects a logic, values, or attitude of domination. Its antinaturist, antisexist, antiracist, and anticlassist (and so forth, for all other "ism" of social domination) stance forms the outer boundary of the quilt: nothing gets on the quilt which is naturist, sexist, racist, classist, and so forth. (p. 333)

Another part of the feminist ethic quilt, Warren noted, is a *contextualist* ethic: "Like any collage or mosaic, the point is not to have one picture based on a unity of voices, but a *pattern* that emerges out of the very different voices of people located in different circumstances . . . [a] central place for the voices of women" (p. 332).

Warren delineated other factors of a feminist ethic quilt. She noted that structural pluralism rather than a unitary or reductionistic perspective rejects the assumption of "one voice." A feminist ethic reconceives theory as theory in process that will change over time. A feminist ethic is more inclusive of the felt experiences and perspectives of oppressed persons. A feminist ethic makes no attempt to provide an "objective" point of view, because it assumes that in contemporary culture there really is no such point of view. A feminist ethic provides a central place for values typically unnoticed, underplayed, or misrepresented in traditional ethics (e.g., values of care, love, friends, and appropriate trust). And a feminist ethic offers a reconception of what it is to be human, what it is for humans to engage in ethical decision-making, rejecting any gender-free or gender-neutral description of *human*, *ethics*, and *ethical decison-making* (pp. 332–333).

Rush worked on a concept known as *global eco-communications* (1989b, 1992, in press), or the global ecology of communications. She defines *global* with at least two meanings. One is the traditional definition of international or intercultural, which has messages, data, or people going across or through some kind of barriers, boundaries or constraints, whether it is the encoding–decoding process from one human being to another, or the artificial borders between nation-states. The other *global* defines issues that are common enough to any group(s) of people in that they share similar problems or meanings. Such global issues often transcend traditional boundaries.

As Rush (1989, pp. 2–4) noted:

Eco-communications as used here stands for the ecology of communications and information—the mutual communicative and informative relations between humans as a species, and their environment. Eco-communications is seen as an integrative, realistic networking force between humans and their concern for the inclusion and well-being of other planetary species' information and communication systems.

Further:

The process of human eco-communications as envisioned and when fully operative in a community will help people to secure important and relational places in a changing, ongoing society, challenging and enhancing their unique contributions. A truly integrative eco-communications system, in application, provides a map of communication and information flows and gaps, and continually works to improve delivery methods, channels, and content for filling the lacunae. It is what this author has elsewhere called a flow-keeping agenda.

Ostensibly, this book is about the integration of theory and research, and this chapter is primarily about the integration of gender and communication (see van Zoonen's, 1994, discussion on feminism's common concepts and unconditional focus on *gender*) Women have taken their careers, their time, their money, their initiatives to bring forth a new knowledge, a new literature—not just now, but many times throughout herstory. Women have been criticized and suffered greatly to advance and enhance their fields of scholarship. It matters little what the scholarship is named or called, but it matters a lot that it is not often included in its current and immense variety and depth: *The academic discipline of communications, because of its potential centrality and mediation in the flow of societal issues, especially needs the benefit of all its scholarship.* The scholarship is needed because of, not in spite of, its drive toward inclusiveness, diversity, and equality.

It seems rather nonsensical to try to integrate theory and research if large parts of it are missing, distorted, or coopted. Such vacuous exclusivity seems analogous to one hand clapping—and perhaps that is about all that needs to be said in favor of the "greening" rather than the "browning" (as in, withering away) of communication scholarship. The greening of communication scholarship means that it is capable of sustaining itself and its scholars in a genotypic—species-centered—community rather than a dying field in the Age of Phenotypes—individual-centered (e.g., Hazel Henderson, 1989). Interestingly, David Orr (1992) provided an environmental focus for 11 academic disciplines, but journalism and communication are not among them (pp. 135-136). Perhaps this should instruct those of us in a discipline conspicous by its absence: The greening, including feminism, of communications is a seemingly *big* "window of opportunity."

In a larger sense, the greening of communications could be important to the survival, sustenance, and enhancement of all global life and that, it seems, should be the focal concern which captures our humanoid (nearly human) imagination, energy, and efforts.[7]

RESEARCH: RECYCLED, NEW, AND AN EXAMPLE

It should be clear that feminist theory and research, like other forms of inquiry, is as varied as those studying it. Shulamit Reinharz (1992) displays a whole range of feminist methods in social research, including traditional methods of research such as survey, experimental, and case studies, as well as original feminist research methods. Feminist research methods are often "feminist-enhanced" in that, as Reinharz noted, the "use of the term 'original' does not signify a method never considered or used prior to the instance discussed here. Rather, it reflects the researcher's effort to create a new approach that met her feminist criteria" (p. 215). Such new methods included consciousness-raising, creating group diaries, drama, genealogy and network tracing, the nonauthoritative research voice or multiple-person stream-of-consciousness narrative, conversation, using intuition or writing associatively, identification, studying unplanned personal experience, structured conceptualization, photography or the talking-pictures techniques, speaking freely into a tape recorder or answering long, essay-type questionnaires.

Reinharz wrote that most feminist researchers who develop original methods do not argue that these methods meet the norms of science "Rather, they ignore the debate about science and strive to find methods that fit their definition of feminism" (p. 238).[8] Perhaps it should be noted here and sprinkled generously throughout this chapter, however, that finding or creating methods suited to feminist ideology is no different in principle than creating conventional science methods to suit a positivist ideology (Wood, 1994). The difference is in the eye of the beholder and beholden when dominant paradigms assure standpoint dependency.

---

[7]Ralph Waldo Emerson said something to the effect that when you travel, do not carry your ruins with you. One of the female graduate students who proofread this chapter provided a smiling face insertion/rejoiner, a quote by Mark Twain, to continue the idea: "Travel is fatal to prejudice, bigotry, and narrow-mindedness."

[8]In "Some Final Thoughts" about original feminist research methods, as the chapter is titled, Reinharz wrote:

Not all feminist social research is innovative with regard to method. In fact, some feminist scholars regard methodological innovation as counterproductive because only studies conducted according to "rigorous" scientific procedures will convince the skeptics. For those who do not share this concern, however, feminism typically leads to the study of new topics that require or allow new forms of study. For these people, the feminist spirit is one of breaking free, including breaking free of methodological traditions.

One of the many ways the women's movement has benefitted women is in freeing up our creativity in the realm of research. And one of the ways feminist researchers, in turn, have benefitted the societies in which we live is by the spirit of innovation. Although I have listed several types of "original" research and writing, there is room for many more. *As feminists gain greater control of publishing opportunities and academic positions, we will undoubtedly see evidence of more of these* (italics added; pp. 238–39).

Autumn Grubb-Swetnam's dissertation's interpretion of women's use of fashion and beauty magazines (1994) serves as a communication research example. In her introduction, she wrote:

> As women, we stand in grocery store lines where magazines beckon us with promises of "thin thighs in thirty days," "meals in a minute," "supermom sagas," and "make your man melt tonight." As we sweat and grunt at the spa, lithe feminine bodies in slick magazine spreads look on. As we sit waiting in doctors' and dentists' offices, these mass-mediated messages entice us to pick them up, promising the secrets to feminine happiness. In middle-and upper-class adolescent female bedrooms and mothers' kitchens, living rooms or sewing rooms, these magazines lie about the place, accessories to the well-decorated home. In school libraries and in female dorm rooms, these magazines become interspersed among academic textbooks and journals. (p. 1)

She noted that the purpose of her research was to apply a feminist interpretive approach to study women's use of mass communication and popular culture. Explication of magazine use was limited to Euro-American and African-American heterosexuals, lesbians, and bisexuals to provide insights into understanding how race, class, gender, and sexuality are experienced by women when they negotiate and interpret mass-mediated images. The second part of her purpose involved *praxis*: to provide understanding about women's use and intepretation of mass mediated images "so that we may be mindful of our media choices" (p. 2).

To ground her research initially, Grubb-Swetnam chronicled the historical evolution of women's magazines in American culture and discussed nuances of the editorial content in women's magazines. In another chapter, she delineated feminist cultural studies approaches to examining women's use of the media, evolution and types of standpoint epistemologies, and research questions pertinent to the study.

In the method chapter, Grubb-Swetnam explained that her relying on the standpoint of women was a methodological choice. She described the general characteristics of the sample, the interview locations and structure, her assumptions approaching the data, and the process of data analysis. Grubb-Swetnam discussed problems she encountered in the elicitation of working class, poor, African-American and lesbian perspectives. Further, she paid particular attention to how traditional methods of data collection limit and restrain the researcher attempting to document women's voices—the other in relation to White, middle-class heterosexual women.

The analysis section of the dissertation provides the reader with information about the individual women that participated in the study, the ways they used magazines, how they defined and described the magazines, and their general criticisms of magazines. She also discussed the women's talk about their bodies in relation to magazine use, and the perspective of the outsider-within as it relates to magazine use.

The magazines in the study included *Cosmopolitan, Ladies' Home Journal, Redbook, Good Housekeeping, Elle, Mademoiselle, Family Circle, Woman's Day, Upscale, Deneuve, Vogue, Essence, Glamour, McCall's, Self,* and *Working Mother.*

Feminist *Praxis* in Research

This section explains how feminist theory and *praxis* (practical application) is integrated into the research process. Earlier, Rush noted specific themes that exist in feminist research, as defined by Reinharz. Five of those themes are addressed in this section.

Theme 1: Feminist research strives to represent human diversity. Typically, traditional sample techniques have been shown to generate a majority of Euro-American, middle-class respondents (Cannon, Higginbotham, & Leung, 1991). This claim is supported in mass communication research generated in the 1970s when academicians studied commercial television's attempts at ascertainment information. These studies found that, typically, White middle-class males were the majority of ascertainment respondents, revealing that researchers do not often gather a diverse population in their sample due to sampling techniques. The techniques did not assure that diverse communities would be accessed, because they were not socially ordered—nor did they utilize the same social structures—as White, middle-class communities (e.g., Heller, 1977; Leroy & Ungurait, 1975; Walker & Rudelius, 1976).

To decrease this tendency, snowball sampling technique (a sampling technique in which respondents are asked to identify other respondents) was used to increase sample diversity. Andrea Press (1991) defended the technique as effective in building samples when respondents are needed from particular social groups. The study on women's magazine use required both African- and Euro-American women of heterosexual, lesbian, and bisexual standpoints as well as from a variety of economic classes. The snowball sampling technique collected diverse voices in the data. To generate the core group of female respondents, electronic mail discussion lists were used. The women who responded were then asked to inform their friends, families, and coworkers about the research. If the women they told seemed interested in participating in the research, they were given a phone number for contact. The snowball sampling that occurred with the core group of women (through word of mouth) secured the majority of African-American respondents, lesbian respondents, and working-class respondents. Because of this sample, the analyses reflected the variety—and sometimes contradictory ways—women use, interpret, and negotiate media messages aimed at them. The diverse sample provided data that made visible the complex ways in which women consume and make sense of media messages.

Theme 2: Feminist research includes the researcher as a person. Theme 3: Feminist research frequently attempts to develop special relations with the people studied. Themes 2 and 3 are incorporated in the discussion of how they were integrated into the research. This section will provide specific examples of how Grubb-Swetnam intertwined themes 2 and 3 into the research process and in writing.

In-depth interviews generated data about the women's lived experience with women's magazines. During these in-depth interviews, stories that were similar to those told by respondents were shared when appropriate by Grubb-Swetnam. Because the questions were open-ended, respondents sometimes seemed unsure about question meanings. At those times, a personal story was provided as an example response to the question. Jenny Nelson (1989) supported this interviewing technique:

> In my own research, I have discovered that disclosure on my part can open the entire interview situation to more explicit descriptions on the part of my co-researchers. When I tell a story, this can help to elicit a story from the other person. The stories may not be

similar (in fact, they often express variations), and my input provides the respondent with a comfortable format by which she can relate her story. (p. 228)

Nelson believed that this interviewing technique minimizes the "perceived authority of the interviewer, and promotes an intersubjective, conversation style to the situation" (p. 228).

Another way Grubb-Swetnam integrated herself into the research process and writing was to illuminate clearly for the respondents and the reader the researcher's personal experiences and knowledge about women's magazines. In the methods chapter section titled *Approaching the Data*, for example, Grubb-Swetnam wrote:

In order to interpret the data, it is important the reader be aware of three assumptions I make. First, I make the assumption that a variety of interpretive (Lindlof, 1988) or epistemological communities exist within the sample. Approaching the data with this assumption allows me to be sensitive to the similarities and differences in women's magazine use. It also affords me the opportunity to explicate the variety of interpretive communities.

Another assumption I hold is that race, class, gender, and sexuality are not simply individual differences but function as sites of experiencing and generating oppression, as well as pleasure, resistance, and creativity. I also believe that these facets of the self interact with one another in an organic fashion, driven by the particular context of each women's life. With this assumption I approach the data for indications of women's magazine use that explicate these sites of oppression, as well as reveal women's enjoyment, resistance and creativity in magazine use.

A third assumption I use when approaching the data is that I have used women's magazines in the past and am familiar with their contents. This will assist me when analyzing data to understand the terminologies the women use to describe particular types of stories, articles, advice columns, or advertisements. These statements about the assumptions I hold when approaching the data are meant to help the reader understand my standpoint in this research. (pp. 78–79)

Grubb-Swetnam also acknowledged her presence in the research process within the analysis section. She did this to help readers make sense of what the women were saying about their magazine use, as well as validate their experiences with magazines. For example, in one of the analysis chapters, after providing the reader with several respondent quotations about negotiating mediated images of feminity that described internal struggle, She wrote:

I am intimately familiar with Libby's struggle with the mediated images of appropriate femininity. In 1992, I wrote in my journal about my negotiation and struggle between self and mediated cultural norms. A portion of this journal entry was: I have come to realize in myself that I could not and did not begin to generate (let alone hear) my original thought and voice until I accepted my natural, wild beauty. Until I quit putting chemicals on my hair and face; until I quit cinching my waist and chest into confining, uncomfortable clothing; until I quit hating myself as an imperfect commodity; until I explored that pain and gently laid it down I could not hear and know and believe in my original thought and voice. I could not breathe in whole breaths; could not see the background for the blinding, neon foreground; and could not move in freedom and grace as long as I accepted the commodity model for myself. Now that I know this, I must constantly recreate this knowing of self-acceptance that struggles against some unseen ideological circle that is maintained in our cultural systems. (pp. 167–168)

This conscious effort to maintain a connection to the reader and respondents by the researcher is one way Themes 2 and 3 were incorporated as feminist praxis in research.

Theme 4: Feminist research is guided by feminist theory. Generally, feminist theorists study, describe, and analyze issues impacting women's lives. This underlying assumption of the worth of women's lived experiences does not tend to be shared in traditional research goals. Specifically, Grubb-Swetnam's dissertation drew from feminist standpoint theorists such as Patricia Hill-Collins (1990), Gloria Anzaldua (1990), bell hooks (1984), and Liz Stanley and Sue Wise (1993). Standpoint theorists discuss the position of individuals in society who must function both in the mainstream and the margins. Explicating and analyzing the political and social positions marginalized individuals must juggle help to illuminate how a society acts out race, class, gender, and sexuality as social relations.

Feminist cultural and media audience theorists provided a second framework for the dissertation. Angela McRobbie (1991) and Janet Radway (1984) provided a theoretical understanding of women as active, complex media users.

Theme 5: Feminist research may be transdisciplinary. The feminist theorists who grounded and guided Grubb-Swetnam's study represent a variety of disciplines. Patricia Hill-Collins, sociology; Gloria Anzuldua and bell hooks, English and literature disciplines; Stanley and Wise, philosophy; Angela McRobbie, media and cultural studies; and Janice Radway, literary criticism. Investigating their theoretical writings, we find their work also represents a transdisciplinary approach that includes Marxism, psychology, semiotics and theology. This trandisciplinary approach allows for new opportunities in communication research. Rakow (1992) posits a cross-discipline approach evident in feminist theories offers an ability to ask new research questions. Additionally, she argued:

Feminist scholarship is essential because it will help transcend the traditional, theoretical boundaries between domains of communication research such as socio-linguistics, speech communication, interpersonal, organizational, and mass communication which are currently informed by incompatible theories and methods. (p. 24)

Summary

In summary, the examples provided in this section have made visible how feminist praxis in the research process calls for an open acknowledgement of the positioning of the reseacher as a person engaged in the research process. Second, these examples made visible how feminist praxis in research strives to break down barriers of authority between the researcher and respondents, and attempts to incorporate ways for the respondents to be coresearchers. Finally, the examples provided in this section have made visible how feminist praxis strives to reveal humanity in all its complex diversity.

SELECTED BIBLIOGRAPHY

Allen, D. (n.d.). *Media without democracy and what to do about it.* (Available from Women's Institute for Freedom of the Press, 3306 Ross Place, NW, Washington, DC 20008)

Bannerji, H., Carty, L., Dehli, K., Heald, S., & McKenna, K. (1992). *Unsettling relations: The university as a site of feminist struggles.* Boston, MA: South End Press.

Beasley, M., & Gibbons, S. (1993). *Taking their place: A documentary history of women and journalism.* Washington, DC: American University Press.

Boulding, E. (1976). *The underside of history: A view of women through time.* Boulder, CO: Westview Press.

Bunch, C. (1987). *Passionate politics: Feminist theory in action.* New York: St. Martin's Press.

Carlsson, U. (Ed.). (1994). Women and the media *The Nordicom Review of Nordic Mass Communication Research 1.* [special issue].

Creedon, P. J. (Ed.) (1994). *Women, media, & sport: Challenging gender values.* Newbury Park, CA: Sage.

DuBois, E. C., Kelly, G. P., Kennedy, E. L., Korsmeyer, C. W., & Robinson, L. S. (1987). *Feminist scholarship: Kindling in the groves of academe.* Chicago: University of Illinois Press.

Einerson, M. J. (1994). *Female pre-adolescent intepretations of popular music experience: An interpersonal perspective.* Unpublished doctoral dissertation, Lexington, University of Kentucky.

French, M. (1992). *The War Against Women.* New York: Ballantine Books.

Gallagher, M. (1989). A feminist paradigm for communication research. In B. Dervin, L. Grossberg, B. J. O'Keefe, & E. Wartella (Eds.), *Rethinking Communication* (pp. 75-87). Newbury Park, CA: Sage.

Grossberg, L., Nelson, C., & Treichler, P. (Eds.). (1991). *Cultural studies.* New York: Routledge.

Griffin, G. B. (1992). *Calling: Essays on teaching in the mother tongue.* Pasadena, CA: Trilogy Books.

Haraway, D. J. (1991). *Simian, cyborgs, and women: The reinvention of nature.* New York: Routledge.

Henderson, H. (1991). *Paradigms in progress: Life beyond economics.* Indianapolis, IN: Knowledge Systems.

Henderson, H. (1969, Spring). Access to the media: A problem in democracy. *Columbia Journalism Review,* 5–8.

hooks b. (1992, July/August). Out of the academy and into the streets. *Ms. Magazine,* 80–82.

Kramarae, C., & Spender, D. (1992). *The knowledge explosion: Generations of feminist scholarship.* New York: Teachers College Press.

Miedzian, M. (1991). *Boys will be boys: Breaking the link between masculinity and violence.* New York: Doubleday.

Rush, R.R. (1989a). Communications at the crossroads: The gender gap connection. In R. Rush & D. Allen (Eds.), *Communications at the crossroads: The gender gap connection* (pp. 3–19). Norwood, NJ: Ablex Publishing Corporation

Rush, R. R. (1989b). From silent scream to silent scheme: The role of women in international communication. In G. Osborne and M. Madrigal (Eds.), *International communication: In whose interest?* (pp. 388–397). University of Canberra, Australia, Centre for Communication and Information Research.

Rush, R. R. (1993). Being all that we can be: Harassment, barriers prevent progress. *Journalism Educator,* 48, 71–79.

Rush, R. R., Buck, E., & Ogan, C. (1982, July–September). Women and the communications revolution: Can we get there from here? *Chasqui* publication of the Centro Internacional de Estudios Superiores de la Comunicacion para America Latina (CIESPAL), Quito, Ecuador.

Schumacher, E. F. (1973). *Small is beautiful: Economics as if people mattered.* New York: Harper & Row.

Stuart, M. (1989). Social change through human exchange: Listening moves people more than telling. In R. Rush & D. Allen. (Eds.), *Communications at the crossroads: The gender gap connection* (pp. 177-192). Norwood, NJ: Ablex.

Steeves, H. L. (1987). Feminist theories and media studies. *Critical Studies in Mass Communication, 4,* 95–135.

Steinem, G. (1992). *Revolution from within: A book of self-esteem.* Boston, MA: Little, Brown.

Steinem, G. (1994). *Moving beyond words.* New York: Simon and Schuster.

Tuchman, G., Daniels, A., & Benet, J. (1978). *Hearth & home: Images of women in the mass media.* New York: Oxford University Press.

Women's Action Coalition. (1993). *The facts about women.* New York: The New Press.

REFERENCES

Anzaldua, G. (Ed.). (1990). *Making face, making soul: Creative and critical perspectives of feminists of color.* San Francisco: Aunt Lute Books.

Anzaldua, G. (1990). La consciencia de la mestiza [The conscience of the Mestiza]: Towards a new consciousness. In G. Anzaldua (Ed.), *Making face, making soul: Creative and critical perspectives of feminists of color* (pp. 377–389). San Francisco: Aunt Lute Books.

Basow, S. A. (1992). *Gender: Stereotypes and roles* (3rd ed.). Pacific Grove, CA: Brooks/Cole.

Belenky, M. F., Clinchy, B. M., Goldberger, N. R., & Tarule, J. M. (1986). *Women's ways of knowing: The development of self, voice and mind.* New York: Basic Books.

Bowen, S., & Wyatt, N. (1993). *Transforming visions: Feminist critiques in communication studies.* Cresskill, NJ: Hampton Press.

Cannon, L. W., Higginbotham, E., & Leung, M. (1991). Race and class bias in qualitative research on women. In M. M. Fonow & J. A. Cook (Eds.), *Beyond methodology: Feminist scholarship as lived experience* (pp. 107–118). Bloomington: Indiana University Press.

Carter, K., & Spitzack C. (1989). *Doing research on women's communication: Perspectives on theory and method.* Norwood, NJ: Ablex.

Chodorow, N. (1978). *The politics of mothering.* Berkeley: University of California Press.

Cirksena, K. (in press). Resistance and circulation of feminist paradigms in communication studies. In D. Allen, R. R. Rush, & S. J. Kaufman (Eds.), *Women transforming communication.* Thousand Oaks, CA: Sage.

Cirksena, K., & Cuklanz, L. (1992). Male is to female as ———— is to ————: A guided tour of five feminist frameworks for communication studies. In L. Rakow (Ed.), *Women making meaning: New feminist directions in communications* (pp. 18–44). New York: Routledge.

Creedon, P. J. (Ed.). (1989). *Women in mass communication: Challenging gender values.* Newbury Park, CA: Sage.

Creedon, P .J. (Ed.). (1993). *Women in mass communication.* Newbury Park, CA: Sage.

Creedon, P. J. (Ed.). (1994). *Women, media, & sport: Challenging gender values.* Newbury Park, CA: Sage.

Daly, M. (1973). *Beyond God the father: Toward a philosophy of women's liberation.* Boston, MA: Beacon Press.

Daly, M. (1989). *Gyn/Ecology: The metaethics of radical feminism.* Boston: Beacon Press.

Eisler, R. (1987). *The chalice and the blade: Our history, our future.* New York: HarperCollins.

Friedan, B. (1974). *The feminine mystique.* New York: Dell.

Frye, M. (1983). *The politics of reality: Essays in feminist theory.* Freedom, CA: The Crossing Press.

Gaard, G., & Gruen, L. (1993). Ecofeminism: Toward global justice and planetary health. Feminism and Ecology issue. *Society and Nature: The International Journal of Political Ecology, 2,* 1–35.

Gallagher, M. (1981). *Unequal opportunities: The case of women and the media.* Paris: UNESCO.

Gilligan, C. (1993). *Meeting at the crossroads.* Cambridge, MA: Harvard University Press.

Gimbutas, M. (1989). *The Language of the goddess,* New York: Harper & Row.

Gray, E. D. (1982). *Patriarchy as a conceptual trap.* Wellesley, MA: Roundtable Press.

Griswold, W. F., & Swenson, J. D. (1991). The greening of the mass media: On the ethics of reporting environmental issues. In G. Bortynk (Ed.), *Earth ethics report* (pp. 313–319). Seminole, FL: The Journal of Earth Ethics Research Group.

Grubb-Swetnam, A. (1994). *Women's use, negotiation and interpretation of women's service, fashion and beauty magazines: Generating gynergetic tales through standpoint epistemology.* Unpublished doctoral dissertation, University of Kentucky.

Harding, S. (1991). *Whose science? Whose knowledge?* Ithaca, NY: Cornell University Press.

Heller, M. A. (1977). Problems in ascertainment procedures. *Journal of Broadcasting, 21,* 427–433.

Henderson, H. (1989). Eco-feminism and eco-communication: Toward the feminization of economics. In R. Rush & D. Allen (Eds.), *Communications at the crossroads: The gender gap connection* (pp. 289–304), Norwood, NJ: Ablex.

Hill-Collins, P. (1990). *Black feminist thought: Knowledge, consciousness, and the politics of empowerment.* New York: Routledge.

Hoagland, S. (1988). *Lesbian ethics: Toward new value.* Palo Alto, CA: Institute of Lesbian Studies.

Holmstrom, N. (1982). Women's work, the family and capitalism. *Science and Society, 42,* 186–211.

hooks, b. (1994, January). Sisters of the yam: Feminist opportunism. *Z Magazine,* 42–44.

hooks, b. (1984). *Feminist theory: From margin to center.* Boston, MA: South End Press.

Jaggar, A. (1983). *Feminist politics and human nature.* Totowa, NJ: Rowman & Allenheld.

Landes, J. (1977). Women, labor and family life: A theoretical perspective. *Science and Society, 41,* 386–409.

Leroy, D. L., & Ungurait, D. F. (1975). Ascertainment surveys: Problem perception and voluntary station contact. *Journal of Broadcasting, 19,* 23–30.

Malos, E. (Ed.) (1980). *The politics of housework.* London: Allison & Busby.

McRobbie, A. (1991). *Feminism and youth culture.* Boston: Unwin Hyman.

Ms. Magazine. (1994, July/August) 50 ways to be a feminist, 33–64.

Nelson, J. (1989). Phenomenology of feminist methodology: Explicating interviews. In K. Carter & C. Spitzack (Eds.), *Doing research on women's communication: Perspectives on theory and method* (pp. 221–241). Norwood, NJ: Ablex.

Orr, D. W. (1992). *Ecological literacy: Education and the transition to a postmodern world.* Albany: State University of New York.

Press, A. (1991). *Women watching television. Gender, class and generation in the American television experience.* Philadelphia: University of Pennsylvania Press.

Radway, J. (1984). *Reading the romance: Women, patriarchy and popular literature.* Chapel Hill: University of North Carolina Press.

Rakow, L. F. (1992). *Women making meaning: New feminist directions in communication.* New York: Routledge.

Rakow, L. F. (1986). Rethinking gender research in communication. *Journal of Communication, 36,* 11–26.

Reinharz, S. (1992). *Feminist methods in social research.* New York: Oxford University Press.

Riano, P. (Ed.). (1994). *Women in grassroots communication: Furthering social change.* Thousand Oaks, CA: Sage Publications.

Rossi, Alice S. (Ed.). (1970). *Essays on sex equality: John Stuart Mill & Harriet Taylor Mill.* Chicago: University of Chicago Press.

Rush, R. R. (1989, May). *Global eco-communications: Assessing the communication and information environment.* Paper presented to the International Communication Association, San Francisco.

Rush, R. R. (1992, August). *Global eco-communications: Grounding and refinding the concepts.* Paper presented to the International Association for Mass Communication Research, Guaruja, Brazil.

Rush, R. R. (in press). Ten tenets of deep communications: Transforming communication theory and research. In D. Allen, R. R. Rush, & S. J. Kaufman (Eds.), *Women transforming communications.* Thousand Oaks, CA: Sage.

Rush, R. R., Oukrop, C. E., & Ernst, S. W. (1972). *(More than you ever wanted to know) about women and journalism education.* Paper presented at the annual meeting of the Association for Education in Journalism, Southern Illinois University, Carbondale, IL.

Spender, D. (Ed.). (1983). *Feminist theorists: Three centuries of key women thinkers.* New York: Pantheon Books.

Stanley, L., & Wise, S. (1993). *Breaking out again: Feminist ontology and epistemology* (2nd ed.). London: Routledge.

Steeves, H. L. (1988, Spring). What distinguishes feminist scholarship in communication Studies. *Women's Studies in Communication, 11,* 12–17.

"Study reports sex bias in news organizations." (1989, April 11). *New York Times,* p. C22.

Theriot, N. M. (1990). The politics of "meaning-making:" Feminist hermeneutics, language and culture. In D. Raymond (Ed.), *Sexual politics and popular culture* (pp. 3–14). Bowling Green, OH: Bowling Green State University Popular Press.

van Zoonen, L. (1994). *Feminist media studies.* Thousand Oaks, CA: Sage.

Walker, O. C. & Rudelius, W. (1976). Ascertaining programming needs of "voiceless" community groups. *Journal of Broadcasting, 20,* 89–99.

Warren, K. J. (1993). The power and the promise of ecological feminism. In M. E. Zimmerman, J. B. Callicott, G. Sessions, K. J. Warren, & J. Clark (Eds.), *Environmental philosophy: From animal rights to radical ecology* (pp. 320–341). Englewood Cliffs, NJ: Prentice Hall.

Wollstonecraft, M. (1975). *A vindication of the rights of women.* In C. H. Poston (Ed.). New York: Norton. (Original work published 1792)

Wood, J. T. (1994). *Gendered lives: Communication, gender, and culture.* Belmont, CA: Wadsworth.

Young, I. (1980). Socialist feminism and the limits of dual systems theory. *Socialist Review, 10,* 173–182.

32

Communication Ethics

Donald K. Wright
University of South Alabama

Philip Meyer (1987), who enjoyed two distinguished professional careers in the communication field—first as a newspaper reporter with *The Miami Herald* and then as a journalism professor at the University of North Carolina-Chapel Hill—called communication ethics "a slippery topic," and likened the assignment of defining ethical behavior to the task of defining art (p. vii).

Ethics—in all aspects of communication study and practice—has attracted a good deal of attention over the past few decades. Many who work in various aspects of communication are bombarded regularly with diverse ethical cues, and too few of these communications practitioners really have developed frameworks for making ethical judgments. This chapter explores the concept of ethics from several perspectives, aiming at a *broad* understanding of the pragmatic, the conceptual, and the practical implications of *communication* ethics across disciplinary areas.

THE DESIRE TO BE ETHICAL

The desire for ethical behavior depends entirely upon the actions of individuals and the assumption that these people wish to act responsibly. Goodpaster and Matthews (1989) addressed three important concerns in terms of the ethical *responsibility* of individuals: someone is to blame, something has to be done, and some kind of trustworthiness can be expected.

The first of these affects an individual's action and whether he or she was responsible for the action. The second exists in circumstances in which individuals are responsible for others: lawyers to clients, physicians to patients; or, in the communication context, journalists to their readers, public relations professionals to their organizations, and the public, and so on. The third meaning of ethical responsibility focuses on the individual's moral reasoning and the intellectual and emotional processes connected to it. Thus, ethical responsibility rests on the decisions people make regarding who is responsible for acting responsibly. These decisions are influenced by a variety of factors, most of which are often beyond the individual's understanding at the time (the individual is unprepared to deal with them for a variety of reasons, including lack of training in ethical reasoning), deal with a relationship with another person, or other persons, or communcation environmental factors. However looked at, communication ethics boils down to making—or not making—a decision.

Ethics and Decision Making

The topic of ethics has attracted a good deal of attention throughout the communication community over the past few decades. Although those working in journalism, advertising, broadcasting, public relations, organizational communication, corporate communications, and communication education are bombarded with many diverse ethical cues, too few really have developed frameworks for making ethical judgments.

Ethics is the division of philosophy that deals with questions of moral behavior. Making ethical decisions in the communication environment is easy when the facts are clear and the choices are black and white. It's a different story when ambiguity clouds the situation along with incomplete information, multiple points of view, and conflicting responsibilities. In such situations, ethical decisions depend on both the decision-making process and on the decision-makers—their experience, intelligence, and integrity.

Much of the applied communication and ethics literature centers on the role of the decision-maker in ethical behavior. Although communication professionals do not always make decisions, their counsel quite frequently enters that decision making process. There are circumstances where the decision-making role rests firmly within the communication function. An important aspect of many communication jobs is trying to help management make decisions.

In this process, the ethical question might be whether or not to say something as much as it might be whether or not to do something. Unfortunately, for some it is easy to say nothing and later blame the unethical results on somebody else's decision. Dick Rosenberg (1991), Chairman of the Bank of America, recently told an audience of corporate communication professionals that "We don't shoot people for bringing us bad news; we shoot them for delivering it too late." This view suggests that communications managers who can head off serious problems before they blow up in the company's face, surface in a newspaper's columns, or ruin an individual's reputation are two steps ahead of the game.

Outside of individual responsibility, people must assume that they work for some-body who wants to be told the truth. Further, that truth should be respected. Some system of ethics must serve as a cornerstone for any civilized society. Communication cannot be effective without being ethical and socially responsible.

Unfortunately, the people who make the decisions in American business do not always possess responsible moral judgments. Harvard business school professor Kenneth R. Andrews (1989) contends that ethical decisions require three qualities that can be identified and developed by individuals. These are:

1. Competence to recognize ethical issues and to think through the consequences of alternative resolutions.
2. Self-confidence to seek out different points of view and then to decide what is right at a given place and time, in a particular set of relationships and circum-stances.
3. "Tough-mindedness," which is the willingness to make decisions when all that needs to be known cannot be known and when the questions that press for answers have no established and incontrovertible solutions. (p. 2)

Some Basic Questions

Most people understand the clear cut differences in moral choice. They can recognize and decide what is good or evil, right or wrong, honest or dishonest. There is, however, a faulty assumption held by many in our society that communication practitioners can be unethical—as long as they resolve conflicting claims in their own hearts and minds. There are people who often resort to certain rationalizations that appear to justify questionable behavior.

Although ethical decisions are often hard enough to make, there is much more to communication ethics than struggling with the short-range decisions on a case-by-case basis. Ethical communication begins with individuals' capacity for socially construct-ing a long-range moral realism.

One way or another, most people break some law at least once every day. Those who fall into that category rationalize away some of their illegal (and morally wrong) behavior. The speed limit is 55 miles-per-hour but a person drives 62 ("everyone's doing it; it would be unsafe to do otherwise"). People jaywalk ("no traffic, why walk to the corner and then back?"). Healthy people sometimes park their cars in places reserved for handicapped drivers. Merely breaking the law, however, is not necessarily equivalent to acting unethically; sometimes adhering to the law can be unethical, as examples of Martin Luther King, Jr., and Mahatma Ghandi illustrate.

DEFINING THE CONCEPT OF ETHICS

As noted earlier, *ethics* is the branch of philosophy that deals with questions of moral behavior. It is similar to a set of principles or a code of moral conduct (Fink, 1988). The study of ethics can provide the tools for making difficult moral choices. Students of communication do not need to know as much about how to make ethical decisions as they need to possess the knowledge and ability to defend critical judgments on some rational basis. Perhaps more than anything else, they need to recognize ethical problems when they arise.

It is inevitable that conflicts among competing values will emerge in this process. The study of ethics and moral reasoning cannot necessarily resolve such conflicts, but they can provide the tools to make it easier to live with difficult ethical choices. And, cutting through the rhetoric, most—if not all—know when we are ethical and when we are not.

According to ethics scholar Richard Johannesen (1983), ethical situations are multifaceted. They usually arise when a *moral agent* (the one making the ethical decision) commits an *act* (either verbal or nonverbal) within a specific *context* with a particular *motive* directed at an *audience*. Johannesen argues that *each* factor must be taken into account before passing judgment on the outcome of any moral scenario.

As a formal field of inquiry, ethics can be further divided into three related subareas (Callahan, 1988). *Metaethics* attempts to assign meanings to the abstract language of moral philosophy. *Normative ethics* provides the foundation for decision making through the development of general rules and principles of moral conduct. *Applied ethics* is concerned with using these theoretical norms to solve real-world ethical problems. Each provides ethics scholars with areas from which to construct ethical frameworks at varying levels of the decision-making process, from the language used in rationalizing an ethical decision to applying an ethical framework in real-world situations.

WHY THIS CONCERN ABOUT ETHICS?

Why this concern about communication ethics? One popular answer suggests that Americans have become morally adrift without traditional anchors. We have compromised our individual ethics so frequently that it sometimes becomes just as easy to compromise our professional ethics.

Followers of Sigmund Freud suggest that the development of moral character and habits of moral thought essentially are complete in early childhood. This Freudian view meets considerable resistance, particularly from Lawrence Kohlberg (1981) and his followers who believe that moral development undergoes significant structural changes well into adulthood.

Despite some huge differences between these two theses, there is strong agreement that moral development is *learned* behavior. The following scenario, filled with communication examples, forces us to think about that:

> A man and his wife take their two children, whose ages are 6 and 13, to a movie. The neighbors think they're great parents. En route to the theatre the man breaks the speed limit, drives through one stoplight after it has turned from green to amber and fails to come to a complete stop at two separate stop signs. He also fails to signal while making turns and changing lanes. Just before purchasing the movie tickets, the wife tells the 13-year-old to claim he is 12, so the parents can pay the less expensive children's ticket rate. After the movie the family eats in a buffet restaurant. The parents ask the 6-year-old

to claims he is 5 so they can pay less. What message do these children learn from these examples?

Does it matter that the man was speeding? Does it matter that there was no other traffic at the intersections where he did not completely stop at the stop signs?

A week later the 13-year-old is arrested for shoplifting at a local mall. The parents, and the neighbors, wonder why.

Many of these decisions present us with difficulty. Some ethical decisions are simple. Others are more complex. If you support abortion you are a killer of babies; if you oppose abortion you do not respect the rights of women. To attempt to justify a principle morally, belief, attitude, policy, or action is to seek good reasons in support of it. *Good* reasons are reasons you are willing to commend to others rather than simply accept privately.

A large portion of our concern about ethics comes from a realization that possessing a systems of ethics is not merely a *sufficient* condition for social intercourse, but is a *necessary* requirement. Ethics is the foundation of advanced civilization, a cornerstone that provides some stability to society's moral expectations. In the communication business it is essential that we enter into agreements with others. As such, we must be able to trust one another to keep those agreements—even if to do so is not always in our best self-interest.

Ethics not only has to be the cornerstone the effective practice of organizational communication, it also must be the cornerstone of any civilization where virtues such as truth, honesty, and integrity are to prevail. A system of ethics is essential for:

1. building trust and cooperation among individuals in society;
2. serving as a moral gatekeeper in apprising society of the relative importance of certain moral values;
3. acting as a moral arbitrator in resolving conflicting claims based on individual self interests; and
4. clarifying for society the competing values and principles inherent in emerging and novel moral dilemmas.

Can Ethics Be Taught?

There are two schools of thought on the question of whether ethics can be taught. One school claims it is a waste of time to study ethics because moral character and habits of moral thought are fully developed even before children begin formal education. Advocates of this position (e.g., Freud, 1923/1961; Simon, 1971) pointed out that knowledge about ethical principles does not always produce moral behavior. These skeptics also believe that the process of moral development is completed in most people before they are 6 years old. They do not believe the teaching of ethics in public schools is needed, much less at colleges and universities.

The other school of thought views ethics as a subject like history, sociology, chemistry or mathematics. Advocates (e.g., Florman, 1978; Jaska & Pritchard, 1994; Toffler, 1986) argue that ethics has its own sets of standards and rules as well as distinctive methods of problem solving.

The study of ethics comes with its own unique set of problems. More than most academic subjects, ethical viewpoints are shaped and molded through a variety of different aspects of society. A person's individual ethical beliefs are the product of many factors, including family, religion, economic status, environment, age, gender, race, and so forth.

One of the strongest arguments in favor of studying ethics comes from scholars who believe in the process of moral reasoning (e.g., Kohlberg, 1981). These scholars believe ethics involves much more than memorizing a list of ethical principles and view ethics instruction as an important component in moral conduct because it provides information and perspectives that people need to make ethical judgments.

Ethical decisions are not made in a vacuum. Day (1991) pointed out these decisions involve a variety of considerations which can be grouped into three categories: (a) the situational definition; (b) an analysis of the situation; and (c) the ethical judgment. Advocates of moral reasoning view it as a structured, systematic approach to ethical decision making. It also provides an intellectual means of defending ethical judgments against criticisms. The Hastings Center (1980), a pioneer in ethics education, recommended these five steps be followed in preparing people to be effective in the process of moral reasoning: stimulating the moral imagination, recognizing ethical issues, developing analytical skills, eliciting a sense of moral obligation and personal responsibility, and tolerating disagreement.

ETHICAL THEORIES

The study of ethics is certainly not new. Anders Wedberg (1982), in his history of philosophy, traces ethical theories to antiquity, to the ancient Greeks. From these early beginnings can be traced the modern moral questions that contemporary communication researchers and theorists now study.

Classical Ethical Theory

The study of ethics began in ancient Greece with Socrates (c. 470–399 BC), who claimed virtue could be identified and practiced. His disciple, Plato (c. 428–348 BC), advocated moral conduct even in situations when responsible behavior might run counter to societal norms. Plato's student, Aristotle (384–322 BC), argued that moral virtue often required tough choices.

Development of the Judeo-Christian ethic brought forward the concept of "love thy neighbor as thyself," which introduced the importance of a love for God and all other people. In the 18th century, Immanuel Kant (1724–1804), a German philosopher, introduced the *categorical imperative* which was a duty-based moral philosophy. Kant (1785/1982) believed in the duty to tell the truth even if it resulted in harm to others. Partially in response to Kant came the progressive relativism school of thought that believes what is right or good for one is not necessarily right or good for another, even under similar circumstances.

Classical ethical theory views ethical obligation in two different ways. *Teleological ethics* underscores the consequences of an act or decision, whereas *deontological ethics* emphasizes the nature of an act or decision.

The teleological approach deals with two basic approaches, *ethical egoism* and *utilitarianism*. Egoists make decisions based on what result is best for them, whereas utilitarianism attempts to foster whatever is best for the entire society. The tradition of egoism dates to Epicurus (c. 342–271 BC), who advocated people should do those things that would lead to their own satisfaction (Albert, Denise, & Peterfreund, 1980). Writings of more contemporary egoism theorists, such as Ayn Rand (1964), are much more a blend of reason and justification of self-interest. Jeremy Bentham (1748–1832) is noted as the founder of utilitarianism, a philosophy that endeavors to provide "the greatest happiness for the greatest number" (Christians, Rotzoll & Fackler, 1987, pp. 12–13). Bentham's "hedonistic calculus" was designed to serve as a manual to direct his followers in taking appropriate actions. Now seen as old-fashioned, the calculus has given way to the broad overview of Bentham's philosophy. The more modern versions of utilitarianism focus on either acts or rules. *Act utilitarianism* places little value in precepts, claiming rules such as "thou shalt not kill," "never lie," and so forth, only provide rough directions for moral and ethical experiences. *Rule utilitarianism*, in contrast, is more concerned with what rule or action, when followed, will maximize the greatest good rather than with what rule or action will result in the greatest good result (Boycc & Jensen, 1978).

In examining the nature of the act in determining the rightness of an action, deonotologists believe there are acts that are moral or immoral by their very nature, regardless of consequences or outcome. Immanuel Kant generally is considered the forefather of deontological ethics. He is especially known as the seminal thinker in *pure rule deontology,* by which people follow a rationally derived duty to tell the truth. Another branch of this thinking, known as *pure act deontology,* asserts that because no two circumstances are alike the nature of acts and decisions constantly change (Kant, 1982). As such, act deontologists reject reason as a means to calculate moral conduct and are influenced more by the urgency of the moment and their innate ethical sense. Some deontologists consider not only the nature of an act in determining its rightness, but also its consequences. These people are known as *mixed deontologists* (Lambeth, 1986).

As ethical theory and research developed in the traditional areas of scholarship—philosophy, the classics, and so forth—*moral rules* came to represent the fuel that powered the ethical system. They provided guideposts for resolving ethical dilemmas and posed moral duties on individuals. In fulfilling moral duties people took into account all parties, including themselves, who may be touched by our ethical decisions.

Moral Reasoning Theories

Four criteria form the basis of any system of ethics. These are shared values, wisdom, justice, and freedom. First of all, an ethical system must have shared values. Before ethical judgments can be made, society must reach agreement on its standards of moral conduct. Second, these standards should be based on reason and experience. They should seek to harmonize people's rights and interests with their obligations to their fellow citizens. Third, a system of ethics should seek justice. There should be no double standard of treatment unless there is an overriding and morally defensible reason to discriminate. Finally, an ethical system should be based on freedom of choice. Moral agents must be free to render ethical judgments without coercion. Only in this way will the individual's ethical level of consciousness be raised.

In the cosmopolitan sense of the terms, ethics and moral values outline the ideals and standards people should live by. However, as those who study ethics quickly realize, no set of principles exists that will solve all ethical dilemmas. Much of the literature involved with communication ethics views ethics with a focus on what too many people refer to as *degrees* of *rightness* and *wrongness*. While ethics certainly deals with truth, fairness, and honesty, in the United States at least, the legal environment has the clear-cut mandate to be concerned with right and wrong.

DIFFERENCES BETWEEN *LAW* AND *ETHICS*

The central core of what ethics and morality are all about deals with differences between what is *good* or *bad*. Laws focus on questions of what is *right* or *wrong*. Although it is possible for a law to be bad, something ethically good always should be right. Societies make and change laws, but ethical principles, theoretically at least, remain constant over time.

For example, for decades in the United States certain laws prevented African-Americans and women from voting. Many considered these laws to be bad because they violated a greater good. And, of course, eventually these laws were changed. Although societies can enact these laws, they are not ethical. Most laws, however, are consistent with ethical philosophy. Few would challenge laws that protect members of a society against those who murder, rape, or commit armed robbery. However, laws frequently are challenged by members of society who do not believe the ordinances are good.

VARIOUS SETS OF LOYALTIES

The morally and ethically responsible person gives each set of loyalties its share of attention before rendering an ethical determination. For most of us the following categories must be examined: duty to ourselves, duty to one's organization or firm, duty to professional colleagues, and duty to society.

These loyalty sets provide interesting questions for professional communicators. Some newspaper journalists might believe their first duty is to their readers, advertising people could think their first loyalty to clients, public relations professionals might think their first loyalty is to client stockholders. An ethical issue could present itself for communicators if actions that might be moral for one public are unethical for another.

ISSUES INVOLVING COMMUNICATION ETHICS RESEARCH

Most research involving ethics and responsibility in communication and related disciplines is concerned with problems of justice and duties—that is, *good*, *truth* and *right*—and with stages of moral judgments and duties. Frankena (1963) claimed the academic study of ethics involves three kinds of normative or moral judgments. These include:

judgments of moral obligation or deontic judgments, which say a certain action is right or obligatory; judgments of morally good or aretaic judgments, which say that certain people, motives, or character traits are morally good, virtuous; and judgments of nonmoral value in which we evaluate not so much actions and persons but all sorts of other things including experiences, paintings, forms of government, and what not. (p. 147)

The study of ethics in contemporary communication public relations research and practice generally reflects some interpretation or judging of value systems and is representative of much contemporary research. As Wilcox, Ault, and Agee (1986) described it, "a person determines what is right or wrong, fair or unfair, just or unjust. It is expressed through moral behavior in specific situations" (p. 108).

Early work involving communication ethics usually considered the basic human need to function in honest and ethical ways. A good number of these articles also combined ethics and professionalism while some concerned themselves with accreditation and licensing. Writings of Appley (1948), Bateman (1957), Bernays (1979, 1980), and Harlow (1951, 1969) justify this claim. Bateman was one of the first to encourage communication practice to develop a philosophic structure to serve as the source of its ethics. The early works of Carr-Saunders and Wilson (1993) and Flexner (Flexner, 1930) suggest that professions be "guided by altruism." Liberman and Greenwood (Greenwood, 1966; Liberman, 1956) were among the first mention a code of ethics as part of the criteria which must be satisfied for an "occupation" to be a "profession."

A Divergence of Communications Viewpoints

Ethics in communication can be confusing especially when scholars and practitioners do not always agree with their colleagues in other segments of the discipline.

Print and broadcast journalists, for example, frequently differ with people who work in public relations. These disagreements can be over simple matters such as whether or not journalists are ethical if they accept free food and beverages at press conferences. They also can entail more complex and serious controversy. For example, some journalists actually believe that anything that happens in public relations is unethical and would deny organizations the right to seek counsel on matters related to public opinion. Izard (1984–1985) reported many journalists believe some forms of deception are permissible "if the situation demands it and circumstances are right" (p. 8). Some public relations people, on the other hand, pointed out that the media's agendas often hurt society, even though they might sell publications and attract broadcasting audiences.

Disagreements of this nature were common during the Watergate scandals in the early 1970s. Although journalists praised the work of *Washington Post* reporters Bob Woodward and Carl Bernstein in exposing the misdeeds of big government, many public relations experts questioned the ethics that appeared to permit these journalists to practice deception while seeking information. In academic research, for instance, ethical perceptions of journalists and public relations professionals have for similar situations been found to differ (Ryan & Martinson, 1984).

Codes of Ethics

Any discussion about communication ethics would not be complete without devoting some time to issues such as licensing, accreditation, and codes of ethics. In some ways, ethical research involving these topics has raised more issues than it has resolved. Rarely, if ever, is the total agreement regarding topics such as licensing, accreditation and codes of ethics.

In all likelihood American communication professionals never will become licensed by the government. One reason for this might be found in the First Amendment. Print and broadcast journalists as well as those who work in public relations, advertising, and organizational communication, hold strong beliefs suggesting free and open communication for all is more important than the restrictions some would face through licensing in any of these areas.

Codes of ethics are fairly commonplace throughout the communication industry. Most communication professional organizations have ethical codes. The most noted of these codes are those of the Society of Professional Journalists, the Public Relations Society of America, and the International Association of Business Communicators. Such codes represent industry self-regulation in the absence of government restrictions and are controversial to say the least (Bernays, 1979, 1980).

Although many have praised the merits of communication codes of ethics, critics point out these codes usually are unenforceable. They also are dismissed by many as being merely cosmetic (Merrill & O'Dell, 1983). Still, supporters claim the field is better with them than without them. Just as the voluntary nature of codes of ethics makes most of them unenforceable, professional accreditation programs have not made ethical codes any more accountable, and this situation is unlikely to change in Western society.

The fact that there are no legal restrictions on the practice of communcation—as there are in law or medicine—pose dilemmas for the communication industry that must be resolved. The problem is that any person—qualified or not—who wants to work in journalism, public relations, broadcasting, advertising, or any other aspect of communication in most Western nations can. Violations of conduct codes have kept a small minority out of some professional organizations, but codes cannot prevent them from working in the field.

Codes of ethics in communication have some strengths and can be valuable, but their voluntary nature—that is, their inability to be enforced—breeds inherent problems. Most codes of ethics for communication-related associations are filled with meaningless rhetoric, do not accomplish much, and are not taken seriously by most of the people who work in organizational communication. These codes might be able to make ethical behavior less likely because of awareness. With or without professional codes of conduct, most who practice communication will choose to be ethical because they behave ethically themselves and want others to respect them. In light of the voluntary nature of these codes, most communicators are ethical because they want to be, not because they have to be. Some claimed that enforcement of these codes often is infrequent and uneven (e.g., Cutlip, Center, & Broom, 1985). Others pointed out that many communications professionals do not belong to professional associations and note the inability of these organizations from prohibiting these nonmember practitioners from violating these codes, even if the organization belongs to or adheres to a professional code of conduct (Grunig & Hunt, 1984).

Is Ethics an Individual Issue?

Our own studies of communicators in a number of contexts—including corporate communications, public relations, broadcasting and journalism—suggest that ethics is an individual issue, claiming it is up to individual practitioners to decide whether or not to be ethical regardless of professional ethical codes (Wright, 1976, 1979, 1982, 1985).

Although not dealing directly with the wide variety of occupational duties in public relations practice—including the four Grunig (1976) models of practice and the Broom–Dozier (Broom & Dozier, 1986) assessment of different practitioner roles—a major assumption of this doctrine of the individual implies press agents could be as ethical as the two-way symmetrical communicators if they had such a desire (see chapter 29). It also would contend that communication managers are not necessarily more ethical than communication technicians. We have suggested many times that public relations and communication never will be any more ethical than the level of basic morality of the people who are in public relations. This is to agree with those who claim the occupational or professional ethics of a person cannot be separated from that individual's personal ethics. Indeed one major sign of ethical and moral maturity, in Kohlberg's (1981) opinion, is the ability to make ethical judgments and formulate moral principles on our own rather than our ability to conform to moral judgments of people around us. Scholars have supported this argument for centuries. Socrates, Plato, and Aristotle all stressed the importance of individual moral convictions in their writings about ethics.

Ethics in Group Decision Making

Most ethical choices center around decision making. Although some decision-making situations in organizational communication involve the individual, most include task-oriented small groups of employees.

Modern-day organizations consider sensitivity to ethical behavior to be a strong leadership attribute. Although management groups are not always able to comprehend the ethical and moral value interpretations of all their decisions, groups try to avoid making unethical decisions. Dennis Gouran (1991) suggested five ideas that help encourage more ethical group decisions:

1. show proper concern for all affected by the group's decision;
2. explore the discussion stage of decision making as responsibly as possible;
3. avoid misrepresenting any position or misusing any information;
4. do not say or do anything that could diminish any group member's sense of self-worth; and,
5. make certain all group members respect each other (pp. 166-167, 222).

Herbert E. Gulley (1968) provided another set of guidelines for ethical communication in small group settings. These suggest:

1. communicators have the responsibility for defending the policy decisions of groups in whose deliberations they have participated;
2. communicators must be well informed and accurate;

3. communicators should actively encourage the comments of others and explore all viewpoints;

4. communicators should openly reveal their own biases and identify their sources of information;

5. communicators should neither lie, deceive, fabricate evidence, falsify facts, nor invent information or sources;

6. communicators should not attempt to manipulate group discussions unfairly so that selfish motives are served at the expense of the group; and,

7. communicators should avoid the use of tactics such as name calling, emotionally "loaded" language, guilt-by-association, hasty generalizations, shifting definitions, and oversimplified either–or alternatives. (pp. 334–366)

EXAMINING COMMUNICATION ETHICS RESEARCH

The contemporary study of ethics in communication research and practice is fairly young and generally reflects some interpretation or judging. Opinions about ethics and moral values in all aspects of communication vary widely. Some of the early research, particularly in journalism, attempted to determine what was right and what was wrong, fair or unfair, just or unjust. Other research approached the study of ethics through moral behavior in specific situations, much of which also considered the basic human need to function in honest and ethical ways.

Most of the research concerning ethics and communication employs a wide variety of quantitative and qualitative methodologies, traceable to three separate and unique areas: journalism and broadcasting, public relations, and speech communication. These studies include survey research, personal interviews, focus groups, experimental, and critical methods.

Journalism and *broadcasting studies* involving ethics have existed for nearly half a century. The Hutchins Commission report on freedom of the press in 1947 criticized print journalism for its lack of social responsibility (Hocking, 1947). Journalism ethics also concerns the First Amendment, business aspects of the mass media, invasion of privacy, the relationship between reporters and a wide variety of news sources, pornography and allegedly morally offensive material, and a variety of case study reports dealing with examples in many of these topical areas.

Most of these ethical topics are discussed thoroughly in four of the foremost books on the topic of journalism ethics. Rivers and Mathews (1988) provided a fairly thorough clarification of ethical issues combined with specific and practical suggestions for solutions. Their work included journalistic virtues, objectivity, basic news gathering, standards for news reporters, press councils, and media codes of ethics. The book also addresses sexism, investigative reporting, privacy, photojournalism, and freedom of the press. Christians, Flacker, and Rotzol (1995) devoted several editions of a book that used commentaries and cases taken from actual media experiences to encourage journalists and other media practitioners to think analytically and to improve ethical awareness.

Lambeth (1986) concentrated on outlining the principles journalists should consider in making ethical judgments. His work also attempts to provide direction on to whom, or what, journalists owe professional loyalty—themselves, the public, an employer, or colleagues. Hulteng (1985) used the case study approach to illustrate the problems media practitioners face in making practical applications of ethical ethical principles and moral standards. Meyer's research (1987) involved a large survey of editors, publishers, and reporters and documents ethical confusion in American journalism during the Watergate and Pentagon Papers controversy. Swain (1978) explored how newspaper reporters handle the delicate questions of ethics that arise repeatedly in their pressured daily routines.

Public Relations ethics research studies began in the 1950s with articles that encouraged public relations to develop a philosophic structure to serve as the source of its ethics. Since then, a number of empirical studies examined various aspects of the public relations process including ethical questions concerning individual practice, dealings with the news media and the overall improvement of professional working standards.

Ferre and Willihnganz (1991) reported that nearly 300 books or articles were published on the subject of public relations ethics since 1922, which—considering that public relations considers itself to be the conscience of corporations and society—is a very low number indeed. Unlike other areas of communication, in which many books were written, Ferre and Willihnganz noted that most of the ethics articles that concern public relations are short essays. The majority also are positive articles, claiming, for the most part, that public relations people believe in honesty, integrity, and in telling the truth.

Public relations ethics receive some coverage, albeit minor, in some of the books concerned mainly with ethics in journalism and mass communication (Christians et al., 1995, pp. 225–262; Day, 1991, pp. 71–75, 89–90, 131, 148–158, 171–174, 273–275, and 313–315). Of the many journal articles, Ryan and Martinson's (1984) comparison of differences between journalists and public relations professionals stands alone, as does Kruckeberg's (1989) research on codes of ethics, Pearson's (1989) work on the theory of public relations ethics, and some of Wright's articles involving communicator analysis studies of individual public relations practitioners (Wright, 1979, 1982, 1985, 1989).

Speech Communication ethics research has been conducted from political, human nature, dialogical, and situational perspectives. The literature in this area also lists studies regarding ethics and various aspects of oral communication skills—public speaking, interpersonal and small group communication.

Much of the speech communication studies involving ethics explore ethical implications of a wide variety of human communication experiences, both oral and written. One of the most prolific scholars in this area is Richard L. Johannesen, whose work also attempts to provide direction to participants in the communication process and to encourage individuals to develop their own working approach to assessing communication ethics (e.g., Johannesen, 1983). Other leading research in this area includes Nilsen's (1974) efforts to provide a general orientation by which to guide communication conduct, Barnlund's (1962) insistence that all human communication theory must include moral standards specifications, and Miller's (1969) perceptions about ethical implications between communicators and audiences.

PRACTICAL APPLICATIONS
OF COMMUNICATION ETHICS RESEARCH

This section examines two practical applications of communication ethics research. One involves journalism; the other corporate communications. Both of these studies could be adapted to other aspects of communication research.

Sample Journalism Ethics Study

The journalism study involves the moral values of journalists that would be measured via a mail questionnaire sent to a large, random national sample of members of the Society of Professional Journalists.

Assuming a 40 percent return rate for studies of this nature, obtaining 350 usable responses would necessitate an initial mailing of no fewer than 875 questionnaires. If funding was available, 1,000 questionnaires would be mailed. Questionnaires, accompanied by a cover letter from a noted journalist encouraging participation in the study, and a self-addressed and stamped return envelope would be mailed to randomly selected participants. Any questionnaire of this nature would need to be extremely user-friendly and probably no longer than three or four pages to enhance the return rate.

In addition to a small number of basic demographic questions, the questionnaire would concentrate on three areas: perceived moral values of subjects themselves; perceived moral values of subjects' peers; and, subjects' job satisfaction. Questions could be arrived from any number of indices and previous research questions measuring these items. Data analysis would compare and contrast scores registered in each of these three areas. If additional funding could be acquired the researcher might wish to test results through five or six focus groups of journalists in various parts of the nation.

Sample Corporation Communication Ethics Study

The corporate communications study is concerned with the impact on corporate public relations professionals of organizational codes of ethics, sometimes known as *corporate vision*, *values*, or *beliefs statements*. The sample would consist of senior-level corporate public relations executives; the most likely sources for the sample's population would be the directories of the Public Relations Seminar or the Arthur W. Page Society, both populated by senior-level public relations professionals.

Data gathering would consist of two parts. First, the researcher would identify several organizations that have corporate ethical codes, value statements, or similar codes. Ideally these would be Fortune 100 companies and should yield no fewer than five and no more than ten organizations. Public relations practitioners in these organizations would be surveyed in an attempt to measure the perceived impact these organizational behavior codes have on professional behavior in their specific organizations.

Second, public relations executives from other organizations would be surveyed to determine how they perceived the impact of these behavior codes. This external study also would attempt to gather information concerning the impact, if any, on corporate communications and public relations behavior caused through codes of ethics of professional societies such as the Public Relations Society of America, the International Public Relations Association and the International Public Relations Association.

Data analysis would test for differences between the perceived effectiveness of various aspects of these codes of ethics.

CONCLUSION

All in all, those who work in various professional aspects of the field of communication have made considerable progress in the direction of more ethical behavior. The field has come a long way, but it still has a long way to go.

When it comes to the bottom line, the final arbiter in separating right from wrong or good from evil in communication is the decision maker. And the authenticity of any decision depends on a universal form of morality. The higher good is purity of motive rather than the good or harm of outcome. The central value in the unwritten contract people make with society is fairness or decision making guided by principles anyone and everyone would agree with.

REFERENCES

Albert, E. M., Denise, T. C., & Peterfreund, S. (1980). *Great traditions in ethics*. New York: Van Nostrand.

Andrews, K. R. (Ed.). (1989). *Ethics in practice: Managing the moral corporation*. Boston: Harvard Business School Press.

Appley, L. A. (1948). The obligations of a new profession. *Public Relations Journal, 4*, 4–9.

Barnlund, D. C. (1962). Toward a meaning centered philosophy of communication. *Journal of Communication, 12*, 198.

Bateman, J. C. (1957). The path to professionalism. *Public Relations Journal, 13*, 6–8, 19.

Bernays, E. L. (1979). The case for licensing and registration for public relations. *Public Relations Quarterly, 24*, 26–28.

Bernays, E. L. (1980). Gaining professional status for public relations. *Public Relations Quarterly, 25*, 20.

Boyce, W. D., & Jensen, L. C. (1978). *Moral reasoning*. Lincoln: University of Nebraska Press.

Broom, G. M., & Dozier, D. M. (1986). Advancement for public relations role models. *Public Relations Review, 12*, 37–56.

Callahan, J. C. (Ed.) (1988). *Ethical issues in professional life*. New York: Oxford University Press.

Carr-Saunders, A. M., & P. A. Wilson. (1933). *The professions*. Oxford: Clarendon Press.

Christians, C. G., Fackler, M., & Rotzoll, K. B. (1995). *Media ethics: Cases and moral reasoning* (4th ed.). White Plains, NY: Longman.

Christians, C. G., Rotzoll, K. B., & Fackler, M. (1987). *Media ethics: Cases and moral reasoning* (2nd ed.). White Plains, NY: Longman.

Cutlip, S. M., Center, A. H., & Broom, G. M. (1985). *Effective public relations* (6th ed.). Englewood Cliffs, NJ: Prentice-Hall.

Day, L. A. (1991). *Ethics in media communications: Cases and controversies*. Belmont, CA: Wadsworth.

Ferre, J. P., & Willihnganz, S. C. (1991). *Public relations & ethics: A bibliography*. Boston, MA: Hall & Co.

Fink, C. C. (1988). *Media ethics: In the newsroom and beyond*. New York: McGraw-Hill.

Flexner, A. (1930). *Universities: American, English, German*. Oxford: Oxford University Press.

Florman, S. (1978, October). Moral blueprints. *Harpers*, 31.

Frankena, W. K. (1963). *Ethics*. Englewood Cliffs, NJ: Prentice-Hall.

Freud, S. (1961). *Civilization and its discontents* (J. Strachey, Trans.). New York: Norton. (Original work published 1923)

Goodpaster, K. E., & Matthews, J. B., Jr. (1989). Can a corporation have a conscience? In K. R. Andrews (Ed.), *Ethics in practice: Managing the moral corporation* (pp. 155–167). Boston: Harvard Business School Press.

Gouran, D. (1991). *Making decisions in groups*. Glenville, IL: Scott Foresman.

Greenwood, E. (1966). The elements of professionalism. In H. M. Vollmer & D. L. Mills (Eds.), *Professionalization* (pp. 9–19). Englewood Cliffs, NJ: Prentice-Hall.

Grunig, J. E. (1976). Organizations and public relations: Testing a communication theory. *Journalism Monographs, 46.*

Grunig, J. E., & Hunt, T. (1984). *Managing public relations*. New York: Holt, Rinehart and Winston.

Gulley, H. E. (1968). *Discussion, conference, and group process* (2nd ed.). New York: Holt, Rinehart & Winston.

Harlow, R. F. (1951). A plain lesson we should heed. *Public Relations Journal, 5,* 7–10.

Harlow, R. F. (1969). Is public relations a profession? *Public Relations Quarterly, 14,* 37.

Hastings Center (1980). *The teaching of ethics in higher education*. Hastings-on-Hudson, NY: Author.

Hulteng, J. L. (1985). *The messenger's motives: Ethical problems of the news media* (2nd ed.). Englewood Cliffs, NJ: Prentice-Hall.

Hocking, W. E. (1947). *Freedom of the press: A framework of principle. Report from the Commission on Freedom of the Press*. Chicago: University of Chicago Press.

Izard, R. S. (1984–1985). Deception: Some cases rate approval if other methods don't work. *Journalism Ethics Report*. Chicago: Society of Professional Journalists.

Jaska, J. A., & Pritchard, M. S. (1994). *Communication ethics: Methods of analysis* (2nd ed.). Belmont, CA: Wadsworth.

Johannesen, R. L. (1983). *Ethics in human communication* (2nd ed.). Prospect Heights, IL: Waveland Press.

Kant, I. (1982). The good will and the categorical imperative. In T. L. Beauchamp (Ed.), *Philosophical ethics: An introduction to moral philosophy* (pp. 3–17). New York: McGraw-Hill. (Original work published 1785)

Kohlberg, L. (1981). *Essays on moral development, vol. 1, The philosophy of moral development: Moral Stages and the idea of justice*. New York: Harper and Row.

Kruckeberg, D. (1989, Summer). The need for an international code of ethics. *Public Relations Review, 6–18.*

Lambeth, E. B. (1986). *Committed journalism: An ethic for the profession*. Bloomington, IN: Indiana University Press.

Liberman, M. (1956). *Education as a profession*. Englewood Cliffs, NJ: Prentice-Hall.

Merrill, J. C., & O'Dell, S. J. (1983). *Philosophy and journalism*. White Plains, NY: Longman.

Meyer, P. (1987). *Ethical journalism*. New York: Longman.

Miller, G. R. (1969). Contributions of communication research to the study of speech. In A.H. Monroe & D. Ehninger (Eds.), *Principles and types of speech communication* (6th brief ed., p. 355). Glenview, IL: Scott, Foresman.

Nilsen, T. R. (1974). *Ethics of speech communication* (2nd ed.). Indianapolis: Bobbs-Merrill.

Pearson, R. (1989, September 20). Remarks to the San Francisco Academy, San Francisco, CA.

Rand, A. (1964). *The virtue of selfishness*. New York: New American Library/Signet Books.

Rivers, W. L., & Mathews, C. (1988). *Ethics for the media*. Englewood Cliffs, NJ: Prentice-Hall.

Rosenberg, R. (1991, September 20). Remarks to the San Francisco Academy. San Francisco, CA.

Ryan, M., & Martinson, D. L. (1984). Ethical values, the flow of journalistic information, and public relations persons. *Journalism Quarterly, 61,* 27–34.

Simon, S. (1971). Value-clarification vs. indoctrination. *Social Education, 35,* 902.

Swain, B. M. (1978). *Reporters' ethics*. Ames: Iowa University Press.

Toffler, B. (1986). *Tough choices: Managers talk ethics*. New York: Wiley.

Wedberg, A. (1982). *A history of philosophy: Antiquity and the middle ages* (Vol. 1). Oxford: Clarendon Press.

Wilcox, D. L., Ault, P. H., & Agee, W. K. (1986). *Public relations strategics and tactics*. New York: Harper & Row.

Wright, D. K. (1976). Social responsibility in public relations: A multi-step theory. *Public Relations Review, 2,* 24–36.

Wright, D. K. (1979). Professionalism and social responsibility in public relations. *Public Relations Review, 5,* 20–33.

Wright, D. K. (1982). The philosophy of ethical development in public relations. *IPRA Review, 9,* 18–25.

Wright, D. K. (1985). Individual ethics determine public relations practice. *Public Relations Journal, 41,* 38–39.

Wright, D. K. (1989, Summer). Examining ethical and moral values of public relations people. *Public Relations Review,* 19–33.

V

Future of Theory and Research
in Communication

33

Communication Theory and Research: The Quest for Increased Credibility in the Social Sciences

Tony Atwater[1]
University of Toledo

From its humble beginnings in the early 20th century to the dawn of the 21st century, the formal study of communication has matured as a social science. However, there is much progress that needs to be made in establishing the field's empirical credibility among its peers in such academic fields as sociology, anthropology, and political science. Only in recent decades have recognized research programs sponsored by the Ford and Fulbright foundations recognized the academic legitimacy of communication. Part of the field's lack of empirical credibility and standing as a social science is related to its youth compared to older, more established disciplines. However, youth does not tell the whole story in the field's continuing quest for credibility.

CHALLENGES ON THE ROAD TO PEDAGOGICAL CREDIBILITY

Earlier chapters in this volume have addressed the value of integrating theoretical propositions with empirical research methods. Another area in which additional

---

[1]Tony Atwater is past president of the Association for Education in Journalism and Mass Communication.

integration is called for is in the theoretical frames of mass communication and human communication. The lack of synthesis and fusion between the two areas poses a significant handicap to the field's theoretical symmetry and empirical credibility. As the 21st century approaches, communication is at an important historical crossroads in developing theoretical and methodological linkages between mass and human communication.

The communication field also faces the challenge of successfully developing synergy and synthesis among its most accepted and popular theoretical frames such as agenda-setting, dissonance theory, cultivation theory, and other research domains. The latter 20th century has seen a host of theoretical frameworks emerge with little attention to how they relate to or build upon existing communication theories and paradigms. More often, new communication theoretical frameworks are linked with older and more established social sciences. This is not, altogether, an undesirable practice. It is important that communication theory demonstrate theoretical compatibility with the other social sciences. However, the time has come for communication scholarship to take a bold step forward in recognizing its own autonomy as a social scientific enterprise, to actively examine how new theoretical frameworks relate to established ones in the field.

Early in its history, communication scholarship borrowed heavily from sociology, social psychology and political science (among others) in building its theoretical frameworks. This was understandable given the interdisciplinary nature of the field and its youthfulness among the social sciences. As we near the 21st century, communication scholarship should set for itself the goal of conceiving more theoretical frameworks that other social sciences will borrow. In the latter 20th century we are seeing some, albeit limited, evidence of this practice. One of the most important signs of the field's increased empirical credibility will be the frequency with which scholars in other social science disciplines cite and employ our theoretical frameworks.

PREACHING TO AN ACADEMIC CHOIR

It is ironic that a discipline devoted to analyzing human perceptions, attitudes and communication behaviors does a such poor job of communicating its own relevance and utility to the public at large. The quest for credibility as a field in the 21st century will require that communication scholars become more active in educating the general public—and specific constituencies—about the import and relevance of communication theory and research. The nature of the communication field is such that its findings and theoretical propositions have broad social, political, and economic implications. We are a field that can hardly afford to be satisfied with preaching to our own academic choir. The choir needs to take to the road and find new ways of demonstrating the relevance of communication to many different constituencies, both private and public.

The quest for credibility inherently involves articulation of the field's validity and salience both in and outside of the academy. More progress is needed in educating publics outside of the academy about how communication theory and research relates to everyday human experience, professional contexts, and shaping public policy. One of the critical risks faced by communication is that commercial and technological currents of the latter 20th century will define and redefine the field to external publics with limited input from the academy. This risk should provide an incentive for communication scholars to take a lead role in telling the world what communication science is, and how it is addressing the new challenges of the 21st century.

How do we get beyond preaching to the choir in the quest for empirical credibility? Because of its broad and pervasive relevance, the communication field carries an additional disciplinary responsibility to make its issues and theoretical tenets comprehensible to the lay public. One way of addressing this responsibility is by publishing journals that impart significant findings and theories in language that nonacademic communities can understand and appreciate. In the professional context, for example, communication research findings and theories could be made more comprehensible for communication professionals such as journalists, advertisers, public relations personnel, as well as our own professional communication educators at the secondary, junior and community college, and college levels. Here our research institutions need to provide leadership in making communication theory and research accessible and available to others.

Additional national foundations and centers that support and promote communication research outside of colleges and universities can further advance the visibility of communication as a viable and respected social science. Centers such as the Annenberg Center and the Freedom Forum Foundation have paved the way for future national support structures which enhance the visibility and political standing of the communication field. The establishment of numerous additional centers which prioritize communication research and interpret it to varied publics will play a key role in promoting the field's credibility into the 21st century.

Third, communication scholars must become more active in the political discourse and policy debates that relate to communication research findings, theories, and agendas. While some academicians are wary of tainting empirical research by examining timely policy questions, others have chosen to use empirical research to help clarify, if not reframe, debates involving public policy. Raging policy debates involving such issues as personal privacy on the information highway, media violence, and concentration of media ownership, as well as communication analysis of political campaigns, and business and technical communication provide opportunities for communication theory and research to assert their salience and validity. Consequently, communication scholars should anticipate and identify policy matters where communication expertise is called for and be ready to respond with studies based on sound theory and methodological procedures. The field has addressed public policy more in the latter 20th century than in the earlier half of the century. To enhance the credibility of the field, a more deliberate and participatory role is called for in contributing to the development of public policy in the information, media, and communication arenas.

MEETING THE CREDIBILITY CHALLENGE

Whereas stronger pedagogical credibility can be achieved by educating external publics about communication theory and research, an internal challenge must be met on college and university campuses. The 1990s may be remembered as the decade when academic departments received a wake-up call as to their centrality to the academic mission in institutions of higher education. Although communication departments were not the only units targeted for consolidation and reallocation of resources, the message was clear. As an academic discipline, communication can and must do a better job of communicating its intellectual significance and establishing its role as a valued academic citizen inside today's university. To accomplish these objectives, we need to take full advantage of our genuinely interdisciplinary character to forge both instructional and scholarly alliances with appropriate units and disciplines throughout the university.

Like most other social sciences, communication continually faces the risk that its theoretical and research agendas will be driven by topical issues of the day as related by the media. However, the communication field faces an additional challenge: commercial and technological trends in the professional sphere also guide our research agenda. Consequently, topical issues and events that become the focus of research can detract from a much-needed larger empirical view of relevant phenomena and dynamics warranting examination and theoretical testing. A trend in communication theory has been to extrapolate from and refine existing theoretical frameworks. While such undertakings are needed and represent legitimate research endeavors, more attention is due to developing and introducing new theoretical frameworks. To do so requires innovation, hard work, and courage. But more and newer theories contribute to a discipline's vitality and credibility. Even when a flawed theoretical framework is introduced, it can become the germ for the evolution of later valid theories. Therefore, the communication field should exercise the courage and assume the risks of identifying and presenting new ideologies and theoretical frameworks, if the field is to enjoy increased credibility in future years.

Although the communication field seldom enjoys the controlled research environments of the natural and physical sciences, communication has ready-made laboratories in many different social and cultural settings. Communication theory and research have been enriched by systematic inquiries in both the human and mass communication areas. In the study of mass communication, we have seen how the research agenda has focused on both media consumer issues, media organizational issues, and media practitioner issues. Media theory and research in or during the 1960s was heavily devoted to the media consumer. In the 1980s and 1990s, more attention was devoted to exploring the dynamics and processes relative to how media fare is produced and framed, providing for the study of media sociology.

For a field that entertains both basic and applied research interests, communication has much to do in generating theoretical frameworks which link both areas of inquiry. Further, there is considerable opportunity for developing new theoretical frameworks in the applied research arena. Often in the academic world, applied research is viewed as second-rate scholarship because it is atheoretical. This perspective is unfortunate; applied research offers an opportunity for the academy to demonstrate the relevance of its research to non-academic communities. Some applied communication research would benefit significantly from theoretical treatment. Further, active theory-building in the area of applied communication research seems long overdue. This arena appears to be a venue that could be better exploited in promoting the scholarly credibility and visibility of the communication field. The communication academy may need to rethink its evaluation of the merit of applied research when it successfully integrates appropriate theoretical frame works.

In the latter 20th century, the communication field has continued to cultivate a growing international academic community. The contributions of international scholars to communication theory and research have been noteworthy, and the future outlook appears bright for continued internationalization of the field. However, agendas for expanding such internationalization are needed to confirm to the world academy that communication is an autonomous social science with a promising intellectual future. Worldwide, as in the United States, the communication field is waging a continuing battle to be recognized as an individual academic discipline, as opposed to an appendage to one or more of the traditional social sciences.

Beyond making a statement to the world academic community, the field has much more to accomplish in broadening its theoretical and research interests across different national cultures, doctrines, and ideologies. While noticeably more published communication studies have involved international subjects, there is a demonstrated need for more comparative studies that assess communication behavior and issues across multiple cultures and longitudinally. Such research needs to become a high priority on the communication research agenda of tomorrow as the global village becomes a reality. International and intercultural communication studies offer excellent opportunities to test the universality of communication theory and research.

FUTURE TRENDS IN MEDIA THEORY AND RESEARCH

As a maturing social science, communication has faced many challenges alluded to earlier in the chapter. It is a field that initially borrowed heavily from the theoretical pastures of the older, established social sciences, as well as the humanities. This early practice has served as a two-edged sword, offering some intellectual credibility in one instance, but connoting theoretical dependence and a subdisciplinary status in another instance. Over the decades of the 1970s and 1980s, and into the 1990s, the field has emerged as an autonomous academic discipline by virtue of its growing body of empirical research and its curricular contributions at many colleges and universities. Still, as a field we have some distance to go in gaining unqualified acceptance of our disciplinary autonomy within the academic community, as well as by some external publics. Additionally, the field's academic credibility continues to be variously impacted by trends and behaviors of professional communication industries. These conditions suggest that now is not the time for complacency in projecting a strong academic identity. Instead, communication scholars and administrators must seize the initiative in articulating their intellectual worth as an autonomous academic discipline.

Further, because more sophisticated research tools are being spawned due to digital technology, it can be expected that communication theory and research will entertain a higher level of precision and validity. Advances in research technology will afford greater use of controlled and field experimentation in exploring communication issues. Fiber optics-based technologies also will contribute to more precision in the most highly utilized data gathering method in communication, the survey. Increased use of cellular technologies to record studied communication behaviors will likely become a more common research tool in coming decades. Consequently, increased precision in testing theoretical propositions will be the result. Such developments further enhance the generalizability of communication studies providing the public at large a new and more applied vision of communication theory and research. This bodes well for promoting the field's empirical credibility.

Another future trend relates to an increased emphasis in research on the processes, roles, and relationships within an organizational context. In the 1960s and 1970s, much attention was devoted to the individual and to groups as captive recipients and consumers in the communication process. Communication studies in the 1990s and into the 21st century are likely to focus on the dynamics that affect communication relationships and the production of communication products within organizations. Communication behavior with two-way interactive communication technologies will continue to be the focus of many empirical studies. Additionally, future studies are likely to analyze how different constituent groups respond to communications and media fare with a precision not possible in earlier decades.

Theoretical precision and research validity are likely to benefit by more extensive utilization of multivariate statistical methods. As data gathering techniques become easier and statistical software more powerful and user friendly, communication research is likely to examine more variables than in the past and routinely will provide options for controlling extraneous variables. Consequently, research in the future will be cleaner, more powerful, and more rigorous in testing theoretical propositions.

To date, much communication research, especially in mass communication, has been satisfied with basing its propositions on relatioships between and among theoretically linked variables. Communication scholarship has aggressively sought to identify causal relationships to predict effects in communication behavior. Limitations in identifying and controlling extraneous variables and in conducting experimental studies have posed obstacles for reporting causality. The advances foreseen in research technology are likely to remove such obstacles, providing for more robust tests of potential causal relationships in the communication process. However, promising results will still warrant that findings be replicated before a causal relationship is confirmed.

In the mass communication area, future research trends will be exciting, if not altogether predictable. Many observers foresee a media environment in which mass communication as we have known it no longer exists. These observers envision a future of interpersonally mediated communications facilitated by the information super highway and fiber optics technology. However, media history suggests that modern media seldom, if ever, replace older existing media. Consequently, our future media environment likely will include both mass and interpersonally mediated communications media. Likewise, media research will entertain both kinds of media, their related issues, and consumption patterns. Future media research likely will address itself to examining a set or portfolio of media behaviors shaped by the media technologies available to most consumers. Comparative analyses of interpersonally mediated communication behavior versus mass communication behavior (by demographic profile) should prove interesting.

A challenge for communication theorists will be to not allow the commercial and technological trends of the early 21st century to dictate the communication theoretical agenda. Theorists must be able to step back to gain a broader view of what new communication needs and problems are emerging. They must see phenomena and dynamics in the communication experience that elude commercial interests but that are vital to a better understanding of human behavior and relationships in the advanced information age. Concomitantly, external communities will be looking for ways to interpret and understand a new communication environment governed by a new set of communication dynamics. Such a scenario provides an awesome challenge and opportunity for the communication academy to demonstrate its inherent intellectual and practical worth.

34

The Future of Theory and Research in Communication: Human Communication

Gustav W. Friedrich[1]
University of Oklahoma

In the preface, Don Stacks and Michael Salwen identify their purpose as "to leave the reader with an appreciation of current theory and research in the various areas of communication study"—a task that this book performs admirably. Accomplishing this task at the deepest level requires that we acknowledge and consider two bifurcations that characterize the communication discipline: theory–research and mass–human communication. Because I share their belief that both bifurcations are often problematic for the discipline, I use the next few pages to provide some thoughts on their origin and on potential strategies for mediating their negative impact.

Let me begin by describing goals and approaches to graduate education in communication. Most of my analysis is aimed at the doctoral student, although my comments also fit the master's student thinking of going on for the PhD. I believe that doctoral education in communication should prepare students for (and socialize students into) careers in the communication discipline. For most students at the doctoral level, these careers are in academia. Thus, a major goal of doctoral programs should be to prepare

---

[1]Gustav W. Friedrich is former president of the Speech Communication Association.

communication scholars—those with generalist orientations to the discipline as well as those with specialty areas (e.g., mass, interpersonal, small groups, health, political, intercultural)—to add to the discipline's knowledge base. (I like these contributions to be both relevant to practitioners, as well as theoretically and empirically sound. Although it is often hard to do both, it is necessary if we are to survive as a scientific yet eminently practical discipline.)

To accomplish this goal of scholarly preparation, the doctoral curriculum exposes students to the content and research methods of the discipline and provides them with research experiences that form a foundation for subsequent careers. The delivery mode of the curriculum for most students is reductionistic and course-based—that is, students learn research methods in courses that devote minimum attention to content; and they take content courses that devote minimum attention to research methods. Furthermore, whereas many students do get research experience either individually or as part of a team (with faculty or other students), these experiences generally are constituted as add-ons to their program rather than central aspects of it.

An additional feature of doctoral education in communication is the fact that few departments are large enough to support concentrations in more than a small number of subdivisions of the discipline. Thus, although most students receive a broad overview of the history and the nature of the communication discipline, this is likely to be a one-time effort—and one targeted to the unique and specific nature of the student's academic unit (e.g., department, school, or college). A student who reads only Herman Cohen's (1994) *The history of speech communication: The emergence of a discipline, 1914–1945* is likely to learn about a very different discipline than does the student who reads only Everett M. Rogers' (1994) *A history of communication study: A biographical approach.* It is also likely that the interrelationships of the subdivisions of the discipline will remain largely unexplored as students take multiple courses in their specialty and in a small number of other major divisions of the discipline.

In short, the bifurcation between theory and research results from a reductionistic approach to teaching. This is an inevitable consequence of conceptualizing the acquisition of the skills of an academic as a building block process—that is, we should break down the necessary skills into smaller units and teach them in appropriately sequenced courses.

The bifurcation between mass and human communication results from similar considerations—that is, a reductionistic model of education. This bifurcation is further complicated, however, by the fact that historically these two subdivisions of the discipline have often been taught in different departments (e.g., journalism and speech or human communication). Even when this is not the case, the typical approach to the doctoral curriculum is to focus on the uniqueness of the discipline's subdivisions (e.g., what is unique about mass communication?) rather than on what that subdivision shares with the communication discipline. Often, this approach creates individuals who identify more strongly with the subdivision (e.g., intercultural, mass, political) than with the discipline. As Stacks and Salwen pointed out in the preface, such territoriality can cause problems when developing a taxonomy for the discipline (including dividing topics among human and mass communication). As someone who is teaching an undergraduate course in small group communication (a subdivision of human communication), must I ignore such mass communication topics as teaching small group discussion via computer-mediated communication, computer support and simulation for the study of small groups, and the effect of electronic meeting systems (teleconferencing, video conferencing, group decision support system, and computer-mediated communication) on small group work?

If my diagnosis is correct (i.e., that bifurcation is a natural outcome of a reductionistic curriculum), what is the remedy? In my view, a more holistic approach to the education of doctoral students is necessary. While a variety of strategies can accomplish this goal, all share a belief that doctoral students will best acquire the theory and research competencies necessary to be communication scholars if they focus on the task holistically rather than by learning isolated, decontexualized skills. This is a lesson that has already been learned in the life and physical sciences. For their doctoral students, such disciplines replace much of the coursework on methods and content with research teams where students learn theory and methods in context under the guidance of a senior scholar. When graduates of such programs enter the job market, they enter with publications, a specialty area of research, and a thorough grounding in theory and research. An additional feature of a holistic approach should be the inclusion of regular seminars and brown-bag sessions that focus on historical and contemporary issues in the communication discipline. Such activities allow faculty and students from a variety of subdivisions of the discipline to share and deepen their appreciation of the nature of the discipline and their role in it.

Before leaving this topic, let me share another bias. The PhD in communication is a research degree, so it is appropriate that doctoral students receive a heavy dose of training in theory and research. However, many new PhDs take positions at colleges and universities that emphasize teaching over research. And most college and university professors spend more of their professional time teaching than doing research. It is also the case that academics spend major portions of their time in service to their college or university, discipline, and the broader community. Thus, I believe that the doctoral program needs to prepare students to be successful in all domains of an academic career—research, teaching, and service. This is best accomplished when the academic unit carefully plans how best to socialize graduate students holistically into an academic career—both inside and outside the classroom. The resulting curriculum is likely to differ from the undergraduate curriculum in the following ways: the undergraduate experience typically covers a broader variety of topics, is career focused, and is teacher and course centered. By contrast, the graduate experience is narrower in focus, discipline based, and student and experience centered.

If you are a graduate student preparing for an academic career, I hope that you are fortunate enough to attend a university that has thought through how best to prepare and socialize its students. If not, you can do what many of your successful predecessors have done—seek out and work with willing faculty and other students to develop the research, teaching, and service competencies that will ensure your success.

REFERENCES

Cohen, H. (1994). *The history of speech communication: The emergence of a discipline, 1914-1945.* Annandale, VA: Speech Communication Association.

Rogers, E. M. (1994). *A history of communication study: A biographical approach.* New York: The Free Press.

About the Authors

Brenda J. Allen (Ph.D., Howard University, 1989) is assistant professor of Communication at the University of Colorado-Boulder, Boulder, CO.

James Anderson (Ph.D., University of Iowa, 1965) is professor and Chair of the Department of Communication at the University of Utah, Salt Lake City, UT.

Charles K. Atkin (Ph.D., University of Wisconsin, 1971) is professor of Communication and doctoral coordinator at Michigan State University, East Lansing, MI.

Tony Atwater (Ph.D., Michigan State University, 1983) is Associate Vice President for Academic Affairs at the University of Toledo. He is also past president of the Association for Education in Journalism and Mass Communication (AEJMC).

Michael Beatty (Ph.D., Ohio State University, 1976) is professor of Communication at Cleveland State University, Cleveland, OH.

Tamara Bell (M.A., University of Texas at Austin, 1993) is a doctoral student at the University of Texas at Austin.

Charles R. Berger (Ph.D., Michigan State University, 1968) is professor of Rhetoric and Communication at the University of California at Davis, Davis, CA.

Jennings Bryant (Ph.D., Indiana University, 1974) is professor of Communication, holder of the Ronald Reagan Chair of Broadcasting, and Director of the Institute for Communication Research at the University of Alabama, Tuscaloosa, AL.

Judee K. Burgoon (Ed.D., West Virginia University, 1974) is professor of Communication and Director of graduate studies at the University of Arizona, Tucson, AZ.

Stephen Busemeyer (B.A., University of Hartford, 1993) is an editor and reporter at *Northwest Colorado Daily Press* in Craig, CO.

Steven Chaffee (Ph.D., Stanford University, 1965) is Janet M. Peck Professor of International Communication at Stanford University, Stanford, CA.

Diane Christophel (Ed.D., West Virginia University, 1990) is assistant professor of Speech Communication at the University of Miami, Coral Gables, FL.

Emmeline G. de Pillis (B.A., University of Southern Califorina, 1984) is a doctoral candidate in Organizational Behavior at the University of Southern California, Los Angeles, CA.

551

Amy S. Ebesu   (M.A., University of Hawaii, 1991) is a doctoral candidate at the University of Arizona and acting assistant professor of Speech at the University of Hawaii, Honolulu, HI.

Larry Erbert   (M.A., Fort Hays State University, 1988) is a doctoral student at the University of Iowa, Iowa City, IA.

Walter R. Fisher   (Ph.D., University of Iowa, 1960) is professor of Communication and Director of the School of Communication at the Annenberg School for Communication, University of Southern California, Los Angles, CA.

Gustav W. Friedrich   (Ph.D., University of Kansas, 1968) is professor and Chair of the Department of Communication at the University of Oklahoma, Norman, OK. He is also past president of the Speech Communication Association.

Carroll J. Glynn   (Ph.D., University of Wisconsin-Madison, 1983) is associate professor and Chair of the Department of Communication at Cornell University, Ithaca, NY.

Cecilie J. Gaziano   (Ph.D., University of Minnesota, 1983) is President, Research Solutions, Minneapolis, MN.

Emanuel Gaziano   (M.A., University of Chicago, 1993) is a doctoral student in the Department of Sociology at Indiana University, Bloomington, IN.

Blaine Goss   (Ph.D., Michigan State University, 1971) is professor and Chair of the Communication Studies Department at New Mexico State University, Las Cruces, NM.

Bradley S. Greenberg   (Ph.D., University of Wisconsin, 1961) is University Distinguished Professor of Communication at Michigan State University, East Lansing, MI.

Autumn Grubb-Swetnam   (Ph.D., University of Kentucky, 1995) is Director of Distance Learning at Morehead State University, Morehead, KY.

Larissa A. Grunig (Ph.D., University of Maryland, 1985) is associate professor of Journalism at the University of Maryland, College Park, MD.

mark Hickson, III   (Ph.D., Southern Illinois University, 1971) is professor and Chair of the Communication Studies Department at the University of Alabama at Birmingham, Birmingham, AL.

Randy Hirokawa   (Ph.D., University of Washington, 1980) is associate professor of Communication Studies at the University of Iowa, Iowa City, IA.

Richard J. Ice   (Ph.D., University of Iowa, 1988) is associate professor of Speech at St. Johns College, Collegeville, MN.

Lynda Lee Kaid   (Ph.D., Southern Illinois University, 1974) is professor of Communication and Director of the Political Communication Center at the University of Oklahoma, Norman, OK.

Timothy R. Levine   (Ph.D., Michigan State University, 1992) is assistant professor of Speech at the University of Hawaii, Honolulu, HI.

Alicia Marshall   (Ph.D., Purdue University, 1990) is assistant professor of Communication at Cornell University, Ithaca, NY.

Maxwell McCombs   (Ph.D., Stanford University, 1966) is Jesse H. Jones Centennial Professor in Communication at the University of Texas at Austin, Austin, TX.

James C. McCroskey   (Ed.D., Pennsylvania State University, 1966) is professor and Chair of the Department of Communication Studies at West Virginia University, Morgantown, WV.

Michael D. Miller   (Ph.D., University of Florida, 1978) is associate professor and Chair of the Department of speech, University of Hawaii, Honolulu, HI.

Michael Morgan   (Ph.D., University of Pennsylvania, 1980) is professor at the University of Massachusetts, Amherst, MA.

Eduardo Nieva   (Ph.D., Federal University of Rio de Janeiro, 1989) is assistant professor and Director of the Communication Research Center in the Communication Studies Department at the University of Alabama at Birmingham, Birmingham, AL.

Stephen D. O'Leary   (Ph.D., Northwestern University, 1991) is assistant professor of Communication at the Annenberg School for Communication, University of Southern California, Los Angeles, CA.

J. D. Rayburn, II   (Ph.D., Florida State University, 1977) is professor of Communication at Florida State University, Tallahassee, FL.

Kathleen K. Reardon   (Ph.D., University of Massachusetts, 1978) is associate professor of Management and Organization and Director of the Presidential Fellows program at the University of Southern California, Los Angeles, CA.

Virginia P. Richmond   (Ph.D., University of Nebraska, 1977) is professor of Communication Studies and and Director of the School of Communication, Kent State University, Kent, OH.

Everett M. Rogers   (Ph.D., Iowa State University, 1957) is professor and Chair of the Department of Communication and journalism at the University of New Mexico, Albuquerque, NM.

Ramona R. Rush   (Ph.D., University of Wisconsin, 1969) is professor of Communications at the University of Kentucky, Lexington, KY.

Abran J. Salazar   (Ph.D., University of Iowa, 1991) is assistant professor of Speech at Texas A&M University, College Station, TX.

Charles T. Salmon   (Ph.D., University of Minnesota, 1985) is Ellis N. Brandt Professor of Advertising at Michigan State University, East Lansing, MI.

Michael B. Salwen   (Ph.D., Michigan State University, 1985) is professor of Communication at the University of Miami, Coral Gables, FL.

Charles Self   (Ph.D., University of Iowa, 1974) is professor and head of the Department of Journalism at Texas A&M University, College Station, TX.

Pamela J. Shoemaker   (Ph.D., University of Wisconsin, 1982) is John Ben Snow Professor of Communication at Syracuse University, Syracuse, NY.

Nancy Signorielli   (Ph.D., University of Pennsylvania, 1975) is professor of Communication at the University of Delaware, Newark, DE.

Arvind Singhal   (Ph.D., University of Southern California, 1990) is associate professor in the School of Interpersonal Communication at Ohio University, Athens, OH.

Don W. Stacks   (Ph.D., University of Florida, 1978) is professor of Communication and Director of Advertising and Public Relations at the University of Miami, Coral Gables, FL.

Thomas Steinfatt   (Ph.D., Michigan State University, 1971) is professor and Director of Speech Communication at the University of Miami, Coral Gables, FL.

Robert L. Stevenson   (Ph.D., University of Washington, 1975) is professor of Journalism at the University of North Carolina at Chapel Hill, Chapel Hill, NC.

Esther Thorson   (Ph.D., University of Minnesota, 1974) is professor of Journalism and Associate Dean of graduate studies at the University of Missouri, Columbia, MO.

Phillip K. Tompkins   (Ph.D., Purdue University, 1962) is professor of Communication at the University of Colorado-Boulder, Boulder, CO.

Donald K. Wright   (Ph.D., University of Minnesota, 1974) is professor of Communication at the University of South Alabama, Mobile, AL.

Dolf Zillmann   (Ph.D., University of Pennsylvania, 1969) is professor of Communication and Senior Associate Dean for Graduate Studies And Research, College of Communication at the University of Alabama, Tuscaloosa, AL.

Author Index

Subject Index